Mastering
Microsoft® Lync®
Server 2013

Keith Hanna

Nathan Winters

SYBEX®
A Wiley Brand

Acquisitions Editor: Mariann Barsolo

Development Editor: Kim Wimpsett

Technical Editor: Lester Hewett

Production Editor: Dassi Zeidel

Copy Editor: Judy Flynn

Editorial Manager: Pete Gaughan

Production Manager: Tim Tate

Vice President and Executive Group Publisher: Richard Swadley

Vice President and Publisher: Neil Edde

Book Designers: Maureen Forys, Happenstance Type-O-Rama; Judy Fung

Proofreader: Amy J. Schneider

Indexer: Ted Laux

Project Coordinator, Cover: Katherine Crocker

Cover Designer: Ryan Sneed

Cover Image: Thomas Northcut/Getty Images

Dear Reader,

Thank you for choosing *Mastering Microsoft Lync Server 2013*. This book is part of a family of premium-quality Sybex books, all of which are written by outstanding authors who combine practical experience with a gift for teaching.

Sybex was founded in 1976. More than 30 years later, we're still committed to producing consistently exceptional books. With each of our titles, we're working hard to set a new standard for the industry. From the paper we print on to the authors we work with, our goal is to bring you the best books available.

I hope you see all that reflected in these pages. I'd be very interested to hear your comments and get your feedback on how we're doing. Feel free to let me know what you think about this or any other Sybex book by sending me an email at nedde@wiley.com. If you think you've found a technical error in this book, please visit http://sybex.custhelp.com. Customer feedback is critical to our efforts at Sybex.

Best regards,

Neil Edde
Vice President and Publisher
Sybex, an Imprint of Wiley

I'd like to dedicate this book to my fantastic wife, Sharon, for allowing me the time out from "family life" to complete this second challenge—evenings are ours again—and also to Rosie and Jamie, who every day continue to amaze me with how quickly they learn and grow up.
—Keith Hanna

I would like to dedicate this book to my parents, who throughout my life have encouraged me to reach my goals and have been there for me both when I have and when I've fallen short.
—Nathan Winters

Acknowledgments

Wow! What started as a simple chat over coffee has now developed into two books! The fact that we've gotten to our second book is as much of a surprise to us as it is to many people who know us! With the first book, *Mastering Lync Server 2010*, we established that writing a book wasn't an easy task. Knowing this, we're not quite sure why we went ahead with this follow-up. (And Nathan is even doing an Exchange book!)

Of course, we learned a lot with the 2010 book, and even more so with this 2013 version. Our approaches were very different this time: Lync 2010 had been released for around a year, and we had involvement in the Technology Adoption Program (TAP) prior to that. This time around, we had only our experiences within the TAP program to drive us and had to rely on our much-valued networks to fill in the gaps—and there were many more gaps!

It's not doing them justice by simply naming those who helped us here; some of this book could simply not have been written without help from those in the following list. Some chapters were being written while the code was still wet and being tested in the TAP program, and indeed one or two of the chapters have undergone complete rewrites during this period, not because the information was wrong, but because the product fundamentally changed prior to release! Some of the people here implemented the first deployments of Lync Server 2013 in the world.

In company alphabetical order, we are extremely grateful to the following people:

Actiance: Robin Smith

AudioCodes: Yaniv Epstein, Ran Inbar

Dell: Ari Protheroe

Formicary: Howard Travers, Angeline Cheng, Daanish Khan

Grey Convergence: Art C Ho, Russ Kirk (MVP for Lync)

HP: Taufique Ahmed, Jeff Leads

Microsoft: Joanne Warden, John McCabe (a key resource!), Gareth Bridges, Chris Stevenson, BJ Haberkorn, Brian Crum, Bryan Nyce, Dave Howe, Nick Smith

Plantronics: Declan Doyle

Polycom: Takeshi Ishimaru, Mike Stacy

Sennheiser: Paul Turner, Charlotte Gaskin

SMART Technologies: Jennifer Thornton, Mark Knowler

SNOM: Tim Koehler, Jan Boguslawski, Paul Jamieson

Big thanks to the sample hardware we were able to use to capture some of the scenarios in the book as well as the early access to firmware for the devices.

Throughout the process, we have been supported, guided, and cajoled (we needed mostly more of this) by a superb team at Sybex: Kim Wimpsett, Dassi Zeidel, Mariann Barsolo, and Pete Gaughan. Apologies again for missing probably every deadline we agreed upon; it was in the best interests to have the book contain the most reliable and accurate information possible!

Of course, no technical book can be released without thorough cross-checking, and for that we are very grateful to Lester Hewitt from Dell, our technical editor, who spent many hours going through the material, replicating our examples to ensure technical accuracy and in several areas correcting our approach as well as advising on many of the examples and real-world usage scenarios.

For all of those who provided feedback, be they verbally or via reviews, corrections, criticisms, and direct email, we thank you; we've tried to incorporate more of what you liked and less of what you didn't in this version. Keep the feedback coming!

We said it in the last book, and repeat it again here because we firmly believe in the power of the user groups and local communities. This is where the knowledge resides. As much as we'd love to cover everything here, we simply don't have the time or the space to do so. The amount of guidance we see coming from the TAP community and the questions being asked directly drove some of the content within this book. Feedback we get from delivering and attending training courses—we listen to it all!

There are many other people we'd like to thank within Microsoft, specifically the community around LCS/OCS and Lync, the Microsoft Certified Master community, and the *original* COE team—guys (and gals), you have helped us many times (and continue to do so); hopefully we can continue to be members of these valuable communities.

Our advice to others: If you work for Microsoft, join these communities; they're invaluable. If you don't, join your local UC user group. These guys reach out via the user groups or Tech Ed. Catch up with these people; they don't bite!

Our thanks go to all involved in helping to create this book.

—*Keith Hanna and Nathan Winters*

About the Authors

Keith Hanna started university life at Sheffield University studying software engineering but finished by graduating from Queen's University, Belfast, in computer science. His first "real" job was with Lucas Aerospace as a software developer working on aircraft engine control systems—it wasn't rocket science, but it was close! Moving to England from Ireland, Keith helped to design and deploy a communications system for the emergency services but found his calling in Windows-based application design and support, eventually making his way to Microsoft, where he has been for over six years, working in a number of roles from engineer to consultant and currently in service delivery. He has contributed several articles to TechNet as well as several chapters in the *Lync 2010 Resource Kit*. He has written training courses for OCS R2 and Lync as well as exam questions. He is a Microsoft Certified Master. He's not aware of any life outside work, and he will be keen to discover if such a thing exists now that the book is finished.

Nathan Winters has worked in IT since graduating from the Royal College of Music (RCM) in 2003, where he studied the clarinet! His first job was at the RCM, migrating from Exchange 5.5 and Windows NT4 to Exchange and Windows Server 2003. Nathan has since worked in a variety of roles for Microsoft partners, including consultancy and practice management. He now works for Microsoft UK as a presales technical specialist. Throughout 2012 and 2013, Nathan has been a regular speaker at industry conferences such as TechEd and Exchange Connections in both Europe and the United States. Before joining Microsoft, Nathan was active in the UK technical community, running the Exchange user group (MMMUG) and writing numerous articles for *Windows IT Pro* magazine and the MSExchange.org website, among others. He was awarded as a Microsoft MVP between 2006 and 2011. Nathan's next book, *Microsoft Exchange Server 2013*: *Design, Deploy and Deliver an Enterprise Messaging Solution*, will be published by Wiley in the summer of 2013. On the rare occasions when he is not working, he enjoys wildlife photography and badminton.

Contents at a Glance

Contents

Introduction

With the release of Lync Server 2010, the Sybex Mastering series has moved into the world of Microsoft's Unified Communications (UC) platform. With the release of Lync 2010, we moved into the third generation of a platform that provides a comprehensive set of functionality, which has placed it consistently in the top right of the Gartner Magic Quadrant for UC.

With the update of Lync Server 2010 to Lync Server 2013, it was necessary to revisit the content. Some will be familiar, but there are significant changes to justify a new version of the book. We've also taken the opportunity to expand the device coverage because devices are very much the heart of a Lync deployment from the user perspective, and after all, without users, there'll be no need for solutions.

With this in mind, we set out to reinforce any prior knowledge you might have of the server platform, but not to assume any, and thereby take you on a journey from the key fundamentals of Lync Server 2013 all the way through deployment and finally to how best to integrate Lync with third-party systems.

We have attempted to ensure that you can gain insight into real-world environments both through the use of lab systems that represent those that might be found in an enterprise network and also through the use of real-world case studies that highlight examples of our day-to-day experience as consultants to some of the world's largest organizations.

What You Need to Run Lync Server 2013

As you read through this book, you will find that there are a range of components that all come together to make Lync function. These include the Lync Server software, the Lync client, and the supporting technology from Microsoft Windows Server 2008 R2 and Microsoft SQL Server 2008 R2. Of course, there are additional pieces that can be integrated, such as gateway devices, telephone devices, and software components such as Exchange and SharePoint.

With this much complexity, you may be wondering how on earth you are going to be able to get started with learning Lync. In addition to all the components, you will find when looking at the published minimum system requirements for Lync that the main Front End (or Standard Edition) servers require a minimum of 32GB of RAM and 12 CPU cores. We cover all this in depth in Chapter 5, but no doubt you will think that is rather a challenge for a lab. Well, don't worry! It is perfectly possible to set up a very capable lab system on a single machine. In fact, while writing this book, we ran our numerous lab systems on a variety of hardware, ranging from Dell desktops with 16GB of RAM and a pair of fast hard drives for the virtual machines to Dell Tower server hardware with 24GB and four hard drives. All in all, this is equipment that is well within the reach of any enterprise looking to get up to speed with Lync and something that anyone studying IT for their career can get hold of for not ridiculous sums.

Within the constraints of the hardware mentioned, we created our labs using Microsoft Hyper-V technology to virtualize many machines. The labs ranged from two machines covering a domain controller and a single Lync server all the way up to the migration lab, which had both OCS and Lync installed with full external communication and Mediation servers for connectivity to the PSTN, where we were running 10 servers on our single piece of hardware. So while for production use you must take care to size things according to best practice, in the lab you can learn a great deal with a single server, Hyper-V, some public IP addresses, public certificates, and a SIP trunk—which are all readily available for affordable amounts of money.

What's Inside

This book is arranged in six main sections, with a couple of appendixes. The six main areas focus on key elements that help build your knowledge of Lync, starting with fundamentals that get you up to speed. We then move through getting your first Lync system up and running to administering your system. At that point, the book takes a deep look into using Lync as your telephony platform before moving on to cover how to integrate Lync into other systems, and we then finish with a look at Lync mobile clients. The appendices wrap up the Bottom Line learning entries from the book and conclude by taking a step back from the technical elements to discuss changes Lync may require to your business and how to make sure you have a successful implementation.

When first picking up a new book, people frequently jump straight to a chapter that answers some immediate need or interest. We have attempted to build concepts throughout this book, with most of the later chapters making the assumption that you are familiar with the previous material. We have, of course, referenced that earlier material wherever possible in case you need to brush up, but as a general recommendation, we suggest that if you're new to Lync, you will have the most success by reading through the chapters in order.

Part 1: Fundamentals

This section covers the background information that will help you understand what makes Lync tick.

Chapter 1: What's in Lync?   This chapter runs through Lync from top to bottom, covering key concepts, features, and where Lync sits in the history of real-time communication products from Microsoft.

Chapter 2: Standards and Protocols   Like any technical product, Lync is underpinned by numerous protocols and standards that enable it to operate and interoperate with other platforms. This chapter focuses in particular on Session Initiation Protocol (SIP), which enables the majority of Lync communications.

Chapter 3: Security   Security is front of mind for all administrators these days. In this chapter, we outline the threats to Lync and explain its architecture in a security-focused manner that will enable you to discuss requirements with your security team. We also cover some of the administrative practices needed to help you administer Lync securely.

Chapter 4: Clients   Without clients, any server product would be pretty useless! In this chapter, we look at the clients available on a PC, Mac, and browser, and we dive deep into how the clients connect to Lync.

Part 2: Getting Lync Up and Running

This section is where you actually get hands on with Lync. We cover planning and sizing and then both the installation and upgrade processes.

Chapter 5: Planning Your Deployment   While we are all keen to dive in and start playing with the nuts and bolts, planning is essential to ensure that you achieve what is required. This chapter shows you how to plan utilizing the available tools, and it helps you understand the Lync prerequisites, enabling you to choose which hardware to use and how high availability in the latest version is implemented.

Chapter 6: Installation   By the end of this chapter, you should have installed your first Lync system. We take you through preparing your underlying server OS to publishing Lync to the Internet with all the steps in between!

Chapter 7: Migration and Upgrades   Lync is the latest in a line of real-time communications products from Microsoft. This chapter shows you how to get from the earlier Office Communications Server 2007 R2 or Lync Server 2010 to Lync Server 2013.

Part 3: Administration

Having planned and installed Lync, we now move on to look at administration. These chapters cover PowerShell, explain admin roles and policies, and even look at troubleshooting.

Chapter 8: Introduction to PowerShell, the Lync Management Shell, and Regular Expressions   PowerShell is what underpins the whole management interface of Lync. In this chapter, you learn what PowerShell is, how to use it, and more important, how to work with Lync using PowerShell.

Chapter 9: Role-Based Access Control   Role-based access control (RBAC) changes the granularity and ease with which an administrator can be granted permissions required for their job and only their job, allowing specific delegation of functionality to groups of people. This chapter shows you how Lync implements RBAC and how to use it to implement secure administration of Lync.

Chapter 10: User Administration   Having looked at PowerShell and RBAC, the two main concepts underpinning administration, in this chapter, we show how to manage users, enabling, disabling, and configuring them both individually and through policy to use the Lync features they require.

Chapter 11: Archiving and Monitoring   Lync enables communication, and in many organizations communications must be archived. This chapter covers how Lync does this with the Archiving role. It also covers the way in which you can inspect the communication passing through Lync, not only for quality but also more traditionally, showing who spoke with whom. Finally, we cover how to monitor the Lync service as a whole using System Center Operations Manager (SCOM).

Chapter 12: Troubleshooting   As with any system, there will be times when things don't work as they should. This chapter works through key troubleshooting concepts and then looks at the tools available in Lync and how to use them when trouble strikes.

Part 4: Voice

Lync is the first product from Microsoft that can truly claim to be a full-fledged telephony system (PBX). This section focuses on using Lync as your PBX, taking you from basic phone calls through to complex automated call distribution systems.

Chapter 13: Getting Started with Voice   Lync provides all the capability needed to be a large enterprise telephony platform. This chapter introduces you to the world of the PBX. It covers the features available in Lync and the architecture that supports them.

Chapter 14: Call Admission Control   One of the biggest considerations when utilizing data networks for audio and video communication is bandwidth usage. Call Admission Control enables you to map out your network and protect it from overuse. This chapter shows you how to do this with Lync.

Chapter 15: E911 and Location Information Services   Especially in North America, the ability to locate the origin of a phone call and provide that information to the emergency services is mandatory. This chapter discusses how to provide this functionality with Lync; it also shows how those outside North America can use this innovative technology.

Chapter 16: Extended Voice Functionality   Lync can be used for far more than just basic phone calls. This chapter looks at how to implement your own audio-conferencing bridge, how to set up your own mini call center or help desk, and how to deal with other voice scenarios, such as the need to park calls for others to pick up and to deal with calls to people who have left your company.

Part 5: Integration

One of the huge benefits of Lync being a software platform is that it is very easy to extend and integrate with other systems. This section covers that extensibility by looking at the way Lync integrates with both Microsoft and non-Microsoft products.

Chapter 17: Exchange and SharePoint   While Lync by itself contains a huge amount of technology, it is enhanced even further through tight integration with other Microsoft products. This chapter covers the provision of voice mail and presence integration with Exchange and presence integration and workflow with SharePoint.

Chapter 18: Hybrid Deployments   In this chapter, we look at a new deployment option with Lync Server 2013, hybrid deployment, where server infrastructure is deployed on premises but the users' accounts are based in the cloud. We look at how to install and configure the on-premises side of things as well as the call flows with different scenarios of user locations.

Chapter 19: Third-Party Integration   In this chapter, we cover Lync as it sits at the center of a unified communications system. We cover integration with third-party PBXs, gateways (including the deployment of Survivable Branch Appliances), and videoconferencing systems. We look at extending Lync with third-party software and show how to deploy the XMPP gateway to allow communication with a wide range of IM clouds, including Jabber and Google.

Part 6: Devices

Chapter 20: Mobility   In this chapter we look at the functionality delivered by the mobile device clients for Windows Phone, iOS (iPhone and iPad), and Android. Cumulative Update 1 is required for the Lync 2013 mobile client, so we also have a look at the functionality received if the Lync 2010 mobile clients are still being used.

Chapter 21: Telephony Devices   The final chapter of this book covers the range of user devices, starting with simple USB headsets all the way through to third-party room-based conference systems. We take a focused look at the Lync Phone Edition and non-Lync Phone Edition (3PIP, Third-Party IP Phone) devices and how to configure the environment to support them.

Appendixes

There are three appendices. The first covers all the learning points from throughout the book, and the second discusses how to successfully adopt Lync in your organization. The third appendix provides examples of how Persistent Chat can be used.

Appendix A: The Bottom Line   Throughout the book, the Bottom Line section appears at the end of each chapter. It asks relevant questions to help test your understanding of the material in that chapter. This appendix covers all those questions and includes the answers so you can verify yours.

Appendix B: Adoption   While this book has focused on the technology that is Lync, there is another major aspect to utilizing Lync: how do you get Lync adopted in your organization? Without a proper plan and a great team that includes people ranging from very senior personnel to those using the technology every day, you may not have great success deploying Lync. This appendix discusses some of the key elements that come together to enable a business to successfully adopt Lync.

Appendix C: Using Persistent Chat Effectively   Previously known as Group Chat and seen by many as the "black sheep" of the application, Persistent Chat now has a fully integrated deployment method as well as a fully integrated single-client approach for users. Here we take a look at several use cases for Persistent Chat and how they can be implemented.

The Mastering Series

The Mastering series from Sybex provides outstanding instruction for readers with intermediate and advanced skills in the form of top-notch training and development for those already working in their field and clear, serious education for those aspiring to become pros. Every Mastering book includes the following:

◆   Real-World Scenarios, ranging from case studies to interviews that show how the tool, technique, or knowledge presented is applied in actual practice.

◆   Skill-based instruction, with chapters organized around real tasks rather than abstract concepts or subjects.

◆   Self-review test questions, so you can be certain you're equipped to do the job right.

Conventions Used in This Book

Before you set off into the world of Lync described in this book, there is one final piece of information that we want you to know.

Throughout the book, we used various methods to describe things. In particular, we had many discussions about how best to describe the tools used to administer Lync. As you will see, there are two main interfaces: a web-based control panel called Lync Server Control Panel (LSCP) and a command-line shell called the Lync Server Management Shell (LSMS), which is based on PowerShell. In the book, we used the terms *Control Panel* and *LSCP* interchangeably to describe the Lync Server Control Panel and *PowerShell* to describe the Lync Server Management Shell. Please don't confuse this use of PowerShell with the standard Microsoft PowerShell shell, which is installed on Windows Server 2008 R2 by default. When working with Lync, unless explicitly stated otherwise, you should be using the Lync Server Management Shell.

HYBRID VOICE

As this book goes to press Microsoft has announced the removal of the Hybrid Deployment functionality (see Chapter 18). The exact reasons behind this are no yet known, however, one of the aims of the deployment scenario was to reduce the amount of hardware required to be deployed on premises, as servers would be hosted in the cloud. With the ability of Lync to collocate Mediation servers and Front End servers on the same physical hardware, this aim is difficult to meet, so it may be simply that the ability to move users to the cloud, whilst working, doesn't provide enough benefits to justify further investment in this functionality.

CAPACITY PLANNING

The capacity planning figures used in this book for Standard Edition quote 2,500 users per server. This is from the Microsoft guidance. Since completing the planning guidance, Microsoft has clarified this to state that the 2,500 users is the preferred number for Standard Edition servers as it allows 2 Standard Edition servers to act as backups for each other, and fully cope with 100 percent of the load in the event of a disaster. By implication, this means that a Standard Edition server can cater for 5,000 users—similar to what we had in previous versions—however, as functional disaster recovery has such a large focus with Lync Server 2013, the numbers have been revised to include this.

How to Contact the Authors

We welcome feedback from you about this book. Obviously, it's always nice to get messages about what you liked about the book, but we also welcome suggestions for improvements we could make in future editions. You can reach Keith by writing to hannakeith@hotmail.com, and you can reach Nathan at nathan@clarinathan.co.uk. If you are looking for information about future articles or speaking engagements, visit Nathan's blog: www.nathanwinters.co.uk.

Sybex strives to keep you supplied with the latest tools and information you need for your work. Please check the website at www.sybex.com/go/masteringlyncserver, where we'll post additional content and updates that supplement this book should the need arise.

Part I

Fundamentals

Chapter 1

What's in Lync?

Lync Server 2013 is the latest in the line of the Communications Server platforms from Microsoft. The platform originally started with Live Communications Server 2003 (some would say with Exchange Conference Server 2000!) and continued through Live Communications Server 2005, Office Communications Server (OCS) 2007, Office Communications Server 2007 R2, and the first incarnation of Lync: Lync Server 2010. This latest version extends the capabilities even further than those introduced with Lync Server 2010.

For those of you experienced with Lync Server 2010 (or indeed previous versions of OCS/ LCS), this chapter will call out some of the core capabilities introduced in previous versions as well as the new capabilities specific to Lync 2013, so some of this content may be a refresher to knowledge you already have.

In this chapter, you will learn to:

◆ Describe the features of the client

◆ Describe the features of the server

◆ Describe the voice features

Understanding the Lync 2013 Client

As an administrator, the first thing you'll see is the Setup tool; however, the users will see the client. Therefore, understanding what the client can and will provide is important for administrators trying to sell the business justification. It is also important in terms of what policies will need to be configured to enable (or disable) features. Lync 2013 is so much more than a simple instant messaging (IM) tool or a phone, and treating it as either end of the messaging scale will impact the way you deploy it to users. At one end, the IM capabilities can be deployed quite simply, whereas the phone integration will take significant planning and should not be underestimated. Some of the additional training capabilities freely provided by Microsoft are covered in Appendix B, "Adoption."

With OCS (and to some extend LCS), the user experience was made up of a number of clients:

◆ Communicator

◆ Live Meeting

◆ Group Chat

Lync 2010 consolidated the Communicator and Live Meeting clients into one; however, that still left the Group Chat client as a separate installation requirement. We know a number of large financial institutions that have a heavy reliance upon the Group Chat functionality and have been asking for some time for the consolidation of this client. Well, it's finally come. Group Chat (now known as Persistent Chat) is incorporated into the Communicator client, so there's only a single installation required. Indeed, more than that is the decision to make Persistent Chat a "full" function of Lync Server 2013 rather than a download add-on as it was previously — more on this later.

Chapter 20, "Mobile Devices," covers in detail the new Lync 2013 Mobility capability; this was first introduced with Cumulative Update 4 in Lync Server 2010.

With the 2013 edition, Lync has had a facelift; new features introduced with Lync 2013, such as user photos, have been further improved, and other features have been moved around to make them easier to find for users.

In addition, device selection has been considered with Lync 2013 clients being adapted to tablet devices as well as the expected mobile and desktop/laptop-style devices.

There is also the expected transition to the Windows 8 user interface (UI). Although Lync is still supported on previous versions of Windows, the look and feel has become more consistent with the Windows 8 UI.

The Communicator client is also now part of the Office suite and is no longer available separately. Figure 1.1 shows the client when a user is first logged in.

FIGURE 1.1
The client startup screen

Connecting via the Lync 2013 Client

To communicate and collaborate, Lync client users need to be able to locate and connect to each other on the network. Over time, users will build their own contacts list (sometimes called a *buddy list*); however, they need to find other users to be able to create and add to the list. The basic search functionality from previous versions has been retained and has been expanded to include integration and key-skills searching within SharePoint as well as the expected Address Book search. Also new with Lync (introduced in Lync 2010) is the ability to remove the Address Book download capability and provide only an online web-based search function. Figure 1.2 shows the client search bar and results window when data has been entered into the search bar.

FIGURE 1.2
The client search bar and results window

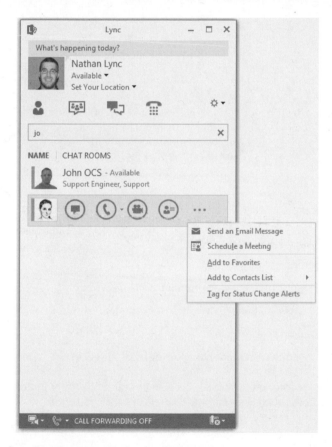

From these results, you can initiate any type of communications modality. The submenu is opened by selecting the ellipsis (…).

Unfortunately, this is one area in which we think the user interface has lost capability when compared with Lync 2010. To find more information from the user (the contact card), you have to at least appear to begin a conversation with them. Starting an IM conversation has the least impact in that until you actually send a message, there is no prompt to the recipient. Figure 1.3 shows the new-style contact card, which you can see once you initiate communications and expand the user data.

FIGURE 1.3
The user contact
card

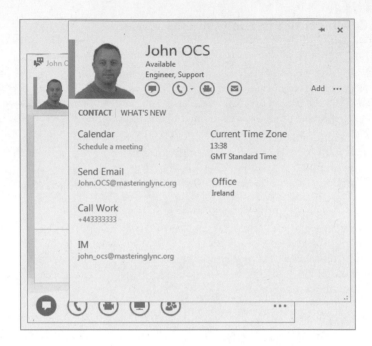

The User Properties box is extended to provide a lot more contextual information:

♦ Department

♦ Office

♦ Phone numbers (work, mobile, home, if permitted)

♦ SharePoint links (to MySite, for example)

♦ Calendar information

♦ Location information (including local time and time zone)

This *contact card* provides a consistent Lync 2013 client interface across all the integrated applications, such as Office and SharePoint. Connecting from other applications preserves context; if you start a conversation from an Outlook email, both the subject and the priority are carried across to the conversation windows and the document title is transferred from SharePoint. The contact card now includes the ability to provide location information, giving users a way to quickly establish where people are currently, which can help them determine whether personal contact or a video call is the more appropriate type of communication. The location information also provides the local time for the user, which can be extremely useful when people are spread across multiple geographies.

You can search across the following locations:

◆ Lync contacts

◆ Active Directory

◆ Outlook contacts (including suggested contacts)

New with Lync 2013, in conjunction with Exchange 2013, is the Unified Contact Store, where all contacts are merged and stored within the user mailbox (specifically within the contacts folder). An additional capability introduced by the Unified Contact Store is the ability to store high-definition (HD) photographs of the users. In the past, photographs were stored in SharePoint or Active Directory; now they are stored within the user mailbox in Exchange 2013.

Searching allows you to easily establish availability and identity (the extended contact card provides more information to help identify the correct recipient) and quickly establish contact using any modality. In addition to searching by name, the SharePoint integration allows you to search by skills (or keywords) to help identify the correct person.

As mentioned, the ability to add contacts (or *buddies*) and group them is retained; in fact, it is expanded to include an auto-populated Frequent Contacts group. This group is automatically populated with your 10 most-frequent contacts, which are weighted based on modality. For example, someone you regularly call is going to be placed higher in the list than someone you IM. You'll learn about other automatically created groups later in this chapter.

The Contacts tab, which is the default, contains a number of subtabs that provide different views (shown in Figure 1.4).

FIGURE 1.4
The Groups subtab
on the Contacts tab

Groups　This is probably the most frequently used subtab; it is where you can find all the contacts sorted alphabetically but also grouped together in user-defined groups.

Status　Under this subtab, all the contacts are sorted by availability, under the following groups:

◆ Away (includes Off Work)

◆ Unknown

♦ Unavailable

♦ Online (includes Busy, In a Meeting, and Do Not Disturb)

Relationships Here, you can manage the permissions assigned to each contact. The default categories are as follows:

Friends and Family This relationship must be assigned manually. It provides the following setting:

"Share all my contact information except meeting details."

Workgroup This relationship must be assigned manually. It provides the following setting:

"Share all my contact information except Home and Other phone; contact can interrupt Do Not Disturb status."

Colleagues Any users from within the same Lync organization (or OCS if in coexistence) are automatically placed within this group and receive the following setting:

"Share all my contact information except Home, Other, and Mobile phone, and meeting details."

External Contacts Any external (federated) users are placed within this group by default and receive the following setting:

"Share only my name, title, email address, company, and picture."

Blocked Contacts This relationship must be manually assigned and provides the following setting:

"Share only my name and email address; blocked contacts can't reach me via Lync."

Auto-Assign Relationship This item is not found in the Relationships tab; however, it can be found on a contact and is used to reset the privacy level:

"Reset this privacy relationship to the Lync default."

New If users have added you to their contact list but you have not (yet) added them to yours, they will appear on the New tab.

Add A Contact Provides a submenu with the following list of options for finding and adding a new contact:

♦ Add A Contact In My Organization

♦ Add A Contact Not In My Organization

♦ Create A New Group

♦ Display Options

VOICEMAIL DISPLAY

The voicemail display within the Lync 2013 client is not as fully featured as the voicemail integration from within Outlook. Lync 2013 allows only basic integration, providing the name of the user (or phone number display, if caller ID could not be matched to a contact), a Play button, and the Lync 2013 interaction options allowing the call to be responded to from the client (using any modality).

Outlook (2007 or higher) provides additional capability such as Notes, Play-on-Phone, and fully integrated media controls for playback. Exchange 2010 and Exchange 2013 also provide speech-to-text translation for certain language packs, the output of which will be displayed in Outlook only.

Communicating via the Lync 2013 Client

As mentioned in the previous section, the Lync 2013 contact card lets users quickly and easily establish any modality from any integrated application. In particular, Lync 2013 allows users to receive phone calls on any device (including non-Lync devices) as well as manage their own (and potentially other users') communications easily and more effectively than before.

The final button (telephone icon) provides a single page for telecom interaction (see Figure 1.5), so users can make calls (from a dial-pad) and display and listen to voicemails. The dial-pad operates exactly as you would expect; for example, press and hold 1 to call your voicemail. If you need to access your voicemail box when it is empty (for example, to set your greeting), this is the only method to do so other than dialing the voicemail access number. The voicemail section allows quick and easy access to voicemails stored in your inbox. When there are voicemails in your inbox, a drop-down menu is available for direct access to set your greeting.

VIDEO CALLING

Since Office Communications Server 2007 R2, high definition has been supported for peer-to-peer video only; however, Lync 2013 now provides the capability for HD (using H.264 SVC codec

support) conference calls (VGA was the default with Lync 2010). In addition to the higher resolution provided by this default codec, the Lync 2013 client supports direct integration with the
Microsoft RoundTable devices, providing a panoramic video strip when used in calls.

FIGURE 1.5
The dial-pad

The video screen can be detached from the client and viewed in a separate window, which
can be extremely useful for users who have multiple monitors because the video channel can
be displayed on a separate display from the main conference window, allowing a more true-life
experience.

H263 codecs are no longer supported with Lync 2013, so organizations may need to upgrade
legacy non-Lync video hardware or look to additional gateway capability to continue operating.

DEVICE MANAGEMENT

New device management functionality allows the Lync client to intelligently select the appropriate device for your calls. Even changing devices within a call is much easier. The Audio And
Video Tuning Wizard is no longer required; you simply use a drop-down menu with all the

devices listed and select a new one to transfer the call to the selected device immediately with no further interaction. Devices can even be added mid-call and the audio (or video) directed to the newly added device.

Audio and video device management and tuning is still possible from within the Options page from the Tools menu; however, doing so is now an optional task, whereas previously it was required every time a device was inserted.

The call-forwarding and team-call settings can now be managed with a single click in the main client window, shown in Figure 1.6.

FIGURE 1.6
Making a call forwarding selection

MANAGING COMMUNICATIONS

Tabbed conversation view allows all conversations to be viewed in a single window. With previous versions, a new conversation window would open for each person. Indeed, the client can be configured to allow this mode of operation if preferred. Figure 1.7 shows the tabbed conversation view.

FIGURE 1.7
Tabbed
conversations

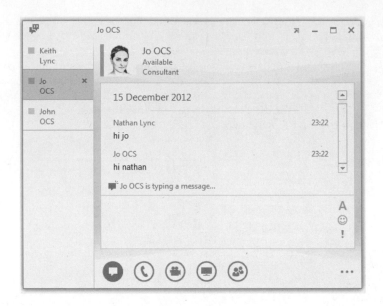

The tabbed conversation view can be very confusing at times. If you move from IM to audio modalities, the new audio window does indeed detach to form a separate "floating" window (containing the previous IM conversation), and when the audio portion is finished and the call ends, the window "pops" back into the tabbed view.

The Conversations tab provides a single location where you can keep track of ongoing communications. From this tab, it is easy to bring up previous conversations, assuming this information has been stored in Outlook (or more accurately, Exchange). Figure 1.8 shows this tab with content.

Each entry contains the history of the interaction, including all attendees and the modalities in use. Conversations can be resumed from this tab, and they will include the information from the previous conversation if it is still available. From the user's perspective, this will look like a continuation of the previous conversation.

A private line can be enabled for a user, in addition to their primary line, and is the equivalent of an incoming-only line. A user can have only a single private line, and when enabled, it is associated with the same Session Initiation Protocol (SIP) address (that is, the user does not get a second SIP address). It is an unlisted number and does not appear within any address books or Active Directory. The Private Line function provides a user with the ability to give out a number that will always get through; any Do Not Disturb or delegated-call scenarios are ignored by an incoming private line, and a different style of *toast* (the name given to the pop-up notification for any incoming communications) will appear, indicating an incoming call on the private line. In addition, a different ringtone is sounded for private line calls.

Lync 2013 provides an easy method to initiate calls on behalf of others. Once you are configured as a *delegate* for someone (as an assistant might be for a boss), additional options are provided for making calls.

FIGURE 1.8
The Conversations
tab

In the delegated-call scenario, incoming calls are displayed on the client for both the delegate and the boss, enabling the delegate to handle any call on the boss's behalf. On the incoming toast, the availability of the boss is also displayed, allowing the delegate to quickly evaluate whether to pick up the call.

When added as a delegate, the user receives a notification indicating who added them. As shown in Figure 1.9, additional groups are also created, showing who the user's delegates are as well as those for whom they act as a delegate.

When a user is designated as a delegate of someone, they can also place calls on their behalf, as shown in Figure 1.9.

Figure 1.10 shows the additional information added to the toast when a call is for someone who has delegates. If the delegate picks up the call, the toast will change to briefly show who picked up the call and an email message will be sent.

Collaboration via the Lync 2013 Client

Finally, a truly unified client!

As mentioned earlier, previous versions of the Microsoft communications platform provided a separate client targeted for group collaboration: Live Meeting. This provided an interface whereby large groups could "meet" and collaborate on shared content (desktop or documents). Also, an additional add-in client, the Conferencing Add-In for Microsoft Office Outlook, was required to provide integration with Outlook, allowing meetings to be scheduled from the Outlook client.

Since Lync 2010, both the additional Live Meeting client and the Conferencing Add-In for Outlook have been removed, simplifying not only the installation process but also the user interaction. In addition, Lync 2013 has removed the need for a separate Group Chat (now called Persistent Chat) client. All functionality from within the Live Meeting client is included in the Lync 2013 client. The single installation package includes the Online Meeting Add-In for Microsoft Lync 2013, which provides the online meeting capability previously provided via the separate installation of the Conferencing Add-In for Outlook.

In some cases, it was difficult for users to understand which client was the correct one to use to join meetings or conferences; consolidating the features into the single client removes any scope for this confusion.

The Online Meeting Add-In for Microsoft Lync 2013 (automatically installed as part of the client) provides a single-click approach to creating a meeting. The user no longer needs to decide whether a meeting will be audio only or whether it will require desktop sharing; the client dynamically adapts and provides the needed resources from the server.

Here are some other collaboration highlights:

◆ The sharing model within Lync 2013 provides a flexible approach to sharing individual applications, screens, or the full desktop as well as enabling the coediting of a document opened from SharePoint.

◆ Meetings now include a *lobby*, where users can wait to join a meeting. Previously users could only enter the conference directly or have their call dropped if the conference had not started or they were not permitted to join.

◆ Presenting PowerPoint sessions enables an Asynchronous Viewing mode, allowing other presenters to navigate through the content and review it.

◆ Media can be embedded into PowerPoint presentations and played back to participants.

◆ Dial-in conferencing supports the use of DTMF (touch-tone) commands for control of the conference as well as providing voice announcements of attendees.

◆ Users can share notes from OneNote during a meeting rather than sharing the app itself.

◆ Web-based access to conferences is provided on the platforms shown in Table 1.1.

Conference call video management has been further improved with the ability to view multiple live video streams (maximum of five) simultaneously. Previously, you could view only active speaker and previous active speaker video streams (and potentially active panorama and previous active panorama if multiple RoundTable devices were present). While this function is limited to five concurrent active streams, any additional users are moved to the "sitting" row in the video view, and these sitting users, rather than display a video stream, provide their photo view. This is also known as the "Gallery View"; see Figure 1.11 for standing and sitting row views.

TABLE 1.1: Web-based access supported by Lync Client 2013

OS	IE 10	IE 9	IE 8	FIREFOX 12.X	SAFARI 5.X	CHROME 18.X
Windows 8 (Intel based)	Yes			Yes*		Yes*
Windows 7 SP1	Yes	Yes	Yes	Yes*		Yes*
Windows Vista SP2	Yes*	Yes*	Yes*	Yes*		Yes*
Windows XP SP3			Yes*	Yes*		Yes*
Windows Server 2008 R2 SP1	Yes	Yes	Yes	Yes		Yes*
Windows Server 2008 SP2	Yes*	Yes*	Yes*	Yes*		Yes*
Mac OS X				Yes*	Yes*	Yes*

* 32-bit-only versions of the browser

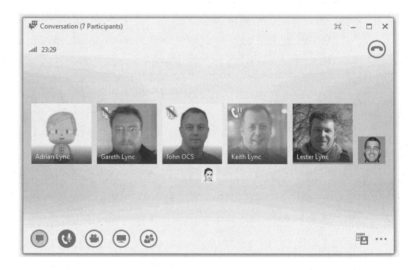

FIGURE 1.11
"Sitting" row and
"Standing" row
viewing

A specific video stream can be locked as the meeting focus for everyone in the conference call if required. This stops the video stream from bouncing from person to person in the event of strong background noise (this was often distracting with older client conference calls).

Understanding Lync Server 2013

Customer feedback played a large role in driving the changes implemented in Lync Server 2013. Some of the issues admins brought to Microsoft's attention in previous versions are listed here:

◆ There was no common store for configuration items, which could be found in Active Directory and SQL Server as well as in individual server metabases or WMI.

◆ There were no methods to validate configuration changes prior to deployment.

◆ Microsoft Management Console (MMC) was becoming complex.

◆ Automation was difficult.

◆ Deploying certificates correctly the first time was complicated.

◆ There was no "proper" support for virtualization.

◆ Multiple-site deployments required too many servers.

These issues were addressed within the Lync Server 2010 release, and further updates were made within Lync Server 2013 to address the following issues:

◆ High-availability options that were unrealistic and unnecessarily complex for multiple sites

◆ Failover from pool to pool, providing only basic voice capability

◆ Federation changes, including PIC and XMPP

◆ Archiving capability not compliant with many industry requirements

◆ Client-side virtualization

◆ Role bloat (too many roles to deploy)

◆ IPv6 support

◆ Cloud-capable/hybrid scenario support

Managing Lync Server 2013

Lync Server 2010 provided a completely new interface compared to any of the previous communications platforms, and this is continued with Lync Server 2013. Gone is the MMC interface used to navigate and manage the configuration of Live Communications Server and Office Communications Server. (Well, the MMC interface is almost gone. The new Topology Builder application is the only application to continue to use it.) Replacing it is a combination of PowerShell and a Silverlight-based Control Panel application.

Following the lead of Exchange Server and other applications, Microsoft built Lync Server 2010 on a base of PowerShell, which you can learn more about in Chapter 8, "Introduction to PowerShell, the Lync Management Shell, and Regular Expressions." When carrying out configuration requests, Lync Server's Silverlight-based Control Panel interfaces directly to PowerShell.

Lync Server 2013 also builds on the initial Lync Server 2010 introduction of role-based access control (RBAC), allowing separate disparate groups to manage separate areas of the application, such as users or telephony. Chapter 9, "Role-Based Access Control," covers the topic in detail.

TOPOLOGY BUILDER

You'll learn how to use Topology Builder in Chapter 5, "Planning Your Deployment," where we'll define the architecture and overall topology of the environment. The actual configuration of policies and implementation, however, is carried out using either PowerShell or the Control Panel application (in some cases, configuration items are available only in PowerShell). As you'll see, Topology Builder provides the first checkpoint for the topology and ensures configuration consistency; it will not allow configuration items to be removed if they are still in use.

The Topology Builder also consolidates all the information required for generating a certificate. It ensures that any additional subject alternative name (SAN) entries are included as required, ensuring that when the Setup program for a server gets to the Certificate Wizard, all the information is already in place. Additional user input and control over the certificate template used is provided using this wizard. The Edge server consolidates the external facing requirements from three separate certificates in previous versions to a single external certificate.

CENTRAL MANAGEMENT STORE

The multiple configuration stores from previous versions have been replaced with the *Central Management Store*. It is the sole location for all the configuration data for the deployment and operation of Lync Server 2013. Combining all the various configuration stores into a single Central Management Store means there is only a single point of failure, which is this database. Replicating this database to all servers in the environment results in the following benefits:

◆ Mitigates the single point of failure

◆ Allows servers to continue operating without access to Active Directory

◆ Removes reliance on Active Directory schema changes

◆ Provides consistency in server configuration (especially the Edge server)

The Central Management Store is stored within SQL Server (in a Standard Edition deployment, this is SQL Express) and can be made highly available by the use of SQL mirroring.

The Central Management Store operates in a master/replica state. In the event of a catastrophic loss of the Central Management Store, a replica can be promoted to be the master database. During an outage of the master database, no changes can be made to the environment; however, Lync Server 2013 will continue to operate based on the configuration at the time of loss (this also includes server restarts).

CENTRAL MANAGEMENT STORE REPLICAS

During a server-role installation, local instances of SQL Express are installed, and the Central Management Store is replicated to this database. The instances are called RTCLOCAL and LYNCLOCAL. This occurs on all server roles installed, including the Edge server.

Some companies are wary about proliferating SQL Express throughout the environment, mostly in the wake of the SQL Slammer virus and similar attacks. (In January 2003, the SQL Slammer virus impacted over 75,000 systems within 10 minutes, causing a large denial of service and Internet slowdown.)

By introducing these additional databases—RTCLOCAL was introduced with Lync Server 2010—Lync Server 2013 gives the admin more to manage and patch (if required). In addition, because the configuration information is replicated to the perimeter network on the Edge servers, availability of the configuration is at greater risk if the Edge servers are compromised.

The advantages provided by the local database replication, as well as the measures taken to protect them (e.g., encryption), outweigh the risks involved in most cases.

Many large financial service companies have already deployed Lync Server 2013 Edge servers. If there were significant risk of compromise, they'd be the first to provide feedback!

LYNC STORAGE SERVICE

The Lync Storage Service (LYSS) provides an abstract storage framework allowing Lync Server 2013 to access storage systems within other applications. Currently the other applications are limited to Microsoft SQL Server and Microsoft Exchange 2013 (via Exchange Web Services). Aside from the Lync databases, it is used for Exchange 2013 archiving integration and the Unified Contact Store.

WINDOWS FABRIC

Another underlying infrastructure change is the implementation of the Windows Fabric system. This provides a background enablement function that places users within a pool. This feature was introduced with Lync Server 2013 and is responsible for defining the user accounts' primary, secondary, and tertiary home server locations.

LYSS uses Windows Fabric for replication.

As a result of the Windows Fabric replication, additional requirements are need to ensure full capability within a Front End pool. The number of servers required to be functional in a pool for the pool to be functional is shown in Table 1.2.

TABLE 1.2:   Servers required in a pool for full functionality

TOTAL SERVERS IN THE POOL	MINIMUM REQUIRED FOR FULL FUNCTIONALITY
1 or 2	1
3 or 4	2
5 or 6	3
7 or 8	4
9 or 10	5
11 or 12	6

What happens if the number of available servers drops below the minimum listed here? Well, the pool goes into survivability mode, and if after 5 minutes the pool is still in survivability mode, it will shut down all Lync services. See `http://technet.microsoft.com/en-us/library/gg412996.aspx` for more information.

DNS LOAD BALANCING

Lync Server 2010 introduced DNS load balancing as a method to provide connection-based resilience to both client and server interactions. DNS load balancing provides functionality only for SIP-based traffic.

Using DNS load balancing reduces the configuration requirements of a hardware load balancer (at the cost of creating a few additional DNS entries), allowing the hardware load balancer to focus on load balancing HTTP traffic (a job for which it is much better suited).

For example, Table 1.3 shows the configuration required when using hardware to load balance a pool of three Front End servers.

TABLE 1.3:   DNS records required when using hardware load balancing

ITEM	DNS FQDN	DNS A RECORD
Pool VIP	Lyncpool.company.com	192.168.0.1
Front End	FE1.company.com	192.168.0.2
Front End	FE2.company.com	192.168.0.3
Front End	FE3.company.com	192.168.0.4

Table 1.4 shows the configuration required when using DNS load balancing on the same pool of three Front End servers.

TABLE 1.4:   DNS records required when using DNS load balancing

ITEM	DNS FQDN	DNS A RECORD
Web VIP	Lyncweb.company.com	192.168.0.1
Pool	Lyncpool.company.com	192.168.0.2
Pool	Lyncpool.company.com	192.168.0.3
Pool	Lyncpool.company.com	192.168.0.4
Front End	FE1.company.com	192.168.0.2
Front End	FE2.company.com	192.168.0.3
Front End	FE3.company.com	192.168.0.4

Figure 1.12 diagrams the process through which a client will connect when using DNS load balancing. It is important to note that this is only for the first connection; once connected, the client will cache the server name and IP address for subsequent connections.

FIGURE 1.12

The client connection process

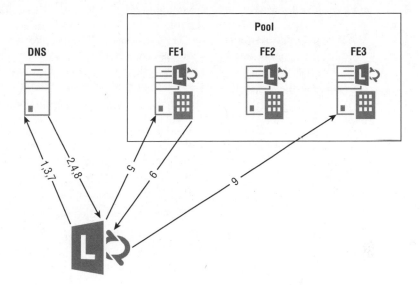

The following steps correspond to the numbered links in Figure 1.12 and describe the actions within each communications step:

1. The client queries DNS for the service record (SRV). (A service that was published using the Domain Name System [DNS] can be discovered through its SRV record. Its SRV record includes information such as protocol, port, priority, and weight in the single record entry.)

2. The DNS server returns the SRV record pointing to the pool fully qualified domain name (FQDN).

3. The client queries DNS for the pool FQDN.

4. The DNS server returns the IP addresses of pool members.

5. The client connects to a randomly selected IP address from the list returned by the DNS server.

6. If this server is not the home server for the client, the server returns the home server name.

7. The client queries DNS for the address of the home server.

8. DNS returns the IP address of the home server.

9. The client connects to the server and registers the user.

INSTALLABLE SERVER ROLES

Lync Server 2013 introduces the Persistent Chat server role, but more importantly it restructures and consolidates the existing roles, allowing organizations to consolidate resources by combining various roles onto a single server deployment. Chapter 6, "Installation," covers the steps required to define and install each role.

Office Communications Server 2007 introduced the concept of an *expanded topology*, whereby a single pool could be separated into its constituent parts: web services, conferencing, and Front Ends. The move to a 64-bit deployment with Office Communications Server 2007 R2 allowed this topology to disappear (it was still supported, although not recommended) due to the capability of the 64-bit hardware to address more memory resources and make them available to the application.

Lync Server 2010 provided the capability to do either, depending on the deployment needs. When the user count was greater than 10,000 in a pool, Microsoft recommended separation of the Audio/Video Conferencing Multipoint Control Unit (MCU) to a separate server/pool.

Lync Server 2013 has once again removed this separation of resources and supports only the consolidated model.

Virtualization is now fully supported for all server roles (except the Survivable Branch Appliance), and more detail is provided in Chapter 5.

The following server roles are provided in Lync Server 2013:

- Front End
- Back End
- Edge
- Director
- Mediation
- Persistent Chat
- Survivable Branch Appliance
- Survivable Branch Server

The next sections describe these roles in detail.

Front End

The Front End server provides the connection point for the client. It is responsible for all registration, via the Registrar service, and routing requests for clients. Because of this routing responsibility, all clients belonging to the same user must register on the same Front End server. In addition, the Front End server holds all the conference MCUs:

- Web
- App sharing
- IM
- Audio/video (unless separated)

The Front End server is also home to the Web component services, such as Address Book, Group Expansion, Control Panel, and Reach, the Silverlight application that provides web-based access to conferences.

High availability is achieved by the deployment of multiple (up to 12) Front End servers into a single pool and the utilization of hardware (with or without DNS) load balancing.

Back End

The Back End role is the SQL Server database, which provides both conference capability and contact/buddy lists. In deployments that also configure the built-in voice applications (Response Group Service, Call Park, and Dial-In Conferencing), their data is also stored within this SQL Server database. The Central Management Store is also stored in the Back End role.

High availability is achieved by deploying SQL Server in a log shipping configuration, with an optional Witness server. The advantage of the Witness server is that it will allow for automatic failover, whereas it's a manual process without the Witness.

STANDARD EDITION SERVER

The Standard Edition server combines both the Front End and Back End roles into a single package. In this scenario only, the Back End role is stored within a SQL Express database. High availability is not possible with Standard Edition. However, two Standard Edition pools can act as backups for each other.

Edge

The Edge role is deployed within the perimeter network and provides remote capability to Lync Server 2013. Remote capability is defined as follows:

◆ Remote access

◆ Federation with other organizations

◆ Public Internet Connectivity (PIC) federation with Windows Live, Yahoo!, AOL, Skype, and XMPP gateways (such as Google's gTalk). In addition, the Edge server provides a method to reroute calls via the Internet if insufficient internal bandwidth is available. In this case, an Edge server (or pool) is required at each location.

Multiple Edge servers may also be deployed to localize Internet conference traffic. For this purpose, each Edge server (or pool) is associated with an internal Front End pool, and users homed on the Front End pool use their locally defined Edge server for all traffic except SIP. SIP traffic (including federation) will travel only via a single Edge location.

High availability of the Edge environment is achieved with the deployment of multiple Edge servers in a single location. High availability of the federation functionality (including PIC) requires the use of a hardware load balancer and is only available in a single location.

Lync Server 2013 includes the ability to communicate with Extensible Messaging and Presence Protocol (XMPP) gateways natively. Previously this was enabled via a separate download and separate server instance. XMPP is used by systems such as Google Talk.

PIC FEDERATION

As this book is going to press, Microsoft has announced plans to enable federation with Skype and also that the Windows Live Messenger/MSN Messenger federation will be discontinued as that service moves to Skype.

The PIC support agreement between Microsoft and Yahoo! Messenger is also coming to an end, and at this time there is no indication this will be renewed. Service will continue until at least June 2013, but the exact date is yet to be determined.

Other services are expected to continue to provide federation as they are today.

Director

The Director role performs authentication and is recommended when you are also deploying an Edge server. You should use the Director role to perform authentication when you are deploying an Edge server. The Director role provides a stop-off point for all external traffic. By placing this function at the first point of authentication, you ensure that all (any) malicious traffic is intercepted here rather than at a Front End (where internal clients may be impacted). When an Edge server is used, the Director server is configured as the next hop and proxies the external traffic to its final destination. Figure 1.13 shows a typical Director placement.

FIGURE 1.13
Typical Director
architecture

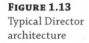 **Real World Scenario**

AUTHENTICATION MODES

Like previous versions of the platform, Lync Server 2013 supports both NT LAN Manager (NTLM) and Kerberos authentication modes. Traditionally, Kerberos was the preferred authentication method for internal client connections, and NTLM was used for external (remote user) access because the client could not receive a Kerberos ticket when it wasn't connected to the domain.

Lync Server 2013 allows clients to log in without access to Active Directory, so NTLM or Kerberos authentication is not required. Instead, a certificate is downloaded to the client upon first successful login (via either NTLM or Kerberos, so those tools are still required).

This certificate is provided by the web services component of the Front End server. By default, it is valid for 180 days, but the time is configurable. The certificate is valid only for sign-in to Lync Server 2013.

A copy of the certificate is shown here. As you can see, the certificate is issued by Communications Server, and further investigation will show it can be used only for client authentication.

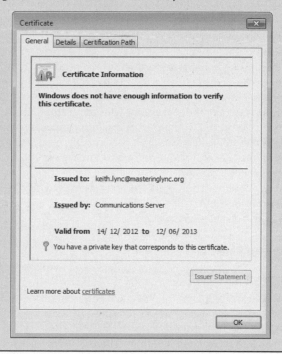

When used for internal traffic, the Director is defined as the result of the DNS SRV query for automatic login and, in this scenario, will redirect traffic to the correct home pool. With the additional support for multiple DNS SRV records, this requirement is redundant within the internal infrastructure.

Unlike the Office Communications Server versions, Lync Server 2013 makes the Director a defined role, not a normal pool with its features disabled.

High availability of the Director role is provided by deploying multiple servers and using DNS (or hardware) load balancing.

Mediation

The Mediation role is the interface into the public switched telephone network (PSTN). Typically, it is used in conjunction with a media gateway device, allowing an interface either into an existing PBX (private branch exchange) or directly to the PSTN. The latter configuration, known as *SIP trunking*, is now becoming more prevalent; it allows the Mediation server to connect directly to the PBX or PSTN without the need for an additional hardware media gateway device.

With previous versions of the Communications Server platform, the Mediation server was used to transcode the codec used internally (typically, RTAudio) into the codec used by the media gateway, whether it was PBX or PSTN (typically, G711). Lync 2010 introduced the concept of *media bypass*, whereby the client can communicate using G711 directly to the media gateway or PBX, alleviating the need for the transcoding to occur and thus removing the need for transcoding by the Mediation role. Media bypass to the PSTN is not possible because there is no termination point to which the client can connect.

By removing (or at worst reducing) the need for transcoding on the Mediation role, media bypass reduces the tasks carried out by this role, which means that less-powerful hardware can be used to run this role. This, in turn, allows for colocation of the Mediation role with a Front End role, reducing the server footprint required.

Office Communications Server 2007 (both versions) had a one-to-one ratio of Mediation servers to media gateways; Lync Server 2010 removed this requirement and supports a many-to-many ratio. Also, introduced with Lync Server 2013 is the concept of *trunks*. These allow for additional configuration to be applied to calls traversing the trunk.

High availability of the Mediation role is provided by deployment of multiple servers. Certain configuration options may perform better with or even require the hardware load balancing.

Persistent Chat

Persistent Chat functionality previously was available via a separate download and was called Group Chat.

Lync Server 2013 incorporates this functionality directly into the client as well as providing a fully fledged role deployed via Topology Builder.

Persistent Chat provides chat room, or channel, capability where the content is not lost after a user has logged out and is retained indefinitely. It also provides a searchable resource to users.

A maximum of four active Persistent Chat servers can be deployed for high availability and load sharing. Channels will be instantiated on a single server initially, and when the load of users trying to connect becomes large enough, the channel will then be created on another server. New clients will be directed to the channel on the new server by the lookup service. This process will continue until the channel is created on all available servers.

Data submitted to a channel is broadcast to all other subscribing servers and then broadcast back to listening clients while at the same time the data is written back to the SQL database for future queries.

Survivable Branch Appliance

The Survivable Branch Appliance (SBA) is a hardware device provided by one of five hardware vendors (all support for these devices is provided by the hardware vendor directly):

◆ Audiocodes

◆ Dialogic

- ◆ Ferrari

- ◆ HP

- ◆ NET

The SBA is an all-in-one device that provides some of the functionality of a pool (specifically, registrar and routing) as well as having a colocated Mediation role and media gateway. The function of this device is to continue to provide local service to users in the event of a wide area network (WAN) or pool outage in the central location.

Users are provided local calling functionality via the device, but they rely on a central pool for conference and contact/buddy list information. In the event of a WAN or pool outage, the local PSTN breakout will continue to operate, allowing both incoming and outgoing calls. However, contact/buddy list information and access to conferencing will be unavailable, and the client will go into *Survivable mode*. Figure 1.14 shows the client feedback when in Survivable mode, and as with OCS 2007 R2, any calls currently in progress will continue. Upon restoration of the failed service (network or server), the client will return to normal operations automatically.

FIGURE 1.14
The client display in
Survivable mode

A Survivable Branch Appliance may only be a primary registrar and must be configured with a backup central pool.

High availability is provided by the backup central pool.

Survivable Branch Server

The Survivable Branch Server provides similar functionality to a Survivable Branch Appliance, except that it includes no media gateway. This option is typically used in locations that already have a media gateway deployed, such as, for example, where OCS 2007 was previously deployed and the cost of replacement cannot be justified.

Like a Survivable Branch Appliance, the Survivable Branch Server may only be a primary registrar and must be configured with a backup central pool.

High availability is provided by the backup central pool.

Monitoring and Archiving

Monitoring and Archiving are no longer separate roles; rather, they are incorporated into the Front End role. In essence, they have been reduced to a feature. The Monitoring feature provides the capability to capture both Quality of Experience and Call Detail Record information objects about all the calls in the environment.

This information is stored in a SQL Server database and evaluated using the provided SQL Reporting Services report pack, which contains almost 50 built-in reports. Additional reports may be created using SQL Reporting Services Report Builder.

The Archiving role provides a capture of all IM traffic and records any file transfers (filename and location, not content) occurring in the environment.

This information, like that captured by the Monitoring role, is stored within a SQL Server database. However, it should be noted that there are no additional compliance checks on this database; it is a store only.

High availability is provided through the use of an Enterprise pool, with multiple Front End servers, and a SQL database configured for high availability using SQL mirroring.

For those organizations with stricter compliance needs, or those that want archiving of all products to be centralized in one location, Archiving can be enabled to use the archiving capabilities built in to Exchange 2013, such as Legal Hold and Compliance Search.

Office Web Applications Server

The Office Web Applications (OWA) server (not to be confused with Outlook Web Access) is used to enhance presentation capability with Lync Server 2013. It is not a part of the Lync Server 2013 media and is not a required role. However, some functionality is available only if it is present (such as video streaming in PowerPoint).

It has separate installation (as well as licensing) requirements, and the detailed installation is out of scope of this book; we do cover how to configure Lync Server 2013 to leverage it, though, in Chapter 6!

Colocation

With previous versions of the Microsoft Unified Communications platform, there were significant limitations on what can be colocated. Table 1.5 calls out the permitted colocation options for Lync Server 2013.

Archiving and Monitoring have not been specifically called out here because, unlike with previous versions, they can no longer be installed as stand-alone servers; their database instances can, of course.

TABLE 1.5: Supported Lync Server 2013 colocation deployments

SERVER ROLE	COLOCATED ROLES	NOTES
Enterprise Edition Front End	Mediation	
Back End database of Front End pool	Database for Persistent Chat Database instance for Archiving Database instance for Monitoring	
Mediation	None	The Mediation server may be colocated with the Front End pool.
Director	None	
Edge	None	
Survivable Branch Appliance	Mediation Media Gateway	
Survivable Branch Server	Mediation	No gateway is included in a Survivable Branch Server.
Persistent Chat Server	Standard Edition server	The Persistent Chat server still requires a separate SQL server installation. This is not a recommended configuration for production environments but is suitable for testing.
Trusted Application servers	None	
Exchange Unified Messaging	None	Exchange Server roles may be colocated with each other but not with Lync Server 2013 roles.
Reverse proxy	None	Reverse proxy may be colocated with other server applications as detailed in the reverse proxy support guidelines; however, no Lync Server 2013 roles may be colocated.

AUTOMATION CAPABILITIES

Lync Server 2013 is built from the ground up on PowerShell. This architecture provides significantly easier scripting and automation capability than Office Communications Server and Live Communications Server, which relied on Windows Management Instrumentation (WMI) for most (but not all) configuration options. You can find more information about the use of PowerShell for Lync 2013 in Chapter 8.

HYBRID AND CLOUD SCENARIOS

Lync Server 2013 will enable hybrid scenarios where some infrastructure is located in the cloud and some infrastructure is located on the customer premises. This is enabled by supporting a split-domain model, whereby the same domain can be shared between two Lync organizations.

As this book goes to press, this functionality is still in beta, and we have covered it in more depth in Chapter 18, "Hybrid Deployments," which includes information received during the early beta process.

Lync clouds scenarios are further expanded with upgraded capability with regard to administration and reporting. This capability comes as a result of the improved tenant management and differentiation. Aside from cloud interaction, administrators of hosting providers will see this enhanced capability within the hosting pack when it is released (due mid 2013).

Understanding the Voice Capabilities

Since the release of Office Communications Server 2007 back in October 2007, Microsoft has been relentlessly developing and pushing the voice capabilities of OCS. Lync Server 2013 takes them to the next level and in most cases fills the gaps from previous versions.

There are still areas in which Lync Server 2013 does not completely address the functionality provided by a traditional PBX. Many of these functions, however, are being made redundant as people move to new ways of communication. One example is ringback. On a PBX, if you call a number and it is busy, you can enter a DTMF code to tell the PBX to call you back when the line becomes free. It can be argued that the use of presence information in OCS/Lync 2013 removes this requirement (if the *callee* is busy initially, the call will not be placed) and provides the capability to notify of presence changes.

The focus points for Lync Server 2013 voice capabilities are as follows:

Resiliency Lync Server 2010 introduced the concept of a backup registrar and also increased the scope of the multidatacenter (Metropolitan) pool scenario supported to include all modalities. Lync Server 2013 expands the resiliency options further by increasing the backup registrar functionality to be more than simply registrar backup but is capable of providing significantly more redundancy.

The Metropolitan pool scenario—single pool stretched between two data centers—is no longer a supported model under Lync Server 2013.

The backup registrar continues to provide telephony functionality in the event of a failure to the primary registrar. The Lync 2013 client will register to the primary registrar when available; however, in the event that either the network connection to the primary registrar or the registrar itself fails, the client (following a configurable time-out) will register to the backup registrar and enter Survivable mode. As mentioned previously, this mode provides only telephony functionality and limited search capability for other users; all centralized services are lost, including conferencing, contact/buddy lists, and voice applications.

Any pool type (Enterprise or Standard) can act as a backup registrar to only a pool of same type (Enterprise or Standard) as well as to a Survivable Branch Appliance (or Server). The Survivable Branch Appliance (or Server) can be designated only as a primary registrar. When you are configuring backup registrars, you need to consider the server specification and overall capacity of the backup registrar, taking into account a potential failure of the primary registrar and the total number of users who could then be homed in on the backup registrar.

In addition to the backup registrar, Lync Server 2013 includes the capability to pair pools. This provides increased functionality in the case of a failure. With the backup registrar, only telephony voice capability was provided; however, with paired pools, significantly more functionality is available, such as conferencing and presence.

Call Admission Control   Call Admission Control (CAC) is the capability to manage the number of Lync 2013 calls being placed on the network at any time. It is covered in detail in Chapter 14, "Call Admission Control."

Call Park   Call Park is the capability to place a call into a parked location for pickup (typically by another person) on another device or even location. Call Park is frequently used in conjunction with paging systems. A call will be received by an operator and put into an *orbit*. Then a notification will go out on the paging system/intercom; the callee can then retrieve the call from orbit simply by dialing the orbit number. Hospitals and manufacturing plants typically use this feature; everyone has heard something like "Call for Dr. Smith on 1234."

Media bypass   The introduction of media bypass in Lync Server 2010 (and client) reduces the role of the Mediation server, which is no longer involved in the transcoding of the codecs, because both the client and the gateway are talking to each other with a common codec (typically, G711). As mentioned, removing this transcoding requirement from the mediation role also means there no longer needs to be one Mediation server per media gateway, allowing a single mediation role to support and control multiple media gateways.

Removing the extra hop of a Mediation server has the side benefit of improving voice quality (because the media traffic has a shorter path to travel) and also removes another potential point of failure.

Enhanced 9-1-1   Enhanced 9-1-1 is the provision of location-based information when calling emergency services within North America. E9-1-1 is covered in detail in Chapter 15, "E9-1-1 and Location Information Services (LIS)."

Analog device management   Although Lync Server 2013 does not directly support and manage analog devices themselves, it does control the signaling information and, as such, can provide controls to restrict the class of service to which the devices have access (for example, you can choose not to permit international dialing and you can place similar restrictions). The device is connected to the environment via a media gateway using an analog terminal adapter (ATA), and Lync Server 2013 does not interfere in the media stream, only the signaling. Not being involved in the media stream allows fax machines to also benefit from this management.

Call detail records can be captured for all these analog devices because the signaling is controlled from the Lync Server 2013 servers.

Private Line   As mentioned previously, the Private Line functionality is a means to assign a second number to a user. Incoming calls to this Private Line number do not follow any delegation rules (or other routing options, such as Do Not Disturb or Call Forward) and will always go through to the recipient. This function is for incoming calls only. The incoming toast, which has a different ringtone associated with it, can be seen in Figure 1.15.

FIGURE 1.15
Private line toast

Routing changes   Lync Server 2013 makes significant changes to the number normalization and outgoing caller ID capability from OCS 2007 R2. Outbound normalization is now possible and can be defined centrally on a per-route (or per-gateway) basis; this allows simplified administration of the media gateways, especially in a global deployment where, perhaps, the same media gateway model (or indeed manufacturer) cannot be used in every country.

Caller ID can be managed on a per-user or per-group basis to suppress or alter the calling party number data presented. This feature is automatically overridden for the simultaneous-ringing scenario, where when the call is forwarded to a mobile device, you want to present the originator number.

Common area phones   *Common area phones* are Lync 2013 Phone Edition devices that are deployed in a communal area such as a lobby. Figure 1.16 shows a Polycom common area phone.

FIGURE 1.16
Polycom CX500
common area phone

Lync Server 2013 provides the capability to manage these devices, even though they are not associated with a user and no one is logged onto them.

The ability to control the functions of these common devices ensures that they cannot be misused (e.g., by placing international calls).

In addition to these functionality changes, the portfolio of devices has been significantly increased, with additional device partners on both the end user and media gateway sides.

A number of additional certification programs have been launched for each of these areas, and all can be found under this URL:

http://technet.microsoft.com/en-us/lync/gg236602

Open Interoperability Program   The Open Interoperability Program is an interoperability testing and certification program not managed by Microsoft. Any devices (not limited to user devices, but also gateways and services such as SIP trunks) qualified through this program are fully supported for interoperability with Lync Server 2013.

Optimized for Lync 2013   The Optimized For program ensures that devices "just work" on installation—meaning there is no user configuration required; they simply need to be plugged in—and provide high-quality audio/video user experience. These devices are built and tested following the Lync 2013 specifications, and they are created by global partners at the Certified or Gold Certified level.

Other Compatible IP Phones   This program is designed for IP phones based on the publicly available Windows protocols and the Microsoft Office protocols documentation. As with the Optimized For program, they are created by global Certified or Gold Certified partners.

Software and hardware load balancers   These applications and appliances are tested by the vendor and reviewed by Microsoft to meet Lync Server 2013 requirements.

Understanding the Unified Communications Managed API Capabilities

The Microsoft approach to unified communications is to remove the islands of legacy technology—the voicemail solution that doesn't integrate with the switchboard solution, and so on—to provide one identity and one mailbox from which all capabilities can be taken.

Microsoft provides the familiarity of both the platform and the infrastructure to build new applications, ensuring that they can fully integrate across the environment.

Lync Server 2013 adds a (Representational State Transfer) REST-ful API and provides extensibility and interoperability by building on the two pillars of development:

◆   .NET

◆   Web services

By building on the Lync Server 2013 infrastructure, developers know they already have an enterprise-class platform; by using the .NET framework and the Web services layer, they have an easily extensible foundation, which can be developed using skills they already have.

Lync Server 2013 allows the creation of presence-aware (known as *Communications-Enabled Business Process*, or *CEBP*) applications; this allows the applications to react and make decisions based on the presence of users in the environment, providing notifications or alerts as needed and in the modality required.

Presence can be embedded in already developed applications, or the Lync 2013 client can be expanded to include the conversation window to show rich context on both sides of the conversation.

Unwrapping the SDK

The Lync Server 2013 software development kit (SDK) allows four scenarios for which developers might need to customize a deployment:

◆ To integrate with existing line-of-business applications

◆ To provide contextual conversations

◆ To add custom applications to the client

◆ To completely customize the client UI

Developers can utilize the Visual Studio Windows Presentation Foundation and Silverlight controls to quickly add Lync 2013 functionality (drag-and-drop controls) into internal applications; this can include functionality such as docking the conversation windows within the application itself.

Deploying the Lync 2013 client and (hopefully!) using it as the main collaboration toolset doesn't mean you're stuck with the feature set provided. *Application launch links* can be sent within conversations, allowing data to be shared in third-party applications; you can see this in the continuation of subject and priority messages started from Outlook. These links also enable developers to extend the menu functionality of both contact cards and the client itself.

An important point with application launch links is that no code is registered on the receiver side; the client simply calls out to existing installed applications. A current example of this functionality is sending of hyperlinks, where clicking the link does nothing other than open the web browser with the address listed in the link; no additional code is executed.

Even scenarios where the client is completely customized are supported; the Lync 2013 controls can be retemplated in Expression Blend.

It should be noted that the Lync 2013 client is still required to be installed in all of these scenarios (with the exception of the web services development); however, it is possible to run the client in UISuppressionMode, whereby only the features from the customized user interface (UI) are presented to a user and all the interaction is behind the scenes.

Further investigation into the customization and development of applications is beyond the scope of this book. See *Professional Unified Communications Development with Microsoft Lync Server 2010* by George Durzi and Michael Greenlee (Wiley, 2011) for more information about developing custom applications.

The Bottom Line

Describe the features of the client.   The Lync 2013 client is designed to achieve three core goals: connect, communicate, and collaborate. This new client makes it is much easier to find people and verify identity, initiate communications (typically, with a single click), and collaborate with full-blown information sharing. Device integration and call management have been greatly simplified, removing the need to run through wizards constantly.

Master It   You are assembling a new product-development team. The new product will be similar to a previously released product, and you want to ask members of the previous team for guidance. How can you find people associated with the previous product team?

Describe the features of the server.   Lync Server 2013 provides most of the server roles included in Office Communications Server and introduces the Survivable Branch Appliance (or Server) to help in the high-availability scenarios. The management approach has changed through the introduction of the Topology Builder application and role-based access control to limit administrative access to defined users and scopes as required. PowerShell and Silverlight combine to provide the day-to-day administration of the environment.

Master It   When deploying high availability, which of the following roles can be a primary registrar?

- ◆   Director

- ◆   Enterprise Edition Front End

- ◆   Standard Edition Front End

- ◆   Survivable Branch Appliance

- ◆   Survivable Branch Server

Describe the voice features.   Significant investment and development have gone into Lync Server 2013's voice feature set. The new set has allowed it to become a match for a large portion of the PBX workload and, in many cases, a viable replacement for a PBX.

New functions (such as Private Line, Call Admission Control, Call Park, E911, and Common Area Phones) provide welcome additions to the user experience. By contrast, behind-the-scenes features (such as Media Bypass, routing improvements, resiliency improvements, and analog device management) provide a more integrated and available solution for the administrator while they help reduce the number of servers required.

Master It   As the network and telephony administrator for your company, you want to invest in SIP trunks rather than legacy PBX-style PSTN connectivity using media gateways.

How should you configure media bypass and deploy mediation servers?

Chapter 2

Standards and Protocols

Any platform that needs to interoperate with other platforms will rely on standards, and a communications platform is no different in that respect. As with previous versions, Lync Server 2013 uses the Session Initiation Protocol (SIP) standard to provide its backbone, and it builds on that backbone by extending SIP to accommodate additional functionality.

Regardless of whether communication is conducted via the public telephone network using voice or via the Internet with other instant messaging products, you need to know the limitations of the protocols used and understand where interface gateways will be needed to extend beyond the edges of the Lync Server 2013 infrastructure. (Communication may include other organizations running Lync Server 2013 and using federation.)

This chapter introduces the history behind the signaling that led to the introduction of SIP. While the protocol itself is interesting, understanding the background network infrastructure will help you design and troubleshoot Lync Server 2013.

In this chapter, you will learn to:

◆ Understand the basics of SIP for signaling

◆ Understand how SIP has been extended to provide additional functionality for Lync Server 2013

◆ Identify additional protocols used by Lync Server 2013

Understanding SIP's Origins

Before the Internet (yes, there was a time when there was no Internet), the only real-time communication was via the public telephone network. This network was extremely easy to use (pick up the phone and dial) and highly reliable, and communications were understandable at both ends (it was just talk). The system was based on a circuit-switched network.

Circuit-Switched Networks

At some time in their youth, most people have played with a tin-cans-on-a-string communications system (see Figure 2.1). The tin-can system essentially is a basic, circuit-switched network. It's extremely basic because there is only a single circuit—and even adding one more user requires significant investment because two additional lines are needed so that everyone can talk to each other. With this type of system, complex signaling isn't needed. Each endpoint is connected to only one other endpoint; therefore, when one endpoint is picked up, the users immediately know where the communication is going.

FIGURE 2.1
A primitive commu-
nication system

FIGURE 2.1
A primitive commu-
nication system

Adding a third person would require two more lines (one for each existing endpoint); adding a fourth person would require three additional lines; a fifth, four more lines; and so on. With this system, any individual must have the number of lines coming to them equivalent to the total number of people in the system minus one. This type of basic system can very quickly become unmanageable.

The solution to this management nightmare was the *switch*. All endpoints terminated at the switch (in a star or hub-and-spoke topology), and it is the responsibility of the switch to determine (or *route*) the call from one endpoint to another. In the early telephony days, the routing was performed by a human switchboard operator who physically connected the two endpoints with a patch cable. Figure 2.2 depicts a manual switchboard.

FIGURE 2.2
A manual
switchboard

As technology improved and automation became more prevalent, the endpoints acquired dialing capability and were allocated unique identifiers (extension numbers). A termination endpoint could be signaled simply by dialing the extension number.

Building up to today's larger, modern telephony infrastructure, these switches were connected to each other (they were beginning to be known as *exchanges*), and this allowed for a wider distribution of calls.

Each exchange was allocated a routing number. When the routing number of the exchange was dialed, followed by the extension of the endpoint, a call could be routed from one location to another. Of course, in the early days, this was achieved by calling and asking the operator to perform the routing manually.

In the rudimentary example shown in Figure 2.3, if you are using Extn 100, connected to Switch 1, you dial only the extension number to reach another internal (connected to the same switch) extension number. However, simply dialing the extension number will not work when you need to reach an extension at another location (switch)—especially when the extensions are duplicates of local extensions—because you will be connected to the local extension on the same switch.

FIGURE 2.3
Endpoint and
switches

This is where the routing number comes into play. To connect to Switch 5, Extension 101, for example, you could dial 5101. You need to ensure that there is no numerical overlap as there could be when you are dialing to Switch 1. This is where the concept of dialing a specific number (typically, 9 or 0) for an "outside line" comes into play. When the switch sees this outside line number first, it knows to route the following digits away from the internal extensions.

This concept of endpoint/exchange numbering and routing has expanded to include national and international routing as well, and it has led to the national and international numbering plans that are so familiar to everyone making telephone calls today.

PROS AND CONS OF CIRCUIT SWITCHING

Circuit switching is so called because to establish a connection from one point to the other, a *circuit* is created, which is in effect a dedicated connection between endpoints—think back to our piece of string between the two cans.

Once this *circuit* has been established, the system is very fast. There are no more decisions to be made or content to be inspected; the call is simply forwarded to the destination (or, on a switch basis, to the next interface).

This dedicated path is perfect for analog transmissions because there is no (or, more accurately, an extremely small) delay between the sending and receiving of the signal. However, there is a delay with the establishment of the path before any transmission can occur.

Once the path is in place, it will stay in use until closed down, even if transmission has stopped. This results in wasted capacity, and although it has not had a big impact in voice transmissions, it has much bigger implications when the move is made to digital transmissions where speed of transmission is much greater than the speed of interpretation, resulting in idle time on the transmission path.

CIRCUIT-SWITCHED SIGNALING

Outside of the tin-cans-on-a-string scenario, signaling information needs to be provided along with a call. As you can see from Figure 2.4, any transmission type is built of at least two parts, signaling and data (there may be more than one data channel).

FIGURE 2.4
Separation of
signaling and media

In the basic scenario, this signaling will establish the call in the first place and then stop it when it's finished. More advanced signaling provides additional features, such as placing the call on hold or transferring the call to another endpoint. For these more advanced features to work, the signaling needs to be parallel to the actual transmission—you couldn't put a call on hold if you had to hang up first!

Early signaling simply completed an electrical current when the receiver was picked up. The operator saw a light being lit on the switchboard and connected to that endpoint; once the operator understood the target, they used a patch cable to connect the caller to the called party. Although manual switchboards were still around into the eighties, they obviously made way for automated switching systems.

Frequency Division Multiplexing (FDM) allowed multiple calls to be provisioned across a single wire connection, but it also required a new method of signaling. The solution to this was *in-band* signaling, using the same connection for both the signaling and the data transmission.

FDM is extremely expensive to operate, requiring the use of analog filters tuned to specific frequencies to allow continued operations.

DIGITAL TRANSMISSION

With the advent of digital transmission in the early sixties, signaling needed to evolve even more. Digital signals comprise discrete 0s and 1s (represented in the system as changes of voltage), whereas analog signals are acoustic and must be translated to digital for transmission and then translated back to analog—sound—at the receiving end to be heard. Many different *codecs* (coder-decoders) are available to do this. Modems (modulator-demodulators) were used to connect to the early Internet; they provided a service similar to codecs except in reverse, converting the digital computer signal to an analog signal suitable for transmission on the telephone network. In actual effect, the telephone network was converting the message back to digital for transmission.

PROS AND CONS OF DIGITAL TRANSMISSIONS

The first advantage to digital transmission is that digital equipment is extremely cheap (relatively speaking) because it uses computers rather than the electromechanical valves in analog switching, resulting in less required maintenance.

Second, quality is much higher with digital transmission. The data is either a 1 or a 0; there are no "in-between" values, and any corrective measure required in a digital signal results in retransmission (newer digital protocols include built-in error correction mechanisms). To have digital data travel farther, it is repeated; conversely, to have analog data transmitted farther, it is amplified. Amplification will increase the signal strength, which will also include any interference (or noise). Repetition will simply repeat the clean signal, meaning it is effectively a new signal.

Of course, there are also downsides to digital. The signal must be processed, resulting in a delay while the transformation takes place. Naturally, this occurs twice—once at each end.

Additionally, delays are introduced through the switching and signaling mechanisms. Typically, for voice transmissions, a delay higher than 250 milliseconds (ms) round trip will make it difficult to follow a conversation. Individually, delays are likely to be negligible, but in a badly designed network with multiple congested hops, they will be major factors.

DIGITAL SIGNALING

Digital transmissions are typically *bursty*; the transmission and idle times have peaks (and consequently an average data rate). Because the data did not flow at a steady stream, a new signaling method, known as Time Division Multiplexing (TDM), was introduced to address the associated issues. TDM, like FDM, allows multiple signals to be transmitted across a single line, but each connection is given a specific time slot during which it is allowed to transmit. Compared with FDM, TDM allows significantly higher bandwidth (number of connections) on the same cable.

TDM requires the use of buffers in the switches, ensuring that the data is stored ready for transmission when the relevant time slot becomes available (time slots always transmit in the same order, 1, 2, 3, 4, and so on; once finished, they restart).

Early transmissions were 64Kbps channels, which exactly matched the output rate of the telephony codecs. Increases to the amount of data that could be sent meant that more options were made available for sending that data. Bits could discretely define letters, words, and sentences, allowing rules to be easily built around a signal—for example, the signaling command to place a call on hold could now be defined as *HOLD*, making it easily understood by people troubleshooting.

Signaling between switches (exchanges) is known as *trunk* signaling, and signaling between an endpoint and the switch is known as *access* signaling, as illustrated in Figure 2.5.

FIGURE 2.5
Switch signaling types

Access Signaling   Trunk Signaling   Access Signaling

ACCESS SIGNALING

Initially, access signaling consisted simply of on-hook/off-hook requesting a dial tone (or hanging up). It has progressed to include pulse signaling, or commonly now Dual Tone Multi-Frequency (DTMF) tones used for signaling. Standard tones have been defined (typically, per country or region) to indicate busy, call waiting, and other common states to the user.

Digital Subscriber Signaling System No. 1 (DSS1), which is used in Europe and elsewhere, is an example of an access signaling protocol.

TRUNK SIGNALING

The trunk signaling used between switches is either Channel Associated Signaling (CAS) or Common Channel Signaling (CCS). The difference between these two methods is that in CAS the signaling travels the same path as the data and in CCS there may be a completely separate signaling path. The CAS data path takes up a single channel; in European systems this is typically channel 16 in a 32-channel link. The CCS separate signaling path allows a signaling network to be completely separate from the data network.

CCS allows advanced network features, such as toll-free calling, to be implemented. For example, a toll-free number on the network translates into the actual number required (seamlessly to a user); this is achieved by the separation of the signaling to allow this number translation/lookup functionality.

SS6 and SS7 are the two main CCS methods in use, and they provide access to supplementary services such as call forwarding; typically, these supplementary services are implemented differently from one telecom provider to another, so the signaling boundary tends to be at the provider level—that is, the specific code used to enable call forwarding is different on Verizon than on AT&T. Typically, these codes are difficult to remember unless frequently used. This is an area where the user interface within the Lync communicator client excels, by removing this complexity from the user; you simply point and click.

Circuit-switched networks work on the principle that the intelligence is in the network rather than the endpoint, meaning that the availability of the network nodes is critical, which implies that added expenses will be accrued to ensure that the network nodes are always available.

Packet-Switched Networks

Packet-switched networks work on the assumption that the intelligence is in the endpoint and the network is purely a routing mechanism. The Internet is the largest public packet-switched network in the world. As mentioned, data networks are bursty, going from busy to idle to busy. Using dedicated circuits to handle this type of traffic wastes resources. By separating the data into sections (packets) and transmitting them separately, you can better utilize resources by mixing packets from multiple sources being sent to multiple destinations through the same resources. The result is a smoother distribution of data. Each packet is tagged with the destination address in the header and sent to the first network node (router). The router analyzes the packet header to determine the route (the next network node) and forwards the packet to this intermediate point. This process is repeated until the packet arrives at its destination, where the packet header is removed and the data remains. (This description is somewhat simplified, but the outlines should be clear.)

Some of the routers may be visible to route analysis, but with *virtual circuits* many more routers may be hidden behind the physical route. *Virtual circuits* can appear similar to a circuit-switched network because they seem to provide a point-to-point link (remember the string from the tin cans?) between two networks. Virtual circuits can be permanent connections or temporary, where the first packet will establish the link and the final one will disconnect it.

PROS AND CONS OF VIRTUAL CIRCUITS

Virtual circuits can be beneficial because they ensure that all packets travel the same path. This means that all traffic is likely to suffer the same delays due to the underlying network conditions, resulting in all traffic being treated equally. However, this consistency comes at a cost: The network will need more resources to ensure that the state is kept.

Like circuit-switched networks, virtual circuits must be established, a task that has an associated delay, and interruptions to the network nodes in the underlying infrastructure will result in interruption to the virtual circuit, requiring the establishment of a new one. Additionally, if a virtual circuit cannot be established end to end, the connection will not be established.

Without the virtual circuit overhead, packets are dynamically rerouted in the event of infrastructure problems, possibly introducing delays or even packet loss.

PROS AND CONS OF PACKET SWITCHING

The use of packet switching provides efficiency to the network, allowing better utilization of the available bandwidth by sharing resources. It also allows differing rates of bandwidth between networks. Routers naturally buffer incoming data, so the outgoing data rate may differ from the incoming; this allows multiple networks of differing speeds to be joined and still communicate with each other.

Packet-switching infrastructure is much cheaper than circuit-switching infrastructure; simply put, the packet-switched infrastructure reads the packet header and forwards it as appropriate, whereas a circuit-switched infrastructure must keep the state of all packets (resulting in more resource overhead, which results in more expense).

However, the delay introduced by analyzing every packet is a weakness compared to circuit switching; with circuit switching, once a connection is established, the data is simply switched from one circuit to another. Compounded with this delay is the queue delay introduced while the packet is being received and waiting to be transmitted. Later, you'll see that this can be mitigated by assigning priorities to packets, but in busy networks, queues can still introduce significant delay.

Finally, every packet has a header attached, adding to the data to be transmitted. The actual impact here depends on the overall packet size because the headers will typically be the same size, resulting in greater overhead if smaller packet sizes are used.

Early packet-switched networks were based on X.25 (for the access signaling) and X.75 (for the trunk signaling). The Internet is based on Internet Protocol (IP), defined in Request for Comments (RFC) 791.

 Real World Scenario

REQUESTS FOR COMMENTS

Requests for Comments (RFCs) are memos published by the Internet Engineering Task Force (IETF) that describe methods and innovations applicable to the working of the Internet and Internet-type systems.

RFCs started as a document circulated among the early pioneers of the Internet (ARPANET) in 1969. As each document was circulated and feedback generated, it eventually became a standard ensuring the interoperability and communications on the Internet as we know it today. Indeed, the RFC process continues to develop new standards. Although not all RFCs become standards, they will be designated as one of the following:

◆ Informational

◆ Experimental

◆ Best Current Practice

◆ Standards Track

◆ Historic

The *Standards Track* can be further broken down into these categories:

◆   Proposed Standard

◆   Draft Standard

◆   Internet Standard

Each RFC is uniquely identified by its number, and within it may refer to previous RFCs to expand or even deprecate that piece of work.

Later in this chapter, you'll see that SIP itself is a combination of multiple RFCs, some of which are still in the draft stage.

Not all RFCs are serious documents; almost every year since 1989 (and first appearing in 1978), April 1 has seen at least one humorous RFC released. (Indeed, we suspect that some tangled networks are genuine implementations of RFC 1149, A Standard for the Transmission of IP Datagrams on Avian Carriers, or Internet by homing pigeon.)

In addition, RFCs can be found here:

```
www.rfc-editor.org/rfc.html
```

As described there, the IP layer traffic travels on top of many different types of underlying infrastructure, and when IP is leveraged as the common infrastructure platform, endpoints can easily communicate with various applications and services. Chapter 5, "Planning Your Deployment," discusses the additional network services that Lync Server 2013 relies on; the use of the common IP networking stack allows these services to interoperate easily.

The main IP network relies on the assumption that intelligent endpoints run the applications and a dumb network is simply routing the packets to their destination. Current-generation IP routers can obviously provide much more functionality than simple routing, such as packet inspection and firewalls; however, the principle of the dumb network remains!

The Internet Protocol makes the network almost stateless; that is, the state of each packet is not stored, only the state of routes. By doing so, it allows high availability to be achieved because there are multiple routes to a destination. In the event of a failure on one circuit, traffic is simply rerouted to another. For example, what would you do if you encountered road maintenance on your commute to work? You would take a different route to the same destination, of course. However, taking a different route would be much more difficult by train than by car. Provision of multiple paths is much easier (and cheaper) than trying to ensure that equipment is always available. IP is considered to be layer 3 in the standard seven-layer Open Systems Interconnection (OSI) network model, illustrated in Figure 2.6. Each layer in the OSI model can request services only from the layer below it. The contents of the layer above become the *payload* of the lower layer and are encapsulated with headers (and/or footers), enabling onward routing to the final destination.

At the destination, the reverse occurs, where each layer will inspect and remove the headers/footers and pass the data up to the layer above it.

Some named protocol definitions comprise more than one layer; for example, Ethernet is both layer 1 and 2.

Here are examples of what you would find at each layer:

◆   Physical cable layout, pins, voltages, and so on

◆   Physical addressing, such as MAC address

◆ Routing protocols, logical addressing, such as X.25

◆ Flow control and reliability functionality, such TCP and UDP

◆ Full-duplex or half-duplex

◆ Establishment of context, such as XML

◆ Synchronization of communications and establishment of resources, such as SIP

FIGURE 2.6
OSI Network layer
model

| 7. Application |
| 6. Presentation |
| 5. Session |
| 4. Transport |
| 3. Network |
| 2. Data Link |
| 1. Physical |

TRANSPORT LAYER PROTOCOLS

The two Transport layer protocols we are interested in are Transport Control Protocol (TCP), RFC 793, and User Datagram Protocol (UDP), RFC 768. The difference between them is that TCP provides a reliable (or connection-oriented) connection. The traffic is acknowledged, and if any packets are not received or errors encountered, they will be retransmitted. The delay introduces an additional overhead to be considered. UDP is considered to use a *fire-and-forget* (or connectionless) approach, meaning that it cares only about transmitting the data. If it gets there, great; but if it doesn't, the data is not retransmitted. There is no guarantee of delivery. Both TCP and UDP require the use of *port numbers* in addition to the IP address to route traffic correctly.

Consider the postal service analogy: You want to send a birthday card (packet) to a friend. For the birthday card to be correctly delivered, it would need a postal/zip code (consider this the IP address) and a house number (the port). Now, suppose you want to send some cash in the birthday card. You would then want to make sure the card was delivered, so you would require proof of delivery, such as with a registered letter. This is equivalent to TCP. On the other hand, if you aren't sending cash, you don't really care as much to confirm delivery; this is UDP.

REAL-TIME DATA

Real-time (or very near real-time) transmission is required for two-way audio and video communications and as such imposes different engineering considerations than non-real-time communications. For example, a delay of minutes when sending an email is typically not significant, whereas a delay of even a second or two can make a conversation (audio or video) unbearable.

As previously mentioned, delay can occur at many points throughout the transmission of audio (or video) data; this delay is normally measured in milliseconds. At a certain point, traffic received can be delayed so much that it is no longer useful and the delay can no longer be ignored.

Both UDP and TCP provide mechanisms to ensure that packets arrive in the correct order when they are received. These ordering mechanisms guarantee only that the packets are replayed in the correct order, not that they appear on time. Packets that arrive late are ignored; however, there are mechanisms within Lync that attempt to cover up these missing packets, as discussed in the section "Understanding Lync 2013 Codecs and Standards" later in this chapter.

When packets are not received in a regular pattern (they may be out of order, or there may be variations in the time to transmit and receive), this variation in the time to receive is called *jitter*, and the amount of jitter can differ based on many factors, such as the devices used for encoding as well as the routers and switches in the network path. The amount of jitter is not necessarily the same for both endpoints involved in a call.

THE JITTER BUFFER

With the Real-time Transport Protocol (RTP), RFC 1889, a jitter buffer is used to attempt to reduce the delay introduced by the different processing required in transmission (if the delay time exceeds the size of the jitter buffer, packets will be lost). The receiving system buffers the incoming data to allow some delay, resulting in the appearance of no delay to the user listening (or watching) because the stream will appear to have a continuous playback. Figure 2.7 shows the impact of the jitter buffer as traffic is sent, received, and played back.

FIGURE 2.7
The operation of the jitter buffer

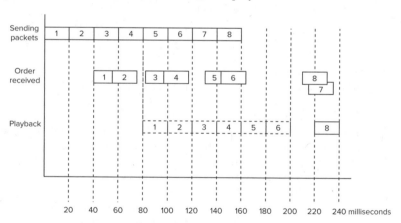

From this example, you can see that the packets are sent in an orderly fashion; however, some delays are incurred through the transmission. Packets 2, 4, and 6 are beginning to be received before the previous packet has finished and packet 7 actually arrives after packet 8.

The jitter buffer allows a way to store these packets until the correct time for them to be played back. Unfortunately, packet 7 arrives after it is due to be played, so it is useless to us. Dealing with this is where the codecs may differ in approach—some may replay the previous packet, others may attempt to "guess" what the packet contained. Remember that individually, these packets are only 20ms in duration, so they are extremely difficult to detect by the human ear.

The jitter buffer size may change throughout the course of a call (this is automatic), but is likely to be around 40ms in most cases for Lync Server 2013.

SYNCHRONIZATION OF TRAFFIC

Until now we've mentioned audio and video separately but have not considered that each is actually a separate media stream in its own right. This provides an additional level of complexity because you have to ensure that the audio and video are synchronized—after all, they were when they were captured at the sender endpoint. However, because they are two separate streams, there is no guarantee that the traffic has followed the same route from source to destination, and indeed Lync Server 2013 provides the capability to prioritize each traffic stream (modality) separately.

Real-Time Transport Control Protocol (RTCP), RFC 1889, is used to associate the time stamps of the data packets with the actual time points in the session. RTCP is also used to track the quality of the RTP transmission, measuring the number of lost packets, total delays, and jitter.

QUALITY OF SERVICE

Being able to prioritize traffic on a network allows you to guarantee a level of traffic delivery. In a busy network, it's a good idea to prioritize voice traffic over file copy traffic, thereby ensuring that the network routers keep any delays to the voice traffic to an absolute minimum. This will result in a longer time to copy a file, but it will at least allow an understandable conversation.

There are two methods to enable Quality of Service (QoS) on a network:

◆ Integrated Services, RFC 1633

◆ Differentiated Services, RFC 2475

Lync Server 2013 supports only the use of Differentiated Services, by marking packets using a Differentiated Services Code Point (DSCP)—effectively, an additional flag in the packet header.

Lync Server 2013 allows you to apply a different packet marker to each modality, as shown in Table 2.1.

TABLE 2.1   Default DSCP marking per modality

MEDIA TYPE	DEFAULT PER-HOP BEHAVIOR	QUEUING AND DROPPING	NOTES
Audio	EF	Priority Queue	Low loss, low latency, low jitter, assured bandwidth. Pair with WAN bandwidth policies on constrained links.
Video	AF41	BW Queue + DSCP WRED	Class 4. Low drop priority. Pair with WAN Bandwidth Policies on constrained links.
SIP signaling	CS3	BW Queue	Class 3. Bandwidth allocation should be sufficient to avoid drops.

TABLE 2.1   Default DSCP marking per modality *(CONTINUED)*

MEDIA TYPE	DEFAULT PER-HOP BEHAVIOR	QUEUING AND DROPPING	NOTES
App sharing	AF21	BW Queue + DSCP WRED	Class 2. Low drop priority. Pair with end-user policy caps.
File transfer	AF11	BW Queue + DSCP WRED	Class 1. Low drop priority. Pair with end-user policy caps.

The Default per-Hop Behavior column indicates the DSCP tag applied to the packet (a numeric value provides further differentiation where listed):

◆ EF: Expedited Forwarding, RFC 2598.

◆ AF: Assured Forwarding, RFC 2597.

◆ CS: Class.

◆ Numeric value: When associated with the same DSCP text, a higher value indicates a higher priority.

It is important to understand that when QoS is used on a network, the same configuration must be on all routers and switches in the path of the traffic; otherwise, the correct priority will fail to be applied at one (or more) hops, thereby introducing unwanted delay.

SESSION DESCRIPTION PROTOCOL

Session Description Protocol (SDP, RFC 2327) provides the information required to enable a media session to be encoded for transmission; it also provides the receiving endpoint with the information required to decode. In many cases, SDP is used to notify users of upcoming Internet broadcasts (webcasts).

It provides the ability to negotiate information such as IP and port addresses, media codecs used, and authentication, and it can be extended further to future needs through the a= information lines.

The SDP syntax is text based and consists of lines of human-readable text, providing an easy-to-understand view for troubleshooting. A sample session (taken from the RFC document) is shown here:

```
v=0
o=mhandley 2890844526 2890842807 IN IP4 126.16.64.4
s=SDP Seminar
i=A Seminar on the session description protocol
u=http://www.cs.ucl.ac.uk/staff/M.Handley/sdp.03.ps
e=mjh@isi.edu (Mark Handley)
c=IN IP4 224.2.17.12/127
t=2873397496 2873404696
a=recvonly
m=audio 49170 RTP/AVP 0
```

```
m=video 51372 RTP/AVP 31
m=application 32416
```

From this sample, you can immediately discern (or at least make an educated guess at) some of the values of this media stream before even knowing what the field identifiers are. Here is a list of some of these values:

- Subject: s=SDP Seminar

- Information: I = A Seminar on the session description protocol

- Email: e=mjh@isi.edu (Mark Handley)

- Media: m=audio/m=video/m=application

The following values taken from the RFC show the valid session description identifiers for SDP; for further descriptions of the fields, see the RFC document (any value marked * is optional):

```
v= (protocol version)
o= (owner/creator and session identifier).
s= (session name)
i=* (session information)
u=* (URI of description)
e=* (email address)
p=* (phone number)
c=* (connection information - not required if included in all media)
b=* (bandwidth information)
z=* (time zone adjustments)
k=* (encryption key)
a=* (zero or more session attribute lines)
t= (time the session is active)
r=* (zero or more repeat times)
m= (media name and transport address)
i=* (media title)
c=* (connection information - optional if included at session-level)
b=* (bandwidth information)
k=* (encryption key)
a=* (zero or more media attribute lines)
```

The Session Initiation Protocol in Depth

What is commonly referred to as Session Initiation Protocol (SIP) is more accurately known as SIPv2. The first version (SIPv1) was submitted to the Internet Engineering Task Force (IETF) as a draft standard for session establishment and was called *Session Invitation Protocol*. Its job was done once the users joined the session, relying on something like SDP to continue control of the established session. SIPv1, which was created by Mark Handley and Eve Schooler, was UDP based.

At the same time, another draft standard, *Simple Conference Invitation Protocol* (SCIP), was also submitted to the IETF by Henning Schulzrinne. SCIP used an approach similar to Hypertext Transfer Protocol (HTTP) for communication and defined a new method to continue the session controls. SCIP was based on TCP.

The outcome of these two proposals was SIPv2, which is based on HTTP but able to use both UDP and TCP. For the remainder of this book, we'll use *SIP* to refer to SIPv2.

RFC 2543 describes the basics of SIP; however, a number of extensions have been defined in other RFCs. In the following list, the values in parentheses indicate the SIP message defined in the RFC:

- RFC 2976 (INFO)
- RFC 3261 (ACK, BYE, CANCEL, INVITE, OPTIONS, REGISTER)
- RFC 3262 (PRACK)
- RFC 3265 (SUBSCRIBE, NOTIFY)
- RFC 3311 (UPDATE)
- RFC 3428 (MESSAGE)
- RFC 3515 (REFER)
- RFC 3903 (PUBLISH)

Each of these extensions shows how flexible SIP is with its ability to operate with early implementations while bringing new functionality to bear where possible. The flip side of this extensibility is that it can be difficult to fully define which version of SIP is actually implemented by an application. Later, you'll learn how you can query an application (or endpoint) to see what is supported.

In addition, Microsoft has provided extensions to the Lync Server 2010 (and subsequently Lync Server 2013) implementation of SIP in the form of message headers, which are all prefixed with ms-. These extensions, which we'll discuss shortly, are supported only within Lync Server (both 2010 and 2013). Although some of them may become standard in a future version, they do not provide any interoperability with other systems at this point.

From this point on, we will focus on the Microsoft implementation of SIPv2 and the architecture within Lync Server 2013 (although in most cases this is also relevant to Lync Server 2010); if you want a wider understanding, please refer to the RFC documentation.

Using SIP

In its basic form, SIP is used to create, modify, and end individual sessions between users (or a user and a server). Let's say Nathan wants to call Keith. At a high level, SIP would begin this process with an INVITE message and finish with a BYE message. However, prior to the INVITE, both Nathan and Keith would have to issue REGISTER messages to the server, providing the address information for the client on which they are logged in. During the message exchange, there are likely to be several ACK messages and possibly more INVITE messages if the call were to change from one device to another or additional functionality were added (such as video or desktop sharing).

SIP is a request-and-response protocol similar to HTTP (on which it is based), meaning that for every request sent out, a response is expected, and within these responses are human-readable *reason phrases*. As you might expect, the response codes are similar to HTTP codes and many will be familiar—for example, 404 - Not Found.

Table 2.2 shows the response classes and some common examples.

TABLE 2.2   SIP responses

RANGE	RESPONSE CLASS	EXAMPLES
100–199	Informational	100 - Trying
		180 - Ringing
200–299	Success	200 - OK
300–399	Redirection	301 - Moved permanently
		302 - Moved temporarily
400–499	Client error	401 - Unauthorized
		404 - Not found
500–599	Server error	500 - Internal server error
		502 - Bad gateway
600–699	Global error	600 - Busy everywhere

The SIP requests each have a different purpose (some are paired) and, as mentioned previously, have been implemented through many additional extensions and new RFCs. We'll look at each of them in turn now.

INVITE   The INVITE message is the initiation of a SIP session, an invitation from one user to another (or more) to begin a communications method. This will proceed any modality, and indeed changing modalities will require additional INVITEs to be sent for each modality. The SDP carried in the INVITE will detail the actual session modality information, and further communications will establish the connection points for the session.

Figure 2.8 shows the INVITE message in the ladder diagram format commonly used to illustrate SIP flows; the latest version of the Lync log analysis tool (snooper.exe) includes the capability to generate a ladder diagram from the log files. You'll see more of this in Chapter 12, "Troubleshooting."

FIGURE 2.8
An INVITE ladder
diagram

The 180 Ringing response shown here is an informational response, and there is no expectation or guarantee of informational responses being received. When the remote user accepts the request, a 200 - OK response is sent.

INFORMATIONAL RESPONSES

The SIP protocol defines that there is no guarantee of informational responses being received and that connections using it should not rely on such data. However, when TCP is used as the transport, as with the Microsoft implementation, there is a guaranteed response, and Microsoft has included additional useful troubleshooting information in these responses. These additional headers are prefixed with ms- (for example, ms-received-port and ms-received-cid).

ACK   The ACK shown in Figure 2.8 is the acknowledgement of the INVITE from the *initiating* user. It is required because the INVITE message may take longer than expected to receive a response. INVITE is the initiation of a session, and at this point the location of the recipient endpoints are not known and the user may not be nearby, resulting in a delay in the acceptance of the call.

In a scenario with multiple receiving endpoints (forking), multiple responses will be received, and each response needs to be acknowledged. This is partly a remainder from the initial SIPv1 implementation, in which the expectation was to use UDP, an unreliable transport protocol.

An ACK message also allows additional information to be sent within its SDP.

CANCEL   The CANCEL message is used to cancel any pending INVITEs. As you can see in Figure 2.9, a CANCEL message is acknowledged through the separate cancellation message (487 - Transaction Cancelled); this is to accommodate the case where the 200 - OK response and the CANCEL happen to cross paths on the network. Finally, even though the INVITE is cancelled, an ACK message is sent to acknowledge the 200 - OK response.

FIGURE 2.9
A CANCEL ladder diagram

BYE A BYE message is used to disconnect an established session. Figure 2.10 shows the SIP ladder diagram including the BYE.

FIGURE 2.10
A BYE ladder
diagram

REGISTER A REGISTER is used to inform the server of the location of a user endpoint. Lync Server 2013 supports Multiple Points of Presence (MPOP), and this requires each endpoint to uniquely provide its location (IP address) so that follow-up messages (INVITE, SUBSCRIBE, or OPTION) can be directed to each endpoint on which the user is logged in. Figure 2.11 shows a ladder diagram for REGISTER.

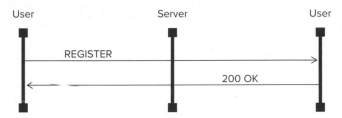

FIGURE 2.11
A REGISTER ladder
diagram

OPTIONS OPTIONS messages provide the capability to query an endpoint (including a server) for the functionality it supports. This is how different SIP applications can still function with differing implementations of the SIP standard. Figure 2.12 shows the ladder diagram, and in this case the 200 - OK response will include the data of the capabilities provided.

FIGURE 2.12
An OPTIONS ladder
diagram

SIP Protocol Formatting

SIP messages are transmitted in human-readable format; however, this means they are required to follow strict formatting to ensure functionality.

For a request, this format is as follows:

◆ Request line

- Several header lines
- Empty line
- Message body

Similarly, a response consists of the following elements:

- Status line
- Several header lines
- Empty line
- Message body

The request line comprises the request, request URI, and finally the version, as shown here:

```
INVITE sip:nathan.lync@masteringlync.org SIP/2.0
```

The response line consists of simply the version, response code, and reason phrase:

```
SIP/2.0 180 Ringing
```

There are many available header lines, and some of the more interesting standard ones are listed here:

- Accept
- Alert-info
- Authorization
- Call-ID
- Contact
- Content-length
- Content-type
- Cseq
- Date
- Encryption
- Error-Info
- From
- In-reply-to
- Max-forwards
- Record-Route
- Route
- Server
- Subject

- ◆ Supported
- ◆ Timestamp
- ◆ To
- ◆ User-agent
- ◆ Via

However, headers can be extended, and as mentioned, Microsoft has added many customized headers, all beginning with ms-. It's worth looking at some of the more useful headers in more detail. Understanding them will dramatically help you when troubleshooting (see Chapter 12 for more about troubleshooting). Here are a few of the standard headers explained:

Call-ID The Call-ID header is unique for each SIP session; it allows the flow of a single session to be monitored across several servers and indeed different systems, ensuring consistency and ease of troubleshooting.

If an original call is transferred, the Call-ID header is changed, and if multiple calls are merged, a new Call-ID header is also generated.

Contact The Contact header is similar to the From header except that it contains the specific IP address and port information for which the user/endpoint can be contacted. This becomes extremely useful when you're dealing with a forked session, which will be delivered to multiple endpoints; you can uniquely identify each one.

Cseq The Command Sequence (Cseq) header is used to keep track of individual requests within a session. For example, the first INVITE will be

    Cseq: 1 INVITE

The corresponding 200 - OK response will include this Cseq value also. If the session is modified to include additional modalities, the next INVITE will be

    Cseq: 2 INVITE

(and it will have a corresponding 200 - OK response). If there are any delays in the first 200 - OK response, the Cseq value will indicate which INVITE is being referenced.

The ACK message will always have the same Cseq value as the INVITE to which it corresponds, as will any CANCEL request. Other request messages will have an incremented Cseq value.

From This header is the SIP URI for the user sending the message, similar to the From field in an email.

Record-Route/Route/Via These three headers indicate the routing through which the SIP message has traversed in terms of SIP proxy servers. The Record-Route header indicates a proxy server that must remain in the return route. This may be for security reasons, where a specific path is required.

The Route header provides the return path, without forcing a specific route hop by hop.

The Via header is used to detect routing loops; it stores each proxy that has handled the request, as shown in this example:

    Via: SIP/2.0/TLS 192.168.2.106:61382;received=192.168.2.10;ms-received-port=63942
    ;ms-received-cid=57738800
    Record-Route: <sip:se01.corp.masteringlync.org:5061;transport=tls;ms-fe=se01.cor

```
p.masteringlync.org;lr;received=192.168.2.10;ms-received-cid=4FCF2601>
Record-Route: <sip:fed.masteringlync.org:443;transport=tls;opaque=state:Ci.D57738800;lr;ms-
rou
te-sig=hhekkICd-Rvcsd8OF--J6yJgk7YJjn8ihOWz0XIb_dEi4gL9pjnDiCAQAA>
```

To   This header is the SIP URI for the recipient of the message, similar to the To field in an email.

Providing Presence

So far you've seen how to register (REGISTER) your endpoints and invite (INVITE) sessions. However, we haven't looked at one of the key features of Lync Server 2013 (and previous versions, including LCS and OCS), which is also implemented via SIP—presence.

Presence in the user sense is the availability and willingness of a user to communicate. Technically, it is the functionality behind knowing how available or how busy a user is. When a user is logged in with multiple sessions, a level of aggregation is provided so that other users will see only the result of this presence, not each individual state. The two SIP messages SUBSCRIBE and NOTIFY are used to indicate this functionality.

NOTIFY is used to update the presence state of an endpoint to the server, and within Lync Server 2013 an aggregation script runs to provide a final updated result of the user's presence based on this change.

For example, assume a user is logged in on both a laptop and a Lync 2013 Phone Edition device. If the user picks up the phone and dials a number, the status of the phone device becomes *busy* (or more accurately *in a call*); at the same time, the user is no longer using the laptop Lync 2013 client, so this client changes to *away*. Any other users who have this user in their own buddy list will simply see the status to be *in a call*; there is no indication of the second client (on the laptop) and certainly no indication of the user being *away*. The Lync Server 2013 server is responsible for this aggregation of presence from all the endpoints and provision of the data out to other users. In fact, the Lync 2013 client (on the laptop) will show *in a call* as the aggregated presence update will also feed back to the user on all logged in clients.

For a user to receive presence updates of contacts (buddies), they must be added to the *contacts list* on the client (see Chapter 4, "Clients"). The background SIP message used by the Lync 2013 client is SUBSCRIBE. This message contains the SIP URI of the user whose presence is to be added to the contacts list.

For presence information outside the Lync 2013 client, an ad hoc request is created for a single view of presence; this is typically the case for email messages or SharePoint sites where the users involved are not necessarily on the contacts list.

Upon login to the Lync 2013 client and download of the contacts list from the server, a *batch subscription* is requested for all the users listed in the contacts list. A batch subscription also sets up a request for permanent updates to any of the presence states of the contacts on the contacts list.

Figure 2.13 shows the ladder view when multiple users log in, change state, and subscribe to presence. Notice that the users also subscribe to their own presence state.

Sending an Instant Message

After presence updates, sending instant messages is probably the second most popular use of Lync Server 2013's SIP features.

Once you have identified the user you want to send a message to, the new IM window will open so that you can type the message. At this point, in the background you will have already logged in (REGISTER) and received the presence status of the user (SUBSCRIBE, NOTIFY). Not surprisingly, the MESSAGE request is used to process the sending and receiving of IMs.

The content (SDP) of the MESSAGE is not visible within the logs of the Lync 2013 client (or server) for privacy reasons. Figure 2.14 shows the SIP message exchange process in ladder format.

FIGURE 2.13

A ladder diagram of presence updates

FIGURE 2.14

A ladder diagram for sending an IM

Understanding Lync 2013 Codecs and Standards

So far we've looked at SIP's background and how SIP is used to provide the IM and presence functionality in Lync Server 2013. Obviously, Lync Server 2013 (like Lync Server 2010 and both versions of OCS) extends the client functionality beyond IM and presence to include peer-to-peer desktop sharing, voice, and video as well as conferencing versions of all of these. These features are not just for internal communication; the Edge server provides the same client functionality to remote users in a secure way. All of these extensions to SIP are implemented in Lync using the codecs we'll discuss next.

Call Admission Control (CAC) can be used to control which codecs are available for communications between endpoints; for more information, see Chapter 14, "Call Admission Control."

USING THE VOICE CODECS

Prior to Lync Server 2010, with all other factors being ignored (network capacity, jitter, etc.), the default codec for peer-to-peer calling was Real-Time Audio (RTAudio); with Lync Server 2010 onward, the preferred codec is G711. From the session setup perspective, the codec used is irrelevant because it is negotiated (via the SDP content) in the initial INVITE, as shown in the following example log:

```
CSeq: 1 INVITE
Contact: <sip:keith.lync@masteringlync.org;opaque=user:epid:rKqM2mMJqV2mDOKTo
UtijwAA;gruu>
User-Agent: UCCAPI/15.0.4433.1506 OC/15.0.4433.1506 (Microsoft Lync)
Supported: ms-dialog-route-set-update
Ms-Conversation-ID: AcyDJ2+hW2+XFkopTdeZrXulwA41yA==
Supported: timer
Supported: histinfo
Supported: ms-safe-transfer
Supported: ms-sender
Supported: ms-early-media
Supported: 100rel
ms-keep-alive: UAC;hop-hop=yes
Allow: INVITE, BYE, ACK, CANCEL, INFO, UPDATE, REFER, NOTIFY, BENOTIFY, OPTIONS
ms-subnet: 192.168.0.0
Accept-Language: en-US
ms-endpoint-location-data: NetworkScope;ms-media-location-type=Intranet
P-Preferred-Identity: <sip:keith.lync@masteringlync.org>,<tel:+44555111122;
ext=11122>
Supported: replaces
Supported: ms-conf-invite
Proxy-Authorization: Kerberos qop="auth", realm="SIP Communications Service
", opaque="4E502AF5", targetname="sip/se01.corp.masteringlync.org", crand="
2257d26a",cnum="12",response="040400ffffffffff00000000000000005c49a725aa991
8f694cf4cec"
Content-Type: multipart/alternative;boundary="----=_NextPart_000_0006_01CC832F.D19DE7F0"
Content-Length: 3304
------=_NextPart_000_0006_01CC832F.D19DE7F0
```

```
Content-Type: application/sdp
Content-Transfer-Encoding: 7bit
Content-ID: <4a9a5f370140470a9bd92a02c4c0f7f2@masteringlync.org>
Content-Disposition: session; handling=optional; ms-proxy-2007fallback
v=0
o=- 0 0 IN IP4 192.168.2.10
s=session
c=IN IP4 192.168.2.10
b=CT:99980
t=0 0
m=audio 53509 RTP/AVP 117 114 9 112 111 0 8 116 115 97 13 118 101 a=candidate:UgthpTzpXdxzN
80OUm7KdqW+4eLzS6ekVGT899b5Tts 1 1azIPAGwsoG5ed3FKOQ/Lg
 UDP 0.830 172.23.24.236 13646
a=candidate:UgthpTzpXdxzN80OUm7KdqW+4eLzS6ekVGT899b5Tts 2 1azIPAGwsoG5ed3FKOQ/Lg
 UDP 0.830 172.23.24.236 13647
a=candidate:33hmkNO0YZHHwWb36Z7XdlW7zI9q1DD8i+HMP054xiI 1 49feTBWu+huGWNQFxBbGWA
 UDP 0.840 192.168.2.10 4680
a=candidate:33hmkNO0YZHHwWb36Z7XdlW7zI9q1DD8i+HMP054xiI 2 49feTBWu+huGWNQFxBbGWA
 UDP 0.840 192.168.2.10 4681
a=cryptoscale:1 client AES_CM_128_HMAC_SHA1_80 inline:ShWUCidF5aWY6EWHAXrWULrPZYJDN8d6cEUD
hP39|2^31|1:1
a=crypto:2 AES_CM_128_HMAC_SHA1_80 inline:UuMge3Oy0ozckMdHhNYpGQGDIcixnEyU0+Q2JNqy|2^31|1:1
a=crypto:3 AES_CM_128_HMAC_SHA1_80 inline:903WFSguPZMR/SPKb+dzLtX+5oH1jzuTVlGrGS6k|2^31
a=maxptime:200
a=rtcp:54489
a=rtpmap:117 G722/8000/2
a=rtpmap:114 x-msrta/16000
a=fmtp:114 bitrate=29000
a=rtpmap:9 G722/8000
a=rtpmap:112 G7221/16000
a=fmtp:112 bitrate=24000
a=rtpmap:111 SIREN/16000
a=fmtp:111 bitrate=16000
a=rtpmap:0 PCMU/8000
a=rtpmap:8 PCMA/8000
a=rtpmap:116 AAL2-G726-32/8000
a=rtpmap:115 x-msrta/8000
a=fmtp:115 bitrate=11800
a=rtpmap:97 RED/8000
a=rtpmap:13 CN/8000
a=rtpmap:118 CN/16000
a=rtpmap:101 telephone-event/8000
a=fmtp:101 0-16
```

Here, you can see the a=rtpmap entries, listing each of the different codecs available; the value after the codec name is the sample rate used, so there may be multiple entries for the same codec but different sample rates (for example, a=rtpmap:114 x-msrta/16000 and a=rtpmap:115 x-msrta/8000).

The line

    m=audio 53509 RTP/AVP 117 114 9 112 111 0 8 116 115 97 13 118 101

shows the order in which the codecs are negotiated, with each number corresponding directly to the number immediately after the a=rtpmap designator. This is not a codec selection preference order. You may notice that the first codec in the list is RTAudio with a sample rate of 16000; although Lync prefers to use the G711 codec, it will only do so once it has confirmed there is suitable bandwidth, and so the first codec negotiation attempt will be RTAudio.

The actual workings of the codec are the interesting parts, and we'll look at how generic codecs operate in the Lync Server 2013 environment.

We've already discussed how the media stream is negotiated via the SDP and is separate from the signaling. Lync Server 2013 includes healing capability to allow recovery from the loss of packets, using Forward Error Correction (FEC). FEC is dynamic, so it will be in effect only when problems are detected on the network.

For example, consider the sound wave shown in Figure 2.15.

FIGURE 2.15
Input audio wave

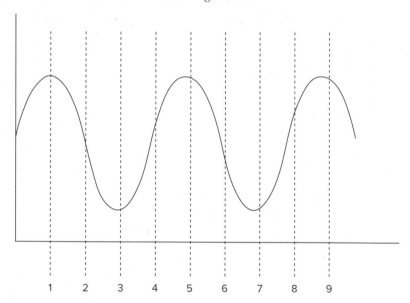

The Lync 2013 client will sample the input, in this example at a rate assumed to be 20ms per packet, and it will output the data in a number of packets to be sent across the network (Figure 2.16).

FIGURE 2.16
Sampled data for packetization

1	2	3	4	5	6	7	8	9

Now suppose that a problem occurs on the network, resulting in packet loss, and some of the data is lost. At this point, the endpoints will be aware of the packet loss and implement FEC on the audio stream. This means that another copy (compressed) of the previous packet will be sent with each actual packet (Figure 2.17).

FIGURE 2.17
Sampled data
for packetization
with FEC

2	1	3	2	4	3	5	4	6	5	7	6	8	7

This will result in additional data on the network; however, it compensates well for packet loss and allows the codec to "heal" the data into a more usable form. Figure 2.18 shows a comparison with and without FEC, assuming packet loss of packets 4 and 5.

FIGURE 2.18
Received audio
wave after packet
loss (top); after
packet loss using
FEC (bottom)

Losing two consecutive packets with FEC means that the healing capability has to try to recover 40ms worth of data; on the other hand, using FEC means that you actually have the information for the second packet, thereby reducing the amount of data the healing algorithm needs to repair.

USING THE VIDEO CODECS

With Lync Server 2010 and video, we only saw a change in the default supported resolution for conferencing, changing from Common Interchange Format (CIF) to Video Graphics Array (VGA). However, in Lync Server 2013, we see the introduction of a new video codec that could dramatically expand the interoperability capabilities.

The announcement of H264AVC/SVC (Advanced Video Coding/Scalable Video Coding) support in Lync 2013 was well received in the Lync user communities but should equally be read with caution—there are many different variations of the H264 standard (of course!).

H264 in Lync Server 2013 uses a layered approach to provide video streams to clients. Each layer builds on top of the previous layer with additional details. This allows multiple resolutions to be delivered without each having to be transcoded separately.

For example, layer 1 will be 15 frames per second (fps), and to provide 30fps at layer 2, layer 2 will include the additional 15fps. See Figure 2.19.

FIGURE 2.19
Video codec
layering

- – – ⟶ 1080p / 30fps
- – – – ⟶ 720p / 30fps
- ·········⟶ 360p / 30fps
- ⟶ 180p / 15fps

In addition to the layering approach for providing different frame rates, different resolutions are provided in separate streams. See Figure 2.20. This gives the ability for a client to request multiple streams, each at different resolutions, and potentially different layering as well.

FIGURE 2.20
Video codec
streaming

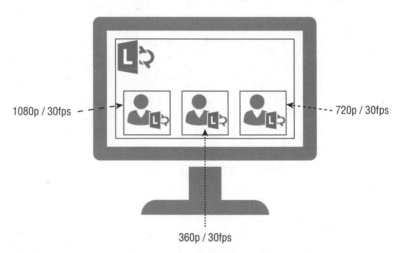

1080p / 30fps

720p / 30fps

360p / 30fps

As mentioned in Chapter 1, "What's in Lync?," the Gallery View allows multiple separate video streams to been seen simultaneously, each of which could potentially be a different resolution. Taking the approach of layering and streaming in the codec reduces the Media Conferencing Unit (MCU) to more of a relay role rather than a transcoding role as with previous versions of Lync and OCS. This allows for high resolution and potentially more users to be able to connect to a conference.

Lync Server 2013 uses compressed video to reduce the amount of data required to be transferred over the network. The video codec is negotiated in the same way as the audio, via the SDP associated with the INVITE. Here's a sample log:

```
CSeq: 1 INVITE
<shortened for brevity, but would include the same audio details as the
previous example>
m=video 57338 RTP/AVP 122 121 123
a=x-ssrc-range:2160803841-2160803940
a=rtcp-fb:* x-message app send:src,x-pli recv:src,x-pli
a=rtcp-rsize
```

```
a=label:main-video
a=x-source:main-video
a=ice-ufrag:SpCz
a=ice-pwd:yxq1Wp8Mi7KW0NTDLhJk+VRF
a=x-caps:121 263:1920:1080:30.0:2000000:1;4359:1280:720:30.0:1500000:1;8455:640
:480:30.0:600000:1;12551:640:360:30.0:600000:1;16647:352:288:15.0:250000:1;2074
3:424:240:15.0:250000:1;24839:176:144:15.0:180000:1
<candidate information removed for brevity>
a=rtcp:58163
a=rtpmap:122 X-H264UC/90000
a=fmtp:122 packetization-mode=1;mst-mode=NI-TC
a=rtpmap:121 x-rtvc1/90000
a=rtpmap:123 x-ulpfecuc/90000
```

In this case, you can see that the `m=video 57338 RTP/AVP 122 121 123` line, listing three codecs and translating via their relevant `rtpmap` entries, results in the codecs being RTVideo (`x-rtcv1`) and H264, with `x-ulpfecuc` actually being an audio codec.

The additional `a=x-caps` line provides the encapsulation details for each codec (as with audio, the number is the identifier). This `x-caps` line definition has the following format for each video quality contained within the protocol:

> *port*:*width*:*height*:*framerate*:*bitrate*;

Therefore, the entry

```
a=x-caps:121 263:1280:720:30.0:1500000:1;4359:640:480:30.0:600000:1;8455:352:288
:15.0:250000:1;12551:176:144:15.0:180000:1
```

corresponds to the following quality definitions: 720p;VGA;CIF;QCIF.

Lost frames are simply ignored because the next frame will provide more info, and frames appearing out of order are useless to the picture. But because some frames are dependent upon others, this approach can lead to a "stuttering" or "artifact" effect in the playback. Figure 2.21 shows a typical sample for a conference video codec using a frame rate of 30 frames per second.

FIGURE 2.21
Video codec frame breakdown

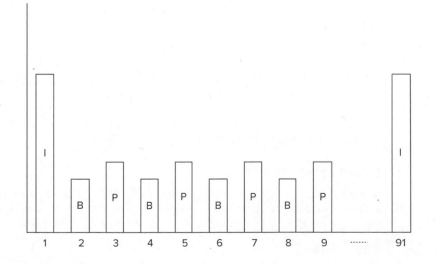

Each full sample will begin and end with an *I-frame* (Intra-coded picture), which appears every 4 seconds for peer-to-peer video and every 3 seconds for conferences; the period between I-frames is known as the Group of Pictures (GoP). No compression is available with this frame.

Within the full sample period is a combination of *P-frames* (Predicted picture) and *B-frames* (Bi-predictive picture). Each of these P-frames and B-frames contains only changes from the previous frame, with the B-frame also containing changes from the *next* frame.

Figure 2.22 shows the content within an I-frame and a P-frame (the dotted line represents the removal of content). Here, the P-frame predicts that the character will next raise her arms. It describes only their new position and the deletion of the old.

FIGURE 2.22
I-frame versus
P-frame

I-frame

P-frame

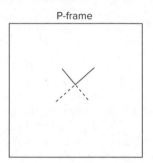

An individual frame loss will not have a massive impact; however, depending on the specific type of frame lost, it may lead to a pause or some ghosting of images, in which a frame has been dropped and some updated information has been missed (such as an artifact not being removed).

A packet loss will cause an artifact to appear until the next same type or larger frame. For example, an I-frame is the largest frame, and losing it will cause a problem until the next I-frame. On the other hand, losing a P-frame will result in a problem until the next P-frame or I-frame (whichever occurs first).

Each P-frame is tagged to allow the SVC profile to either decode or discard as needed.

USING DESKTOP SHARING

Desktop sharing uses Remote Desktop Protocol (RDP) as its media stream. The Desktop Sharing function has been improved dramatically in Lync 2013, providing users with more control; they can now specify individual applications for sharing, individual screens, or the full desktop.

From the communications perspective, Lync leverages only the RDP protocol and uses SIP as the signaling method, as it does with all other communication functions. Apart from permissions and workstation configuration, there is nothing specifically different between an RDP session within the Lync 2013 client and a direct RDP session.

CONNECTING REMOTELY

During the session establishment process of the INVITE, the SDP will carry information of the IP address on which the client can be reached. This will always be the direct interface address from the client because the clients will always try to connect peer to peer.

This scenario fits perfectly into an enterprise environment, where all clients share a network (likely via a WAN connection) and can be directly reached. However, it doesn't work as well when firewalls have been implemented and even less so when clients are connecting via the Internet.

The solution to this is the Edge server, which will act as a SIP proxy server but also as a media termination point. Where clients previously connected directly to each other, they can now use the Edge server to provide a common termination point to exchange media.

The establishment of this termination point is a multistep process:

1. Log in to the Front End server using SIP via the Edge server (as a proxy).

2. Request the Media Relay Authentication Service (MRAS) credentials via the Front End server.

3. Request the Edge endpoint details.

4. Send the INVITE to another user, populating the SDP with Edge endpoint details.

5. Negotiate which endpoint to use for media communications.

6. Begin the session.

When an endpoint is located remotely, it can be directly connected to the Internet or connected behind a Network Address Translation (NAT) device, effectively hiding its direct IP address (Figure 2.23).

FIGURE 2.23
Remotely
connected devices

Public IP addresses

Internet

NAT device

Private IP addresses

Even though the endpoint may be behind a NAT device, it will not automatically be aware of that and will continue to include its local IP address in the SDP exchange. If it is behind a NAT device, it needs to have a method to determine that and also to determine the actual IP address (and port) to use on the Edge server.

This is where Internet Connectivity Establishment (ICE), RFC4091; 5245/Session Traversal Utilities for NAT (STUN), RFC 3489; and 5389/Traversal Using Relay NAT (TURN), RFC 5766 come into play. All of them provide methods to overcome the problem of hidden IP addresses with NAT when using media connectivity.

Simply put, using STUN and TURN methods allows the endpoint to identify addresses via the Edge server; STUN provides a reflexive address (on the NAT device), and TURN provides a relay (on the Edge server). Figure 2.24 shows this in detail.

FIGURE 2.24
STUN and TURN
addressing

Once the endpoint has identified its own available addresses, it can populate the SDP and begin negotiating which address to communicate.

Once the SDPs have been exchanged, the negotiation of connection addresses will begin and follow this order:

1. UDP direct

2. UDP NAT (STUN)

3. UDP Relay (TURN)

4. TCP Relay (TURN)

Once bidirectional connectivity is established, the INVITE is stopped and reissued, this time including only the valid address information. From here the session will begin as normal.

The SDP is the best place to find information for troubleshooting because it contains the complete call flow as well as all the negotiation steps. More detailed information on troubleshooting can be found in Chapter 12.

The Bottom Line

Understand the basics of SIP for signaling. SIP originates from an extensive background of telephony signaling. Although knowing that background is not strictly required for Lync administration, understanding how we have gotten to where we are today will help you overcome some of the challenges you'll face when integrating with legacy telephony environments.

Master It For what is a jitter buffer used?

Understand how SIP has been extended to provide additional functionality for Lync Server 2013. In its plainest form, SIP provides session-based signaling; however, with some of the extensions for SIP, you can extend this session-based signaling approach to incorporate additional functionality within the SIP request itself, such as IM and presence information.

Master It Assuming a user is not yet logged in, describe the SIP requests required to log in and establish an IM session with another user.

Identify additional protocols used by Lync Server 2013. Lync Server 2013 uses many different protocols for its various modalities as needed by the user. It can also tie many of these modalities together, providing an integrated solution running on top of SIP. Microsoft has also been able to successfully (and securely) extend this functionality to the Internet.

Master It What is the new codec used in video calling and conferencing?

Chapter 3

Security

In today's world, where security breaches are all too common, the ability to secure your Lync Server 2013 deployment is critical. In particular, your key focus should be protecting external access to Lync, especially as federation capability has been further extended, allowing interaction with a wider range of systems. The Lync Edge role and its supporting components deliver the ability to communicate with billions of people worldwide. However, the possibility of communicating with that many people entails risk. When correctly configured, Lync's design will help you mitigate that risk.

Of course, its various core capabilities provide security. For example, Lync encrypts all its communications, both the signaling and the media, which means that as a platform it can be used in highly secure environments where systems that leave the media unencrypted on the wire would be less useful. With Lync, there is no need to implement another security system, such as IP Security (IPsec), just to secure media traffic. Indeed, adding an additional security layer on top of the encryption used typically results in a deterioration of audio and video quality. The authentication mechanisms available constitute another key element to securing Lync. While the standard username and password (NTLM and Kerberos) options, as well as a Lync certificate authentication, are used for several clients (the PC-based ones), PIN and extension authentication (in conjunction with certificate authentication) are used on some of the Lync Phone Edition devices. Non–Lync Phone Edition devices (such as the SNOM range) can use NTLM or PIN and extension authentication—certificate-based authentication is not available on these devices. Finally, many Lync policies enable you as an administrator to run a secure platform. Chapter 10, "User Administration," covers policies in depth; this chapter covers security-based policy topics. For example, you'll learn how to determine PIN policies, you'll learn about the length and complexity of the PIN, and you'll learn how to define who can federate with external parties.

In this chapter, you will learn to:

- ◆ Secure external access
- ◆ Understand core security
- ◆ Provide security administratively

Securing External Access

One of Lync's most exciting features is its ability to provide communication functionality not only to users within your network but to those outside it, whether they are employees working from home or while mobile, or perhaps partners, or even the general public. Lync makes it possible to communicate with millions of people worldwide through a variety of networks, including Windows Live, Yahoo!, Google, AOL, and now Skype. Table 3.1 summarizes the available types of communication based on the different types of external users.

TABLE 3.1: Communication types available to different types of external users

SCENARIO	REMOTE USER	FEDERATED USER	PUBLIC IM CONNECTIVITY/ INTEROP	ANONYMOUS USER
Presence	Yes	Yes	Yes	No
Instant messaging (IM) peer-to-peer	Yes	Yes	Yes	No
IM conferencing	Yes	Yes	No	Yes
Collaboration	Yes	Yes	No	Yes
A/V peer-to-peer	Yes	Yes	Yes, if using the latest version of Windows Live Messenger	No
A/V conferencing	Yes	Yes	No	Yes
File transfer	Yes	Yes	No	No

USING AV WITH WINDOWS LIVE MESSENGER

If you require audio/video (AV) to work with Live Messenger, you must use the latest Live Messenger client and alter the encryption policy used by Lync from `required` to `supported`. You can do that using the following command from the Lync Server Management Shell (LSMS), also known simply as PowerShell. PowerShell will be covered in depth in Chapter 8, "Introduction to PowerShell, the Lync Management Shell, and Regular Expressions."

```
Set-CsMediaConfiguration Global -EncryptionLevel SupportEncryption
```

When this command is issued, Lync will no longer insist on encrypting all media traffic; it's needed because the Live Messenger cloud can't perform encryption. Lync will try to negotiate encryption, but if that fails, it will fall back to unencrypted media.

Finally, to enable AV with cloud providers, you must use the following command:

```
Set-CsExternalAccessPolicy Global -EnablePublicCloudAccess $true
  -EnablePublicCloudAu
dioVideoAccess $true
```

This code will alter the Global CsExternalAccessPolicy to allow AV to the cloud (PIC). Of course, the external access policy can also be configured through Lync Server Control Panel (LSCP).

All of this communication potential can send security professionals running scared! Think about opening up all that traffic through firewalls … and what about information leakage?

If you look closely, you will see that the way Lync has been designed combined with the best practices for its deployment will go a long way toward mitigating the risks of broad communication. Clearly, though, you need to get your security guys to understand that. The next few sections will help you do so!

Edge Security Components

Like other elements of Lync architecture, the way you provide external access offers choices—but not as many as back in the Office Communications Server (OCS) 2007 days, when it was possible to have a whole range of different roles split onto different servers. Now with Lync, all the Edge roles are consolidated onto a single Edge server, and your main choice is whether to have one or many of these servers and, if there will be many, how to load balance them to provide high availability. The deployment options for an edge topology are as follows:

- Single consolidated Edge with private IP addresses and NAT
- Single consolidated Edge with public IP addresses
- Scaled consolidated Edge, DNS load balancing with private IP addresses using NAT
- Scaled consolidated Edge, DNS load balancing with public IP addresses
- Scaled consolidated Edge with load balancers

Each of these options has been developed to cater for different needs of deployments, notably high availability and the use of Network Address Translation (NAT). The first two listed are solitary server deployments, whereas the final three consider multiple servers in a "load balanced" form. Only the final option (using the load balancers) is truly load balanced, as external devices (hardware or software) are used to balance the load among available Edge servers.

Of course, the Edge server is not the only element that comes into play in enabling external access to Lync functionality; there are also many supporting components, which are detailed throughout the chapter.

THE EDGE SERVER

The Single Consolidated Edge model takes all the Edge roles—Access Edge, AV Edge, and Web Conferencing Edge—and runs them on a server. This provides all the external access capabilities of Lync in a single box. Each of these roles provides specific security capabilities and has specific requirements. In particular, each requires certificates that have the correct name entries to be provided and firewalls to be configured with the relevant ports open.

The Access Edge role is a specially designed proxy concerned with passing Session Initiation Protocol (SIP) signaling traffic. It is a routing solution in that two Network Interface Cards (NICs) are used and traffic is terminated on the way into the external NIC and then reestablished through the internal NIC on the way out. This creates a barrier between external and internal components. The Access Edge role doesn't carry out authentication, and so it is not required to be a member of the Active Directory (AD). Remote user authentication traffic is passed through to the next internal hop, either the Director pool or the Front End pool, which, being a member of AD, carries out the authentication. The Access Edge role is responsible for all kinds of federation traffic: SIP, PIC, eXtensible Messaging and Presence Protocol (XMPP), and Skype.

The Web Conferencing Edge is a proxy for Persistent Shared Object Model (PSOM) traffic. This protocol is used to provide access to conferencing content such as slides, whiteboards, and poll pages shared between internal and external users. It works in conjunction with the Access Edge for SIP session setup and the reverse proxy for slide/attachment content downloads.

The AV Edge is where Lync implements the Interactive Connectivity Establishment (ICE) protocol, which provides the ability to enable media traffic to traverse a Network Address Translation (NAT) environment, using STUN or TURN. In Lync Server 2010, the AV Edge role also introduced the ability to allow file transfers through NAT via the Edge server, whereas in previous OCS versions, clients had to be on a directly routable network between them for transfers to work.

The key benefits of combining these three roles into a consolidated Edge server are simplicity and fewer hardware requirements. As mentioned, each Edge server will have, at least, two NICs, one of which is on the external side of the demilitarized zone (DMZ) and the other on the internal side; additional NICs can be used for the other external facing roles, AV and Web Conferencing, for additional capacity. The external NICs will require three IP addresses assigned, one for each of the Edge roles. This will equate to three separate URLs, one for each role. The internal interface requires a single IP on a different subnet that is routable from the internal LAN; this internal interface may not be configured with NAT.

Using a Single External IP Address

Although it is possible to use a single IP address on the external Edge interface, doing so is not recommended because it would require the ports on which each Edge role listens to be reconfigured. By default, Lync was designed (where possible) to require only well-known ports, such as TCP/443, to be opened. This port is required by all the Edge roles, and so having a single IP only would cause clashes as these ports overlapped. You would, therefore, have to change to other ports, thereby complicating deployment (by moving away from the defaults) and making the system harder to understand for other administrators who might not be aware of the changes.

Another advantage of using the well-known ports is the likelihood that corporate proxy servers already allow client requests on these ports. For example, most corporates will allow traffic to leave the organization with a target port of 443—after all, this is what secure websites will use.

As mentioned, four IP addresses and, therefore, four FQDNs will be on each Edge server (except in a load balanced environment, where some of the URLs will be shared between Edge Servers, and they will be directed to the load balancer). When you're setting up Edge servers, choose these FQDNs carefully. For example, if OCS (or Lync Server 2010) is already deployed, you must consider the FQDNs already in use. To enable the Lync Server 2013 Edge role to be deployed side by side with existing Edge Servers, you should use new FQDNs. For more information about these options, see Chapter 7, "Migration and Upgrades." The specifics of topology are discussed later in this chapter.

When you are deploying Edge servers, another key consideration is where they will be deployed. If you have a single central site, the choice is simple because the Edge server will be there; however, once you scale out to several central sites, perhaps in a global deployment, you need to consider how best to route external traffic. Keep in mind that there is only one path to the external world for all federation traffic for a particular SIP domain. As discussed in the "DNS Entries" section later, a specific DNS Service (SRV) record is needed for federation, and it can point only to one fully qualified domain name (FQDN)—namely that of the Access Edge, which provides the route for federation traffic. Either this would be a Virtual IP (VIP) on a load balancer device or load balancing would be provided through DNS load balancing, as discussed later in the chapter. Other Edge traffic (based on the nature of its content, such as real-time audio) is typically better being localized to where the Front End pool is, reducing network hops and therefore improving audio and video quality. In such cases, you can have multiple Edge pools, each paired with their respective Front End pools.

THE DIRECTOR

The Director role in Lync is now a full-fledged role in its own right. Prior to Lync Server 2010, the Director was a modified Front End server that had to be manually customized by turning off certain services; it was, however, still possible to accidentally end up with users homed to the Director. From Lync 2010 onward, this is no longer possible. The Director role provides user authentication and redirects users to their home pool. The ability to provide authentication and redirection means that the Director is essentially an additional layer sitting between the Edge servers and the Front End servers and is, therefore, in the path of external users coming through the Edge servers to the internal Front End servers. This functionality provides a range of benefits.

First, in Lync organizations with multiple pools deployed in a central site, the Director is configured as the first point of contact for users who are signing in. This means that all user registration/authentication requests first arrive at the Director, which can then authenticate and route the traffic to the relevant Lync Front End server pool rather than having the Front End servers burdened with all this traffic when they could be providing resources for all the other functions they support.

The second area where the Director role comes into play is in providing a stopgap between external users and the Front End servers. As traffic is passed on from the Edge to the Director, it is the Director that does the authentication. Therefore, if your Lync system were to be subjected to an externally sourced denial of service (DoS) attack, where large quantities of malformed authentication traffic were blasted at your Edge, the Director would take the brunt of the attack rather than the Front End servers that serve the internal users. Admittedly, external users would no longer be able to gain access, but internal users who were already logged onto the system would be able to continue working.

Like many of the other Lync roles, the Director can be installed either as a stand-alone server or as a pool of Directors that have some form of load balancing. As with the Edge and Front End servers, this load balancing can be either DNS load balancing or hardware load balancing, about which you'll learn more shortly.

The Director is an optional role, and with the ability of the Lync Communicator client (2010 onward) to support multiple DNS SRV responses, the first scenario highlighted earlier becomes less necessary, and the Director becomes only useful in a scenarios with external user connectivity (either remote or federated users).

THE REVERSE PROXY

While the Edge server and the Director provide access to the SIP and media facilities within Lync, another type of remote access is required by Lync clients. This is the requirement for access to the various web-based elements provided by Lync through IIS websites. The role of the reverse proxy is to publish the required URLs on the Front End and Director pools. The process by which it does so is discussed in depth in Chapter 6, "Installation."

The external access to web services allows remote users to connect to meetings or dial-in conferences using simple URLs, to download meeting content when in a conference, to expand distribution groups, to obtain a user-based certificate for client certificate–based authentication, to download files from the Address Book server, to submit queries to the Address Book Web Query service, and to obtain updates to client and device software.

Table 3.2 shows the URLs that are published through the reverse proxy and describes the certificates that are needed.

TABLE 3.2:　　　URLs that must be published through the reverse proxy

ROLE/SUBJECT NAME	USED TO PUBLISH	SUBJECT NAME SYNTAX EXAMPLE
External Web Services/ FQDN of the Front End pool	Address Book files Distribution group expansion Conference content Device update files	Se01webext.masteringlync.org
External WebServices/ FQDN of the Director pool	Address Book files Distribution group expansion Conference content Device update files	Directorwebext. mastering-lync.org
Simple URL/AdminFQDN	AdminFQDN is not published externally. It is only used internally.	N/A
Simple URL/DialinFQDN	Dial-in Conferencing information	dialin. masteringlync.org
Simple URL/MeetFQDN	Meeting URL	meet. masteringlync.org
Office Web Apps Server	Enhanced meeting content, such as PowerPoint streaming capability	

Multiple areas of functionality are listed in the "used to publish" column of Table 3.2; however, best practice is to publish them all using a single rule in TMG (Forefront Threat Management Gateway 2010), which uses FQDN/* in the Paths field.

PUBLISHING HTTP EXTERNALLY

You may notice that the bulk of external connections come over HTTPS. However, HTTP is still required for device updates to work.

One of the elements published is the *simple URL*. Simple URLs are a method of making the URL used in conferencing a lot easier for end users to understand. Where there is a Director pool in place, the URLs are published on the Director because this gives a single point of ingress to the network. You can configure the simple URLs in a variety of ways. You should consider this configuration carefully during your planning phase; once the URLs are set, changing them will require rerunning setup on the Front End server and can also require certificate changes.

You will need three simple URLs: the Meet URL, the Dial-in URL, and the Admin URL. The Admin URL is optional, but it simplifies internal access to the Lync Control Panel. It is never published externally. One thing to be aware of is that the Meet URL is set per supported SIP domain, while only one Admin and Dial-in URL are needed per organization. The following three examples demonstrate different ways you can configure your simple URLs.

The simplest option is to have a dedicated simple URL for each site:

```
https://meet.masteringlync.org
https://dialin.masteringlync.org
https://admin.masteringlync.org
```

You will need additional Meet URLs for any additional SIP domains:

```
https://meet.anotherdomain.com
```

This method requires a significant number of certificates or subject alternative names to support each URL and many different DNS entries.

In the next option, the simple URL is essentially presented as a virtual directory under the external web services URL. This is called the *shared simple URL* syntax:

```
https://directorwebext.masteringlync.org/meet/
```

and additional domains as

```
https://directorwebext.anotherdomain.com
https://directorwebext.masteringlync.org/dialin/
https://directorwebext.masteringlync.org/admin/
```

Here you benefit from using the same base URL as the external web services and, therefore, the same DNS records and certificate.

Finally, to make the most efficient use of URLs, you can tweak the shared format, as shown here:

```
https://directorwebext.masteringlync.org/abc/meet/
https://directorwebext.masteringlync.org/anotherdomain/meet/
https://directorwebext.masteringlync.org/dialin/
https://directorwebext.masteringlync.org/admin/
```

This technique uses the least number of certificates or subject alternative names and DNS entries and is, therefore, the simplest to configure and most cost effective.

Now that you've seen the various types of simple URLs, here's a summary of when you would use each one:

FORMAT	USED FOR
Shared	Single-pool deployments
	Multiple-pool deployments where each pool shares global simple URLs
	Multiple-pool deployments where each pool has dedicated simple URLs and public certificate cost is an issue (you can save one certificate per pool by using shared simple URLs).
Dedicated	Multiple-pool deployments where each pool has dedicated simple URLs.
	Deployments where you do not want to potentially display internal server names externally.

When a reverse proxy publishes sites, it actually intercepts the traffic from the external source, inspects it, and then sends it to the internal server. This process has two elements with specific requirements. First, one important step during this process is for the reverse proxy to translate incoming requests on the public ports 80 and 443 to internal requests for the Lync external websites on ports 8080 and 4443. Second, certificates are used to terminate the encrypted traffic and then send it on again also encrypted. Externally, these should be trusted certificates from a public certificate authority (CA). The reverse proxy uses them to identify itself externally. When re-encrypting the traffic to pass on to the internal server, it uses the certificates on the Front End or the Directors, which come from the internal CA. If this is not possible because the reverse proxy cannot trust additional internal CAs, then you need to set up the external web services site on the Lync servers with trusted public certificates.

In Table 3.2, you can see that both the Director and the Front End pools have external web URLs that must be published. The Director must be published because it plays a role in web ticket authentication, about which you'll learn more later. The Front End must be published because the URLs of the Front End are sent in-band to the client for operations such as distribution group expansion.

High Availability

Because all the Edge roles are provided on a single server, making them highly available is a relatively simple case of adding more Edge servers. Of course, when you do this, you need some way to balance and route the traffic between the different Edge servers accordingly, so that they can present a single identity. In Lync, you have two ways of doing this: DNS load balancing and load balancing using either a hardware device (HLB) or a software implementation (SLB). Both have advantages and disadvantages. In a migration or when you need to communicate externally with earlier versions of OCS, using hardware or software load balancing is still the way to go.

In OCS, it was a challenge to set up HLB devices correctly to support both the web and SIP traffic that needed to be load balanced (OCS did not support the use of SLBs). In order to simplify the load balancing requirements, DNS load balancing was introduced in Lync to deal with non-web-based traffic (HTTP/HTTPS). Another benefit is that DNS load balancing supports the *server draining* feature, which allows a server to be prepared for shutdown by not accepting any new connections but still allowing existing ones to come to a natural conclusion.

Due to the way in which Lync is implemented, HLB and SLB do not provide the application layer mechanisms required to support the server draining feature correctly.

The simplicity of DNS load balancing comes from the fact that it is application based and uses client intelligence to determine which traffic can and can't be load balanced. Each Front End server in a pool registers its FQDN as an A record in DNS, and then the pool FQDN is configured in DNS with an entry of each of the Front End IP addresses.

The client will then try each record as required (in a random order) until it receives a response from the server. This response will be either a successful login or a redirect to the client's home pool.

If a Director pool is in place, this will work in exactly the same way: The client will receive a redirect to the home pool.

Once directed to the home pool, the client will follow the same process using DNS load balancing as before, only this time it will be directed (if needed) to the home server within the pool.

For Edge servers using DNS load balancing, the client will continue until it gets a response. This response will be the proxied login attempt, which is further directed internally by the Edge server next-hop configuration (either a Front End pool or Director pool).

When you're using an HLB/SLB device to load balance the internal NIC of the Edge server, you must ensure that traffic to the Web Conferencing Edge role is not load balanced, even though the rest of the traffic to the other two Edge roles should be load balanced.

When using DNS load balancing, another benefit of the client intelligence is that the Lync client knows how to handle the traffic flow and setup is simpler.

Another key consideration is compatibility. Although DNS load balancing is simpler to set up, you must ensure that the clients and third parties to which you will be connecting can use the new method. As mentioned, DNS load balancing requires intelligence in the client. For example, the RTM version of Exchange 2010 Unified Messaging (UM) doesn't understand DNS load balancing; therefore, if you provide remote access to UM, you could end up with remote users always hitting a single server. If that single server were down, no redundancy would kick in. Also, legacy clients from OCS/LCS don't understand DNS load balancing, which must be considered in a migration, as discussed in Chapter 7. When referring to things specifically related to the Edge role, Public Internet Connectivity (PIC) providers, eXtensible Messaging and Presence Protocol (XMPP) clouds, and older OCS/LCS networks as federated partners all have issues with DNS load balancing. All in all, you may find DNS load balancing useful inside the network; however, for external communication, you may still need to use an HLB/SLB.

If HLB/SLB is chosen, the configuration must still allow a direct connection to each server in the pool—the servers cannot be "hidden" behind the load balancer. In some cases, the clients will still need a direct SIP connection; however, in *all* cases the client needs a direct connection to the server for conferencing.

DNS LOAD BALANCING DOES NOT LOAD BALANCE

When configuring Lync Server 2013 and clients using DNS load balancing, it would not be unreasonable to expect the connections to be load balanced across the Edge server (or Front End pool) to which the clients are connecting. However, if you look at the performance counter showing the number of connections on each server, you will see they are not balanced. And indeed, in some cases they are extremely unbalanced!

This has created cause for concern in the Lync Server 2010 time frame, and for unsuspecting administrators, could do so again with Lync Server 2013.

Basically, because the "load balancing" is carried out by the DNS server (in the order in which the IP addresses relating to the Edge/Front End pool are returned) and the client (in the order in which it attempts each connection), there is no correlation of load on the servers, and therefore there is no load balancing carried out.

Based on the "randomness" of the DNS server and the client decisions, there "should" be an even spread of initial connections to the servers, but in the case of Front End pools, these may be redirected after that initial connection, and this is where the "load balancing" falls down.

Of course, you may not realize that whatever you do, HLB/SLB devices are still required to implement high availability. They are, as mentioned, required only for the HTTP and HTTPS traffic unless you need some of the elements listed earlier, which are not possible with DNS load balancing. This is because the web traffic is stateful and, therefore, the session must be maintained between a single client and server. Currently, there is no way to build this technology into the client (essentially the browser), unlike the way it is built into the Lync client for the other traffic streams.

MIXING LB TYPES

You cannot mix and match load-balancing methods on the internal and external interfaces of the Edge server.

The traditional option for making the web service and reverse proxy components highly available requires an HLB/SLB device in front of an array of reverse proxies.

GETTING THE RIGHT LOAD BALANCER

Given that so many load balancer devices are available, it is important to make sure you follow proper procedures and use one that is qualified for use with Lync. To find out which models are certified, see this TechNet article:

    http://technet.microsoft.com/en-us/lync/gg131938.aspx

CERTIFICATES

There are two types of certificates used by Lync Server 2013:

◆ Client-based certificates

◆ Server-based certificates

Client-based certificates are used in conjunction with/instead of username and password login for authentication; they will be discussed later in this chapter.

Server-based certificates are what we are discussing now.

As well as being required on all internal servers, certificates play an important role in publishing Lync externally. They establish trust between the client and server so that the client knows it is talking to the correct server and not one that is spoofing its identity. Certificates are used on both interfaces of the Edge server. On the external interface, a public certificate authority (CA) trusted certificate should be used to identify all three roles. A public CA is suggested because, in most cases, the root CA will already be trusted by the underlying operating system, ensuring a seamless connection experience.

Another change in Lync is that a single, public trusted certificate can now be used for all these roles, as long as it has the right names. Getting the names on the certificate correct is critical. Thankfully, the Certificate Wizard within the Setup application helps you do this, as shown in Chapter 6.

The subject of the external certificate is the Access Edge name. The subject name should also be the first subject alternative name (SAN), and then further SANs should be used to include the other required URLs, such as the FQDN of the Web Conferencing Edge. When running the wizard, you may notice that the AV Edge FQDN is not included on the certificate. This is because it doesn't need the name to use the certificate for encryption. This saves you the cost of an additional SAN.

For client autoconfiguration to work, the SANs should contain the sip.*domainname*.com URL for each SIP domain supported because this is one of the failback URLs used by the clients. See Chapter 4, "Clients," to learn more.

As a rule, you should create the external certificate with an exportable private key. This is a requirement if you are running a pool of servers because the certificate used for the AV Edge authentication on the external interface must be the same on each server in the pool. It is also needed if you create the certificate request on a server other than where it will be used.

You must also take into account that certificates are required on the reverse proxy. This is covered in depth in Chapter 6, where you will configure these components. Briefly, the reverse proxy needs a certificate to identify all the websites it must publish. The certificate should come from a trusted CA. This certificate should cover the simple URLs and the external web services URLs, which are published as described in the section "The Reverse Proxy" earlier. The certificates you require will vary depending on your defined topology. If you split out simple URLs, each will need to be published with a certificate. If not, and the simple URLs all point to a single central location, then the URLs can be published via the standard URL used for external web services for that location. For example, you would publish meet.masteringlync.org with a certificate that has the same subject name rather than using the se01webext.masteringlync.org/meet version, which could be published using the same external certificate at the reverse proxy.

DNS ENTRIES

Of course, all of the components just described are useless unless you can locate them, which is where DNS comes in. Lync uses two types of DNS entries, the A record and the SRV record, and is generally deployed in a *split-brain* DNS implementation where the same zones are configured internally as well as externally but have different entries to give different results based on where the query originates.

Split-brain ensures that externally, the client will receive information only for the external servers (Edge), whereas, internally, the same DNS entry will point to a Front End pool. For example, for autoconfiguration of Lync clients to work, you would configure _sipinternaltls._tcp.masteringlync.org to point to se01.corp.masteringlync.org internally, whereas externally you would configure _sip._tls.masteringlync.org to point to accessedge.masteringlync.org.

With this configuration, you need to make sure that the machines in your network resolve the correct addresses. In particular, it is important to consider where Edge servers resolve their DNS queries.

Essentially, they can point either internally or to external-facing DNS servers. Either way, what is really important is that they can resolve the correct addresses for queries. You may, therefore, find that a combination of DNS and HOSTS file entries are needed. It is important to note that internal clients and servers must resolve the external address for the AV Edge service.

The Lync Edge server should resolve as follows:

FQDN	EXPECTED BEHAVIOR
Accessedge.masteringlync.org	Public IP of Access Edge (or VIP)
sip.masteringlync.org	Public IP of Access Edge (or VIP)
webconf.masteringlync.org	Public IP of Web Conferencing Edge (or VIP)
avedge.masteringlync.org	Public IP of AV Edge server (or VIP)
se01.corp.masteringlync.org	Private IP of Front End server (or VIP)

A computer on the internal network should resolve as follows:

FQDN	EXPECTED BEHAVIOR
avedge.masteringlync.org	Public IP of AV Edge server (or VIP)
edge01.corp.masteringlync.org	Internal IP of Edge server

The Lync Front End server should resolve as follows:

FQDN	EXPECTED BEHAVIOR
avedge.masteringlync.org	Public IP of AV Edge server (or VIP)
edge01.corp.masteringlync.org	Internal IP of Edge server

A computer outside your network should resolve from external DNS as follows:

FQDN	EXPECTED BEHAVIOR
Accessedge.masteringlync.org	Public IP of Access Edge (or VIP)
sip.masteringlync.org	Public IP of Access Edge (or VIP)
webconf.masteringlync.org	Public IP of Web Conferencing Edge (or VIP)
avedge.masteringlync.org	Public IP of AV Edge server (or VIP)
se01.corp.masteringlync.org	Not resolved (internal only record)

As long as the name resolution laid out here is possible, Lync will work correctly.

Of course, there are scenarios where split-brain DNS simply isn't possible. For example, suppose your internal AD domain is not the same as your external presence, such as `corp.masteringlync.org` rather than `masteringlync.org`; in this case, you would need to either create a zone internally for `masteringlync.org` and populate it with entries for your external resources or use another type of Lync client autoconfiguration, as described in Chapter 4.

The problem here is that you might not be able to create an internal zone matching your external zone because you might have hundreds of entries in the external `masteringlync.org` zone that you don't want to have to transpose to the internal zone and continue to keep up-to-date.

In that case, what can be done? Well, you can create something called a *pin-point zone*. This internally created zone is essentially the specific SRV record we wanted to create in the `masteringlync.org` zone we were not allowed or were unable to create. To create it, you must use the command line because the Windows DNS server GUI doesn't allow you to create pin-point zones. Therefore, open `cmd.exe` as an administrator on your DNS server and run the following commands:

```
dnscmd . /zoneadd _sipinternaltls._tcp.corp.masteringlync.org. /dsprimary
dnscmd . /recordadd _sipinternaltls._tcp.corp.masteringlync.org. @ SRV 0 0 5061
se01.corp.masteringlync.org.
dnscmd . /zoneadd .corp.masteringlync.org. /dsprimary
dnscmd . /recordadd .corp.masteringlync.org. @ A 192.168.1.223
```

Note that if you were performing DNS load balancing, you would need to add the additional A records for each Front End. Here's an example:

```
dnscmd . /zoneadd _sipinternaltls._tcp.corp.masteringlync.org. /dsprimary
dnscmd . /recordadd _sipinternaltls._tcp.corp.masteringlync.org. @ SRV 0 0 5061
eepoo l01.corp.masteringlync.org.
dnscmd . /zoneadd eepool01.corp.masteringlync.org. /dsprimary
dnscmd . /recordadd fe01.corp.masteringlync.org. @ A 192.168.1.223
dnscmd . /recordadd fe02.corp.masteringlync.org. @ A 192.168.1.224
dnscmd . /recordadd fe03.corp.masteringlync.org. @ A 192.168.1.225
```

Although these commands are shown for a Windows-based DNS solution, the concepts apply equally to other DNS server products; simply the implementation will differ.

FIREWALLS

Given the extent of external communication that Lync allows through use of machines in the DMZ, it is not surprising that firewalls come into play. In a Lync deployment, the recommended route is to have two firewalls as part of the topology. There should be a front firewall that sits between the Internet connection router and the Lync DMZ subnet. There should then also be a back firewall, which sits between the Lync DMZ subnet and the LAN. This means that there are routed connections between the LAN and the DMZ and between the DMZ and the Internet, and it ensures that all external traffic passes through two firewalls before entering the LAN. This configuration is shown in Figure 3.1.

FIGURE 3.1
The Lync Edge
Network layout

After you establish the location of firewalls, you must look at what holes need to be poked in them. As with any product that communicates using TCP/IP or UDP/IP, Lync requires specific firewall ports to be open. The improved Lync is much more frugal with the ports that need to be opened, especially if you are talking only to other Lync systems externally.

 Real World Scenario

DEALING WITH THREE-TIERED NETWORKS

In Figure 3.1, you can see that Lync is essentially a two-tiered system. The Edge server sits in the first tier in a DMZ and is exposed to the Internet, while the LAN containing the Front End servers is on the second tier. Throughout our consulting experience, we sometimes come across organizations that operate systems where there is a middle tier between the DMZ and LAN. These organizations are commonly in highly secure or regulated industries such as financial services.

This causes problems for Lync. The issue is that Lync has no out-of-the box way of working in these networks. The Edge would have to be in the middle tier, and therefore, the Internet would have to be opened into that tier (not supported by the organization in question) or the Front End would have to be moved to the middle tier with the Edge in the first tier (DMZ). Again, having LAN-based servers with all their AD requirements in the middle tier was not supported in such cases.

Fortunately for these installations, a company called Sipera has come up with a range of gateway devices that can act as a super proxy for all traffic destined for a Lync Edge server. The gateway device sits in the first tier (DMZ), allowing the Lync Edge to sit in the middle tier and the Front End to sit securely in the third tier (LAN). For more information, check out `www.sipera.com/company/`.

As an example, the following series of figures illustrates an enterprise perimeter network configuration in which Lync is deployed with a single Consolidated Edge server and the ports that need to be opened for Lync to work externally. Figure 3.2 shows the Reverse Proxy server and its external and internal connections. Figure 3.3 shows the external Internet port connections to the Consolidated Edge server, and Figure 3.4 shows the internal network connections. This configuration forms the basis of the ports needed even when load balancing is introduced.

FIGURE 3.2
The Reverse Proxy server and its required connections

Note that a range of ports is required for the AV Edge server role. If you look closely, you may also notice that the Access Edge role is enabled for port 53 outbound to resolve DNS. If instead you allow DNS resolution to the internal DNS servers, port TCP 53 and UDP 53 access for DNS queries would be needed through the other side of the DMZ network via the back firewall.

Because the AV Edge role has the most complex port requirements (and possibly the most concerning security), it is worth exploring those requirements in more detail. Another reason this is worth doing is that while the external ports required by the other external services stay the same no matter who you are communicating with or how, the AV Edge requirements can change—for example, if you talk with an OCS 2007 system rather than a Lync system. These requirements are detailed in Table 3.3.

FIGURE 3.3
Internet connections with the Lync Server 2013 Consolidated Edge server

TABLE 3.3:   Ports required under different circumstances by the AV Edge role

FEDERATION WITH	FEATURE	TCP/443	UDP/3478	RTP/UDP 50000–59999	RTP/TCP 50000–59999
Windows Live Messenger 5.0	Point to Point Audio/Video (A/V)	Open in	Open in and out	Not open	Open in
Lync Server 2010/2013	Lync Server 2010/2013	Open in	Open in and out	Not open	Open in
Lync Server 2010/2013	Application sharing/desktop sharing	Open in	Open in and out	Not open	Open in

TABLE 3.3: Ports required under different circumstances by the AV Edge role

FEDERATION WITH	FEATURE	TCP/443	UDP/3478	RTP/UDP 50000–59999	RTP/TCP 50000–59999
Lync Server 2010/2013	File transfer	Open in	Open in and out	Not open	Open in
Office Communications Server 2007 R2	A/V	Open in	Open in and out	Not open	Open in
Office Communications Server 2007 R2	Desktop sharing	Open in	Open in and out	Open in and out	Open in and out
Office Communications Server 2007 R2	File transfer	N/A	N/A	N/A	N/A
Office Communications Server 2007	A/V	Open in	Open in	Open in and out	Open in and out
Office Communications Server 2007	Desktop sharing	N/A	N/A	N/A	N/A
Office Communications Server 2007	File transfer	N/A	N/A	N/A	N/A

As you can see, generally it is best practice to open the range TCP 50000–59999 from the AV Edge interface outbound to any remote hosts because this allows the widest level of communication. UDP 50000–59999 is required only if you need to communicate with those on OCS 2007. It is required both inbound and outbound. The requirements for opening large port ranges have significantly improved since the early days of OCS. If you don't need the ability to talk to partners running OCS 2007, only three ports require opening inbound: TCP 5061 for SIP traffic, TCP 443 for a variety of traffic (this port is usually open for other services anyway), and UDP 3478, which is for STUN traffic, which provides external access to AV traffic.

Support for NAT on the Edge interfaces has been a long-running topic for OCS administrators. When OCS 2007 first shipped, administrators were faced with the need for large numbers of externally routable IP addresses. NAT was not supported for all interfaces (in particular the AV Edge interface/IP address). OCS 2007 R2 improved matters by allowing all the Edge interfaces to sit behind a NAT device (whether a router or firewall), but only in the single consolidated Edge server mode. Since Lync Server 2010, NAT can be used for all external Edge server interfaces, including Scaled Consolidated mode. NAT is still not supported on the internal Edge interface. This must be routable from the internal LAN.

FIGURE 3.4
Internal corporate network connections with the Lync Server 2013 Consolidated Edge server

To implement NAT on the Edge interfaces, some specific requirements must be met, in particular for the AV Edge address. These requirements cover how the destination and source addresses of the IP packets are modified when passing through the NAT device. Essentially, the principle is that traffic coming from the outside (that is, the Internet) should have its destination address in the packet header changed and traffic coming from the inside should have its source address in the IP header changed. This means that both types of traffic maintain a return path; the outside traffic maintains its source, and the internal traffic changes its source. If the internal traffic did not change its source, then return traffic would try to reach the internal NAT address, which would not be routable from the Internet.

RUNNING LYNC WITH FIREWALLS ON YOUR INTERNAL NETWORK

It is not uncommon to find networks on which Lync needs to be installed and that have firewalls separating the various internal elements of the LAN. For example, a company may have a LAN/WAN system with elements in which certain sites are less trusted than other sites. Frequently, there is a firewall between a branch site and the central site. In such cases, it is very important to fully understand which ports need to be opened. Although written for Lync Server 2010, this useful blog goes into some depth on this subject and is also relevant for Lync Server 2013:

```
http://ucmadeeasy.wordpress.com/2011/04/26/deploying-a-lync-sba-watch-out-for-
port-444/
```

One final element worth noting is that although it is not a firewall as such, the use of IP Security (IPsec) on a network affects Lync traffic—particularly the media components of Lync, which carry real-time communications. IPsec creates a delay as security is negotiated. Therefore, you should turn off IPsec for all media traffic as outlined in Table 3.4.

TABLE 3.4:   Media traffic for which IPsec needs to be disabled

RULE NAME	SOURCE IP	DESTINATION IP	PROTOCOL	SOURCE PORT	DESTINATION PORT	FILTER ACTION
A/V Edge Server Internal Inbound	Any	A/V Edge Server Internal	UDP and TCP	Any	Any	Permit
A/V Edge Server External Inbound	Any	A/V Edge Server External	UDP and TCP	Any	Any	Permit
A/V Edge Server Internal Outbound	A/V Edge Server Internal	Any	UDP and TCP	Any	Any	Permit
A/V Edge Server External Outbound	A/V Edge Server External	Any	UDP and TCP	Any	Any	Permit
Mediation Server Inbound	Any	Mediation Server(s)	UDP and TCP	Any	Any	Permit
Mediation Server Outbound	Mediation Server(s)	Any	UDP and TCP	Any	Any	Permit
Conferencing Attendant Inbound	Any	Any	UDP and TCP	Any	Any	Permit
Conferencing Attendant Outbound	Any	Any	UDP and TCP	Any	Any	Permit
A/V Conferencing Inbound	Any	A/V Conferencing Servers	UDP and TCP	Any	Any	Permit

TABLE 3.4:   Media traffic for which IPsec needs to be disabled   *(CONTINUED)*

RULE NAME	SOURCE IP	DESTINATION IP	PROTOCOL	SOURCE PORT	DESTINATION PORT	FILTER ACTION
A/V Conferencing Server Outbound	A/V Conferencing Servers	Any	UDP and TCP	Any	Any	Permit
Exchange Inbound	Any	Exchange Unified Messaging	UDP and TCP	Any	Any	Permit
Application Sharing Servers Inbound	Any	Application Sharing Servers	TCP	Any	Any	Permit
Application Sharing Server Outbound	Application Sharing Servers	Any	TCP	Any	Any	Permit
Exchange Outbound	Exchange Unified Messaging	Any	UDP and TCP	Any	Any	Permit
Clients	Any	Any	UDP	Specified media port range	Any	Permit

Understanding Core Security

By its very nature, Lync was designed to fulfill Microsoft security standards. That is, it is secure by default both in the way it is designed and in the way a deployment using default settings will work. When designing any feature in a product, Microsoft product groups conduct threat assessments to determine how the feature could be subverted to create problems. With this in mind, we will look at some of the key elements that make Lync secure, starting with media security and moving on to authentication and certificates.

Media and Signaling Security

Because it is a wide-ranging communication platform, Lync Server 2013 is subject to a lot of threats. Many of them involve someone trying to hijack traffic and manipulate it to gain access to the system. For example, common threats include *spoofing* (where someone pretends to be someone they are not), *eavesdropping* (where an attacker tries to look at traffic to ascertain its contents), and *replay* (where an attacker takes the traffic and changes it to gain access or alter content). All of these threats can be mitigated through the use of Mutual Transport Layer Security (MTLS) between trusted servers and Transport Layer Security (TLS) between client and server.

TLS and MTLS allow both encryption of traffic and authentication of endpoints. Lync clients must validate a certificate on the server; the certificate is issued by a CA that the client trusts and identifies that the server is indeed who it says it is. When MTLS is used between servers, both servers exchange certificates from a trusted CA so they can verify (trust) each other's identity. This security is in place between internal servers, and it is used when talking to gateway devices and Edge servers.

So far we have described *signaling traffic*—that is, SIP between servers or clients. There are other types of traffic, including AV media, traffic from gateways to a Mediation server, traffic from the reverse proxy to Lync servers, clients downloading content from meetings, and traffic between Lync and the Monitoring and Archiving servers. All of this traffic is also encrypted. The reverse proxy traffic is encrypted using SSL or TLS as normal, secure web traffic. The traffic from the Mediation server to the gateway can be encrypted, assuming the gateway is capable of supporting a certificate to use for MTLS. The client content download uses standard HTTPS.

One use case warrants a further comment—media traffic uses a different protocol, known as Secure Real-Time Transport Protocol (SRPT), a specialized media transfer protocol that supports encryption and traffic authentication.

FIPS SUPPORT

Readers in the United States may be pleased to know that Lync supports the Federal Information Processing Standard (FIPS) 140-2 algorithms. Each Lync server would need to be configured to use the correct FIPS algorithms, a process that is described in the following KB article:

```
http://go.microsoft.com/fwlink/?linkid=3052&kbid=811833
```

In summary, all Lync media and traffic is encrypted. This has enabled companies that were concerned with the use of traditional Voice over IP (VoIP) systems, which didn't encrypt traffic, to use Lync in secure environments, such as trading floors. Table 3.5 details the security methods for the different types of Lync traffic.

TABLE 3.5:   The protection methods used to secure Lync traffic

LYNC COMMUNICATION TYPE	SECURITY METHOD
Server to server	MTLS
Client to server	TLS
Instant messaging and presence	TLS (if configured for TLS)
Audio and video and desktop sharing of media	SRTP
Desktop sharing (signaling)	TLS
Web conferencing	TLS
Meeting content download, address book download, distribution group expansion	HTTPS

Authentication

One of the most fundamental aspects of security is authenticating those who try to access a system. In Lync, there are many ways in which a user can attempt to access the system:

◆ Through an internal Lync client

◆ Through an external Lync client

◆ Via a web application

◆ Anonymously (conferencing or via a web application)

◆ Through an IP phone device

◆ Through a mobile device

The most obvious is through the standard desktop Lync client, which operates based on authentication against credentials stored in Active Directory whether the client is internal or external to the network. Earlier in the chapter, we laid out the external authentication path via the Director, so let's look at how the authentication itself occurs. If the client is on the internal LAN, Kerberos V5 is used. For details of Kerberos and the way it operates, see the following URL:

http://msdn.microsoft.com/en-us/library/aa378747(VS.85).aspx

If the client is outside the network, NT LAN Manager (NTLM) is used because Kerberos requires direct access to the AD. NTLM is not as secure as Kerberos for many reasons. It doesn't allow mutual authentication; also, with Kerberos, passwords are never sent across the wire, thereby protecting them from man-in-the-middle attacks. Another benefit of Kerberos is that it is an open standard, whereas NTLM is not. Finally, in most recent operating systems, including Vista and Windows Server 2008 and later, Kerberos supports AES encryption but NTLM doesn't. More information about NTLM can be found here:

http://msdn.microsoft.com/en-us/library/aa378749(VS.85).aspx

Because NTLM is less secure, some companies no longer allow it to be used as a method of authentication. This restriction may mean you need to prevent remote access to Lync or you may need to use an alternative, such as Direct Access, to provide connectivity to AD.

That covers the initial default authentication of the main Lync client both inside and outside the network. However, by default, once authenticated, the client will download a Lync certificate, signed by the Front End server (this is not associated with any internal or external CAs) that can only be used to authenticate against the same Front End server from this single client. Each client will have a different certificate associated with it (see Figure 3.5 for a sample certificate).

Note that a certificate is generated for each individual client, not each user. A user using multiple clients will have multiple certificates generated. Even using the same client version on different computers (or same phone software version on different devices) will result in additional certificates being generated.

This certificate is valid for 180 days by default and can allow a user to continue to log in even if the user account in AD has been disabled. This method of login can be used on all Lync clients (PC or phone) and was developed to cater to the branch disaster scenarios in which access to AD was unavailable due to a network outage (or similar).

FIGURE 3.5
Client login
certificate

However, other types of clients with their own types of authentication are used in Lync.

The Lync Web App provides remote access to conferences. It allows you to authenticate using your corporate credentials using either NTLM or Kerberos, depending on where your client is located. Anonymous authentication can also be made available. This works using the Digest authentication protocol and requires the client/user to have a meeting ID, which can be passed as part of the authentication process. For more information about Digest authentication, go to the following location: http://technet.microsoft.com/en-us/library/cc778868(WS.10).aspx

For anonymous authentication to be allowed, you must enable it in a couple of places, first on the default Access Edge configuration as follows:

```
Set-CsAccessEdgeConfiguration -AllowAnonymousUsers $True
```

This allows anonymous connections to the Access Edge. However, you must also enable it on one or more of your conferencing policies, as follows:

```
Set-CsConferencingPolicy Identity Global -AllowAnonymousParticipantsInMeetings
    $True
```

This would allow anonymous participants in meetings governed by the global conferencing policy. Both of these steps can also be carried out through the Control Panel under the External Access and Conferencing sections, respectively.

The final type of authentication available is PIN authentication. This is part of what allows users to authenticate using just a PIN and extension combination (instead of a full username and password) on IP phone handsets and when signing into conferences. Once authenticated via PIN, a certificate is downloaded to the device and is retained on the device until the user logs out.

DISABLING A USER

Using certificate authentication has many advantages. However, one disadvantage is that users can continue to log in even when their account has been disabled. This requires an additional step to be considered for any "user leaving" process.

From PowerShell, the command to view the certificates is as follows:

```
Get-CsClientCertificate -Identity <userID>
```

This results in the following (one entry for each certificate):

```
Identity         : sip:keith.lync@masteringlync.org
CertificateType : OcsSigned
DeviceId         : {5ae27c22-4127-5e1c-8a95-0d4f8dcd2aed}
PublicationTime : 14/12/2012 14:23:32
ExpirationTime  : 12/06/2013 15:08:30
```

Removing the certificates from a user requires this command:

```
Revoke-CsClientCertificate -Identity <userID>
```

This action can also be carried out from the GUI, as shown in the following image.

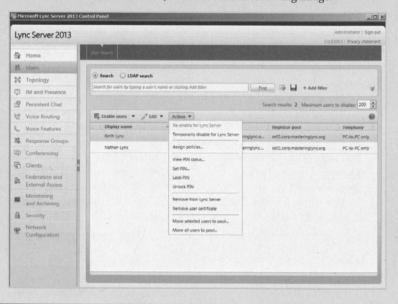

How do these certificates get to the phone devices, and how are they associated with the user? The devices are configured to look at AD for an object with the category of certifica-tionAuthority. If one is found, the caCertificate attribute is checked and the root CA certificate is installed on the device.

To load the relevant certificate into the caCertificate attribute, you must use the following command from an administrative CMD prompt:

```
certutil -f -dspublish "c:\lyncbookCA.cer" cn=corp-DC01-CA, cn=Certificate Autho
rities, cn=Public Key Services, CN=Services, cn=Configuration, dc=corp, dc=maste
ringlync, dc=org
```

This command will insert the `lyncbookCA.cer` certificate, which is the `corp-DC01-CA` root certificate, into the directory.

As long as the device is able to locate and install the relevant root CA certificate, authentication progresses as follows:

1. Obtain the root CA.

2. Verify the web services certificate using the root CA trust.

3. Store the certificate chain.

4. Take the credentials from the user, consisting of conferencing PIN and phone number.

5. Check the credentials.

6. Request a certificate for the user.

7. Receive the certificate on the device and publish it in the user store.

8. Use the certificate for all further authentications for the user.

Because the certificate needs to be obtained from AD, this procedure must be performed on the LAN the first time a user sets up the phone device. After it is set up, the device can be used remotely.

For devices that are "tethered"—that is, connected to a PC via USB—a username/password prompt will appear on the PC screen, allowing for authentication via Kerberos and onward access to information stored in Exchange. For more information, see Chapter 21, "Telephony Devices."

Two-Factor Authentication

In some environments, *two-factor authentication* is a must for any externally accessible system. Two-factor authentication is a system whereby the user has to authenticate with both something they have and something they know (for example, a PIN provided through a token device as well as a username and password). Of course, Lync is often available externally. However, providing two-factor authentication is not all that simple. In cases where extreme security is a must, various steps can be taken. You could remove external anonymous access so that all conferences require users to know both the conference ID and PIN. Second, you could ensure that only business-owned laptops are used to connect to the system externally. This could be done by using an internally signed certificate on the Edge server, which would require you to install the root CA as a trusted certificate on any remote machines. This would sacrifice the availability of PIC federation, but it would provide security. Finally, you could provide two-factor authentication on the remote laptops by using BitLocker and requiring a smart card to boot the machines.

Certificates

We have examined certificates in various contexts in this chapter already, but there are still a couple of areas that need to be addressed to ensure that Lync can use certificates.

First, public certificates should be obtained from a suitable CA. Table 3.6 lists a few of the more familiar CAs that have been validated by Microsoft as properly supporting Lync and Exchange.

TABLE 3.6:   Familiar CAs supported by Lync

CERTIFICATION AUTHORITY	URL
Entrust	www.entrust.net/microsoft/
Comodo	www.comodo.com/msexchange
DigiCert	www.digicert.com/unified-communications-ssl-tls.htm
GlobalSign	www.globalsign.com/ssl/buy-ssl-certificates/unified-communications-ssl/

Second, it is important that you set up the required certificate revocation list (CRL) distribution points for internal CAs. A CRL distribution point allows systems to validate whether a certificate has been revoked and, therefore, is no longer valid. More information about this process can be found here:

```
http://technet.microsoft.com/en-us/library/cc753296.aspx
```

Third, it is important to configure the relevant Enhanced Key Usage (EKU) settings for certificates. All Lync certificates must support the Server Authentication EKU, which is essential for MTLS to function. Also, while previous versions of Microsoft OCS required the Client Authentication EKU, now it is required only on Edge servers that connect to the AOL cloud.

Finally, as discussed earlier in the section on authentication, it is possible to allow certificate-based authentication. This can be enabled or disabled externally using the following PowerShell cmdlet:

```
Set-CsProxyConfiguration -UseCertificateForClientToProxyAuth
```

It can be enabled or disabled entirely using this cmdlet:

```
Set-CsWebServiceConfiguration -UseCertificateAuth
```

See Chapter 8 for more information about working with PowerShell.

Providing Security Administratively

No matter how secure a system is "out of the box," without correct administration, holes can easily be created through which attackers can penetrate. In the following sections, you will see how policies can be used to prevent attacks, how a company can meet regulatory requirements through the use of disclaimers, how users can protect their presence information, and how to use antivirus software with Lync.

Client-Version Filtering

To create a secure environment, narrowing down the variables in that environment can be useful. One way of doing this in Lync is to restrict access to a known set of clients. Lync allows you to do this by using CsClientVersionPolicy. This policy is composed of a collection of rules that specify which particular clients, based on their identity in SIP headers, are allowed to connect. By default, a global policy is in place. You can also set policies in a more granular way—for example, at the site or registrar level. This would allow you to have a group of users who must continue to use a legacy OCS client, perhaps because of desktop OS compatibility issues, while most of your other users are mandated to use the latest Lync client. For more information about how policies work, see Chapter 10. For more information about PowerShell, see Chapter 8.

To investigate the global policy, you must first `Get` it using the PowerShell:

```
Get-CsClientVersionPolicy -Identity global
```

This will return the policy, and you will see a blob of text showing the rules. To see each rule individually, you must use the following command:

```
Get-CsClientVersionPolicy -Identity global | Select-Object -ExpandProperty Rules
```

This first gets the policy and then pipes the output to `Select-Object`, which then extracts all the information from the `Rules` attribute and lists them separately. Following is an example of one of the rules:

```
RuleId             : d957a4a4-6053-4f70-b28b-335145a4c53f
Description        :
Action             : Allow
ActionUrl          :
MajorVersion       : 4
MinorVersion       : 9999
BuildNumber        : 9999
QfeNumber          : 9999
UserAgent          : OC
UserAgentFullName  :
Enabled            : True
CompareOp          : LEQ
```

From this output, you can see the elements that go into a rule.

To create a new policy, enter the following command:

```
New-CsClientVersionPolicy -Identity site:EMEA
```

This simple command creates a new policy with the default settings and links it to the EMEA site. However, if you wanted to amend the default rules while creating the policy, you could. To do so, you may use either the `CsClientVersionPolicyRule` cmdlet or the Control Panel, as shown in Figure 3.6.

Whether you use the cmdlet or the GUI, the requirements are relatively complex, so it is important to understand them.

First, each rule must have a *unique identifier*. This means it must have a reference to where it will be attached—that is, the scope of the policy to which it will be applied. It must also have a globally unique identifier (GUID).

Next, you must specify the client type from those shown in Figure 3.6 and Table 3.7, along with the version that will be referenced in the policy, and whether the client will be allowed or blocked or one of the other actions will be chosen. For example, you could allow the client to be blocked and show the user a URL where they can get more information about why the client has been blocked or even download a newer version. Equally, you could have the client blocked and then automatically upgraded based on software available through Windows Update or Windows Software Update Services. Whether it is enabled or not, you can also configure how the rule is matched; that is, versions equal to that specified, or less than or equal to, and so on. For the full list, see Figure 3.7.

FIGURE 3.6

The client types available in Rules

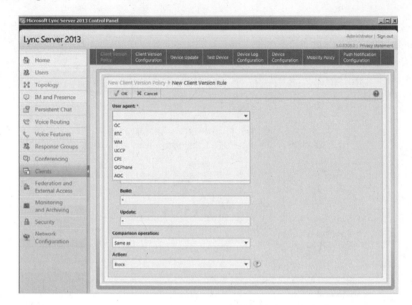

FIGURE 3.7

The match types available in Rules

TABLE 3.7:   Client codes and associated clients

CLIENT CODE	CLIENT DETAIL
OC	Office Communicator or Lync client
RTC	LCS clients
WM	Live Messenger
UCCP	Applications such as response groups
CPE	IP Phone
OCPhone	IP Phone
AOC	Attendee only client
iPadLync*	iPad Lync client
iPhoneLync*	iPhone Lync client
WPLync*	Windows Phone Lync client
NokiaLync*	Nokia Lync client
AndroidLync*	Android Lync client
McxService*	Mobility service

Items are available for configuration only in the Lync Management Shell.

Finally it is important to note that the rules in a policy are listed in order of precedence. This is why you have the option to specify the priority of the rule. If you specify a priority that is already in use, the new rule will take the priority number given and all the other rules will move down one.

Now that you've seen the possibilities, let's create a couple of rules for different scenarios. We will do the first one in the Control Panel.

1. Log into the Control Panel with an account that is a member of the CsAdministrator RBAC group (for more information, see Chapter 9, "Role-Based Access Control").

2. Locate the Clients tab and then double-click the Global policy in the right pane. This will open it for editing.

3. Click New. On the page that opens, specify the client type in the User Agent drop-down shown earlier in Figure 3.7. Select OC, which is the client type for Lync and Office Communicator clients. This becomes the identifier of the rule. Figure 3.8 shows the completed rule.

FIGURE 3.8

The finished rule

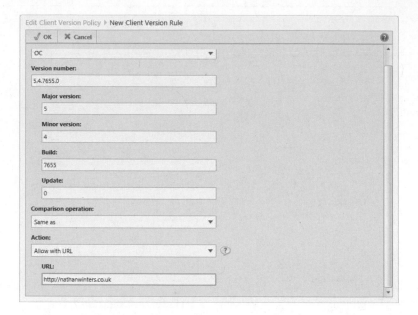

4. Enter the relevant version information to match the client—for example, Lync client version 15.0.4420.1017. Newer versions are released each quarter.

5. Set the action, which in this case is to allow and launch a URL. Enter the URL as shown in Figure 3.9 and then click OK.

6. On the main policy page, locate the rule, which by default will be at the bottom of the list of rules in the policy. Use the green up and down arrows to position it where needed. Once you are satisfied, click Commit.

Now when users log in using the specified Lync client version, they will be presented with a pop-up in the Windows Taskbar, which suggests that a new version of the client is available. If they click the pop-up, they will be taken to the appropriate website.

To create a similar rule from PowerShell, do the following. First, create a GUID for the rule:

```
$g = [guid]::NewGuid()
```

This generates a GUID and stores it in the $g variable. Next, create the rule using the following command:

```
New-CsClientVersionPolicyRule -Parent "Global" -RuleId $g -MajorVersion 15 -Minor
Version 0 -BuildNumber 4420 -QfeNumber 1017 -UserAgent OC -Action AllowWithUrl -A
ctionUrl "http://nathanwinters.co.uk/LyncRuleAllow.htm" -CompareOp EQL -Priority
0
```

This will create the same rule as the one created through the GUI. Do *not* do this if you've already created the rule in the GUI; you will get an error if you do. You will need to change the version details to prevent a duplicate entry to get it to run.

Now you can create new rules and add them to existing policies. You need to understand that the way all Client Version policies are applied is governed by the cmdlet `CsClientVersionConfiguration`. Among other things, `CsClientVersionConfiguration` allows you to modify the default action for clients not specifically mentioned in the active policy, to enable or disable Client Version checks entirely, and to specify the default URL to which clients are pointed if the action of a rule is set to point users to a URL but no URL is specified. The following is an example:

```
New-CsClientVersionConfiguration -Identity site:EMEA -Enabled $True
-DefaultAction Block
-DefaultURL "http://nathanwinters.co.uk/LyncRuleBlock.htm"
```

This command creates a new Client Version Configuration policy for the Europe Middle East and Africa (EMEA) site; it enables version checking, blocks any clients not specifically listed on Client Version policies, and points any users that match rules with an action pointing to a URL, if they do not have their own URL defined, to the `http://nathanwinters.co.ukLyncRuleBlock.htm` site.

Note that both the new Client Version policy rule and the new Client Version configuration can be configured from the Clients tab in the Control Panel.

Message Hygiene

The Lync IM functionality has many uses, and it frequently cuts down on email usage by implementing a quick efficient method of communicating. One element of an IM conversation is the ability to send files and links. Of course, this ability has the potential to open users up to malicious or inadvertent threats because files can contain viruses and links can point to unsafe files or sites. Lync, therefore, allows administrators to control what can and can't be sent in an IM conversation.

The `CsImFilterConfiguration` cmdlet allows you to control what happens when a user attempts to send a link through IM. By default, links are allowed in IM messages. To control this, you can enable the `CsImFilterConfiguration` policy. These settings can be manipulated either as shown (through PowerShell) or in the Control Panel on the IM & Presence section.

Once set, all messages sent by those users within the scope of the policy (for more information about scope, see Chapter 10) will be checked for links. The options are to block the link so that the message will not be sent, allow it but disable the link by inserting an underscore (_) character at the beginning of the link, or warn the user with a specific message but still allow the link to operate. By default, the `CsImFilterConfiguration` settings pick up the following link types:

- `callto:`
- `file:`
- `ftp.`
- `ftp:`
- `gopher:`
- `href`

- ◆ http:
- ◆ https:
- ◆ ldap:
- ◆ mailto:
- ◆ news:
- ◆ nntp:
- ◆ sip:
- ◆ sips:
- ◆ tel:
- ◆ telnet:
- ◆ www*

For example, to create a new policy for the EMEA site, use this command:

```
New-CsImFilterConfiguration -Identity site:EMEA -Action Warn -WarnMessage "This
link could be dangerous, make sure you know where it is taking you!"
-Prefixes http: -Enabled $true
```

This will create a new policy for the EMEA site. When it sees a link starting with the `http:` prefix, it will warn users with the text shown next to the `WarnMessage` parameter. Note that if you wanted to have all the prefixes listed as defaults here, you would not specify the `Prefixes` parameter. Figure 3.9 shows the client result with this rule in place.

FIGURE 3.9
Warning message on Communicator client after sending an IM containing a URL

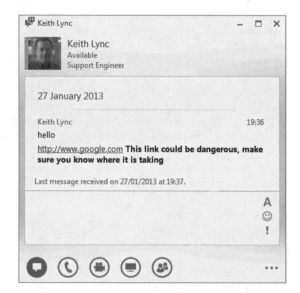

One issue with this process is that if the link is sent as the first message in a conversation and would appear in the "toast," then no warning message is attached, simply the link itself.

To remove the newly created policy, use the following command:

```
Remove-CsImFilterConfiguration -Identity site:EMEA
```

This command removes the CsImFilterConfiguration policy assigned to the EMEA site. Basic enabling and disabling of hyperlinks, which you can do through CsClientPolicy using the EnableURL setting, is another way to block URLs in IM.

Now that we've looked at how to mitigate one threat, let's look at the threat associated with file transfer via IM. Just as with email attachments, normal antivirus scanning on client machines will provide a lot of protection. However, you can also control whether all or no attachments are allowed and whether specific file types are allowed. This is done using the CsFileTransferFilterConfiguration cmdlets.

The New-CsFileTransferFilterConfiguration cmdlet is relatively simple. It enables you to create a policy that affects a certain scope of users, defined using the Identity parameter as discussed in Chapter 10. The key parameters that make up the policy settings are Action, Enabled, and Extensions. The Extensions parameter is simply a list of the allowed (or disallowed) file types. By default, the following file types are part of a policy:

```
.ade, .adp, .app, .asp, .bas, .bat, .cer, .chm, .cmd, .com, .cpl, .crt, .csh, .exe, .fxp,
.grp, .hlp, .hta, .inf, .ins, .isp, .its, .js, .jse, .ksh, .lnk, .mad, .maf, .mag, .mam, .maq,
.mar, .mas, .mat, .mau, .mav, .maw, .mda, .mdb, .mde, .mdt, .mdw, .mdz, .msc, .msi, .msp,
.mst, .ocx, .ops, .pcd, .pif, .pl, .pnp, .prf, .prg, .pst, .reg, .scf, .scr, .sct, .shb, .shs,
.tmp, .url, .vb, .vbe, .vbs, .vsd, .vsmacros, .vss, .vst, .vsw, .ws, .wsc, .wsf, .wsh
```

The Enabled parameter lets you turn filtering on or off entirely. By default, file transfers of the types just listed are blocked. The Action parameter controls what happens when a file type listed in the Extensions parameter is detected. It has two possible settings, BlockAll and Block. The default is Block, which blocks file types listed in the Extensions parameter; by contrast, BlockAll simply prevents any file transfers.

To create a new file transfer configuration policy for the EMEA site, use the following command:

```
New-CsFileTransferFilterConfiguration -Identity site:EMEA
```

This command creates a new policy for the EMEA site with default extension values. Alternatively, you could specify different file types as shown here:

```
New-CsFileTransferFilterConfiguration -Identity site:EMEA -Extensions .moo, .too
```

If you only want to add to the default types, enter the following:

```
New-CsFileTransferFilterConfiguration -Identity site:EMEA -Extensions @{
Add=".moo",".too"}
```

Finally, you can also add to an existing CsFileTransferFilterConfiguration policy, using this command:

```
Set-CsFileTransferFilterConfiguration -Identity site:EMEA -Extensions @{
Add=".doo",".foo"}
```

Configuring Antivirus Scanning

As with other Microsoft server–based systems, having an antivirus product in place on both the servers and the clients is sensible. On the client, antivirus scanning will be most relevant to Lync when using the file transfer and content download features, because these elements will be scanned and protected by the antivirus software. On the server side, there are no such features; however, as a best practice, AV software should still be deployed. It is important to configure that software correctly so that scanning does not compromise Lync performance. To do so, you must configure the following exclusions:

Lync Server 2013 processes:

- ◆ ABServer.exe
- ◆ ASMCUSvc.exe
- ◆ AVMCUSvc.exe
- ◆ ClsAgent.exe
- ◆ DataMCUSvc.exe
- ◆ DataProxy.exe
- ◆ Fabric.exe
- ◆ FabricDCA.exe
- ◆ FabricHost.exe
- ◆ FileTransferAgent.exe
- ◆ IMMCUSvc.exe
- ◆ LysSvc.exe
- ◆ MasterReplicatorAgent.exe
- ◆ MediaRelaySvc.exe
- ◆ MediationServerSvc.exe
- ◆ MeetingMCUSvc.exe
- ◆ MRASSvc.exe
- ◆ OcsAppServerHost.exe
- ◆ QmsSvc.exe
- ◆ ReplicaReplicatorAgent.exe
- ◆ RTCArch.exe
- ◆ RtcCdr.exe

- RtcHost.exe

- RTCSrv.exe

- XmppTGW.exe

IIS processes:

- %systemroot%\system32\inetsrv\w3wp.exe

- %systemroot%\SysWOW64\inetsrv\w3wp.exe

SQL Server processes:

- %ProgramFiles%\Microsoft SQL Server\MSSQL11.LYNCLOCAL\MSSQL\Binn\SQLServr. exe

- %ProgramFiles%\Microsoft SQL Server\ MSSQL11.LYNCLOCAL\Reporting Services\ ReportServer\Bin\ReportingServicesService.exe

- %ProgramFiles%\Microsoft SQL Server\ MSSQL11.LYNCLOCAL\OLAP\Bin\MSMDSrv.exe

Directories:

- %systemroot%\System32\LogFiles

- %systemroot%\SysWow64\LogFiles

Disclaimers

In many countries, regulations specify how a company should identify itself in business communications. IM is just another form of business communication, and, like email, it can be used to communicate with other companies. Therefore, applying disclaimers or footnotes to messages is often required. In the United Kingdom this footnote should, for example, contain the company's registration details.

Lync has a couple of places where you can add disclaimers. One is applicable to those who join conferences and is configured using the Set-CsConferenceDisclaimer. You could, for example, use the following command to set up a disclaimer that will be shown to anyone joining the conference using a web link, such as the Join URL.

```
Set-CsConferenceDisclaimer -Header "MasteringLync.org Conference Service" -Body
"Please Note: Conferences can be recorded. You will be notified if a conference
is recorded in the client and can choose to leave."
```

This displays the text in the Body parameter to users joining conferences.

The more common disclaimer used in Lync is the one added to IM messages. To apply disclaimers to IMs, you need to use the CsClientPolicy cmdlets. In particular, the IMWarning parameter must be set as follows:

```
Set-CsClientPolicy -Identity Global -IMWarning "IM message from Company Mastering
Lync"
```

This command simply applies the warning text to all users. However, it is possible to target different `IMWarning` text at different users using the standard method of creating new policies with specific User scopes, as described in Chapter 10.

PIN Policy

As discussed in the section "Authentication" earlier in this chapter, you can log into Lync using a PIN in conjunction with your extension or phone number. This is used when connecting to conferences via a phone line rather than using the Lync client and also when using a Lync IP phone device. As with any other authentication method, controlling the form of credentials that can be used is important. PIN policies allow you to define the minimum length for a PIN and also to configure whether or not to allow common patterns, such as consecutive digits (for example, a PIN like 123456 or 111111). You can also define the length of validity for a specific PIN and the number of PINs the system remembers, so a user can't continually use the same one.

To create a new PIN policy, use the `New-CsPinPolicy` cmdlet. The next command shows how to create one for the EMEA site:

```
New-CsPinPolicy -Identity "site:EMEA" -MinPasswordLength 7 -PINHistoryCount 5
-PINLifetime 60
```

This command will create a new PIN policy and assign it to the EMEA site. The minimum length will be seven digits, five previous PINs will be remembered, and the PIN will expire in 60 days. As described in Chapter 10, these policies could be assigned to either the site or the per-user scope. This feature can also be configured in the Control Panel under the Security section.

Federation and How to Control It

We'll end with a discussion of *federation*. This feature enables you to communicate using Lync not only internally but also externally with those who also have Lync and even those on public IM services such as Windows Live Messenger, Yahoo!, and Skype. Lync Server 2013 also introduces built-in XMPP federation capability—previous versions required a separate download and also a separate server installation for XMPP.

Being able to talk not only within your company but with others over voice, video, and of course IM is a great benefit; however, some companies have concerns about the level of flexibility this brings. For example, while it is usually possible to email companies outside your own, your organization may have detailed controls in place to monitor such traffic. These restrictions may not be in place for Lync; therefore, your company may want to restrict your ability to federate entirely or limit it to specific external parties.

By default, federation is disabled. You can enable it during the setup of the Edge server or afterward using this command:

```
Set-CsAccessEdgeConfiguration -AllowFederatedUsers:$True
```

This command configures the Access Edge role to allow federation. There is one more step to enable federation. You need to ensure that the users you want to be able to communicate with federated contacts are covered by a `CsExternalAccessPolicy` that enables federation for those users.

To edit the default global policy, use a command like this:

```
Set-CsExternalAccessPolicy -Identity Global -EnableFederationAccess:$True
-EnablePublicCloudAccess:$True
```

This command enables standard external federation with other companies and also access to public clouds such as Messenger, assuming they have been allowed globally using the `Enable-CsPublicProvider` cmdlet as shown here:

```
Enable-CsPublicProvider -Identity "Messenger"
```

This would enable global access to Messenger; other options would be Yahoo!, AIM, and LyncOnline.

Of course, you may not want to simply enable all federation. This can be controlled using the `Set-CsAccessEdgeConfiguration` cmdlet. Here's an example:

```
Set-CsAccessEdgeConfiguration - EnablePartnerDiscovery:$True
```

This command enables essentially open federation where companies looking to federate will locate each other through DNS SRV records and connect automatically, while setting `EnablePartnerDiscovery` to `$False` would restrict federation to those domains specified manually. This leaves us with how to manipulate the list of allowed or blocked federation domains, which is done using the `CsAllowedDomain` and `CsBlockedDomain` cmdlets. Here's an example:

```
New-CsAllowedDomain -Identity "masteringlync.info"
-ProxyFqdn "edgeserver.masteringlync.info"
-MarkForMonitoring $True
-Comment "Contact: Nathan Winters (nwinters@masteringlync.info)"
```

Here we created a new entry to allow the domain `masteringlync.info` to participate in a federated relationship. We also specified the URL for the Edge server in the federated domain and that we want to monitor the traffic. Finally, we added a comment labeling the domain with a contact person.

The method of blocking domains is similar.

```
New-CsBlockedDomain -Identity "masteringlync.com" -Comment "Blocked by Nathan
Winters."
```

This simple command blocks the `masteringlync.com` domain from federating with our system and lists Nathan Winters as the person who carried out the configuration. Again, note that although PowerShell is used in this section to perform the configuration, these settings could have been set from the Control Panel in the External Access section.

The Bottom Line

Secure external access.   Lync utilizes the Edge server and supporting components to provide external access to communications modalities. The Edge server sits in the DMZ and is a proxy between internal and external users. Many layers of security are in place to ensure that communicating externally won't cause security breaches.

Master It Describe the role the Director plays in external access. Why would you use one?

Understand core security. Lync is designed to be secure by default. It does this in many ways, not least of which is by encrypting all traffic and using certificates as part of mutual authentication of connections.

Master It In different circumstances, Lync can use five different authentication mechanisms. What are they and where are they used?

Provide security administratively. No matter how secure a product is by design, an administrator can easily open up holes in its defenses. Lync provides many ways in which administrators can participate in tightening or relaxing security. Numerous policies are available to control users, including the clients they are allowed to use and the length and complexity of PINs. Equally, you can configure Lync to block links in IMs and prevent the transfer of files. Finally, Lync can be set up to add disclaimers to messages so that regulatory issues can be managed.

Master It You have been asked to ensure that users in the EMEA site can send only files with extension .txt in IM messages and that any links in the messages will be prefixed with an underscore character so they must be copied into a browser manually. How would you do this?

Chapter 4

Clients

Client applications tend to be one of the most important aspects of a Lync deployment, and they can cause the most pain if they are not fully understood. Lync 2013 includes several significant changes from the previous release, updating the main Lync 2013 desktop client with new features such as multiparty video and integrated Persistent Chat, introducing a new client specifically designed for Windows 8 and optimized for touch-screen devices, and significantly changing the Lync Web App client, resulting in Lync Attendee now being deprecated.

Understanding the features the various clients have to offer, how they should be configured, and how they coexist and interoperate with each other and previous versions ensures that the correct clients are deployed to the correct people at the correct phase of the Lync deployment project.

In this chapter, you will learn about:

- ◆ Usage scenarios for and features of each of the Lync clients

- ◆ Customizing and configuring Lync clients using Group Policy and in-band provisioning

- ◆ Changes to the Desktop and Web App clients to support new features such as multiparty video, Persistent Chat, and IP audio and video

- ◆ How clients discover and communicate with various server roles, such as the Director, Front End, Persistent Chat, and the various Multipoint Control Units (MCUs) for conferencing

Lync User Clients

In Lync Server 2013, there are four main clients that we will focus on for the remainder of this chapter:

- ◆ Lync 2013 and Lync 2013 Basic, which are both Windows desktop clients

- ◆ Lync Web App, the significantly redesigned Lync Web App found in Lync Server 2010; now supports IP audio and video

- ◆ Lync Windows Store app, which is designed specifically for Windows 8 and Windows RT devices and is optimized to work with touch screens

Lync for mobile devices (including iPad) is covered in Chapter 20, "Mobility," and the Lync Attendee and Attendant clients have not been updated for Lync Server 2013. Furthermore, use of the Lync 2010 Attendee client is no longer recommended in Lync Server 2013 because Lync Web App is now the preferred meeting experience client.

Lync 2013

Lync 2013 is the updated version of the Lync 2010 client and provides access to all of the functionality of Lync Server 2013. Unlike previous versions of the UC platform the latest client can be used against a *legacy* infrastructure, meaning Lync 2013 can also be used against a Lync Server 2010 pool, allowing you to deploy the latest client (which is included as part of Microsoft Office 2013) without having to migrate everybody to Lync Server 2013 first.

The Lync 2013 client is a full-featured client for Lync Server 2013. The user interface has been redesigned to incorporate new features, such as Persistent Chat (previously a separate client with Lync Server 2010), tabbed conversations, video preview, and multiparty video. At a high level, the client provides the following features:

- Contacts: Similar to Lync 2010, the contact list displays the name, presence, photo, and communication modalities available for users.

   - **Contact photos**: Lync 2013 makes a couple of changes to contact photos. The first noticeable change from Lync 2010 is that the option to set your photo using a user-specified URL has been removed from the Lync 2013 client. Lync 2013 will still honor the URL if it is included in another user's presence document (e.g., if Alice subscribes to Bob's presence, and Bob has previously set his Facebook or LinkedIn photo as his contact photo, Alice would still see that photo). Lync 2013 also introduces support for HD photos, although this feature requires Exchange Server 2013 (more in the section "High-Resolution Photos" later in this chapter). This is particularly useful when you're in a conference and are not sharing video: instead of showing an up-scaled version of the low-resolution photo in Lync 2010, Lync 2013 can now display an HD-quality photo. Photos are capped to ~300Kb and are shared across Office (e.g., Outlook, Outlook Web App, Lync, etc.). A small version of the photo is also written back to the *thumbnailPhoto* attribute in Active Directory, for backward compatibility with Lync 2010.

   - **New Contacts view**: Lync 2013 includes a New Contacts view to allow you to easily see who has added you to their contacts list recently.

- **Presence**: Lync includes two new presence statuses, Off Work and Presenting, which are triggered automatically when sharing PowerPoint slides.

- **Instant messaging**: Similar to Lync 2010, instant messaging is supported between users in the same organization as well as in other organizations running Lync Server or Office Communications Server via federation.

   - **XMPP**: While no different to the end user, XMPP (Extensible Messaging and Presence Protocol) is now natively supported in Lync 2013. You can add an XMPP user to your contacts list and engage in IM/Presence conversations with them the same way you could before, but this no longer requires the separate Office Communications Server 2007 R2 XMPP Gateway role. This functionality is built into the Lync Server 2013 Edge and Front End servers.

   - **Tabbed Conversations**: One change from Lync 2010 is the support for Tabbed Conversations. This allows the user to have all IM conversations appear in a single window, with tabs representing each conversation for easy switching. This feature also extends to Persistent Chat, which is now natively supported in the Lync 2013 client (see the section on Persistent Chat later in this chapter for more information).

- **Voice**: While there have been some investments in voice in Lync Server 2013, the majority of these are "under the covers" and are server-side or topology changes rather than being exposed through the Lync 2013 client.

- **Video**: Lync 2013 represents a major investment in video. At a technical level, the video codec used by Lync 2013 is now the standards-based H.264 AVC/SVC codec rather than RTVideo. Additionally, a number of user interface changes are apparent in the Lync 2013 client:

  - **Multiview video**: Instead of being based on *active* and *last active* speaker, Lync 2013 now features multiview video for more natural integrations, showing you the video stream of the 5 most active users in the conference, with support for up to 75 users being promoted from the Seating Row to the Standing Row.

  - **HD in conference**: Lync 2013 now supports HD video of up to 720p for conferences as well as 1080p for room-based systems.

- **Collaboration**: Similar to the investments in video, Lync 2013 has been significantly redesigned to incorporate new features related to collaboration:

  - **PowerPoint viewing**: Lync 2010 relied on the Microsoft Office PowerPoint viewer, embedded in the Lync client, to render PPT slides with animations and transitions. This limited PowerPoint sharing to platforms where the PowerPoint viewer was available. In Lync 2013 and Lync Server 2013, the Office Web Apps companion server role is used to render PowerPoint slides. For more details, see the section "Lync Conferencing Clients" later in this chapter.

- **Application and Desktop Sharing**

  - **DRM**: Following customer feedback, Lync 2013 now supports and honors DRM in a desktop sharing session. If a user opens a DRM-protected document, it will appear blacked out in a desktop sharing session.

  - **Lync Web App**: Application and desktop sharing are now supported in Lync Web App. This requires a browser plug-in, which can be installed in user mode. See later in "Lync Web App."

  - **Whiteboard**: Lync 2013 supports sending whiteboard images directly to OneNote. Additionally, touch is supported for whiteboards when viewed on Windows 7 or Windows 8 as well as Smart Board devices.

  - **Recording**: Lync 2013 removes the intermediate file format it had for recording in Lync 2010 and instead records natively into MP4 format. Additionally, Lync 2013 supports active speaker recording, which will record the video or photo of the active speaker, unlike Lync 2010, which would record one person for the whole meeting if they were the only person sharing video. Recordings are also in HD format.

- **File Transfer**: File transfer is unchanged from Lync 2010.

- **Persistent Chat**: Another large area of investment in Lync 2013 is the integration of Persistent Chat, formerly Group Chat, into both the server architecture (although it is still a separate pool, it is defined and managed through standard tools now, such as Topology Builder and Lync Server Management Shell) and the client user interface:

◆ **Built-in Persistent Chat**: In Lync 2013, there is no longer a separate Persistent Chat client, as was the case in Lync 2010. The Lync 2013 desktop client is a truly unified client, providing IM and presence, audio, video, conferencing and collaboration, desktop and application sharing and Persistent Chat in a single user interface. See the section on Persistent Chat later in this chapter for more details.

OTHER CHANGES FROM LYNC 2010

The following are other changes from Lync 2010:

◆ **Integration with Office Setup**: Lync 2013 and the Online Meeting add-in for Lync 2013, which supports meeting management from within Microsoft Outlook, are both included with Office 2013. In addition to including the client as part of Office 2013, this change allows administrators to customize and control the installation using the Office Customization Tool (OCT), `Config.xml`, and set up command-line options. Additionally, Lync 2013 installs side-by-side with the previous version (either Lync 2010 or Office Communicator 2007 R2).

◆ **Group Policy deployment**: Lync 2013 introduces the Lync ADMX and ADML administrative templates that are provided with Office Group Policy administrative templates.

◆ **Outlook Scheduling Add-in updates**: Administrators can now customize the organization's meeting invitations by adding a custom logo, a support URL, a legal disclaimer URL, and custom footer text. These can be enabled and customized using Lync Server Control Panel or Lync Server Management Shell, specifically the `CsMeetingConfiguration` cmdlets. Additionally, new controls allow the meeting organizer to schedule conferences that have attendee audio and video muted by default.

◆ **Virtual Desktop Infrastructure (VDI) plug-in**: Lync 2013 supports all modalities, including audio and video, when deployed in a Virtual Desktop Infrastructure (VDI) environment, with some caveats. Users can connect an audio or video device (e.g., a USB headset) to the local computer (e.g., thin client). The user can connect to the virtual machine, sign in to Lync 2013 running inside the virtual machine, and participate in real-time audio and video as though the client is running locally. This is achieved by using the VDI plug-in, a standalone application that installs on the local computer and allows the use of local audio and video devices. The plug-in does not require Lync 2013 to be installed on the local computer. Lync 2013, running inside the virtual machine, will prompt the user to enter their credentials to establish a connection to the VDI plug-in. The caveats are as follows:

  ◆ The virtual machine must be running Windows 8, Windows 7, or Windows Server 2008 R2 with the latest service pack.

  ◆ The user's local computer (e.g., thin client) must be running Windows Embedded Standard 7 with SP1, Windows 7 with SP1, or Windows 8.

  ◆ If Remote Desktop Services is used, the Lync VDI plug-in platform architecture (32-bit or 64-bit) must match the local computer's operating system platform architecture.

  ◆ On the local computer (e.g., thin client), the remote desktop client settings must be configured so that audio plays on the local computer. Remote recording must be disabled.

In addition to the caveats listed here, there are a number of limitations of the Lync 2013 VDI plug-in. There is limited support for call delegation and Response Group Agent anonymization, and there is no support for integrated audio and video device tuning, multiview video, recording of conversations, joining meetings anonymously (e.g., joining a Lync meeting hosted by an organization that does not federate with your company), pairing a Lync Phone Edition device, call continuity in the event of a network outage, or customized ringtones and music on hold (MOH).

SIGN-IN CHANGES

Lync 2010 introduced certificate-based authentication using TLS-DSK. Clicking Save Password when signing in results in Lync Server issuing you a certificate, which is then saved in the Personal certificate store on the individual computer, as shown in Figure 4.1. This certificate is then used to authenticate future sign-in requests, allowing Lync to sign in without communicating with an Active Directory domain controller, which is useful in branch office scenarios during a WAN outage. Certificate authentication is also faster than Kerberos or NTLM authentication.

FIGURE 4.1

The user certificate in the Personal certificate store

Lync 2013 continues the support for TLS-DSK authentication but with a couple of changes in the client. First, when you check the Save Password check box when signing in for the first time, you are now clearly prompted to indicated whether you want to save your Lync sign-in info for use in the future, as shown in Figure 4.2.

FIGURE 4.2

User being prompted about saving sign-in credentials

Second, the option to delete sign-in information, effectively asking Lync 2013 to forget you, is now displayed at the sign-in screen, as shown in Figure 4.3. Clicking this will provide a prompt asking you to confirm. Clicking Yes will remove the Lync certificate from the user's certificate store. It will also remove a number of files listed below from the `AppData` folder, located in `%userprofile%\appdata\local\microsoft\office\15.0\lync\<sipuri>`.

- ABS cache file

- `CoreContact.cache`

- `EndpointConfiguration.cache`

- EwsFolder cache file

- MfuGroup cache

FIGURE 4.3
The link allowing
you to ask Lync to
forget your sign-in
details

INSTALLATION CHANGES

One significant difference with Lync 2013 is the way administrators can deploy the Lync client to their users. While it is possible to obtain a separate stand-alone installer for Lync 2013, the preferred option is to deploy Lync 2013 as part of Office 2013. There are two methods of doing this:

- **Office 2013 Windows Installer**: This is the traditional Windows Installer package that contains multiple MSI files.

- **Office 2013 Click-to-Run**: Primarily intended for Office 365 customers, this is an installation method that streams Office 2013 setup files from the Office 365 portal or another installation source. Administrators can download the Office 2013 Click-to-Run application and language source files to an on-premises location. Details on Click-to-Run can be found in the Office 2013 Resource Kit.

DEPENDENCY ON EXCHANGE SERVER 2013

A number of new features in Lync 2013 rely on the user's mailbox being hosted on Exchange Server 2013. These features are Unified Contact Store, high-resolution photos, and Exchange archiving, and each is introduced here and covered in more detail in Chapter 17, "Exchange and SharePoint."

Unified Contact Store

Unlike in previous versions, in Lync Server 2013, Exchange Server is the Unified Contact Store across Office. This is enabled by policy when Exchange Server 2013 is deployed in the environment. Unified Contact Store can be enabled only when both Lync Server 2013 and Exchange Server 2013 are deployed in the environment. Communication between Lync and Exchange are handled by Exchange Web Services (EWS). Lync 2010 can leverage the Unified Contact Store in read-only mode, but only Lync 2013 clients can modify the contact list once Unified Contact Store is enabled by policy for a given user. The benefits of this are that it provides a single repository of contact data—Exchange, which is utilized across Office as well as Windows Phone.

High-Resolution Photos

Lync 2010 supported contact photos that could be stored either in Active Directory or as a user-specified URL, referencing a public website. Whether the photo was stored or not depended on the photo's source. If the photo was from Active Directory, it would be stored in the *thumbnail-Photo* attribute and replicated to other domain controllers in the environment. If the photo was from a user-specified URL, the photo was not stored in the environment. Instead, the URL was stored and communicated to other presence watchers via the user's presence document.

The size of photos stored in Active Directory was limited by the size of the thumbnailPhoto attribute in Active Directory, which needed to remain relatively small so as not to negatively impact replication traffic.

Lync 2013 supports the ability to use photos with resolutions ranging from 48 × 48 up to 648 × 648 pixels, provided your mailbox is hosted on Exchange Server 2013. This is because the photos are now stored in Exchange as one of three typical resolutions:

- ◆ 48 × 48, which is also used for the thumbnailPhoto attribute in Active Directory

- ◆ 96 × 96, which is the format Outlook 2013, Outlook Web App, Lync 2013, and Lync Web App will use in various places

- ◆ 648 × 648, which is the format used by Lync 2013 and Lync Web App in specific scenarios, such as when you're the active speaker in a conference and you're not sharing your video

As mentioned, a change in Lync 2013 is that the ability to specify a photo from a URL has been removed from the client. If a user still has a photo from a user-specified URL stored in their presence document, Lync 2013 will honor it. However, as soon as a high-resolution photo is stored in the user's Exchange Server 2013 mailbox, this replaces the URL and also triggers the 48 × 48 version of the photo being stored in Active Directory for backward compatibility. Additionally, because the photos are now stored in the Exchange mailbox rather than being a URL referenced in the presence document, photos will no longer be displayed to federated users. This was always the case in Lync 2010 for photos stored in the thumbnailPhoto attribute in Active Directory. Users can change their photos via Outlook Web App. One thing to keep in mind is that changing the photo in Active Directory does not trigger an up-scaled version of that photo to replace the one stored in the Exchange Server 2013 mailbox. Due to Lync 2013's use of photos in places such as multiparty conversations, it is recommended that users have a photo to replace the default icon and display name that Lync 2013 will use instead.

Archiving

The final new feature where Lync 2013 has a reliance on Exchange Server 2013 is archiving. When this is enabled, Lync archive data is written to the Exchange Server 2013 mailbox instead of the Lync archiving database (in SQL). This does not mean you can only enable archiving in Lync 2013 once everybody is on Exchange Server 2013; users who do not have an Exchange Server 2013 mailbox can continue to use the Lync archiving database store (SQL) instead. However, the benefit of using the Exchange integrated archiving feature is that it results in a single archive repository—the Exchange Server mailbox—and makes legal hold and compliance easier to administer.

MULTIPARTY VIDEO

As mentioned earlier, a significant amount of investment in Lync 2013 is around video and the collaboration experience in general. One of the most noticeable and striking differences in this area in the Lync 2013 client is multiparty video.

In Lync 2010, active speaker switching was used to switch the video stream between whoever was speaking. It was not possible to see the video streams of other participants in the meeting, with the exception of using a room-based system or a RoundTable device for video panorama, but that relied on all participants being in the same physical location.

Lync 2013 supports multiparty video, allowing the video stream (or high-resolution picture if no video is shared) to be displayed for 5 speakers, plus yourself, in the "standing row," with support for up to 75 participants in total, with the others making up the Seated Row.

In Figure 4.4, we see three users who are taking part in a Lync meeting. The screen shot shows Nathan's view of the conversation, indicated by the fact that his is the smallest of the three tiles in the window.

FIGURE 4.4
A multiparty call showing the user experience

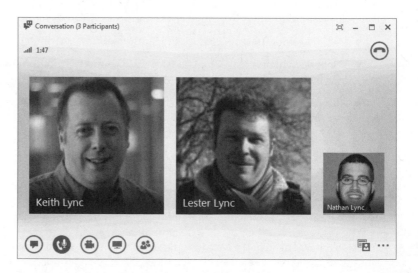

Video Preview

Another new feature in Lync 2013 is the video preview. This allows you to hover your cursor over the video icon in the Lync 2013 client and display a "peek," showing you what your video looks like to others, before you actually start sharing it. If you're happy with what you see (within reason), you can click Start My Video to start sharing your video. In Figure 4.5 and then Figure 4.6, you can see Lester's video replacing the photo currently displayed on Lester's tile in the conversation window.

FIGURE 4.5
Viewing a video preview

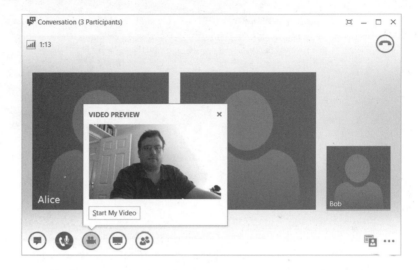

FIGURE 4.6
Video now shown in the call

Figure 4.6 actually shows this conversation window from another participant—Keith in this case; he sees the video of Lester as one of the (up to) five people in his Standing Row. Nathan is

represented by a high-resolution photo, if available, or as in Figure 4.7, the default tile if no photo is uploaded for Alice.

FIGURE 4.7
Default tile view

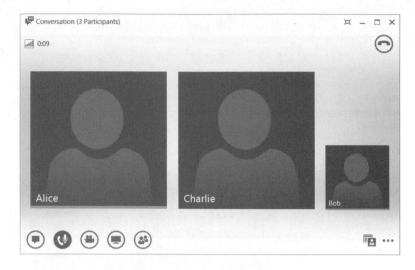

Smart Framing

Video framing and smart sizing ensure that the video feed automatically centers the participant in the frame. When in a Lync Meeting, the client will expand the video tile for a particular user if two people are in the frame. It will expand to include the second person so both are centered properly. It automatically shrinks if the second person leaves.

Lync Web App

Lync Web App is a browser-based meeting client that allows users to join Lync Meetings. Clicking the Join Lync Meeting link in a meeting invite will cause Lync Web App to start, assuming either one of the following is true:

◆ The computer you are using does not have Lync 2013 installed.

◆ You're using an Apple Mac.

Lync Web App has been significantly redesigned in Lync Server 2013 to provide a richer meeting experience across different platforms. It does not provide IM and presence or contacts lists outside a Lync Meeting, however.

In Lync 2010, if you did not have the full Lync client installed and wanted to join a meeting with computer audio and video, you needed to download and install the Lync 2010 Attendee client. In Lync 2013, Lync Web App supports computer audio and video, meaning the Attendee client is no longer required. Furthermore, Lync 2010 Attendee is not supported against a Lync Server 2013 pool.

Lync Web App is also preferred over Lync 2010 when joining a meeting hosted on Lync Server 2013 because Lync Web App will support features in Lync Server 2013, such as multiparty video and additional conference controls that are not supported when joining from Lync 2010. This is an important change in people's perception that web-based clients are second-class citizens to the full Windows application client. This may have been the case in Lync 2010, where Lync Web App was restricted to Windows due to its use of Silverlight and did not support computer audio and video, but this is not the case in Lync 2013.

Audio and Video in the Browser

The major change required to help achieve voice and video in the browser in Lync Server 2013 is that Lync Web App is based on HTML5 and JavaScript instead of Silverlight, meaning it can be used on Windows, Mac, and other platforms that support these web standards.

It should be noted that audio, video and desktop sharing require a client plug-in. The good news is that this plug-in can be installed in user mode rather than requiring administrative permissions. You can still join a meeting without the plug-in and will still be able to participate in IM and PowerPoint viewing.

Prior to joining the meeting from Lync Web App, the user will be prompted to install the plug-in. This is the default option and the user must clear the check box if they do not want to install the browser plug-in. In Figure 4.8, Dave is joining the meeting from Lync Web App on Windows 8. Notice that the check box to install the Lync Web App plug-in is already checked.

Figure 4.8
Joining a meeting
with Lync Web App

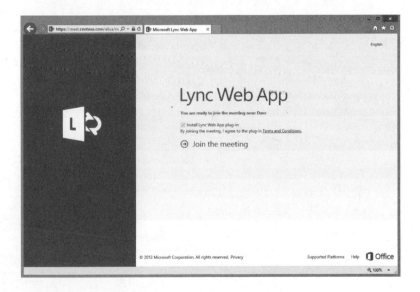

Exactly the same behavior can be observed when using Lync Web App on a Mac. The user needs to provide their username and password, and the check box to install the Lync Web App plug-in is checked by default.

How the user is notified about installing the plug-in differs slightly depending on whether you're using Windows or Mac, as illustrated in Figure 4.9 and Figure 4.10.

Both Windows and Mac clients will display a warning about the Lync Web App plug-in when it is first installed, as shown in Figure 4.11.

FIGURE 4.9
Installing the Lync
Web App plug-in on
Windows

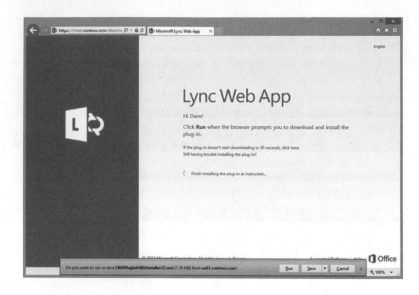

FIGURE 4.10
Installing the Lync
Web App plug-in on
a Mac

FIGURE 4.11
Lync Web App plug-
in warnings

JOINING WITHOUT THE PLUG-IN

Of course, it is also possible to simply not install the plug-in. When joining a meeting without the plug-in installed, the user has three options to choose from, as shown in Figure 4.12.

FIGURE 4.12
The browser-based meeting join options without a plug-in

The options are as follows:

◆ **Using My Computer**: This will install the plug-in.

◆ **Have The Meeting Call Me**: This will initiate a call to the number you specify in the box. In Lync Server 2010, this required the organizer to be Enterprise Voice enabled (or it required a potentially unsafe and definitely unsupported workaround by adding a static route to the Mediation server, allowing Lync Server to place calls to any number). In Lync Server 2013, it is possible for the administrator to assign a voice policy to users not enabled for Enterprise Voice, so dial-out conferencing is still possible without introducing the risk of toll fraud.

◆ **I Will Dial Into The Meeting**: This will close the prompt. The user will manually dial in using another phone (mobile, PSTN) using the dial-in conferencing numbers provided in the meeting invite. If the organizer is hosted on Office 365, dial-in conferencing numbers will be provided only if the tenant has configured audio conferencing provider (ACP) integration.

LYNC WEB APP EXPERIENCE (MAC)

Once the user is joined to the meeting via Lync Web App, the experience is so similar in terms of feature parity with the Lync 2013 desktop client that it's difficult to tell the two apart. It is worth highlighting that this experience is not just restricted to Windows, however. It's even difficult to tell the difference when viewed on a Mac. Figure 4.13 shows Alice, Bob, and Charlie in a Lync Meeting. Alice and Charlie are using Lync 2013 desktop clients on Windows, whereas Bob is using Lync Web App on Mac OS X running in the Safari browser.

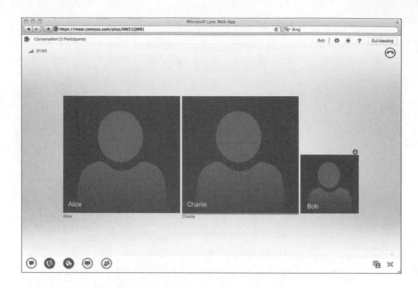

Bob is connected to the meeting audio via his browser and can preview and start video sharing, as shown in Figure 4.14 and Figure 4.15.

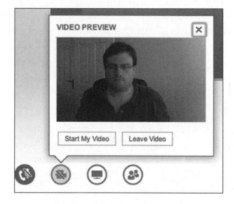

Because Bob did not clear the check box to install the Lync Web App plug-in when he joined the meeting, he can also add desktop sharing to the meeting, as shown in Figure 4.16. This causes the video feed of Alice, Bob, and Charlie to move up to the top row, allowing content and video to be presented at the same time.

Alice's point of view is shown in Figure 4.17. She can see Bob's Apple Mac desktop, with About Finder clearly visible, being shared inside the meeting.

SIGNALING

For all signaling, Lync Web App communicates via HTTPS to the Unified Communications Web API (UCWA), which acts as a web relay and in turn communicates with the Focus and all MCUs using C3P/HTTP.

Lync Web App does not support connecting to a RoundTable (e.g., Polycom CX5000) device, although it does support viewing the video panorama stream.

Windows Store App

Lync Windows Store app is a new Lync 2013 client designed specifically for Windows 8 and Windows RT and is optimized for touch-screen devices.

FIGURE 4.15
Bob's video in the call

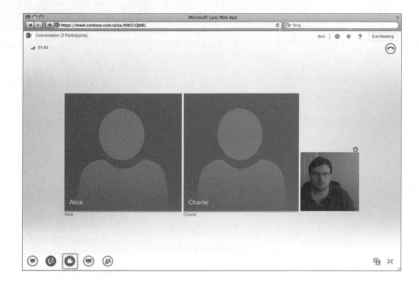

FIGURE 4.16
Bob adding desktop sharing

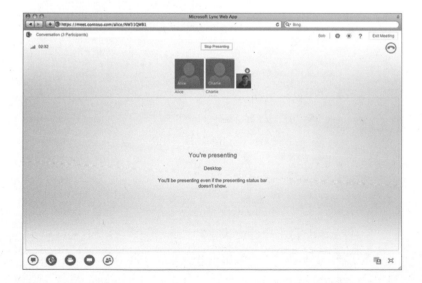

FIGURE 4.17
Alice's view of Bob's
Mac desktop

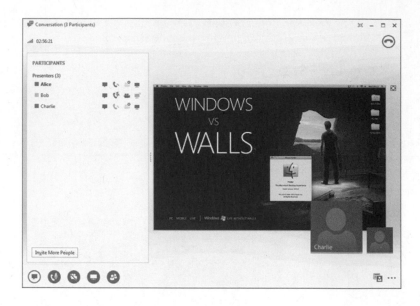

FEATURES OF LYNC WINDOWS STORE APP

As you would expect for an app focused on Microsoft's newest user interface, Lync Windows
Store app is fully featured as outlined in the following list:

- Enhanced presence support
  - Publish and view status
  - View status based on calendar free/busy information
  - View status notes and Out of Office messages
  - Add a custom note
- Contacts and contact groups
  - View contacts lists
  - Modify contacts lists
  - Search the corporate address book
  - Manage contact groups
  - Expand distribution groups
  - Display alternative contact views (e.g., title)
- IM and presence support
  - Initiate IM with contacts
  - Switch between multiple IM conversations

- ◆ Log IM conversations in Outlook

- ◆ Initiate an email to contact, using the Windows 8 Mail app on Windows RT devices

- ◆ Skills Search, when Lync Server is deployed with SharePoint Server integration

- ◆ Conferencing

  - ◆ Add computer audio

  - ◆ Add video

  - ◆ View multiparty video

  - ◆ View the detailed meeting roster

  - ◆ Participate in multiparty IM conferences

  - ◆ Use dial-in audio conferencing

- ◆ Telephony

  - ◆ Start a voice call

  - ◆ Select contact to start a call

  - ◆ Transfer calls

  - ◆ Manage Call Forwarding options

  - ◆ Support emergency services dialing (E911 where available)

  - ◆ Connect to voice mail

- ◆ External Users

  - ◆ Initiate IM with public contacts

  - ◆ Initiate IM with federated contacts

  - ◆ Conduct two-party or multiparty calls with external users

Note that desktop sharing, application sharing, and file transfer are not supported in Lync Windows Store app.

LYNC WINDOWS STORE APP REQUIREMENTS

The Lync Windows Store app can be used against on-premises deployments of Lync Server 2010 and Lync Server 2013 as well as Office 365. Prior to installing Lync Windows Store app, there are a number of system requirements you must meet.

For Lync Server 2010, two different cumulative updates are required to enable Lync Windows Store app to be fully functional. First, ensure that the Lync Server 2010: February 2012 cumulative update is installed on all servers. Second, to enable users to join meetings, you need to apply the Lync Server 2010: October 2012 cumulative update.

Unlike the Lync 2013 desktop client, Lync Windows Store app will not fail back to using DNS SRV records to discover the Lync Server SIP registrar. Therefore, the Autodiscover service must be enabled and configured in the environment. Additionally, Lync Web App and the Web Ticket services must be enabled in Lync Server 2013. We will cover the Autodiscover service in the "Discovery and Connection" section later in this chapter. DNS (CNAME) resource records for the Autodiscover service are also required.

Other requirements are that certificates used by Lync Server need to have a valid certificate revocation list (CRL) distribution point, which should be configured for HTTP instead of LDAP.

Finally, any HTTP proxies in the environment should allow Lync Server–related HTTP traffic. Exceptions should be used to exempt the Autodiscover, Lync Web App, and WebTicket services from the HTTP proxy if necessary.

Installing Lync Windows Store App

You can install the Lync Windows Store app from the Windows 8 Store. Using the Search charm, search for "Lync" as shown in Figure 4.18.

FIGURE 4.18
Searching in the Windows Store for the Lync Windows Store app

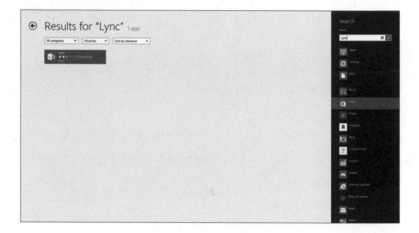

Once you have opened the app page, click Install, as shown in Figure 4.19. Once installed, the Lync Windows Store app will be listed on your Windows Start screen and you can also find it listed under Apps in the Windows 8 search box.

FIGURE 4.19
The app page for the Lync Windows Store app

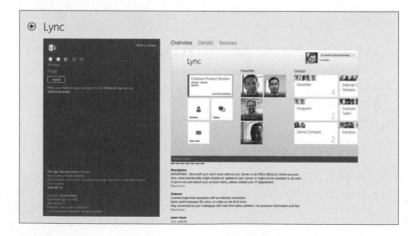

Lync will sign in automatically if you're logged on to your computer with your domain credentials. If not, or you're signed in to a Windows RT tablet, you may need to enter your sign-in address and password and choose what presence setting you require before signing in, as shown in Figure 4.20.

FIGURE 4.20
Signing into the
Lync Windows
Store app

Once signed in you will be presented with the Home screen, which allows you to access Lync Meetings, Contacts, Conversation History, and Voice Mail as well as allowing you to make changes to your Presence, Note, and Call Forwarding settings.

To switch between screens, either right-click in the app (non-touch-screen devices), or swipe down from the top to reveal the bars at the top and bottom of the screen, shown in Figure 4.21.

FIGURE 4.21
The action bars at
the top and bottom
of Lync Windows
Store app

You can return to the Home screen at any time by tapping the Lync tile.

SNAPPED VIEW

As a Windows 8 application, Lync Windows Store app supports being snapped to either the left or right of the screen, allowing you to access Lync while working in other apps in the main view. To enter Snapped view, click/tap and drag with your mouse or finger to the side of the screen you want Lync to snap to.

You can switch between the applications in Snapped view by dragging the divider.

SEARCHING FOR PEOPLE

If the person you want to communicate with is not already visible on your Home screen, switch to Contacts (right-click or swipe from the top and select the Contacts tile, shown in Figure 4.22).

FIGURE 4.22
The Contacts tile

If the person is not in your Contacts, swipe from the right to show the Charms bar, then select the Search charm. In the search box, type the name or phone number of the contact you're looking for. If the person you're looking for is outside your company, search using their email address.

ADDING AUDIO AND VIDEO TO CONVERSATIONS

When in a conversation, you can easily add audio or video. Swipe down from the top (or swipe up from the bottom) to display icons for the roster, dial pad, IM, audio, video, and presentation features, as shown in Figure 4.23.

FIGURE 4.23
The AV controls in a call

Before adding audio or video, make sure you have a webcam and speakers and a microphone or a compatible headset connected to your computer. Note that it is not possible to change the audio and video device used by Lync Windows Store app as you can in the Lync 2013 desktop app.

CHANGING OPTIONS

To change settings for Lync Windows Store app, use the Charms bar. Swipe from the right and select the Settings charm, and then select Options.

You can change the following options via the Settings charm:

◆ **Call Forwarding**: Displays the current Call Forwarding settings and allows you to change them. This can also be done from the Home screen by tapping your photo.

◆ **Personal Information Manager**: With this option, you can choose to save IM conversations and call logs in the Outlook Conversation History folder. Note that this feature relies on Exchange Web Services and will work on Windows 8 and Windows RT devices.

◆ **Avoid Metered Connections**: On by default, this option keeps Lync signed out when the computer is connected to a metered connection that might charge extra (e.g., Internet sharing or tethering on a compatible phone).

◆ **Customer Experience Improvement**: Off by default, this option allows you to opt in to the Microsoft Customer Experience Improvement Program.

◆ **Phone Accessibility**: Off by default, this option allows you to use Lync with a compatible connected TTY device.

◆ **Automatically Start Lync With Windows**: This option is on by default, although it will only work if Lync is set as a Lock Screen application (see the next section for further information).

◆ **Logging**: There are two options for logging:

  ◆ Sign-In Logs: On by default, this option will send your sign-in error info to Microsoft.

  ◆ Diagnostic Logs: Off by default, this option allows diagnostic information to be collected for use by your support team when troubleshooting.

SETTING LYNC WINDOWS STORE APP AS A LOCK SCREEN APP

For Lync Windows Store app to start automatically when Windows starts, it must be configured as a Lock Screen app. To do this, from the Windows Start screen, swipe right to reveal the Charms menu, then tap Settings and then Change PC Settings.

The PC settings should default to display the Personalize and Lock Screen view. Scroll down to Lock Screen Apps, and if Lync is not already listed, tap one of the available slots, which will be identified by a + sign instead of an app icon, and select Lync from the Choose An App pop-up menu.

LOGGING

Logs generated by the device can be used for troubleshooting Lync Windows Store app issues. The logs are stored in the following location:

```
%LocalAppData%\Packages\Microsoft.LyncMX_8wekyb3d8bbwe\LocalState\Tracing
```

Prior to sending log files, the user should make sure that all data stored in memory on the device is also written out to the log files on the hard drive. This is done by saving the log files, as follows:

To turn on logging, follow these steps:

1. Open Lync Windows Store app on the device.

2. Swipe from the right to reveal the Charms bar, then select Settings.

3. Select Options and scroll down to Diagnostic Logging.

4. Use the slider to turn on Diagnostic Logging.

5. If Diagnostic Logging was previously off, which is the default, you must restart Lync for the change to take effect.

To save logs, follow these steps:

1. Open Lync Windows Store app.

2. Attempt to sign in.

3. If the sign-in attempt fails, swipe from the right to reveal the Charms bar, then select Settings.

4. Tap About and then tap Save Logs.

TROUBLESHOOTING

There are a couple of known issues that can prevent Lync Windows Store app from successfully signing in to Lync Server:

◆ **Time and date:** The time setting on the device must be synchronized with the time setting on the server. This is especially important on Windows RT devices such as Microsoft Surface, which are not domain joined so will not synchronize their time with a domain controller. Time should be set manually on Windows RT devices using the command w32tm /resync. This command should be run from an elevated command prompt.

◆ **Network**: Some network adapters, such as 4G LTE USB modems, do not register with Windows 8 as physical devices. Lync Windows Store app may have issues when using such devices.

Lync 2013 Basic

Lync 2013 Basic provides IM, audio, and video plus the ability to join a Lync Meeting. It is a cut-down version of the Lync 2013 client; however, it provides the same core functionality. It is primarily intended as a downloadable client for customers with an Office 365 subscription that does not include the full Lync 2013 client, although it can also be used against an on-premises deployment of Lync Server 2013. It is provided as a free download to customers with Office 365 Plan P1, E1, or E2 as well as customers with Lync Online Plan 1, 2, or 3.

As the name implies, not all of the features available in Lync 2013 are available in the Lync 2013 Basic client. The following advanced features require the full desktop client, Lync Windows Store app, or Lync Web App:

◆ Advanced call features, specifically call forwarding, team calls and delegates. You cannot initiate a call to a Response Group, and Enhanced 911 is not supported. Additionally, you cannot connect to voice mail or make calls on behalf of another user (e.g., Manager/ Delegate scenario). You also cannot handle calls on behalf of another user. Lync-to-Lync calling is supported, however.

◆ Gallery video view in Lync Meetings is not available.

◆ OneNote and SharePoint integration (e.g., Skill Search) are not available.

◆ You cannot use the Virtual Desktop Infrastructure (VDI) plug-in with Lync 2013 Basic. This feature is not supported in Office 365.

Here are some other things to note about Lync 2013 Basic when used with Office 365:

◆ Conversation history is available only if you're also using Exchange Server and Outlook.

◆ At the time of writing, you can't interact with customers who are using an IM service other than Lync Server.

◆ Setting up meetings without Outlook requires the Lync Web Scheduler, which can be accessed at http://sched.lync.com.

◆ Dial-in conferencing requires that your Office 365 subscription be configured to integrate with an audio conferencing provider (ACP). If, when you send a meeting invite, the invitation does not include a dial-in number, then ACP integration is not deployed.

◆ Persistent Chat is not available in Office 365, so the Chat Room functionality will not be displayed in the Lync 2013 Basic client.

◆ Telephony integration (e.g., Remote Call Control) is not supported in Office 365, so these features are disabled in the Lync 2013 Basic client.

◆ Finally, the ability to make and receive calls to and from standard PSTN phone numbers (instead of using Lync-to-Lync computer audio) is available only with Lync Online Plan 3 when configured with a Lync-to-phone service provider.

Client Configuration

As was the case with Lync 2010, in Lync 2013, the majority of client configuration takes place in Lync Server policies, applied via in-band provisioning, instead of Group Policy. Some client bootstrapping policies are still available in Group Policy, however. These are typically settings that need to apply before a user signs in to Lync, and as they are usually generic and apply to the whole environment, they can be set at a higher level using Group Policy in Active Directory. Details are below.

Lync Server policies provide the Lync administrator with greater control and more flexibility over the settings they need to configure. Additionally, the settings can be applied more granularly because they can be scoped to Global, Site, and User in the Lync Server environment.

Group Policy Settings: Client Bootstrapping

In previous versions of Lync and Office Communicator, a stand-alone `Communicator.adm` administrative template was available for configuring client Group Policy settings. As Lync 2013 is included as part of Office 2013, new administrative templates (`*.admx` and `*.adml`) are included with the Office Group Policy Administrative template, which is available here:

`www.microsoft.com/en-us/download/details.aspx?id=35554.`

Details of the client bootstrapping policies can be found in the Lync Server 2013 Help file. Of interest in Lync 2013 is the Disable Automatic Upload Of Sign-In Failure Logs setting.

This setting automatically uploads sign-in failure logs to Lync Server for analysis. No logs are uploaded if sign-in is successful, however. This setting is applied differently depending on whether you are trying to connect to an on-premises or online version of Lync Server 2013. For Lync Online, sign-in failure logs are automatically uploaded. For Lync on-premises, a confirmation window is displayed prompting the user to upload the logs, as shown in Figure 4.24.

Figure 4.24
The user being prompted to upload logs

Client Policies: In-Band Provisioning

Client policies can be created, modified, and deleted by the administrator using Lync Server Management Shell. They are passed to the client during sign-in. The Lync 2013 client will request in-band provisioning settings in a SIP SERVICE message. The settings are returned in a SIP 200 OK message. Using a tool such as Snooper from the Lync Server Resource Kit or Lync Server Debugging Tools, it is possible to read the XML body of the SIP conversation and observe the settings that were actually passed to the client.

Lync Server 2013 provides a number of new client management parameters that can be used by the Lync 2013 client. A full list can be found in the Lync help file, but the following two, configured via `CsClientPolicy`, are explained here:

EnableMediaRedirection When set to `true`, this setting allows audio and video streams to be separated from other network traffic. This allows client devices to do encoding and decoding of audio and video locally, resulting in lower bandwidth usage. This setting is required for the Lync 2013 VDI plug-in to work.

TracingLevel When set to `true`, this setting allows the tracing level in Lync 2013 to be configured by the administrator. Tracing in Lync can be off, light, or on:

◆ **Off**: Tracing is disabled and the user cannot change the setting.

◆ **Light**: Tracing is enabled and minimal tracing is performed. The user cannot change this setting.

◆ **On**: Verbose tracing is performed. The user cannot change this setting.

Additionally, some of the policies available in Lync Server 2010 have been deprecated in Lync Server 2013:

EnableSQMData This parameter has been removed from Lync 2013 `CsClientPolicy` and is instead controlled by the shared Group Policy setting for Software Quality Management, which is part of the Office Group Policy template. It relates to the following key in the Windows Registry and can be either enabled (1) and the user can clear the check box or disabled (0), which prevents the user from modifying the check box:

HKEY_CURRENT_USER\Software\Policies\Microsoft\Office\Common\QMEnable

AllowExchangeContactStore This parameter has been removed from Lync 2013. Instead, when you deploy Lync Server 2013 and publish the topology, Unified Contact Store is enabled for all users by default. This means users' contacts are stored in their Exchange Server 2013 mailbox. You can change this functionality using `Set-CsUserServicesPolicy` if you want to enable/disable Unified Contact Store for all users or by site, by tenant (Office 365), or by individual users or groups.

MAPIPollInterval This parameter is no longer used by Lync 2013. In Lync 2010, this parameter specified how frequently the client retrieved MAPI data from Exchange public folders.

Discovery and Connection

Having learned the different clients, it is important to know how they connect to Lync so that you can troubleshoot any issues in this area. The following sections will cover not only how the Lync client discovers the Lync server to connect to but also how it connects.

DISCOVERY

Cumulative Update for Lync Server 2010: November 2011 (CU4) added support for Lync Mobility. One of the features this Cumulative Update includes is the Lync Autodiscover Service, which is used by mobile clients to locate the Lync Server.

Unlike in Lync 2010, in Lync 2013, the Autodiscover service is favored over DNS SRV records as a method of resolving the SIP registrar—the Lync Server 2013 Front End, Director, or Edge—for all clients. The Lync 2013 desktop client will fail back to using DNS SRV if the Autodiscover method fails; however, the Lync Windows Store app and Lync Mobile clients will not.

All clients will attempt to use the Autodiscover service as their preferred method of discovering their SIP registrar. The discovery and connection process is outlined here:

1. The client will attempt to resolve `lyncdiscoverinternal.<sipdomain>` This DNS (A) Host record would typically be available only on the internal DNS server(s), so the inability to resolve it suggests that the client is external (or Lync Discover has not been configured!).

2. If the previous attempt is unsuccessful, the client will attempt to resolve `lyncdiscover.<sipdomain>` instead.

If neither of the Lync Discover records work, then Lync 2013 will fail back to using DNS (SRV) and (A) records, which will be resolved in parallel and tried in the following order, in the same way as in Lync 2010:

1. Internal DNS SRV using TLS, specifically `_sipinternaltls._tcp.<sipdomain>`

2. Internal DNS SRV using TCP, specifically `_sipinternal._tcp.<sipdomain>`

3. External DNS SRV using TLS, specifically `_sip._tls.<sipdomain>`

Lync Windows Store app and mobile clients will not fail back and the sign-in will be unsuccessful.

CONNECTION

Once the client has successfully resolved one of the preceding DNS SRV records, it will attempt to connect. The DNS SRV record informs the client of the fully qualified domain name (FQDN) and the port number the SIP registrar is listening on. This will be TCP/5061 for internal connections and TCP/443 for external connections. The client will issue a SIP REGISTER message to begin the sign-in process.

The DNS (A) record(s) returned to the client depend on whether DNS load balancing or hardware load balancing is being used in the environment. If hardware load balancing is being used, the client will be returned a single IP address—this is the virtual IP (VIP) of the Hardware Load Balancer. If DNS load balancing is being used, which is the preference, then the client will be returned the IP address of each server in the pool. The ordering of the IP addresses changes in a round-robin fashion and is not important because the chances are the client will still require redirecting, which happens via a SIP 301 Redirect once it successfully registers. This is because all endpoints for a single user must be registered on the same SIP registrar.

Once the client has successfully registered, it will receive a SIP 200 OK message, which will trigger the creation of the `EndpointConfiguration.cache` file. The client will use this local file to avoid having to do the autodiscover or DNS lookup again.

Persistent Chat Client

Persistent Chat, formerly Group Chat, is an optional role in Lync Server 2013. If your topology includes Persistent Chat, you can now use the Lync 2013 client to access chat rooms, without the need for a separate client.

Lync 2013 communicates with the Persistent Chat service using a combination of Session Initiation Protocol (SIP), for registration, and the Extensible Chat Communication Over SIP (XCCOS) protocol, for chat.

SIGN-IN

The following sequence describes the sign-in process in detail:

1. Lync 2013 sends a SIP SUBSCRIBE message to retrieve in-band provisioning from the server. This document includes a number of client settings in XML format, one of which indicates if Persistent Chat is enabled or disabled for the user, as shown in Figure 4.25. If it is enabled, in-band provisioning also provides the list of SIP URIs for the Persistent Chat pool, as shown in Figure 4.26.

FIGURE 4.25
The SIP messages showing whether Persistent Chat is enabled for the user

FIGURE 4.26
The in-band provisioning messages the client received showing the Persistent Chat pool

2. The settings requested in the SIP SUBSCRIBE message are provided in the accompanying SIP 200 OK message.

3. Lync 2013 will then send a SIP INVITE message to the SIP URI of the Persistent Chat server that was obtained in step 1, as shown in Figure 4.27. The INVITE should be followed by a 200 OK and associated ACK, which means that Lync 2013 has established a SIP session with the Persistent Chat server.

    For the remainder of this SIP dialog, Lync 2013 and the Persistent Chat server will communicate via SIP INFO messages, which contain either chat messages or commands requesting that the server take action.

    For comparison, this is similar to how conferencing works in Lync. Conferencing uses the Centralized Conference Control Protocol (C3P) for signaling between the client and server. The C3P messages are embedded in the body of SIP messages. Persistent Chat works in the same way, utilizing the XCCOS protocol to send signaling commands to, and receive responses from, the Persistent Chat server. These XCCOS messages are embedded inside SIP INFO messages.

4. Once a SIP session has been established between Lync 2013 and the Persistent Chat server, Lync 2013 will send a SIP INFO message that contains the XCCOS `getserverinfo` command, as shown in Figure 4.28.

5. The Persistent Chat server replies with a new SIP INFO message containing information about the Persistent Chat service configuration, as shown in Figure 4.29.

FIGURE 4.27
Sending the SIP
INVITE message to
the Persistent Chat
server

```
01/11/2013 15:49:08.902 A9C:8BC INFO  :: Sending Packet - 10.0.0.10:5061 (From Local Address:
10.0.0.101:63890) 1301 bytes:
01/11/2013 15:49:08.902 A9C:8BC INFO  :: INVITE sip:GC-1-PersistentChatService-2
@contoso.com SIP/2.0
Via: SIP/2.0/TLS 10.0.0.101:63890
Max-Forwards: 70
From: <sip:alice@contoso.com>;tag=f265eed0e9;epid=97afa84934
To: <sip:GC-1-PersistentChatService-2@contoso.com>
Call-ID: 6646a513cf6842ff83bd26e1c91ca605
CSeq: 1 INVITE
Contact: <sip:alice@contoso.com;opaque=user:epid:G3FH0WD29FGI-lkqIhWeHwAA;gruu>
User-Agent: UCCAPI/15.0.4420.1017 OC/15.0.4420.1017 (Microsoft Lync)
Supported: ms-dialog-route-set-update
Supported: timer
Supported: histinfo
Supported: ms-safe-transfer
Supported: ms-sender
Supported: ms-early-media
Roster-Manager: sip:alice@contoso.com
EndPoints: <sip:alice@contoso.com>, <sip:GC-1-PersistentChatService-2@contoso.com>
Supported: com.microsoft.rtc-multiparty
ms-keep-alive: UAC;hop-hop=yes
Allow: INVITE, BYE, ACK, CANCEL, INFO, MESSAGE, UPDATE, REFER, NOTIFY, BENOTIFY
ms-subnet: 10.0.0.0
Proxy-Authorization: TLS-DSK qop="auth", realm="SIP Communications Service",
opaque="D9E810AF", targetname="SE01.contoso.com", crand="2daa0c4a", cnum="8",
response="af3711430099ecc6be0e21436d80b1bf220e1d05"
Content-Type: application/sdp
Content-Length: 147

v=0
o=- 0 0 IN IP4 10.0.0.101
s=session
c=IN IP4 10.0.0.101
t=0 0
m=message 5060 sip null
a=accept-types:text/plain application/ms-imdn+xml

01/11/2013 15:49:08.902 A9C:8BC INFO  :: End of Sending Packet - 10.0.0.10:5061 (From Local
Address: 10.0.0.101:63890) 1301 bytes
```

FIGURE 4.28
The SIP INFO
message that con-
tains the XCCOS
`getserverinfo`
command

```
01/11/2013 15:49:09.168 A9C:8BC INFO  :: Sending Packet - 10.0.0.10:5061 (From Local Address:
10.0.0.101:63890) 1114 bytes:
01/11/2013 15:49:09.168 A9C:8BC INFO  :: INFO
sip:pc01.contoso.com@contoso.com;gruu;opaque=srvr:PersistentChat:-
tcbmmHSU1O3pUB3ofZF5wAA SIP/2.0
Via: SIP/2.0/TLS 10.0.0.101:63890
Max-Forwards: 70
From: <sip:alice@contoso.com>;tag=f265eed0e9;epid=97afa84934
To: <sip:GC-1-PersistentChatService-2@contoso.com>;tag=492c6184d8;epid=40D3F228D8
Call-ID: 6646a513cf6842ff83bd26e1c91ca605
CSeq: 2 INFO
Route: <sip:SE01.contoso.com:5061;transport=tls;opaque=state:T:F.Ci.R36500;lr;ms-route-sig=barWFft-
uKwzqX7XbQWBGM4wr75O45sqUTMMnq0ALhf_LiSV46Ok1xHAAA>
User-Agent: UCCAPI/15.0.4420.1017 OC/15.0.4420.1017 (Microsoft Lync)
Supported: ms-dialog-route-set-update
Supported: timer
Proxy-Authorization: TLS-DSK qop="auth", realm="SIP Communications Service",
opaque="D9E810AF", targetname="SE01.contoso.com", crand="c83fc0af", cnum="11",
response="179a1904f1bd439ed64761692dcf1257ff17dac1"
Content-Type: text/plain
Content-Length: 218

<xccos xmlns="urn:parlano:xml:ns:xccos" ver="1" envid="38071391">
<cmd id="cmd:getserverinfo" seqid="1">
<data>
<sib domain="contoso.com" infoType="2047" clientVersion="15.0.4420.1017"/>
</data>
</cmd>
</xccos>

01/11/2013 15:49:09.168 A9C:8BC INFO  :: End of Sending Packet - 10.0.0.10:5061 (From Local
Address: 10.0.0.101:63890) 1114 bytes
```

In Figure 4.29, you see that the server response code was "200", which is SUCCESS_OK, and you see the requested information from the Persistent Chat server. For example, you can see that Search Limit is "999" and Message Size Limit and Story Size Limit are both "8000". We also see the database and server version numbers and the display name of the Persistent Chat server, which in this example is Persistent Chat.

FIGURE 4.29
The SIP INFO messaging containing configuration info about Persistent Chat

01/11/2013|15:49:09.731 A9C:8BC INFO :: Data Received -10.0.0.10:5061 (To Local Address: 10.0.0.101:63890) 1674 bytes:
01/11/2013|15:49:09.731 A9C:8BC INFO :: INFO sip:10.0.0.101:63890;transport=tls;ms-opaque=6eca485f33;ms-received-cid=36500;grid SIP/2.0
Via: SIP/2.0/TLS
10.0.0.10:5061;branch=z9hG4bKD7A28FBB.6175619F4FBEFB85;branched=FALSE;ms-internal-info="cagdGgnlCrrffbMfK61aczyP0cmABWzCuuyOhlev-nE27efYXVhMDK1CgAA"
Authentication-Info: TLS-DSK qop="auth", opaque="D9E810AF", srand="D855185F", snum="14", rspauth="b01cb0bf9dea38fa527ffede03e6804572e18d6e", targetname="SE01.contoso.com", realm="SIP Communications Service", version=4
Max-Forwards: 69
Via: SIP/2.0/TLS 10.0.0.40:49364;branch=z9hG4bK80e7cae7;ms-received-port=49364;ms-received-cid=36600
FROM: <sip:GC-1-PersistentChatService-2@contoso.com>;epid=40D3F228D8;tag=492c6184d8
TO: <sip:alice@contoso.com>;epid=97afa84934;tag=f265eed0e9
CSEQ: 1 INFO
CALL-ID: 6646a513cf6842ff83bd26e1c91ca605
CONTACT: <sip:pc01.contoso.com@contoso.com;gruu;opaque=srvr:PersistentChat:-tdxmmHSU1O3pUB3ofZF5wAA>
CONTENT-LENGTH: 658
SUPPORTED: gruu-10
USER-AGENT: RTCC/5.0.0.0 PCS/5.0.8308.0
CONTENT-TYPE: text/plain

<xccos xmlns:xsd="http://www.w3.org/2001/XMLSchema"
xmlns:xsi="http://www.w3.org/2001/XMLSchema-instance" ver="1" envid="377932198379190054"
xmlns="urn:parlano:xml:ns:xccos">
 <rpl id="rpl:getserverinfo" seqid="1">
  <commandid seqid="1" envid="38071391" />
  <resp code="200">SUCCESS_OK</resp>
  <data>
   <sib infoType="1787" serverTime="2013-01-11T15:49:09.042504Z" searchLimit="999"
messageSizeLimit="8000" storySizeLimit="8000" rootUri="ma-cat://contoso.com/f2b85903-44b6-41dd-bf5a-3783627e9b95" dbVersion="5bf0458a-868d-49f6-bad2-fcfa008b5ac9" serverVersion="5.0.8308.0"
displayName="Persistent Chat" />
  </data>
 </rpl>
</xccos>
01/11/2013|15:49:09.731 A9C:8BC INFO :: End of Data Received -10.0.0.10:5061 (To Local Address: 10.0.0.101:63890) 1674 bytes

6. Lync 2013 sends a SIP INFO message containing the XCCOS getassociations command, as shown in Figure 4.30.

FIGURE 4.30
Sending the SIP INFO message containing the XCCOS getassociations command

01/11/2013|15:49:09.731 A9C:8BC INFO :: Sending Packet - 10.0.0.10:5061 (From Local Address: 10.0.0.101:63890) 1244 bytes:
01/11/2013|15:49:09.731 A9C:8BC INFO :: **INFO**
sip:pc01.contoso.com@contoso.com;gruu;opaque=srvr:PersistentChat:-tdxmmHSU1O3pUB3ofZF5wAA SIP/2.0
Via: SIP/2.0/TLS 10.0.0.101:63890
Max-Forwards: 70
From: <sip:alice@contoso.com>;tag=f265eed0e9;epid=97afa84934
To: <sip:GC-1-PersistentChatService-2@contoso.com>;tag=492c6184d8;epid=40D3F228D8
Call-ID: 6646a513cf6842ff83bd26e1c91ca605
CSeq: 3 INFO
Route: <sip:SE01.contoso.com:5061;transport=tls;opaque=state:T:F:Ci.R36500;lr;ms-route-sig=barWFft-uKwzqX7XbQWBGM4wr75O45sqUTMMnq0ALhf_LJSV46Ck1xHAAA>
User-Agent: UCCAPI/15.0.4420.1017 OC/15.0.4420.1017 (Microsoft Lync)
Supported: ms-dialog-route-set-update
Supported: timer
Proxy-Authorization: TLS-DSK qop="auth", realm="SIP Communications Service", opaque="D9E810AF", targetname="SE01.contoso.com", crand="3a9b2fc8", cnum="14", response="b09db19493f78c138f198c137a0223e2be0209ff"
Content-Type: text/plain
Content-Length: 348

<xccos xmlns="urn:parlano:xml:ns:xccos" ver="1" envid="38071392">
<cmd id="cmd:getassociations" seqid="1">
<data>
<association domain="contoso.com" type="MEMBER" maxResults="100"/>
</data>
</cmd>
<cmd id="cmd:getassociations" seqid="2">
<data>
<association domain="contoso.com" type="MANAGER" maxResults="100"/>
</data>
</cmd>
</xccos>

01/11/2013|15:49:09.731 A9C:8BC INFO :: End of Sending Packet - 10.0.0.10:5061 (From Local Address: 10.0.0.101:63890) 1244 bytes

7. This causes the Persistent Chat server to respond with a new SIP INFO message providing a list of rooms of which the user is a member, as shown in Figure 4.31. Lync 2013 repeats this process to obtain a list of rooms for which the user is a manager.

FIGURE 4.31

Lync responding with the rooms of which the user is a member

In Figure 4.31, you can see that Alice is a member of the Persistent Chat room called Room 1, with a description of "This is a test room." An additional SIP INFO message, not shown for brevity, provides the same information because Alice is both a member and manager of Room 1.

8. Lync 2013 obtains the list of followed rooms from the presence document, whereby each followed room is represented by a `roomSetting` category. All followed rooms are joined by a single SIP INFO message that contains the XCCOS `bjoin` command, which contains the list of room URIs. The list of followed rooms is stored on the server, meaning any client on any computer has the same list of rooms for the specified URI. Additionally, Lync 2013 will cache a list of open rooms (if this option is enabled by the user) in the local computer Registry. Lync 2013 will join each of these rooms at sign-in by sending a SIP INFO message containing the XCCOS `join` command for each opened room. This will differ between the computers the user may use because the information is stored in the local Registry.

9. For each room joined, Lync 2013 sends a SIP INFO message containing the XCCOS `bcontext` command. The Persistent Chat server replies with a new SIP INFO message containing the most recent chat message in the room.

10. Finally, Lync 2013 sends a SIP INFO message containing the XCCOS `getinv` command (short for Get Invitation) to request any new room invitations that the client has not yet seen. The Persistent Chat server responds with a list of rooms in a separate SIP INFO message.

PERSISTENT CHAT CLIENT EXPERIENCE

When configured in the topology and enabled via policy, clients will show an additional icon in the row of tabs in Lync 2013, as shown in Figure 4.32.

FIGURE 4.32
The Lync Persistent
Chat tab

The Persistent Chat tab includes the following additional views:

◆ **Followed**: This displays all the rooms that the user is following. It is also where the *ego* feed and *topic* feeds will be displayed—in bold—when there is new content requiring attention.

◆ **Member Of**: This displays all of the rooms that the current user is configured as a member of. Following a room is optional and results in notifications being displayed for the room in the client. Membership of a room is not optional; if you're configured as a member of a Persistent Chat room, that membership will be reflected in Lync 2013 here.

◆ **New**: This displays a menu with the options shown in Figure 4.33.

FIGURE 4.33
Options for creat-
ing a new room

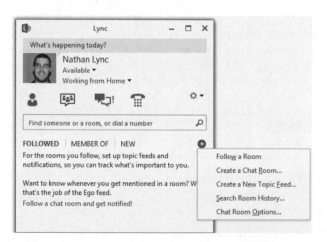

One of the New area menu items that you will see is Chat Room Options. This displays global options for chat rooms. These can be changed here to affect all chat rooms or can be changed on a per-room basis as rooms are created or as you choose to follow a room or receive topic feeds about the room.

CREATING A CHAT ROOM

Another option on the New area menu shown in Figure 4.33 is Create A Chat Room. End users (rather than administrators) will typically create chat rooms, and the user will see this menu option regardless of whether they have permission to create a chat room. Clicking Create A Chat Room will open Internet Explorer and, if necessary, after you provide credentials, will display the Persistent Chat Management website, shown in Figure 4.34.

FIGURE 4.34

The Persistent Chat Management website

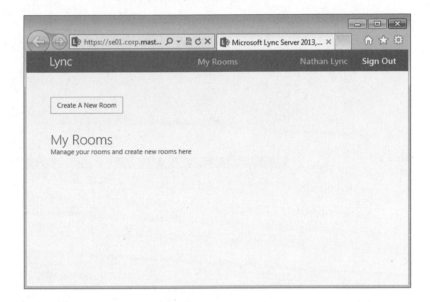

Users create rooms by clicking Create A New Room. They can also modify rooms they have already created here. In this example, Charlie does not have permission to create rooms, so when she clicks Create A New Room, she'll receive the error shown in Figure 4.35.

When Alice, who does have permission, is logged in, clicking Create A New Room will display the page shown in Figure 4.36.

From here, Alice can specify the following details:

◆ **Room Name**: This uniquely identifies the room.

◆ **Description**: An optional description to tell people what the room is for.

◆ **Privacy**: This can be one of three settings:

   ◆ **Open**: Anybody can find the room and read the contents.

   ◆ **Closed**: Anybody can find the room and see the room's membership, but only members can read posts in the room. This is the default.

   ◆ **Secret**: Only members can find the room, view membership, and read posts.

FIGURE 4.35
The error shown
when you don't
have permissions to
create a room

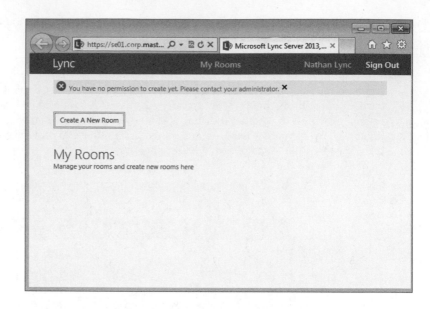

FIGURE 4.36
The Create A Room
page

- ◆ **Add-In**: Allows a web application add-in to be configured for your room.

- ◆ **Managers**: This is automatically populated with Alice as the creator of this room. She can add other users by typing their names or SIP URIs. Users entered here have management capability of the room.

- ◆ **Members**: This is automatically populated with Alice as the creator of this room. She can add other users by typing their names or SIP URIs. Users added here can access the room to read or post, but not manage it.

◆ **Invitations**: By default, the invitation setting is inherited from the category that applies to this room on the Persistent Chat server. The other option is to not send invitations to members.

At this point Alice will see the newly created room on her My Rooms page, as shown in Figure 4.37.

FIGURE 4.37
My Rooms page now that Room 1 has been created

The Persistent Chat tab in Alice's Lync 2013 client now shows a number next to the icon, indicating there is unread content. Clicking the Persistent Chat tab shows Room 1 in bold, to identify that this room is new. The same will happen on Bob and Charlie's Lync 2013 clients because they were added as members and invitations were enabled for the category of room that was just created.

Lync Conferencing Clients

The following clients can be used as conferencing clients in Lync Server 2013:

◆ Lync 2013: The full, unified Windows desktop client is preferred for meetings.

◆ Lync Web App: The web-based browser version of Lync 2013 can be used in meetings.

◆ Lync Windows 8 store app: The Windows 8 store app can be used to join audio and video and view PowerPoint slides being presented in a meeting.

As mentioned earlier in this chapter, Lync Web App now supports audio and video natively in the browser through the use of a browser plug-in, which can be installed in user mode rather than administrator mode. Because of this change, Lync Web App is now considered a first-class meeting client and is actually preferred rather than continuing to use the Lync 2010 desktop application in a coexistence scenario because it supports new features such as multiparty video and conference controls, as described in the following sections.

JOIN LAUNCHER

The Join Launcher—the component responsible for accepting requests to the Meet simple URL and processing theme—has been updated in Lync Server 2013 to provide support for additional conferencing clients, including Windows Phone, Android devices, Apple iOS devices, Windows 8, and Internet Explorer 10.

VIDEO SPOTLIGHT

Presenters can configure a conference, using either Lync 2013 or Lync Web App, so that only the video stream from a selected participant is seen by others in the meeting. When configured, this also applies to video captured and provided by conferencing devices for Panoramic video (e.g., RoundTable). This is useful in a classroom-like scenario, where a single speaker should be the focus of the participants' attention.

LIVE MEETING MCU

One change on the server side that affects the client application used for meetings in Lync Server 2013 is the removal of the Web Conferencing Compatibility Service MCU from the Front End server. This MCU simulated the Live Meeting MCU from the Office Communications Server time frame and made it possible for a user migrated from OCS 2007 R2 to Lync Server 2010 to continue to participate in meetings using the Live Meeting client.

Live Meeting would connect to the Web Conferencing Compatibility Service MCU on the Front End, which would simulate being a Live Meeting server, tricking the client into thinking it was connected to Live Meeting instead of Lync Server 2010.

In Lync Server 2013, this MCU has been removed, meaning Live Meeting is no longer a supported meeting client when running against a user who is hosted on Lync Server 2013. As such, all meetings must be upgraded to Lync meetings when the user is migrated. If the user will not have the Lync 2013 desktop client installed immediately following migration, they can use Lync Web App to join the meeting instead.

OFFICE WEB APPS AND POWERPOINT SLIDES

As mentioned earlier, Lync 2013 changes the way PowerPoint slides are rendered on the client, making this more standards based to support a wider number of platforms, including Windows, Windows RT, Windows Phone, iOS, and Android.

When you upload a PowerPoint presentation to a meeting using Lync 2013, the file is uploaded to the Data Multipoint Control Unit (MCU) on the Front End server. The Data MCU returns a broadcast URL representing the file you just uploaded, causing Lync 2013 to start an embedded browser frame inside the client. The URL returned to the client is actually the URL of the Office Web Apps server, which will retrieve the file from the Data MCU using the Web Open Platform Interface (WOPI) protocol and will then render the slides into web-based presentable data. Every second, the embedded browser frame will ping the Office Web App server using AJAX (Asynchronous JavaScript and XML) to confirm which slide it should be viewing. This information is then sent back to the Lync 2013 client's embedded browser frame, moving the presentation along.

Legacy Clients

Lync Server 2013 supports a number of previous versions signing in against a Lync Server 2013 pool. Table 4.1 shows which legacy clients are supported against which type of Lync Server pool.

TABLE 4.1:   Coverage of which clients can connect to which server versions

CLIENT	LYNC SERVER 2013	LYNC SERVER 2010	OFFICE COMMUNICATIONS SERVER 2007 R2
Lync 2013	Supported	Supported	Not Supported
Lync Web App (2013)	Supported	Not Supported	Not Supported
Lync 2010	Supported	Supported	Not Supported
Lync 2010 Attendant	Supported	Supported	Not Supported
Lync 2010 Group Chat	Supported	Supported	Not Supported
Lync Web App (2010)	Not Supported	Supported	Not Supported
Lync 2010 Attendee	Not Supported	Supported	Not Supported
Office Communicator 2007 R2	Supported	Supported	Supported
Office Communicator 2007 R2 Attendant	Supported	Supported	Supported
Office Communicator 2007	Not Supported	Supported	Supported
Live Meeting 2007	Not Supported	Supported	Supported

It is worth highlighting that the Lync 2010 Attendee client is not supported against a Lync Server 2013 pool. This is because the new Lync Web App supports IP audio and video, making it a fully featured client.

There is no new Lync for Mac client with this release, and Lync 2013 is only available for Windows. However, Lync Server 2013 supports the following legacy Mac clients (when running on Mac OS 10.5.8 or later on an Intel processor), in addition to Lync Web App:

◆ Microsoft Lync for Mac 2011

◆ Microsoft Communicator for Mac 2011

Lync 2013 supports integration with the following previous versions of Microsoft Office:

◆ Outlook 2013 and Outlook 2010 when running against Exchange Server 2013 or Exchange Server 2010.

◆ Some integration features will work with Office 2007 and Office 2003 Service Pack 3, but an update may be required for Outlook. The update is described in Knowledge Base article 936864.

◆ Online Meeting Add-in for Lync 2013 is supported with Office 2013, Office 2010, Office 2007, and Office 2003.

Some Lync 2013 features such as high-resolution photos, Unified Contact Store, and Exchange archiving require the user's mailbox to be on an Exchange Server 2013 server.

Finally, the minimum supported operating system for the Lync 2013 clients is Windows 7; none of the clients are supported on Windows XP. Additionally, some of the clients specifically require Windows 8 or Windows RT (e.g., Lync Windows Store app).

The Bottom Line

Understand usage scenarios for each client.   Each of the Lync clients discussed in this chapter is designed for a specific usage scenario. For example, Lync 2013 allows IM and presence with other users.

Master It   You have been engaged by a graphic design company to design and deploy Microsoft Lync Server 2013. The company already has Lync Server 2010 and will be migrating to Lync Server 2013 over the next six months. The company has 300 employees who are split almost 50/50 between Apple Mac computers and Windows PCs running Lync 2010. All users need to be able to participate in meetings with partners and customers during this coexistence phase.

Understand changes in Group Chat.   In Lync 2013, Group Chat has been built into the main products and called Persistent Chat.

Master It   You are working with a large financial services company that is in the process of migrating from Lync Server 2010 to Lync Server 2013. The company's employees are heavy users of Group Chat in Lync Server 2010. What benefits does Lync Server 2013 and Lync 2013 introduce in this area?

Part 2

Getting Lync Up and Running

Chapter 5

Planning Your Deployment

You're probably eager to start implementing Lync Server 2013 in your network and you want to dive in right away.

Stop! Take a step back, breathe deeply, and think about what you want to achieve. Is this a throwaway lab deployment (perhaps virtualized?) utilized just to see what the management interface is like and what changes have been made since Office Communications Server (OCS) 2007 R2? Is this a pilot deployment in a production environment that will be removed once the decision to go ahead with full deployment is made? (Of course, everyone knows the pilot is never thrown away; it's just built on, right?) Are you planning to move from an existing Lync Server 2010 environment and want to investigate the subtle changes first?

The easiest (and best) way to deploy a solid system is to take the time to plan properly. By all means, jump right into a throwaway system deployment, but for any type of test or production system, proper planning will almost always save time in the long run. Even though many of us want to be "doing stuff" such as installing, troubleshooting, and so on, the best deployments are the ones for which the appropriate amount of time was spent in the planning phase.

Also remember that having a separate test environment will justify its cost in the long term, and it will allow you to catch patches or changes that could inadvertently bring down the system.

In this chapter, you will learn to:

◆   Use the planning tools available

◆   Determine when virtualization is appropriate

◆   Understand the prerequisites

Capturing the Requirements

You would never build a house by starting at the builder's yard, buying some bricks and mortar, and taking them back to a field. The same is true for a deployment. To ensure that you are not wasting and repeating work, it is extremely important to plan ahead. For example, if you configure and deploy Lync Server 2013 and later decide to change or add SIP domains, you will have to revisit every pool server and every request certificate again (a significant waste of time, especially if you have a manual certificate requisition process).

Experience tells us that most Lync deployments grow organically; they often start with a proof of concept or pilot and others outside the initial test groups latch onto the excitement of a new product and want to be involved. Next thing you know your 200-user pilot ends up with

1,000 users, and if proper planning hasn't occurred, issues will start to arise with the exponential growth.

In the same sense, there are two ways to approach any project:

◆ Define the end goal and then determine how to get there.

◆ Define the current state and then determine what you want.

Understanding What Is Wanted

The preferred approach is to know the end goal first; then you can work out the best route to get there (considering time, cost, or function) rather than building on what is already in place and trying to "morph" something into something else (the "organic growth" option).

Typically, the result ends up being some sort of migration or coexistence state. The longer that coexistence is in place, the longer (and more complicated) a project will be. By planning toward the end goal, you can reduce the time of coexistence and therefore reduce the risk.

Broadly, high-level needs can be divided into four areas:

◆ Core (instant messaging and presence, including Persistent Chat, peer-to-peer audio/video, internal conferencing)

◆ Remote access (and/or federation)

◆ Telephony integration

◆ High availability

Once you've established (or confirmed) these four key areas, you can begin to get an idea of the infrastructure required. Here's an example of what you might need:

◆ You need at least one pool (it's obvious, but it still needs to be stated!).

◆ Remote access means you'll need at least one Edge server.

◆ Telephony integration means you'll need Mediation servers (possibly colocated) and possibly gateways or direct SIP support.

◆ High availability requires Enterprise pool(s) and hardware load balancers.

Now the infrastructure design is taking shape. As you go further into the discovery process, you'll consider things such as the number of users to determine how many servers (and potentially pools) are needed and the location of users to determine how many pools and where they will be located.

Once you have determined the functional requirements, you can build the detailed design. For example, if you have a peak requiring 1,200 concurrent telephony calls through the public switched telephone network (PSTN), this will translate into a requirement of two Mediation servers (plus another for high availability). However, to get to this level of detail requires a lot of investigation and discovery, and it means the organization must already be capturing that type of information from the current telephony system via Call Data Records (CDRs) and it must be able to report the information. Bear in mind that many PBX systems are incompatible with others, resulting in a lot of work to consolidate data across different PBX vendors. Some companies provide consolidation software for reporting purposes on CDRs; however, the software is expensive, so it probably won't be used for a migration unless it is already in place.

Understanding What Is Currently in Place

Once the endgame is established, it's important to take a step back and establish what you have already. In some cases, you may be further along than you expect.

When deploying Lync Server 2013, you will typically be coming from one of the following scenarios:

- Greenfield (a deployment to a company that has never had an instant messaging product in use)

- Lync Server 2010

- OCS 2007 R2

- OCS 2007/LCS 2005 (or an earlier Microsoft instant messaging product)

- Other non-Microsoft instant messaging products

The *greenfield* scenario is the easiest and most straightforward of the options because you start with a clean slate and don't need to plan for migration or coexistence.

Migrating from Lync Server 2010 or OCS 2007 R2 to Lync Server 2013 is the only migration path supported by Microsoft. For details, see Chapter 7, "Migration and Upgrades."

Migrating from versions prior to OCS R2 and non-Microsoft instant messaging products are similar processes. Because no (current) toolsets are available to simplify the process, dealing with these migrations requires extremely detailed planning to handle the user-experience aspects. For example, are buddy lists migrated or are users expected to re-create them? Will meetings be migrated?

A nonsupported migration approach can be successful, but more likely it will involve problems that result in a nonoperative system or a system that appears to work initially but is hiding a more serious problem. These serious problems tend not to be obvious at first and may take some time to manifest. When they finally do arise, Microsoft may refuse to provide support to resolve them because an unsupported approach was used.

Now that you have established where you want to go (the features required) as well as where you are (the current state), you can begin planning the more detailed aspects of the design and deployment.

Using the Capacity Planning Toolset

With the launch of OCS 2007, Microsoft provided a Planning Tool application, which guides the administrator to a suggested topology based on a number of questions. Typically, they are feature driven, such as "Do you wish to use Enterprise Voice?"

From the resulting answers, the Planning Tool draws a recommended topology for each identified site, suggesting the types and quantities of hardware needed. In addition, it provides links to the specific planning and deployment tasks required to implement the suggested topology.

With the release of OCS 2007 R2, the Planning Tool was updated to take into account the new architecture and features provided in this updated version. In addition, a separate Edge Planning Tool application was released, specifically focusing on the Edge role and the complications involving the certificates and DNS and firewall entries required.

As expected, the Planning Tool was updated again with the release of Lync Server 2010, and the latest version for Lync Server 2013. In addition to supporting the updated topology of

Lync, the Lync Server 2010 version incorporated the Edge Planning Tool, previously a separate download.

The Lync Server 2013 Planning Tool now also includes functionality for mobile clients as well as Persistent Chat.

DOWNLOADING THE PLANNING TOOL

You can find the Lync Server 2013 Planning Tool at www.microsoft.com/downloads/, along with versions of the tool for OCS 2007, OCS 2007 R2, OCS 2007 R2 Edge, and Lync Server 2010. Each version of the Planning Tool is specific to the version of the product. Because you have chosen a book on mastering Lync Server, you probably will not need to download previous versions of the tool; however, if you are migrating from Live Communications Server 2003 or 2005, you will need to first migrate to a version of OCS.

In addition to the Planning Tool, Microsoft has provided the following tools to help you plan:

◆ Edge Server Reference Architecture Diagrams

◆ Stress and Performance Tool

◆ Capacity Calculator

◆ Bandwidth Calculator

With the exception of the Edge Server Reference Architecture Diagrams (simply a package of Visio diagrams), we will cover all of these tools in this chapter.

The Planning Tool will install and run on the following operating system versions:

◆ Windows 7 Service Pack 1

◆ Windows 8

◆ Windows Server 2008 R2

◆ Windows Server 2012

Defining a Topology with the Planning Tool

Once downloaded and installed, the Planning Tool will be located in the Lync Server 2013 folder in the Programs menu. Starting the application will take you to the Welcome screen, where you will have two options for planning, Get Started and Design Sites, as well as the option to open a saved topology.

As you'll see, Design Sites is more efficient when you know what features you need to implement, but Get Started provides you with a little more guidance, so it is more helpful. If you follow the Get Started path, you will be prompted with the following questions:

◆ Would you like to enable audio and video conferencing for your organization?

◆ Would you like to deploy dial-in conferencing within your enterprise?

◆ Do you want to locally host Web conferencing?

- Do you want to deploy Enterprise Voice?

- Do you want to deploy Exchange UM?

- Would you like to deploy Call Admission Control?

- Do you want to enable monitoring?

- Do you want to enable archiving?

    - Enable Exchange Archiving Integration and use Exchange data store as archiving storage

    - Deploy Archiving SQL Database as archiving storage

- Do you want to deploy Persistent Chat?

- Do you want to deploy mobility?

- Do you want to enable federation with other organizations or with public IM service providers?

    - Yes, I want to enable Lync to Lync cross-enterprise federation through SIP.

    - Yes, I want to enable Lync to OCS cross-enterprise federation through SIP.

    - Yes, I want to enable Lync to other public cloud IM providers federation through SIP.

    - Yes, I want to enable federation via XMPP.

- Is high availability of communications critical to you? If so, do you want to deploy standby servers for failover support?

- Which IP infrastructure do you want to deploy your Microsoft Lync Server 2013 on?

    - IPv4 Only

    - IPv6 Only

    - Both IPv4 and IPv6

- Do you want to enable Disaster Recovery?

Once you have answered these questions, you will be taken to the Central Sites page, shown in Figure 5.1. If you choose the Design Sites button on the Welcome page, this is where you will be taken directly.

On this page, you can provide the site name along with the number of users located at this site. In addition, you can modify the answers to any of the previous questions simply by checking (or unchecking) the boxes next to each option. If you use the Design Sites button, a default of Yes will be assumed for all questions except "federation with previous versions." Using this quick-start approach will save at least 10 clicks of the mouse to get to the same point.

You also have the opportunity to define users having W15 Exchange mailboxes (which equates to Exchange 2013). Even though integration with Exchange archiving was selected, you still need to select it again for the users here.

If you follow the wizard and answer the prompted questions, the output will provide a great starting point for a design topology; however, it shouldn't be taken as the only option.

FIGURE 5.1
The Central Sites
page

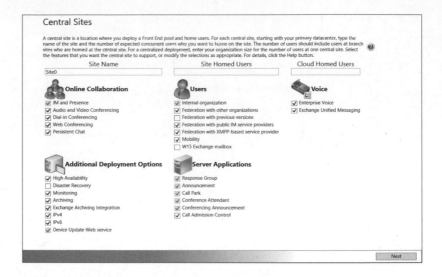

A lot of the questions are simply "enable/disable this feature" questions; however, some values will already have default suggestions based on the planning profile used to capture the statistics for recommended hardware. Details of these values can be found in the help file provided with the Lync Server 2013 installation media.

Here are some of the questions you'll be asked in each category:

SIP Domain You'll need to provide a listing of all the SIP domains supported by the deployment. Entering a SIP domain will help generate more accurate output in later sections (such as with the DNS or certificate requirements).

Conference Settings This section will provide the following prompts with their defaults:

Meeting Concurrency: **5%**
Meeting Audio Distribution
What percentage of conferences are dial-in? **15%**
What percentage of conferences have no audio (IM-only)? **10%**

Media Mix for Web Conferences
What percentage of conferences are web conferences with audio plus some other collaboration modalities? **75%**
Video is enabled. **Selected**
Multi-view is enabled. **Selected**
Application Sharing is enabled. **Selected**
Data Collaboration is enabled. **Selected**

Voice Settings You'll be provided with the following prompts:

Enabled users
What percentage of users at this site will be enabled for Enterprise Voice? **60%**
Enable All Users **Not Selected** (This item will force all Enterprise Voice user selection entries to 100%.)

External Phone Traffic
>On average, how many calls to the public telephone network do you think that each user at this site will make during the busy hour? **4 calls per hour**

Media Bypass
>What percentage of all phone calls will use media bypass? **65%**
>Enable All Calls **Not Selected** (If all the locations will have local gateways, this should be selected.)

Types of Calls
>What percentage of calls will be UC-PSTN calls? **60%**
>Enable All Calls **Not Selected**

Response Group
>What percentage of users use Response Group? **0.15%**

Call Park
>What percentage of calls will be parked? **0.05%**

Voice Infrastructure   You'll be provided with the following prompts:

Infrastructure
>I plan to deploy gateway using a direct PSTN connection. **Default**
>I plan to use SIP trunking.
>I have an existing voice infrastructure with a PBX deployed.

PBX (The default is unavailable unless the previous option includes PBX.)
>I have an IP-PBX that is qualified with Microsoft Lync Server (Direct SIP).
>I plan to deploy an IP-PBX that requires gateways.
>I have already deployed a TDM-PBX.

Infrastructure Supportability (The default is unavailable unless the previous option includes PBX.)
>My IP-PBX supports DNS local balancing.
>My IP-PBX supports media bypass.

Network Line
>Are you using a T1 line or an E1 line? **T1**

Type of Gateway
>What type of gateway will you deploy? **4 ports**

Exchange Unified Messaging Settings   You'll be provided with the following prompts:

Enabled users
>What percentage of users at this site will be enabled for Exchange Unified Messaging? **50%**
>Enable All Users **Not Selected**

Exchange Unified Messaging Voicemail Traffic
>On average, how many times per day do you think users will check their voicemail? **4 times per day**

External User Access   You'll be provided with the following prompts:

Do you want to enable external user access?
    Yes, and I want to deploy Edge Servers in my perimeter network. **Default**
    Yes, but I want to use Edge Servers deployed at another site.
    No.

What percentage of users are external? **30%**
Enable high availability for my external users. **Selected**
Which type of load balancer do you want to use?

    DNS load balancer using NAT.
    DNS load balancer using public IP addresses.
    Hardware load balancer using public IP addresses. **Default**

I want to deploy a Director at this site. **Unselected**
What percentage of users who have XMPP contacts? **30%**

Persistent Chat Settings   Only a single prompt for the number of users to enable.

What percentage of users will use Persistent Chat? **20%**

Client Settings   This section is asking what percentage of clients are using mobility or web access.

What percentage of users will be enabled for mobility? **40%**
Enable all users. **Unselected**
What percentage of users will be almost exclusively use LWA? **50%**
Enable all users. **Unselected**

Colocation Options   You'll be asked how you want to deploy your Mediation servers: colocate them on your Front End servers or deploy them as stand-alone Mediation servers. The default value is for Mediation servers to be colocated.

Branch Sites   You'll be asked to define your branch sites, including the number of users, whether there is a resilient WAN connection, and whether Media Bypass is available.

Add Another Central Site?   Finally, you'll be asked whether to add another central site. Selecting Yes at this point will repeat the entire question set for the next site; the default is No.

That finishes the Planning Tool data collection; on the next page click Draw to generate the topology.

GLOBAL TOPOLOGY

Once the site definition is completed, the Planning Tool will present the Global Topology page, shown in Figure 5.2.

FIGURE 5.2
The Global Topology
page

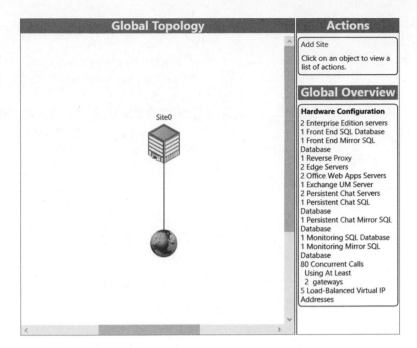

From this page, the Global Topology view provides the total hardware recommendations for all sites defined based on your answers to the questions on the Central Sites page. The hardware includes not only servers but also the number of hardware load-balanced IP addresses required as well as the concurrent call expectation and required gateways. If a single site is selected, the actions list changes to show these items:

◆ Add Site

◆ Add Branch Site

◆ View Site

◆ Edit Site

If more than one site is added, the actions list adds a Delete Site item.

Only additional sites may be deleted; the first site created can never be deleted. If it was designed incorrectly, you will need to start fresh or go back and modify the answers.

◆ Add Site will take you back through the Planning Wizard questions and provide an additional site configuration once completed. You can define a maximum of eight sites.

◆ Add Branch Site will provide the opportunity to define additional branch sites associated with this site.

◆ Edit Site will take you back through the questions you already answered for this site and allow you to make changes.

◆ Selecting a site and then choosing View Site from the actions list, or simply double-clicking a site, will open the Site Topology page, shown in Figure 5.3.

FIGURE 5.3
The Site Topology page

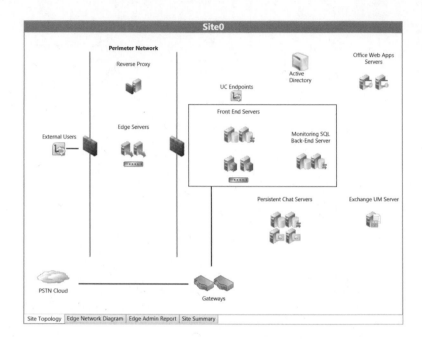

SITE TOPOLOGY

The Site Topology page displays the servers and devices required to support the site as defined in the Planning Wizard. It also provides a breakdown of the specific configuration required (for non-Lync servers this will be the generic rules).

On the Site Topology page, the actions list includes these items:

◆ View Global Topology

◆ View Planning Steps

◆ View Deployment Steps

When you select a specific server on the page, a View Server Information item will be added to the actions list. Clicking this action item (or double-clicking the server) will provide a response similar to Figure 5.4. The specific details provided will vary based on the actual server role selected. As you can see, the recommended hardware is displayed in addition to configuration information.

FIGURE 5.4
The Server
Information page

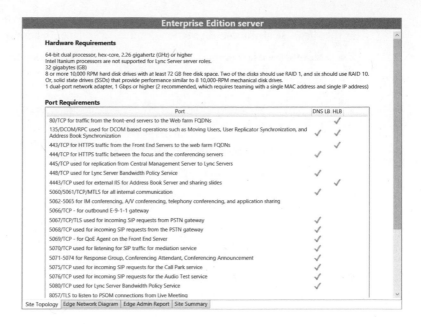

To add a View Firewall Diagram item to the list, select a firewall on the Site Topology page. To display the new firewall rule, as shown in Figure 5.5, select it from the actions list.

FIGURE 5.5
The firewall
diagram

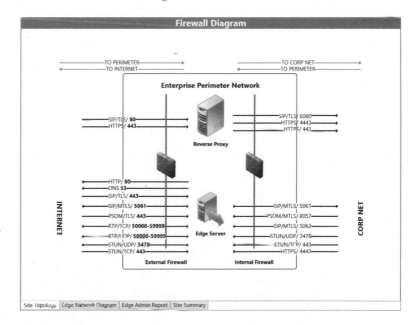

Like the Global Topology page, Site Topology displays the hardware requirements, but only for the site. A site information section describing some of the definition criteria is also included:

- Number of users (split between "site" homed and "cloud" homed)
- Percentage of voice-enabled users
- Percentage of Exchange UM users
- Percentage of Archiving users
- Percentage of "on-notification" users (mobility)
- Percentage of Lync Web App users
- Percentage of Monitoring users
- Percentage of Persistent Chat Users
- Number of external users

EDGE NETWORK DIAGRAM

Selecting the Edge Network Diagram tab on the bottom will display the network diagram view of the Edge infrastructure. This will include IP addresses as well as server names, as shown in Figure 5.6.

FIGURE 5.6
Viewing the Edge network diagram

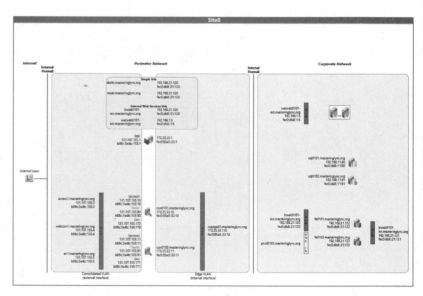

At this point, you can populate the detail behind the topology. Double-clicking any of the server icons or the data (server names or IP addresses) will provide a pop-up (also shown in Figure 5.6) through which the server names and IP address information can be added.

Providing this information now allows the topology from the Planning Tool to be exported to a file and directly imported into any design documentation, which will save time because all the firewall rules are already defined.

Edge Admin Report

The Edge admin report has four sections providing information about the Edge infrastructure. Figure 5.7 shows the beginning of a Summary report.

Figure 5.7

The Summary tab of the Edge admin report

The four tabs are as follows:

Summary Report This report provides the information such as server role, FQDN, IP address, and specific guidance where required (such as static route requirements).

Certificates Report The Certificates report provides the detailed certificate requirements for each of the roles involved with the Edge infrastructure (Edge and Reverse Proxy as well as the Next Hop pool). This one is very useful for the Reverse Proxy certificate because the Installation Wizard will generate the Edge and Next Hop certificates. Also included on this report are whether the certificates are required to be internal or public and which specific Enhanced Key Usages (EKU) are required.

Firewall Report The Firewall report provides all the information required to generate the rules allowing the external configuration. This information is broken down by internal, external, and reverse proxy interfaces.

DNS Report The DNS report provides all the records required, both A and SRV, along with the actual FQDNs to be assigned and the resulting IP address mappings.

In large organizations, the Lync Server 2013 administrator typically is not also the DNS or firewall administrator, so each of these reports can be extremely useful when configuration information needs to be provided to another team.

Site Summary

This page, illustrated in Figure 5.8, provides the list of enabled features as well as the capacity details. In some cases, it may make more sense to adjust the number of servers based on the information here.

FIGURE 5.8
A site summary

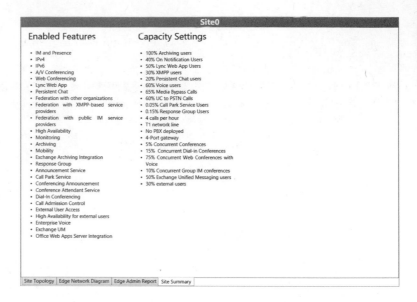

EXPORTING THE TOPOLOGY

Once the topology has been identified in the Planning Tool, you have several methods to extract that information:

◆ Exporting to Visio

◆ Exporting to Excel

EXPORTING TO VISIO

Selecting the Export To Visio option (via the icon or the File menu) provides a prompt for saving the file as a Visio drawing.

The Visio file opens to show the following worksheets as a minimum:

◆ Global Topology

◆ Site0

◆ Site0 Edge Network Diagram

Each additional site (and if defined, associated Edge network diagram) will also be represented on individual worksheets.

These aids are great for inclusion in any design documentation being organized and gathered.

EXPORTING TO EXCEL

Selecting the Export To Excel option (via the icon or the File menu) provides a prompt for saving the file as an XML 2003 spreadsheet.

By default, opening an XML file will launch Internet Explorer to display the content; however, if you launch Excel and then load the file, Excel opens to show the following worksheets as a minimum:

Summary   This worksheet provides a summary of the sites and server hardware required as well as a per-site breakdown of the features and capacity provided.

Hardware Profile   This worksheet provides a summary hardware count and specifications as well as a detailed breakdown per site and role.

Port Requirements   This worksheet summarizes the port requirements per role and provides a list of which ports require hardware load balancing and which can use DNS load balancing.

Summary Report-Site0   This worksheet summarizes the role of each server as well as the FQDN and IP address of each network card. In addition, there are comments associated with each entry detailing the role of each FQDN and IP address as well as information as to whether it should be added to DNS.

Certificates Report-Site0   This worksheet provides a breakdown of each certificate needed, including information such as Subject Name, Subject Alternative Name, CA (internal or public) and what Enhanced Key Usage (EKU) settings are required.

Firewall Report-Site0   This worksheet summarizes the firewall rules required, including FQDN, port, protocol, and direction of traffic.

 Real World Scenario

USING THE PLANNING TOOL OUTPUT IN YOUR DESIGN

As you've seen up to this point, the Planning Tool provides an extremely quick way to determine your design requirements. However, there's no such thing as a free lunch. The output should *not* be used as the definitive design. It should instead be used as a starting point. Because the scenarios are rule based, they do not (and cannot) deal with small variations in the requirements.

For example, using all the default settings, a single Front End server (without high availability enabled) will support 6,666 users. If you change the number of users to 6,667, the Planning Tool will indicate that two Front End servers are required. A third Front End server is not required until you reach 13,333 users.

According to the help file, a single Front End server can support up to 6,666 users, and two front ends can support up to 13,332 users.

For most of the customers we work with, we round the number of users to the nearest thousand. We typically start with the Planning Tool output and adjust as needed using the information from the help file and planning documentation.

The Planning Tool does have some inconsistencies within it. For example, it is possible to disable high availability for the pool but enable it for the Edge environment. However, doing so would cause the internal environment to become a single point of failure, and it would affect the external environment too.

Note that the help file and planning documentation are updated more frequently than the Planning Tool; therefore, this documentation is more likely to incorporate user feedback than the Planning Tool.

The Stress and Performance Tool

Of course, the only true way to confirm whether your design meets the defined performance requirements is to stress-test it using the Stress and Performance Tool, which can be downloaded from

```
www.microsoft.com/en-us/download/details.aspx?id=36819
```

The Stress and Performance Tool can be used to simulate load for the following modalities:

◆ Instant messaging and presence

◆ Audio/video/multiview conferencing

◆ Application sharing

◆ Peer-to-peer audio (including PSTN)

◆ Web Access Client conferencing

◆ Conferencing Attendant

◆ Response groups

◆ Address book download and address book query

◆ Distribution list expansion

◆ Emergency calling and location profiles

The Stress and Performance Tool can support multiple pools and federation.

When you deviate from the recommended hardware specifications or usage model, you should carry out performance testing to ensure that the planned design is capable of handling the expected load. This is the only way to validate a deployment prior to deploying in production with live users.

The toolset contains a number of applications to carry out the testing:

UserProvisioningTool.exe   Used to generate user accounts and contacts information used during the testing; these will be created within Active Directory.

UserProfileGenerator.exe   Enables the wizard to build the input criteria for the tests.

LyncPerfTool.exe   The Client Simulation Tool, which will consume the data created by the other two tools and carry out the testing.

There are also a number of associated files: Default.tmx and some example scripts.

STRESS AND PERFORMANCE TOOL PREREQUISITES

The LyncPerfTool.exe tool is capable of simulating the load of 4,500 users for every machine matching the following hardware:

◆ 8GB RAM

◆ Two dual-core CPUs

In addition, `LyncPerfTool.exe` requires Windows Server 2008 R2 SP1 (64-bit) or Windows Server 2012 (64-bit) with the following software installed:

◆ Microsoft .NET Framework 4.5

◆ Desktop Experience (Windows Server 2008 R2 only)

◆ Microsoft Visual C++ 2008 redistributable package (x64)

The following criteria must also be met:

◆ The admin running it must be logged on using an account that is a member of the Domain Admins group.

◆ `LyncPerfTool.exe` cannot be run on a server with Lync Server installed.

◆ PowerShell V3 must be installed on the server running `UserProvisioningTool.exe`.

◆ `UserProvisioningTool.exe` must be run on the Front End server where the user accounts will reside (Standard Edition or Enterprise Edition).

◆ Each test account must have a unique phone number.

◆ The server page file must be system-managed or at least 1.5 times the size of RAM.

◆ Windows Server 2008 R2 (or Windows Server 2012) must have Active Directory Remote Admin tools installed.

◆ The `CapacityPlanningTool.msi` file must be executed on each server being used to simulate clients.

◆ The Lync Server environment must be enabled for the scenarios being tested.

RUNNING THE LYNC STRESS AND PERFORMANCE TOOL

The Lync Stress and Performance Tool is not supported when run in a production Active Directory environment.

Because of the tool's requirements, and the tool's high-risk security requirements needed to access the accounts in Active Directory, it should be run only in test environments.

As a general best practice, any sort of performance testing should be carried out in a separate environment on hardware identical to that which will be used in production.

CREATING USERS

Because you'll be running the stress test in a test environment, you'll need to configure some users before you begin testing. To do that, you'll use the `UserProvisioningTool.exe` tool. When you run it, the first thing you'll see is the screen shown in Figure 5.9. The information you'll need to provide on each tab is outlined here. Upon first load, the fields will be grayed out and you'll need to load a configuration file, either the sample or a newly created one.

We have to admit to being slightly disappointed in the latest iteration of the stress testing tools. There's so much more that could've been achieved, even simple things like having a single button to run each section in turn rather than having to manually define and then create each section or the fact that the default entries populated (shown in Figure 5.9) are different from those used in the tools to actually generate the tests!

FIGURE 5.9
UserProvisioningTool
.exe

User Creation   Here you'll provide the following information to generate the users:

- ◆ Front-End Pool FQDN: The pool on which the users will be provisioned.

- ◆ User Name Prefix: All usernames will begin with this prefix.

- ◆ Password: This must meet the domain password complexity rules.

- ◆ SIP Domain: This field is for users' URIs.

- ◆ Account Domain: The user account domain.

- ◆ Organizational Unit: OU in which to create the objects (both user accounts and distribution lists).

- ◆ Phone Area Code: This is the starting prefix for users. Please note that when you're assigning phone numbers to new users, the tool does not "pad out" the number to be truly E.164 compliant. It simply joins this phone area code with the user index ID.

- ◆ Voice Enabled: Check box to indicate whether the users should be enabled for Enterprise Voice.

- ◆ Number Of Users: Enter the number of users you expect to have.

- ◆ Start Index: Used to uniquely identify users.

Once all the information has been entered, click the Create Users button to begin the process of creating them; depending on the number of users selected, this will take some time.

When your testing is complete, you can populate the tool with the same information as when you created the users, and then select Delete Users to remove the accounts.

Contacts Creation   Here you'll define how the user contacts lists are populated.

- ◆ Average Contacts Per User
- ◆ Fixed (Checking this doesn't allow for variation in number of contacts; the average is given to all.)
- ◆ Average Contact Groups Per User
- ◆ Federated/Cross Pool Contacts Percentage
- ◆ Federated/Cross Pool User Prefix
- ◆ Federated/Cross Pool User SIP Domain

When you're ready, click the Create Contacts button to populate the already provisioned users.

There is no option to remove the contacts—when you delete the users the contacts list will automatically be removed.

Distribution List Creation   Here you'll define and populate the distribution lists to be used:

- ◆ Number Of Distribution Lists
- ◆ Distribution List Prefix
- ◆ Minimum Members in a Dist. List
- ◆ Maximum Members in a Dist. List

Clicking Create Distribution List will create and populate the distribution lists. Oddly there is no option to delete the distribution lists, so this will have to be manual; deleting an account will remove it from the distribution list, but in the end, you'll be left with a number of empty distribution lists.

Location Info Service Config   Here you'll enter the address information to populate the Location Information Services (LIS) database.

- ◆ Number Of Addresses
- ◆ Offices Per Address
- ◆ Number Of WA Ports
- ◆ Number Of Subnets
- ◆ Number Of Switches
- ◆ Number Of Ports

Also the *Civic Address Details* section needs to be populated; this has the fields listed below, although not all are needed for each address.

- ◆ Company Name
- ◆ Street Name
- ◆ Street Name Suffix

- ◆ Post Directional

- ◆ City

- ◆ State

- ◆ Zip Code

- ◆ Country

As you'd expect, the Generate LIS Config Files button will generate the configuration information for importing into LIS.

Correctly defining the Location Information Services (LIS) content can be quite complicated (especially for locations outside North America where different address definitions are used), so it's best to simply use the sample data given in the documentation and vary the following data based on the specific number of addresses and access points you want to define:

CONFIGURING PROFILES

After you've created the users, you can configure their user profiles. To do that, you'll run `UserProfileGenerator.exe`, which displays the screen shown in Figure 5.10. (You'll need to display the profile generator on your own screen to see the details.) The information you'll provide on each tab is outlined next.

FIGURE 5.10
The screen displayed by
`UserProfileGenerator`
`.exe`

Common Configuration   Here you'll provide the following information to enable the stress testing to be performed. (At startup, all the information is defaulted to `contoso.com`, so you will have to reenter it).

- Number Of Available Machines (for running the stress testing)
- Prefix For User Names
- Password For All Users
- User Start Index
- Number Of Users
- User Domain
- Account Domain
- MPOP Percentage (Multiple Points of Presence support—i.e., how many users will log in via multiple clients)
- Sign In Per Second (Per Instance)
- Internal Network Server Settings
  - Access Proxy Or Pool FQDN
  - Port
- External Network Server Settings
  - Access Proxy Or Pool FQDN
  - Port

General Scenarios   Here you'll provide the following information to determine the level of testing performed:

- IM Load Level*
- Audio Conferencing Load Level*
- Application Sharing Load Level*
- Data Collaboration Load Level*
- Distribution List Expansion Load Level
- Address Book Web Query Load Level
- Response Group Service Load Level
- Location Information Services Load Level

Items marked * have the ability to be configured with additional settings:

- External
- AdHoc
- Large Conf

Each modality can be configured as follows:

◆ Disabled

◆ Low

◆ Medium

◆ High

◆ Custom

The Advanced button allows you to specifically configure each modality as required (detailed information on the default user profile is available in the Lync Server 2013 help file).

Voice Scenarios   Here you'll provide the following information specifically detailing the voice modalities:

◆ VoIP Load Level

◆ UC/PSTN Gateway Load level

◆ Conferencing Attendant Load Level

◆ Call Parking Service Load Level (requires the phone number to be configured)

◆ Mediation Server and PSTN

As with the options on the General Scenarios tab, these options can be configured as follows:

◆ Disabled

◆ Low

◆ Medium

◆ High

◆ Custom

The Advanced button allows you to specifically configure each modality, such as length of call, which location profile to use, and so on.

Reach   Here you'll provide the following information for remote and federated users:

◆ General Reach Settings

◆ Application Sharing Load Level

◆ Data Collaboration Load Level

◆ IM Load Level

◆ Voice Conferencing Load Level

Again, as with the options on the General Scenarios tab, these options can be configured as follows:

◆ Disabled

◆ Low

- ◆ Medium
- ◆ High
- ◆ Custom

The Advanced button allows you to specifically configure each modality, such as URLs, lobby time-out, and the like.

Mobility   Here you can configure the settings available for the mobility modality; this is new with the Lync Server 2013 implementation of these tools:

- ◆ General Mobility Settings (This includes definition of the URLs, Autodiscovery enabled, and other mobile specific settings.)
- ◆ Presence and P2P Instant Messaging/Audio Load Level

Summary   This tab provides an overall summary of the data and allows you to generate custom user ranges.

By default, the system will allocate user ranges for each of the load tests to be performed (see Table 5.1 for an example); tests not being performed will not be listed in the table. To allow the User Range column to be manually edited, check the Enable Custom User Range Generation check box.

TABLE 5.1:   User range generation

NAME	LOAD LEVEL	USER RANGE
Distribution List Expansion	Low	0–9
Audio Conferencing	Medium	10–46
Application Sharing Sharer	Low	47–50
Application Sharing Viewer	Low	1–64
Data Collaboration	Medium	65–71
Instant Messaging	High	72–999

When you're ready, click the Generate Files button and indicate where the files should be placed. The test case files will be generated and stored in the specified folder. This folder needs to be copied to each of the client systems that will be executing the stress tests (this folder must be copied to the same folder in which the Stress Tools are installed).

An option is provided to insert an initial sign-in delay when starting up; having a significant number of clients attempt to sign in at the same time can cause unexpected (and potentially unrealistic) delays to the testing.

Now that you've created the users and the profiles and have generated the client test cases, you can execute `runclient x.bat` (where *x* is replaced by the client ID—for example, `runclient0.bat` for the first client) on each of the client computers to begin the execution tests.

Be sure to enable performance counter capturing (using Performance Monitor or `perfmon.exe`) before starting the stress testing.

A number of command prompts will report the testing status (one prompt for each test), as shown in Figure 5.11.

FIGURE 5.11

Client view of stress test execution

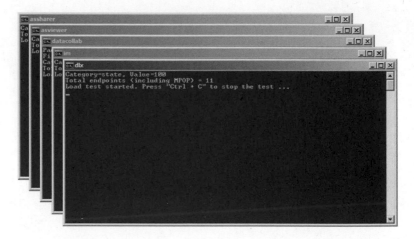

INTERPRETING THE RESULTS

Now that you've run the performance tests and the servers haven't turned into smoldering lumps of metal and plastic, what's next?

You'll need to analyze the performance during the testing. It's not enough to say the servers didn't crash and therefore it must be fine. You need to determine if there was any impact, such as dropped connections or busy responses.

Experience indicates that success counters don't really add value in this scenario; the failure rates are where you can establish when the servers start to come under pressure.

The following counters provide the most information to determine if the pool(s) can cope with the load expected:

- ◆ Failed Logons

- ◆ 5*xx* Responses for SetPresence

- ◆ 6*xx* Responses for SetPresence

- ◆ 5*xx* Responses for GetPresence

- ◆ 6*xx* Responses for GetPresence

- ◆ ABS Full/Delta File Downloads Failed

- ◆ ABS WS Calls Failed

- ◆ Calls Failed

- ◆ Calls Declined

- ◆ Calls Received 5*xx* (separate counters for IM, VOIP, App Sharing)

- Calls Received 6xx (separate counters for IM, VOIP, App Sharing)

- Conference Schedule Failure

- Join Conference Failure

If these failure numbers are significant, then the load is probably beyond the bounds of the environment's capacity and further investigation is needed. Typically, the causes will be due to poor or inadequate disk or memory performance on the SQL Server machine.

On the other hand, if the numbers are minimal, it is a good indication the servers are reaching their peak capacity and any further load would put them over the top.

There are no specific guidelines for what values constitute "significant" or "minimal" numbers; they will vary dramatically based on the number of users and the types of customers. For example, a call center will require better consistency from GetPresence-type responses than from Join Conference Failure because the call-center capability, Response Groups, relies on the presence states of users to direct calls. Equally, a failure of one call in a 100-user company will have a larger impact than one failure in a 50,000-user company.

In an ideal world, you would run tests to confirm that the servers are capable of supporting the load expected and then go further to establish the maximum the design can support. By doing that, you will determine the design's capability for future expansion.

Capacity Calculator

The Capacity Calculator Tool provides a way to establish the specific requirements for a server based on a scenario rather than based on the standard user profile as defined by Microsoft. This calculator can be downloaded from

```
www.microsoft.com/en-us/download/details.aspx?id=36828
```

This particular tool is aimed at people who have detailed knowledge of their environment. The answers they supply (things like average calls per user per hour, call duration, and so on) should be factual (or very close approximations) rather than simple guesses.

The calculator is capable of adjusting the server count based on the actual CPU clock speed and processor cycles. The sample server used is a dual-processor, hex-core 2.6GHz system, with 32GB of memory. If your server specifications differ from this, enter and calculate the appropriate values to provide a true reflection of your server's capability.

From Figure 5.12, you can see some of the configuration options as well as the output recommendations for a physical deployment. The output recommendations for a virtualized deployment are not shown here but are displayed beside the physical outputs in the tool.

Items in the tool colored orange are the configuration items and profile definitions to be changed based on your own expectations. They are listed here:

- Number of users enabled

- Average number of calls per user per hour

- Users enabled for Enterprise Voice

- Average number of UC-PSTN calls per user

- Percentage of calls that use media bypass

- Percentage of voice users enabled for UC-PSTN calls

◆ Percentage of voice users enabled for UC-UC calls

◆ Percentage of users in concurrent conferences

◆ Percentage of conferences with group IM only (no voice)

◆ Percentage of users using dial-in conferencing

◆ Percentage of conferences using voice (web conferences)

    ◆ Including video

    ◆ Including Multi-View

    ◆ Including applications sharing

    ◆ Including web conferencing

◆ Percentage of users enabled for mobility

FIGURE 5.12
The Capacity Planning Calculator

Microsoft Lync Server 2013 Capacity Calculator

Author: Pramod Jaisalmeria   Version 1.0
Contributor: Walid Boumerdassi, Andrew Frantsuzov

Legal Information: © 2013 Microsoft. All rights reserved. This tool is designed to assist you for your internal determination of server requirements based on users and traffic patterns. Results generated may vary based on the parameters you elect to use. This tool is provided AS IS; there are no express warranties, guarantees, or conditions.

	Modality/Workload	Workload	Number of users	Front End CPU*	Network in Mbps	Memory in GB
IM/P	Users enabled for Instant messaging (IM) and presence	100.0%	80000	176%	226	26.02
	Average number of contacts in Contacts list	80	NA			
Enterprise Voice	Users enabled for Enterprise Voice	60.0%	48000			
	Average number of calls per user per hour (peak)	4	NA			
	Percentage of calls that use media bypass	65.0%	NA			
	Percentage of voice users enabled for UC-PSTN calls	60.0%	28800	137%	314	9.10
	Percentage of voice users enabled for UC-UC calls	40.0%	19200	24%	25	1.83
Conferencing	Percentage of users in concurrent conferences	5.0%	4000			
	Percentage of conferences with group IM only (no voice)	10.0%	2200	15%	23	0.15
	Percentage of users using dial-in conferencing	15.0%	600	40%	14	1.17
	Percentage of conferences using voice	90.0%	3600	91%	479	3.21
	Including video (No Multi View)	☐	0	0%	0	-
	Including Multi View	☑	600	7%	272	1.17
	Including application sharing	☑	1500	25%	551	10.27
	Including web conferencing	☑	600	4%	123	0.37
Mobility	Percentage of users enabled for Mobility	40.0%	32000	96%	2.34	14.76

Recommendations	Physical			
	Servers*	Average CPU Load	Network in Mbps	Memory in GB
Total Front End Servers Required	12	57%	169	20
Edge Servers (based on 30% external)	2	NA	NA	NA
Archiving/Call Detail Recording/Quality of Experience services Store	1	NA	NA	NA
Back End Database Server Required (Pools Required)	1	NA	NA	NA

Mediation Server Perf counters

Call duration in minutes	3
Concurrent calls	2616
Calls on consolidated Mediation Server	218
Maximum calls on a stand-alone Mediation Server	1500

Input	Calculation	No Input/Output

The values shown in the tool in yellow are the specific resource requirement breakdowns per modality. They are as follows:

◆ Workload

◆ Number of users

- Front End CPU
- Network in Mbps
- Memory in GB

What is extremely useful about the Capacity Planning Calculator is its ability to break down per modality to view the impact on CPU and RAM simply by changing the usage profile.

As with any planning guide and calculator, you should perform a load test before deploying into production.

Bandwidth Calculator

A major piece of feedback that the Lync development team received from OCS deployments was that with the earlier version, admins were unable to determine the bandwidth requirements prior to installation, at which point it was typically too late to do anything. This inability posed a major problem because when there isn't enough bandwidth, users are impacted and other lines of business applications can be too. Call Admission Control (see Chapter 14, "Call Admission Control") helps provide a level of control on this; however, again it provides it after the fact.

You can use the Bandwidth Calculator to estimate the bandwidth prior to deploying and configuring Lync Server 2013, thereby allowing additional bandwidth to be purchased before rollout if necessary. It is very similar to the calculator for Lync Server 2010, obviously adjusted for the new bandwidth values for the codecs and also for the Multi-View capability of conferencing. Some additional new calculations are listed here:

- H.264 support
- Multi-View Gallery support
- Both Lync 2010 and Lync 2013 clients
- Internet traffic calculations
- Traffic aggregation per user-definable QoS traffic classes
- Scalability to 300 branches

To calculate those estimates, the Bandwidth Calculator requires the following information:

- Number of sites
- Number of users per site
- Persona of the users (The persona can be thought of as the user profile. A separate worksheet allows the personas to be customized to indicate low/medium/high usage rates for each modality.)
- Usage model
- WAN connectivity and any restrictions placed on traffic
- Thresholds

Figure 5.13 shows a sample of some of the output generated by the Bandwidth Calculator.

FIGURE 5.13
Output from
the Bandwidth
Calculator

At least for the first few times you use it, you should follow the steps in the flowchart guide (located on the Start Here worksheet) to set up the input values (shown reduced to fit the page in Figure 5.14).

FIGURE 5.14
Bandwidth
Calculator
flowchart

Using Topology Builder

So far in this chapter, we've been working purely with planning tools. The Topology Builder is the first deployment tool from the Lync 2013 installation media that you will probably use. When you get to this stage, the planning is complete (unless, of course, this is a test or development environment). This stage is where you define the architecture for your deployment; it is also where the first set of automated checks are performed.

The Chicken or the Egg?

Once you have planned your topology, you need to run the Topology Builder, and once you've input the topology, you need to publish it into the Central Management Store (CMS), a SQL database. However, the CMS must be in place prior to publishing, and you can't create the CMS until you have defined a SQL database in the topology.

Fortunately, there is a way to get around this chicken-or-egg scenario. Run setup.exe to go to the Deployment Wizard screen shown in Figure 5.15. On it you will find an item labeled Prepare First Standard Edition Server, which if selected will install the CMS portion into a SQL Express instance on the server on which it is run.

FIGURE 5.15
The Deployment Wizard includes the option Prepare First Standard Edition Server.

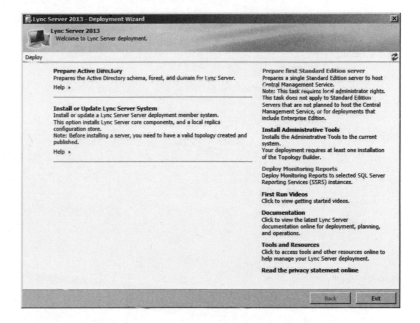

What about high availability in an Enterprise Edition deployment? Here you have two options. If the plan is to start with a pilot where you are deploying a Standard Edition server first, you could choose Prepare First Standard Edition Server. When it's time to move to production, define and publish the SQL Server instance and then move the CMS to it.

Or you could create the Enterprise pool as the initial pool and deploy to that using Topology Builder, although with additional options available for an Enterprise pool, we find it easier to start simple and then move up.

As an alternative, you could use PowerShell to install and create the database, as the following cmdlet shows:

```
Install-CsDatabase -CentralManagementDatabase
-SqlServerFqdn <FQDN of SQL Server> -SqlInstanceName <named instance>
-DatabasePaths <logfile path>,<database file path>
-Report <path to report file>
```

Then, when you want to define the topology, the location is already defined and the database has already been created.

Using Topology Builder

It might make more sense to include this information on the Topology Builder in the chapter on installation (Chapter 6, "Installation"); however, the Topology Builder is included here because its additional functionality makes it an appropriate tool for planning.

Specifically, although Topology Builder is used to configure, the largest part of its job is to define, *check*, and publish the topology. This ability to check the topology offers a significant advantage over what was available in previous versions.

By verifying that the configuration and dependencies are in place *prior* to making any changes, you can achieve an additional, higher level of verification of your changes. For example, Topology Builder will not let you delete a database or share a file that is still being used. (Of course, it can't stop someone from going to the server itself and deleting the database or share. However, even if someone did that, there would still be a record of what it should be.)

In addition to the checks carried out, after publishing, Topology Builder will provide a To Do list of actions to be carried out and the servers on which they need to performed (see Figure 5.16).

FIGURE 5.16
To Do list

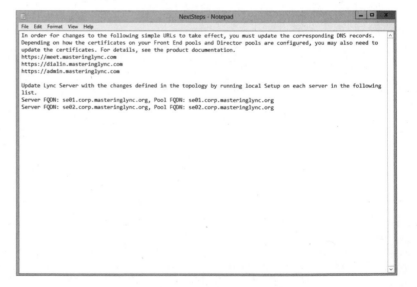

PUBLISHING MULTIPLE CHANGES WITH TOPOLOGY BUILDER

The To Do list is an extremely useful feature because it provides the next set of steps (rerun setup, request new certificates, etc.) required to complete any configuration changes.

One thing to note is that no records of the completed actions are kept. For example, if you make a change to the SIP addresses supported in the organization, there will be a reminder to request new certificates for each Front End server (and possibly Directors and Edge servers, if they are in the environment). If you remove (or add) the Mediation Server role to a specific Front End server before updating the certificates, the To Do list will report only the last change (the specific Front End server) and the need to request new certificates may be lost.

Therefore, we recommend that you make all your changes in a single topology publishing step.

When you start Topology Builder, it opens with the dialog shown in Figure 5.17. Here you are prompted with the following options for dealing with the topology:

Download Topology From Existing Deployment: This option will read the topology from Active Directory.

Open Topology From A Local File: This option will read a topology from a file.

New Topology: This option will create a blank topology to work with.

Whichever option you choose, the next window prompts for a filename; this is used to save the work in progress and any changes, prior to *publishing* the topology. Publishing the topology commits those changes.

FIGURE 5.17
Starting Topology
Builder

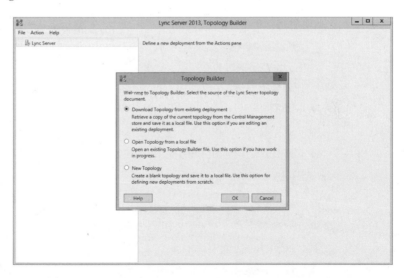

The Topology Builder comprises a number of wizards, one for each role. The following lists show the information captured by each wizard. In addition, where a wizard is dependent upon another role (for example, Enterprise pool requires SQL and a file share), it is possible to launch the new role wizard from within the running wizard; there is no need to predefine all the dependencies prior to running a wizard.

NEW TOPOLOGY

In the New Topology section, you'll provide the following information:

- Primary SIP domain
- Additional SIP domain(s)
- First site name
- First site description
- First site address—city
- First site address—state/province
- First site address—country/region code

Once the organization and site is defined, Topology Builder starts with four top-level sections under each site:

- Lync Server 2010
- Lync Server 2013
- Shared Components
- Branch Sites

LYNC SERVER 2013

The following items are all found under the Lync Server 2013 section of Topology Builder.

Enterprise Edition Front End Pools   Here you'll provide the following information:

- FQDN of pool
- FQDN of computer(s)
- Features—Conferencing
- Features—Conferencing, dial-in
- Features —Enterprise Voice
- Features—Call Admission Control
- Feature—Archiving
- Features—Monitoring
- Colocation—Mediation
- Associations—Edge
- SQL

- File share
- Web services URL—override internal FQDN
- Web services URL—External base URL
- Office Web Apps Server

Standard Edition Front End Servers   Here you'll provide the following information:

- FQDN of pool
- FQDN of computer(s)
- Features—Conferencing
- Features—Conferencing, dial-in
- Features —Enterprise Voice
- Features—Call Admission Control
- Feature—Archiving
- Features—Monitoring
- Colocation—Mediation
- Associations—Edge
- SQL
- File share
- Web services URL—override internal FQDN
- Web services URL—External base URL
- Office Web Apps Server

Director   Here you'll provide the following information:

- Pool FQDN
- Multiple or single computer pool
- FQDN of computer(s)
- Monitoring
- File share
- Web services URL—override internal FQDN
- Web services URL—External base URL

Mediation   Here you'll provide the following information:

- Pool FQDN
- Multiple or single computer pool
- FQDN of computer(s)

- ◆ Next Hop pool
- ◆ Edge server
- ◆ PSTN gateways

Persistent Chat Pools   Here you'll provide the following information:

- ◆ Pool FQDN
- ◆ Multiple or single computer pool
- ◆ FQDN of computer(s)
- ◆ Pool Properties—Display Name of Persistent Chat pool
- ◆ Pool Properties—Persistent Chat port
- ◆ Pool Properties—Enable compliance
- ◆ Pool Properties—Use backup SQL Server stores for DR
- ◆ Pool Properties—Use this pool as default for site <sitename>
- ◆ SQL
- ◆ File Share
- ◆ Next Hop pool

Edge   Here you'll provide the following information:

- ◆ Pool FQDN
- ◆ Select Features—Single FQDN and IP address
- ◆ Select Features—Enable federation
- ◆ Select Features—Enable XMPP federation
- ◆ IP options—Enable IPv4 on internal interface
- ◆ IP options—Enable IPv6 on internal interface
- ◆ IP options—Enable IPv4 on external interface
- ◆ IP options—Enable IPv6 on external interface
- ◆ IP options—External IP address uses NAT
- ◆ External FQDNs and Ports—SIP Access
- ◆ External FQDNs and Ports—Web Conferencing
- ◆ External FQDNs and Ports—Audio/Video
- ◆ Multiple or single computer pool
- ◆ Internal—IP

- ◆ Internal—FQDN

- ◆ External IP—SIP access

- ◆ External IP—web conferencing

- ◆ External IP—A/V conferencing

- ◆ Define the computers that make up the pool

- ◆ Next Hop pool

- ◆ Associate internal pools

Trusted Application Servers   Here you'll provide the following information:

- ◆ Pool FQDN

- ◆ Multiple or single computer pool

- ◆ FQDN of computer(s)

- ◆ Next Hop pool

SHARED COMPONENTS

The following items are all found under the Shared Components section of Topology Builder.

File Stores   Here you'll provide the following information:

- ◆ File server FQDN

- ◆ File share

SQL Server Stores   Here you'll provide the following information:

- ◆ SQL Server FQDN

- ◆ Named instance (Name) or default instance

IP/PSTN Gateway   Here you'll provide the following information:

- ◆ FQDN

- ◆ IP Address—Enable IP v4

- ◆ IP Address—Use all configured IP addresses/Select IP address

- ◆ IP Address—Enable IPv6

- ◆ IP Address—Use all configured IP addresses/Select IP address

- ◆ Define root trunk—Trunk Name

- ◆ Define root trunk—Listening port

- ◆ Define root trunk—SIP Transport Protocol

- ◆ Define root trunk—Associated Mediation Server

◆   Define root trunk—Associated Mediation Server port

Trunk   Here you'll provide the following information:

◆   Trunk Name

◆   Listening port

◆   SIP Transport Protocol

◆   Associated Mediation Server

◆   Associated Mediation Server port

Office Web Apps Server   Here you'll provide the following information:

◆   Office Web Apps Server FQDN

◆   Office Web Apps Server discovery URL

◆   Office web apps server deployed internally or externally?

BRANCH SITES

On this tab, you'll provide a name and description for the branch site along with its address comprising city, state/province, and country/region code.

Each branch site entry has another representation of the main site environment, this time without the Branch entry:

◆   Lync Server 2010

◆   Lync Server 2013

◆   Shared Components

Both the Lync Server 2010 and Lync Server 2013 sections only allow the creation of Survivable Branch Appliances (SBAs), and the Shared Components section only PSTN gateways and trunks.

SURVIVABLE BRANCH APPLIANCE

Here you'll provide the following information:

◆   FQDN

◆   Front end pool

◆   Edge pool

◆   PSTN Gateway—FQDN

◆   PSTN Gateway—root trunk name

◆   PSTN Gateway—Listening port

◆   PSTN Gateway—SIP Transport Protocol

Topology Builder also includes the capability to import an OCS 2007 R2 environment via another wizard (this requires the backward-compatibility module to be installed, `OCSWMIBC.msi`). Publication of this information is required to ensure that all the Lync Server 2013 servers are aware of and can communicate with any legacy servers.

Most of the data can be captured automatically; however, the Merge Legacy Wizard requires information regarding the legacy Edge servers because in OCS R2 environments, the Edge configuration information is stored only on each Edge server. (Lync Server 2010 and 2013 instead store all the information for all the roles in the CMS and require the CMS to be replicated to all servers.)

Once the OCS infrastructure data is imported, Topology Builder defines the legacy environment as BackCompatSite; it may be viewed for information about server names and roles, but detailed information is not available in Topology Builder and it must still be managed using the legacy management toolset.

Lync Server 2013 Topology Builder allows for management of a Lync Server 2010 environment from the same console; this is remarkably different from the previous approach by Microsoft when it comes to upgrading; typically two sets of management tools are required during coexistence/migration.

Installation Prerequisites

Once you have completed the planning stage, you are nearly ready to install Lync Server. Before you do, though, you'll need to take care of a few prerequisites for both the infrastructure and the operating system.

Recommended Hardware

The term *recommended hardware* is always a little confusing. Does it mean this is the minimum hardware needed or something else? In the past, it has tended to be a relatively high specification. If you are working for a small company, does this mean Lync Server 2013 is unsuitable for your needs? Can you use lower-spec hardware? Should you virtualize?

The recommended hardware values are based on the tested profiles used by Microsoft (available from the Lync Server 2013 help file) and feedback from the beta release programs.

By using the capacity tools mentioned earlier, it is possible to downsize the scalability of Lync Server 2013 for companies that do not meet the minimum size of 2,500 users and do not want to pay extra to meet the recommended hardware guidelines (especially when based on a usage profile that does not match their own).

Physical Hardware

The best way to determine your hardware needs is to consider the performance characteristics and profiles provided. The recommended hardware is the hardware that has provided the values used in the Microsoft-provided planning tools and guidance, based on the default user profile (which can be found in the Lync Server 2013 help file). If you deviate significantly from the defaults, you should consider more detailed planning.

Table 5.2 shows the recommended hardware for each role.

TABLE 5.2:   Recommended hardware

ROLE	CPU	MEMORY	DISK	NETWORK
Front End, Back End, Standard Edition, and Persistent Chat servers	64-bit dual processor, hex core 2.6Ghz	32GB	72GB free disk space 8+ disks, 10,000 RPM Two configured with RAID-1 and remainder RAID-10	Two NICs, 1Gbps
Edge, Stand-alone Mediation, Director servers	64-bit quad core, 2.0Ghz Or 64-bit dual processor, dual core, 2.0Ghz	16GB	72GB free disk space Four+ disks, 10,000 RPM	Two NICs, 1Gbps

A single pool will support up to 80,000 users with 12 Front End servers (using all modalities). The recommended approach is 6,660 users per Front End server; be careful to cater for this number when planning with server failures in mind.

VIRTUALIZATION

Based on feedback (from the Lync Server 2013 beta program, previous versions of Lync, and general computing trends), Lync Server 2013 supports virtualization of any of the server roles.

The following virtualization machine managers (also known as *hypervisors*) are supported at the time of writing:

◆ Windows Server 2008 R2 Hyper-V

◆ Windows Server 2012 Hyper-V

◆ VMware ESX 4.0

See http://go.microsoft.com/fwlink/?linkid=200511 for updated details of other hypervisors that may be supported.

If Windows Server 2008 R2 is being used as the host, the hotfix described in Knowledge Base article 981836 is required (http://go.microsoft.com/fwlink/p/?linkid=201212). This hotfix must be installed on both the host and all virtual machines.

A mix of virtual and physical servers in the same pool is not supported. For this purpose, Microsoft defines a pool as "two or more servers of the following roles—Front End, Director, Mediation, and Edge." Front End servers are considered separate from Back End servers, so you can virtualize Front End servers and have physical Back End servers and vice versa, physical Front End servers with virtualized Back End servers.

You can, however, mix virtual and physical pools in the same enterprise deployment (for example, servers in one region could be virtual while servers in another region could be physical). Within the topology, they would be configured in separate pools (and most likely separate central sites).

There is no requirement to host all types of server roles on the same physical server, such as all virtual Mediation servers on one physical node and all virtual Front End servers on another.

However, you should mix the types of roles deployed on physical nodes to reduce the single points of failure introduced by having all of one role on one physical node.

Quick/live migration is not supported and can introduce additional complexity to the client connectivity.

As a rough rule of thumb, 4GB of memory should be assigned to the host OS, and the remaining memory allocated as if dealing with physical machines. There are many reasons to virtualize (green computing, cost reduction, etc.); however, there are also reasons not to virtualize. Don't assume that virtualization is the correct answer in every environment.

Software Prerequisites

In addition to the hardware requirements just discussed, a number of software prerequisites must be met before you can begin installation. Some of them are at the operating system or application level; others are at the component level.

ACTIVE DIRECTORY

Of course, before you can install Lync Server 2013, you need to update Active Directory to support Lync.

The following Active Directory topologies are supported:

◆ Single forest with single domain

◆ Single forest with a single tree and multiple domains

◆ Single forest with multiple trees and disjoint namespaces

◆ Multiple forests in a central forest topology

◆ Multiple forests in a resource forest topology

The Active Directory forest version must be Windows Server 2003 Native Mode or higher, and all the domains in which Lync Server 2013 will be deployed must also be Windows Server 2003 Native Mode or higher.

The domain controllers must be Windows Server 2003 (32-bit or 64-bit) or higher, and the Schema, Forest, and Domain prep actions must be performed from a 64-bit machine. There are no tools capable of running the required Lync Server 2013 Active Directory updates from a 32-bit machine.

Don't forget permissions! The account used to install Lync is required to be a member of the CsAdministrator group or, if the installation permissions have been delegated, a member of the delegation group. In addition, when changes are published to the topology, the account used to publish must be a member of the CsAdministrator group as well as the Domain Admins group or, if delegated setup has been configured, only a member of CsAdministrator. Permissions are also required on the SQL database being installed.

SUPPORTED OPERATING SYSTEM AND SQL SERVER VERSIONS

Lync Server 2013 is supported on the following Windows Server versions:

◆ Windows Server 2012 Standard

◆ Windows Server 2012 Datacenter

◆ Windows Server 2008 R2 Standard (with SP1)

◆ Windows Server 2008 R2 Enterprise (with SP1)

◆ Windows Server 2008 R2 Datacenter (with SP1)

Only the 64-bit version of the OS is supported, and they must not be Server Core versions.

An update is required for Windows 2008 R2: See Knowledge Base article 2646886, "FIX: Heap corruption occurs when a module calls the InsertEntityBody method in IIS 7.5" at the following location:

```
http://go.microsoft.com/fwlink/p/?linkid=3052&kbid=2646886
```

A question commonly asked is whether service pack updates are supported. Service packs are supported upon release, but full version updates are not supported until explicitly tested and confirmed. For example, if SP2 for Windows is released, Lync Server 2013 will automatically be supported with this service pack applied to the operating system. However, if instead of SP2, Windows 2008 R3 is released, Lync Server 2013 will *not* be supported until testing has been confirmed on this new operating system.

In addition to the OS, this rule of thumb also applies to the SQL Server version, of which the following are supported (only 64-bit versions are supported):

◆ SQL Server 2008 R2 Standard

◆ SQL Server 2008 R2 Enterprise

◆ SQL Server 2012 Standard

◆ SQL Server 2012 Enterprise

◆ SQL Server Express 2012 (for Lync Server 2013 Standard Edition and the local server databases).

Lync Server 2013 does not support the use of SQL Server failover clustering. New functionality within Lync Server 2012 uses native database mirroring for high availability functions.

The administrative tools may also be installed on the following client OSs (they must also be 64-bit):

◆ Windows 7 with SP1

◆ Windows 8

Remote PowerShell administration does not require installation of the administrative toolset. As discussed in Chapter 8, "Introduction to PowerShell, the Lync Management Shell, and Regular Expressions," you can instead remotely connect to a Lync Server 2013 Front End server and access the Lync Server 2013 PowerShell cmdlets as if you were remotely logged into the server and running the cmdlets directly.

REQUIRED OPERATING SYSTEM COMPONENTS AND DOWNLOADS

In addition to the base operating system version, a number of other components are required:

◆ Windows PowerShell 3.0

◆ .NET Framework 4.5

♦ Windows Identity Foundation

♦ Windows Communication Foundation (WCF)

Depending on your OS, some of these items might be installed already, or they may need to be downloaded. Pay special attention to the .NET Framework. Each version does not replace previous versions, so it is possible (and this is fine!) to have multiple different versions of the .NET Framework installed.

Individual roles have different additional component requirements based on their configuration:

Front End Servers and Directors   These require IIS and the following modules installed:

♦ Static content

♦ Default document

♦ HTTP errors

♦ ASP.NET

♦ .NET extensibility

♦ Internet Server API (ISAPI) extensions

♦ ISAPI filters

♦ HTTP logging

♦ Logging tools

♦ Tracing

♦ Windows authentication

♦ Request filtering

♦ Static content compression

♦ Dynamic content compression

♦ IIS management console

♦ IIS management scripts and tools

♦ Anonymous authentication

♦ Client certificate mapping authentication

If you attempt an installation without any of these, the response shown in Figure 5.18 will be displayed.

Unfortunately, this is one of the few generic error messages within Lync Server 2013. The error itself states the problem, but it does not mention which modules are not installed. It simply states that all are needed.

The following PowerShell commands will install all the required Windows IIS modules:

```
Import-Module ServerManager
Add-WindowsFeature Web-Static-Content, Web-Default-Doc, Web-Http-Errors,
```

```
Web-Asp-Net, Web-Net-Ext, Web-ISAPI-Ext, Web-ISAPI-Filter, Web-Http-Logging,
Web-Log-Libraries, Web Http-Tracing, Web-Windows-Auth, Web-Filtering,
Web-Stat-Compression, Web-Dyn-Compression, Web-Mgmt-Console,
Web-Scripting-Tools, Web-Basic-Auth, Web-Client-Auth –Restart
```

FIGURE 5.18
When IIS modules are not installed, an error message appears.

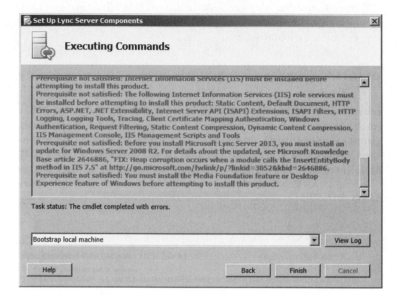

In addition to the IIS modules previously listed, the following Windows features are needed:

- Remote System Administration Tools

- Desktop Experience

The following PowerShell commands will install all the required Windows features:

```
Import-Module ServerManager
Add-WindowsFeature RSAT-ADDS, Desktop-Experience
```

Mediation Servers   No additional components must be installed.

Edge Servers   No additional components must be installed.

Persistent Chat Servers   No additional components must be installed.

Servers Running Conferencing Components   If conferencing is configured on a server, the Windows Media Format Runtime component must be installed, and this requires a reboot.

For Windows Server 2008 R2, use this command:

```
%systemroot%\system32\pkgmgr.exe /quiet /IP /m:%windir%\servicing\Packages\Microsoft-
Windows-Media-Format-Package~31bf3856ad364e35~amd64~~6.0.6001.18000.mum
```

Or install the Desktop Experience feature using this command:

```
Import-Module ServerManager
Add-WindowsFeature Desktop-Experience
```

Archiving and Monitoring Components   No additional components must be installed.

Other Components or Server Roles   Aside from the Lync-specific programs (installed ones will differ based on actual Lync installation choices), Lync Server 2013 will also install the following software if it is not already installed:

- Microsoft Visual C++ 2012 x64 Redistributable, 11.0.50727

- Microsoft Visual C++ 2010 x64 Redistributable, 10.0.40219

- Microsoft Visual C++ 2010 x86 Redistributable, 10.0.40219

- SQL Server 2008 Setup Support Files

- SQL Server 2012 (64-bit)

- SQL Server 2012 Management Object (x64)

- SQL Server 2012 Native Client

- SQL Server 2012 Setup (English)

- SQL Server 2012 Transact-SQL ScriptDom

- System CLR Types for SQL Server (x64)

- VSS Writer for SQL Server 2012

- SQL Server Browser for SQL Server 2012

- URL Rewrite Module version 2.0 Redistributable

- Windows Fabric

High Availability

One of the main architectural changes with Lync Server 2013 is the high availability model. As mentioned previously in this chapter, SQL failover clustering is not supported; up until this version, SQL clustering was the de facto high availability model. However, increasing customer demands on the availability of service, especially between physically separate data centers, made this option unusable.

Lync Server 2010 introduced the concept of a backup registrar, but this capability provided only limited failover for voice functionality. A lot of additional functionality was missing (such as IM and presence, conferencing, etc.).

Lync Server 2013 leverages SQL mirroring technology to provide significantly more capability, and the only issue remaining is the automation in smaller environments; a third SQL Server instance is required, two for the mirrored pair and one for the witness.

Client failover uses DNS load balancing and was discussed in Chapter 1, "What's in Lync?"

In simple terms, SQL mirroring provides a method for replication of the primary databases to a secondary location. With the inclusion of a witness server, this can enable automatic failover for the pool to the secondary databases. Without the Witness server, this failover is a manual process.

The SQL mirroring architecture is shown in Figure 5.19.

SQL mirroring involves only a single pool, but with the new high availability/failover capability with Lync Server 2013 allowing for failover between pools, we need to look at how that process is achieved.

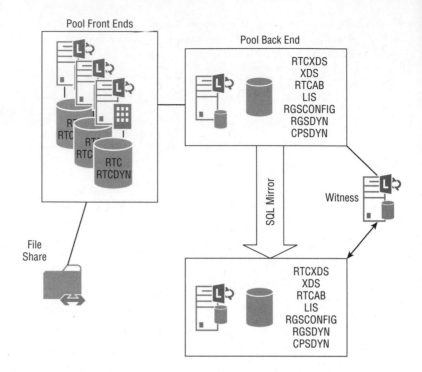

FIGURE 5.19
SQL mirroring
architecture

When the resiliency option is configured in Topology Builder and the Lync Server 2013 setup process is run again to update the Front End servers in the pool, a new service is installed: the Lync Backup Service. This service is responsible for ensuring that each database is replicated across to the other pool. Although the service is installed on all the front ends in the pool, only a single front end is running it at any time; this is determined by the pool itself in a random manner.

Figure 5.20 shows the architecture with the backup service dealing with the data replication between pools, and also the file share using Distributed File Sharing (DFS) for its replication.

It's important to note that changes are first written locally, then replicated to the pool SQL mirror, and then across to the backup pool. Due to the time delays configured in Topology Builder, it is possible that some changes will not be available on the backup pool in the event of a disaster occurring.

It is important to understand that this data loss is likely to be of the following functionalities:

◆ Change to buddy list

◆ Meeting creation/modification

◆ Meeting content (stored in the file share)

◆ Setting of call forwarding settings

Settings such as presence are dynamic and as such are not replicated.

Due to this multiple pool architecture, it's important to scale the pools for the perceived load in a disaster; for this reason, each pool is expected to hold 50 percent of the user base so that in the event of a disaster, 100 percent of the users will be hosted on a single pool and this pool will have the hardware to cope with the scenario.

FIGURE 5.20
Lync Backup
Service architecture

The Bottom Line

Use the available planning tools.   Lync Server 2013 is an extremely complex application, even when only some of the modalities are being used. Being able to plan for capacity, not just the number of servers but also bandwidth, is extremely critical.

> **Master It**   Which of the planning toolsets would you use to determine the required bandwidth on the network?

Determine when virtualization is appropriate.   Lync Server 2010 introduced support for all modalities when virtualized. Lync Server 2013 has increased the performance capabilities and supported options. In certain cases, this enables administrators to reduce the server footprint, giving a better "green computing" deployment.

> **Master It**   What virtualization support improvements have been introduced with Lync Server 2013?

Understand the prerequisites.   Like most applications, Lync Server 2013 has a number of prerequisites that must be met prior to installation. These range from Active Directory requirements to individual server role requirements, at both the OS level and the component level.

> **Master It**   Which operating systems are supported for deployment of Lync Server 2013?

Chapter 6

Installation

Now you're ready to get up and running with a Lync deployment. If you've deployed OCS, you'll see that Lync deployment is dramatically different but simpler. In Chapter 5, "Planning Your Deployment," you learned that the key difference is in the planning of the topology and how this information is used in deployment.

Lync utilizes a Central Management Store (CMS), which holds information about all the roles and settings in the deployment. This replaces the various data stores that were used in OCS. The benefit of this Central Management Store is that once the topology is defined and published, every installation simply pulls from the defined configuration. This minimizes administrator input and allows automated deployment. The CMS has been updated between Lync Server 2010 and Lync Server 2013, and once Lync Server 2013 has been introduced to the environment, only the Lync Server 2013 version of the tools should be used to manage the environment.

Other improvements include the process by which certificates are requested and deployed and the fact that the Edge server role can now be centrally managed; the administrator no longer has to connect remotely to that server to manage it locally.

Like many Microsoft server applications, Lync has a Standard and an Enterprise Edition. The Standard Edition is fully functional but runs on a single server, using a SQL Express backend database. It is still supported by other roles, such as the Edge, Monitoring, and Archiving roles, some of which would still run on other server installations. The supporting roles don't have a definition of Standard or Enterprise; they simply support the deployed Front End servers.

The Enterprise Edition allows for higher availability and more scalability of the roles to support organizations with hundreds of thousands of users. Both versions of the software can be installed only on a Windows Server 2008 R2 (SP1) or Windows Server 2012 64-bit operating system (OS) and must be installed on the full GUI version of those OSs rather than the Server Core version.

In this chapter, you will learn to:

- Configure Windows Server for a Lync installation

- Prepare Active Directory for a Lync installation

- Install your first Standard Edition server

- Get your first users up and running

- Implement external access through the Director, Edge server, and reverse proxy server

- Understand the differences in an Enterprise Edition installation

Getting Up and Running with Standard Edition

In the previous chapters, we explored what Lync is, so you're familiar with its components and the underlying protocols that enable it to function. We also discussed clients and security. Now it's time to get things up and running so you can start to experience Lync hands on!

Lync Standard Edition is designed to support up to 2,500 users on its single server, so it is more than capable of supporting an enterprise. However, it doesn't scale beyond those 2,500, nor does it provide full high availability (HA). That said, it is perfect for smaller enterprises or branch deployments with significant numbers of users to support. For now, though, Standard Edition provides the best environment to learn the key deployment concepts without needing tons of hardware to support it. This is true in home learning or training class scenarios, although in the more complex scenarios you may need hardware that will enable the progression to Enterprise-class deployments.

Configuring Windows Server 2008 R2 SP1

The first step to installing Lync is to prepare the supporting server OS with the prerequisites to support Lync. In Chapter 5, we touched on the major elements required from a planning point of view, such as OS version support and capacity planning. Here we will discuss the specifics required on each server before Lync can be installed.

> **OS SUPPORT**
>
> Lync is supported on Windows Server 2008 R2 (SP1) and Windows Server 2012, both 64-bit operating systems. For the bulk of this chapter, we will concentrate on Lync running on Server 2008 R2 SP1, which is the most widely deployed version of Windows supported at the time of writing (and also because the screenshots display better in a book from Windows Server 2008—some windows in Windows Server 2012 have a gray background!). If you are installing Lync on another OS, see "Preparing for Lync Server on Other Operating Systems" later in the chapter for the differences.

The software prerequisites differ for the various Lync roles. The prerequisites for the Standard Edition server are very similar to those for the Director and Front End server roles used in enterprise deployments. We will discuss the specific requirements of each role as we install it in this and later chapters.

The prerequisites fall into a few different areas. The first requirement is the .NET Framework v4.5; it is required because Lync is written as *managed code*, a program that will run only under Common Language Runtime. For more information, see the wiki page at the following location:

```
http://en.wikipedia.org/wiki/Managed_code
```

Second is the Microsoft Visual C++ 11 x64 Runtime requirement, with a minimum version number of 11.0.50531. Fortunately, the Setup program will install this if it is not already installed.

A new requirement for Lync Server 2013 is PowerShell V3.0. If this is not already installed on the OS (such as with Windows Server 2012), it will need to be installed. PowerShell v3.0 is part of the Windows Management Framework 3.0, and can be downloaded from here:

```
www.microsoft.com/en-ca/download/details.aspx?id=29939
```

An additional requirement introduced for Lync Server 2013 is Windows Identity Foundation, which can be downloaded from the following location:

`www.microsoft.com/en-us/download/details.aspx?id=17331`

The next area of software to install is IIS 7.5 (on Server 2008 R2) or 8 (on Server 2012). Lync has many elements that use IIS, which provides access to the Address Book, client updates, meeting content that is stored in the file store and exposed to users via a virtual directory in IIS on the Lync Front End servers, and of course the Meet, Dial-in, and Admin URLs, which provide access to conferences, the dial-in conferencing settings, and the Lync Control Panel.

Table 6.1 lists the IIS modules required by Lync Server Standard Edition.

TABLE 6.1:　　IIS modules required by Lync Server Standard Edition

MODULE	DESCRIPTION
Web-Static-Content	Static content
Web-Default-Doc	Default document
Web-Http-Errors	HTTP errors
Web-Asp-Net	ASP.NET
Web-Net-Ext	.NET extensibility version 3.5
Web-ISAPI-Ext	Internet Server API (ISAPI) extensions
Web-ISAPI-Filter	ISAPI filters
Web-Http-Logging	HTTP logging
Web-Log-Libraries	Logging tools
Web-Http-Tracing	Tracing
Web-Client-Auth	Client certificate mapping authentication
Web-Windows-Auth	Windows authentication
Web-Filtering	Request filtering
Web-Stat-Compression	Static content compression
Web-Dyn-Compression	Dynamic content compressions
Web-Mgmt-Console	IIS management console
Web-Scripting-Tools	IIS management scripts and tools
Anonymous Authentication	Installed by default when IIS is installed

TABLE 6.1: IIS modules required by Lync Server Standard Edition *(CONTINUED)*

MODULE	DESCRIPTION
Web-Asp-NET45*	.NET extensibility version 4.5
NET-WCF-HTTP-Activation45*	Windows Communication Foundation (WCF) web activation

* for Windows Server 2012 only (they are installed by default with the WCF installation for Windows Server 2008 R2)

As well as the IIS components, Windows Communication Foundation requires some components to be installed:

◆ NET-WCF-HTTP-Activation45 - Windows Communication Foundation (WCF) web activation

◆ NET-WCF-TCP-PortSharing - Installed by default

Finally, some elements are required in specific cases. If your Lync Front End (FE) or Standard Edition server is going to run conferences and you intend to provide music on hold, you will also need the Windows Media Format Runtime (as well as deploying an Office Web Apps server).

Likewise, if you are installing your first Lync server, from which you intend to prepare your domain, or if you want to be able to manage Active Directory (AD) through the Active Directory Users and Computers (ADUC) snap-in or for that matter PowerShell, you need to install Remote Server Administration Tools–Active Directory Domain Services (RSAT-ADDS). We will include both of them in the Standard Edition configuration in this chapter.

A LAB TO FOLLOW

Chapter 5 covered the system requirements and prerequisites to deploy Lync Server 2013 in your network; however, if you want to follow along with this chapter but don't think you will be able to because the specs are so high, don't worry!

Here is what will work (and what we used to write this book): We have a single laptop-class tower machine, with an Intel Core i7 Quad Core CPU and 16GB of RAM, running Windows 8 with Hyper-V.

This formed the platform for deployment and testing. We ran a domain controller (DC), Exchange, Lync, SQL, and clients on this system, with a single virtual CPU allocated to each. The Standard Edition Lync Server that we are about to install had 4GB of RAM. Supporting roles had 2GB of RAM, and the DC had a single CPU and 1GB of RAM. SQL had 2GB of RAM. Only servers used for the specific piece of deployment were enabled at that time to ensure that memory requirements were suitable.

No, that isn't the supported minimum, and it won't let you run many users, but it works very nicely for learning, whether in a training class or at home. To prepare the server on which you plan to install Lync Standard Edition, you will need to log into the server as at least a local administrator. Later you will need top-level domain and forest permissions like Schema

Administrator and Enterprise Administrator. For this exercise, you will perform the steps as the built-in domain administrator account. We will discuss more complex systems where different accounts have different rights later.

The server should already be running Windows Server 2008 R2 SP1, and it should be joined to your test domain and have all the latest Microsoft Update patches installed. This can include .NET Framework v4.5 if that is part of your build.

BE SAFE, SEGREGATE!

Please, please, please don't install Lync for the first time in your production network! This has a great chance of becoming an RGE (a resume-generating event). Lync installation will make significant changes to your Active Directory schema that can't be undone. It also creates a bunch of groups and ACLs/ACEs on many objects in your forest, so you should create a safe environment in which to learn by spinning up a test lab.

As you have just seen, preparing the server for the installation of Lync requires various pieces of software. Lync Setup will actually install some of them automatically if they are not in place; however, many must be manually configured. The first you will install is the .NET Framework 4.5. If you try to run Lync Setup before it is installed, you will be prompted to install it, as shown in Figure 6.1.

FIGURE 6.1
Warning to install
.NET 4.5 on your
server before
installing Lync

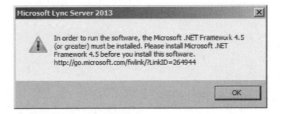

NOTE   We like to use PowerShell to do these installations because they can be done with a couple of simple commands and all Lync prerequisites can be installed in a simple script.

For versions of Windows prior to Windows Server 2012, .NET Framework 4.5 must be installed manually via the download

`www.microsoft.com/en-us/download/details.aspx?id=30653`

or executable file provided on the Lync Server 2013 media.

For Windows Server 2012, there are a few ways to install .NET Framework 4.5, including through the GUI's Server Manager Features section or through PowerShell. To perform the installation using PowerShell, you must open up Windows PowerShell as an administrator. Assuming you are logged on as an administrator, type **PowerShell** in the Start menu search area and click on the result, the Windows PowerShell command shell. (You may want to skip to Chapter 8, "Introduction to PowerShell, the Lync Management Shell, and Regular Expressions," if you need an introduction. You'll use PowerShell for numerous installation tasks in this chapter.)

Once in PowerShell, follow these steps:

1. Run the following command:

```
Import-Module ServerManager
```

This command will import the module `ServerManager`. You will learn much more about modules in Chapter 8, "Introduction to PowerShell, the Lync Management Shell, and Regular Expressions"; however, for now, all you need to know is that it is a way to extend PowerShell with additional functionality. In this case, you are adding the ability to install roles and features on the server.

2. Run the following command:

```
Add-WindowsFeature NET-Framework-Core
```

This installs the core .NET Framework code needed to run Lync.

3. Install Visual C++ Runtime.

Manual installation will require Visual C++ Runtime version 11.0.50531 to be installed; it can be found in the `\setup\amd64` folder of the installation media and is a file called `vcredist_x64.exe`.

Running `setup.exe` will result in the screen shown in Figure 6.2 being displayed, and assuming you click Yes, the Visual C++ Runtime will be installed. Once the Runtime is installed, the Setup application will launch.

FIGURE 6.2
Automatic installation of Microsoft Visual C++ Runtime by the Setup application

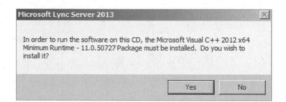

Now that the non-OS-specific prerequisites have been installed, we can start with the web components listed earlier. These can be installed in a single PowerShell command.

On versions of Windows prior to Windows Server 2012, the ServerManager module must be imported:

```
Import-Module ServerManager
```

4. To install all the required web and .NET elements, use the following command:

```
Add-WindowsFeature Web-Static-Content,Web-Default-Doc,Web-Http-Errors,Web-Asp-
Net,Web-Net-Ext,Web-ISAPI-Ext,Web-ISAPI-Filter,Web-Http-Logging,Web-Log-Librar
ies,Web-Http-Tracing,Web-Windows-Auth,Web-Filtering,Web-Stat-Compression, Web-
Dyn-Compression,Web-Mgmt-Console,Web-Scripting-Tools,Web-Client-Auth
```

If installing on Windows Server 2012, you can also add the following modules to the list:

```
Web-Asp-Net45,Net-HTTP-Activation,Net-WCF-HTTP-Activation45
```

Having run the previous command, you should check the output, which should be as shown here:

```
Success Restart Needed Exit Code Feature Result
------- -------------- --------- --------------
True    No                       Success    {IIS Management Scripts and Tools, IIS Man...
```

5. At this point, all the required IIS components should be installed on your Lync server. This just leaves RSAT-ADDS, which can be installed with the following command:

```
Add-WindowsFeature RSAT-ADDS
```

Running this command will get a slightly more detailed output than the web component installation because you are warned that a reboot is needed:

```
WARNING: [Installation] Succeeded: [Remote Server Administration Tools] AD DS
Snap-Ins and Command-Line Tools. You must restart this server to finish the ins
tallation process.
WARNING: [Installation] Succeeded: [Remote Server Administration Tools] Server
for NIS Tools. You must restart this server to finish the installation process.
WARNING: [Installation] Succeeded: [Remote Server Administration Tools] Active
Directory module for Windows PowerShell. You must restart this server to finish
the installation process.
WARNING: [Installation] Succeeded: [Remote Server Administration Tools] Active
Directory Administrative Center. You must restart this server to finish the ins
tallation process.
Success Restart Needed Exit Code Feature Result
------- -------------- --------- --------------
True    Yes                      Succes... {AD DS Snap-Ins and Command-Line Tools, Se...
```

AUTOMATING THE REBOOT

You have seen that a reboot is needed. If you don't want to wait and manually reboot, you can add the `restart` parameter to the command to make the system reboot immediately after completing the RSAT-ADDS install.

6. Now that you have installed .NET, ADDS tools, and the web components, reboot the server.

The last piece of preparation needed is to install the Windows Media Format Runtime or Desktop Experience (depending upon the version of Windows).

Windows Media Format Runtime is installed in a slightly different manner. You should run the installation command from the CMD.exe shell as an administrator:

1. To run the CMD prompt, type **CMD** into the Start menu search box, right-click the result, and select Run As Administrator. Having done so, run the following command:

```
%systemroot%\system32\dism.exe /online /add-package /packagepath:%windir%\serv
icing\Packages\Microsoft-Windows-Media-Format-Package~31bf3856ad364e35~amd64~~
6.1.7601.17514.mum /ignorecheck
```

2. This command will install the Runtime and then exit as shown in Figure 6.3. As shown, you will need to restart, so type **Y** to do so.

FIGURE 6.3
Installing the
Windows Media
Format Runtime
from the CMD.exe
shell

The Desktop Experience is a Windows feature and can be added in the same way as the IIS components.

```
Add-WindowsFeature Desktop-Experience
```

This will also add in the dependency for Ink Support, and a reboot is required.

Real World Scenario

PREPARING FOR LYNC SERVER ON OTHER OPERATING SYSTEMS

If you are installing Lync Server on an OS other than Windows Server 2008 R2 SP1, note the following differences.

INSTALLING THE WMFR ON OTHER WINDOWS OPERATING SYSTEMS

To install the Windows Media Format Runtime on servers running Windows Server 2008 R2 RTM, use the following command:

```
%systemroot%\system32\dism.exe /online /add-package /packagepath:%windir%\servicing\Pac
kages\Microsoft-Windows-Media-Format-Package~31bf3856ad364e35~amd64~~6.1.7600.16385.mum
 /ignorecheck
```

PREREQUISITES FOR OTHER SUPPORTED OPERATING SYSTEMS

In general, we refer to Windows Server 2008 R2, and specifically SP1, as the platform on which Lync is installed. That is because it is the most deployed Microsoft operating system that is supported. However, in the real world, you may not be able to install Lync on the latest and greatest OS or at the latest service pack level. This can occur for a number of reasons, including licensing; your company simply may not have purchased the client access licenses (CALs) for Server 2012. Not having the proper CAL could make deploying Lync cost prohibitive. Another compelling reason could be that your company has a restricted set of customized OS builds and has yet to prepare one for Server 2012. If such were the case, you may have to install Lync on Windows Server 2008 R2 SP1.

To do so, you must realize that there are other differences (beyond Windows Media Format Runtime) in the prerequisites required and how they are installed.

The key difference is that the following elements, installed by default on Server 2012, are not in Server 2008 R2:

◆ PowerShell V3

◆ .NET Framework 4.5 manual download

To install Windows PowerShell 3.0 on a server running Windows Server 2008 R2, see the following link:

    http://www.microsoft.com/en-us/download/details.aspx?id=34595://go.microsoft.com/
    fwlink/?linkid=197390

To install .NET Framework manually, download Microsoft .Net 4.5 Framework from the Microsoft Download Center at this link:

    www.microsoft.com/en-us/download/details.aspx?id=30653

That is nearly all the prep work that needs to be done manually. All you must do now is run Windows Update again to check for any updates and ensure that the system is fully patched.

You are now ready to start the Lync setup process. Throughout setup, additional pieces of supporting software will be installed. As mentioned, on your first run of Setup, you will install the Microsoft Visual C++ v11.0.50727.1 Redistributable. If, for example, you've run Setup to install Topology Builder, this will already be installed. As part of the rest of Lync installation, these other elements will be installed:

◆ URL Rewrite Module version 2.0 Redistributable

◆ SQL Server 2008 Express SP1

◆ SQL Server 2008 Native Client

◆ SQL Server 2012 and components

◆ Microsoft Identity Extensions

◆ Silverlight

◆ Windows Fabric

Most of them are not likely to cause any problems with your server team; Visual C++ is simply a programming interface that allows Lync to operate, and the URL Rewrite module is used by the simple URLs, discussed further in Chapter 4, "Clients," and Chapter 15, "E911 and Location Information Services."

However, you may notice that SQL Server Express and its client pieces are installed, which may cause your SQL team some concern. SQL Express is installed on each Lync server and is part of the replication and data storage mechanism used to ensure that each server has a local copy of the CMS. For more information about the CMS and its replication, see Chapter 5. You may need to discuss SQL and Lync Server requirements with your database administrators

(DBAs). For Lync Server 2010, this was SQL Express 2008, and for Lync Server 2013, this is now SQL Express 2012.

Having set up the prerequisites, the next thing you need to do is prepare Active Directory.

Preparing Active Directory

Active Directory (AD) is absolutely critical to your network. It is the central authentication point, so any changes to it should be carried out with appropriate care and attention. As with other Microsoft server applications, Lync makes significant changes to AD as part of setup. There are three key elements to these changes. First, the schema is extended with classes and attributes in which to store information about Lync and its users. Second, the forest is prepared; it creates global settings and universal groups that are used in the management of Lync. Finally, each domain where Lync users or servers will be deployed must be prepared. Let's look at each stage in more depth.

THE SCHEMA

Schema preparation is run against the holder of the schema master Flexible Single Master Operation (FSMO). That doesn't actually mean you must be running at the console of the box, but you do need to be a member of the Schema Administrators group and the Enterprise Administrators group in the root domain.

In this simple installation of Standard Edition, we will be running in a single-forest, single-domain model and the installation will be carried out as the default administrator, so no worries there. Later in the chapter, we will discuss what happens in more complex AD environments, where permissions are heavily locked down or where different teams manage AD and Lync.

As you learned in Chapter 5, most of the Lync configuration information is now stored in the CMS; however; there is still some information written into AD. The schema extension adds attributes to user objects to store information such as the SIP Uniform Resource Indicator (URI) of a user (the Lync equivalent of an email address); it also creates classes and attributes for backward compatibility with OCS 2007 R2.

There are two ways to extend the schema during installation. One is through the Lync Setup program; the other is through the command line. The cmdlets that handle this are installed as part of the administrative tools package during the Topology Builder installation.

At this point let's prepare the schema. We will use the Setup Wizard for this and come back to the cmdlets later in the chapter when we talk about automating setup.

1. Run setup.exe from within the install media $X:\Setup\amd64$ directory. If you followed the instructions in Chapter 5 to install the Topology Builder, you will not face any prompts and will land at the home page of the Setup Wizard application, shown in Figure 6.4.

2. On the home page, click Prepare Active Directory, which will take you to the area where all the AD preparation tasks are chosen. In the Prepare Schema section, click Run to kick off Schema Prep.

3. Follow through the wizard, clicking Next to kick off the process. This will take only a minute at most in this exercise.

FIGURE 6.4
The Setup Wizard
home page, from
which all setup
activities are run

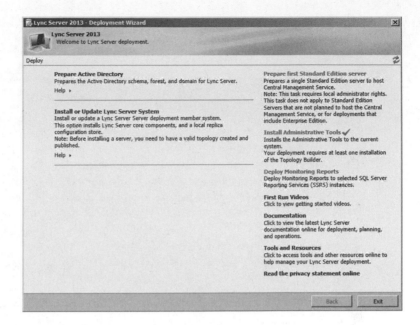

On completion, you will see a summary screen of the cmdlet that ran in the background, allowing you to view the log of the process. As long as there were no warnings shown on the summary screen, there is no need to check the log unless you want to know a little more about what happened during the process.

If you do want to check the log, click the View Log button next to the drop-down, which will allow you to select a log based on the activity you want to investigate. The log will open in the web browser. If you are using an older version of Internet Explorer, you may need to click Allow Blocked Content to explore the log. Click Expand All Actions in the top right of the page to see details of the log.

IT'S ALL POWERSHELL

As mentioned, a PowerShell cmdlet ran in the background during the schema-extension process. As you will see in Chapter 8, Lync is entirely controlled through PowerShell. The GUI simply calls the relevant cmdlets and indeed does not expose all of the PowerShell cmdlets; some capability is available only via PowerShell.

---

4. If you click the Log button, the log will open in Internet Explorer (IE). You may need to allow IE to run the blocked content, at which point you will be able click Expand All

Actions in the top right of the window to show the entire file. Once satisfied, close the browser and click Finish in the wizard to complete schema preparation and return to the AD preparation wizard page.

CHECK SCHEMA REPLICATION

In our small lab with one DC, checking replication is irrelevant because there are no other DCs with which to talk. However, in a larger AD, it is critical to ensure that replication of the schema changes has occurred on all DCs before moving on to the forest preparation.

To do this, log into a server as a member of the Enterprise Admins group and then load `asdiedit.msc`. Note that ADSI Edit is not installed by default and comes either with the Windows Server 2003 resource kit tools or as part of the RSAT ADDS tools on Windows Server 2008, Server 2008 R2, and Server 2012 systems. On the Action menu, click Connect To. In the Connection Settings dialog box under Select A Well Known Naming Context, select Schema, and then click OK.

Under the schema container, search for `CN=ms-RTC-SIP-SchemaVersion`. If this object exists, and the value of the `rangeUpper` attribute is 1150 and the value of the `rangeLower` attribute is 3, then the schema was successfully updated and replicated. If not, wait a little longer for replication to occur.

THE FOREST

Now that the schema has been extended, it is time to prepare the forest in which Lync is to be installed. The AD *forest* is a collection of trees (which contain domains) that share a common global catalog and directory schema. The forest represents the security boundary within which users, computers, groups, and other objects reside.

The process of forest preparation is what creates the permission structure by which Lync is managed. It creates a bunch of universal groups, whose names all start with the characters *RTC* and *CS*. These groups are combined to provide administrative rights over Lync objects and are shown in Table 6.2.

TABLE 6.2:   RTC and CS groups created by ForestPrep

RTC GROUPS	CS GROUPS
RTCComponentUniversalServices	CSAdministrator
RTCHSUniversalServices	CSArchivingAdministrator
RTCProxyUniversalServices	CSHelpDesk
RTCSBAUniversalServices	CSLocationAdministrator
RTCUniversalConfigReplicator	**CsPersistentChatAdministrator**
RTCUniversalGlobalReadOnlyGroup	CSResponseGroupAdministrator
RTCUniversalGlobalWriteGroup	**CSResponseGroupManager**

TABLE 6.2: RTC and CS groups created by ForestPrep *(CONTINUED)*

RTC GROUPS	CS GROUPS
RTCUniversalReadOnlyAdmins	CSServerAdministrator
RTCUniversalSBATechnicians	CSUserAdministrator
RTCUniversalServerAdmins	CSViewOnlyAdministrator
RTCUniversalServerReadOnlyGroup	CSVoiceAdministrator
RTCUniversalUserAdmins	
RTCUniversalReadOnlyGroup	

Items in bold are new for Lync Server 2013; also note that CsPersistentChatAdministrator is the only group with a lowercase for the s in CS.

This is covered in much more depth in Chapter 9, "Role-Based Access Control." The forest prep also creates various objects in the configuration partition of AD, which is replicated to all domain controllers in the forest.

THE CONFIG PARTITION

The config partition is used as a store of information, which is readily available to all DCs because it is part of the information set of which all DCs hold a replica. In OCS 2007, this configuration information was by default stored in the System container in the root domain of the forest; however, this often caused issues in large distributed ADs where access to the root forest was slow. Therefore, in OCS 2007 R2, the default was changed to the configuration store, and this is maintained in Lync.

Because you ran the schema preparation from the setup GUI, you will run the forest preparation in the same way. Again, you need to be a member of the Enterprise Admins group, but this time not Schema Admins. You will continue running as the default administrator.

1. Either start Setup again, if you closed it after schema prep, or carry on from where you left off. This time click Run on the Prepare Current Forest section of the wizard to start the process. Once the wizard starts, follow through with the defaults. Notice that there is an option to specify a different domain in which to create the universal groups; however, for now there will be only the single domain. We will cover this further in the section "Enterprise Deployments" later in this chapter.

2. Once the wizard completes, you must recheck replication. This time there is a Lync cmdlet to do this. Open the Lync Server Management Shell by navigating through Start, All Programs, Microsoft Lync Server 2013, Lync Server Management Shell. Run the following cmdlet:

```
Get-CsAdForest
```

This will check that your Active Directory forest has been correctly configured to allow installation of Microsoft Lync Server 2013. As long as the output is as shown here, you are fine to proceed:

```
LC_FORESTSETTINGS_STATE_READY
```

3. If you want more detail about what the `Get-CsAdForest` cmdlet has checked, run the following command to output results to the log file specified:

```
Get-CsAdForest -Report C:\ForestPrep.html
```

This outputs a log file in HTML format that you can open in your browser, and it looks something like Figure 6.5.

FIGURE 6.5
The deployment log file shows the steps to verify forest prep

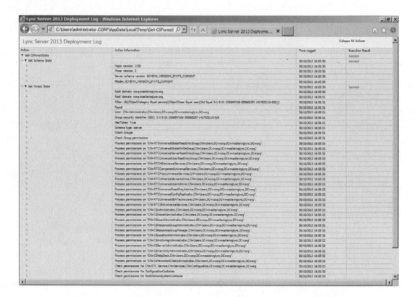

For detailed info about PowerShell and Lync, see Chapter 8.

THE DOMAIN

The final step in AD preparation is the domain preparation. This step must be carried out in every domain with Lync users and/or servers. To run domain prep, you must be either an enterprise admin or a domain admin in the domain being prepared.

The access control entries (ACEs) that allow members of the RTC groups to manage Lync objects and manipulate user objects in the domain are actually created during domain preparation. The permissions are set on the default containers, users, and domain controllers and at the root of the domain.

Again, this step can be run either through the shell or through the setup GUI:

1. Continuing from the completion of forest prep, you should be back in the AD Prep home page section of the Setup application. To start domain prep, click Run in the Prepare Current Domain section of the page. Run through the wizard, selecting the defaults and clicking Next to progress and Finish to end.

2. At this point, you once again need to check that things have completed correctly. Run the following command:

`Get-CsAdDomain -Report "C:\DomainPrepReport.html"`

This will check the domain prep steps and output a report with the `Get-CsAdForest` cmdlet. The expected output is

`LC_DOMAINSETTINGS_STATE_READY`

Assuming this all checks out, you are ready to move on. If things didn't quite work, your next step will be to leave more time for replication; if that doesn't work, then try rerunning the preparatory steps. If this still isn't successful, then use the logs to localize the area of failure. To identify more ways of fixing common problems, see Chapter 12, "Troubleshooting."

Installing the Standard Edition Server

As you learned in Chapter 5, the Lync installation is driven by the topology you define using Topology Builder and publish to the CMS. In Chapter 5, you defined a simple topology for a Standard Edition deployment, so let's retrieve that topology, create the CMS, and publish the topology. Once that is done you can begin the actual installation.

PERMISSIONS

In these exercises, we are running all the steps as the default domain administrator account. It has Schema, Enterprise, and Domain admin rights, which give full access to allow setup to be performed. Later in the process, we will create a Lync Admin account, which we will use to administer Lync. At the end of the chapter, the section "Enterprise Deployments" covers environments where permissions are locked down more tightly.

RETRIEVING THE TOPOLOGY AND CREATING THE CMS

To retrieve the topology, take the following steps:

1. On the Lync server, open the Topology Builder (this should have been installed in Chapter 5).

2. When you open the Topology Builder, you are prompted to load a topology, by downloading from a CMS, by opening from a saved file, or by creating a new topology. For this example, select Open From File and find the file saved in Chapter 5.

   Once it is opened, all the settings defined in the topology will be visible and you can make any final tweaks. At this point, you need to publish the topology to the CMS, but you haven't actually created the CMS yet.

3. To create the CMS, you need to prepare a SQL database. SQL is installed on each Lync server, but you can't install Lync without having published the topology—the "chicken and the egg" or catch-22 scenario.

To get around this with the Enterprise Edition (more later), you could have already created the SQL instance and prepared the database using PowerShell.

On the Standard Edition, where SQL Express is installed on the same box, you must use the Prepare First Standard Edition option in the Setup application. This installs SQL Express on the Standard Edition server, which gives you access to a database engine that Topology Builder can use to create the CMS to which you then publish the topology.

4. To prepare the first Standard Edition (and yes, it is only the first, because once the CMS is created you are no longer in the Catch-22 situation mentioned earlier), you must once again run setup.exe. On the home page in the top-right corner, you should click Prepare First Standard Edition Server (see Figure 6.6). This will launch a wizard, and after you click Next, the wizard will start to install SQL Express. Once the installation completes, click Finish to exit the wizard and return to the home page of Setup.

FIGURE 6.6
Click Prepare First Standard Edition Server

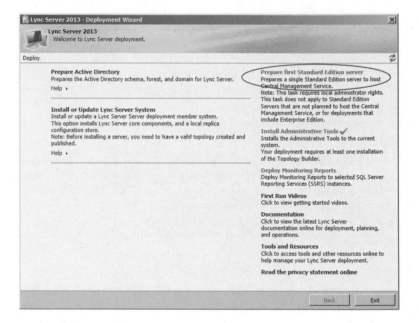

Once this is done, you don't need to run this portion of Setup again on any other servers. If you do, all it will do is leave you with an empty SQL Express installation.

PREPARING THE FIRST STANDARD EDITION SERVER MIGHT TAKE A WHILE

You may well find that the preparatory steps take a while, even as long as 10 to 15 minutes on slower systems while nothing much seems to be happening on the console. Don't worry at this point! If you are really concerned, fire up Task Manager and take a look at the following processes:

```
Deploy.exe
TrustedInstaller.exe
```

> ```
> Setup.exe
> SQLEXPR_x64.exe
> ```
>
> You will find that these processes require a fluctuating amount of CPU resources and that the memory consumed by the Setup100.exe and SQLsrv.exe processes grows.
>
> As long as you see these fluctuations, all is well and you should just keep waiting.

The preparation process not only installs SQL, it ensures that remote computers have access to it; that access is provided by creating relevant firewall rules using the following NetSH commands:

```
> Creating firewall exception for SQL instance
netsh advfirewall firewall add rule name=" SQL RTC Access" dir=in action=allow pro
gram="c:\Program Files\Microsoft SQL Server\MSSQL11.RTC\MSSQL\Binn\sqlservr.exe" e
nable=yes profile=any
> Creating firewall exception for SQL Browser
netsh advfirewall firewall add rule name="SQL Browser" dir=in action=allow protocol
=UDP localport=1434
```

At this point, you have one final task to perform before returning to the Topology Builder to publish the topology. You must set up the file share, which Lync will use, depending on configuration, to store some or all of the following elements:

◆ Application server files

◆ Archiving server

◆ CMS file store

◆ Web services (including elements like the Address Book files, meeting content, and device updates)

To create the file share on the server where you are about to install Lync Standard Edition, follow these steps:

1. First run cmd.exe to open a command prompt and then enter the following commands:

```
Mkdir c:\share
```

This will create a folder named share on the C: drive, which you will share using this command:

```
NET SHARE share-c:\share /GRANT:Administrators,FULL
```

This will share the c:\share folder with Full permissions for the Administrators group, which is all that is needed to allow you to publish the topology. Now you're ready to publish the topology and install Lync.

2. Move back to the Topology Builder and check through the topology opened earlier in the chapter. Verify the following elements:

◆ Check all simple URLs.

◆ Confirm that the file share is available and has the proper permissions defined.

◆ Ensure that you've defined the server roles you need at this time.

◆ Confirm that any servers defined are online and joined to AD.

Given that you are installing a very simple topology on a single server at this point, and have literally just created the file share, there should be no problems here. If you are uncertain, revisit Chapter 5 for more information.

3. The final thing to check is that the topology references the correct CMS. To do this, right-click at the root of the topology where it says Lync Server 2013 and select Edit Properties, and then on the page that opens, select from the left pane Central Management Server. In the drop-down, select the Standard Edition server as the CMS.

DNS ENTRIES

Before publishing the topology, you must make sure all servers are available. One aspect of this is setting up the relevant DNS entries. These entries are detailed in Chapter 4 and Chapter 5; however, the basics are that you need an A record for the FQDN of the Standard Edition server and SRV records to enable automatic sign in for each SIP domain.

```
A = se01.corp.masteringlync.org = IP of the Standard Edition server

SRV = _sipinternaltls._tcp.masteringlync.org over port 5061 that maps to
the FQDN of the Standard Edition server (se01.corp.masteringlync.org)
```

You also need to create the Meet, Dial-in, Admin, and Lyncdiscover records:

```
A = meet.masteringlync.org = IP of the Standard Edition server

A = dialin.masteringlync.org = IP of the Standard Edition server

A = admin.masteringlync.org = IP of the Standard Edition server

A = lyncdiscover.masteringlync.org = IP of the Standard Edition server

A = Lyncdiscoverinternal.masteringlync.org = IP of the Standard Edition
    server
```

PUBLISHING THE TOPOLOGY

Once you are satisfied with the topology, it is time to publish it:

1. In Topology Builder, right-click Lync Server and select Publish Topology on the drop-down menu (it is also located under the Action menu).

2. This will kick off a wizard that first gives you a list of requirements to follow before you can publish the topology. You have met all of them, but take a quick read to verify and then click Next to continue.

3. You will be presented with a screen that asks you to select the Front End server on which to create the CMS. It should be prepopulated with the server on which you are installing. If it isn't, select the correct server in the drop-down. You may notice the Advanced button, which is used to be more specific about the directories used when creating SQL databases. It will be covered in more depth later in the chapter. Click Next to begin publishing.

Once publishing completes, Lync gives you the option to check the logs; it also links to a to-do list, a text file telling you which actions need to be performed on other servers. This is something you will see repeated throughout the setup stages and is very useful. In this case, you are reminded that you need to create the relevant DNS records for the Meet and Dial-in URLs, as shown in Figure 6.7.

FIGURE 6.7
The actions required after the topology is completely published

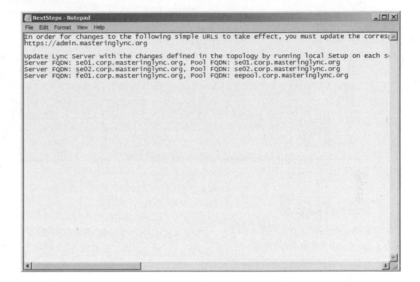

The topology is now published, which means that the relevant configuration has been entered into the CMS. This means that when you install Lync, the configuration can be pulled to the Local Configuration Store and used to configure the local server.

FURTHER PREPARATION

The remaining setup steps are relatively straightforward. First, you need to install the Local Configuration Store. This will create a new SQL instance on the server that holds a read-only replica of the CMS.

1. To install the Local Configuration Store, start `setup.exe` from the `\setup\amd64\` folder of the media, and on the Setup home page, click Install Or Update Lync Server System.

2. This takes you to a setup page that runs through all the tasks to get the server up and running. Click Run in the Install Local Configuration Store section.

3. This kicks off a wizard where you will first be asked from where you want to pull the config. In this instance, you will pull it from the CMS. The other option would be to pull from a file that you will see later when you configure the Edge server. Click Next to begin creating the Local Configuration Store.

This process will take a few minutes, after which you will get the familiar completion page that allows you to view the steps taken and to launch the log in a browser to delve further into any details. One nice touch to note is that if multiple logs were created for different steps of the process, all of them are available from a drop-down menu.

4. To end the wizard, click Finish.

HOW THE LOCAL CONFIGURATION STORE IS POPULATED

We've discussed that the Local Configuration Store is pulled from the CMS. However, you might be wondering how this is actually done.

What happens is that an `Export-CsConfiguration` command is run against the CMS, which creates a ZIP file. Because this is our first Standard Edition server, this file is stored locally; however, if we were building a server remote from the CMS, this would be sent by SMB over port 445 to the remote server. Once it is received, an `Import-CsConfiguration` is carried out with the `-LocalStore` parameter, which imports the configuration into the local configuration database. At this point, the HTTPS SQL replication process kicks in to maintain consistency between the databases.

INSTALLATION

Let's return to the Install or Update Lync Server Settings setup page. The next element to complete is the Setup Or Remove Lync Server Components section. This is what actually installs the Lync binaries onto the server.

1. To begin the process, click Run in the Setup Or Remove Lync Server Components section. This kicks off the Setup Lync Server Components Wizard.

In the background, Setup will look in AD to find a Service Connection Point (SCP), which will provide the location where the CMS is held. Setup will review the data in the CMS and then install any required components by checking the local server name against the name of the server listed in the topology.

2. On the first page of the wizard, click Next to kick off Setup. On completion, click Finish.

The next element to configure is certificates. This has been simplified somewhat compared to the OCS installation process.

3. Back at the Install Or Update Lync Server System setup page in the Certificates section, click Run to start the Certificate Wizard. This will open the page shown in Figure 6.8.

You can see that by default the Lync server requires two certificates:

Default certificate

OAuthTokenIssuer

However, if you click the drop-down by the default certificate, you will see that it is possible to install a certificate for each component, including Server default, Web services internal, and Web services external. This flexibility is particularly useful when providing external access through a reverse proxy that cannot trust an internal certificate authority (CA), which would cause you to need a trusted public certificate on the Web services external component. In this case, keep the simple, standard installation because you will be using Forefront Threat Management Gateway as the proxy, as you will see later in the chapter.

FIGURE 6.8
The Certificate
Wizard

4. To create the required certificate, minimize the drop-down and highlight Default Certificate. Click Request and then follow the wizard that opens. Click Next to progress to the selection of an online or offline CA.

Here, you can choose whether to use a CA that is internal (private) to your organization and is online to issue certificates automatically or save the request to a file and submit it to a CA manually. This could be the case either if you use trusted public certificates or if your own CA can't provide certificates automatically.

PUBLIC VS. PRIVATE CAs

You will regularly see recommendations for Lync to use certificates from either a public CA or a private (internal) CA. Which is best for you?

Well, the recommendation for the use of an internal CA pretty much comes down to cost—once installed, each certificate is free, and the overhead of managing them is relatively minimal (unless you are using certificates on a large scale, at which point you probably already have a solution in place to manage them).

If all (or the vast majority) of your users are internal AD users, with AD-joined machines, then an internal Enterprise CA will be a better choice as it will automatically be trusted by all the AD-joined machines.

On the other hand, if you are not running Windows as your main OS, or your users are connected to a different forest than the Lync deployment, it may be better to use a public CA because you can select a CA that is in the default trusted root CA list of the OS, ensuring no additional overhead to manage trusted root CAs.

External certificates for the Edge server role are recommended to be from public CAs because (in most cases) they provide the automatic trust from the underlying OS to the certificate provided.

5. In this case, keep it simple and go for the internal CA, which is running as an Enterprise Root CA on Windows Server 2008 R2. Because this is the only CA in the environment, it is the only one in the drop-down, so click Next to continue.

6. On the next page, you can opt to select different credentials to use to access the CA. This can be useful if you are using an account with only enough rights to install Lync so it cannot access the CA. In this case, leave the defaults in place and use the account you are using to run Lync Setup (the built-in domain administrator account) which has plenty of rights. Click Next to continue to the next page.

7. Here you can select a custom certificate template instead of using the default Web Server template on the CA. This could be useful if, for example, later you need to be able to export the private key and your default certificate template doesn't allow that. Leave this blank and thus use the default template. Click Next to continue.

8. You are prompted to give the certificate a "friendly name," as shown in Figure 6.9. Make it something meaningful. It is not obviously presented to users but will show up if they view the certificate that is used by the internal Web components.

FIGURE 6.9
Setting the certificate friendly name

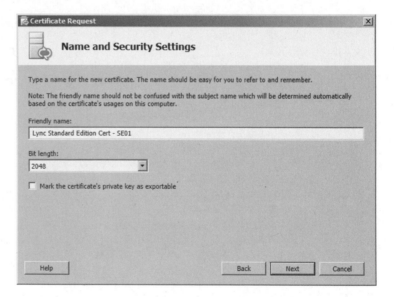

9. Click Next to progress and then follow the next couple of pages entering information about your organization and location, which will be stamped on the certificate.

Once the information has been entered and you have clicked Next a couple of times, you will get to a summary page that displays the subject alternative names (SANs), which will be used to create the certificate. In Figure 6.10, you can see how this contains the URLs for the simple URLs defined, URLs used for mobile connectivity alongside the server FQDN and also the external web services FQDN, which will be used later in the chapter when you provide external access to Lync.

FIGURE 6.10
The summary page shows all the URLs entered on the certificate.

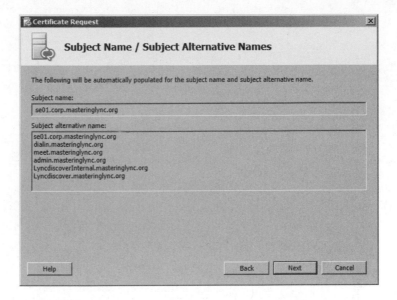

10. To complete the request, click Next to move on to choose whether to set up any further subject alternative names on the certificate.

11. Ensure that you complete the check box in the box next to your SIP domain. As noted on the dialog, this would be required because of the way devices connect to Lync and was described in depth in Chapter 4. Again click Next to proceed.

12. On the next screen, you will not need any more SANs, so click Next again to reach the summary page.

13. Take a look and note how the settings you have entered throughout the wizard are represented. Once you are happy, click Next to create the certificate.

    On completion, you will be presented with the familiar page showing the commands that ran, and you will be given the option to look at the log file that was generated.

14. Finally, you need to assign the certificate. Click Next, and then on the next page, click Finish to start the Certificate Assignment Wizard.

    The Certificate Assignment Wizard opens and gives you a chance to view the certificate. The View Certificate Details button displays the default info about the certificate, such as the expiration date and where it was issued. On the Details tab, shown in Figure 6.11, you can scroll down to view the subject alternative names.

15. In the wizard, click Next to get to the summary page and then Next to assign the certificate. Finally, click Finish to exit the Certificate Assignment Wizard.

Now you return to the main Certificate Wizard, where you can see that you have assigned the certificate you just created.

Follow the previous process to create an OAuth certificate. This is used for interserver communications with other applications, such as Exchange and SharePoint.

Clicking Close takes you back to the Lync Server Deployment Wizard, where you will see that you are now ready to start the services.

FIGURE 6.11
The certificate shows both the issuing CA (left) and the details of the SANs (right).

16. Finally, click Run in the Start Services section to start the Services Wizard. Click Next to start the services, after which you can review the log or simply click Finish to exit. This process simply executes a start service command to each Lync service installed and exits immediately afterward. There is no check to see if the services have started or not; this must be checked manually. The remaining button on this page will start `Services.msc`, from which you can view the results of the start services commands.

When Lync is being installed, a service may occasionally fail to start, as shown in Figure 6.12. If that happens, check the log and find which service hasn't started. In this case, it simply timed out, so it can be manually started using `Services.msc`.

At this point, you are done installing the main Lync components for your first Standard Edition server. You can exit from the Deployment Wizard and run one final check to see if there are any Windows Updates. Install anything you find and then reboot the server. Although the process was lengthy to describe, once you have done it a couple of times you can whip through setup easily, especially if you have taken a suitable amount of time in the planning phase using Topology Builder. Now you're ready to move on to what to do after setup.

FIGURE 6.12
The summary
page of Start
Services, showing
a warning about
the RTCASMCU
service.

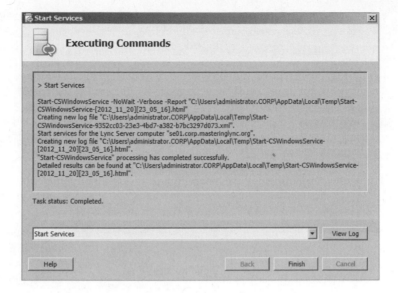

Post-Deployment Tasks

Now that you've completed setup of the Standard Edition server, there are several steps you
need to perform before you can get users up and running. You need to create an account with
basic administrative permissions before you can do anything else. Then you need to test the
installation, install any needed updates, and finally configure Kerberos authentication. The following sections discuss each of those steps.

Basic Administrative Permissions

Once you've finished setup, your first task is to give an account full administrative rights to the
server. Up to this point, you've been using the administrator account to perform the setup, but
by default Lync includes no accounts in the administration groups created by forest prep. Now
you'll create a Lync administrator account and use it to manage the system in the future.

First, you need to create a new user in Active Directory.

1. Open Windows PowerShell by typing **PowerShell** into the Start menu search area and
running the top result.

2. Import the Active Directory module. This can be done with the following command:

   ```
   Import-Module ActiveDirectory
   ```

3. This imports all the cmdlets needed to manage AD. Now that you have the cmdlets to
manage AD objects, run the following command to create the new administrative user.

   ```
   New-ADUser -SamAccountName "lyncadmin" -UserPrincipalName "lyncadmin@mastering
   lync.org" -GivenName "Lync" -Surname "Admin" -DisplayName "Lync Admin" -Name "
   ```

```
Lync Admin" -Enabled $true -path "CN=Users,DC=corp,DC=masteringlync,DC=org" -A
ccountPassword (Read-Host -AsSecureString "AccountPassword")
```

This will create a new user Lync Admin in the default Users container, and it will prompt you to enter a password. On completion, the account will be enabled. Having done this, you need to add the account to two groups, which will give you all the rights you need to perform basic administration on Lync 2013.

4. The following command adds the Lync Admin account to the required groups:

```
Add-ADGroupMember RTCUniversalServerAdmins lyncadmin; Add-ADGroupMember CsAdmi
nistrator lyncadmin
```

This command will first make Lync Admin a member of the RTCUniversalServer Admins group and then, when it is run again, make Lync Admin a member of the CsAdministrator group.

5. The last thing you need to do to ensure that Lync Admin can make any necessary changes to the local server is to add Lync Admin to the local administrators group. You can do this by copying the next six lines of code into the Windows PowerShell on the Standard Edition server and running them:

```
$computerName = $env:COMPUTERNAME
$Group = "Administrators"
$LocalGroup = [adsi]"WinNT://$computerName/$Group,group"
$Domain = "corp"
$UserName = "lyncadmin"
$LocalGroup.Add("WinNT://$Domain/$userName")
```

Once these commands are run, the Lync Admin domain user account will also be a member of the Local Administrators group.

POWERSHELL AND PERMISSIONS FOR MANAGEMENT

At this stage, don't worry if the PowerShell commands you've just seen are unfamiliar. Not only is all of Chapter 8 about PowerShell, but Chapter 9 focuses on setup and delegation of management.

Testing the Installation

Now that you've created the Lync Admin user, you are ready to log into the Standard Edition server as that user and begin testing the installation. The aim is to validate that all server components are installed and communicating correctly and that all services are started before you move on to any complex system configuration.

1. Log into the Standard Edition server as Lync Admin.

2. Once you're logged in, type **l s c p** (yes, with the spaces) in the Start menu search bar and press Enter.

This will run the Lync Server Control Panel (LSCP), which allows you not only to administer the majority of Lync settings but also to validate that Setup has completed properly. In this case, start with validation.

CONTROL PANEL REQUIREMENTS

You thought you'd finished all the installation prerequisites, didn't you? Well, Control Panel requires Silverlight to be installed prior to running. If Silverlight is not installed, you'll still get prompted for credentials, and then the response will be "Silverlight is not installed; please install Silverlight."

This may cause concern for those environments in which servers are highly locked down and the installation of additional software is not permitted. In these cases, the only option is to install the admin tools on a client machine along with Silverlight or to use PowerShell.

---

3. If prompted, log into the Control Panel with the Lync Admin user credentials and click the Topology tab. This will bring up a view of all the deployed services, as shown in Figure 6.13.

FIGURE 6.13
A warning appears on the Topology tab in Lync Server's Control Panel.

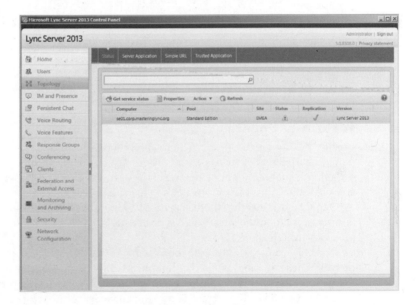

You can see information about the status of the server you installed. Hopefully, everything will have a green tick/icon. However, in the figure, you can see a warning denoted by the yellow triangle in the Status column.

4. Double-click the row to drill into the services to find out what is wrong. You can see in Figure 6.14 that the Conferencing server is stopped.

FIGURE 6.14
Drill into the components to determine the error.

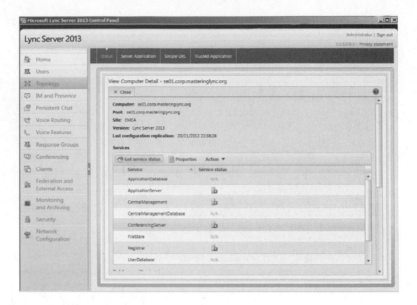

5. To rectify this, select the service row and then click the Action drop-down and select Start Service. The service will start.

6. Once the service is started, click Close to move back to the first page and you will see all green icons, meaning that the service is healthy.

Installing Updates

Within a Cumulative Update (CU) release, there are various files to download, each of which patches a different element of Lync. There can be patches both for the server side and the various clients, including phone devices. However, not all CU releases will have patches for all Lync components.

One nice thing is that there is no need to install the patches from each subsequent CU. Simply download the latest patches and install them, and that will get you all the patches from previous updates.

One very important thing to look out for is that some CU releases will include a database update. These are not installed automatically! People frequently overlook this element of the update and then can't figure out why things aren't working properly. The most important thing you can do in this regard is make sure you carefully read the release notes and knowledge base (KB) articles associated with the patch before installation and ideally test this in a lab environment.

In terms of installing the patches, each of these pages has a link to the relevant download site. For the main Lync Server update, you can download patches for each component separately or, more sensibly, download the LyncServerUpdateInstaller.exe file, which will provide all the server-side updates in one file and install them for you in the correct way.

As mentioned, LyncServerUpdateInstaller.exe will not patch the database, so you will need to do this manually, typically using the Install-CsDatabase cmdlet as described in the KB article (there will always be a KB article describing how to apply the update).

Before you install the patches, make sure you log on as the user you installed Lync with, in our case the default domain administrator account, and ensure that all Lync apps like the Control Panel and Topology Builder are shut. Even having done this, you may find that while installing some updates you will be prompted that Setup needs to stop and restart one of the services. As with all patches, test them in your lab environment before rolling them out in production.

Kerberos Authentication Configuration

The last piece of post-setup work to be done on this Standard Edition installation is to set up Kerberos authentication. Lync can use either NT LAN Manager (NTLM) or Kerberos for web services authentication; however, everyone knows that Kerberos is more secure than NTLM because it uses mutual authentication, so it is important to perform this setup.

This difference in the Lync configuration process compared to that of OCS is because Lync now runs under the Network Service account. OCS ran using service accounts like RTCService. Kerberos relies on the correct service principal names (SPNs, which are used for mutual authentication) being assigned to accounts; however, it is not possible to link SPNs to the Network Service account under which Lync runs. To work around this, Lync creates a dummy computer account on which to place the SPNs needed by IIS. This is used instead of a user account to get around the default password policy, which might require irritating regular changes of password.

It is only necessary to have a single Kerberos computer account, but it is possible to create multiple accounts to provide one for each site. This might be needed if you have a large distributed topology with many sites because the process whereby a password change is communicated to each site happens via Distributed Component Object Model (DCOM), which is a set of Microsoft standards allowing distributed software components to talk to each other. If you have a large network, this password reset may take quite some time to complete; therefore, having local Kerberos accounts may be more sensible.

Just so you get an idea of what SPNs look like, let's check to see what SPNs exist currently for the SE01 computer before you start. Do this by running the following command from an administrative command prompt (CMD.exe):

```
SetSPN -L SE01
```

When this is run, you should see output similar to the following, which is a listing of Kerberos SPNs linked to the Standard Edition computer object:

```
Registered ServicePrincipalNames for CN=SE01,CN=Computers,DC=corp,DC=masteringlync
,DC=org:
        MSSQLSvc/se01.corp.masteringlync.corp:49463
        MSSQLSvc/se01.corp.masteringlync.corp:LYNCLOCAL
        MSSQLSvc/se01.corp.masteringlync.corp:49319
        MSSQLSvc/se01.corp.masteringlync.corp::RTCLOCAL
        http/se01.corp.masteringlync.corp
        sip/se01.corp.masteringlync.corp
```

```
MSSQLSvc/se01.corp.masteringlync.corp:49257
MSSQLSvc/se01.corp.masteringlync.corp:RTC
WSMAN/se01
WSMAN/se01.corp.masteringlync.corp
RestrictedKrbHost/SE01
HOST/SE01
RestrictedKrbHost/se01.corp.masteringlync.corp
HOST/se01.corp.masteringlync.corp
```

The bold entries indicate new entries compared with Lync Server 2010; some of the port number on other entries have also changed.

Next, create the Kerberos account:

1. To create the account, log on to the Lync server as a domain administrator and open the Lync Server Management Shell. Run the following command to create your first Kerberos account.

   ```
   New-CsKerberosAccount -UserAccount "corp\LondonLyncKerb" -ContainerDN "CN=User
   s,DC=corp,DC=masteringlync,DC=org"
   ```

   This command creates an account in the corp domain, called LondonLyncKerb, within the default Users container. Obviously, you would use your domain name and create an account name that is meaningful to you. You can also put the account in a different container or OU if you want to keep it separated from the main Users container.

2. Next, you need to assign the account to the site, which you do with the following command:

   ```
   New-CsKerberosAccountAssignment -UserAccount "corp\LondonLyncKerb" -Identity "
   site:EMEA"
   ```

   This will assign the LondonLyncKerb account to the EMEA site, which is the only one you have at the moment.

3. At this point, you need to update the topology, so use the following cmdlet:

   ```
   Enable-CsTopology
   ```

   This registers all the relevant SPNs against the newly created Kerberos account based on the sites you have assigned to it. The penultimate step is to ensure that all machines in the site have registered the password assigned to the account. The account is assigned a random password on creation, but each machine running IIS needs to know it! This is done using the following command:

   ```
   Set-CsKerberosAccountPassword -UserAccount "corp\LondonLyncKerb"
   ```

   Once you've run this command, all the IIS instances in the site on Front End servers, Directors, or Standard Edition servers will get the password.

4. Finally, run SetSPN -L again, but this time with the computer account you just created as the target:

   ```
   SetSPN -L LondonLyncKerb
   ```

Now, you will see output similar to this:

```
Registered ServicePrincipalNames for CN=londonlynckerb,CN=Users, DC=corp,DC=ma
steringlync,DC=org:

        http/se01.corp.masteringlync.org
```

This is the SPN, which will allow the LondonLyncKerb account to be used for Kerberos authentication for web services rather than using the local Network Service account.

5. Having created the account and assigned and enabled it, you can run the following command, which will test whether it is operating properly:

```
Test-CsKerberosAccountAssignment -Identity "site:EMEA" -Report "c:\logs\Londo
nKerberosReport.htm" -Verbose
```

This runs through a number of tests and outputs to the familiar HTML format log file in the directory you specify.

Before we move on, there are various considerations worth mentioning about Kerberos accounts. One recommended methodology is that before you configure Kerberos, you complete your deployment, or at least all the elements that are going to use web services, namely Standard Edition, Director, and Front End servers. Realistically, this may not be possible, which means that when you add a server, like a Director, after setting up Kerberos authentication you need to configure IIS and set the password on the server. This is described later in the chapter, as part of the process of setting up a Director server, but briefly, you use the Set-CsKerberosAccountPassword cmdlet to do this.

Similarly, each time you create a new site, you need to decide whether to create a new Kerberos account and link it to the site or reuse an existing one. As mentioned, this depends on the size and scale of your topology. If you choose to use a new Kerberos account, then go ahead and create it and link it as described earlier.

Enabling Your First Pair of Users

Lync is installed and ready to use, but there aren't any users enabled to test it. You can create a couple of test users either manually through Active Directory Users and Computers or using PowerShell much as you did when creating the administrative user. For this example, we will use PowerShell, so do the following:

1. Open Windows PowerShell and ensure that you are running it as a domain administrator. Next, import the Active Directory module. This can be done with the following command:

```
Import-Module ActiveDirectory
```

This imports all the cmdlets needed to manage AD.

2. Now that you have the cmdlets to manage AD objects, run the following command to create the new administrative user:

```
New-ADUser -SamAccountName "Keith_Lync" -GivenName "Keith" -Surname "Lync" -Di
splayName "Keith Lync" -Name "Keith Lync" -EmailAddress "keith_lync@masteringl
ync.org" -Enabled $true -path "CN=Users,DC=corp,DC=masteringlync,DC=org" -Acco
untPassword (Read-Host -AsSecureString "AccountPassword"); New-ADUser -SamAcco
```

```
untName "Nathan_Lync" -GivenName "Nathan" -Surname "Lync" -DisplayName "Nathan
 Lync" -Name "Nathan Lync" -EmailAddress "nathan_lync@masteringlync.org" -Enab
led $true -path "CN=Users,DC=corp,DC=masteringlync,DC=org" -AccountPassword (R
ead-Host -AsSecureString "AccountPassword")
```

This will prompt you for two passwords, one for each account, and will then create two new, enabled test user accounts in the default Users container. Importantly, these accounts will have email addresses, which will then be used as the SIP addresses when you're enabling for Lync

3. To enable users, log into the LSCP as the Lync Admin account created earlier. Select the Users tab and click Enable Users. This opens the page shown in Figure 6.15.

FIGURE 6.15
The New Link
Server User dialog

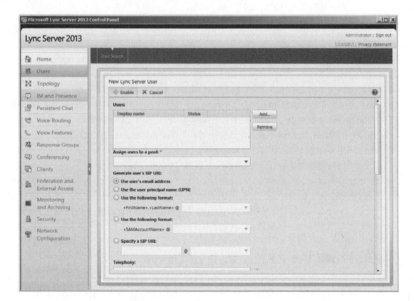

4. Click the Add button and then search for "Lync" to find the Keith and Nathan accounts.

5. While holding down the Shift key, select both the users so they are highlighted in yellow, and click OK. Back on the first page, assign the users to the SE01.corp.master-inglync.org pool and leave the default setting of Using The Email Address to generate the SIP URI. There are many other settings, but we will cover them in Chapter 10, "User Administration." For now, click Enable to accept all the defaults and enable the two test users for Lync. On completion, you will see the new users, as shown in Figure 6.16.

Rolling Out the Client

Finally, you are just about ready to test with actual users. Before you can do that, however, you need to roll out the Lync client. Most likely at this stage, you will simply perform a manual install of the Lync client on a couple of test machines, but you also need to consider how you will install the Lync client on hundreds of machines in your organization. First, we'll run through the manual setup and then discuss options for a wider deployment.

FIGURE 6.16
The newly enabled
users

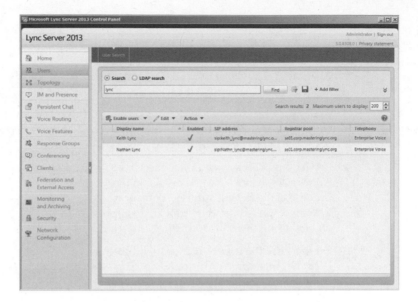

A MANUAL LYNC CLIENT INSTALLATION

Installing Lync manually is a simple process. You must first prepare a client machine with the relevant prerequisites. The Lync client supports Windows desktop OS Windows 7 and Windows 8, and there is also a Mac version. It also installs fine on the following server versions: Server 2008 R2 and Server 2012. Silverlight 4.0 is included as part of the install. The client can be installed on a Windows server running Lync.

For Windows 8 clients (including Windows 8 RT), a Modern Interface client is available for download from the Store. It is a free download and is called Lync MX.

For full integration with Exchange and Office, you will need Office 2010 or 2013 installed and Outlook configured with an Exchange user profile. The Office install is not mandatory, although the client is now part of Office 2013, and for now we will simply install on a blank Windows 7 install.

Office 2003 (SP3) and Office 2007 provide limited integration functionality.

CLIENT VERSIONS

The Lync client has both 32-bit and 64-bit versions. Setup will automatically choose the relevant version for your OS. Lync Server can accept connections from various client versions including OCS 2007 R2 and Lync 2010 with different updates applied. It is possible to set up Lync to allow only certain versions of the Lync client to connect, as discussed in the section "Client-Version Filtering" in Chapter 3, "Security."

The Lync 2013 communicator client is the first "newer" version client that can connect to a previous version of the server; that is, the Lync 2013 client can connect to Lync Server 2010.

Installation can be carried out by following the steps shown:

1. Copy the Office client setup program to the X:\ drive of the machine on which you intend to install and double-click it.

2. Check the install location, and if you want, check the box to allow information about your usage of Office to be passed back to Microsoft to help drive improvements in the future. Click Install.

3. Once Setup completes, leave the Start Lync check box enabled and click Close. At this point, the Lync client will start, and you will need to enter the details of the user to log on.

4. Repeat this process on another client machine and log in as a second user. Test that Address Book lookup works by using the search bar to search for a user enabled for Lync. Because of the default Address Book download synchronization delay, until the download is completed (random time up to approximately 1 hour), you can search for users only by using their SIP address.

   Double-click the user found and send them an IM. This should show up on your other client test machine. At this point you can be satisfied because you have a working Lync installation.

WIDER DEPLOYMENT OF LYNC CLIENTS

Clearly, it would be possible in a small deployment to go around to each PC and manually install Lync, but in an organization with hundreds or even thousands of PCs all around the world, this approach isn't practical. Thankfully, there are several ways to deploy the Lync client in large or managed IT environments. First, you can use tools such as Microsoft System Center Configuration Manager 2007 R3 or Microsoft System Center 2012 Configuration Manager to package and deploy the client. This gives the benefits of scheduling, reporting, and specific features to mitigate the bandwidth challenges associated with pushing packages over a WAN. Other options are the use of the traditional login policy or using the deployment options available in Group Policy.

To dive deeply into the methods available for mass deployment of software would be outside the scope of this book. In many ways, deploying the Lync client is no different from deploying any other piece of Microsoft software. So at this point, we will simply lay out a few of the options and considerations specific to deploying the Lync client through the methods just outlined.

First, you may have noticed that the Lync client Setup program is an EXE file (filename extension .exe) rather than an MSI package (filename extension .msi). The key benefits of this are that the EXE installer performs a series of prerequisite steps required to ensure a successful installation of the Lync client. For example, the installer will let the user know if any apps need to be closed, and it will install relevant versions of Visual C++ components and also Silverlight. The installer will also remove previous versions of Lync or OCS clients and it will notify the user that Windows Media Player is needed for certain functions to work properly. This simplifies the deployment because it doesn't require you to automate these steps yourself.

The Lync 2013 client comes as part of the Office 2013 package and the x86 or x64 versions are located in their appropriate directories.

To deploy Lync from a command line, you could try running the following command:

```
lyncmui.msi /install
```

This will kick off the full graphical user interface (GUI) version of the installer and allow the user to customize settings, which you probably don't want. Instead, you are likely to be better off running this version of the command:

```
lyncmui.msi /install /silent
```

This will carry out the install but use all the default setup options and run predominantly in the background without user interaction. Table 6.3 lists other setup options using the office setup.exe file and customization.

TABLE 6.3:   Lync client deployment options

COMMAND-LINE ARGUMENT	DESCRIPTION
/admin	Runs the Office Customization Tool to create a setup customization file (MSP file).
/adminfile [path]	Applies the specified setup customization file to the installation. You can specify a path of a specific customization file (MSP file) or to the folder where you store customization files.
/config [path]	Specifies the Config.xml file that Setup uses during the installation. Use the /config option to specify the Config.xml file you customized for Lync 2013 installations—for example, /config \\server\share\Lync15\Lync.WW\Config.xml.
/modify Lync	Used with a modified Config.xml file to run Setup in maintenance mode and make changes to an existing Office installation. For example, you can use the /modify option to add or remove Lync features.
/repair Lync	Runs Setup from the user's computer to repair Lync.
/uninstall Lync	Runs Setup to remove Lync from the user's computer.

INSTALLING FOR MULTIPLE USERS ON ONE PC

The Lync client, once installed, is accessible by everyone who uses the PC; it cannot be restricted to a single profile/user on that PC.

The final method of installing Lync is using the MSI file through Group Policy. As Lync is part of the Office 2013 suite, its installation can be controlled in the same way that Office installations can be deployed through Group Policy—the files on the media are ready to be packaged into Group Policy objects because they come as MSI files.

LOCKING DOWN THE LYNC CLIENT

There are many ways in which you can configure and lock down the Lync client. It is important to understand key policies and settings and how these settings are applied, a user administration topic that is covered in Chapter 10.

Configuring External Access

If you've been following along, you now have a full-fledged Lync installation that is perfectly capable of letting people within your organization communicate and collaborate in a wide variety of ways. However, these capabilities are currently limited by the confines of your firewall. It would be so much better if you could access these tools from anywhere and communicate and collaborate in exactly the same way whether you were in your office or in a coffee shop with Wi-Fi halfway around the world. That is exactly what these next sections are about: configuring the Lync Edge server and supporting components to allow external access.

Three main components are involved in providing external access to Lync:

◆ The Edge role, which does the majority of the work

◆ The Director, which is an optional stopgap between the Front End and the Edge server

◆ The reverse proxy, which allows you to publish externally the various Web components of Lync, such as the Address Book and the software update service

The process for deploying external access consists of the following major steps:

1. Define/update the topology.

2. Prepare for deployment.

   a. Meet the software prerequisites.

   b. Set up networking, DNS, and firewalls.

   c. Set up/prepare certificates.

   d. Provision public IM connectivity.

3. Set up the reverse proxy.

4. Set up a Director (optional).

5. Set up the Edge server.

6. Configure users for external access.

7. Test.

The first of these steps is already done because you defined the topology in Chapter 5. The specific prerequisites for each server are outlined in the following sections.

PROVISIONING PUBLIC IM CONNECTIVITY

Public IM connectivity (PIC) requires specific licensing from Microsoft, and while some of the licensing is covered already in the purchase of the Lync CAL, there is still an onboarding process required. Therefore, it's not something that is often able to be tested in a lab. There is an online provisioning process, which is covered in depth in the following TechNet article:

http://technet.microsoft.com/en-us/library/ff945947.aspx

Installing the Director

The Director role is frequently dismissed in designs as just another server overhead and so it is left out. However, the Director does have an important role to play, albeit an optional one. Essentially, a Director is a barrier between the Edge and the Front End server. In this role, it is the Director that performs authentication of users coming in across the Edge server, and thus, it not only takes a load off the Front End server but also helps to isolate the Front End server from any malicious traffic generated as a denial-of-service attack. If, for example, an attacker were to send large amounts of malformed authentication traffic toward the Edge server, it would be passed on to the Director, which would potentially be overloaded. However, the Front End server would be unaffected, so internal users would be able to continue working with limited disruption.

There are a couple of other roles where the Director server plays a part. One is as part of a large enterprise deployment, as discussed later in the chapter. The other is by way of a method of distributing information to clients about a backup registrar that was covered in Chapter 4 but is worth reviewing briefly now.

When a Lync client registers with the pool it finds through autodiscover, or is pointed to through manual configuration, if that pool is not its home pool, the Lync client is sent a SIP redirect message and is provided the details of the user's primary and backup registrar.

If the client were to connect first to its home server instead of the Director, or indeed, any other pool, then if the home pool was unavailable, it would never get the redirect request telling it about the backup registrar and thus failover wouldn't work. However, if the SRV DNS records are configured correctly, upon time-out and re-query for connection, the client would fail to connect to its home pool because it is unavailable, and then it would try another pool via the DNS load balancing process, resulting in a connection eventually.

Directors, like other components, can be deployed either as a single server or in a pool. If they are deployed in a pool, load balancing must be configured. In this Standard Edition deployment, you will simply deploy a single Director. To do so, you will need a server that is running a supported OS as described in Chapter 5. In this network, you will use another Windows Server 2008 R2 SP1 machine that is fully patched and joined to the domain.

Since Lync Server 2010, the Director is finally a role in its own right. It used to be in OCS that it was a Front End pool with various services turned off. The cool thing about having a definite role is that now you no longer have to worry about users getting accidentally homed on the Director server because it simply isn't an available option as it was when it was a cut-down Front End in OCS. Although a separate role, the Director and the Front End (or Standard Edition server) have very similar prerequisites. In fact, there are only a couple of differences. The first is that the Windows Media Format Runtime (or the Desktop Experience) is not required. Similarly, neither are the Active Directory tools (RSAT-ADDS).

Because we spent quite some time detailing the installation of prerequisites on the Standard Edition server, at this point, we will simply list the commands that should be run from a PowerShell command prompt with administrator credentials on the local server:

```
Import-Module ServerManager
Add-WindowsFeature NET-Framework-Core
Add-WindowsFeature Web-Static-Content,Web-Default-Doc,Web-Http-Errors,Web-Asp-Net,
Web-Net-Ext,Web-ISAPI-Ext,Web-ISAPI-Filter,Web-Http-Logging,Web-Log-Libraries,Web-
Http-Tracing,Web-Windows-Auth,Web-Filtering,Web-Stat-Compression,Web-Dyn-
Compression,Web-Mgmt-Console,Web-Scripting-Tools,Web-Client-Auth
```

If installing on Windows Server 2012, you can also add the following modules to the list:

```
Web-Asp-Net45,Net-HTTP-Activation,Net-WCF-HTTP-Activation45
```

Running these commands will first import the cmdlets needed to install software and then install the .NET Framework 4.5, PowerShell v3.0, Windows Identity Framework, and the Web components. If asked, reboot the server and then perform one final check for patches from Windows Update, and install any that are found.

At this stage, you are ready to deploy the Director role:

1. When you insert the media, Setup will autorun, and as with the Standard Edition server, you will be prompted about installing Visual C++ Redistributable. Click Yes and then click Install to agree to the location for install files. Obviously, you can change from the default if you choose to place the installation on another drive. Accept the license agreement by placing a check in the check box and then click OK to progress with setup.

2. Once installation bootstrapping is complete, you will be at the Setup home page. Click Install Or Update Lync Server System, which takes you to the steps for deploying the new role.

3. Then, as with all other roles, click Install Local Configuration Store to begin the wizard that installs the SQL Express database to hold the local replica of the CMS.

4. On the first page of the wizard, opt to retrieve directly from the Central Management Store and click Next to start the installation.

5. On completion, you can view the log as in previous installs or click Finish to return to the deployment steps page and continue.

6. Next, you will install the Lync files by clicking Setup Or Remove Lync Server Components.

7. This takes you to another wizard, where you click Next to kick off a process of installing all the specific services needed for the Director role. On completion, click Finish to return to the setup steps page.

Next, you provision certificates, a procedure very similar to that of the Standard Edition install:

1. Once again there is the option to be very specific about certificates. However, for this example you will request a single certificate with multiple SANs by clicking the Request button.

2. When the wizard opens, click Next and then choose Send Your Request Immediately To An Online Certification Authority and click Next.

3. Select the same CA as for the Standard Edition install and click Next.

4. Assuming you are logged on as the default domain administrator account, there is no need to specify different credentials, so click Next and then Next again to use the default certificate template.

5. On the next page, give the certificate a friendly name such as Lync Director Cert and click Next.

6. On the next couple of pages, enter your organizational information and click Next until you reach the Subject Name And Subject Alternative Names page. Here you will notice the simple URLs, the FQDN of the Director pool, and the external name for the Director of web services all in the SAN. The subject is the Director pool FQDN. Click Next.

7. Select the check box next to the SIP domains, to ensure that the sip.masteringlync.org entry gets populated on the certificate for use later by phone devices, and click Next.

8. There are no other SANs to add, so click Next and then review the summary page and click Next to make the request. Once it is completed, click Finish to run the Certificate Assignment Wizard, which after you click Next twice and then click Finish will have assigned the certificate to the relevant services within Lync.

9. At this point, click Close on the certificate page and then again back on the Install Steps page, and finally, click Run in the Start Services section to start the Director services.

10. You can check that all services have started by launching Services.msc using the Run button in the Service Status (Optional) section. This is worth doing especially in a situation where limited RAM may make things start rather slowly. Assuming everything has started as expected, you should have a running Director.

As mentioned in the earlier Kerberos section, anyone who has configured Kerberos authentication needs to configure it for use on the new Director. Do this from the LMS on a server that has Kerberos already set up (in this case, the Standard Edition SE01), using the following command:

```
Set-CsKerberosAccountPassword -FromComputer SE01.corp.masteringlync.org -ToCompute
r dir01.corp.masteringlync.org
```

This command will synchronize the password and account information from the SE01 server to the new Director.

Perform a final check for Windows Update and install the same level of Lync CU as described in the Standard Edition install, and then you'll be nearly ready to move to the next stage, setting up the reverse proxy.

Before you move on, you should check the topology again as you did after installing the Standard Edition server. Open Lync Control Panel as the Lync Admin user created earlier, and on the Topology tab, check that replication has a tick next to both the Standard Edition server and the Director and that the status is green.

NEW PROMPT WHEN OPENING LSCP

After installing the Director (and indeed any additional pools), note that there is now a prompt for the URL to use when you open Control Panel from the Start menu. This is because both Director and Standard Edition servers have a set of web URLs to offer to users. You can run the Control Panel from either URL successfully.

Configuring the Reverse Proxy

Deploying and configuring a reverse proxy server or farm is outside the scope of this book and in fact warrants a book of its own. We will, therefore, focus only on setting up the rules needed to publish Lync to the Internet. This installation chapter will assume that you have a Forefront Threat Management Gateway (TMG) 2010 server up and running and configured to allow publishing of websites from the internal network. There are, of course, many other supported reverse proxies, but for now we will stick with TMG because it's the one with which we're most familiar!

USE OF REVERSE PROXIES

During the beta program and the creation of this book there were many discussions regarding the use of reverse proxies and supported versus unsupported versions. TMG is reaching end of life. By the time this book is in print, it will no longer be possible to purchase it, although it will continue to be supported until 2020. The concepts shown here, while shown through TMG, are valid with any reverse proxy solution, although terms may differ from product to product.

To begin the process of publishing Lync, it is important to understand what you need to publish via a reverse proxy. As discussed at the beginning of the chapter, Lync makes heavy use of web services to provide access to meeting content, to expand distribution lists, to publish the Address Book, and for many more uses. These services are all provided to external users by publishing virtual directories through TMG for external access. You also need to publish the simple URLs, which provide access to meetings and dial-in conferencing settings.

In general, because of the number of virtual directories involved, it is recommended to publish all virtual directories on a given Front End (or Front End pool), Standard Edition, or Director (or Director pool) through a single rule. For example, we will be publishing https://directorwebext.masteringlync.org/*.

In the simplest deployments (a single Standard Edition server internally and an Edge and reverse proxy in the perimeter network), where a Director is not deployed, you would simply publish all the required URLs from the Standard Edition server. However, given that you followed best practice and deployed the Director, you should use it. Therefore, you need to publish two URLs, one for the Standard Edition and one for the Director.

Because the role of the Director is to redirect traffic to the appropriate pool, you will publish the simple URLs from the Director, which will then pass the traffic on to the appropriate internal resource. The Director will also be where the web ticket authentication occurs (as discussed in Chapter 3, "Security," and Chapter 4), before the connection is passed to the pool where the user is homed. This pool will then give out its distinct URL for the web services elements mentioned earlier. This is why both the Director and internal pool URLs need to be published.

Before you can publish the internal servers, it is important that the reverse proxy resolve the servers to be published. This can be done either through DNS or by editing the HOSTS file on the reverse proxy. Because the TMG server is a member of the internal AD, DNS is pointing to an internal server, which can resolve the Director and Standard Edition servers. For an example of how to edit the HOSTS file, see the section "Installing the Edge Server" later in this chapter.

Another thing you need to do to prepare the reverse proxy server is to make sure it has an external IP address assigned to its external NIC for each of the servers or pools you intend to publish. In this case, you will be publishing the Standard Edition server SE01 and the Director Dir01. Therefore, you need two external IP addresses for the TMG box.

The final step before actually creating the publishing rules is to ensure that you have the correct certificates on the TMG server. You may remember the flexibility Lync allowed in the certificates you installed on the Standard Edition and Director boxes; there was the option either to install a single certificate or to break out the certificates for each component. The reason for this flexibility is that for TMG to successfully publish the virtual directories on the Standard Edition and Director servers, it needs to trust the certificates used to authenticate and identify those servers.

A single certificate can be used on the internal servers, and it can be requested from the internal CA on the domain controller. This works fine when using TMG connected to the domain because it therefore trusts the AD Enterprise CA.

However, if you were using another reverse proxy, which couldn't be made to trust the internal CA, then it might be a problem. You would need to use public certificates instead, which the reverse proxy could trust on the external web services portion of the internal servers. But because the TMG server does trust the internal CA, you have only one final piece to configure, which is the certificates to be used by TMG to identify itself to external users. You need a certificate on the TMG server that corresponds to each URL you publish. In this case, this will be as follows (note the use of SAN certificate for the simple URLs published on the Director):

Standard Edition (SE01)

Subject: `se01webext.masteringlync.org`

Director (Director01)

Subject: `dir01webext.masteringlync.org`

SAN: `dir01webext.masteringlync.org`

SAN: `meet.masteringlync.org`

SAN: `dialin.masteringlync.org`

These externally trusted certificates are needed so that TMG can terminate the connection from the external user, view the traffic to check it for threats, and then open a new encrypted connection from TMG to the internal server, this time using the internal certificate.

To get the certificate on the TMG server, you have various options. However, the cleanest one to use is the command line's `certreq.exe` utility. A lot of detailed information on the subject of using `certreq.exe` is available at the following links:

http://technet.microsoft.com/en-us/library/ff625722(WS.10).aspx

http://technet.microsoft.com/en-us/library/cc725793(WS.10).aspx

Essentially, the process is to create a request template file for each certificate needed and then to use the `certreq.exe` utility, which is installed by default on Windows Server 2008 R2, to create a certificate request file. The template file for the Standard Edition URL is shown in Listing 6.1. You can see that it requests only the one URL. In Listing 6.2, you can see the request template for the Director URLs certificate. Here you can see that the Extensions section is added to create the needed SANs.

LISTING 6.1: INF file text used to create Standard Edition certificate

```
[Version]
Signature="$Windows NT$"
[NewRequest]
Subject = "CN=se01webext.masteringlync.org,OU=IT,O=Corp,L=Croydon,S=Surrey,C=GB"
Exportable = FALSE
KeyLength = 2048
KeySpec = 1
KeyUsage = 0xA0
MachineKeySet = True
ProviderName = "Microsoft RSA SChannel Cryptographic Provider"
RequestType = PKCS10
FriendlyName = "Standard Edition Ext Web Services"
[EnhancedKeyUsageExtension]
OID=1.3.6.1.5.5.7.3.1 ; Server Authentication
```

LISTING 6.2: INF file text used to create Director certificate

```
[Version]
Signature="$Windows NT$"
[NewRequest]
Subject = "CN=dir01webext.masteringlync.org,OU=IT,O=Corp,L=Croydon,S=Surrey,C=GB"
Exportable = FALSE
KeyLength = 2048
KeySpec = 1
KeyUsage = 0xA0
MachineKeySet = True
ProviderName = "Microsoft RSA SChannel Cryptographic Provider"
RequestType = PKCS10
```

```
FriendlyName = "Director Ext Web Services"
[EnhancedKeyUsageExtension]
OID=1.3.6.1.5.5.7.3.1 ; Server Authentication
[Extensions]
2.5.29.17 = "{text}"
_continue_ = "dns=dir01webext.masteringlync.org&dns=meet.masteringlync.org&dns=dia
lin.masteringlync.org"
```

Take the following steps to create the certificates:

1. From an Administrator CMD.exe prompt, change to the folder where the request template INF file is stored and run the following command:

   ```
   certreq -new se01csr.inf se01.req
   ```

   This will pull settings from the se01.csr.inf file and output to the se01.req file in the same directory.

2. Then carry out the same step for the Director certificate:

   ```
   certreq -new dir01csr.inf dir01.req
   ```

   Having run these commands, you have created the certificate request for each required certificate on the TMG. You will need to copy the contents of the REQ file and send it to your third-party CA, such as DigiCert or VeriSign. There are too many third-party CAs to describe all the processes in detail.

3. Once the CA has created the certificate for you, follow its procedure to install it on the TMG machine, making sure the certificate is in the Computer Account>Personal>Certificates store and that you have imported any required intermediary root CAs so that you trust the certificate path.

Once the certificates are installed, you can create the required rules to publish Lync. First, you will publish the Standard Edition server:

1. To do so, open up the TMG management tool, and in the left-hand pane, expand the server Forefront TMG (TMG), right-click Firewall Policy, point to New, and then click Web Site Publishing Rule.

2. On the Welcome To The New Web Publishing Rule page, type a display name for the publishing rule, such as SE01 Lync External, and click Next. On the Select Rule Action page, select Allow and click Next.

3. On the Publishing Type page, select Publish A single Web site Or Load Balancer and click Next.

4. On the Server Connection Security page, select Use SSL To Connect To The Published Web Server Or Server Farm and click Next.

5. On the Internal Publishing Details page, you will enter the Standard Edition server FQDN, which in this case is **SE01.corp.masteringlync.org**, in the Internal Site name

box and click Next. See the accompanying discussion for what to use in more complex scenarios.

DETERMINING THE INTERNAL SITE NAME URL

The internal site name URL will vary depending on whether your internal server is a Standard Edition server or an Enterprise Edition Front End pool. If it is a Standard Edition server, the FQDN is the Standard Edition server FQDN. If your internal server is an Enterprise Edition Front End pool, this FQDN is a hardware load-balancer virtual IP (VIP) that load balances the internal web farm servers.

It is critical that the TMG server be able to resolve the FQDN to the IP address of the internal web server. There are various ways to achieve this; you can use DNS in the perimeter network or point the TMG server to an internal DNS server with the relevant records. Other methods are using the HOSTS file on the TMG server or selecting Use A Computer Name Or IP Address To Connect To The Published Server, and then, in the Computer Name Or IP Address box, type the IP address of the internal web server.

---

6. On the Internal Publishing Details page, in the Path (Optional) box, type **/*** as the path of the folder to be published and then click Next.

   It is worth noting that you are publishing only one URL (path) in this section of the wizard. That's fine in this case for the Standard Edition server because it is the Director that will host the simple URLs, which require additional paths to be published. These additional paths will be added for the Director by modifying the publishing rule once it is created; the steps are described at the end of this section.

7. On the Public Name Details page, confirm that This Domain Name (Type Below) is selected next to Accept Requests For and then type the external Web Services FQDN (in the example, **se01webext.masteringlync.org**) in the Public Name box and click Next.

8. On the Select Web Listener page, click New to open the New Web Listener Definition Wizard, and on the Welcome To The New Web Listener Wizard page, type a name for the web listener in the Web Listener name box (in the example, **LyncPublishingListener**).

9. Click Next to open the Client Connection Security page, and then select Require SSL Secured Connections With Clients and click Next.

10. On the Web Listener IP Address page, select External, and then click Select IP Addresses.

11. On the External Network Listener IP Selection page, select the Specified IP address for the Forefront TMG computer (please note there may be more than one network listed, so be sure to select the correct network address). Because you will use the same listener to publish the Director server shortly, select two of the available public IP addresses and click Add. Click OK to move back to the Web Listener IP Address page and click Next.

12. On the Listener SSL Certificates page, select Assign a certificate for each IP address, select the IP address that is associated with the Standard Edition external web FQDN (se01webext.masteringlync.org), and then click Select Certificate.

13. On the Select Certificate page, select the certificate that matches the SE01 FQDN and click Select.

14. Repeat steps 1 to 13 for the other IP addresses, except this time select the certificate that has the names published on the Director server and then once done, click Next.

15. On the Authentication Setting page, select No Authentication and then click Next.

16. On the Single Sign On Setting page, click Next.

17. On the Completing The Web Listener Wizard page, verify that the web listener settings are correct, and then click Finish.

18. Back on the Select Web Listener page, click Next.

19. On the Authentication Delegation page, select No Delegation, But Client May Authenticate Directly and click Next.

20. On the User Set page, click Next.

21. On the Completing The New Web Publishing Rule Wizard page, verify that the web publishing rule settings are correct, and then click Finish.

22. Click Apply in the details pane and then enter any required notes in the Configuration Change Description page. Click Apply again to save the changes and update the configuration.

Now that you've created the basic rule and listener to publish the Standard Edition web services externally, you must edit the rule to tweak a couple of the settings, which will complete the configuration:

1. To edit the properties of the web publishing rule, locate the rule in the Firewall Policy section of the TMG management tool, right-click it, and select Properties.

2. On the Properties page, on the From tab in the This Rule Applies To Traffic From These Sources list, click Anywhere and then click Remove. Click Add.

3. In Add Network Entities, expand Networks, click External, click Add, and then click Close.

4. On the To tab, ensure that the Forward The Original Host Header Instead Of The Actual One check box is selected.

5. On the Bridging tab, select the Redirect Request To SSL port check box, and then specify port 4443.

Changing this port number is required because in Lync the internal servers (Front End, Standard Edition, and Director) all have two websites, one listening on the standard SSL port 443 for internal users and the other on port 4443 for external users published via the reverse proxy.

6. Click Apply to save changes, and then click OK.

7. Click Apply in the details pane and then enter any required notes in the Configuration Change Description page. Click Apply again to save the changes and update the configuration.

Now you need to repeat the procedure just outlined, but this time to publish the Director. There are a few slight differences when publishing the Director:

♦ Obviously, you need to give the rule a new name, which in this case you can call the Director Lync External.

♦ On the Web Listener page, instead of creating a new listener, select the existing one and click Next.

♦ Finally, when editing the newly created rule at the end, make sure that on the Public Name tab you click Add and enter the first simple URL, in this case **meet.masteringlync.org**. Click OK and then repeat the process to add the second simple URL, **dialin.mastering-lync.org**.

One other consideration is that if you have phone devices externally, then for device updates and for logging purposes you will need to publish on port 80 as well as 443. This means you will need to configure your existing listener to listen on port 80 and bridge to port 8080 on the internal servers. To do this, on the Firewall Policy section of the TMG management console, in the right pane select the Toolbox tab and drill down into Network Objects and through to the Web Listeners folder. Right-click the LyncPublishingListener web listener created earlier and select Properties. On the Connections tab, check the box next to Enable HTTP Connections On Port and click OK.

Apply these changes in the normal way. Next, open the properties of the Lync publishing rules you created. On the Bridging tab, check the check box next to Redirect Requests To HTTP Port and enter **8080** in the port box. Click OK and then perform this on each Lync server publishing rule you have created. Then apply the changes in the normal way. At this point Lync phone devices will be able to be updated and carry out logging externally.

DNS ENTRIES

Of course, for all this publishing to work, you will need to create A records in DNS for the external URLs and point them to the IP external public addresses through which TMG publishes the URLs.

Having completed the configuration needed, you can carry out various tests to prove that everything is working properly. You can test the connection to the Address Book, the Conferencing URL, the distribution group expansion URL, and the dial-in conferencing URL. To do so, follow these steps:

1. Open Internet Explorer from a machine on the Internet outside your local network. To test the Address Book service enter the following URL:

```
https://se01webext.masteringlync.org/abs
```

You should receive an HTTP authentication challenge because directory security on the Address Book Server folder is configured to Windows authentication by default.

2. To test conferencing, use the following URL:

```
https://se01webext.masteringlync.org/meet
```

This URL will display the page used when joining conferences.

3. For distribution group expansion, use this URL:

```
https://se01webext.masteringlync.org/GroupExpansion/service.svc
```

As with the Address Book, you should receive an HTTP authentication challenge.

4. In these examples, we haven't configured dial-in conferencing yet, so this URL won't currently work; however, for future reference, you can test external access to the dial-in conferencing site by typing the simple URL for dial-in conferencing shown here, after which the user should be directed to the dial-in page:

```
https://dialin.masteringlync.org
```

If you have published both Director(s) and Front End or Standard Edition server(s), you should run these tests on each of the published servers.

Installing the Edge Server

The Edge server role is slightly different from the other Lync roles in that it is the only one not connected to your Active Directory domain; it is installed in the perimeter network.

EDGE BEST PRACTICES

The Edge server should not be connected to your internal Active Directory. Microsoft supports connecting it to an Active Directory forest specifically for use in the perimeter network. The size of your DMZ will determine if it requires an AD to manage or whether each server can be managed independently.

This difference raises various challenges about how best to manage the installation. Lync does a vastly better job than OCS in this regard, as you will see. Now that Lync has the CMS, once the first replication of the configuration is complete (done manually as part of setup), secure push replication is carried out so that all management can be performed from the Topology Builder and Lync management tools. This ensures that all Edge servers are consistent with their configurations, a major headache for OCS!

The first step to deploying an Edge server is to set up a server meeting the prerequisites described in Chapter 5. In this case, you will use another Windows Server 2008 R2 SP1 server, which you will not join to the domain. The server will be called Edge01. Once the server is built and fully patched, it then needs the relevant prerequisites installed.

First, it is important to configure the primary DNS suffix to match the internal domain suffix of the Lync server pool; in this case it will be `corp.masteringlync.org`. To do this, follow these steps:

1. Open the Properties page of the computer and click Change Settings In The Computer Name, Domain And Workgroup Settings section.

2. On the Computer Name tab, click Change, and then on the Computer Name/Domain Changes tab, click More.

3. Enter the required suffix, and click OK until prompted to reboot, which you should do.

Next, you need to configure the NICs. As we discussed in Chapter 5, the Edge server must have at minimum two NICs, each on a different subnet. One is public facing and the other closer to the internal LAN. In this exercise, you will use public IP addresses on the external interface instead of using NAT, as discussed in Chapter 3 and Chapter 5. Ensure that the external NIC has the default gateway defined pointing to the external firewall or router and that this NIC is at the top of the NIC binding order. To do this, take the following steps:

1. Type **Network and Sharing** into the Start menu search bar and open the Network And Sharing Center.

2. Click Change Adapter Settings. When the window opens, press the Alt key. This will bring up menu options from which you should select Advanced and then Advanced Settings.

3. The Adapters And Bindings window opens, where you should ensure that the Internet/external NIC is at the top of the bindings, as shown in Figure 6.17.

FIGURE 6.17
The NIC bindings
on the Edge server

Because you have pointed the default gateway to the external firewall, you may have to create static routes to allow communication with the internal network. This is achieved via the ROUTE command, within a command prompt. The syntax is as follows:

```
route ADD <destination subnet> MASK <mask> <gateway> METRIC <metric> IF <interface>
```

More information can be found by typing **route /?** within a command prompt window.

The next step is to ensure that the Edge server can resolve the internal servers by name. There are a couple of options here: using DNS servers you control in the perimeter network or using external DNS servers.

If you have DNS servers in the perimeter network, they must contain A records for the internal servers the Edge server needs to talk with—the next-hop server, which will be the Front End, Standard Edition, or Director server. If there is a pool of servers, each should have an individual record under the same FQDN to provide for DNS load balancing.

If you are using external DNS servers, these should be defined purely on the external NIC and should point to public DNS servers. This option will not provide name resolution for the internal server, so you will need to provide entries in the HOSTS file. Figure 6.18 shows how to open the HOSTS file, which should be done from Notepad running as Administrator. Figure 6.19 shows the entries in the HOSTS file in our environment.

FIGURE 6.18
Opening the HOSTS file using the All Files option

FIGURE 6.19
The HOSTS file entries

At this stage, the basic preparatory steps are done. Now you need to install the prerequisite software, which for the Edge is simply the .NET Framework 4.5:

1. Install this as with the Standard Edition server process.

2. Having installed the .NET Framework, start the Lync Setup program and allow Setup to install Visual C++. As with the previous roles, Setup follows the same format, first installing the Local Configuration Store.

   The difference in the Edge installation is that instead of pulling the first config synchronization from the CMS, you have to pull it from a file. This means that you need to create the file, which is done by exporting the CMS on one of the internal servers with the admin tools installed. In this case, go to the Standard Edition server and open the PowerShell. Use the following command to export the topology to a file:

   ```
   Export-CsConfiguration -FileName c:\toplogyexport.zip
   ```

3. Locate the file and copy it over to the Edge server. Next run the local setup, and when prompted, select Import From A File and specify the location of the ZIP file copied from the Standard Edition server, as shown in Figure 6.20.

FIGURE 6.20
Importing the topology from a file into the Edge server

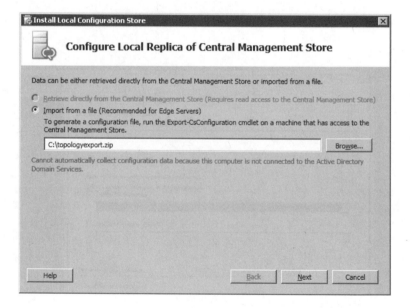

Again, as with other roles, you need to install certificates. The specific requirements were discussed in Chapter 5, so for now we will simply list what you need to install on the Edge server:

Cert request for external NIC:

Subject: Accessedge.masteringlync.org

SAN: `Accessedge.masteringlync.org`

SAN: `Webconf.masteringlync.org`

SAN: `Sip.masteringlync.org`

Note that the first SAN entry must be the same as the subject name of the certificate because TLS encryption is in use and it simply looks at the SANs of the certificate rather than the subject name.

Cert request for internal Edge NIC:

Subject: `Edge01.masteringlync.org`

Another difference in the process of requesting the certificates for the internal servers is that this time, you will not be able to submit the requests to an online CA. The external NIC certificate request should be submitted as an offline request to a public trusted CA such as DigiCert or VeriSign, and although the internal certificate can and should be issued from the internal CA used for the internal servers, that will also need to be done offline because it is unlikely that relevant ports will be open from the DMZ to the internal network for online enrollment.

To create the manual requests, take the following steps:

1. Start with the Edge Internal certificate highlighted and click Request. Elect to prepare the request now and click Next.

2. Enter a name and path for where to save the request file and click Next.

3. Click Next on the Specify Alternative Certificate Template window, and then on the Name And Security Settings page, enter a friendly name for the certificate. Use something in the name that will help you identify the server and interface.

4. Click Next to proceed. On the next couple of pages, enter organizational information. Accept the default subject name on the Subject Name / Subject Alternative Names page and then click Next.

5. Don't enter additional SANs, and click Next.

6. Finally, check the summary and click Next to create the certificate request. As long as the request is created without error, click Next, and then on the Certificate Request File page, click View to look at the certificate request data. This is the text data that must be sent to the CA.

7. Click Finish to return to the first Certificate Wizard page.

8. Once you have received the certificate and installed it into the personal store of the local computer account, return to the first Certificate screen, and with the Edge Internal certificate still highlighted, click Assign.

9. On the first page of the Certificate Assignment Wizard, click Next, and then on the Certificate Store page, locate the certificate to assign by friendly name, as shown in Figure 6.21.

FIGURE 6.21
Choosing the certificate to assign

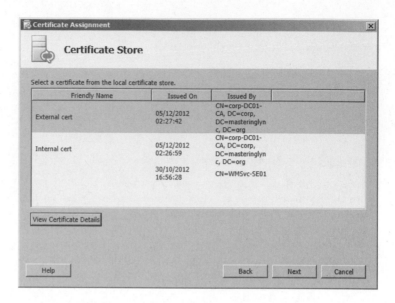

10. Click Next twice to assign the certificate. On the Executing Commands page, check for any errors and view the log if required, and then click Finish to exit.

CA TRUST FOR INTERNAL CERTIFICATES

One step to carry out before requesting the certificates is to ensure that the Edge server trusts the internal CA that issues certificates to the internal servers. This is achieved by importing the root CA certificate into the certificate store on the Edge server.

When creating the external certificate, follow the same process. As before, when prompted, select the check box to create the sip.masteringlync.org SAN entry for later use by phone devices. This certificate request will be sent to an external CA, which will generate and return the certificate. As with the installation of externally trusted certificates on the TMG box, you must follow the installation instructions carefully. Once the certificate is in the personal store of the local computer, go back to the Certificate Wizard, and with the external interface certificate highlighted, click Assign and follow the wizard to assign the externally trusted certificate.

Now that you've completed the certificate setup, all that remains is to start the services, install any remaining Windows patches, and update Lync to the same CU version as the other servers in the organization.

Enterprise Deployments

So far in this chapter, we installed Lync Standard Edition and enabled external access with a single Edge server. In essence, this has been a simple, small-business installation. That is not to say that this system can't support a large number of users; it can.

Standard Edition will, when run on the right hardware, support up to 2,500 users; however, there are companies with many more users than that. Another aspect of the installation that was simpler than many deployments is the domain and network.

We set up a single site and single-forest/-domain Active Directory. Even some small businesses with far fewer than 5,000 users have many sites that need support.

In these more complex environments, there are additional considerations that may change the way deployment is carried out. In the remainder of this chapter, we will look at these issues, starting with installing into a large Active Directory, which potentially has restricted rights for different administrators.

Other topics will include specifying how you want install to work with SQL, working in environments with multiple sites (including both small branch offices and those with tens of thousands of users), and finally, a discussion of setup automation.

Working in Large Active Directories

As discussed in the section "Preparing Active Directory" earlier in this chapter, Lync uses AD less than its predecessor OCS did. That said, there is still a need for schema changes and the creation of a significant number of new objects, which, therefore, requires careful collaboration between all those working with the Active Directory environment.

So what exactly constitutes a large/complex directory? Anything larger than a single forest, single domain, and single site warrants some discussion. Traditionally, there are various types of structures that form large directories:

◆ Single forest with a single tree and multiple domains

◆ Single forest with multiple trees and disjoint namespaces

◆ Multiple forests in a central forest topology

◆ Multiple forests in a resource forest topology

The requirements for these directories were discussed in Chapter 5, so this section covers what is needed from an installation perspective. The key rule is to remember the following:

Schema prep needs to be run once in each forest where Lync servers will be deployed.

Coming back to the structure of the forest mentioned earlier, you do not need to run this directly on the schema master (which is likely to reside in the root domain in the forest), so long as the account you run schema prep under has rights to the schema master. This is good news because it means that you don't need to gain access to a machine in the root domain, which is likely to be heavily locked down. In a resource forest model, schema prep is run in the resource forest where the Lync servers are, not in the user forest.

The forest prep procedure, which creates the universal group, is run once in a forest that will host Lync servers. It is forest prep that creates the universal groups used to assign permissions to the various Lync components. In a large directory environment you may want to take advantage of the opportunity to create these groups in a domain other than the forest root. You might particularly want to do this if you operate an empty forest root domain and, therefore, want to keep access as limited as possible to the forest root domain. In a resource forest model, forest prep is run in the resource forest where the Lync servers are, not in the user forest.

Domain prep should be run in each domain where Lync users will be enabled. In a resource forest model, domain prep is run in the resource forest where the Lync servers are not in the user forest. This is because although there will be users in the user forest accessing Lync, they will be linked via the disabled user objects in the resource forest, which are what will hold the Lync properties.

SINGLE-LABEL DOMAINS

It should be noted that unlike Exchange 2010, Lync cannot be installed in a *single-label domain*. That is, for example, a domain called .masteringlync rather than .masteringlync.org.

When working in an environment that has a complex AD, it is likely that AD will be managed by a dedicated team of directory experts. Before making changes to the AD, you will often need to describe the details behind all the changes Lync will make. One of the biggest and most permanent is the schema update. A great deal of detail can be found in the Lync help file; however, in summary what happens is that schema prep imports information from four LDF files in the order shown here:

ExternalSchema.ldf   This file creates the classes and attributes that allow integration of Lync with Exchange for UM and OWA IM.

ServerSchema.ldf   This is the primary Lync schema file and contains the majority of classes and attributes associated with Lync.

BackCompatSchema.ldf   This file provides for interoperability with components from prior releases.

VersionSchema.ldf   The changes in this file set the version of the schema, making it possible to check which version is installed.

If you want to take a closer look at these files, you can find them in the \Support\schema folder on the installation media. It is even possible to import these files manually in AD with the LDIFDE utility. You would no longer need to provide the directory teams with the ability or training needed to run the Lync Setup program, and you'd have a workaround in cases where the only option available is to run the process from a machine that is not 64-bit, which is what Lync Setup needs.

Another difference with a large directory is that once you have run the schema and forest preparation, more care is needed to ensure that the changes have replicated around all domain controllers in the forest. It is also worth noting that making these changes will create replication traffic, so it is worth carrying out these changes over a period of low usage to ensure a smooth replication process.

Delegating Setup Permissions

Closely related to the topic of AD is that of administrative permissions needed to carry out setup in an enterprise deployment.

Delegation of setup permissions is much simpler than in OCS 2007 R2. Running local setup now requires only Local Administrator permissions on the Lync server and the ability to read domain-based information and CMS information. These are granted by the Domain Users and RTCUniversalReadOnlyAdmins groups, respectively. This simplification is possible because so much work has already been carried out in the Topology Builder. Of course, a greater level of permissions is needed to publish and enable the changes in a new topology, as discussed in Chapter 5.

The other permissions issue you may come up against when running Setup is that of a locked-down AD. This might occur, for example, if your directory team has turned off inheritance on certain sections of the directory to enable delegated security. When Lync Setup is run, both the domain prep and server activation steps set permissions on objects within the domain. Not having the relevant security entries can prevent Lync from properly understanding the topology of the system and will prevent user administration. Therefore, if inheritance is blocked on a particular OU, you can use the following command to manually set the required security entries for Lync after domain prep is run:

```
Grant-CsOuPermission -ObjectType "User" -OU "ou=testusers,dc=corp,
dc=masteringlync,dc=org" -Domain "corp.masteringlync.org"
```

This will set the required permissions on the user objects within the testusers OU in the corp.masteringlync.org domain.

If instead this were a Computer OU, which held Lync computer accounts, you could run the following command:

```
Grant-CsOuPermission -ObjectType "Computer" -OU "ou=Servers,dc=corp,
dc=masteringlync,dc=org" -Domain "corp.masteringlync.org"
```

This would set the permissions on Computer objects in the servers OU in the corp.mastering-lync.org domain.

Granting permissions means that members of the RTC groups can access the objects without being members of the Domain Admins group because these groups are used to control access for user accounts as well as machine accounts (now that Lync has moved to a local user approach rather than the service account approach used by OCS).

Stand-alone SQL

One major area that is different in an Enterprise Edition installation is SQL. As you know, SQL is used to store various databases, the most important being the CMS. In Standard Edition, the CMS and other databases are installed on the Standard Edition server and run on SQL Express. However, when you're using Enterprise Edition, SQL must be run on a separate server, which is often a SQL cluster to provide suitable resilience.

In Lync Setup there are two main ways to install the required databases; they offer different levels of control. The Setup Wizard provides some capacity for specifying database file location but often does not select the correct disks for the correct database roles in a server with multiple disks installed. For full control you need to revert to the command line.

The Install-CsDatabase cmdlet lets you create databases from the command line. It is a cmdlet with many parameters and a lot of intelligence. For example, you can use it to determine automatically the best available deployment path for the database on the SQL server. However, this works only on a stand-alone SQL server and not on SQL clusters. Therefore, it makes sense to learn how to use the cmdlet to deploy databases in a syntax that specifies the path for the data and log files.

Before attempting to run any of the commands listed next, make sure that the server you are attempting this from has the following components installed and that Lync AD preparation has completed successfully.

COMPONENT NAME	FILE LOCATION ON MEDIA
Lync Server 2013 Core components (OCSCore.msi)	\Setup\amd64\Setup
SQL Server 2012 Management Objects (SharedManagementObjects.msi)	\Setup\amd64
SQL Server 2012 Native Client (sqlncli.msi)	\Setup\amd64
System CLR Types for SQL Server 2012 (SQLSysClrTypes.msi)	\Setup\amd64

To prepare the Lync CMS database, open LMS and first run this command:

```
Set-ExecutionPolicy -RemoteSigned
```

This allows local PowerShell scripts to run unhindered while also ensuring that those not created locally need signing to prove their authenticity.

Next, run a command similar to the following:

```
Install-CsDatabase -CentralManagementDatabase -SqlServerFqdn sql01.corp.
masteringlync.org -SqlInstanceName rtc -DatabasePaths "E:\LyncDB-Logs",
"D:\LyncDB-CMS" -Report "C:\Logs\InstallDatabases.html"
```

This will install the CMS database on the SQL server SQL01. The database named `rtc` will be placed in D:\LyncDB-CMS while the logs will on E:\ in the LyncDB-Logs folder. Finally, a log file will be written to the C:\Logs folder.

REFERRING TO SQL SERVERS BY NAME

When you are using the SQL server name in commands, it is important to use the FQDN and not the short (NetBIOS) name. For example, use sql01.corp.masteringlync.org rather than SQL01.

Having created the CMS database just shown, you can continue through the processes discussed in Chapter 5 to create and publish the topology. Once Lync deployment progresses to the point of installing the server, you should use the following command to create the databases defined in the topology:

```
Install-CsDatabase -ConfiguredDatabases -SqlServerFqdn sql01.corp.
masteringlync.org -Report "C:\Logs\InstallDatabases.html"
```

This command will install all the databases defined in the topology for the SQL server sql01.corp.masteringlync.org.

An alternative to using the PowerShell commands to create the databases is to allow the Publish Topology Wizard to do it for you, as mentioned earlier. The wizard does not provide much control over where the databases will be placed–it will use its judgment! Figure 6.22 shows the Publish Topology Wizard Create Databases page. Selecting Advanced will bring up the screen shown in Figure 6.23. Note the section at the bottom where it says. "Due to performance optimization, actual file paths may be different than the file paths that you specified" Basically, you can choose paths, but it may change them!

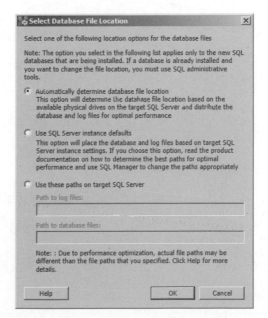

Mirrored SQL

In an enterprise environment, most likely there will be requirements for high availability (HA). As mentioned in Chapter 1, "What's in Lync?," SQL clustering is no longer supported as a HA solution; instead, SQL mirroring is the available option.

This is configured during the SQL configuration steps in Topology Builder, either for an Enterprise Pool, Archiving, or Monitoring store or for a Persistent Chat store. Figure 6.24 shows the definition of these stores during creation.

FIGURE 6.24

SQL mirror store definition

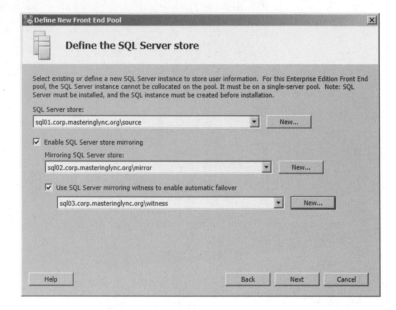

Once you start the Publish Topology Wizard and get to the Create Databases page (shown in Figure 6.22), rather than display all databases on one page, the wizard shows each individually.

Figure 6.25 shows the Create Mirror Databases page. Here you also have to define a file share. This is used to replicate the log files for replay. Click Settings and provide the file share name.

For our installation, we have created a share on the sql02.corp.masteringlync.org servers (called share). Nothing is required for the Witness server.

Figure 6.26 shows the state of the databases within SQL Server Management Studio, showing both principal and mirror states.

The PowerShell cmdlet Get-CsDatabaseMirrorState shows the following output when mirroring is operational:

```
DatabaseName             : rtcab
StateOnPrimary           : Mirror
StateOnMirror            : Principal
MirroringStatusOnPrimary : synchronized
MirroringStatusOnMirror  : synchronized
```

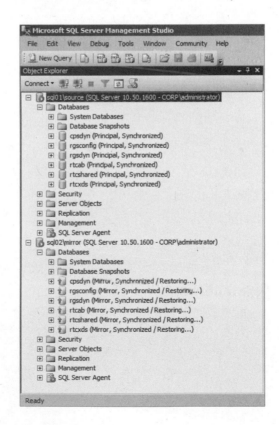

This output is repeated for each additional database (pool databases are shown here):

◆ rtcxds

◆ rtcshared

◆ rgsconfig

◆ rgsdyn

◆ cpsdyn

The third server (the Witness) is used to enable automatic failover. With this third server in place, a quorum can be reached in the event of a failure and it can enable the mirror to become the primary data source.

In the event a manual failover is required (perhaps to perform hardware maintenance), the PowerShell cmdlet to use is `Invoke-CsDatabaseFailover`, with the following parameters:

```
Invoke-CsDatabaseFailover -PoolFqdn <poolfqdn> -DatabaseType "User" -NewPrincipal
"Mirror"
```

`DatabaseType` can be any of the following types:

◆ Archiving

◆ Monitoring

◆ User

◆ Provision

◆ CentralAdmin

◆ Lyss

◆ Registrar

◆ Edge

◆ PersistentChat

◆ PersistentChatCompliance

◆ CentralMgmt

`NewPrincipal` can be either Mirror or Primary, depending upon whether the database is being failed over or back.

Installation of Persistent Chat

With previous versions of Lync (and indeed, OCS R2), Persistent Chat was known as Group Chat. It has its origins as a product called MindAlign from a company called Parlano (which was acquired by Microsoft in 2007).

For both OCS R2 and Lync Server 2010, Group Chat was a separate optional download and not seen as core to the product. Lync Server 2013 has changed this by bringing the installation into Topology Builder and giving the management the same integration and look and feel as the rest of the Lync Server 2013 product.

As with the rest of the roles in Lync Server 2013, installation is carried out using Topology Builder and must be published prior to use.

Opening Topology Builder and selecting New Persistent Chat Pool will open a wizard similar to that for the Standard Edition server we have already installed.

The wizard includes the following steps:

◆ Define the FQDN (multiple or single computer pool)

◆ If multiple, then define each member

◆ Define the properties of the Persistent Chat pool:

　◆ Display name

　◆ Port (default 5041)

　◆ Enable compliance

　◆ Use this pool as default for site <currently selected sitename>

　◆ Use this pool as default for all sites

◆ Define the SQL store (mirroring is supported; see the previous section)

◆ Define the file store

◆ Select the next-hop server (actually asking for a pool)

The only difference with this wizard (compared to a regular pool) is the properties of the Persistent Chat pool page. In this case, if you select Enable Compliance, you will be asked another question regarding the location of the SQL server for compliance.

LOCATION OF THE COMPLIANCE DATABASE

The compliance database may be located in the same SQL instance as the main Persistent Chat database. However, permissions are likely to be assigned at the instance level, so this may cause potential issues because the same user DBA permissions will be applied to the original source as well as to the compliance database.

Therefore, to ensure separation, it is better to have a separate instance (and possibly SQL server) to contain the compliance database.

Figure 6.27 shows both the Persistent Chat (mgc) and compliance (mgccomp) databases.

Once the topology has been published, the Setup And Deployment Wizard can be run as with any other servers and will automatically install the required components.

Persistent Chat servers require a certificate, which the Setup and Deployment Wizard can request and assign.

As before, services will need to be started manually.

FIGURE 6.27
Persistent Chat
and compliance
databases

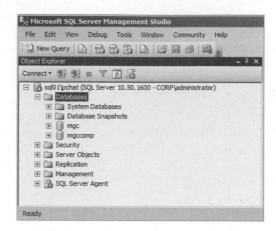

Configuring an Office Web Apps Server

Actual installation and base configuration of the Office Web Apps server is beyond the scope of this book (detailed info can be found at http://go.microsoft.com/fwlink/p/?linkid=257525); however, you do need to integrate Lync Server 2013 with it, so the integration aspects are covered here.

Like any Lync infrastructure, the Office Web Apps server needs to be defined and published in the topology, so you need to run Topology Builder to do this.

An Office Web Apps server is associated with a pool, so open the pool definition page, select a pool, right-click, select Edit Properties On the Edit Properties page (see Figure 6.28), scroll down, and select Associate Office Web Apps Server. This option is not visible unless conferencing is available as a selected feature on the pool.

FIGURE 6.28
Define an Office
Web Apps server
using Topology
Builder

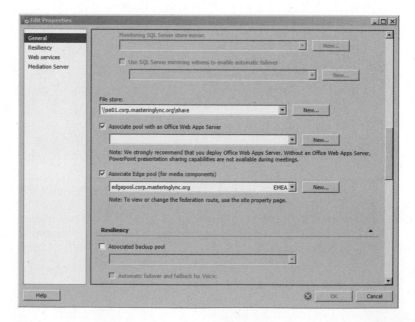

Selecting New will open the prompt for the server and the server discovery URLs (see Figure 6.29).

FIGURE 6.29
Prompt for Office
Web Apps server
URLs

If the Office Web Apps server is deployed on the internal network, then the check box should be left blank; otherwise, if the Office Web Apps server is in a perimeter network, this check box should be selected.

Once the definition is completed, the topology should be published as before.

Depending on whether you wish external users (federated users, etc.) to access this Office Web Apps server, you may need to create associated web publishing rules on your reverse proxy. This will also be dependent upon whether your Office Web Apps server is located internally or in the perimeter.

Although the screenshots for the Office Web Apps server are shown associated with the Enterprise Pool (you'll have to look closely), the Office Web Apps server can also be associated with Standard Edition servers.

Considerations for Branches

As discussed in Chapter 5, there are various aspects to consider when deploying Lync in branch offices, including the bandwidth available and the reliability of that bandwidth back to the central site, the number of users in the remote site, and the availability of local IT staff.

Planning might determine that a local server capable of supporting all workloads is needed at the branch office. This would, therefore, not be a survivable branch appliance but would instead be a Standard Edition server.

Deploying a Standard Edition server in a branch site is very similar to deploying one in a central site. The main difference is that instead of running the "Prepare first Standard Edition server" step, you can progress straight to installing the Local Configuration store. That is because you will already have a CMS in the topology, which is used to define the updated topology required for the deployment of Standard Edition server in the branch office.

TYPE OF SITE FOR STANDARD EDITION DEPLOYMENT IN A BRANCH

Contrary to common sense, to deploy a Standard Edition server in a branch office, you don't create a branch site—which would be the case for a SBA deployment. Instead, you create another central site.

It is possible to create an additional Standard Edition server in the existing central site and Lync Server 2013 would function perfectly.

The advantage, however, of creating a separate central site is one of management and the ability to define policy specific to that site—for example, emergency calling options.

Automating Installation Using PowerShell

Throughout this chapter, if you looked carefully at the summary pages at the end of the various installation steps, you have seen the PowerShell commands that ran. As stated earlier, Lync is entirely underpinned by PowerShell, which means that it is entirely feasible to carry out the installation directly from the command line without using the GUI setup at all. Although it may not be the most user-friendly option, it is great for documentation and repetition.

So if you are rolling out Lync globally, we highly recommend taking a look at this option and working to build a deployment script that will enable you to deploy Lync servers in a known manner without any administrative errors. Given that we have yet to dive into PowerShell in depth, we will leave the details of this script until we introduce PowerShell in Chapter 8. If you are keen, then feel free to skip ahead now.

The Bottom Line

Configure Windows Server for a Lync installation.   Installing Lync is relatively simple, but many steps are involved. One of the most important is the preparatory work needed. If you get this wrong, it will slow down your installation and you may find that certain features will not work later on down the line.

> **Master It**   Lync can be installed on several subtly different operating systems. You have been asked to lay out which OS requires the least amount of preparatory work and what the main preparatory stages are before Lync can be deployed.

Prepare Active Directory for Lync installation.   Like many Microsoft server applications, Lync has tight ties with AD. Lync Server 2010 was the first version of Microsoft's real-time communications product to start moving away from the reliance on AD, but nevertheless, with both Lync Server 2010 and Lync Server 2013 there are still hard requirements and preparatory steps that must be carried out, which include schema, forest, and domain prep.

> **Master It**   You are working in a large corporation with a single forest and multiple domains. You have been instructed to work with your directories team to help them understand the changes that need to be made to the schema as part of setup.

Install your first Standard Edition server.   A Lync Standard Edition server is a complex environment requiring careful deployment. It has numerous prerequisites that need to be installed. Once you have completed the installation of prerequisites, setup is relatively straightforward, following a standard process.

> **Master It**   You have been tasked with installing the first Standard Edition Lync server in your network. What is one of the unique preparatory steps required for this Standard Edition, and why? Following that, what are the standard steps that setup takes?

Get your first users up and running.   Getting the first users on Lync is slightly more involved than it first sounds. Of course, you need a couple of users with which to test. Enabling them for Lync is straightforward, especially if they already have an email address defined that matches the SIP uniform resource identifier (URI) you want the user to have. The more interesting challenge is getting the client deployed. Of course, this can be done manually, but once things scale out that won't be feasible.

Master It You are rolling out the Lync client to thousands of users. How would you do this, and what are some of the considerations you need to make?

Implement external access through the Director, Edge, and reverse proxy servers. There are many elements that come together to provide external access. The Edge server and reverse proxy server sit in the perimeter network and provide access to media and web components, respectively. The Director sits on the LAN and acts as a routing and security buffer between the external users and the Front End pools. The deployment of the Director is very similar to the deployment of Standard Edition or Front End servers and requires similar prerequisites.

Master It You are deploying an Edge server as part of providing remote access to your network. What is different about the install compared to the Standard Edition and Director installs?

Understand the differences in an Enterprise Edition installation. There are many differences when working on an Enterprise deployment of Lync compared to a Standard Edition install. For example, there is the potential for a complex directory to be present, which requires close cooperation with a directories team. Another change is that SQL is installed separately from Lync and does not coexist with the Lync server as it does with Standard Edition. Finally, there is the challenge of scalability and branch offices to overcome.

Master It You have been asked to work with the database team to ensure that everything is in place for the Lync installation. What do you need to explain and how would you instruct the database team to create the databases?

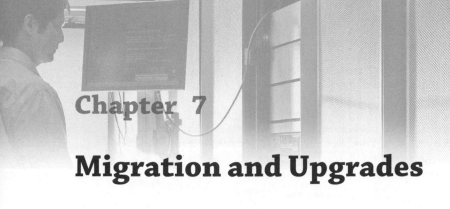

Chapter 7

Migration and Upgrades

If you've followed along in the book so far, you should have a good understanding of much of Lync, including how to deploy it. However, if you already have a Microsoft real-time communication platform in your environment, things are slightly more complex than if you don't. You will need to consider how to upgrade or migrate from one system to the next and negotiate a period of coexistence. Only migrations from Office Communications Server (OCS) 2007 R2 and Lync Server 2010 are supported. Any other older versions will require a "stepping-stone" approach to migrate to a supported start point prior to the final move to Lync Server 2013.

Of course, throughout this period you'll need to work with your users to make sure the transition period is as painless as possible for them as they move from clients they know to the new Lync client.

The main focus in this chapter will be moving from OCS 2007 R2, although we will briefly cover Lync Server 2010 because the more complex migrations will be from the older product.

In this chapter, you will learn to:

◆ Understand migration considerations

◆ Consider client pain points

◆ Migrate to Lync Server 2013 from OCS 2007 R2

◆ Migrate to Lync Server 2013 from Lync Server 2010

Understanding Migration

Migration to Lync can take a variety of forms. Possibly the simplest would be to install a new Lync system, not have it talk to the old system, and ask users to re-create all their contacts and meetings. Clearly, this isn't possible very often! The disruption would simply be too great.

Therefore, a move to Lync from one of the previous Microsoft real-time communication platforms needs to include a period of coexistence. At the time of writing, this period of coexistence can include only two versions of the product at any one time; Lync Server 2013 is one, and the other is either OCS 2007 R2 or Lync Server 2010. Migration from OCS 2007 (or earlier versions) directly to Lync 2013 is not supported, tested, or documented, and neither is having both OCS 2007 R2 and Lync Server 2010 deployed in the same organization and adding Lync Server 2013 to that. If you have a complex environment with a mix of OCS 2007 and OCS 2007 R2, or even an old Live Communications Server (LCS) system, you have to perform some intermediary steps before you can get to Lync Server 2013.

In order to get to a state where Lync Server 2013 can be integrated and coexist with your existing environment, you need to make sure that any LCS deployments are upgraded to at least OCS 2007 R2 and that LCS is completely decommissioned. Equally, if you have a mixed OCS 2007 and OCS 2007 R2 deployment, then you'll need to complete the move to OCS 2007 R2 and remove all of the OCS 2007 pools so that you have only OCS 2007 R2 left, and of course if you're partway through a move to Lync Server 2010, you'll have to either roll back (assuming it's from OCS 2007 R2) or complete the move to Lync Server 2010. Once you've done that, you are ready to move to Lync Server 2013—not as easy as first thought perhaps!

Coexistence

This chapter is called "Migrations and Upgrades" because people use both words interchangeably to describe moving to the latest versions of Microsoft software. In general, the term *upgrade* refers to an in-place upgrade, which only really occurs with operating systems or databases these days, and the term *migrate* refers to deploying a parallel system side by side and moving the configuration and users to the new system. You are *upgrading* in the sense that you are moving from one Microsoft real-time communication product to the next version; however, you are *migrating* in the method that you carry out the move. We describe it this way because there is no way to simply put the install media into the existing servers and click Upgrade.

The only way to get to Lync Server 2013 (aside from a greenfield install) is through a side-by-side migration, in which you install Lync on new servers in your existing Active Directory (AD) and then configure it to coexist with your current product, OCS 2007 R2 or Lync Server 2010.

NOTE Although we mentioned that Lync would be installed on new hardware into the existing AD, you must still install a new Lync pool. Lync servers cannot be installed in OCS pools, nor can Lync Server 2013 servers be installed into Lync Server 2010 pools.

One key piece of coexistence is the ability for Lync to talk to OCS. Because there has been a significant architecture change from OCS 2007 R2 to Lync Server 2013, particularly in the move to the Central Management Store, some configuration is needed to make this possible. Once you are happy that you have Lync Server 2013 installed and running satisfactorily on your pilot pool, you must then merge the OCS 2007 R2 configuration data from Windows Management Instrumentation (WMI) and Active Directory (AD) into the Lync Server 2013 topology. Then, once everything is configured correctly so that communication can flow, you start the process of moving services and then users over to the new Lync system and then finally decommission the old OCS setup.

Another key element of coexistence is the way the Edge and Director roles are handled. The first principle is that the Lync Server 2013 Edge and Lync Server 2013 Director roles should always be deployed together. You should not have an OCS 2007 R2 Edge talking to a Lync Server 2013 Director, for example. Another similar requirement is not to mix the Lync Server 2013 and OCS 2007 R2 versions of the Edge and Mediation roles. For example, a Lync Server 2013 Mediation server should have a route out of a Lync Server 2013 Edge, not an OCS 2007 R2 one.

In addition to the major issue of version support, you need to be aware of a couple of more detailed points about coexistence. First, when moving to Lync Server 2013, there are a variety of options involving the SQL database. You can either create and use an entirely new SQL Server infrastructure or reuse an existing SQL Server installation. Obviously, you must size the SQL infrastructure correctly in either case so that it can perform adequately for Lync Server 2013.

One thing that is highly discouraged is using an existing SQL Server instance that is supporting another application. Although it is possible to make this work theoretically, you would not be able to control the way CPU and memory resources were assigned even though you could control where the database resided on the disk. Also, if the existing instance is supporting OCS 2007 R2, you would have a clash of default database names, which is definitely something to avoid! You can find more information about SQL Server sizing for Lync Server 2013 at the following locations.

To configure SQL Server for Lync Server 2013, refer to

http://technet.microsoft.com/en-us/library/gg425848.aspx

For information on server hardware platforms, refer to

http://technet.microsoft.com/en-us/library/gg398835.aspx

THE OCS ENHANCED PRESENCE BIT

OCS 2007 introduced the concept of *enhanced presence*, which allowed users to set different levels of access to their presence information, including blocking access altogether. When you're migrating, you need to make sure that Enhanced Presence is turned on for each OCS 2007 R2 user when you are configuring. This must be done before you migrate users to Lync Server 2013. If this is the first time you have turned Enhanced Presence on in OCS, you need to make sure that users have logged on at least once to an OCS client because this is what completes the Enhanced Presence setup in the OCS database. If they haven't logged on, the migration will produce an error and they will lose their blocked contacts list.

Another aspect of migration to be aware of is that Lync Server 2013 brings some new roles that didn't exist in OCS 2007 R2. Both Standard and Enterprise versions of Lync can utilize the new Survivable Branch Appliance, which provides resilience to branch offices. It is recommended to complete the deployment of Lync Server 2013 and the removal of OCS 2007 R2 before deploying new roles.

A final piece to consider about coexistence involves applications that have been written in United Communications Managed API (UCMA). Apps that use v2.0 and are running on OCS 2007 R2 servers can be called into by users migrated to Lync Server 2013 servers; however, if you still have UCMA v1 apps that are running on OCS 2007, they will not work. Either way, for apps to run on Lync Server 2013, they need to be written using UCMA v4.0, so as part of your migration, you will need to consider how best to get this done and have the new apps deployed on the Lync Server 2013 servers. This custom development work is outside the scope of this book, so you should contact whoever created the application for you and discuss specific requirements and process for migration with them.

Considering Client Pain Points

When a move to Lync Server 2013 is being planned, one of the most important considerations is how the migration will affect users. After all, it would be a shame to create a negative feeling about such a great new platform. To ensure that things go smoothly, you need to be aware of common issues and problems that inevitably occur as new functionality is introduced that works differently than its predecessor. This topic is discussed more broadly in Appendix B, "Adoption."

The first consideration is the client. The OCS 2007 R2 client can connect to the Lync 2013 server, but not the other way around; therefore, the client is the last thing to be upgraded. This helps to simplify how things work, but it also means that in a large deployment, if you stick rigidly to the old client, users who have been migrated could miss out on the new features of Lync Server 2013 (such as the new conferencing features of document and program sharing) for a long time until everyone is moved. To avoid that, you might decide to move people and then upgrade their clients, which would mean that you will have two different versions in place and that people will have access to different functionality. It is critical to communicate to users exactly what is happening and when and how it will affect their ability to do what they always have done. It also means that you as an administrator will have two different clients to support and manage using the policies available. Indeed.

The Live Meeting client is unable to connect to a Lync Server 2013 conference. This will mean that users are unable to participate in conferences without using the Lync 2013 Web App. The reverse is also true; the Lync 2013 client cannot take part in meetings created with Live Meeting, so you may wish to consider keeping the Live Meeting client installed until the migration is complete!

The exception to this point is with migrations from Lync Server 2010; the new Lync Server 2013 client *can* connect to the Lync Server 2010 servers. This backward compatibility from the client is rare in the LCS/OCS/Lync world!

Policies

In OCS 2007 R2, there are many policies available to control the client. Lync Server 2010 introduced a fairly significant change in how policies are applied and this continues with Lync Server 2013. It is covered in depth in Chapter 10, "User Administration." However, in the context of a migration, you need to understand a few things. In particular, you need to know how a certain group of settings, which provide client configuration and lockdown for OCS 2007 R2 users and clients, should be translated into the new Lync Server 2013 policy mechanisms.

In Lync Server 2013, the majority of policy settings are now set through in-band provisioning. However, there are also a number still provided via Group Policy, which enables settings to be configured before the client logs on. Fortunately for these bootstrapping policies, the same group policy used for an OCS client will work for Lync clients. For example, you might have been using Group Policy to configure an OCS client to connect to a specific server, to use TCP rather than TLS, and to not display the client first run splash screen; this policy will still work with Lync.

Of course, there are differences based on the new policy engine. There are also many new policies to cover new Lync Server 2013 features. Before you complete your rollout of Lync, be sure to read Chapter 10, which covers the policy engine in depth. Also take a look at the "Client Policies and Settings" topic in the help file, which can be found here:

```
http://technet.microsoft.com/en-us/library/jj205204.aspx
```

This discussion provides a useful reference point for policies that have the same name, involve a name change, or are new altogether.

Meetings

The biggest change in client functionality in Lync (introduced with Lync Server 2010) is that Live Meeting is removed. As part of this move, the old meeting URLs are replaced. In OCS, conference URLs start with `conf://` and Live Meeting URLs start with `meet://`. In Lync, all meeting URLs start with the `HTTPS://` format, which means that participants can access a meeting via the Meeting Join website.

If they already have a suitable client installed (either Lync or Lync Attendant), they will be taken directly into the meeting. The Lync Attendant provides access only to the audio part of the meeting.

With Lync Server 2010 they were given the option to join via Lync Web App or to download the Lync Attendee client and use it instead. Lync 2013 only provides a Web App client (see Figure 7.1), although if a user already has a Lync 2010 Attendee client installed, they will be able to connect to the meeting using this client.

FIGURE 7.1
Lync Web App

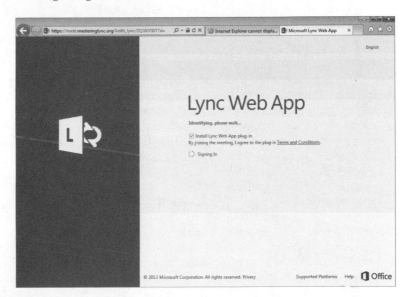

CONFIGURING THE MEETING JOIN PAGE

Previously with Lync Server 2010, it was possible to configure the Meeting Join page to allow access by legacy clients. However, this option has been removed with Lync Server 2013 because the preference now is for connectivity via Lync Web App (now providing audio and video) rather than a legacy client.

Indeed, the only configuration now available is via PowerShell, and it only allows you to download the Lync 2010 Attendee client. You can configure this setting by using the `New-CsWebServiceConfiguration` or `Set-CsWebServiceConfiguration` PowerShell cmdlet with the `ShowDownloadCommunicatorAttendeeLink` parameter.

As part of the migration, there is also a change from creating a Live Meeting for sharing to creating a new Lync meeting. When creating these new Lync Meetings, it is important to realize that there are differences in the default settings for meetings. Specifically, with OCS scheduled meetings, anonymous participants could enter straight into the meeting (subject to conferencing policy); since Lync 2010, this is not the case. The Lobby feature is enabled to capture people who enter a meeting and are not part of your company; this information is ascertained by checking the supported SIP URIs of your organization. In comparison, Lync ad hoc meetings that are set up using Meet Now from the Lync client by default allow anyone directly into the meeting without waiting in the lobby. You need to be aware of these changes so that you can communicate the new system to your users or change the defaults to better meet your needs.

PINS AND IDS

As with other elements of migration, some things change and others don't. One thing that won't change is a user's PIN to get into conferences from a phone device; one thing that will change is your conference ID. It is changed when you start using the new Lync client Online Meeting add-in to Outlook to schedule meetings. The ID is covered in more depth in Chapter 16, "Extended Voice Functionality." However, the key thing to note is that although your old ID will continue to work for meetings already scheduled, all new ones will use your new ID.

Of course, not all meetings will be new. It is important to address what happens to recurring meetings or those that are already set up for the future. For meetings that were created on OCS 2007 R2, when a user is migrated to Lync, the meetings are carried over but remain either conf:// (Conferencing) or meet:// (Live Meeting). For conf:// URLs, a migrated user will use the Lync client. For meet:// URLs, the Live Meeting client will still be attempted. However, there is no longer a "legacy" MCU that will allow the Live Meeting client to connect, and so the user will fail to connect (see Figure 7.2).

Also note that users migrated to the new Lync client cannot create new Live Meetings hosted on OCS. Conferences or Live Meetings that have been migrated to Lync will need to be updated or re-created. Most meeting settings remain editable as usual; however, if a user modifies the end date, subject, or attendee list of a meeting created on OCS, that meeting will be migrated to the new Lync Meeting format. Given that you can create only new Lync meetings once you have been migrated and are using the new client, it may well make sense to move those who are heavy conference users to Lync early in the process so they can begin using the benefits.

MEETING CONTENT

Content in existing meetings that are migrated is not brought across. For example, if your salespeople have already set up regular meetings with uploaded PowerPoint slides and polls, even though the meetings will be migrated, the decks and polls will not. You will need to set up this information again.

You also need to understand that although a user migrated to Lync can easily join a meeting set up on OCS, the new features available in Lync Server 2013 meetings will not be available.

So far we have focused on moving to Lync when the new Lync client is in place. The other aspect of migration is when you have been moved to Lync but the new clients have not rolled out. In this instance, a user would not be able to continue to use the Live Meeting conferencing add-in to schedule meetings and would not have access to new features such as lobby management in the meeting or to new Lync Server 2013 collaboration features as provided by the Lync 2013 client. Equally, before a user is moved to Lync Server 2013, they have access to conferences created on Lync but will not get access to the new conferencing functionality unless they use the Lync 2010 Attendee or Lync 2013 Web App client. This is similar to when users still on OCS 2007 R2 are invited to meetings hosted on the Lync Server 2013 server. They will find that there are various methods of joining. They can use the browser-based Lync 2013 Web App or download and install the Lync 2010 Attendee, or they can be dialed in using the legacy OCS client. However, they will end up with reduced functionality. If coexistence is going to be in place for any length of time, the Lync 2010 Attendee client should be rolled out to all users and then replaced with the Lync client as users are migrated or accepted to use the Lync 2013 Web App client.

FIGURE 7.2
Attempting to join via Live Meeting client

You may also need to provide access to the new Lync Server 2013 meetings to those outside your company. Instead of using the Live Meeting client, you need to make sure people use the Lync 2010 Attendee or the Lync 2013 Web App to join your meetings. These clients are covered in Chapter 4, "Clients." When access is provided to a federated party, if the meeting organizer uses the Lync Server 2013 feature to lock a meeting so participants come into the lobby, the meeting can't be accessed by federated users using the LCS 2005 or OCS 2007 client. Participants need to use the Lync 2010 Attendee or Lync 2013 Web App to enter.

Interoperability

As touched on previously, one of the bigger challenges of your move to Lync Server 2013 is making sure things work as expected for users. A big part of this challenge is determining how those users still on the old client can work with those on the new client.

MULTIPLE POINTS OF PRESENCE

By default, OCS and now Lync offer the potential for a user to sign in from many different places. For example, a user could be signed in on a phone device, a cell phone, a Mac laptop, a Windows desktop, and a web browser! Once a user is moved to Lync, there are few limits to which clients they can be signed in from simultaneously. They can use all forms of the Lync client and be signed in with both the current and older Lync clients and OCS 2007 R2 client at the same time, subject to your client version policy.

There is, however, one important exception. A Lync *2010* Attendant user can be signed in simultaneously only with phones running the Lync Phone Edition client. Simultaneous sign-in with other Lync 2010 or Lync 2013 clients is not supported. For example, a user signed in using Lync 2010 Attendant cannot go to another computer and sign in on another client without first signing out of the Lync 2010 Attendant client.

DELEGATING

In OCS 2007 R2, a new feature called *call delegation* enabled managers to delegate phone call handling to one or more administrative assistants or other delegates. When a delegate answered a call, the manager was notified that the call had been answered and given the name of the delegate who answered. In Lync Server 2013, delegation has been improved significantly. In OCS 2007 R2, the administrative assistants needed to use the Attendant console; in Lync, all of this is now integrated into a single Lync 2013 client as part of the push toward a real-time communications client. Of course, for this new functionality to work, both the manager and delegate must be using Lync 2013, so it is very important that you move managers and delegates to Lync 2013 at the same time; otherwise, you will disable the delegates' ability to manage their bosses' calls.

FUNCTIONALITY

A few functional areas need to be addressed, especially if you are moving from OCS 2007 R2 but occasionally if you are moving from Lync 2010 as well. These areas particularly affect some of the Enterprise Voice functionality, which is understandable given the rate of development from OCS 2007 R2 to Lync Server 2013.

As a starting point, let's look at basic communication between different client versions. First, it is important to note that Lync Server 2013 users can only talk to those on the LCS 2005 or OCS 2007 client if they are federated users, that is, not in the same organization/AD forest. Lync 2013 clients are fully supported to communicate with OCS 2007 R2 or Lync 2010 clients in the same organization, and Lync 2013 provides the ability to communicate via IM, voice, and video. The limitations involve specific voice features. For example, it is not possible to retrieve a call parked on Lync (see Chapter 16 for more information) from a non-Lync client. Equally, response group anonymization when using OCS 2007 R2 clients is unavailable. With these caveats aside, most communications scenarios will work just fine during your period of coexistence.

On a different but related note, it is important to acknowledge that although Lync provides a feature called Lync Web App (LWA) installed on each Front End server, LWA no longer provides the full IM functionality that Communicator Web Access (CWA) in OCS 2007 did. LWA is supported only to gain access to conferences in Lync. Therefore, if you still require the functionality of CWA as an individual client, you must either deploy CWA and connect it to Lync Server 2013, which is still supported, or go without this functionality until Microsoft provides a replacement. An alternative may be to use the IM client built in to Outlook Web Access within Exchange.

Migrating to Lync

Now that you're familiar with a broad outline of the migration process and understand how a migration affects users, it's time to dive in and actually migrate a system. The rest of this chapter will discuss moving from a system on OCS 2007 R2 to Lync 2013.

NOTE   Although the migration-related aspects of the process will be discussed in depth, this chapter assumes that you have read and understand other areas of the book. Given that a migration touches many elements of Lync, if we covered every piece of the process in depth, this chapter would be huge!

The elements involved in the migration consist of the following machines:

◆   DC01: The domain controller, which hosts the DNS and certificate services; domain name `corp.masteringlync.org`

◆   EX01: The Exchange 2010 SP1 server (We're using this specific version of Exchange in the migration because it supports both OCS 2007 R2 as well as Lync 2013.)

◆   OCS01: Our OCS 2007 R2 Standard Edition server running Cumulative Update 11

◆   OCSMed01: Providing Enterprise Voice functionality via a SIP trunk

◆   OCSCWA01: The Communicator Web Access server providing web-based access to IM, presence, and conferencing dial-in

◆   OCSEdge01: Providing full external access and federation for user domain names:

    ◆   `OCSEdge.corp.masteringlync.org`

    ◆   `OCSAccess.masteringlync.org`

    ◆   `OCSConf.masteringlync.org`

    ◆   `OCSAV.masteringlync.org`

The Director role hasn't been deployed, but otherwise this is a great representation of a standard OCS deployment. As part of the migration, you will add two more servers:

◆   SE01 will be your Standard Edition Lync server; domain name `se01.corp.masteringlync.org`

◆   Edge01 will provide remote access to Lync users. Domain names area as follows:

    ◆   `Lyncedge.corp.masteringlync.org`

    ◆   `LyncAccess.masteringlync.org`

    ◆   `LyncConf.masteringlync.org`

    ◆   `LyncAV.masteringlync.org`

MONITORING AND ARCHIVING DURING MIGRATION

Although a Monitoring or Archiving server isn't defined in the migration scenario in this chapter, it is something you may need to take into account. This is especially the case when your company relies on archiving for compliance reasons or perhaps monitoring for billing purposes. The main principle is that each version of OCS or Lync works with only the Monitoring and Archiving server from the same version. Therefore, if you are migrating and maintaining these capabilities is critical, you must implement the Monitoring and Archiving roles in your Lync pool before you move any users to Lync. For more information on the Monitoring and Archiving roles, see Chapter 11, "Archiving and Monitoring."

As the migration progresses, when you merge the topology to allow Lync and OCS to communicate, you will find that the existing Archiving and Monitoring policies come across into Lync. Similarly, when users are migrated, if their communications were archived in OCS, they will also be in Lync.

Finally, you should note that the new Lync Server 2013 Archiving and Monitoring roles don't use the same databases as the OCS roles (or indeed the Lync Server 2010 roles), so if you need to maintain the legacy data, you should back up the databases and keep them available for reporting.

Before you get going with the migration, there are a few things you must pay close attention to throughout the process. First, test at all stages; don't simply plow on after each step without validating that the changes you have made were actually applied correctly.

It is also very important to use the correct tools to manage both systems during coexistence. As you might expect, you should (and can only) manage the Lync elements using the Lync Server Control Panel (Control Panel) or Lync Server Management Shell (PowerShell) and OCS using the OCS Management tools. Migrations should all be carried out from the Lync Management tools.

Preparing

When all your planning is complete, the final stage before starting the actual migration steps is to prepare your OCS 2007 R2 environment. This takes several forms; some of it is technical and some of it relates to documentation.

The most important step is to ensure that your OCS 2007 R2 installation has the latest patches installed. Realistically, this should have been part of normal operations, so most likely it is already complete. However, if it is not, you must at the very least ensure that you have installed OCS 2007 R2 CU11. These patches should be installed across all servers and clients, including phone devices.

Once you've completed the updates, it is worth downloading the OCS Best Practices Analyzer (BPA) from the following link:

```
www.microsoft.com/downloads/en/details.aspx?FamilyId=1B90993C-072A-4C84-B385-
B76D23B2F27C&displaylang=en
```

The BPA tool is a way of scanning your environment to check that it is configured correctly and will highlight any issues that you need to either address or acknowledge. Figure 7.3 shows the interface as you kick off the scan.

FIGURE 7.3
Beginning a BPA
scan

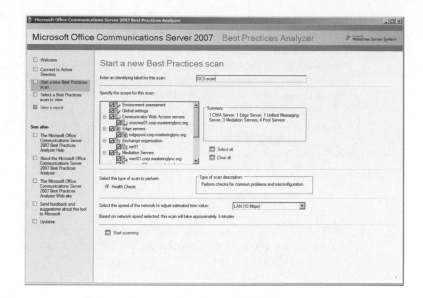

Once you are satisfied that you have resolved any issues the BPA reveals, you should perform your usual backup to ensure that in the event of any unforeseen problem, you have the ability to roll back to a known working state. This should, of course, include an Active Directory system state backup and any OCS databases. At this point, it is also well worth making sure you have up-to-date documentation of the OCS system, showing IP addresses, DNS FQDN and certificate details, pool locations, policies, and any custom configuration.

You may also want to export the user data prior to migrating, just as an additional backup! You can use the dbimpexp.exe tool to do this.

The final element is to choose which clients should be able to connect to OCS during the coexistence and migration phase. It is highly recommended to make sure that only the clients with the latest updates can connect. Equally important is to ensure that no Lync 2013 clients can connect to OCS. This is done using client version filtering on OCS as follows:

1. On the OCS Standard Edition (or Front End in an Enterprise Edition deployment) in the OCS management console, drill down to the pool name, right-click, hover over Filtering Tools, and then select Client Version Filter.

2. Once in the tool, your first objective is to block Lync clients from connecting to OCS. This is done by adding the following elements as Blocked:

Client	User Agent Header	Version
Lync 2013	OC	15.*.*.*
Lync Web App	CWA	5.*.*.*
Lync Phone Edition	OCPhone	4.*.*.*

3. Your second objective is to ensure that only the latest versions of the OCS clients can connect to the OCS pool. This is done by entering the following elements and setting them so that if the client version is less than (<) the running version, it will be blocked. Note that this is current as of the May 2011 Live Meeting and January 2012 (CU11) Office Communicator R2 updates. (Two different version numbers were released for CU11—.244 and .253—using .244 allows both version numbers of the client to connect.)

Client	User agent header	Version
Office Communicator	OC	3.5.6907.244
Live Meeting	LMC	8.0.6362.202

4. Once you have entered this information and removed conflicting elements, your client version policy should look something like Figure 7.4. Once you are finished, click OK to apply the policy.

FIGURE 7.4
The newly updated Client Version policy on OCS

If you want more details about some of the available options, see the following TechNet articles.

For a discussion of OCS 2007 R2, see the following:

`http://technet.microsoft.com/en-us/library/dd572488(office.13).aspx`

Deploying the First Lync Pool

Now that all the checks have been performed and the rollback plans are in place, it's time to install Lync. The procedure follows the same steps described in Chapter 6, "Installation." You'll begin by installing the Lync Standard Edition server, which will also host a colocated Mediation server in time. You'll also be adding a Lync Edge server later in this process. The new servers will be as follows:

◆ SE01.corp.masteringlync.org (hosts Lync Web App and includes the colocated Mediation server)

◆ Edge01.corp.masteringlync.org

The key thing about deploying the first pool is that you should install the elements that match what you have in OCS. In other words, you should not add the newer Lync roles (for example, the SBA) until you have removed OCS. This first pool can be used to pilot Lync and thoroughly test integration. It is generally built with minimal hardware, as shown earlier. Once functionality testing is complete, you build out the pool to support the required number of users and provide resilience through load balancing. At that point, the pool will be taken into production.

LARGE-SCALE DEPLOYMENTS

In large-scale deployments, you'll need to choose which pool you want to move to Lync first. Whether you are migrating from Lync Server 2010 or OCS 2007 R2, you should start with a pool that does not hold the Edge servers that perform federation. This allows you to test functionality while keeping the existing federation routes!

NOTE Adding the first Lync pool is performed as a new deployment; therefore, you can follow the steps outlined in Chapter 5, "Planning Your Deployment," and Chapter 6. For the Voice elements, you can follow the steps explained in Chapter 13, "Getting Started with Voice," and Chapter 16. Given that those chapters cover deployment of Lync in depth, this chapter will focus on what is needed for a successful migration and will provide step-by-step guides only when doing so will not cause extensive duplication.

During the process of creating your topology, you will maintain the same primary and secondary SIP domains. When you create the Lync pool, you must give it a unique pool name. Do not attempt to reuse the OCS pool name. In this case, it is called Se01.corp.masteringlync.org.

Given that Enterprise Voice and Dial-in Conferencing are enabled in OCS 2007 R2, you will enable them here. The Lync documentation talks about using a colocated Mediation server during migration, even if you will eventually move to a dedicated Mediation server. Experience indicates that this is not essential. You should do whatever you feel is suitable, based on best practice Mediation server design principles. Best practice states that when using SIP trunks to an ITSP (Internet Telephony Service Provider), you should configure the SIP trunks to terminate on a dedicated Mediation server in Lync because you can frequently end up having to pay for a trunk per Front End member of a load-balanced pool. Given that this migration is in a test environment, not in a real environment, for the sake of minimizing resource requirements and because there is only one Front End server, you will maintain the colocation. You will come back to the EV migration shortly.

Although you'll deploy a Lync Edge server later, at this point you're deploying only the Standard Edition box, so don't use the "Enable an Edge pool to be used by the media component of this Front End pool" option.

Because you opted for a colocated Mediation server, the Topology Builder will prompt you to specify PSTN gateways. At this stage, you will enter none. This is something you will create at the relevant point of the migration. The SIP trunk (like many others) is configured to allow sending and receiving from a specific public IP address and to have certain DDI numbers assigned to it. This trunk is currently assigned to the OCS 2007 R2 Mediation server. Therefore, moving it to Lync at this point is not an option. You must first move all the users to Lync. At that point, you'll need to move the specific external IP address onto the Lync Mediation server and then set up the relevant routes. This, of course, will require an element of downtime, which can be scheduled well in advance. If this is not an option, an alternative would be to set up a second trunk homed on the Lync Mediation server and then gradually reassign the DDI numbers to the second trunk as users are moved. Clearly, this is more administratively complex and requires a second trunk; however, it would ensure that the service remains available throughout the migration.

Having configured the topology, complete the deployment of the Lync pool as covered in Chapter 6. To take care of permissions, remember to add the user installing Lync to the RTCUniversalServerAdministrators group and also add a Lync admin user to the CsAdministrator group.

CREATING THE CENTRAL MANAGEMENT STORE (CMS)

Even though you already have an OCS Standard Edition server, you still need to run the Prepare First Standard Edition Server Wizard to prep the SQL database on SE01 for the Central Management Store (CMS). Of course, you still need to have completed the Active Directory updates first!

Once you have finished, make sure that everything on OCS is still working and that you can add a pair of new users to the Lync pool and have them communicate between themselves. They will, of course, not be able to communicate externally or to users on the OCS system because you haven't enabled coexistence yet.

Merging the OCS and Lync Topology

At this point, you are ready to introduce the OCS and Lync systems to each other. As previously discussed, OCS and Lync use different structures to store configuration information, so to enable coexistence, you must enable these structures to interoperate. Otherwise, users in each environment will be unable to contact each other and will receive a Presence Unknown response as shown in Figure 7.5.

To do this, you must first install the Windows Management Instrumentation (WMI) Backward Compatibility Package on the Lync server. OCS stores configuration information in WMI, and this package enables Lync to understand that information and merge it into the Central Management Store (CMS).

FIGURE 7.5
Presence Unknown

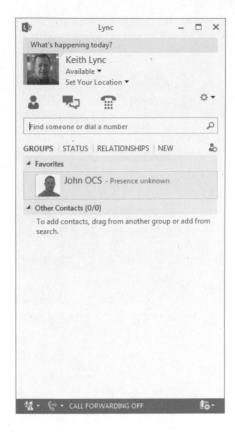

For this exercise, you will install the required component on the machine where the topology merge will be performed. In this case, you have only one, so it will be on the SE01 machine.

The component is located on the install media in the directory setup\amd64\setup\ ocswmibsc.msi. Running the MSI is a very quick process and doesn't require a reboot.

1. Open Topology Builder and have it pull down the configuration from the Central Management Store in the normal way. Under the Action menu, click Merge OCS 2007 R2 Topology.

2. When the Merge OCS 2007 R2 Topology Wizard opens, click Next.

3. The Specify Edge Setup window opens. This wizard allows you to specify the configuration of the Edge servers on OCS, where you should add all OCS Edge servers in the environment. To begin, click Add.

4. You are presented with a screen giving a choice of Edge configuration: Consolidated, Load Balanced, or Expanded. The Expanded Edge configuration was a potential OCS 2007 design where the different Edge roles (Access, Conferencing, and AV) were placed on separate servers. This design could have been carried over to OCS 2007 R2 as part of a migration. Lync does not support interoperating with this type of Edge setup, so if you have this setup, you will need to convert it back to either a load-balanced or single con-solidated Edge setup before you can migrate. In this case, select Single Edge Server and then click Next.

5. On the next page, specify the ports and fully qualified domain name (FQDN) at which you want to talk to the Edge. The default ports are populated automatically. For the FQDN, specify OCSEdge01.corp.masteringlync.org as shown in Figure 7.6, and then click Next.

FIGURE 7.6
Specifying the Edge server FQDN and ports

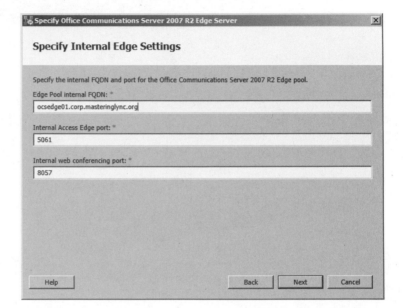

6. On the next screen, enter the FQDN of your external conferencing Edge NIC and the associated port, which again is populated with the default of 443. Assuming the Edge server to which you are connecting is your federation and Public IM connectivity host, check the box as shown in Figure 7.7.

7. Click Next and then enter the details of the next hop. Often this will be a system or pool of machines running as Directors, but in this small network you will connect directly to the OCS Front End on OCS01.corp.masteringlync.org, as shown in Figure 7.8. To com-plete the configuration, click Finish.

8. You will return to the Specify Edge Setup page, where you should click Next to continue or repeat the process if you have other OCS Edge installations.

9. The final step is to specify the internal SIP port on which Lync will communicate with OCS. Assuming you haven't changed this, stick with the default of 5061. If you have changed the ports for any of your internal pools, make sure they are all available and allow remote WMI access, and opt for the Automatic Discovery option. The automatic discovery service will attempt to locate your pools via the automatic discovery SRV records; if you use manual definitions for clients to locate servers, this will fail.

FIGURE 7.7
Selecting the Edge server/pool for federation

FIGURE 7.8
Configuring the next hop to the internal servers

10. To move to the Summary page, click Next, and click Next again to begin merging the topologies.

11. Once it is complete, click Next to review the process. You are given the option to view the XML config file, shown in Figure 7.9. Finally, click Finish to exit the Merge Wizard.

FIGURE 7.9
The XML representation of the configuration imported to Lync

```
<?xml version="1.0"?>
<TopologyInput xmlns="urn:schema:Microsoft.Rtc.Management.Deploy.LegacyUserInput.2008">
  <EdgeClusters>
    <EdgeCluster FederationEnabled="true" Version="OCS2007R2" DP="true" MR="true" AP="true">
      <LoadBalancer ExternalDPFqdn="ocswebconf.masteringlync.org" InternalFqdn="ocsedge01.corp.masteringlync.org"/>
      <Machines>
        <Machine InternalFqdn="ocsedge01.corp.masteringlync.org"/>
      </Machines>
      <DirectorOrEdgeNextHop IsDirector="false" Fqdn="ocs01.corp.masteringlync.org"/>
      <Ports InternalDPPort="8057" ExternalDPPort="443" InternalAPPort="5061"/>
    </EdgeCluster>
  </EdgeClusters>
  <RegistrarClusterPort Port="5061" EnableAutoDiscoveryOfPorts="false"/>
</TopologyInput>
```

Having completed the Merge Wizard, you will now see in Topology Builder a new element on the left pane, called BackCompatSite. This is the representation of the OCS environment in Lync topology format. You should check that it lists all the OCS pools in your environment and that it contains the Edge servers you defined in the wizard. Now that it is in the topology, you must publish the topology (a process described in Chapter 5), which will write it to the CMS and allow it to replicate among the Lync servers.

The Merge Wizard has given Lync the knowledge of the basic shape of the OCS deployment; for example, it now knows about OCS pools and Edge servers. However, what hasn't yet been brought across are the policies and configuration information, which is set on OCS. For example, version policies, dial plans, dial-in conferencing numbers, and voice routes are all configured in OCS but Lync knows nothing about them yet. To bring these settings across to Lync, you have to move into the PowerShell and run the Import-CsLegacyConfiguration cmdlet. (For more about PowerShell, see Chapter 8, "Introduction to PowerShell, the Lync Management Shell, and Regular Expressions.") Note when you run the command that if you have any policies in OCS that contain illegal characters such as the colon (:), you will see the warning shown in Figure 7.10. This is nothing to worry about and is simply for information.

FIGURE 7.10
Warning on import about illegal characters in OCS policy names

Once the command is run, when you're looking through the relevant areas of the Lync Server Control Panel (Control Panel) such as Voice Routing, Conferencing, and External User Access, you will see that the various objects mentioned now have configuration data from OCS. You will also see the OCS element show up on the Topology – Status section of the Control Panel. Of course, policies in Lync are more granular than those in OCS (as discussed in Chapter 10), so generally the global policy in Lync will be what has been updated. Elements to pay careful attention to are the dial-in conferencing numbers. They are also copied across to Lync; however, at this point, they are still homed on the OCS system and should continue to be modified there. Most important, with the dial-in conferencing numbers and other policy settings on OCS, anytime you change the configuration on OCS, you should again run the Import-CsLegacyConfiguration cmdlet.

If you want to see more details about your newly merged pool, run the following command:

```
Get-CsPool -Identity ocs01.corp.masteringlync.org
```

This will provide you with similar information to that shown in the LSCP Topology–Status section, and it will add information about services running on the pool.

Finally, check that the conferencing directories merged properly, by running this command:

```
Get-CsConferenceDirectory
```

This will show all conferencing directories where content is stored both on Lync and OCS. Sample output from the exercise environment is shown in Figure 7.11.

FIGURE 7.11

Displaying both OCS and Lync conferencing directories

Configuring the First Lync Pool

Now that the Lync pool knows about OCS, you need to configure Lync to properly utilize the OCS components, most importantly the Edge and Mediation servers. As with other major configuration changes, you do this in the Topology Builder with a user account that is a domain administrator and member of the RTCUniversalServerAdmins group.

To enable the Lync pool to use the OCS Edge server, you need to define a route for federation traffic:

1. To proceed, open the Topology Builder and download the configuration from the CMS. Next, right-click the site (in this case, EMEA) and select Edit Properties.

2. On the window that opens, in the left pane click Federation Route. In the Site Federation Route Assignment section at the bottom of the right pane, click Enable SIP Federation, and in the drop-down, select the OCS 2007 R2 Edge server you entered in the Merge Wizard previously, in this case ocsedge01.corp.masteringlync.org BackCompatSite Edge. See Figure 7.12. Click OK to save the settings.

3. At this point you must again publish the topology, as described in Chapter 5, to lock the changes into the CMS.

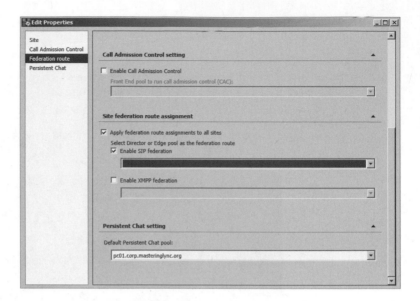

4. Once the topology is published, check the Notepad file for the next actions to see if you need to run local setup on any of your Lync servers. (You might need to run local setup on the Standard Edition server.)

If when trying to configure the federation route you see federation listed as Disabled, as in Figure 7.13, this is due to Lync Server 2013 determining federation as being disabled; check the configuration on the OCS servers to ensure that it is correctly enabled and that all the OCS servers have been imported into the topology (especially the Edge servers).

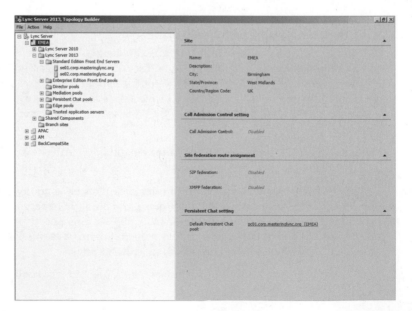

Having configured Lync, you must now move to the OCS side of things and ensure that the OCS servers actually trust the Lync Front End pool or Standard Edition server to communicate with it.

To do this, on your OCS Edge server run `Compmgmt.msc` to open the administrative console where you access the OCS Management tools under the Services And Applications node. Right-click the Office Communications Server 2007 R2 node and select Properties. Navigate to the Internal tab, and then at the bottom of the window in the Internal Servers Authorized To Connect To This Edge Server section, click Add Server. Add the FQDN of the internal Lync Standard Edition server (or Front End pool) as shown in Figure 7.14 and click OK. If you have more than one Lync server pool that will use this Edge server, you will also enter those server FQDNs at this time. Likewise, if you are using Directors in your Lync pool, the FQDN of the Director (or Director pool) will need to be added here. Once you have added all the necessary server FQDNs, click OK to complete the process. At this point, the new Lync pool is configured to use the OCS Edge server. Of course, you will also need to make sure the OCS Edge server can resolve the new Lync servers. If you are using an internal DNS server on your OCS Edge, that shouldn't be a problem. However, if you are using a HOSTS file, be sure to add entries for the new Lync servers. Finally, make sure communication is not blocked by firewalls, as discussed in Chapter 3, "Security."

FIGURE 7.14

Authorizing the new Lync server on the OCS Edge

At this point, you can address the other element of configuration, ensuring that the Lync servers can access the OCS Mediation server. Of course, if you are not using Enterprise Voice in your environment, you can skip this step.

Because you already have functional voice routes on OCS 2007 R2, they will have been brought across to Lync by merging the topology and configuration. You can check that this was the case by opening the Control Panel and selecting the Voice Routing tab. You should see your location profiles on the Dial Plan tab and the route to your gateway or SIP trunk on the Route tab.

The final step before you move on to user migration is Unified Messaging integration with Exchange. Given that you have UM-enabled users in this environment, it is important that this functionality continues to work once users are migrated to Lync. To ensure that this is possible, on your Exchange UM server you must rerun the ExchUCUtil.ps1 script, which you ran as part of UM setup. This script and its function are described in Chapter 17, "Exchange and SharePoint." For now, though, you will see that it creates a new IP gateway representing the new Lync Front End server and maps it to the existing dial plan. Now that you have carried out this configuration, voice mail will continue to work once you migrate users.

Testing and Migrating Pilot Users

Now you're ready to see if the coexistence really works and begin migrating a handful of users over to the new Lync pool.

The first thing you need to verify is that simple communication is possible between the Lync users you created earlier in the chapter. Test the basic Lync installation and the OCS users. You should test all normal communication methods such as IM, voice, and video. Equally, you should test with combinations of users internal to the network and external to the network for both Lync and OCS users.

Obviously, testing will be different for different organizations because you will use a variety of features and functions. As a starting point, refer to the test plans at the following location:

```
http://technet.microsoft.com/en-us/library/gg425729.aspx
```

Please be aware that this URL points to content created for Lync Server 2010. As the time of writing, this content was not available for Lync Server 2013; however, because these test are primarily integration tests, the fact that there are new workloads introduced with Lync Server 2013 is irrelevant because you cannot test these new workloads using old clients. So, this test plan is still valid.

Once you are sure that basic communication is possible, it is time to migrate your first user from OCS to Lync. This can be done either through PowerShell or in the Control Panel. Note that users are essentially pulled across to Lync using the Lync tools rather than being pushed across using the OCS tools.

To move a user in the Control Panel, you must open and log on to Control Panel as a member of either the RTCUniversalServerAdmins group or the CsAdministrator or CsUserAdministrator RBAC roles. Once in Control Panel, navigate to the Users tab. On the right pane, don't enter any search text and click Add Filter. Make sure the query drop-downs read Office Communications Server User (for migrations from OCS 2007 and OCS 2007 R2, this drop-down referred to Legacy User), Equal To, and True. Click Find. This will return a list of all users on Lync, as shown in Figure 7.15.

At this point you should choose a suitable user or group of users to migrate to Lync. Once you have selected the user or users that you want to move, click the Action drop-down and select Move Selected Users To Pool. This opens a dialog in which you select the pool to move to from the drop-down and then click OK.

MOVING BACK TO OCS

You can, of course, also move users back to Lync by locating the user in the Control Panel and then, instead of selecting the Lync pool when prompted, moving the user to the OCS pool.

FIGURE 7.15
Using Control Panel
to search for legacy
users

If instead you want to perform the migration from PowerShell, you can use the following commands. First, get a list of all OCS users, using this command:

```
Get-CsUser -OnOfficeCommunicationServer | Select-Object SamAccountName,
SipAddress
```

This will output a list of accounts and display only the SamAccountName parameter and the important SipAddress, as shown here:

```
SamAccountName   SipAddress
--------------   ----------
jo_OCS           sip:jo_ocs@masteringlync.org
john_ocs         sip:john_ocs@masteringlync.org
                 sip:OCSAA.OCSDialPlan.corp.masteringlync.org@masteringlync.org
                 sip:OCSDialPlan.corp.masteringlync.org@masteringlync.org
```

Next, choose the user you want to migrate. In this example, you'll migrate jo_ocs. To move the user, run the following command:

```
Move-CsLegacyUser -Identity "sip:jo_ocs@masteringlync.org"
-Target "se01.corp.masteringlync.org"
```

If the user is logged on at this time, they will be logged off and then Office Communicator will automatically log them back on. When the user does get logged back on, they will still use DNS entries that point users to the OCS server to log on. OCS will redirect them to the Lync server so the user can log on. Later in the process, you will change these DNS records to point users to the Lync server.

To validate that the move occurred correctly, run this command:

```
Get-CsUser sip:jo_ocs@masteringlync.org
```

In the output shown here, you can see that the RegistrarPool is now our Lync server:

```
Identity                   : CN=Jo OCS,OU=Users,DC=corp,DC=masteringlync,DC=org
VoicePolicy                :
VoiceRoutingPolicy         :
ConferencingPolicy         :
PresencePolicy             :
DialPlan                   : OCSDialPlan.corp.masteringlync.org
LocationPolicy             :
ClientPolicy               :
ClientVersionPolicy        :
ArchivingPolicy            :
ExchangeArchivingPolicy    : Uninitialized
PinPolicy                  :
ExternalAccessPolicy       : Allow No Access
MobilityPolicy             :
PersistenChatPolicy        :
HostedVoiceMail            :
HostedVoicemailPolicy      :
HostingProvider            : SRV:
RegistrarPool              : se01.corp.masteringlync.org
Enabled                    : True
SipAddress                 : sip:jo_ocs@masteringlync.org
LineURI                    : tel:+445554444444
EnterpriseVoiceEnabled     : True
ExUMEnabled                : True
HomeServer                 : CN=Lc Services,CN=Microsoft,CN=1:1,CN=Pools,
CN=RTC Service,CN=Services,CN=Configuration,DC=corp,DC=masteringlync,DC=org
DisplayName                : Jo OCS
SamAccountName             : jo_ocs
```

Finally, if you want to move multiple users or even all OCS users using LSMS, the following two commands should be used. First, to move a selection of users:

```
Get-CsUser -Filter {DisplayName -eq "Jo OCS" -or DisplayName - eq "John OCS"} |
Move-CsLegacyUser -Target "se01.corp.masteringlync.org"
```

That command would move both Jo OCS and John OCS to se01.corp.masteringlync.org pool. Alternatively, if you want to move all OCS users to Lync, then the following command would be needed:

```
Get-CsUser -OnOfficeCommunicationServer | Move-CsLegacyUser -Target
"se01.corp.masteringlync.org"
```

This command gets all the OCS users and pipes them to the Move-CsLegacyUser cmdlet, which moves them to Lync.

As you may recall, once the user has been migrated, they won't have access to a bunch of new functionality until the clients are updated. Another thing to remember is that policies and configuration from OCS are brought across to Lync during the configuration import and topology merge. While you are testing, you should make sure that policies that were brought across are working as expected for both Lync and OCS users and that any archiving and monitoring servers (see Chapter 11) are performing adequately.

USER REPLICATION ERROR PREVENTS MIGRATION

If a migration fails with an error including the text "...the user is not provisioned," you may find that user replication from AD to Lync hasn't finished. This is particularly likely if you have a large number of users in AD and you haven't waited very long since getting Lync up and running before starting the migration. To verify that replication has completed, use the following steps:

1. Log on to the computer where Topology Builder is installed as a member of the Domain Admins group and the RTCUniversalServerAdmins group.

2. Click the Start menu, and then click Run.

3. Type **eventvwr.exe** and then click OK.

4. In Event Viewer, click Applications And Services Logs to expand it, and then select Lync Server.

5. In the Actions pane, click Filter Current Log.

6. From the Event sources list, click LS User Replicator.

7. In <All Event IDs>, enter **30024** and then click OK.

8. In the filtered events list, on the General tab, look for an entry stating that user replication has completed successfully.

JOINING CONFERENCES CREATED BY A LYNC USER

Lync Server 2013 conferences have different connectivity requirements than previous versions (including both OCS and Lync), so it's important that once you have migrated users to the new server infrastructure, you also start to update the clients.

The preference is for users using legacy clients to connect via Lync Web App because they will get better user experience and functionality than by continuing to use their legacy client.

Another conferencing issue is the ability of federated users to attend Lync meetings. You must verify that the conferencing policy assigned to the Lync user has the Allow Participants To Invite Anonymous Users check box selected.

Adding Lync Edge and Director Roles

At this point, you can happily leave the system running. Users are now working on Lync and can communicate with users on OCS both internally and externally and with federated users. Equally, if you have rolled out the Lync client to the newly migrated Lync users, those who have been migrated to Lync can now use the new Lync functionality—for example, the enhanced conferencing and sharing capabilities. However, you are now essentially supporting two systems, OCS and Lync, so you need to begin the process of making sure Lync can start to take up all workloads. The first step to that end is to configure the components that will allow native Lync external access. Most of the configuration steps were discussed in depth in Chapter 6; we'll highlight the important steps of the migration process here.

The first step will be to configure the Reverse Proxy server to publish the Lync web services externally. Key elements to consider are that you will need a second public IP address on the reverse proxy to publish the Lync components and that you must have the required certificates. In this case, you are not using the Director role, so you will simply put the Meet and Dial-in URLs on the main Lync Standard Edition certificate and publish them on the main Lync web publishing rule as you did for the Director in Chapter 6. Had we been deploying an Enterprise Edition pool, we'd also need to publish the pool external web services URL also.

Next, you must configure the Lync Edge server. The first part of this is to define a Lync Edge server in the Lync topology using Topology Builder, as described in Chapter 5. While defining this topology, it's important that you do not configure this Edge pool to be the route for federation; leave the option unchecked as shown in Figure 7.16.

FIGURE 7.16
When configuring the Edge topology, don't enable federation.

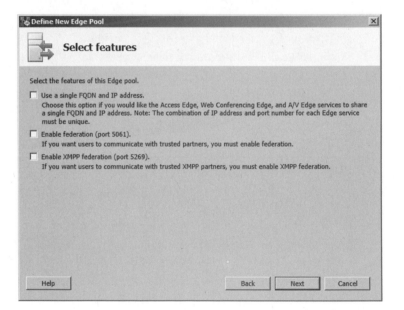

To continue, progress through the Topology Builder (described in Chapter 5), entering the URLs and IP addresses. When prompted, select the Lync Standard Edition (or Front End pool) as the next hop. When prompted on the Associate Front End Pools page, do not associate the Edge server with the Lync Front End. You'll do this later, so leave the settings as shown in Figure 7.17.

Once the Edge installation is complete, make sure as always that the servers are patched and that the latest Lync CU is installed on all Lync boxes including the Edge.

FIGURE 7.17
Make sure you don't associate the Edge with the Lync Front End pool.

 Real World Scenario

WHAT ABOUT MIGRATION FROM LYNC SERVER 2010?

This chapter covers migrating to Lync Server 2013 from OCS 2007 R2. However, it is also possible (and significantly easier) to migrate from Lync Server 2010. If you are doing that, there are a few differences and quite a few similarities to the process and some real-world tips that can help you avoid trouble.

First, schema, forest, and domain prep all still need to be executed; the changes with Lync Server 2013 are above and beyond those deployed in Lync Server 2010.

Lync Server 2010 servers will all need to be updated to a minimum of Cumulative Update (CU) 5.

Upon installing the Lync Server 2013 admin tools, Topology Builder will show the "new" topology tree format rather the Lync Server 2010 view:

- Lync Server
  - \<sitename\>
    - Lync Server 2010
    - Lync Server 2013
    - Shared Components
    - Branch Sites

However, using Lync Server 2010 Topology Builder *after* publishing any changes from the Lync Server 2013 Topology Builder will result in the following error: "The topology is from a later version of the product. Use the correct version of Topology Builder to open this topology."

This experience is similar to administration in that only Lync Server 2013 tools can be used to manage Lync Server 2013; however, Lync Server 2010 tools (PowerShell and Control Panel) must be used to continue to manage the Lync Server 2010 environment.

The actual migration steps and process are very similar to those outlined in this chapter for migrating from OCS 2007 R2.

Moving users, contacts, and other objects is much easier because the commands are the same as the commands you would use if you were moving to another Lync Server 2010 pool; that is, `move-csuser` rather than the individualized `move-cslegacyuser` as used when migrating from OCS 2007 R2.

Some data cannot be migrated, such as Archiving and Monitoring databases. These have slightly different database schemas and therefore are incompatible with Lync Server 2013. If you need to store the data for a period of time, the recommended approach is to create new database instances for Lync Server 2013 and leave the Lync Server 2010 data in its current databases until no longer needed.

Pilot first, and test thoroughly, before moving the main infrastructure such as Edge (federation and remote access), media routes. and finally, simple URLs.

Because users will be using a Lync client already, meetings will continue after migrations and the user experience should be relatively painless.

Once migrated, then it's time to introduce new features such as XMPP federation, Persistent Chat, and so on, and obviously these are the feature sets that rely upon the client being upgraded.

For a more detailed view of the migration from OCS 2007 to Lync 2010, see the following TechNet article:

```
http://technet.microsoft.com/en-us/library/gg412976.aspx
```

Moving the First Lync Pool from Pilot to Production

Now you are at the stage where the majority of the Lync components are installed and configured and you are ready to start moving the bulk of services and the remaining users across to Lync. The first thing you'll need to do is enable the Lync Edge server as the route out for federation and media traffic. Make sure you schedule a little downtime for external access and federation. As noted earlier, the FQDNs for all services on the OCS Edge differ from those on the Lync Edge. Although this means that you need an additional certificate, it does keep things clean and allows you to have everything set up and ready to move, without having to juggle service names and DNS entries.

1. To begin the process, log on to the Lync Front End (or Standard Edition) box as a member of the RTCUniversalServerAdmins and Domain Admins groups.

2. Open Topology Builder and download the topology from the CMS. Right-click the site with your first Lync pool in it (in this case, the EMEA site) and select Edit Properties.

3. In the window that opens, in the left pane, click Federation Route. Then in the right pane under Site Federation Route Assignment, uncheck Enable SIP Federation, as shown in Figure 7.18. Then click OK, and publish the topology. This has disabled the route for the Lync pool to federate out through the OCS Edge server.

FIGURE 7.18
Disabling the federation route for the Lync pool

Next, you need to rerun the Merge 2007 R2 Topology Wizard so you can reconfigure the legacy Edge defined within it:

1. To do this, while still in Topology Builder in the Actions pane, click Merge 2007 R2 Topology.

2. On the first page, click Next; this takes you to the Specify Edge Setup page. Select the Edge server defined (in this case ocsedge01.corp.masteringlync.org) and click Change.

3. Then click through the wizard until you get to the Specify External Edge page. Clear the check box by This Edge Pool Is Used For Federation And Public IM Connectivity, as shown in Figure 7.19, and then click Next through to the end of the wizard, keeping the default settings.

Once the merge completes, you will likely see the following warning:

```
No Office Communications Server 2007 / Office Communications Server 2007 R2
Edge Has Been Enabled For Federation.
```

This is expected. Again, you need to publish the topology.

FIGURE 7.19
Ensuring that the
OCS Edge isn't used
for federation

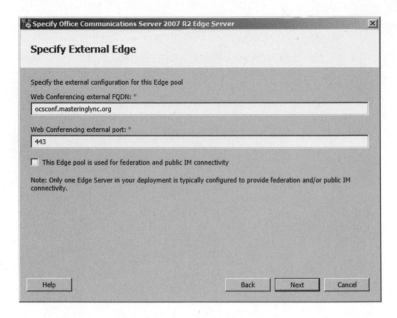

Now you are ready to move across to the OCS system and configure it to use the Lync Edge for federation:

1. Log on to the OCS Front End server (OCS01.corp.masteringlync.org) as a member of the RTCUniversalServerAdmins group.

2. Open the OCS Admin tool, and in the left pane, right-click the forest and select Global Properties. In the window that opens, navigate to the Federation tab and enter the internal URL of the Lync Edge server, in our case edgepool.corp.masteringlync.org, as shown in Figure 7.20. To complete the process, click OK.

FIGURE 7.20
Reconfiguring OCS
to federate through
the Lync edge

You're almost done; what remains is to make the Lync Edge server live. You do this back in Topology Builder:

1. Right-click the Standard Edition server and click Edit Properties.

2. In the window that opens, scroll down to the Associations section, and on the drop-down in the Associate Edge Pool (For Media Components) section, ensure that the Lync Edge is selected, as shown in Figure 7.21.

FIGURE 7.21
Routing Lync pool media traffic out of the Lync Edge

3. Click OK, and then back in the Topology Builder, in the left pane right-click the Lync Edge pool and select Edit Properties.

4. In the General section, check the box next to Enable Federation For This Edge Pool (Port 5061), as shown in Figure 7.22. Then click OK and republish the topology.

5. Finally, we need to re-enable federation at the site level. Right-click the site, and select Edit Properties, then Federation Route. Select Enable SIP Federation, and in the drop-down box, select the Edge server. See Figure 7.23.

6. On the Publishing Wizard Complete page, check whether any further steps are needed and carry them out. For example, you might be requested to run local setup on the Lync Edge server.

Now it is time to ensure that your firewalls and DNS entries are configured correctly for the Lync Edge server as described in Chapter 3.

Then you'll need to reconfigure the DNS SRV records so that all external traffic for federation and remote access will be pointed at the Lync Edge server. This will involve updating the _sip._tls.masteringlync.org SRV record and the _sipfederationtls._tcp.masteringlync.org SRV records so they will be served by the accessedge.masteringlync.org host.

FIGURE 7.22
Enabling federation
on the Lync Edge
pool

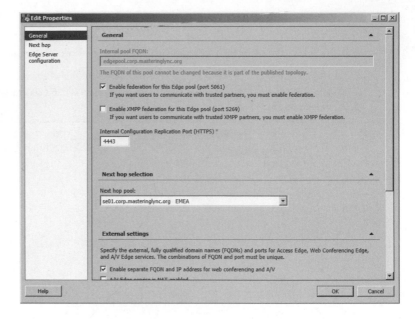

FIGURE 7.23
Re-enabling federa-
tion at the site level

All that remains is to log onto the OCS Edge server, where you can stop and disable all the Office Communications Server services. You can also remove the entries allowing access for the OCS Edge from your firewalls and the external DNS entries for the box.

POLICIES TO ENABLE EXTERNAL ACCESS AND FEDERATION

We've already said it a number of times, but just to be absolutely clear, once you move the federation and media over to travel through the Lync Edge server, the Lync policies governing external access and federation come into play. In the Control Panel on the External Access policy, make sure you enable external access and federation on both the External Access policy and the Access Edge configuration.

Now that you've configured the Edge so that federation and media traffic flows through it, you are ready to move the Exchange UM contact objects to Lync. This is a two-step process. First, you move the Subscriber and Auto Attendant contact objects over to the Lync server and then update the Exchange UM server so it knows about the new Lync pool. To move the contact objects, log onto the Lync Front End (or Standard Edition) server as a member of at least the RTCUniversalUserAdmins group or CsUserAdministrator RBAC role and open PowerShell.

Get the contacts that exist, using the cmdlet `Get-CsExUmContact`. This will bring back all Exchange UM contact objects in the forest, so to narrow it down, use the following command to specify objects for migration by display name:

```
Get-CsExUmContact | where {$_.DisplayName -eq "OCSDialPlan" -or "OCSDialPlanSA"}
```

This will get only the objects named `OCSUMAuto` and `OCSUMSubscriber`, as shown in the following output:

```
Identity             : CN=OCSDialPlan,OU=Contacts,DC=corp,DC=masteringlync,
DC=org
RegistrarPool        :
HomeServer           : CN=LC Services,CN=Microsoft,CN=OCS-SE01,CN=Pools,CN=RTC
                       Service,CN=Services,CN=Configuration,DC=corp,
                       DC=masteringlync,DC=org
Enabled              : True
SipAddress           : sip:OCSAA.OCSDialPlan.corp.masteringlync.org@
masteringlync.org
LineURI              : tel:+445554410000
OtherIpPhone         : {sip:OCSAA.OCSDialPlan.corp.masteringlync.org@
masteringlync.org;opaque=app:exum:OCSDialPlan.corp.masteringlync.org:OCSAA}
AutoAttendant        : True
IsSubscriberAccess   : False
Description          : Exchange UM Auto-Attendant
DisplayName          : OCSDialPlan
DisplayNumber        : +445554410000
HostedVoicemailPolicy :
ExUmEnabled          : False

Identity             : CN=OCSDialPlanSA,OU=UMContacts,DC=DC=corp,
DC=masteringlync,DC=org
RegistrarPool        :
HomeServer           : CN=LC Services,CN=Microsoft,CN=OCS-SE01,CN=Pools,CN=RTC
                       Service,CN=Services,CN=Configuration,DC=corp,
```

```
                                    DC=masteringlync,DC=org
Enabled                 : True
SipAddress              : sip:OCSDialPlan.corp.masteringlync.org@masteringlync.org
LineURI                 : tel:+44554420000
OtherIpPhone            : {sip:OCSDialPlan.corp.masteringlync.org@
masteringlync.org;opaque=app:exum:OCSDialPlan.corp.masteringlync.org}
AutoAttendant           : True
IsSubscriberAccess      : False
Description             : Exchange UM Subscriber Access
DisplayName             : OCSDialPlanSA
DisplayNumber           : +445554420000
HostedVoicemailPolicy   :
ExUmEnabled             :
```

At this point, you have confirmed that you have the correct objects and you will pipe the output of the previous command into the `Move-CsExUmContact` cmdlet as follows:

```
Get-CsExUmContact | where {$_.DisplayName -eq "OCSDialPlan" -or "OCSDialPlanSA"}
| Move-CsExUmContact -Target "se01.corp.masteringlync.org"
```

This will move the previously mentioned contact objects to the `se01.corp.masteringlync.org` pool. Now that the contact objects have been moved, you need to run the `ExchUCUtil.ps1` script on the Exchange UM server again to ensure that all entries are updated as described in Chapter 17. Having run the script, restart the Lync Front End service on all the Lync Front End or Standard Edition servers so they'll pick up the changes.

The next components that need to be moved across to Lync are your response groups. Response groups are covered in depth in Chapter 16, so we'll simply cover the migration steps here. First, download and install the SQL Server 2005 native client on the Lync server where you will perform the migration, in this case the Standard Edition server. This is required because the database where the configuration is held on the OCS 2007 R2 server is running on SQL 2005. If another version were being used, you would need to use the appropriate client. The required version of the SQL 2005 native client is part of the feature pack for Microsoft SQL Server 2005 – December 2008. Specifically, it is the `sqlncli.msi` package, and it can be downloaded from the Microsoft Download Center here:

```
http://go.microsoft.com/fwlink/?LinkId=204105
```

Because your Lync server is running Windows 2008 Server R2, which is a 64-bit OS, you should download the 64-bit version. The installation process consists of simply accepting the defaults and clicking through the installation.

Once that process is complete, make sure you are logged on as a member of the RTCUniversalServerAdmins group and then open PowerShell. Then run the following command to migrate the configuration across to the new Lync pool:

```
Move-CsRgsConfiguration -Source ocs01.corp.masteringlync.org
-Destination se01.corp.masteringlync.org
```

This command will read the Response Group service configuration from the database on the OCS pool and bring it across to the Lync pool. You should note that the command will bring all the information from the OCS source pool over to the Lync destination pool. There is no way to be more granular. If you need to move any more components around, perhaps to split up pools, do it after you have moved everything across to Lync. Once you have run the command, in typical PowerShell fashion there will be no output if it is successful. To verify that the configuration has moved correctly, you can run the following commands. First, run:

```
Get-CsRgsAgentGroup
```

This brings back the agent groups you set up, and its output will be as follows:

```
Identity                  : service:ApplicationServer:se01.corp.masteringlync.
org/58db633d-179c-4681-ac29-5478deb0f134
Name                      : Agent Group 1
Description               :
ParticipationPolicy       : Informal
AgentAlertTime            : 20
RoutingMethod             : RoundRobin
DistributionGroupAddress  :
AgentsByUri               : {sip:jo_ocs@masteringlync.org,sip:john_ocs@
masteringlync.org}
```

Here is the next verification cmdlet:

```
Get-CsRgsQueue
```

This will bring back a list of the queues that you had set up, which in this case is RG Queue 1, as shown in the following output:

```
Identity          : service:ApplicationServer:se01.corp.masteringlync.org/
0584762b-b2f7-4562-87a7-09159f686944
TimeoutAction     : Action=Terminate
OverflowAction    : Action=Terminate
Name              : RG Queue 1
Description       :
TimeoutThreshold  :
OverflowThreshold :
OverflowCandidate : NewestCall
AgentGroupIDList  : {service:ApplicationServer:se01.corp.masteringlync.org/
58db633d-179c-4681-ac29-5478deb0f134}
```

Finally, check on the workflows:

```
Get-CsRgsWorkflow
```

This command brings back a list of the workflows you have set up, which includes the IT Helpdesk workflow set up in the example.

```
Identity               : service:ApplicationServer:se01.corp.masteringlync.org/
2682ac21-7df7-454a-a272-52089640f92d
NonBusinessHoursAction : Action=Terminate
HolidayAction          : Action=Terminate
DefaultAction          : Prompt=Hi, Welcome to the IT Helpdesk.
                         Action=TransferToQueue
                         QueueId=0584762b-b2f7-4562-87a7-09159f686944

CustomMusicOnHoldFile  :
Name                   : Helpdesk
Description            : IT Helpdesk
PrimaryUri             : sip:helpdesk@masteringlync.org
Active                 : True
Language               : en-US
```

```
TimeZone              : GMT Standard Time
BusinessHoursID       : Service:1-ApplicationServer-1/2242b88a-168e-4ba4-a218-
                        2cc7ac2421d1
Anonymous             : False
DisplayNumber         : +445554490000
EnabledForFederation  : False
LineUri               : tel:+445554490000
HolidaySetIDList      : {}
```

Of course, if you want, you can see all this from the Control Panel, as shown in Figure 7.24.

FIGURE 7.24
Verify that the Response Group settings have migrated into the Control Panel.

The last test is performed by making a call into the newly created IT Helpdesk workflow to see if it still works for both internal and external OCS and Lync users, where both Lync and OCS users are agents and calling parties.

MORE COMPLEX RESPONSE GROUPS WITH AGENT SIGN ON

The Response Group system in OCS and now Lync is a very flexible application, and we've only scratched the surface. One thing worth mentioning, and covered in depth in Chapter 16, is that agents can be required to log into an agent group via a tab added to the OCS client—in which case, users will still be using the OCS 2007 R2 client after they move to Lync. As part of the migration, you will need to make sure users log into the new URL by updating the customer tab definition file with the new URL, which in a Standard Edition deployment will be similar to this:

    https://ocs01.corp.masteringlync.org/RgsClients/Tab.aspx

(If you are using Enterprise Edition, use the Web URL for the pool.)

Once users move to the Lync client, that client will pick up the URL automatically and prompt the users to sign in.

Now that you have moved all the main pieces across to Lync, there will be limited disruption from here on. You are ready to migrate the remaining OCS users across to Lync; do that following the procedure covered previously in the section "Testing and Migrating Pilot Users."

Postmigration Steps

Congratulations! Having moved all your users and main services across to Lync, you are now in production. Of course, a few areas still need to be tidied up a bit. The most disruptive of these is the migration of the Mediation server to Lync, alongside moving the dial-in access numbers.

TELEPHONY

Because telephony is usually a critical subsystem, it is important to schedule a period of downtime for this piece of the migration. The outage should be very short, but give yourself peace of mind and do it on a weekend or late evening. Start by moving the dial-in conferencing access numbers over from the OCS 2007 R2 pool:

1. The first step is to log on to your OCS Front End or Standard Edition server as a member of the RTCUniversalServerAdmins group and open up the OCS administrator console.

2. In the left pane, right-click the forest and select Conferencing Attendant Properties. On the window that opens, on the Access Phone Numbers tab, sort the entries by clicking the Service By Pool column heading. Double-click any entries serviced by the legacy OCS pool to open the Edit Conferencing Attendant Number window.

3. In the new window, copy the SIP URI, shown in Figure 7.25, which you will need to use in the PowerShell command used to migrate the conferencing attendant number to Lync. Once you have copied all the Sip URIs, close the Properties page.

FIGURE 7.25
Making a note of the SIP URI of the conferencing attendant number

4. Now that you have the SIP URI for all conferencing attendant numbers, move over to the Lync Front End server and open PowerShell. Run the following command, making sure to use your SIP URI rather than the example shown here:

```
Move-CsApplicationEndpoint -Identity sip:Microsoft.Rtc.Applications.Caa-
7ACD4071-F209-4469-91D7-1FF131EA6697@masteringlync.org
-TargetApplicationPool se01.corp.masteringlync.org
```

5. Repeat this process for each of the conference attendant numbers. When you're done, move back to the OCS server and reopen the Conferencing Attendant Properties window to check that none of the conferencing attendant numbers are serviced by the legacy OCS pool.

This should complete the move of the conferencing attendant numbers. Now you still need to move the conferencing directories hosted on OCS over to Lync. This step is important because it enables all migrated meetings to continue working. If you miss it, users will have to set up all their meetings again.

1. Verify that you can correctly access the relevant directories. To do so, run the following command:

```
Get-CsConferenceDirectory | Where-Object {$_.ServiceID -match
"ocs01.corp.masteringlync.org"}
```

This gets the conference directories that are hosted on the OCS pool as shown here:

```
Identity          : 3
ServiceId         : UserServer:ocs01.corp.masteringlync.org
TargetServerIfMoving :
Id                : 3
Fingerprint       :
Element           : <ConferenceDirectory Id="3"
xmlns="urn:schema:Microsoft.Rtc.Management.Settings.PstnConf.2008">
                    <ServiceId xmlns="urn:schema:Microsoft.Rtc.
Management.Deploy.Topology.2008" SiteId="BackCompatSite" RoleName="UserServices"
Instance="1"/>
                    <UpaSeparator xmlns="urn:schema:Microsoft.Rtc.
Management.BaseTypes.2008"></UpaSeparator></ConferenceDirectory>
```

2. Make a note of the Identity (a numeric value) because you will need it to migrate the directory. To migrate the conference directories, use the following command:

```
Move-CsConferenceDirectory -Identity 3 -TargetPool se01.corp.masteringlync.org
```

This command moves the conference directory over to the Lync pool. That completes the conferencing number and directory migration, so you are ready to migrate the Mediation server across to Lync.

3. You already have the Mediation server enabled on the Lync Front End server, so you need to configure it. Open the Topology Builder, making sure you are logged on as a member of the RTCUniversalServerAdmins and Domain Admins groups, and download the configuration from the CMS. In the left pane, locate the Front End server, right-click it, and select Edit Properties. In the left pane of the new window, click Mediation Server. Depending on your PSTN connection, you will need to configure this section

appropriately. (See Chapter 13, "Getting Started with Voice," and Chapter 19, "Third-Party Integration," for more information.) You are connecting to a SIP trunk, which needs to listen on port 5060, so first check the box to enable the TCP port and enter **5060** in the data entry box, as shown in Figure 7.26.

The default listed will be 5067 as this is a secured SIP connection; however, in our case we have been told by the provider to use 5060.

FIGURE 7.26
Configuring the
Mediation server

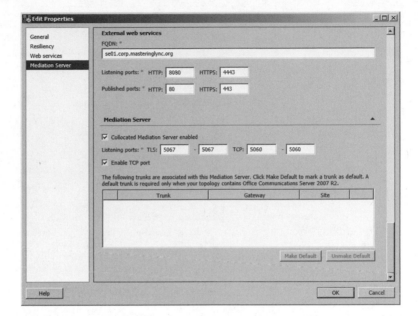

4. Next, open the Shared Components section, right-click PSTN gateways, and select New IP/PSTN Gateway. In the dialog that opens, configure the IP or URL for the gateway and select Next. The next page is for defining the IP address in use (and whether IPv6 is enabled). Clicking Next will take you to the Define The Root Trunk page. Here you need to define and enter the relevant port and protocol information (for this example, that is TCP port 5060, as shown in Figure 7.27), as well as define the associated mediation server (or pool).

5. Click Finish to accept the changes and then publish the topology. If prompted at the end of publishing, rerun local setup on the Lync Front End server.

You are now ready to swap the external IP address, which is the endpoint for the SIP trunk, from the OCS Mediation server over to the Lync Front End server. Your downtime will begin now. Once you have configured the networking on the Lync Front End server appropriately, as it was on the OCS Mediation server, go back into the Topology Builder and download the configuration from the CMS. Then, in the left pane, right-click the Front End server and click Edit Properties.

We're modifying the Front End server entry in this case because it is a collocated Mediation server. If we had a stand-alone Mediation server, we'd be carrying out this step on the Mediation server.

FIGURE 7.27
Setting up a new
PSTN gateway

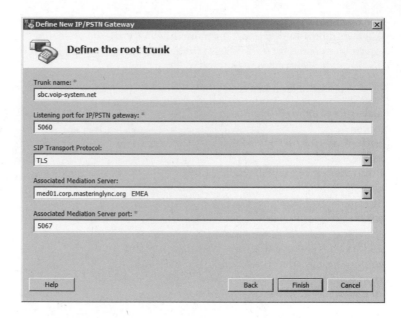

In the General section, click Limit Service Usage To Selected IP Addresses. In the Primary IP address box, enter the LAN address of the server, and in the PSTN IP Address box, enter the newly moved SIP trunk public IP address, as shown in Figure 7.28. Click OK and then publish the topology.

FIGURE 7.28
Configuring the
Lync server service
IP addresses

Now you have a functioning Mediation server that is set up to communicate with your PSTN gateway using the external NIC. The final step is to set up a new voice route so that traffic knows to use the new gateway. This is done in Control Panel, and you need to be logged on as a user who has at least the CsVoiceAdministrator role.

1. In the Control Panel on the left pane, click the Voice Routing tab and then navigate to the Route tab on the right pane. Click New to start creating a new route. Give the policy a name and then scroll down to the Associated Trunks section and click Add.

2. In the window that opens, select the new PSTN gateway you just created and click OK. Next, scroll down to the Associated PSTN Usages section and click Select.

3. On the Select PSTN Usage Record page, select Default Usage or another appropriate usage and then click OK. For more information about usages and when and where they should be used, see Chapter 13.

4. Back on the New Voice Route page, click OK to create the voice route. Select the newly created route and click Move Up until the newly created route is at the top of the list.

5. Finally, click Commit and then select Commit All. On the Summary page, click Commit to apply the changes and then click Close.

OCS GATEWAYS AND LYNC

If you are using media gateways to connect your OCS server to the PSTN, you will need to upgrade them with either new hardware or new software when you move to Lync because OCS gateways don't support the necessary encryption features that Lync requires. For more on gateways, see Chapter 19, "Third-Party Integration."

WEB

Having completed the telephony-related aspects of the migration, you can finish the web aspects. Specifically, you will reconfigure the CWA server to work with the Lync pool and enable the Lync pool for integration with Exchange 2010 SP1 (or greater) Outlook Web App (OWA) to provide IM and presence access in OWA. You'll begin by redirecting Communicator Web Access (CWA). As you know, Lync doesn't provide a native fully functional IM and presence web application as of CU3, so you must maintain the use of the OCS 2007 R2 CWA server until this functionality is added to Lync natively.

1. To do so, log on to your CWA server as a member of the local Administrators group and the RTCUniversalServerAdmins group, and open the CWA MMC snap-in.

2. In the left pane, expand the name of the computer that hosts the virtual server for which you want to specify a next-hop server (in this case, OCSCWA01.corp.masteringlync.org), and then right-click the name of the virtual server and select Properties.

3. In the window that opens, navigate to the Next Hop tab. From the Next Hop Pool drop-down, select the Lync pool (se01.corp.masteringlync.org). Unless you have changed it, you can leave the listening port at the default of 5061.

4. Click OK. You have now repointed CWA to the Lync pool. To verify functionality, you should log on to CWA to test.

To complete the web elements of the migration, you need to enable Lync integration with Exchange OWA. See Chapter 17 for an in-depth description of the process.

THIRD-PARTY APPLICATIONS

The last server-based piece of the migration concerns third-party applications. There are a variety of types; some, such as videoconferencing units, are defined in Lync as trusted application pools. They need to be configured so that they point to the Lync pool as the next hop. This is performed in Topology Builder and is covered in Chapter 19. The other type of application is the type built on a version of UCMA earlier than v3.0. These applications cannot be run on Lync Server and so must be rewritten and then deployed on Lync. That topic is beyond the scope of this book, and you should speak with the vendor who built the application to migrate them.

Now that everything is migrated, you can move the internal SRV records that currently direct clients to the OCS pool so that they point to the Lync pool.

CLIENT ROLLOUT

The final piece of the migration is to complete the rollout of the Lync client along with the same level of cumulative update as is deployed on your Lync servers. Some considerations for the rollout of the Lync client are as follows:

◆ Use client version filtering rules on the Lync Front End to ensure that only clients with the correct updates installed are able to sign in, as described in Chapter 3.

◆ As discussed earlier in this chapter, you may need to configure the Group Policy settings that are required for client bootstrapping.

◆ Ensure that you have all the required policies in place on Lync and that they are correctly targeted at the necessary Lync users.

Decommissioning Legacy Systems

Now that you've migrated everything to the Lync pool, you are ready to remove the legacy OCS pool. We won't cover the required steps in detail here, but the following documentation will help:

◆ Decommissioning OCS 2007 R2 Standard Edition Servers and Enterprise Edition Pools:

http://go.microsoft.com/fwlink/?LinkId=205889

◆ Removing OCS 2007 R2 servers and server roles:

http://go.microsoft.com/fwlink/?LinkId=205887

◆ Removing an OCS 2007 Enterprise pool:

http://go.microsoft.com/fwlink/?LinkId=205888

Once you have completely removed the OCS servers from your network (except of course for the OCS CWA server you pointed at Lync earlier), you need to rerun the Merge OCS 2007 R2 Topology Wizard. Running through the wizard will remove all the aspects of the OCS topology except for the CWA server under the Trusted Application Servers node. Of course, if you are no longer using CWA, then running the merge will also remove the BackCompatSite.

Finally, once you've removed all the OCS servers, rerun the `ExchUCUtil.ps1` script on the Exchange UM server to remove the OCS IP Gateway entries.

The Bottom Line

Understand migration considerations.   The process of migrating to Lync involves many aspects of an organization, not the least of which are the end users who will have new functionality to exploit and skills to learn. It is very important to thoroughly evaluate all the phases of a migration and communicate clearly and efficiently to the staff. This is particularly true for any phase of coexistence where some users will be on Lync and others on OCS, potentially with different versions of the client in place.

> **Master It**   You have been asked to prepare a short presentation covering the key elements of the migration. List areas you would cover.

Consider client pain points.   During Lync migration, your primary concern should be for your users. Throughout the migration users will face a changing environment. How you deal with this and control the changes both through careful process and configuration of policy will have a large impact on the successful completion of the migration.

> **Master It**   You have been asked to prepare a short presentation covering the key difficulties faced by users during migration. List the areas you would cover.

Migrate to Lync.   Migrating to Lync is a complex set of processes that will move you from a stable OCS environment to a stable Lync environment with minimal downtime.

> **Master It**   You have been asked to lay out the steps to migrate to Lync. What are they?

Part 3

Administration

Introduction to PowerShell, the Lync Management Shell, and Regular Expressions

PowerShell was introduced by Microsoft in 2006 as the long-term plan to unify various scripting languages. It is a framework built on and integrated with the .NET Framework and consists of a command-line shell and scripting environment. The first product to take advantage of PowerShell natively was Exchange 2007, and the scope has grown dramatically since then to include almost all of the Microsoft collection of server and system administration products: Windows Server 2008, SQL Server 2008, System Center Operations Manager 2007, System Center Virtual Machine Manager 2007, System Center Data Protection Manager 2007, Windows Compute Cluster Server 2007, SharePoint 2010, and first with Lync Server 2010 and now also Lync 2013. As PowerShell was initially released in 2006, the hope was that Office Communications Server (OCS) 2007 R2 would natively integrate with PowerShell; instead, a number of PowerShell scripts were provided as part of the Resource Kit toolset, and these PowerShell scripts simply call VBScript or Windows Management Instrumentation (WMI) to perform their tasks. Outside the Microsoft products, a significant number of third-party vendors, including IBM, Quest, VMware, and NetApp to name a few, provide modules to allow PowerShell integration.

If you are already familiar with PowerShell, you can skip this chapter.

In this chapter, you will learn to:

◆ Use PowerShell command syntax

◆ Employ tips and tricks to get more out of PowerShell

◆ Get help using PowerShell

◆ Understand PowerShell remoting and scripting

Why Use PowerShell?

If you're wondering why you should use PowerShell, the answer is simple: scripting.

In today's large-scale enterprise environments, it is extremely common to perform the same task on a number of servers or on a number of users. With its proliferation and integration across the Microsoft suite of products (as well as the third-party integration), PowerShell is extremely easy to connect to any of these products using the common shell interface.

Looking to the future and cloud computing, Microsoft is providing PowerShell management capabilities for the cloud interface, again meaning that a single interface is now capable of providing management both on premises and in the cloud.

Coming back to the current world and the now-legacy versions of Lync (that is, OCS), there are multiple integration points such as WMI and COM. Developing scripts to simplify administration quite often results in extremely large, complex, and difficult-to-maintain VBScript. Tasks that previously required tens (or even hundreds) of lines of code can now be performed with a single command, and in addition, PowerShell allows the results of one command to be piped into another, providing an even more resourceful environment.

The final reason is that there are some cases in which the only way to achieve a task is via the shell, so even in single-server, 20-user environments, there are scenarios in which the shell *must* be used.

PowerShell is very modular; in Windows Server 2008 R2, the base PowerShell V2 installation has more than 200 individual cmdlets. Lync Server 2010 extended this by more than 500 more cmdlets specific to Lync, and Lync Server 2013 has added another 200 on top! Of course, with PowerShell V3 itself starting with more than 500 cmdlets, this means there are more than 1,200 PowerShell cmdlets to help manage your environment!

Understanding Command Syntax

Unfortunately, every scripting language is different—and typically, as they get more powerful, they become more complicated and, in some cases, more cryptic.

One of Microsoft's goals for PowerShell is to make this language more intuitive, and as a result each PowerShell command typically consists of a verb and noun combination; the verb provides the action and the noun provides the object—for example, Get-CsUser. This combination of verb and noun is referred to as a *cmdlet*. The verb will always come first and the noun will follow, separated by a hyphen. The noun begins with a prefix indicating which tool the PowerShell cmdlet belongs to; for Lync, every cmdlet includes Cs to indicate it is part of the Lync PowerShell command set. Why Cs? It is a reference back to Communications Server. During the Lync Server 2010 beta program, the code name for Lync was "Communications Server 14"—abbreviated to CS. The cmdlets were not changed upon release (and rename) of Lync Server 2010 and have continued this naming convention in the release of Lync Server 2013.

PowerShell is not case sensitive; however, you'll see that cmdlets use a mix of case to make them easier to read.

Table 8.1 shows some of the common verbs and nouns in Lync.

The code

```
Get-CsUcPhoneConfiguration
```

returns the following information about all Lync 2013 UCPhoneConfiguration objects (to return only a single object, specify the UCPhoneConfiguration ID as the only parameter):

```
Identity             : Global
CalendarPollInterval : 00:03:00
EnforcePhoneLock     : True
PhoneLockTimeout     : 00:10:00
MinPhonePinLength    : 6
SIPSecurityMode      : High
```

```
VoiceDiffServTag    : 40
Voice8021p          : 0
LoggingLevel        : Off
```

To update a `UCPhoneConfiguration` object, use the following cmdlet:

`Set-CsUcPhoneConfiguration`

To create a new `UCPhoneConfiguration` object, use the following cmdlet:

`New-CsUcPhoneConfiguration`

The list goes on. You can see that in most cases the cmdlets are self-explanatory; however, there are some scenarios where you'll need to use some trial and error to find the right combination. Alternatively, you can use the help file, which is described next.

TABLE 8.1:   Common Lync management shell verbs and nouns

CMDLET PORTION	VERB/NOUN	DESCRIPTION
Get	Verb	Probably the most commonly used verb. It will return information as specified by the object.
Set	Verb	Next in line of the verbs comes Set. It is used to update an object.
Enable	Verb	Enable is used to turn on functionality.
Disable	Verb	Disable is used to turn off functionality.
New	Verb	Used to create new objects, typically policies.
Move	Verb	Typically used to manipulate the home server (or pool) attribute for an object.
Remove	Verb	Used in the deletion of objects.
CsUser	Noun	The user object when homed on a Lync pool.
CsLegacyUser	Noun	The user object when homed on an OCS pool.
CsAdUser	Noun	Additional AD attributes of a user.
CsConferencingPolicy	Noun	The object dealing with conference policy.
CsCertificate	Noun	The object properties of a certificate.

Finding Help

Figure 8.1 shows the help file index of cmdlets (shown on the left). It also includes a listing by category (on the right), which most people find easier to navigate, at least initially. (You know what you want to achieve, and a category-based grouping makes it easier to find these types of cmdlets.) As time goes by and you become more familiar with cmdlets, you'll probably find that searching directly for the cmdlet is the easiest way to get to the information you want.

FIGURE 8.1
Use the help file
to find cmdlets by
name (left) and by
category (right).

Selecting a specific cmdlet within the help file will display more detailed information regarding the cmdlet itself as well as some examples of its usage. Figure 8.2 shows a snippet of the display for the `Move-CsUser` cmdlet. In a helpful approach, the order of the help file content has been changed to begin with examples rather than the list of parameters as with Lync Server 2010.

The help file consists of the following sections for all cmdlets:

◆ Syntax

◆ Parameters

◆ Detailed description

◆ Input types

◆ Return types

◆ Example

◆ See also

It can be quite time-consuming to leave the shell environment to go to the help file and then go back to the shell to continue scripting or running cmdlets (not everyone has two screens!). The solution to this problem is to run a favorite cmdlet: `Get-Help`. There are several other related cmdlets or associated methods of retrieving help, all of them documented in Table 8.2.

FIGURE 8.2
View the Move-CsUser cmdlet in the help file.

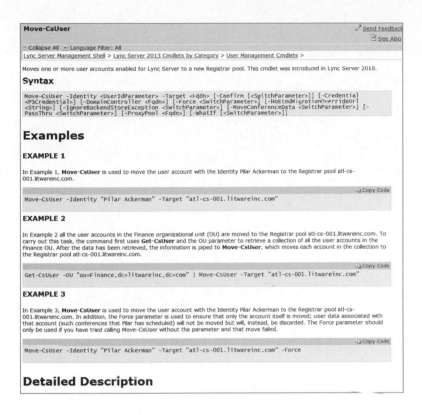

TABLE 8.2: Methods of finding help

METHOD	DESCRIPTION
Get-Help	Lists the help information for the Get-Help cmdlet itself.
Get-Help *Cmdlet*	Lists the help information for the cmdlet specified.
Get-Help *Keyword*	Lists the help information for the keyword specified. This is typically in Table format, so it is not actually very helpful because the columns are truncated.
Help	Same as Get-Help.
Help *Cmdlet*	Same as Get-Help *Cmdlet*.
Help *Keyword*	Same as Get-Help *Keyword*.
Get-Command	Lists all the cmdlets, aliases, and functions in the PowerShell process (including any imported sessions).
Get-Command *keyword*	Lists all cmdlets, aliases, and functions that contain the keyword. Example: Get-Command *-Cs* will return all commands that include *-Cs*.
Cmdlet -?	Lists help specifically for the cmdlet listed.

From within PowerShell, there are different views, or output options, providing a method to control the information returned from the `Help` command:

◆ `Default`

◆ `Detailed`

◆ `Example`

◆ `Full`

◆ `Parameters`

To use these parameters, enter the `Get-Help` cmdlet in the following format, including the view option:

```
Get-Help Disable-CsUser -Detailed
```

Because you specified `Detailed`, you should get the following output:

```
NAME
      Disable-CsUser
SYNOPSIS
      Modifies the Active Directory account of the specified user or users; this
modification prevents users from using Microsoft Lync Server clients such as Microsoft Lync
2013. Disable-CsUser only restricts activity related to Lync Server; it does not disable or
remove a user's Active Directory account. This cmdlet was introduced in Lync Server 2010.
SYNTAX
      Disable-CsUser -Identity <UserIdParameter> [-Confirm [<SwitchParameter>]]
[-DomainController <Fqdn>] [-PassThru <SwitchParameter>] [-WhatIf [<SwitchParameter>]]
[CommonParameters]
DESCRIPTION
      The Disable-CsUser cmdlet deletes all the attribute information related to Lync Server
from an Active Directory user account; this prevents the user from logging on to Lync
Server. When you run Disable-CsUser all the Lync Server-related attributes are removed from
an account, including the Identities of any per-user policies that have been assigned to
that account. You can later re-enable the account by using the Enable-CsUser cmdlet.
However, all the Lync Server-related information (such as policy assignments) previously
associated with that account will have to be re-created. If you want to prevent a user from
logging on to Lync Server, but do not want to lose all of their account information, use
Set-CsUser instead. For details, see the Set-CsUser help topic.
<cut for brevity>
```

The output will continue, providing information on each of the following sections:

◆ Parameters (including details on each parameter)

◆ Examples

◆ Remarks (this typically refers to other links for more information)

The `-Examples` option provides only the example information (only one example is included; however, multiple examples will be displayed):

```
NAME
      Disable-CsUser
```

```
SYNOPSIS
      Modifies the Active Directory account of the specified user or users; this
modification prevents users from using Microsoft Lync Server clients such as Microsoft Lync
2013. Disable-CsUser only restricts activity related to Lync Server; it does not disable or
remove a user's Active Directory account. This cmdlet was introduced in Lync Server 2010.
------------------------ Example 1 ------------------------
Disable-CsUser -Identity "Ken Myer"
The preceding Example disables the Lync Server account for the user Ken Myer. In this
example, the user's display name is used to indicate his Identity.
```

Knowing about this option is important if, like a lot of technical people, you learn by looking at examples and changing the code to do what you need. This Examples view provides only the NAME, SYNOPSIS, and EXAMPLES sections.

On the other hand, running Get-Help Disable-CsUser -Full will display all the sections. From the full output, you can see additional information based on the types of input accepted and output generated. With each parameter, you can also see its associated metadata. Table 8.3 explains each item.

TABLE 8.3:   Get-Help cmdlet metadata

VALUE	DESCRIPTION
Required?	True or False based on whether this parameter is needed.
Position?	Specifies the position of the parameter. Most parameters are Named, which means the parameter value must be prefixed by the parameter tag. The -Identity parameter is always 1, which means the tag is not required.
Default	The value used if none is provided. For most parameters, this is blank.
Accept pipeline input?	True or False based on whether input is accepted from another cmdlet (more on this later in the chapter).
Accept wildcard characters?	True or False and determines whether or not wildcards (such as * or ?) are accepted.

The -Default parameter will return the following sections:

```
NAME
SYNOPSIS
SYNTAX
DESCRIPTION
RELATED LINKS
REMARKS
```

Finally, the -Parameter option will return only the specific information regarding the parameter specified, including the metadata.

Cmdlet versus Command

Understanding the difference between *cmdlet* and *command* is important. Both terms are used frequently when talking about PowerShell.

◆ A cmdlet is the verb-noun combination that takes parameters as input, carries out a task, and in most cases provides output.

◆ A command is the complete string comprising the cmdlet and a specific set of parameters.

For example, Get-CsUser is a cmdlet, and Get-CsUser "sip:keith_lync@masteringlync. org" is a command.

WHEN IS A CMDLET ALSO A COMMAND?

In some cases (such as the previous one), the cmdlet can stand as a command in its own right. Get-CsUser executed on its own will produce the output for every user enabled for Lync. Typically, we refer to a *cmdlet* when we are talking only about generics, and a *command* is the full string of cmdlet and parameters.

Shells versus the Prompt

Opening the wrong shell is a common mistake. You can see why because a Lync server can have some or all of the following installed (see Figure 8.3):

◆ Command prompt (also known as the command shell or DOS prompt)

◆ Windows PowerShell

◆ Lync Server Management Shell

◆ Windows PowerShell modules

FIGURE 8.3
Common command shells installed on a Lync server

The command prompt has been around since before Microsoft itself was first formed. The version on a Lync 2013 server is the latest incarnation of the old DOS prompt (see Figure 8.4). From a Lync administration perspective, it is almost useless. Yes, there are a few utilities that can be run from the command prompt (mostly from the Resource Kit); however, day-to-day administration requires PowerShell, not a command prompt.

FIGURE 8.4

The command prompt

Next up are Windows PowerShell and the Windows PowerShell modules (see Figure 8.5). Windows PowerShell is the basic shell, with over 200 cmdlets; however, the Windows PowerShell modules add significantly more cmdlets to help administer Windows itself. The ability to incorporate additional modules to extend the capabilities of the shell is an extremely powerful function—and it is exactly what the Lync Server Management Shell does. Its additional cmdlets are specific to Lync management.

FIGURE 8.5

Windows PowerShell

Figure 8.6 shows the Lync Server Management Shell, and if you open both it and a base Windows PowerShell window, you will notice a difference in the speed at which they start up; the Lync Server Management Shell is loading the Lync-specific cmdlets in the background.

FIGURE 8.6
The Lync Server
Management Shell

As you can see, the Lync Server 2013 Management Shell window looks extremely similar to a command prompt, so it's quite easy to use the wrong one; however, very quickly you're going to see errors returned if you try to execute PowerShell commands in a Command Prompt window or Lync 2013 cmdlets in a basic PowerShell window.

NOTE   In the book, we use the term *PowerShell* to describe the Lync Server Management Shell. Please don't confuse this use of *PowerShell* with the standard Microsoft PowerShell shell, which is installed on Windows Server 2008 R2 by default. When working with Lync, unless explicitly stated otherwise, you should be using the Lync Server Management Shell. The Lync Server Management Shell can be launched either directly from the Lync Server program group or by importing the Lync module into a standard PowerShell session, using the `Import-Module Lync` command.

Introducing PowerShell Coding

So far, we've looked at individual cmdlets and how to execute them. By linking multiple cmdlets together or working on (or with) the same object, you can develop code (or scripts), which can be saved in a file with a `.ps1` filename extension and rerun at a later date. By introducing and using variables, along with logic controls based on the values of those variables, the script can adapt to different environments, or indeed different conditions in the same environment. We'll now look at how you can begin to build up from cmdlets into scripts that can query the environment and perform additional tasks based on the results of those queries.

Windows PowerShell has over 500 cmdlets, whereas the Lync Management Shell has over 700 Lync-specific cmdlets. A brief PowerShell introduction will explain the difference. You've already seen the `Get-Command` cmdlet and how it displays details for a specific command. By providing it with the parameter `*-Cs*`, you can instruct it to return a list of all the cmdlets that include `-Cs` in their name—that is, all the Lync Management Shell cmdlets.

```
Get-Command *-Cs*
```

In the Windows PowerShell prompt, four entries are returned:

```
ConvertFrom-Csv
ConvertTo-Csv
Export-Csv
Import-Csv
```

In the Lync Management Shell, this same command returns too many entries to read. You need to modify the command to the following:

```
$total = Get-Command *-Cs*
```

This is the first piece of PowerShell coding. By specifying `$total`, you define a variable and assign the results of the `Get-Command *-Cs*` command to it.

The array, which can be thought of as a list, is `$total`. In itself it produces no output; however, you can manipulate it. For example, the variable name alone

```
$total
```

will produce onscreen the same output as if you simply ran `Get-Command *-Cs*`. Specifying the index, or numeric position within the array

```
$total[0]
```

will produce the first entry in the list—in this example, an Alias, `Test-CsClientAuth`.

Finally, adding the count parameter

```
$total.count
```

will return the total number of items in the list—in this example, 752.

TAB COMPLETION

An extremely useful feature of PowerShell is that you can press Tab to complete a cmdlet. This is especially helpful with some of the longer cmdlets. Once you have typed enough to define a unique cmdlet, pressing Tab will complete it. If you haven't reached a unique point in the cmdlet, pressing Tab will cycle through the cmdlets that match what you have typed so far. In actual fact, it will first cycle through any files and folders in the current directory, then applications in the path environmental variable, *then* it will begin cycling through cmdlets.

For example, if you type **A** and then press Tab until you get to the first cmdlet, the cmdlet will complete to `Add-ADComputerServiceAccount`, pressing tab again will move to the next cmdlet, and so on.

But if you start typing `Clear-CsDeviceUpdate` and press Tab (when you reach `Clear-Cs`, you will cycle through `Clear-CsDeviceUpdateFile`, `Clear-CsDeviceUpdateLog`, and `Clear-CsPersistentChatRoom` because you have not reached a unique point.

The tab-completion feature also works with parameters for cmdlets.

Although pressing Tab cycles forward through the cmdlets, if you press Tab too many times and miss the cmdlet you're looking for, you can simply press Shift+Tab to cycle backward to the cmdlet you missed.

PowerShell Variables and Data Types

A variable is a placeholder for a value and can be a string, number, or object. You access the values stored in a variable simply by referencing the variable name. In PowerShell, every variable begins with a dollar sign ($) and is an object. Defining the variable as an object means that you can assign any value to it; however, you can force a specific data type if required. This is called *casting*. For example, the command

```
$x = [int]5
```

would assign the `integer` value 5 to the variable x rather than the `string` "5".

Assigning the output of a cmdlet to a variable creates an *object*, which in turn can be passed to another cmdlet. For example, the command

```
$users = Get-CsUser
```

the `$users` variable will contain all of the user objects in the environment. This will result in an array with each entry being an individual user.

In PowerShell, the first item in an array is always numbered 0; therefore, the first user object would be accessed by using the following notation:

```
$users[0]
```

PowerShell can define and use any .NET framework data type as a value. There are too many to list here; however, the following are the more commonly used ones:

- String

- Integer

- Boolean

- DateTime

- XML

Script Control

So that decisions can be made by the script, PowerShell includes a number of standard constructs that check conditions and that control loops.

Conditions are typically checked in this format:

```
If <something> then <do something> else <do something else>
```

Within PowerShell this format becomes

```
If (condition) {code} else {more code}
```

This can be further extended using `elseif` statements, such as

```
If (condition1) {code} elseif (condition2) {code2} else {more code}
```

PowerShell also includes the `Switch` construct (known as `Case` in some other languages). It is used in the following format:

```
Switch (variable)
{
Value1 {code}
Value2 {code}
Value3 {code}
Default {code}
}
```

Control loops allow a script to parse through multiple values (such as an array). Combined with condition checking, these loops are the logical flow and execution of the script. PowerShell supports a number of different control loops:

- For looping

- ForEach looping

- While looping

- Do While looping

- Do Until looping

The basic syntax of each of these control loops is as follows, with each of the *code* sections repeated within the loop:

```
For (startvalue;condition;nextvalue) {code}
ForEach (Item in collection) {code}
While (condition) {code}
Do {code} While (condition)
Do {code} Until (condition)
```

Functions allow for good organization and segmentation of scripts as well as the ability to have a section of repeated code simplified down to being written once and "called" when needed. For example, the following code definition provides simple mathematical results on a pair of numbers:

```
Function maths{
Param ($x, $y)
$sum = $x + $y
$diff = $x - $y
$product = $x * $y
$div = $x/$y
Write-Host "Sum: $sum"
Write-Host "Difference: $diff"
Write-Host "Product: $product"
Write-Host "Division: $div"
}
```

This function is called using the form below and would give the output shown in Figure 8.7:

```
Maths 10 5
```

It's beyond the scope of this book to go into each of these in detail, but a few of them will be used in the examples later in this chapter.

FIGURE 8.7

Output from a function

Input Parameters

You've already been introduced to the concepts of cmdlet parameters and how to query the help (by passing a parameter!) to find out which parameters a cmdlet needs as well as the metadata definitions of each parameter. Now let's look in more detail.

In Lync 2013, -Identity is the most-used parameter and will always be the first parameter in the cmdlet list, so it doesn't need to have the tag included. For example,

```
Get-CsUser -Identity "sip:keith_lync@masteringlync.org"
```

provides the same result as

```
Get-CsUser "sip:keith_lync@masteringlync.org"
```

Other parameters must be tagged with the parameter name as part of the cmdlet. As mentioned previously, the list of parameters for a cmdlet can be queried using the Get-Help cmdlet, with the specific parameter -Parameters.

The Get verb cmdlets are interesting because the -Identity parameter is optional; if it isn't provided, the cmdlet will work on all objects of that type, so Get-CsUser will return all enabled users.

The groups of Set verbs, on the other hand, require you to provide an -Identity tag to determine the object on which to execute changes. What happens if you forget this (or indeed, any) required parameter? Well, PowerShell is intelligent enough to know the parameters that are required, so it will prompt for them; any optional parameters will be left out of the command. Figure 8.8 shows the prompt from running the Enable-CsUser cmdlet without a specific -Identity parameter.

FIGURE 8.8
Prompting for missing parameters

```
PS C:\Users\administrator.CORP> enable-csuser -RegistrarPool se01.corp.masteringlync.org

cmdlet Enable-CsUser at command pipeline position 1
Supply values for the following parameters:
Identity: _
```

Output Parameters

Because PowerShell is based on the .NET Framework, it uses an object model for data. This means the responses from commands are not text based (although they will display onscreen as text); instead, they are objects. Cmdlets will have a default display (content and format) of the data being returned, but because the data takes the form of objects, you can easily override this default and display the data you want to see. You do that by specifying output parameters. For example, here's the default output of Get-CsPool for the example system:

```
Get-CsPool
Identity  : se01.corp.masteringlync.org
Services  : {UserServer:se01.corp.masteringlync.org, Registrar:se01.corp.masteringlync.org,
            UserDatabase:se01.corp.masteringlync.org, FileStore:se01.corp.masteringlync.org...}
Computers : {se01.corp.masteringlync.org}
Fqdn      : se01.corp.masteringlync.org
Site      : Site:EMEA
Identity  : sql01.corp.masteringlync.org
```

```
Services  : {MonitoringDatabase:sql01.corp.masteringlync.org,
      ArchivingDatabase:sql01.corp.masteringlync.org,
      UserDatabase:sql01.corp.masteringlync.org,
      ApplicationDatabase:sql01.corp.masteringlync.org}
Computers : {sql01.corp.masteringlync.org}
Fqdn      : sql01.corp.masteringlync.org
Site      : Site:EMEA
Identity  : dc01.corp.masteringlync.org
Services  : {FileStore:dc01.corp.masteringlync.org}
Computers : {dc01.corp.masteringlync.org}
Fqdn      : dc01.corp.masteringlync.org
Site      : Site:EMEA
Identity  : lyncpool.corp.masteringlync.org
Services  : {UserServer:lyncpool.corp.masteringlync.org,
      Registrar:lyncpool.corp.masteringlync.org,
      WebServer:lyncpool.corp.masteringlync.org,
      ConferencingServer:lyncpool.corp.masteringlync.org...}
Computers : {fe01.corp.masteringlync.org, fe02.corp.masteringlync.org}
Fqdn      : lyncpool.corp.masteringlync.org
Site      : Site:EMEA
Identity  : ocsse02.corp.masteringlync.org
Services  : {Registrar:ocsse02.corp.masteringlync.org,
      UserServer:ocsse02.corp.masteringlync.org,
      ApplicationServer:ocsse02.corp.masteringlync.org}
Computers : {ocsse02.corp.masteringlync.org}
Fqdn      : ocsse02.corp.masteringlync.org
Site      : Site:BackCompatSite
```

You can manipulate this output by changing the format. The default format for many cmdlets is `Format-Table`, which typically results in a minimal set of parameters being displayed in the output:

```
Get-CsPool | Format-Table
Identity                           Services
--------                           --------
se01.corp.masteringlync.org        {UserServer:se01.corp.masteringlync.org,
                                     Registrar:se01.c...
sql01.corp.masteringlync.org       {MonitoringDatabase:sql01.corp.masteringlync.org,
                                     Archivi...
dc01.corp.masteringlync.org        {FileStore:dc01.corp.masteringlync.org}
lyncpool.corp.masteringlync.org    {UserServer:lyncpool.corp.masteringlync.org,
                                     Registrar:ly...
ocsse02.corp.masteringlync.org     {Registrar:ocsse02.corp.masteringlync.org,
                                     UserServer:ocs...
```

As you can see, the content of the field may be truncated with `Format-Table`. Depending on the size of your window, you may get more columns than shown here, and if you export the output to a file (using `Output-File`), you will get the full column content; however, the individual columns may still be truncated.

`Format-List` will provide all the properties of the returned object:

```
Get-CsPool | Format-List
```

`Format-List` is the default output of many `*-Cs*` commands, so in this case the output is the same as shown for `Get-CsPool` alone, as if you did not include the `Format-List` cmdlet.

In addition, you can specify only the parameters you are looking for, reducing the amount of screen clutter:

```
Get-CsPool | Ft Site, Fqdn
Site                        Fqdn
----                        ----
Site:EMEA                   se01.corp.masteringlync.org
Site:EMEA                   sql01.corp.masteringlync.org
Site:EMEA                   dc01.corp.masteringlync.org
Site:EMEA                   lyncpool.corp.masteringlync.org
Site:BackCompatSite         ocsse02.corp.masteringlync.org
```

ALIASES

In the previous example, the `Format-Table` has been replaced by `Ft`. This is known as an *alias*. Aliases are shortcut references to longer cmdlets. In the native PowerShell installation, almost 150 aliases are predefined.

You can create your own aliases for frequently used commands by using the `Set-Alias` cmdlet.

WHEN OUTPUT EQUALS INPUT

Often it is useful to run one command to retrieve information and directly use that information as the input for another command. You have already seen this in the previous couple of examples, where one command's output is directed to a second command using the pipe (|) symbol:

```
Get-CsPool | Format-Table
```

Here you are sending the output of the first cmdlet into the `Format-Table` cmdlet as well as providing additional information in the form of parameters to filter the results.

Not all cmdlets will support piping between them; however, where the noun portions of the cmdlets match, it will always work, as in the following example:

```
Get-csuser <something> |set-csuser <something>
```

Using the `Get-Help` cmdlet with the `-Full` parameter will provide the details to describe each parameter and whether it will accept pipeline input or not.

When interacting between cmdlets that do not support piping, the `ForEach` cmdlet can usually be used to process the data in a loop:

```
ForEach  ($user in $users)
{
        Write-Host $user.Name
}
```

This code snippet would cycle through each `$user` object in the `$users` collection and output the `Name` parameter.

FILTERING THE OUTPUT

Rather than limiting the properties returned, you may be interested only in a subset of the objects. For example, you may want to select only the users on a particular Lync pool and apply a change to them. This is where filtering comes in. You are running the command on the full environment; however, you then provide a filter across this complete data showing a view of only the data in which you are interested. Here's an example:

```
Get-CsUser | Where-Object {$_.poolname -like 'SE01'}
```

Breaking down this command, run the Get-CsUser command (in this form it is a command rather than cmdlet) to return all the users. This output is piped to the Where-Object cmdlet, and using the filter parameters enclosed in {}, you will retain only the objects that match the criteria. In this case, the $_.poolname property must match the 'SE01' value provided. Here, you have introduced another new concept, because $_ refers to the current object and is used when you want to iterate through a complete list of objects, in this case comparing each one to the filter criteria. Table 8.4 lists common operators that can be used with filtering.

TABLE 8.4:   Shell values and operator descriptions

SHELL VALUE	OPERATOR	DESCRIPTION
-eq	Equal	The property must match exactly the value.
-ne	Not Equal	The property must not match the value.
-gt	Greater Than	Integers only. The property must be greater than the value.
-ge	Greater Than or Equal To	Integers only. The property must be greater than or equal to the value.
-lt	Less Than	Integers only. The property must be less than the value.
-le	Less Than or Equal To	Integers only. The property must be less than or equal to the value.
-Like	Contains	Text. The string can match exactly or wildcards can be used to indicate the string being a substring.
-Notlike	Does Not Contain	Text. The string must not match exactly or wildcards can be used to indicate the string must not be a substring.

PowerShell V3

Until now we've been discussing functionality that is contained within versions 1, 2, and 3 of PowerShell. Windows 7 and Windows Server 2008 R2 introduced PowerShell version 2, bringing some fantastic new features, such as remoting and the Integrated Scripting Environment (ISE). For older operating systems, PowerShell version 2 is available as a download from this link (separate downloads are available for each operating system):

```
www.microsoft.com/download/en/search.aspx?q=powershell+2.0
```

Lync Server 2010 required the use of PowerShell V2, but Lync Server 2013 requires PowerShell to be upgraded to V3.

```
www.microsoft.com/download/en/search.aspx?q=powershell+3.0
```

Version 3 provides significant increases in the number of cmdlets available and thus a wider range of items that can be managed via native PowerShell—some of which are directly helpful to Lync, others not so.

In the following sections, we'll look specifically at some of these new features introduced with V2 and updated with V3, or purely native to V3.

Remoting

Remoting is the term given to managing an environment from a remote shell. You launch a local PowerShell prompt and initiate a remote PowerShell session against the machine (or environment) you want to manage, and then you import that session to your current session:

```
$session = New-PsSession -ConnectionUri https://se01.corp.masteringlync.org
/ocspowershell -Authentication NegotiateWithImplicitCredential
Import-PsSession $session
```

At this point, the remote PowerShell modules become available in the local session.

This is an extremely useful function because it means that you don't need to install local administration tools and you can provide separate administration credentials (ensuring a separation of user and admin roles) through the connection session.

MANAGING MULTIPLE ENVIRONMENTS FROM A SINGLE POWERSHELL SESSION

By taking advantage of PowerShell's remoting capabilities, you can connect a single PowerShell session to multiple environments, which will allow you to modify users for Lync and Exchange at the same time. This concept will work with services located both on the premises and in the cloud; PowerShell doesn't care where the services are located, only that it can reach the administration point.

Take the following script:

```
$ExchangeSession = New-PsSession -ConfigurationName Microsoft.Exchange -ConnectionUri
    http://ex01.corp.masteringlync.org/PowerShell -Authentication Kerberos
Import-PsSession $ExchangeSession
$CsSession = $CsSession = New-PsSession -ConnectionUri https://se01.corp.masteringlync
    .org/ocspowershell -Authentication NegotiateWithImplicitCredential
Import-PsSession $CsSession
Enable-Mailbox corp\PS_DemoUser
Enable-CSuser -identity corp\PS_DemoUser -SipAddress sip:ps_demouser@masteringlync.org -
    RegistrarPool se01.corp.masteringlync.org
Enable-UMMailbox corp\PS_DemoUser -UMMailboxPolicy "UK Default Policy" -
    SipResourceIdentifier PS_DemoUser@masteringlync.org -Extensions "1234"
```

By running this script in a Windows PowerShell session, you first connect to and import an Exchange session (`$ExchangeSession` and `Import-PsSession`) and then connect to and import a Lync session (`$CsSession` and `Import-PsSession`). Then you have a single PowerShell session connected to both Exchange and Lync, you can enable a user with a mailbox and Lync account, and finally, you enable Exchange Unified Messaging—all from within the remaining three lines of code.

The Integrated Scripting Environment

PowerShell v2 introduced the graphical user interface called the Integrated Scripting Environment (ISE), which includes a handy debugging tool. PowerShell v3 improved on the capabilities of the ISE. On Windows Server 2008 R2, the ISE must be installed by adding the Windows PowerShell Integrated Scripting Environment feature from Server Manager. The ISE can be launched by typing **ISE** in a PowerShell window. Figure 8.9 shows the PowerShell v3 ISE when started.

FIGURE 8.9

The Integrated Script Environment

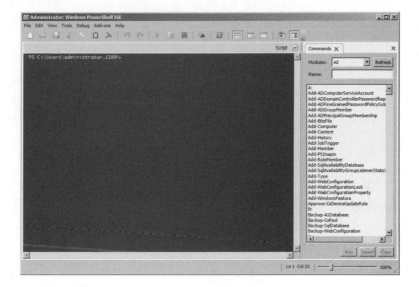

Initially, only a single pane opens with command help on the right-hand side. When dealing with scripts, the single pane moves to the bottom and the scripts are displayed in a tabbed window (see Figure 8.10). This is the normal operating mode.

The bottom pane is simply a PowerShell prompt, in which commands can be entered directly and/or result of scripts viewed. Figure 8.10 shows the working environment where the Get-Service cmdlet was entered in the command line and the results appeared (the screen has scrolled to the end of the output).

ISE does not include any PowerShell extensions (such as Lync 2013 or Exchange) and is required to use the remoting feature to connect to and import a Lync 2013 (or Exchange) session or to import the modules directly if they are available locally.

Figure 8.11 shows the script introduced in the example (to open, select File ➤ Open). Each script is opened in a separate tab, which allows multiple scripts to be opened at the same time.

Although you can't see it in the figure, the scripting section uses color highlighting to make it easier to write scripts and view variables, functions, and cmdlets. The color highlighting allows you to easily spot where the script blocks start and end. When code is written, quote marks (") are frequently placed in the wrong location (or forgotten), starting or ending a string in the wrong place. The highlighting makes it obvious that this has occurred.

Each line in the script area is numbered, as are any errors from PowerShell. This allows you to easily locate an error (use Ctrl+G to jump to a specific line in the script).

FIGURE 8.10
The ISE is working

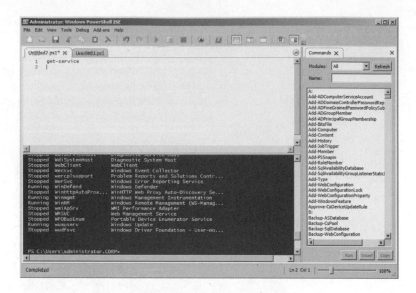

FIGURE 8.11
Scripting via ISE

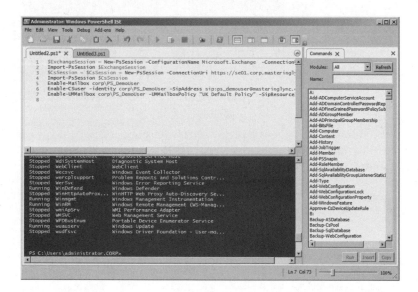

Once the script has been saved (File ➤ Save), debugging is enabled. This allows breakpoints to be set in the script by placing the cursor on a line of code and pressing F9 (or selecting Debug-Toggle Breakpoint). A *breakpoint* is a point in the code where execution will pause, allowing detailed interrogation of the script to determine specific values of the variable at that stage. This technique is used to help resolve errors in the code that may otherwise be difficult to find. Breakpoints are highlighted in dark red. Once a breakpoint has been configured and the script executed, assuming the line of code is reached, the script will pause.

At this point, you can interrogate any variable simply by entering the variable name in the command window; you can also execute PowerShell cmdlets in it. Additional commands become available once the script is paused:

Step Over (F10)   Allows line-by-line execution of the script, and if the line is a function, will not step into the function, but will execute it.

Step Into (F11)   Allows line-by-line execution of the script, and if the line is a function, will continue debugging the function line-by-line.

Step Out (Shift+F11)   Continues execution of a function, and pauses once the function is completed.

Continue (F5)   Continues executing the script until the next breakpoint.

Stop (Shift+F5)   Stops the execution of the script.

Figure 8.12 shows the ISE running a basic script, which will count from 0 to 10, outputting the value each time, and when the value is equal to 5, it will write the text "the value is five" rather than the number. At the point of capture of the screen shot, the *breakpoint* has been reached. The [DBG] indicates that the output screen and the command window are in Debug mode.

FIGURE 8.12
ISE in Debug mode

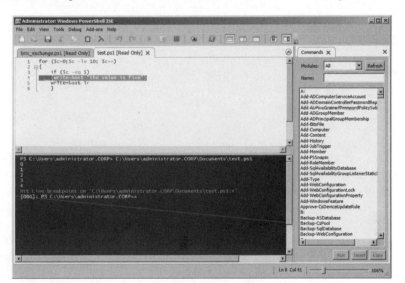

Managing Output

Although PowerShell is the interface used to configure and administer Lync, more often than not it will be used to provide data in a form either for human consumption or for input to other applications. As a result, it is often necessary to massage the results of the command output.

Lists and Tables

You've already seen how to display the output as a list (`Format-List`) or a table (`Format-Table`), and you've seen how to limit the properties displayed by using the `Format` cmdlet.

The next thing you may need to do is sort or group the output. Sorting is provided by the Sort-Object cmdlet, which can take a number of parameters. Here it is receiving the output of Get-CsUser:

```
Get-CsUser | Sort-Object
```

The output will be sorted in ascending alphabetical order, by the default sort property, and return the following:

```
Identity    : CN=Keith Lync,CN=Users,DC=corp,DC=masteringlync,DC=org
SipAddress  : sip:keith.lync@masteringlync.org
DisplayName : Keith Lync
Identity    : CN=Jo OCS,CN=Users,DC=corp,DC=masteringlync,DC=org
SipAddress  : sip:jo.ocs@masteringlync.org
DisplayName : Jo OCS
Identity    : CN=Nathan Lync,CN=Users,DC=corp,DC=masteringlync,DC=org
SipAddress  : sip:nathan.lync@masteringlync.org
DisplayName : Nathan Lync
Identity    : CN=John OCS,CN=Users,DC=corp,DC=masteringlync,DC=org
SipAddress  : sip:John.ocs@masteringlync.org
DisplayName : John OCS
```

LIMITING OUTPUT

Actually, we cheated a little in the sorted output and throughout this chapter. To ensure brevity, we appended

```
| fl identity, sipaddress, displayname
```

at the end of the command to display only those fields—otherwise, this chapter would contain lots of not very useful content! In fact, the command we entered was this (remember that fl is a default alias created for the Format-List cmdlet):

```
Get-CsUser | Sort-Object | Fl Identity, SipAddress, DisplayName
```

To sort in ascending alphabetical order, by the named property (this would show the same output as the previous command), you would enter the following:

```
Get-CsUser | Sort-Object -Property <property name>
```

To sort in descending alphabetical order, by the named property:

```
Get-CsUser | Sort-Object -Property Identity Descending=$True
```

This gives the following output:

```
Identity    : CN=Jo OCS,CN=Users,DC=corp,DC=masteringlync,DC=org
SipAddress  : sip:Jo.ocs@masteringlync.org
DisplayName : Jo OCS
Identity    : CN=John OCS,CN=Users,DC=corp,DC=masteringlync,DC=org
SipAddress  : sip:john.ocs@masteringlync.org
DisplayName : John OCS
Identity    : CN=Nathan Lync,CN=Users,DC=corp,DC=masteringlync,DC=org
SipAddress  : sip:nathan.lync@masteringlync.org
```

```
DisplayName : Nathan Lync
Identity    : CN=Keith Lync,CN=Users,DC=corp,DC=masteringlync,DC=org
SipAddress  : sip:keith.lync@masteringlync.org
DisplayName : Keith Lync
```

`Sort-Object` also has the capability to return only the unique values in a list:

```
Get-CsUser | Sort-Object -Unique
```

You can sort by multiple fields (and in differing directions if required) with an extension to the `Sort-Object` cmdlet. This is typically used to provide a specific format to output. To sort first by `Enabled` in descending order and then by `DisplayName` in ascending order, the command would be as follows:

```
Get-CsUser | Sort-Object -Property @{Expression="Enabled";Descending=$True},
@{Expression="DisplayName";Descending=$False}
```

This command will display the full user object for each order, sorted with the `Enabled` users first and each of them sorted based on the `DisplayName`. The output isn't included because it would stretch to several pages!

This last example is a method of grouping. You can also use the `Group-Object` cmdlet to give a slightly different output.

```
Get-CsUser | Sort-Object -Property SipAddress| Group-Object -Property Enabled
Count Name    Group
----- ----    -----
    4 True    {CN=Jo OCS,CN=Users,DC=corp,DC=masteringlync,DC=org,
               CN=John OCS,CN=Users,DC=corp,DC=masteringlync,DC=org,
               CN=Keith Lync,CN=Users,DC=corp,DC=masteringlync,DC=org,
               CN=Nathan Lync,CN=Users,DC=corp,DC=masteringlync,DC=org}
```

As you can see, the `Sort-Object` and `Group-Object` cmdlets provide extremely powerful output manipulation features in PowerShell.

Output to File

So far you've seen the command output on the screen in table or list formats. In many cases, it is useful to store data in files. PowerShell provides a number of cmdlets to let you do just that. In the following sections, we'll look at the `Out-File`, `Export-Csv`, and `Export-CliXml` cmdlets.

Out-File

`Out-File` captures the command output and stores it directly in a file:

```
Get-CsUser -Identity "keith lync" | Out-File c:\get-csuser.txt
```

Opening the file `c:\get-csuser.txt` shows this:

```
Identity            : CN=Keith Lync,CN=Users,DC=corp,DC=masteringlync,
DC=org
VoicePolicy         :
VoiceRoutingPolicy  :
ConferencingPolicy  :
PresencePolicy      :
DialPlan            :
LocationPolicy      :
```

```
ClientPolicy           :
ClientVersionPolicy    :
ArchivingPolicy        :
ExchangeArchivingPolicy: Unitialized
PinPolicy              :
ExternalAccessPolicy   :
MobilityPolicy         :
PersistentChatPolicy   :
HostedVoiceMail        :
HostedVoicemailPolicy  :
HostingProvider        : SRV:
RegistrarPool          : se01.corp.masteringlync.org
Enabled                : True
SipAddress             : sip:keith.lync@masteringlync.org
LineURI                :
EnterpriseVoiceEnabled : False
ExUmEnabled            : False
HomeServer             : CN=Lc Services,CN=Microsoft,CN=1:1,CN=Pools,CN=RTC
 Service,CN=Services,CN=Configuration,DC=corp,DC=masteringlync,DC=org
DisplayName            : Keith Lync
SamAccountName         : keith_lync
```

Export-Csv

Export-Csv exports the data into CSV format:

```
Get-CsUser -Identity "keith lync" | Export-Csv c:\get-csuser.csv
```

Opening the file c:\get-csuser.csv shows this:

```
#TYPE Microsoft.Rtc.Management.ADConnect.Schema.OCSADUser
"SamAccountName","UserPrincipalName","FirstName",<other fields cut for brevity>

"keith_lync","keith_lync@corp.masteringlync.org","Keith",
<other fields cut for brevity>
```

Export-CliXml

Export-CliXml exports the data into XML format.

```
Get-CsUser -Identity "keith lync" | Export-CliXml c:\get-csuser.xml
```

Opening the file c:\get-csuser.txt shows this:

```
<Objs Version="1.1.0.1" xmlns="http://schemas.microsoft.com/powershell/2004/04">
  <Obj RefId="0">
    <TN RefId="0">
      <T>Microsoft.Rtc.Management.ADConnect.Schema.OCSADUser</T>
      <T>Microsoft.Rtc.Management.ADConnect.Schema.OCSADUserBase</T>
      <T>Microsoft.Rtc.Management.ADConnect.Schema.OCSEndPoint</T>
      <T>Microsoft.Rtc.Management.ADConnect.ADObject.ADObjectBase</T>
      <T>Microsoft.Rtc.Management.ADConnect.ADObject.ADRawEntry</T>
      <T>Microsoft.Rtc.Management.ADConnect.Core.ConfigurableObject</T>
      <T>System.Object</T>
```

```
  </TN>
  <ToString>CN=Keith Lync,CN=Users,DC=corp,DC=masteringlync,DC=org</ToString>
  <Props>
    <S N="SamAccountName">keith_lync</S>
    <S N="UserPrincipalName">keith_lync@corp.masteringlync.org</S>
    <S N="FirstName">Keith</S>
    <S N="LastName">Lync</S>
    <S N="WindowsEmailAddress">keith.lync@masteringlync.org</S>
<remainder cut for brevity>
```

Graphical Display and Filtering with *Out-GridView*

Keeping with the output types, `Out-GridView` was a new cmdlet introduced with PowerShell V2 and updated with PowerShell V3. With this cmdlet, the output appears (as shown in Figure 8.13 with `Get-CsUser | Out-GridView` as the command) in a graphical display that provides its own filtering interaction. This reduces the need to use other cmdlets to sort and filter data, such as the `Where-Object` and `Sort-Object` cmdlets mentioned previously.

FIGURE 8.13
Out-GridView

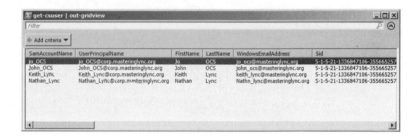

Running Scripts

So far we've been looking at individual cmdlets or in some cases piping the output from one command to another. As you become more proficient with PowerShell, the commands will get more complex, and you won't want to keep working out complex commands every time you need to repeat the same task. This is where scripting comes in.

POWERSHELL SCRIPT FILES

The names of PowerShell script files have the `.ps1` extension and must always be prefaced with the directory path. If you want to run a script in the local directory, preface it with `.\`, as shown here:

   `.\listusersscript.ps1`

Running Scheduled Scripts

The advantages of scripting really come into play when you consider scheduling. If, for example, you want to move a user from one pool to another, use this command:

```
Move-CsUser -Identity "keith lync" -Target "eepool01.corp.masteringlync.org"
```

However, you probably don't want to risk interrupting users during the working day (of course, as an admin you don't want to work overnight). You can save the move command in a file with a .ps1 filename extension (let's call it move_user.ps1) and leverage the Windows Task Scheduler to schedule the command to run after working hours.

You can find the Windows Task Scheduler by choosing Start ➤ Administrative Tools ➤ Task Scheduler; the Microsoft Management Console (MMC) shown in Figure 8.14 will appear.

FIGURE 8.14
The Windows Task Scheduler

Click Create Task in the right Actions panel to open the Task Wizard (shown in Figure 8.15).

FIGURE 8.15
Create a new task

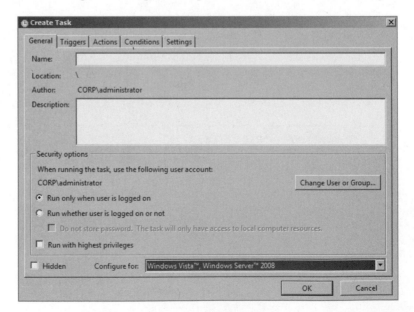

Using this wizard, you can define the task and the triggers that initiate it. You can also put conditions in place—for example, to ensure the task does not run too long. Each of the sections is explained here:

General   Define the name of the task, along with the security controls associated with it, including which user account to use and whether the user must be logged on or not.

Triggers   This is where you define how the task will be started; the options include On A Schedule, At Log On, At Startup, and so on. You can further modify this to include repetition options and expiry dates.

Actions   This is where you define the actual task to be executed; the options include Start A Program, Send An Email, and Display A Message.

Conditions   The Conditions section allows you to check to ensure that the system is in a capable state; for example, you could decide to start the task only if the computer is running on AC power or only if a particular network connection is available.

Settings   This section includes miscellaneous settings that do not fit anywhere else, such as Allow Run On Demand, Restart If The Task Fails, and settings for what to do if the task is already running.

The Task Scheduler does not allow PowerShell scripts to be run directly, so you must create a *batch* file (a list of executable commands for the command prompt, whose name ends with a *.bat* extension) and have the PowerShell script called from the batch file. You would create a new file and call it `move_user.bat`; this batch file would contain the following code:

```
PowerShell -command "& 'move_user.ps1'"
```

Now within the Task Scheduler, you call the task `Move User` and define the trigger to be scheduled for 8:00 p.m., with the action to be executed `Move_user.bat`. Figure 8.16 shows the results of creating the task (with the Actions tab highlighted).

FIGURE 8.16
Create a scheduled task.

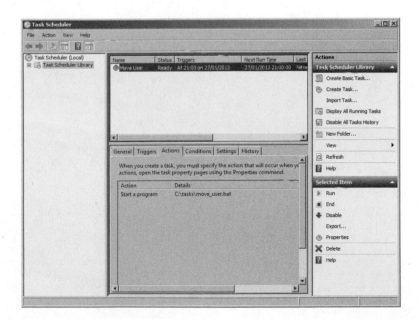

Now you can leave for the night and come back in the morning to view the report showing the user move information. Of course, scheduling a single user move is not a very useful scheduled script; more likely you would move multiple users, perhaps as shown to move all users to a new pool:

```
Get-CsUser | Move-CsUser -Target "eepool01.corp.masteringlync.org"
```

CHANGING POLICY BASED ON TIME

A customer recently needed to limit the number of calls permitted on their network during the day; for the evenings, this limit was lifted. The Call Admission Control (see Chapter 14) functionality within Lync does not provide any time-based policy controls.

However, by using the PowerShell scripting functionality, combined with Windows scheduling, and having two scripts—one to enable the restrictions and one to remove them—we were able to meet this requirement quite easily.

The restriction script runs at 08:00 every day, and the unrestricted script runs at 18:00.

Learning from the GUI

Unlike Exchange 2007 and Exchange 2010, the Lync Server Control Panel does not provide a user-friendly view of the PowerShell script being executed. With Exchange, the GUI allows you to cut and paste from the Exchange Console into your own scripts, making script creation simpler. However, that said, the naming system used on the Control Panel screens in most cases is easily understood and translated into the PowerShell cmdlet parameters. For example, Figure 8.17 shows a sample screen from the Control Panel, and Table 8.5 shows the corresponding parameters.

TABLE 8.5:   PowerShell versus Control Panel naming

CONTROL PANEL	POWERSHELL PARAMETER
Scope	No direct parameter—it is included in the Identity parameter.
Name	Identity
Description	Description
Enable communications with federated users	EnableFederationAccess
Enable communications with XMPP federated users	EnableXmppAccess
Enable communications with remote users	EnableOutsideAccess
Enable communications with public users	EnablePublicCloudAccess
N/A	EnablePublicCloudAudioVideoAccess

The final entry in the PowerShell column highlights again the fact that the shell is more powerful than the GUI; more functionality is exposed using PowerShell than through the GUI (approximately 80 percent of the PowerShell capability is presented within the GUI). For example, in Figure 8.17 you are looking at the External Access configuration and the `New-CsExternalAccessPolicy` (or in the case of changing an existing policy, `Set-CsExternalAccessPolicy`).

FIGURE 8.17
A sample Control
Panel screen

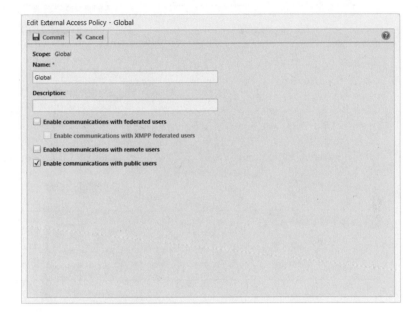

To determine the cmdlet parameter names from within PowerShell, use the following command:

```
Get-Help New-CsExternalAccessPolicy
```

As described previously, the help information is returned for the particular cmdlet selected (in this case `New-CsExternalAccessPolicy`). You're only interested in the Syntax section, so the rest has been omitted for clarity.

```
SYNTAX
    New-CsExternalAccessPolicy -Identity <XdsIdentity> [-Confirm [<SwitchParameter>]]
    [-Description <String>] [-EnableFederationAccess <$true | $false>] [-
    EnableOutsideAccess <$true | $false>] [-EnablePublicCloudAccess <$true | $false>]
    [-EnablePublicCloudAudioVideoAccess <$true | $false>] [-EnableXmppAccess <$true |
    $false>][-Force <SwitchParameter>] [-InMemory <SwitchParameter>] [-WhatIf
    [<SwitchParameter>]] [<CommonParameters>]
```

Here you can see the full list of parameters that can be provided, and if you want to see further detail about a specific parameter, you can use the following command:

```
Get-Help New-CsExternalAccessPolicy -Full
```

As previously shown, this has been shortened for clarity, to show only the information from a single parameter.

```
-EnablePublicCloudAccess <$true | $false>
Indicates whether the user is allowed to communicate with people how have SIP accounts
with a public Internet connectivity provider such as MSN. The default value is False.
Required?                       False
Position?                       Named
Default value
Accept pipeline input?          False
Accept wildcard characters?     False
```

So what have you learned here? From the GUI, you can see the option Enable Communications With Public Users, and from the cmdlet help you can see that the equivalent parameter is EnablePublicCloudAccess. This example was chosen to illustrate that although not all parameters are an exact match (without spaces), enough information should be provided in the GUI to infer a match with a parameter.

How can this help you? While Exchange administrators may be used to cutting and pasting their PowerShell into scripts from the GUI, Lync 2013 administrators can still learn from the GUI. However, creating a script from the actions taken is a manual process—but it is achievable with a little thought and effort!

THE 80 PERCENT RULE

One of the aims of the Lync Server development team was to provide 80 percent functionality via the Control Panel interface. As a result, some functionality is available only by using PowerShell.

Example Script Development

In the following sections, you're going to look at some real-world examples of scripts and how to develop them from scratch, putting into practice some of what you learned in this chapter. The scripts shown here are available to download from this link:

```
www.sybex.com/go/masteringlync2013
```

UPDATING USER INFORMATION

A reasonably common task is to update users' information details; this may be due to a change in name of the department, a building move, or similar occurrences.

In this example, you'll look at updating the Lync 2013 user phone information (we won't consider updating any Active Directory information in this script). This may happen when users move between buildings or when a telephone provider changes the area code (because they need a larger numbering scheme). So, the principle here is to change each user from area code 555 to area code 556.

This high-level approach is as follows:

1. Get a user.

2. Check the user's phone number.

3. If the number includes area code 555, change it to 556.

4. Get the next user.

Let's start with `Get-CsUser`. It allows you to retrieve user information (remember that `Get-CsUser` will return all the users, unless you supply a specific `-Identity` parameter). Because you want to check the user phone number details, you'll want to store the returned information in a variable ($users). The script so far looks like this:

```
$users = Get-CsUser
```

Next, you want to take each individual user in turn; to achieve this, you'll use the `ForEach` control-loop capability:

```
ForEach ($user in $users) {code}
```

Now, you want to look at the phone number field for a user; this is called `LineUri` and can be accessed by using `$user.LineUri` (the `$user` variable is used only within the `ForEach` loop and refers to the current user object).

Next, you want to check that this will include the area code in the number and ensure that you are dealing only with the users from a specific country (you don't want to change users with the same area code but a different country). You need to define the area code as +44555. Indeed, the `LineUri` parameter contains `Tel:` at the beginning, so you'll be looking for an entry that begins with `Tel:+44555`. The script line looks like:

```
If ($user.LineUri.Startswith("Tel:+44555")) {code}
```

Once you have identified a user that needs to be updated, you'll need to generate the new number for that user, and you can use the `Replace` function in PowerShell to do that. You also need to store this new number in a variable ($newnumber):

```
$newnumber = $user.LineUri.Replace("Tel:+44555","Tel:+44556")
```

Then you'll update the user object with the new value, using this command:

```
Set-CsUser -Identity $user.SipAddress -LineUri $newnumber
```

Bringing this all together, the script will look like this:

```
$users = Get-CsUser
ForEach ($user in $users) {
    If ($user.LineUri.Startswith("Tel:+44555")) {
        $newnumber = $user.LineUri.Replace("Tel:+44555","Tel:+44556")
        Set-CsUser -Identity $user.SipAddress -LineUri $newnumber
    }
}
```

Indentation is normally used to make the script more readable—each indentation refers to a control loop or a condition check. The closing brackets line up with the starting command.

Of course, this script updates only the `LineUri` field. What about users who have private lines? Now that you've worked through this section, you can update the script for those users on your own for extra practice. (Look for the `PrivateLine` field.)

Installing Prerequisites

The first script you examined dealt with updating user information, something that probably happens rarely in batches. This script will look at something significantly more useful, especially if you regularly build a lot of Lync 2013 servers for demos or test labs.

Here, you're going to look at configuring the prerequisites for a Lync 2013 Front End server installation, either a Standard Edition or Enterprise Edition. It's worth noting that this procedure can also be used to install other server roles; however, the other roles will have fewer prerequisites, so they should be used only in a lab environment; you don't want to install unused services if you don't need them.

The server is assumed to have only Windows Server 2008 R2 installed and be part of the domain, which matches the SIP domain. The goal is to finish with a deployed and functional Lync 2013 front end.

In addition, there is no way to manage the topology using PowerShell, so the topology is assumed to be already configured and published, with the file share definitions available.

From Chapter 5, "Planning Your Deployment," you know you should make a list of server features you'll need to install Lync Server 2013. First, you need to import the servermanager module to modify the feature list:

```
Import-Module servermanager
```

Next, you need to install the required features using Add-WindowsFeature. The actual names of the features can be found by running Get-WindowsFeature if you want to learn more:

```
Add-WindowsFeature Web-Static-Content, Web-Default-Doc, Web-Http-Errors, Web-Asp-Net,
Web-Net-Ext, Web-ISAPI-Ext, Web-ISAPI-Filter, Web-Http-Logging, Web-Log-Libraries,
Web-Http-Tracing, Web-Windows-Auth, Web-Filtering, Web-Stat-Compression, Web-Mgmt-
Console, Web-Scripting-Tools, Web-Basic-Auth, Web-Client-Auth -Restart
Add-WindowsFeature MSMQ-Server, MSMQ-Directory -Restart
Add-WindowsFeature Net-FrameWork
Add-windowsfeature RSAT-ADDS-Tools, RSAT-AD-AdminCenter
Add-windowsfeature IH-Ink-Support, Desktop-Experience
```

The final line adds support for media playing, which is necessary for any server running the A/V conference Multipoint Control Unit, or MCU (assuming the deployment will have it enabled). Unfortunately, this will typically need a reboot, and further installation will fail if a reboot is pending, so you need to check for a reboot.

In addition to listing all the available features, the Get-WindowsFeature cmdlet will tell you if a reboot is pending, so you can use the following commands to query the state and issue the Restart-Computer cmdlet to reboot if there is a pending reboot:

```
$features = Get-WindowsFeature
if ($features.restarttneeded -eq "yes"){Restart-Computer}
```

Once the computer has rebooted, you can rerun the script, and it will execute to this stage with no ill effects. Even though you are starting to add features, if they are already added, nothing will happen, and the check for reboot this time will return FALSE, so it will not issue the reboot.

Next, you'll register the DNS records, but first you need to query and capture the domain name. In this example, you'll use a system call to get the domain information. If you establish that the server is not domain joined, you'll exit the script (using exit); however, do expect to be domain joined, so you'll store the domain name in the variable $dn_name:

```
$domain = [system.directoryservices.activedirectory.domain]::GetComputerDomain()
if ($domain -eq $null){
    $domain_joined = $false
    exit
}
```

```
else{
    $dn_name = $domain.name
}
```

Capture your own server name from the WMI object `Win32_ComputerSystem`, using the following query, with the hostname stored in the Name field of the variable:

```
$computer = Get-WmiObject -Class Win32_ComputerSystem
$hostname = $computer.name
$seserverfqdn = "$hostname.$dn_name"
```

As you can see from the hostname (`$computer.Name`) and the domain name queried earlier (`$dn_name`), you build the server FQDN (`$seserverfqdn`).

You can't manipulate a DNS record directly within PowerShell; you need to use the `ndscmd.exe` executable. Of course, you first need to find out your own IP address so that you can register it. To do that, query a WMI object, `Win32_NetworkAdapterConfiguration`. You're interested only in enabled network interfaces, assuming the first enabled interface is the one you want to use (remember, the first item in an array is numbered 0):

```
$ip = (get-wmiobject win32_NetworkAdapterConfiguration -filter "IpEnabled=True")
$seserveripaddress = $ip.IPAddress[0]
```

You're going to need the address of the DNS server, and fortunately, the same WMI object holds that data:

```
$dnsserver = $ip.dnsserversearchorder[0]
```

For the actual DNS entries, you want to create the SRV record along with the `meet`, `admin`, and `dialin` entries too:

```
Dnscmd $dnsserver /recordadd $dn_name _sipinternaltls._tcp srv 5 0 5061
$seserverfqdn
Dnscmd $dnsserver /recordadd $dn_name meet a $seserveripaddress
Dnscmd $dnsserver /recordadd $dn_name admin a $seserveripaddress
Dnscmd $dnsserver /recordadd $dn_name dialin a $seserveripaddress
Dnscmd $dnsserver /recordadd $dn_name lyncdiscoverinternal a $seserveripaddress
```

The following prerequisites are not available on the Lync media, so they need to be installed separately:

- .NET 4.5
- Silverlight
- PowerShell v3
- Windows Identity Foundation
- HotFix 2646886

```
$prereq_media_directory = "c:\pre-reqs"
#Install .NET 4.5
$prereq_media_directory\dotnetfx45_full_x86_x64.exe
start-sleep -s 240
#Install Silverlight
$prereq_media_directory\silverlight_x64.exe
start-sleep -s 120
#Install PowerShell v3
```

```
$prereq_media_directory\Windows6.1-kb2506143-x64.msu
start-sleep -s 120
#Install Windows Identity Foundation
$prereq_media_directory\Windows6.1-kb974405-x64.msu
start-sleep -s 120
#Install HotFix 2646886
$prereq_media_directory\Windows6.1-kb2646886-x64.msu
start-sleep -s 120
```

Now that the script has installed the prerequisites and created the necessary DNS entries, you need to install the appropriate software from the Lync 2013 DVD. For this example, we'll assume you are using drive X: for the DVD. You need to install the following:

◆ Visual C++ Redistributable

◆ SQL Native Client

◆ SQL System CLR Types

◆ Unified Communications Managed API (UCMA)

◆ Lync Core Components

◆ Lync Admin Tools

To install them, you can use the following commands. Each software package may take some time to complete, and because you rely upon the package being installed later, you will want to pause while the installation is under way using the Start-Sleep cmdlet (ensuring that the package has completed installation by the time you need it):

```
$lync_media_directory = "x:"
#Install Visual C++ Redistributable
$lync_media_directory\setup\amd64\vcredist_x64.exe /q
start-sleep -s 120
#Install SQL Native Client
$lync_media_directory\setup\amd64\sqlncli.msi -quiet
start-sleep -s 60
#Install SQL System CLR Types
$lync_media_directory\setup\amd64\SQLSysClrTypes.msi -quiet
start-sleep -s 60
#install ucma
msiexec /qn /i $lync_media_directory\setup\amd64\Setup\ucmaruntime.msi
REBOOT=ReallySuppress /QN EXCLUDETRACING=1 BOOT=1
start-sleep -s 60
#Install Lync core components
msiexec /qn /i $lync_media_directory\setup\amd64\Setup\ocscore.msi
INSTALLDIR=`"C:\Program Files\Microsoft Lync Server 2013\`" ADDLOCAL=Feature_OcsCore
start-sleep -s 60
#Install Lync admin tools
msiexec /qn /i $lync_media_directory\setup\amd64\Setup\admintools.msi
start-sleep -s 60
```

At this point, you've done all you can do without running the Lync 2013 PowerShell, so you need to import that module:

```
Import-Module -name 'C:\program files\common files\microsoft lync server 2013\modules\lync'
```

These examples have assumed the topology was published; however, you can check this by using `Get-CsTopology`, and in this case you'll exit the script if it has not. This will allow the script to install all the prerequisites (including Topology Builder) for you and then wait until you define and publish the topology. This is useful if you're deploying only one server. Simply rerun the script after the topology is published and the script will continue:

```
$topology = Get-CsTopology
If ($topology -eq $null){exit}
```

Now you're getting to the actual deployment stages, the first part of which is to install the local SQL Express for the replica of the Central Management Store (CMS). Next, start the Lync Replica Service to allow the data to replicate from the CMS to the new server:

```
"C:\Program Files\Microsoft Lync Server 2013\Deployment\Bootstrapper.exe"
/BootstrapLocalMgmt /SourceDirectory:$lync_media_directory\setup\amd64\
start-sleep -s 120
Enable-CsReplica
Start-CsWindowsService Replica
```

You could wait for replication or use PowerShell to speed it up. Naturally, you'll want to speed it up! Exporting the configuration file from the CMS and importing it locally has the same effect as waiting, but it is quicker! Here, you're temporarily storing the data in the `$config` variable:

```
$config = Export-CsConfiguration -asbytes
Import-CsConfiguration -byteinput $config -LocalStore
```

Now you've reached the stage where the prerequisites (both server side and Lync 2013 specific) are installed, the DNS entries are created, and the topology is replicated to the local CMS replica. All you need to do is run the installation routine, get certificates, and start the services.

The Lync 2013 installation routine checks the local topology to see which roles are defined for the current server, and it will install only what is needed. Because this process is part of the installation, the script does not need to determine which roles are required to be installed; you can simply run the installer:

```
"C:\Program Files\Microsoft Lync Server 2013\Deployment\Bootstrapper.exe"
/SourceDirectory:$lync_media_directory\setup\amd64\
```

At this point, a reboot may be required to complete the installation; however, you still need to get certificates, and this will succeed whether a reboot is pending or not.

Requesting a certificate is relatively easy using Lync PowerShell; the tricky part is to find the certificate authority (CA) details, which are held in Active Directory. You have to connect to Active Directory and search specifically for the `pKIEnrollmentService`, and from the response you need to determine the DNS name of the server. There may be multiple entries of this type; however, this script simply takes the final entry as the one to use:

```
$root = [ADSI]"LDAP://CN=Configuration,$dn_name"
$query = new-object system.directoryservices.directorysearcher($root)
$query.filter = "(&(objectClass=pKIEnrollmentService)(cn=*))"
```

```
$query.SearchSCope = "subtree"
$result = $query.findall()
```

If the results of the Active Directory search are empty, set the $ca_found variable to $false (you'll use this later), and if they're not empty, capture the CA name in the correct format (*dnsname\cnname*) and set the $ca_found variable to $true:

```
if ($result -eq $null){
$ca_found = $false
}
else{
        foreach ($ca in $result) {
         $o = $ca.getdirectoryentry()
         $dnsname = $o.dNSHostName
         $cn = $o.cn
         $ca_name = "$dnsname\$cn"
         $ca_found = $true
}
}
```

Now that you have the certificate details, you can request and assign the certificate and finish starting the services. If the $ca_found variable is set to $true, you will automatically request and assign the certificates using the CA; however, if it is $false, the process will be manual. Once the certificate is assigned, the services can be started:

```
If ($ca_found){
    $Certificate = Request-CsCertificate -New -Type
Default,WebServicesInternal,WebServicesExternal -CA $Ca_Name -FriendlyName Default
-AllSipDomain
    Set-CsCertificate -Thumbprint $Certificate.Thumbprint -Type
Default,WebServicesInternal,WebServicesExternal
    Enable-CsComputer
    Start-cswindowsService
}
```

In summary, this script has achieved the following:

◆ Installed the server prerequisites for Lync Server 2013 Front End

◆ Installed Lync Server 2013 prerequisites

◆ Created the DNS records

◆ Installed SQL Express for the RTCLocal instance

◆ Installed SQL Express for the LyncLocal instance

◆ Replicated the topology

◆ Installed Lync Server 2013 to the configuration specified in the topology

◆ Requested an application of a certificate

◆ Started the Lync Server 2013 Services

At this point, users can be enabled and clients will be able to connect.

Regular Expressions

Regular expressions (also known as *regex*) can be defined as to "provide a concise and flexible means to 'match' strings of text, such as particular characters, words or patterns of characters." In Lync (both versions, as well as OCS), regular expressions are used to manipulate numbers (outgoing as well as incoming) to their base level to better identify best (or permitted) routes as well as to "normalize" numbers, which is converting a number (possibly only an extension) into a fully defined number that can be understood and routed by Lync.

Regular expressions can be very complex; some examples can be seen in the OCS address book normalization sample file. Fortunately Lync has improved significantly on how to manage number normalization!

So, what's the point of regex? And why do we need to understand it?

Well, we've already given one example: providing users with the ability to simply dial an extension and have Lync understand the final target number intended to be dialed and route accordingly. Other examples would be to add in country code information or indeed the number for an outside line. It's much easier to have a user continue their existing dialing habits than have to retrain users to understand the dialing habits of a new system.

Understanding Regex

Let's start with an example outside the world of Lync completely. Say you want to describe your pets—a cat and a dog—using regular expressions.

You could use the following:

<consonant><vowel><consonant>

That matches for both *cat* and *dog*.

Now, let's assume you get another pet: a bird. How can you define all your pets now? Well, it turns out you don't need to do anything. The definition above only defines the *order* in which the consonants and vowel appear; it doesn't define anything regarding numbers or position. As long as somewhere in the word you have the <consonant><vowel><consonant> pattern, you will match upon it.

So, how can you be more specific and match only *cat* and *dog*?

Well, you can have a number of special characters that within regex provide meaning or context, such as, for example (we'll describe these further as we go):

^

$

*

+

?

|

[]

(Please note that different implementations of regex may have different meanings to these symbols; in this example we are referring to the Lync implementation).

The symbol ^ matches against the *beginning* of the string, in other words 'the string MUST start with' the pattern.

So, would ^<consonant><vowel><consonant> help our scenario? Well, no, because each item—*cat*, *dog*, and *bird*—starts with this pattern, so you'd still get a match on all of them.

The symbol $ matches against the *end* of a string. Would that fit?

<consonant><vowel><consonant>$ would be fine for *cat* and *dog* and would exclude *bird*, so looks like it is a good choice for you. However, it does leave you open to matching against *rabbit* because you are looking for the pattern in only the final three characters in this example.

To be more specific, you'd have to match against both the *start* and the *end*, using both ^ and $.

^<consonant><vowel><consonant>$—this ensures that you only look for a pattern that is three characters long.

Now, how about introducing some flexibility? Well, by using a + you can call for a match of the preceding element one or more times.

So, ^<consonant><vowel><consonant>+$ would look for patterns that matched three or four characters, with the pattern <consonant><vowel><consonant> or <consonant><vowel><consonant><consonant>. From your list, this would be *cat*, *dog*, and *bird*.

A ? could also give you similar flexibility. This time you will match the preceding element zero or one times.

You pattern would be: ^<consonant><vowel><consonant><consonant>?$

If you didn't care how many time the final preceding character appeared, you could use *; this would equate to zero or more times.

The characters [] allow for options contained within the brackets, and each option is separated by |.

You could have ^[<consonant><vowel><consonant>|<consonant><vowel><consonant><consonant>]$ to give you another option to represent the three- or four-character selection in the previous cases.

Regex within Lync

In most cases you will encounter regex only if you want to use the address book normalization file to help normalize numbers stored in Active Directory. However, it is used extensively in the background by Lync for the normalization rules for users and their dialing patterns; it's just presented differently to the admin via the GUI, as shown in Figure 8.18.

You may have a complex scenario that cannot be handled by the simple GUI approach and require direct manipulation of regex, or alternatively you may wish to use PowerShell to deploy and configure Lync completely.

Aside from the string-based examples shown earlier, Lync uses \d to represent a digit, so the pattern ^\d\d\d\d$ would represent an entry that is four digits long (as it also includes the start and end characters).

Table 8.6 shows some examples of regex and their descriptions.

TABLE 8.6:   Sample regex expressions for Lync

REGEX	DESCRIPTION
^555\d\d\d\d$	Seven-digit entry, beginning with 555
^555\d{4}$	Seven-digit entry, beginning with 555 (more human readable)
^[555|123]\d{4}$	Seven-digit entry, beginning with either 555 or 123

TABLE 8.6: Sample regex expressions for Lync *(CONTINUED)*

REGEX	DESCRIPTION
^[555|123]\d{*}$	Minimum three-digit entry, beginning with either 555 or 123
^555\d+$	Minimum four-digit entry, beginning with 555
^(555\d{4})$	Seven-digit entry, beginning with 555, including marking the data within the () to be carried to the next stage

FIGURE 8.18
Representation of regex in the Lync GUI

The last example here includes an entry within parentheses. The data enclosed in the parentheses is marked as an item to be carried to the next stage in the manipulation—similar to how a variable would be in a script; indeed, in this case it would be assigned the name $1.

The majority of regex patterns are to manipulate the number dialed by users. This normally involves taking some (or all) of the number entered and modifying it before sending to a gateway for dialing (or matching internally). To allow for these numbers to be taken and passed to the next stage (normally called *translation*), we use parentheses.

A translation pattern would be something similar to +1425$1. In this case, it would take the number represented by $1 and precede it with +1425. Ultimately, here, it's creating an E164 number by adding the area code as well as the international country code. This number could then be passed to a gateway (or PBX) for dialing.

The Bottom Line

Use the PowerShell command syntax.   PowerShell is an easy-to-use command-line interface that provides more control over the manipulation and configuration of Lync (as well as other Microsoft and third-party products).

PowerShell cmdlets consist of a verb, indicating the process (New, Enable, Set, and so on), and a noun, indicating the object (CsUser, CsPool, CsExternalAccessPolicy, and so on).

Master It You need to assign a conference policy to a user. Which is the correct cmdlet to use?

- ◆ Grant-CsConferencePolicy
- ◆ Set-CsUser
- ◆ New-CsConferencePolicy

Employ tips and tricks to get more out of PowerShell. PowerShell has many built-in capabilities, and extensions such as Lync provide the specifics to manage an application environment.

One of its most powerful features is the ability to pipe output from one command to another. This ability lets you easily and quickly perform repetitive tasks.

Master It You want to enable all users for Enterprise Voice. How would you do this?

Get help using PowerShell. The ability to get detailed help information on any cmdlet, as well as use case examples, without leaving the PowerShell environment is an invaluable time-saver.

Master It You need to manipulate some conference configuration items but you can't remember which cmdlet to use. How can you identify possible cmdlets to use?

Understand PowerShell remoting and scripting. PowerShell provides a wealth of scripting capability, allowing relatively easy automation of everyday tasks which previously could be very complex.

Remoting extends PowerShell even further. Now you don't need to install individual administration toolsets for every application on an administrator's workstation; simply connect remotely to a PowerShell session and you can use the cmdlets.

Master It You want to administer the Lync Server 2013 configuration from your local workstation without installing any local administration tools and without using Remote Desktop. How would you connect to a remote PowerShell?

Understand regular expressions. Regular expressions are used to help manipulate user dialing habits, to ensure that the correct numbers (from a Lync Server perspective) are provided to the gateway. In the majority of cases, this regex approach is hidden by the Lync Control Panel GUI; however, it may be required to manipulate regex in some complex scenarios (as well as to implement the address book normalization file).

Master It You want to create an entry that will match only upon a six-digit entry, starting with 12. Which is the best approach from those shown?

^12\d{6}

\d{6}

^12\d{4}$

^[12|\d{4}]$

[12]\d{4}$

Chapter 9

Role-Based Access Control

Implemented first in Exchange Server 2010, then in Lync Server 2010, and now enhanced in Lync Server 2013, role-based access control (RBAC) changes the granularity and ease with which an administrator can be granted permissions required for their job and only their job, allowing specific delegation of functionality to groups of people.

In this chapter, you will learn to:

◆   Use PowerShell to list the standard RBAC groups

◆   Understand the permissions available to each role

◆   Undertake planning for RBAC roles

◆   Create custom RBAC roles and assign them to administrators

◆   Carry out general administration, including granting and removing RBAC roles

◆   Report on the use of RBAC roles

RBAC Overview

In medium to large organizations, the same person does not necessarily administer every system. RBAC was created to address the problems that can arise as a result. In addition, Microsoft and security professionals in general espouse the principle of *least privilege*, whereby each administrator is granted only the minimum permissions needed to carry out their job. Until RBAC was built into the product, companies were forced to work within the constraints of the rather lackluster delegation often provided by Microsoft server applications, or they had to look for a third-party delegation product. This led to the development of rather complex and costly products such as Active Roles, from Quest, which enabled more granular delegation based on the need to perform certain tasks, which grouped together formed roles. If you didn't have the time or budget for such products, you were left with native tools and the myriad possibilities of manually hacking access control lists (ACLs) and below them, individual access control entries (ACEs) in Active Directory (AD).

Administration of Microsoft server products has long been intertwined with permissions. Administrators need rights to modify, create, and delete objects. Until recently, this required granting complex levels of permissions on Active Directory and file system objects. OCS 2007 R2 RTCUniversalReadOnlyAdmins made a token gesture toward granting permissions based on job role. However, membership in the AD group aligned to the role didn't give all the permissions necessary to do the job because other AD group memberships to allow basic account access were required.

Thankfully, in Wave 14 (the 2010 release of Microsoft products), Microsoft answered the call to build in this type of functionality. Starting with Exchange 2010 and then Lync 2010, an implementation of role-based access control (RBAC) was provided. It allowed delegation of tasks based on role and targeting of objects so the administrator can carry out tasks without the need to manually set ACLs. Lync Server 2013 takes the capability introduced in Lync 2010 and enhances it, allowing significantly more granular delegation of administrative commands as well as a couple of new roles that we will cover shortly.

Roles and Scopes

The concept of RBAC is very simple. An administrator is granted the rights to run certain PowerShell cmdlets (a *role*) on a certain group of users or servers (a *scope*).

An RBAC role is built up by defining a set of cmdlets that can be run. Generally, these cmdlets are grouped together to form a set related to a job role. A scope defines the target objects where those cmdlets can be run. For example, a scope could be defined to servers (grouped within a site), a group of users (in an OU), or to the whole organization using a *global scope*.

Each role has a config and a user scope. This means that you can delegate a role both to a set of users and to a site where servers are contained, allowing you great granularity in the way delegation is carried out.

Each role membership is controlled by a linked AD group, which is specified at the creation of the role. The AD groups linked to the standard roles are created in the Users container of the domain specified during AD forest preparation. Although forest preparation must be run from a machine in the root forest, the domain specified for the groups can be anywhere in the forest and doesn't have to be the root. Given that the membership of these groups governs the roles an administrator holds, if your company heavily locks down the root domain of the forest, you may decide to create these groups in a child domain. Figure 9.1 shows the key elements of role, AD group, and scope in diagram form for the standard role AD group CSAdministrator.

FIGURE 9.1
The key elements of
RBAC: role, group,
and scope

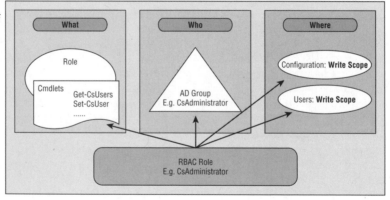

Lync Roles and PowerShell

Chapter 8, "Introduction to PowerShell, the Lync Management Shell, and Regular Expressions," covered PowerShell basics and showed how Lync utilizes its cmdlets. As you learned, all administration can be undertaken through PowerShell in Lync 2013. In fact, even when you are using the Lync Server Control Panel (LSCP), you are actually calling PowerShell commands in the background. This chapter relies primarily on PowerShell because, as in Lync 2010, it provides the only way to manipulate Lync roles.

It is this reliance on PowerShell that enables RBAC to work. When you access PowerShell remotely—as described in Chapter 8—either through the LSCP or through remote PowerShell rather than directly on the Lync server via the Lync Server Management Shell (LSMS), Lync parses the commands to which you have access based on the roles you are assigned. In fact, when accessing Lync through remote PowerShell, when you run `Get-Command` you see only the commands you can run. This is also reflected in the GUI, as shown in Figure 9.2, which shows the LSCP accessed by a full administrator and an archiving administrator logged on. The difference is clear to see, with far less functionality being made available to the archiving administrator.

LYNC 2010 CU2 UPDATES BRING CROSS-DOMAIN SUPPORT

One nice improvement that was made in Lync Server 2010 Cumulative Updates 2 (CU2) was the ability to scope to a child domain. When Lync 2010 was first released, its inability to flexibly use scope caused problems; the common name (CN) of the organizational unit (OU) to be delegated under the control of a scope could only be in the root domain. Thankfully, this was fixed, so it is possible to let different groups of administrators, from different child domains, control the users in the domains they administer.

FIGURE 9.2
The Control Panel accessed by an administrator holding the CSAdministrator role, with full administrative rights (top); the CSArchivingAdministrator role, with limited admin rights (bottom)

So how does this actually work? When an administrator connects to Lync, either through remote PowerShell or via LSCP, they are authenticated. At this point, the Lync Management Web Service will create a run-space for the user, which contains only the cmdlets the user has access to run as assigned by their role membership. When the administrator then runs a command, authorization is performed to confirm that indeed the administrator does have rights to run that cmdlet and that the cmdlet is targeted at a location (scope) where the administrator has been granted access. At this point, assuming all checks are passed, the CS Management Web Service executes the cmdlet.

COMMAND FILTERING IN THE LYNC SERVER CONTROL PANEL

You can actually see this filtering of commands in action in the Lync Server Control Panel. On a slow system, when you log on to LSCP as an administrator with limited permissions, you can see the various elements of the graphical user interface (GUI) to which you don't have access disappear as the role is applied.

How does this work, given that the administrator doesn't need special permissions in AD? Each RBAC role has an associated Universal security group in Active Directory (AD). The groups for the standard roles are shown in Table 9.1.

TABLE 9.1: Details of the standard RBAC role groups

GROUP NAME	GROUP TYPE	DESCRIPTION
CSAdministrator	Security Group - Universal	Members of this group can perform all administrative tasks in Lync Server 2013.
CSArchivingAdministrator	Security Group - Universal	Members of this group can create, configure, and manage archiving-related settings and policies in Lync Server 2013.
CSHelpDesk	Security Group - Universal	Members of this group can view the deployment, including user properties and policies, and can execute specific troubleshooting tasks in Lync Server 2013.
CSLocationAdministrator	Security Group - Universal	Members of this group have the lowest level of rights for E911 management. They can create E911 locations and network identifiers and associate them with each other in Lync Server 2013.
CsPersistentChatAdministrator	Security Group - Universal	Members of this group can run the persistent chat admin cmdlets for Categories/Rooms/Addins.
CSResponseGroupAdministrator	Security Group - Universal	Members of this group can manage the configuration of the Response Group application in Lync Server 2013.

TABLE 9.1: Details of the standard RBAC role groups *(CONTINUED)*

GROUP NAME	GROUP TYPE	DESCRIPTION
CSResponseGroupManager	Security Group - Universal	Members of this group can manage limited configuration of assigned Response Groups in Lync Server 2013.
CSServerAdministrator	Security Group -Universal	Members of this group can manage, monitor, and troubleshoot Lync Server 2013 and services.
CSUserAdministrator	Security Group - Universal	Members of this group can enable and disable users for Lync Server 2013, move users, and assign existing policies to users.
CSViewOnlyAdministrator	Security Group - Universal	Members of this group can view the Lync Server 2013 deployment, including server information, in order to monitor deployment health.
CSVoiceAdministrator	Security Group - Universal	Members of this group can create, configure, and manage voice-related settings and policies in Lync Server 2013.

However, the role group in AD doesn't grant any special permission; it is just a placeholder provided so Lync can manage membership of the role. How are the cmdlets run? They are run under the local machine account of the server to which the administrator has the remote connection. This works because that local machine account is itself a member of various AD groups. These groups will be familiar to anyone who has installed any form of Office Communications Server (OCS)—the Real Time Communications (RTC) groups—and they are still the groups that govern what happens when you don't use remote PowerShell. If you access the console of the Front End server and run the Lync Server Management Shell, for example, you will not be authenticated and managed by RBAC. When the admin logs on locally and uses LSMS on the console of the Lync server, administration rights are governed by membership of the RTC named groups, which are created by Lync forest prep. This system is almost identical to that which was in place with OCS 2007 R2. There is no simple provision for scoping of access.

RBAC ONLY WORKS USING REMOTE CONNECTIONS

If you rely on RBAC to delegate administrative access, you must be careful to protect console access, either via RDP or physically at the server. RBAC only works remotely, so anyone who gains physical access will be governed by membership of the RTC groups, not RBAC roles. It is, therefore, also very important to monitor and manage access to the relevant AD group memberships.

So how are these groups and the RBAC role groups intertwined? The RBAC groups are not granted permissions on anything directly. As mentioned earlier, what actually happens when an RBAC user runs a command is that the CS Management Web Service first confirms that the user is entitled to run the cmdlet and then runs it under the local Lync Server machine account.

These machine accounts get their rights to run cmdlets from membership in the various RTC groups shown in Table 9.2, such as RTCUniversalServerAdmins and RTCUniversalUserAdmins.

TABLE 9.2: RTC groups in the Users container in Active Directory Users and Computers (ADUC)

GROUP NAME	GROUP TYPE	DESCRIPTION
RTCUniveralUserReadOnlyGroup	Security Group - Universal	Members have read access to RTC-related user attributes or property sets.
RTCUniversalUserAdmins	Security Group - Universal	Members can manage RTC users in this forest.
RTCUniversalServerReadOnlyGroup	Security Group - Universal	Members have read access to RTC-related server AD objects in the forest.
RTCUniversalServerAdmins	Security Group - Universal	Members can manage all aspects of RTC servers in this forest.
RTCUniversalSBATechnicians	Security Group - Universal	Members have read access to Lync Server 2013 configuration and are placed in the Local Administrators group of survivable branch office appliances during installation.
RTCUniversalReadOnlyAdmins	Security Group - Universal	Members can only read RTC-related server and user properties in this forest.
RTCUniversalGlobalWriteGroup	Security Group - Universal	Members have write access to RTC global settings.
RTCUniversalGlobalReadOnlyGroup	Security Group - Universal	Members have read access to RTC global settings.
RTCUniversalConfigReplicator	Security Group - Universal	Members can participate in configuration replication.
RTCSBAUniversalServices	Security Group - Universal	Members have read access to Lync Server 2013 configuration for survivable branch office installation.
RTCProxyUniversalServices	Security Group - Universal	Members can be used as RTC proxy service logon.
RTCHSUniversalServices	Security Group - Universal	Members can be used as RTC IM service logon.
RTCComponentUniversalServices	Security Group - Universal	Members can be used as RTC MCU and web component services logon.

The RTC groups are then assigned permissions through the setup process on objects in AD. Figure 9.3 shows the Security tab for a user account, which clearly shows the access control entry (ACE) for the RTCUniversalUserAdmins group.

FIGURE 9.3
The Security tab of a standard user showing the ACE for RTCUniversalUserAdmins

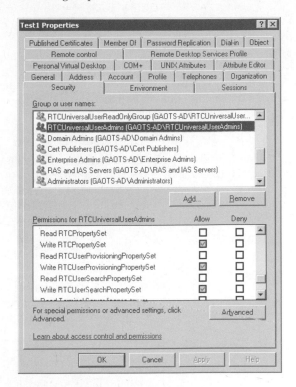

Now that we've looked at the building blocks, let's move on and examine the roles available in Lync out of the box.

Understanding Lync's Standard Roles

Out of the box, Lync 2013 ships with 11 roles, a range that gives you a fair amount of flexibility in grouping your administrators. However, you may find that you don't want to split things quite as they are out of the box. This is one area where Lync 2013 makes significant improvements over Lync 2010. Lync 2013 makes it possible not only to give administrators several of the standard roles but also to utilize the ability to create custom roles, as described later in this chapter. It is the ability to create custom roles that has changed in Lync 2013. Previously, while you could create custom roles, you were limited to making use of the existing groupings of cmdlets. All you could change was the scope and the target group. What you couldn't do was carve up the cmdlets yourself to make custom roles. Thankfully that has now changed and you can not only create custom roles with the any cmdlets you choose, you can also create roles that are only allowed to run specific pre-created scripts. This new approach gives the ability to be extremely granular and controlled about the permissions you give to different groups.

Let's dive into some PowerShell and see how to view the roles. On the Lync Standard Edition server you installed in Chapter 6, "Installation," make sure you are logged on locally either through RDP to the console or physically at the server console. Ensure that you are logged on as a member of the RTCUniversalServerAdmins group in AD. Open up the Lync Server Management Shell (LSMS). This is the simplest command you can use to get Lync to output a list of the roles:

```
Get-CsAdminRole
```

This will bring back any roles, including those you might have created yourself.

You can then be a little more specific and bring back just a single role—for example, the CSAdministrator role as follows:

```
Get-CsAdminRole -Identity CSAdministrator
```

The output, as listed next, shows you the role identity, the security identifier (SID) of the group it is linked to in AD, that it is a standard role, the beginning of the list of cmdlets that are available to those holding the role, and the scopes of the role. At the bottom of the output you will see the template. For the default roles, this is empty; however, as you will see later, when you create custom roles, this is something that you will have to specify.

```
Identity       : CSAdministrator
SID            : S-1-5-21-1336847106-355665257-1417932119-1130
IsStandardRole : True
Cmdlets        : {Name=Get-CsClientPolicy, Name=Set-CsClientPolicy,
                 Name=Remove-CsClientPolicy, Name=New-CsClientPolicy...}
ScriptModules  : {}
ConfigScopes   : {Global}
UserScopes     : {Global}
Template       :
```

To bring back a nicely formatted list of just the standard roles, you need to extend the first PowerShell cmdlets as follows:

```
Get-CsAdminRole | Where-Object {$_.IsStandardRole -eq $True} | fl Identity
```

This pipes the output of the plain `Get-CsAdminRole` cmdlet into `Where-Object`, which checks each role to see if the attribute `IsStandardRole` is set to True. It then pipes those role objects into the `Format-List` cmdlet and shows only the `Identity` attribute.

Having done this, you will have successfully listed all 11 standard roles and will obtain the following output:

```
Identity : CSAdministrator
Identity : CSVoiceAdministrator
Identity : CSUserAdministrator
Identity : CSResponseGroupAdministrator
Identity : CSLocationAdministrator
Identity : CSArchivingAdministrator
Identity : CSViewOnlyAdministrator
Identity : CSServerAdministrator
Identity : CSHelpDesk
Identity : CSResponseGroupManager
Identity : CsPersistentChatAdministrator
```

As mentioned, a Lync role is a group of cmdlets. As you can see, the list of cmdlets is begun but then tails off in an ellipsis. In order to see all of the cmdlets that make up each role, you need to jump back into PowerShell. For example, to see all the cmdlets assigned to the CSAdministrator role, you would use the following command:

```
Get-CsAdminRole -Identity CSAdministrator | Select-Object -ExpandProperty Cmdlets ↵
| Out-File c:\csadminrolecmdlets.txt
```

This command first gets the CSAdministrator role, pipes its attributes to `Select-Object`, and then expands the `Cmdlets` attribute. The results are then piped to the `Out-File` cmdlet, which will write them to a text file. Later in this chapter, in the section "Planning Combinations," you'll see a script created by a member of the Lync product group that lists all the cmdlets available to each role.

Now that you've seen how to list the standard roles, let's take a closer look at each one.

CSAdministrator

Of all the RBAC roles, CSAdministrator is the most powerful. It gives the assigned user the full range of Lync functionality, including the ability to carry out user, server, and device administration and to create and assign RBAC roles and other policies. This is the role to which the setup process asks you to add a user, who will become the first Lync administrator. Essentially, this role would be given only to the most senior administrators who require access to deploy and control all aspects of Lync.

One final thing to note about the CSAdministrator role is that although it gives the most functionality available in a role, it doesn't enable you to run all the commands that exist in the Lync PowerShell module.

POWERSHELL MODULES

For more on the use of PowerShell modules and in particular the Lync module, see Chapter 8. To output all the commands in the module to a text file called `AllLyncCmds.txt`, you would run this version of `Get-Command`:

```
Get-Command -Module Lync -CommandType All | Out-File c:\AllLyncCmds.txt
```

If you compare the cmdlets available in the Lync module and those available to the CSAdministrator role, you will see that many are not included in the CSAdministrator role. These are generally system-altering cmdlets like those that allow the preparation of the domain, such as `Prep-Domain`. They, therefore, need greater permissions than granted through Lync groups alone—for example, Domain Administrator permissions. They are also required to be run locally on the Lync server through LSMS rather than through remote PowerShell.

RELATED EXCHANGE ROLE

Given that Exchange 2013 also implements RBAC, it is useful to understand the similar roles available. If your administrators run both Exchange and Lync, then you will understand how to assign the standard RBAC groups in Lync to match those in Exchange.

A similar role in Exchange to Lync's CSAdministrator role would be the Organization Administrator role.

CSUserAdministrator

The CSUserAdministrator role enables the holder to manage users. Specifically, it can enable users for Lync, although it cannot create new AD users, and it can move users between Lync pools and disable Lync users. It also allows the holder to assign policies to users but not to create policies. This role also allows the management of devices such as analog and common area phones. Interestingly, the role also allows the creation of the contacts used when integrating Lync with Exchange Unified Messaging (UM) for voicemail provision. For more information about UM, see Chapter 17, "Exchange and SharePoint."

It is likely that this role would be given to second-level support engineers who were specifically focused on end-user support rather than support of the server infrastructure, which might be left for third-level support and higher.

RELATED EXCHANGE ROLE

A similar role in Exchange would be Mail Recipients.

CSServerAdministrator

The CSServerAdministrator role is the most far-ranging role outside the CSAdministrator role. It allows control of a significant amount of Lync functionality.

In general, the main thing that this policy can't do is grant policy to end users. For that, you need the CSAdministrator role or the CSUserAdministrator role. It can't enable or disable users either. The other key thing it can't do is create new RBAC roles for which the CSAdministrator role is needed.

Other than that, this role does give the ability to manage and monitor the backend aspects of Lync. It allows the management of services, testing of services, and ability to bring servers up and down through the draining process.

This role is likely to be granted to senior or third-level admins who are focused on maintaining and managing Lync on a day-to-day basis.

RELATED EXCHANGE ROLE

A similar role in Exchange would be the Server Management role.

CSViewOnlyAdministrator

The CSViewOnlyAdministrator role grants the holder the ability to monitor the Lync implementation. It is made up almost entirely of `Get-` cmdlets that pull back information about a wide variety of Lync elements, such as policies, server configuration, voice configuration, call admission control, and users. The one exception is the `Debug-CsLisConfiguration` cmdlet, which allows you to pull back detailed configuration information about Location Information Services (LIS).

This role is intended to give reporting powers and would perhaps be granted to architects or compliance officers to enable them to monitor the progress of deployment or see the settings of various policies.

RELATED EXCHANGE ROLE

There is a very similar role in Exchange: View-Only Organization Management.

CSArchivingAdministrator

The CSArchivingAdministrator role in Lync gives the holder the ability to run a limited set of cmdlets pertaining only to managing the archive and archive policies in Lync. This is the only role other than CSAdministrator that is able to create, grant, and alter archiving policies.

This role is most likely to be delegated to a security/compliance officer who would be specifically tasked with managing archiving by creating and assigning policies to users.

Related Exchange Role

In Exchange, there is the Discovery Management role; however, it is more about performing searches than configuring journaling and retention policy. More similar roles would be the Retention Management role.

CSHelpDesk

In some ways, the CSHelpDesk role is similar to the CSViewOnlyAdmin role in that it is made up of mostly Get- cmdlets giving visibility of configuration. However, the CSHelpDesk role also has many Test- cmdlets, which can be run to validate end-to-end functionality and thus troubleshoot user issues, and also three PIN-related cmdlets (Set-CsClientPin, Lock-CsClientPin, and Unlock-CsClientPin), which allow control over user access. This role is likely to be given to first-line support to enable them to fix basic issues like resetting the user PIN and then to provide a useful report to the more senior engineers after running the relevant Test- cmdlets.

Related Exchange Role

There is a very similar role group in Exchange: HelpDesk.

CSVoiceAdministrator

The CSVoiceAdministrator role is a wide-ranging one; it allows configuration and control over the PBX elements of Lync, including phone devices, response groups, location setup, and call routing. In many organizations where unified communication systems haven't been deployed, the teams who manage the PBX and those who manage servers are different. This role allows that type of split to continue.

Related Exchange Role

There is no equivalent role in Exchange. These teams are often separate. The only possible consideration is whether these administrators might take control over aspects of Unified Messaging (UM) on Exchange. If there were still a "hard" division between those working on telephony and those on servers, UM would probably be handled by the Exchange team in collaboration with the telephony team, who would be assigned the Exchange UM Management role.

CSResponseGroupAdministrator

The CSResponseGroupAdministrator role is another role related to the telephony side of Lync. It gives holders the ability to manage response groups to manage call flow and agents who are members of each queue. This role might be given to a suitably trained contact-center administrator so they can change queues and implement working-hour automation as necessary without troubling the wider support team.

RELATED EXCHANGE ROLE

As with the CSVoiceAdministrator role, there is no equivalent role in Exchange.

CSResponseGroupManager

The CSResponseGroupManager role is new to Lync 2013 and is a telephony-related role. It was created to give greater control over delegation of complex response group deployments where instead of central control, individual response group queues are managed by department or group leads. This role doesn't give rights to manage the response group application as a whole.

RELATED EXCHANGE ROLE

As with the CSVoiceAdministrator role, there is no equivalent role in Exchange.

CSLocationAdministrator

The CSLocationAdministrator is another limited role, much like the archiving role. It allows the holder to manage location information and, as such, might be used by a facilities or networking administrator who would be tasked with managing and maintaining the mapping of locations to subnets, switches, and buildings.

RELATED EXCHANGE ROLE

As with the CSVoiceAdministrator role, there is no equivalent role in Exchange.

CsPersistentChatAdministrator

The CsPersistentChatAdministrator role is new to Lync 2013. As covered in Chapter 1, "What's in Lync?" what was called Group Chat in Lync 2010 is now fully integrated into Lync 2013. This role grants the holder rights to manage and maintain the persistent chat components of Lync. This role would be used to provide a specific team of administrators who previously managed Group Chat (or Mind Align, the predecessor to Group Chat) administrative capabilities in the new environment.

RELATED EXCHANGE ROLE

There is no equivalent role in Exchange.

DIFFERENCES FROM EXCHANGE RBAC

With the release of Lync 2013, RBAC is relatively similar in capabilities in Exchange and Lync. Both allow you to create custom roles defining specific cmdlets to be delegated. There are, however, still some differences. For example, in Lync, roles are assigned to administrators only. In Exchange, roles are granted not only to administrators but to users, which allows users to undertake basic admin tasks such as updating contact information and carrying out message tracking. No doubt with effort something similar could be achieved in Lync, but there are fewer options (such as message tracking) for which Lync users could be enabled, so this may not be entirely relevant.

Creating New Roles

We have covered what Lync offers out of the box, and you have a lot to consider. It is critical to plan the use of RBAC carefully. Taking the easy road will end up with administrators having too many permissions, which as everyone knows, can lead to disaster. Therefore, at this stage you really need to think through how you want administration to work in your organization. The following sections will outline various options and then take you through the steps required to create new roles and perform RBAC management tasks.

Planning Combinations

Now that you've seen the standard roles, you can understand that there is a fair amount of flexibility in the way administrative power can be delegated. One thing to consider is that the structure of the administrative teams in many organizations won't necessarily fit the exact way the standard roles are laid out. It is, therefore, possible to use the standard roles as templates for custom roles that will give more flexibility in what each administrator can do. This is the starting point even if you want to use the new functionality in Lync 2013 that allows creation of roles based on a group of cmdlets you define.

Also bear in mind that each of the standard roles has a global scope, so one recommendation is to follow the process of applying least privilege and create custom roles based on the standard roles but with more suitably targeted scope. For example, if there were a group of administrators on a help desk who needed to administer only users in one OU, you would configure a new custom role with a user scope for that specific OU and use the CSUserAdministrator role as the template.

 Real World Scenario

SPLIT ADMINISTRATORS FOR A SINGLE SITE: TRADERS AND RESEARCHERS

Throughout our consulting work, we have seen certain organizations in which there were significant regulatory reasons to keep groups of users from communicating, and therefore, there were separate IT teams to manage those groups. In these cases, users could be in the same site, but separation of admin rights was needed.

Lync RBAC can deal with these types of situations through the creation of custom roles. Instead of using the global scope, you can create two new roles, one for each set of administrators. Each group's config (site) scope will be the same, but you can apply different user scopes, specifically focused on the OU containing the users to be administered. This will enable the administrators to manage the servers in the site as needed but not to access each other's users.

In addition to the role template and role scope, you must plan the naming of custom roles. First, it is important to realize that the name of the RBAC group must match the SAMAccountName of the group created to hold the members of the role. Therefore, if you have an AD group-naming policy, you must consider how this will affect the name of the RBAC group. Second, to follow best practices, the name of the RBAC role should enable an administrator to easily understand what the role does, identifying, for example, the role template and scope. You could, for example, call your group CSAdministrator-EMEA.

Another consideration is how you might group roles. To help you decide how you might group roles, one of the Lync program managers, Cezar Ungureanasu, put together the following script. It will run through all the standard roles in Lync and output which cmdlets they contain to a tab-separated values file. This file can be opened in Excel, where it provides an easy reference and comparison method to see which cmdlets are in each role and how they overlap. You can download the script from www.sybex.com/go/masteringlyncserver.

```
$roles = Get-CsAdminRole  | where-object { $_.IsStandardRole -eq $true} | Sort Identity
$d = "Cmdlet"
foreach($role in $roles)
    {
        $d = $d + "`t" + $role.Identity
    }
Out-File -FilePath "C:\cmdlettorole.tsv" -InputObject $d
$x = Get-Command -module Lync -commandType cmdlet | Sort Name
foreach($i in $x)
    {
        $a = $i.Name
        $c = $a +"`t"
        foreach($role in $roles)
            {
                if ($role.cmdlets -match $i.Name)
                    {
                        $c = $c + "yes" + "`t"
                    }
                else
                    {
                        $c = $c + "no" + "`t"
                    }
            }
        Out-File -FilePath C:\cmdlettorole.tsv -InputObject $c -Append
    }
```

To run the script, you should enter it into your favorite text editor (Notepad will do) and save it as a PowerShell PS1 file (.ps1). You would then run it from your Lync Front End server. For more details about saving and running PowerShell scripts, see Chapter 8. An extract from the file is shown in Table 9.3. Of course, for space reasons, we have cut this down because it is a large sheet encompassing all the roles and cmdlets available. You can find the entire spreadsheet at www.sybex.com/go/masteringlyncserver.

TABLE 9.3: An extract from the roles analysis spreadsheet

CMDLET	CSADMINISTRATOR	CSARCHIVINGADMINISTRATOR	CSHELPDESK
Approve-CsDeviceUpdateRule	Yes	No	No
Clear-CsDeviceUpdateFile	Yes	No	No
Clear-CsDeviceUpdateLog	Yes	No	No
Debug-CsLisConfiguration	Yes	No	Yes
Disable-CsAdDomain	No	No	No
Disable-CsAdForest	No	No	No
Disable-CsComputer	No	No	No

By looking at the spreadsheet in Excel, you can clearly see that certain roles overlap in functionality, which may mean that if you have a fairly small administrative team where there aren't so many tightly focused roles, you can use the more broadly scoped roles. For example, the CSResponseGroupAdministrator role is entirely a subset of the CSServerAdministrator, CSVoiceAdministrator, and of course, the CSAdministrator roles. Therefore, this might be one role that you can do without if you have a relatively small administrative team and don't need one person to manage only response groups.

In addition, the CSLocationAdministrator role is a subset of the CSVoiceAdministrator role; so again, where there is not one person or group of people specifically responsible for management of network locations (for example, network engineers), then granting the CSVoiceAdministrator role would cover all functionality.

On a different note, and as mentioned previously, CSAdministrator and CSArchivingAdministrator are the only roles that can create and grant archiving policy.

Finally, and rather more obviously, CSViewOnlyAdministrator is a subset of the CSAdministrator role.

This type of analysis, in conjunction with your understanding of how administration works in your organization, should help you decide how you will use RBAC roles in your Lync deployment.

The final planning consideration is the new functionality Lync 2013 brings to the party. As mentioned previously, it is now possible to create custom roles using a set of cmdlets of your choosing and also to add scripts of cmdlets to the allowed tasks of custom roles. Of course, there is the potential to create untold complexity through using the new features, so consider them only after you have worked through the planning stages.

 Real World Scenario

DIFFERENT ORGANIZATION TYPES

Through our consulting experience, we have found that organizations come in all shapes and sizes. In general, administration is organized in one of two ways.

Some organizations centralize their administrative efforts. This may be representative of a company in a single site or simply that they have a central team to deal with all users or systems for a particular application. In such cases, a single group controls the entire Lync organization, and there are likely to be tiers of administrators, starting with first-line help desk personnel who take basic queries and attempt immediate fixes, such as resetting passwords or PINs. More difficult problems are passed up to second-line support, who may visit users at their desks, and this is followed by third- and fourth-level support, who mainly deal with the backend servers and architecture as a whole. Given this type of organization, a global scope would be assigned to the roles, so the default roles could be used.

The second type of organization is a highly distributed environment. In this case, the company might have grown from various acquisitions or be a global company where different regions operate as somewhat separate entities; however, they have chosen to merge their IT systems. These companies often have multiple child domains underneath an empty root forest. To work in this environment, Lync roles would be targeted at specific sites and specific end-user OUs. There would likely still be the same type of tiered support, but it would be regional.

Finally, another issue we have seen occurs when an organization is simply not structured to manage a unified communications system. Lync is an application that brings together two different worlds: that of Windows servers and that of telephony. In many cases, these are managed by totally separate groups of people, each of whom want to keep control and fear change. In these cases, Lync has the ability to delegate the telephony administration to the telephony group without requiring the telephony administrators to have full domain-admin rights or other extensive infrastructure permissions.

Creating the Role

Once you have completed planning and understand what custom roles, if any, you will need in your organization, you are ready to create your custom roles. You need to collect various pieces of data to create a role. First, you need a name for the role. As mentioned previously, it is worth sticking to a naming convention that helps identify the role. Having decided on the name, you must create a new Universal security group with the same name as the new role. For example, if your new RBAC role is to be called EMEA-CSAdmin, you can create the group using the following command:

```
New-AdGroup -Name "EMEA CSAdministrator" -GroupScope Universal ↵
-SamAccountName emea-csadmin -GroupCategory Security
```

Notice how this command creates a Universal security group with a display name containing spaces, but SamAccountName, which is what must match the RBAC role name, is without spaces and is shorter than 20 characters.

With this command, the group will be created in the Users container in the domain to which you are connected. Unlike the standard roles, whose related groups are always in the Users container of whichever domain was specified during forest preparation, the groups created for custom roles can be placed in any OU in any domain in the forest. To do this, specify the common name (CN) of the parent container as follows:

```
New-AdGroup -Name "EMEA CsAdministrator" -GroupScope Universal ↵
-SamAccountName emea-csadmin -GroupCategory Security ↵
-Path "ou=EMEA,ou=Groups,dc=corp,dc=masteringlync,dc=org"
```

That command will create the same group as before, but this time in the Groups OU under the EMEA OU.

Once you have created the relevant group in AD, you can create the new custom RBAC role using this command:

```
New-CsAdminRole –Template CSAdministrator –Identity emea-csadmin
```

This will create a role with all the power of the CSAdministrator role and with a global scope and output as follows:

```
Identity        : emea-csadmin
SID             : S-1-5-21-1336847106-355665257-1417932119-1144
IsStandardRole  : False
Cmdlets         : {Name=Get-CsClientPolicy, Name=Set-CsClientPolicy,
                   Name=Remove-CsClientPolicy, Name=New-CsClientPolicy...}
ScriptModules   : {}
ConfigScopes    : {Global}
UserScopes      : {Global}
Template        : CSAdministrator
```

Of course, the reason for creating custom roles is to be specific about where you want them to apply—in other words, to set the scope. To do this, you need to add one or two more parameters to the command used to create the group. For example, if you want to create a role with a specific site scope to control objects only in an EMEA site, run the command as follows:

```
New-CsAdminRole –Template CSAdministrator –Identity emea-csadmin ↵
-ConfigScopes Site:1
```

This will create the same role as before, but this time those granted the role will only be able to carry out administration in the EMEA (SiteID:1) site. Note that the site is referred to by its numerical site ID, which you can get by running the command Get-CsSite. This will give you output similar to the following for each site you have:

```
Identity              : Site:EMEA
SiteId                : 1
Services              : {UserServer:se01.corp.masteringlync.org,
                         Registrar:se01.corp.masteringlync.org,
                         UserDatabase:se01.corp.masteringlync.org,
```

```
                                FileStore:se01.corp.masteringlync.org...}
        Pools                 : {se01.corp.masteringlync.org,
                                seo2.corp.masteringlync.org}
        FederationRoute       :
        XmppFederationRoute   :
        DefaultPersistentChatPool :
        Description           :
        DisplayName           : EMEA
        SiteType              : CentralSite
        ParentSite            :
```

Once you have created the new role, the output is different in the ConfigScopes area, as you can see next:

```
        Identity      : emea-csadmin
        SID           : S-1-5-21-1336847106-355665257-1417932119-1144
        IsStandardRole : False
        Cmdlets       : {Name=Get-CsClientPolicy, Name=Set-CsClientPolicy,
                        Name=Remove-CsClientPolicy, Name=New-CsClientPolicy...}
        ScriptModules : {}
        ConfigScopes  : {Site:1}
        UserScopes    : {Global}
        Template      : CsAdministrator
```

Assuming that you are using a template group that has user-related commands (perhaps CSAdministrator or CSUserAdministrator), you could instead lock down the new role to a specific OU that contains users. That would allow those allocated the role to manage only those users in the OU specified. In that case, you would run the following command:

```
New-CsAdminRole -Template CSAdministrator -Identity emea-csadmin ↵
-UserScopes "OU:ou=TestUsersOU,dc=corp,dc=masteringlync,dc=org"
```

This command would create the same new role, but administration would be possible only on users in TestUsersOU. Note that when specifying the OU, you must preface the distinguished name with the OU: keyword.

Again, this produces different output, this time in the UserScopes area:

```
        Identity      : emea-csadmin
        SID           : S-1-5-21-1336847106-355665257-1417932119-1144
        IsStandardRole : False
        Cmdlets       : {Name=Get-CsClientPolicy, Name=Set-CsClientPolicy,
                        Name=Remove-CsClientPolicy, Name=New-CsClientPolicy...}
        ScriptModules : {}
        ConfigScopes  : {Global}
        UserScopes    : {OU:ou=TestUsersOU,dc=corp,dc=masteringlync,dc=org}
        Template      : CSAdministrator
        dc=corp,dc=masteringlync,dc=org
```

Finally, if you want to scope to multiple sites or user OUs to enable one group of administrators to have permissions over a range of objects but not the entire deployment, run a command like the following one:

```
New-CsAdminRole -Template CSAdministrator -Identity emea-csadmin ↵
-UserScopes "OU:ou=TestUsersOU,dc=corp,dc=masteringlync,dc=org", ↵
" OU:ou=AnotherTestUsersOU,dc=corp,dc=masteringlync,dc=org" ↵
-ConfigScopes "Site:1","Site:2"
```

This more complex-looking command will create the same old role but this time scoped for user administration on users in TestUsersOU and AnotherTestUsersOU and for Site 1 and Site 2.

BE CAREFUL WITH SCOPES

One thing that is worth highlighting is that the default scope for a new role is global. Therefore, if you create a new role and scope it for a site using the `ConfigScopes` parameter but do not specify a user scope for that role, the administrative permissions will apply to all users. Don't expect the users to be scoped to the site just because you apply a config scope!

Now that you know how to create new custom roles based solely on the template role provided, we can investigate the creation of custom roles where you define a specific set of cmdlets to use. In this instance, you are still required to specify the template that you want to use as the basis of the role. This gives you the base list of cmdlets and script modules. Of course, if you were using an already-existing custom role as the template, you can now choose either to add additional cmdlets or to specify only the ones you want, as follows.

First create the group SimpleOneCmdletRole. Then run the following command:

```
New-CsAdminRole -Template CSHelpDesk -Identity SimpleOneCmdletRole ↵
-Cmdlets Set-CsUser
```

This command will create a new custom admin role called SimpleOneCmdletRole that will only have permission to use the `Set-CsUser` cmdlet. The scope will be carried over from the template CSHelpDesk role.

You might think this is pretty basic, and it is! It is perhaps more likely that you would want to maintain the general list of cmdlets provided through the template role but with a few modifications. This can be done as follows.

First create the group AddingToHelpDesk. Then run the following command:

```
New-CsAdminRole -Template CSHelpDesk -Identity AddingToHelpDesk ↵
-Cmdlets @{Add="Set-CsUser"}
```

This would create the new custom admin role AddingToHelpDesk, which would have all the cmdlets of the original template role but with the addition of the `Set-CsUser` cmdlet. Of course, you could also remove cmdlets or create a role that has specific access to a certain script. In the next sections, we will cover these scenarios and more of the basic day-to-day administration tasks of either the standard or custom RBAC roles.

Manipulating Roles

Now that we've discussed how RBAC works in Lync and how to create custom roles, let's finish this chapter by reviewing the key ways of manipulating roles: assigning users to and removing them from roles, deleting roles, filtering specific roles, adding and removing cmdlets and scripts from roles, and reporting on them.

Assigning and Removing Roles

You assign a role by adding the user who needs to carry out the role's tasks to the relevant AD group. This is a Universal security group and for the standard roles is named equally to the role and is found in the Users container of whichever domain was specified during forest prep. Table 9.1 shows the groups for the standard RBAC roles.

Because granting a role is as simple as placing the new member's user account in the relevant group, it is important to consider the security of Active Directory as well as that of other systems, such as Lync itself; otherwise, the roles could easily be overridden.

Helpfully, the users who are assigned roles do not necessarily need to be Lync enabled. This is good, because it means that the separate administrative accounts, which should be used to follow the principle of separation of powers, do not need to be Lync enabled and, therefore, will not show up in address books and the like.

In the same way that assigning roles is done through membership of an AD group, the removal of a role is as simple as removing the member from the relevant administrative group.

Deleting Roles

You may find that over time sites get decommissioned or OUs are removed, and this means that RBAC roles that were scoped to those areas are no longer needed. To remove the role, use the following command:

```
Remove-CsAdminRole -Identity nameofroletoremove
```

This command will prompt you to verify that you really want to remove the RBAC role; if you enter **Y**, it will remove the role with the name *nameofroletoremove*.

DOES REMOVING A ROLE REMOVE THE AD GROUP?

No! So what can you do? You could remove the group manually, but perhaps you want a command-line method.

If you have the Active Directory module loaded as shown in the CSAdministrator section earlier, you can do something like the following:

```
$Name = nameofroletoremove
Remove-CsAdminRole -Identity $name; Remove-ADGroup $name
```

This first sets a variable, denoted by the $ sign, with the name of the role to remove. It then runs two PowerShell commands on one line, through the use of the semicolon delimiter (;), and thereby first removes the RBAC role as shown previously and then uses the Active Directory module cmdlet `Remove-ADGroup` to remove the AD group.

Filtering Specific Roles

You've already seen a few examples of how to view the roles; once you have built up a significant group of roles with a suitable naming convention, you might want to pull back all the roles
for, say, a certain site. As is often the case in PowerShell, there are a few ways in which you can
achieve this. One is to use the –Filter parameter:

```
Get-CsAdminRole -Filter "*EMEA*"
```

This will bring back all the roles with *EMEA* in the identity as shown here:

```
Identity        : emea-csadmin
SID             : S-1-5-21-1336847106-355665257-1417932119-1144
IsStandardRole  : False
Cmdlets         : {Name=Get-CsClientPolicy, Name=Set-CsClientPolicy,
                  Name=Remove-CsClientPolicy, Name=New-CsClientPolicy...}
ScriptModules   : {}
ConfigScopes    : {Global}
UserScopes      : {OU:ou=TestUsersOU,dc=corp,dc=masteringlync,dc=org}
Template        : CSAdministrator
dc=corp,dc=masteringlync,dc=org
```

Note the use of the wildcard (*) within the quotes to allow the return of any roles that contain
the word EMEA.

Adding and Removing Cmdlets or Scripts from Roles

We showed how to create a new role with only specific cmdlets and touched on the fact that
Lync 2013 now allows the ability to assign the use of specific scripts to a role. We will now look
at those capabilities in more depth. You will see that the methods used are the same as those
used when creating new groups.

Both the Set-CsAdminRole cmdlet and then New-CsAdminRole cmdlet have two new parameters in Lync 2013: -Cmdlets and -ScriptModules.

Manipulating existing roles is done with the Set-CsAdminRole cmdlet in the following ways.
If you wanted to wipe out all the cmdlets assigned to the MyRole1 role and create your own list,
you could do so using the following command:

```
Set-CsAdminRole -Identity MyRole1 -Cmdlets "Set-CsUser","Set-CsAdminRole"
```

This command would change the cmdlets assigned to the MyRole1 custom admin role to only
the two listed, Set-CsUser and Set-CsAdminRole.

If instead of replacing all existing cmdlets assigned to a role you want to add cmdlets, then
you would proceed as follows:

```
Set-CsAdminRole -Identity MyRole1 ↵
-Cmdlets @{Add="New-CsAllowedDomain","New-CsAdminRole"}
```

This would add the New-CsAllowedDomain and New-CsAdminRole cmdlets to the existing cmdlets assigned to the role.

On the other hand, if you wanted to remove some cmdlets, the following would be needed:

```
Set-CsAdminRole -Identity MyRole1 ↵
-Cmdlets @{Remove="New-CsAllowedDomain","New-CsAdminRole"}
```

This command would remove the cmdlets added in the preceding command.

That brings us to assigning scripts to custom roles. This functionality is great if you want to allow a group of administrators to perform a specific task that is defined as a function in a script. The script could even be "hidden" behind a nice custom web console that you create. For more information on functions, see Chapter 8.

To add a script to a role, you use steps that are very similar to those used to manipulate cmdlets available to a role, as shown in the examples that follow. For example, to add a script, follow this process:

```
Set-CsAdminRole -Identity MyRole1 -ScriptModule MyScript.PS1
```

This command replaces any current scripts assigned to the MyRole1 role with the MyScript.PS1 file.

If you noticed that when specifying scripts you specify only the name of the script, you might ask yourself if these scripts that you are defining have to be placed anywhere special. If you thought the answer is yes, then you would be right! The scripts have to be placed in the %Commonprogramfiles%\Microsoft Lync Server 2013\AdminScripts folder and must have the .ps1 or .psm1 filename extension. This folder may well not exist, so go ahead and create it.

Next, we will add a second script to those that the MyRole1 role can execute using the following command.

```
Set-CsAdminRole -Identity MyRole1 -ScriptModule @{Add="MyScript.PS1","AnotherScript.PS1"}
```

This command adds both the MyScript1 and AnotherScript scripts in addition to whatever is already defined.

Removing individual scripts is done in exactly the same way as manipulating cmdlets, as described earlier; however, if you want to remove all scripts, you can use this command:

```
Set-CsAdminRole -Identity MyRole1 -ScriptModules $Null
```

This sets the ScriptModules parameter to $Null.

It is also possible to create admin roles with access to scripts instead of amending existing roles. This would be done by using the parameters shown earlier except with the New-AdminRole cmdlet instead of the Set-AdminRole cmdlet.

Having added scripts to cmdlets, it may well be useful to check up on which roles have which scripts assigned at a later date. You can gather this information in a couple of places. First, you can run a Get-AdminRole cmdlet as follows:

```
Get-AdminRole -Identity MyRole1 | fl
```

This command will output the details of the role, including the scripts assigned, as shown here:

```
Identity       : MyRole1
SID            : S-1-5-21-2281681827-1062710998-2061251255-1145
IsStandardRole : False
Cmdlets        : {Name=set-csuser, Name=Set-csadminrole}
```

```
ScriptModules  : {script1.ps1}
ConfigScopes   : {Global}
UserScopes     : {Global}
Template       : CSHelpdesk
```

Second, the scripts (or more correctly, the functions within the scripts) will be shown to holders of that role when they connect through remote PowerShell:

```
ModuleType Name                          ExportedCommands
---------- ----                          ----------------
Script     tmp_431mkvne.qzg              RunGetCsPool
```

One thing to bear in mind when adding scripts is that the cmdlets used in the script should be available to the admin role. Adding a script is not a magical way to get around not having certain cmdlets available to a role.

Here are a couple of final things to take into account. You would need to replicate this scripts folder to any Front End server that the user could connect to via the remote PowerShell URL. Also note that you need to make sure that this folder is protected. Those delegated roles should not have the ability to edit the scripts; otherwise, clearly they could make changes that may grant them additional permissions.

Reporting on Roles

During the day-to-day management of a Lync system, it is very likely that the following questions will arise:

◆ What roles does a specific user have?

◆ Which users have a specific role?

◆ Which roles have access to certain users?

◆ Which roles have access to certain sites?

Thanks to PowerShell, it is relatively easy to find the answers.

WHAT ROLES DOES A SPECIFIC USER HAVE?

This can be answered with the following command:

```
Get-CsAdminRoleAssignment -Identity "Useralias"
```

This command will return a list of all the roles for the user Useralias.

WHICH USERS HAVE A SPECIFIC ROLE?

To answer this question, in the PowerShell console you must first import the Active Directory module:

```
Import-Module ActiveDirectory
```

This command will import all the cmdlets related to AD management, such as group creation, deletion, and manipulation.

Once the AD module has loaded, you can use the following command to list the members of the group linked to a specific role, in this case the CSAdministrator:

```
Get-ADGroupMember -Identity CSAdministrator | Select name
```

This command brings back all the members of the group CSAdministrator, as shown here:

```
name
----
Administrator
```

To list members of all the roles, try this:

```
Get-CsAdminRole | ForEach-Object ↵
{$_.Identity; (Get-ADGroupMember -Identity $_.Identity) | fl name}
```

This final command gets all the admin roles and then iterates through them by identity. Within the iteration, another command is run within the parentheses to get the AD group membership of each of the corresponding roles in the AD group. Finally, the output is passed to the Format-List format cmdlet, and the name of each member is printed as shown here:

```
CSAdministrator
name : Administrator
CSVoiceAdministrator
CSUserAdministrator
name : RTCUniversalUserAdmins
CSResponseGroupAdministrator
CSLocationAdministrator
CSArchivingAdministrator
name : ArchiveAdmin
CSViewOnlyAdministrator
CSServerAdministrator
name : RTCUniversalServerAdmins
CSHelpDesk
CSResponseGroupManager
CsPersistentChatAdministrator
emea-csadmin
name : Test User1
```

WHICH ROLES HAVE ACCESS TO CERTAIN USERS?

To list which roles can access a certain OU, run the following command:

```
Get-CsAdminRole | Where-Object ↵
{$_.UserScopes -match "OU:ou=TestUsersOU,dc=corp,dc=masteringlync,dc=org"}
```

This command first gets all the admin roles and then lists each role that has a user scope of the OU common name (CN) entered.

WHICH ROLES HAVE ACCESS TO CERTAIN SITES?

In a similar way, you can also find roles that have access to certain servers, based on the site, as follows:

```
Get-CsAdminRole | Where-Object {$_.ConfigScopes -match "site:1"}
```

This command first gets all the admin roles and then lists where any of the roles has a config scope of the site entered.

THE IMPORTANCE OF SECURING CONNECTION METHODS

Now that we've reviewed RBAC, it is worth one final reminder that RBAC does nothing to prevent access on the local machine. It is fundamentally something that protects remote PowerShell connections. Therefore, if an administrator gets access to the local server console, they can run any cmdlets that their AD group membership allows. You need to ensure that delegated administrators can only connect in the way you want so they remain within the scope of RBAC.

The Bottom Line

Use PowerShell to list the standard RBAC groups.   RBAC in Lync 2013 is administered through the Lync Server Management Shell (LSMS). There are 11 standard roles that ship with Lync; they provide an organization with the ability to delegate administration with a reasonable degree of granularity.

> **Master It**   You are in the middle of planning your enterprise Lync deployment and have been asked by the senior architect to research the available options for administrative delegation. You have been asked to provide a list of standard RBAC roles.

Understand the permissions available to each role.   There are 11 RBAC roles in Lync. These roles range from granting high-level administrative access using the CSAdministrator role to granting read-only access with the CSViewOnlyAdministrator. To use them properly, you need to know what each role does and understand any overlaps where different roles provide the same capability.

> **Master It**   As part of an investigation into how to make the best use of RBAC, you have been asked to identify a list of cmdlets each role grants access to so that it can be analyzed to see which RBAC role best fits the way your administrative teams work.

Undertake planning for RBAC roles.   Your implementation of RBAC roles should relate to the way your organization is set up for administration. Some organizations are centralized and others are distributed. You must understand your organizational structures and take them into account when planning RBAC roles. It is also important to follow the principle of least privilege, granting only the rights necessary for an administrator to do the job. This may mean utilizing custom roles and targeted scopes at either user OUs or Lync sites.

> **Master It**   You are in the middle of planning your enterprise Lync deployment and have been asked by the senior architect to plan the RBAC deployment in your organization. What should you consider?

Create custom RBAC roles and assign them to administrators.   Lync allows the creation of custom RBAC roles. These are not as flexible as in Exchange because you cannot grant access to specified single cmdlets. When creating a custom RBAC role, you must specify a template role from one of the eleven standard roles and then set an appropriate scope.

> **Master It**   Having carried out a planning exercise, you have decided that the standard Lync roles are not adequate for your organization. Because you have a separate site supported by a separate team of junior admins who only need to manage users in one site,

you need to be more specific about the areas that certain administrators can manage. How would you create an RBAC role to ensure that the junior admins don't have too many permissions?

Manipulate the cmdlets assigned to a role. One of the new capabilities of Lync 2013 is the ability for RBAC to be far more flexible that it was in 2010. We can now manipulate roles right down to the cmdlet level, enabling far greater granularity of permissioning.

Master It You have an existing RBAC role created called MinimalRole1. Holders of the role need to be allowed to use only the Get-CsUser and Get-CsAdminRole cmdlets.

Later on you decide that the role should be expanded to include the use of the Get-CsAdminRoleAssignment **cmdlet.** Finally, you realize that allowing the Get-CsUser cmdlet was a mistake.

Outline the separate steps you would take to carry out each configuration. You should end up with three commands.

Carry out general administration, including granting and removing RBAC roles. There are a few cmdlets that allow management of RBAC roles in Lync 2013 and most use the CsAdminRole verb. All PowerShell roles are assigned through the membership of a linked Active Directory Universal security group.

Master It A colleague who administered Lync has moved to a new role, and his replacement starts on Monday. You have been asked to ensure that the new staff member has the appropriate rights to do his job.

Report on the use of RBAC roles. Given that the purpose of RBAC is to provide people with administrative access to a system, there will always be a need to review and provide reports to management on who has what access. Reporting on RBAC takes various forms but can all be done through LSMS.

Master It You have been asked to provide details on which roles have access to the APAC site and list the membership of those roles. How would you proceed?

Discuss what is new in RBAC in Lync 2013. Lync 2010 provided the first iteration of RBAC in the Lync product range. Now Lync 2013 adds some key new capabilities that start to bring the Lync RBAC implementation closer to that of Exchange in flexibility.

Master It You have been asked to produce a short report on what Lync 2013 brings to the table in new RBAC functionality. What would you cover?

Chapter 10

User Administration

"The job would be easy if it weren't for the users!" Or so the saying goes. This chapter is all about how Lync handles users. There are simple elements, such as the ability to use Lync Server Control Panel (LSCP) and Lync Server Management Shell (LSMS, commonly known as PowerShell) to find, enable, disable, and generally manipulate users both individually and collectively. Then there are more complex elements, such as understanding how to set the wide variety of policies available in Lync. Lync 2010 changed this aspect dramatically compared with OCS 2007 R2. The vast majority of Lync policy is now set using in-band provisioning rather than the mix of Group Policy objects (GPOs), in-band provisioning, and Registry settings required in OCS 2007 R2. This means you now have a single place to configure and assign policy, making things far simpler to manage. In addition to the changes in of the way you apply policy, many more settings are available to give organizations plenty of control over exactly what users can and can't do with Lync.

In this chapter, you will learn to:

- ◆ Search for users in the LSCP and PowerShell

- ◆ Carry out basic user administration in the LSCP and PowerShell

- ◆ Understand Lync policies

- ◆ Manipulate Lync policies

- ◆ Choose the right policy for the job

User Configuration Basics

The starting point for user configuration in Lync is the Lync Server Control Panel (LSCP). As detailed in Chapter 9, "Role-Based Access Control," to carry out the full range of user administration, you must be logged in with an account that has been delegated the CSAdministrator or CSUserAdministrator RBAC role through membership of the CSAdministrator or CSUserAdministrator group or a new role with a superset of these capabilities that you have created yourself using the new RBAC features in Lync 2013.

LYNC USER ADMIN

To make the screen shots of the LSCP in this chapter cleaner, we decided to create a Lync user administrator (LyncUserAdmin) account the same way we created the Lync Admin account in Chapter 6, "Installation." However, this time, instead of granting the Lync Administrator role (CSAdministrator), we added the user to the CSUserAdministrator group to make him a Lync user administrator. This is the account we will be using throughout the chapter.

LSCP can be accessed in various ways. You can do so directly on the Lync server using the LSCP icon by clicking Start and choosing All Programs ➤ Administrative Tools ➤ Microsoft Lync Server 2013 ➤ Lync Server 2013 Control Panel.

You can also install the administrative tools on another machine; this approach gets you not only the icon from which to launch the LSCP but also the Topology Builder and PowerShell. Essentially, the workstation must meet the following prerequisites:

◆ OS as supported by Lync Server with the addition of Windows 7 SP1 x64 or Windows 8 x64.

◆ Browser with Silverlight plug-in version 5 or later

◆ .NET Framework 4.5 64 bit version

◆ Windows Installer version 4.5

◆ PowerShell v3.0

IE SUPPORT

Interestingly, at the time of writing, there is a support message in LSCP that states that when running in the latest Chrome browser, "you are using a web browser or operating system that is not supported for use with Lync Server Control Panel. We recommend upgrading to the latest version of Windows Internet Explorer. At a minimum, use Windows Internet Explorer 7." Given that a similar error was shown when using Firefox and Chrome with Lync 2010, it seems unlikely that this will change, and therefore we suggest using Internet Explorer to run the LSCP.

Finally, you can use the admin simple URL defined in Topology Builder. For the examples used in this chapter, that was https://admin.corp.masteringlync.org. To actually access the LSCP from the admin URL, you must append /cscp, which is the required virtual directory. Following these steps allows you to log into the LSCP from any computer with a supported browser.

Once you have logged in with our LyncUserAdmin account, you will see the LSCP with only the interface elements related to user administration visible, as shown in Figure 10.1.

Now that you've gained access to the LSCP, the first task you need to master is searching; this will allow you to locate users for administration. Each tab of the LSCP has a search interface, and all of them except the one on the Users tab are very basic. The first thing to note about the searches that can be performed is that they only return objects that are Lync enabled. Don't get caught out by this if you are looking for users to enable! This is done in a similar way but in a different location, which we will discuss shortly.

FIGURE 10.1

Logged into the Lync Server Control Panel as LyncUserAdmin

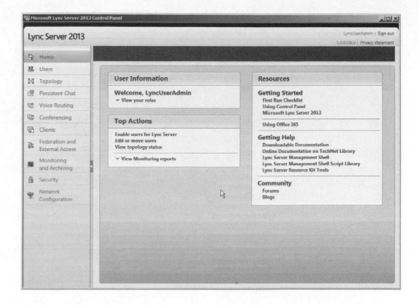

To carry out a search, first switch to the Users tab. At this point, if you click Find, you will simply bring back all Lync-enabled users. Thankfully, the search interface on the Users tab allows you to customize certain search parameters. For example, you can perform a standard or LDAP search. The standard search will search for users by display name, first name, last name, Security Accounts Manager (SAM) account name, SIP address, or line Uniform Resource Identifier (URI). Wildcards appear to work only in part. For example, you can search for *2013, which would bring back any user with a name ending in 2013. However, you can't search for *2013* to bring back users with 2013 in the name and neither would 2013* bring back all users starting with 2013. However you can enter 2013 and have that bring back all users that start with 2013. If you want to search on SIP or line URI fields, you must include the **tel:** or **sip:** preface to the attribute data; otherwise, no results will be returned. The LDAP search allows even greater flexibility. You can use any attribute available through an LDAP query to be very granular about which objects are returned. For example, to start with you could use the following filter to bring back only user objects:

```
(objectclass=user)
```

Selecting the radio button next to LDAP Search and entering this filter brings back all Lync-enabled users. That's not very exciting, so how about this:

```
(description=Marketing)
```

This brings back all users with a description of Marketing. This next one brings back users with the letter *U* in their common name:

```
(cn=*u*)
```

Finally, this last one is much more complex:

```
(&(objectCategory=person)(objectClass=user)(userAccountControl:1.2.840.113556.1.4.803:=2))
```

This brings back all Lync users who have a disabled AD account—as might be the case if the AD team had disabled a user in preparation for deletion but not told you yet.

As you can see, there is a huge amount of flexibility with which you can experiment. For more information about the syntax of the search query for LDAP filter, look at the resource here:

```
http://msdn2.microsoft.com/en-us/library/aa746475.aspx
```

Another feature of the Lync search capability is its ability to create quite complex searches using only the GUI. Clearly a lot is possible through LDAP searches, but if you just want to put together something without needing to research LDAP, you can use the Search Filter feature. Search filters allow you to add various operators to a basic search and only operate in basic search mode rather than LDAP mode. You cannot use wildcards in the search filters, but you can use the operators that PowerShell allows:

◆ Starts with

◆ Ends with

◆ Equal to

◆ Not equal to

◆ Contains

◆ Not contains

To add a filter, click the Add Filter button on the search bar. You can add up to 15 filters to build significantly complex queries. These queries can be saved and reloaded at a later date if this search is regularly used. Saved searches are stored as USF files (filename extension .usf). This approach might be useful if, for example, it is needed to regularly check whether a certain group of users have the correct PIN policy. You could set up the relevant saved query, perform the search, and then use the assign policy action to ensure that all the users had the relevant policy.

Figure 10.2 and Figure 10.3 show the filter interface and some of the attributes that can be used in searches built with filters.

Once the results are returned, you can perform actions on the resulting set of users by selecting one or many of them using either Shift+click or Ctrl+click and using the Actions drop-down; you'll learn more about this shortly.

When you are searching in LSCP, you might run into a couple of issues, one of which is that by default the search interface will return only 200 users. However, it is straightforward to change that using the Maximum Users To Display entry box. The other issue is more of a problem; it is that you can't customize the way data results are displayed. For example, you couldn't perform a simple LSCP search to find and display all the DDI numbers deployed. You could search and return all users with a DDI; however, to see the DDIs you would have to go into the properties of each user because it is not possible to edit the columns of data that are shown. For this level of data manipulation, you would have to dive into PowerShell.

If you want to search using PowerShell, a couple of useful PowerShell cmdlets are available for finding users to manipulate: Get-CsUser and Get-CsAdUser. Get-CsAdUser retrieves all user accounts in Active Directory Domain Services (AD DS), Lync enabled or not, whereas Get-CsUser retrieves only Lync-enabled users inside AD DS.

FIGURE 10.2
The Filter interface
showing the AND
operator, the Add
Filter option, and
the Save and Import
query buttons

FIGURE 10.3
Some of the attri-
butes that can be
added to searches
based on filters

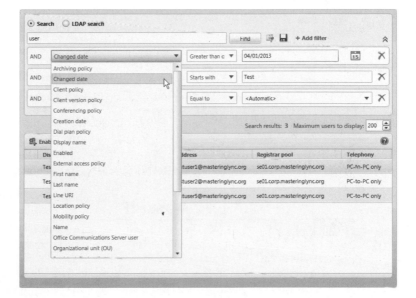

In this section, we will discuss `Get-CsUser`, a cmdlet that focuses on Lync-enabled objects and Lync-specific attributes. `Get-CsUser` allows similar searches to those described in the preceding section. We will cover `Get-CsAdUser` in the next section, on enabling user accounts for Lync.

To run these cmdlets, you need to be connected via a remote PowerShell console to the Lync server using our Lync user admin account. You can do this manually as described in Chapter 8, "Introduction to PowerShell, the Lync Management Shell, and Regular Expressions," or if you've installed the administrative tools, you can use LSMS, which is a little simpler because the connection is made automatically. Once at the prompt, you have even more flexibility than you had in the LSCP. For example, you can search for all Lync-enabled users in a specific OU and return up to two billion results, which should be enough for most people!

CREDENTIALS

Both the `Get-CsUser` and the `Get-CsAdUser` cmdlets have a rather useful parameter that allows you to run them under a user account other than the one with which you are connected to remote PowerShell. To do this, you must first create a PSCredential object using the `Get-Credential` cmdlet, which prompts for credentials and stores them in a variable. Use the following command:

```
$cred = Get-Credential
```

This will bring up a standard credential dialog, which will capture the credentials, including username and password, and store them in the variable `$cred`.

Then, by using the `-Credential` parameter and passing those stored credentials, the `Get-CsUser` or `Get-CsAdUser` cmdlet will run using those credentials. An example would be as follows:

```
Get-CsUser -Credential $cred
```

This would run the command under the credentials stored in the `$cred` variable and return all Lync-enabled users.

To get started, simply run `Get-CsUser`, which will return a list of all Lync-enabled users. Next, you can be more specific about which user or users you will return, by using the `-Identity` parameter as follows:

```
Get-CsUser -Identity "Test User1"
Get-CsUser -Identity "Test User*"
```

The first command brings back only `Test User 1`, and the second brings back any user starting with `Test User`.

WILDCARDS

PowerShell accepts wildcards a little more flexibly than LSCP in that you can use them throughout the search string rather than just in front of a specific ending as in LSCP. It does, however, only accept the asterisk (*) wildcard. You cannot use the whole range of wildcards, such as ? and so on. Another thing to bear in mind is that wildcards work only on the Display Name attribute of a user rather than the department and other names.

You could, for example, use the following command, including the wildcard, to find all users starting with *test*:

```
Get-CsUser -Identity test*
```

Of course, you can also be more specific and search within an OU:

```
Get-CsUser -Identity "Test User1" -OU "cn=users,dc=corp,dc=masteringlync,dc=org"
```

Again, as with the LSCP, you can use filters. They can be of the usual PowerShell filter, as implemented in a `Where-Object` command, or they can be LDAP filters. You should note that only one of these parameters can be used in any one `Get-CsUser` command. The next command shows the use of a PowerShell filter via piping to `Where-Object`:

```
Get-CsUser | Where-Object {[String]$_.Registrarpool ↵
-eq "se01.corp.masteringlync.org"}
```

This command will bring back all users homed on the `se01.corp.masteringlync.org` pool. As you have seen, the simple `Get-User` command outputs all of the properties on which the user can be filtered. The previous filter was simply performed with only one parameter. You can expand the filter to create complex searches. For more specifics about how to format the filter string, see the article at the following location:

```
http://technet.microsoft.com/en-us/library/ee177028.aspx
```

The other type of filter is the LDAP filter. It works in much the same way as through the LSCP but through PowerShell:

```
Get-CsUser -LDAPFilter Description="Office Based"
```

This command will pull back all users where the description contains the text `"Office Based"`. Here's another:

```
Get-CsUser -LDAPFilter "!(Department=Marketing)"
```

This will pull back all users who are not in the Marketing department. As you can see, a great deal of flexibility is available to enable you to retrieve only the users you want.

Now that you know how to search and filter users in the LSCP and in PowerShell, let's move on to what you can do to the users you find.

Enabling and Disabling

Enabling users in the LSCP is relatively straightforward:

1. Open the LSCP as a user with CSAdministrator or CSUserAdministrator rights and click the Users tab. In the main pane, click Enable Users, which will open the main page to select and enable users, as shown in Figure 10.4.

2. Click Add and locate the user or users you want to enable through the searching methods that were described earlier in the chapter. Once you have located and selected the relevant users, click OK.

   Note that multiple users can be selected either in one block using the Shift+click method or individually using the Ctrl+click method, which should be familiar from Windows Explorer.

3. You should be back in the main configuration page shown in Figure 10.4, this time with users listed in the Users section. You must assign the users to a Registrar pool. In Figure 10.4, this will be `se01.corp.masteringlync.org`, which is the only pool available in the drop-down; however, your organization may have pools in different

locations around the world. You must also select a method to generate a SIP URI (uniform resource identifier). We will cover these choices in more depth later when discussing how to enable the user from PowerShell. At this point, you will simply select Use User's Email Address because you know the email address field is populated with an address that fits the naming scheme of the SIP domain, @corp.masteringlync.org.

You could now simply accept the defaults and click Enable to finish setting up the users; however, you should be aware of a few other settings.

FIGURE 10.4

The main configuration page with options for enabling users

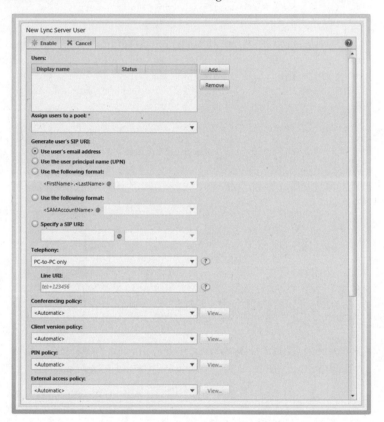

4. The Telephony section allows you to configure the way in which the user can use Lync features to make telephone calls. The default is PC-To-PC Only, which is what you should leave set for the user. This setting allows Lync voice and video calls to be made only within the Lync system between machines with the relevant Lync client installed. Other options are to enable coexistence with a third-party PBX, to configure the user to use Lync as a PBX, or to disable audio and video entirely. These settings will be covered in more detail in Chapter 13, "Getting Started with Voice."

5. The rest of the settings you can configure on this page enable you to assign immediately the various policies Lync provides to enable control of the user environment. For now, leave them at the default settings. We will discuss many of the policies in much more depth later in this chapter; at that point, you can come back and change those policies assigned to users if you like.

6. After you've looked through all the settings available, click Enable to make the users selected live on Lync.

MANAGING USERS WHO ARE DOMAIN ADMINS

We've used LSCP throughout this chapter to manage users; however, domain admins can't be managed this way. At this point, we would like to emphasize what a bad idea it is to have domain administrator permissions on users who are enabled for services like Lync and Exchange and who do "regular" work like web browsing. Of course, it does happen in organizations. You may, therefore, come across an LSCP limitation: Because of the rights it runs under, LSCP cannot manage domain admins; it can only present information about them in a read-only manner. Therefore, to manage domain admin Lync users, you must use LSMS and be logged on as a domain admin to do so.

Although the LSCP is fine for enabling a single user, and even acceptable for doing them in bulk, some people just love to do things from the shell. For those people, here's how you enable a user from PowerShell. As discussed earlier, you need to locate the relevant user or users. When working in PowerShell that means using the `Get-CsAdUser` cmdlet, unless you know the display name of the user, in which case you can simply start with the `Enable-CsUser` cmdlet. In this case, you know the display name is `Test User1`, so you can move right on; but if you didn't know the name, you could use the `Get-CsAdUser` cmdlet to bring back the relevant user or users and pipe the output of `Get-CsAdUser` into the `Enable-CsUser` command, discussed next.

As you saw in the LSCP, certain fields are mandatory. First, of course, you must identify the user or users, using the AD Display Name, SIP address, user Principal name (UPN), or domain\SamAccountName. Again, in this case, you can stick with AD Display Name. Next, you need to specify the Registrar pool and the SIP address. In this simple example setup, this is pretty straightforward because there is only one Registrar pool (`se01.corp.masteringlync.org`). The choice of SIP address is possibly more complex. As a rule of thumb, the SIP address should match the email address of the user if at all possible. However, unless Exchange is installed, the email address field might not be populated. Make sure it is for the user account you will be creating so you can use it later. In this example, `Test User1` is set up with the email address `testuser1@corp.masteringlync.org`.

To enable the user, use the following command:

```
Enable-CsUser -Identity "Test User1" -RegistrarPool ↵
se01.corp.masteringlync.org SipAddressType EmailAddress
```

This command will enable the user `Test User1` for Lync on the `se01.corp.masteringlync.org` pool with a SIP address matching the email address `testuser1@corp.masteringlync.org`. The one parameter here that may not be immediately obvious is the `SipAddressType`. It could have been very specific, used the `SipAddress` parameter, and manually specified the SIP address `testuser1@corp.masteringlync.org`; however, the `SipAddressType` parameter is potentially more useful because it allows various options to form the SIP address. One thing you will note is that when you use certain of the `SipAddressType` settings, you will need another parameter, `SipDomain`. In this environment, things are simple with only the one SIP domain: however, large organizations commonly need to support multiple domains, perhaps to represent different brands or company units.

The options for `SipAddressType` are as follows:

`EmailAddress`: As shown previously, this uses the email address from the user in AD and doesn't require the `SipDomain` parameter.

`SamAccountName`: This uses the SamAccountName from AD and does require the `SipDomain` parameter to specify the suffix of the name after the @ sign.

`UserPrincipalName`: This uses the UPN of the user in AD and, because the UPN is in the same form as an email address, doesn't require the use of the `SipDomain` parameter.

`FirstLastName`: This takes the first and last name of the user and puts a period between them—for example, `nathan.winters`. It requires the use of the `SipDomain` parameter.

PIPING OUTPUT FROM THE `Enable-CsUser` CMDLET

One thing that you may be used to in PowerShell is the ability to pipe the output from one command into the input of the next. This is one of PowerShell's most useful features. It allows you to do the following:

```
Get-CsAdUser -OU "cn=users,dc=corp,dc=masteringlync,dc=org" | ↵
Enable-CsUser -RegistrarPool se01.corp.masteringlync.org ↵
SipAddressType EmailAddress
```

This would enable all the users in the Users container in AD using their email addresses as the SIP address. However, you may not be aware that piping from the output of the `Enable-CsUser` cmdlet doesn't work by default. This is by design, because `Enable-CsAdUser` enables the given User object for Lync and doesn't pass the User object. Thankfully, if you add the `-PassThru` parameter, it will enable the output to be piped to other cmdlets so that you can set specific settings for the newly enabled user—for example, enabling them for Enterprise Voice.

You now know how to find and enable users for Lync. As you have seen, the SIP address is key. This forms the unique ID and is what makes users show up in searches carried out for Lync-enabled users. On occasion this can cause unintended results, as you might ask yourself what happens if a user already has a SIP address populated in their msRTCSIP-PrimaryUserAddress attribute. This could happen as part of a previous deployment when the user maybe became orphaned. Thankfully, there is a PowerShell command that can help identify these users and get them all set up for Lync:

```
Get-CsUser -UnassignedUser | Select-Object DisplayName
```

When run, this command will identify any users who have a SIP address but are not assigned to a Registrar pool. It will then output their display name. You could, of course, simply pipe the output to the `Enable-CsUser` cmdlet and get them set up directly for Lync.

Making Changes to Lync Users

Now that you've enabled some users for Lync, you no doubt feel suitably pleased. However, it won't be very long before the changes start rolling in. For example, someone might move to a different office or even a different country and be served from of a different Lync pool. Another typical occurrence is when a name changes due to marriage, and of course, people will leave your organization temporarily or permanently and their accounts will need to be disabled and then deleted. As with all the other Lync user administration tasks, the first requirement is to make sure you target the relevant user or users; that is where the search skills you've learned early come in handy.

The LSCP is well laid out, so by now you should be pretty familiar with it. On the Users tab, search for the user you need to alter. Once you've selected it, you can explore the available options and find the Edit and Action drop-downs.

The Edit drop-down is very straightforward. It gives you an easy option to select all the users returned by a search, after which you can move to the options on the Action menu, which we'll discuss shortly. Other than that, the only option is Show Details, which takes you to the configuration page for that particular user. This will look familiar from the steps taken to enable the user in LSCP described earlier. The Action drop-down gives many more options, as shown in Figure 10.5.

FIGURE 10.5
The options on the
Action drop-down

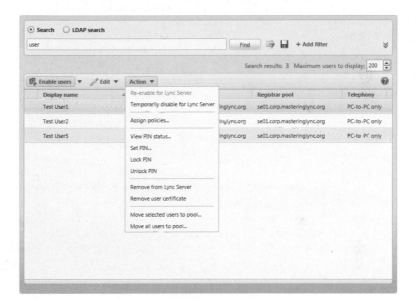

MOVING USERS

As you can see, moving users to another pool is simple. You select the relevant user or users and then, on the Action menu, click the Move Selected Users To Pool entry. This opens a dialog box where you can choose the pool in the drop-down shown in Figure 10.6. There is also a check box labeled Force that should be used if the standard process for moving fails. The standard process of moving users between pools will take across their conferences and buddy lists. If for some reason the source pool is unavailable, you would have to use the Force check box to move the user without this data from the source pool. This is discussed in more detail in Chapter 12, "Troubleshooting."

FIGURE 10.6
The Move Users dia-
log box allows you
to move selected
users to a pool.

Selecting the Move All Users To Pool option will bring up a dialog that allows you to select both a source and destination pool and enables moving all users from the source to the destination, as shown in Figure 10.7. Again, the Force check box allows scenarios where the source pool isn't available.

FIGURE 10.7
The Move Users dia-
log box allows you
to move all users
between pools.

To perform these moves from PowerShell, you would use the Move-CsUser cmdlet, a very simple cmdlet. The required parameters are -Identity to target a specific user and -Target to specify the pool to which you want to move the user. There is also the -Force parameter, which provides the same functionality to move users in failure scenarios without taking user data across to the new pool. This command moves Test User1 to the Newpool pool:

```
Move-CsUser -Identity "Test User1" -Target "newpool.corp.masteringlync.org"
```

Instead of having a separate cmdlet to allow all users to be moved from one pool to another, this time the PowerShell pipe is used for functionality:

```
Get-CsUser | Where-Object {[String]$_.Registrarpool -eq ↵
"se01.corp.masteringlync.org"} | ↵
Move-CsUser -Target "newpool.corp.masteringlync.org"
```

This command first runs the Get-CsUser command you are familiar with, and using a filter it selects all users on the Se01.corp.masteringlync.org pool. These are then piped to the Move-CsUser cmdlet, which moves them to the Newpool.corp.masteringlync.org pool.

CHANGING USERNAMES

In addition to moving users between pools, another commonly needed task is to change usernames, usually after a marriage. In this case most of the work will be done by other teams, namely the AD and Exchange teams. (Of course that might be you, but that's a topic for a whole other book!) In Lync terms, when the AD team have made changes, the user will show up in Lync searches with a new display name. However, what won't have changed is the SIP URI, which as we have said should match the primary email address of the user. To ensure that is the case, in LSCP locate the user, and on the Edit drop-down, click Show Details. In the configuration pane that opens, edit the SIP Address field as required and then click Commit. To do the same process from PowerShell, use the `Set-CsUser` cmdlet as follows:

```
Set-CsUser -Identity "Test User1" -SipAddress testmarried1@corp.masteringlync.org
```

This command will update the SIP address of Test User 1 to `testmarried1@corp.mastering-lync.org`.

Disabling and Removing Users

There are actually a couple of ways of disabling users, which have slightly different effects. On the Edit drop-down, if you click Show Details, one of the options on the user configuration page is an Enabled For Lync Server check box. If this check box is cleared, a Lync user cannot log on to Lync, but it doesn't remove any of the user's settings from Lync and doesn't remove Lync attributes, like the SIP URI, from the user object. This is a sensible option if the user in question is going to be out of the organization for a period of time but will return. In PowerShell, this is the same as running the following command:

```
Set-CsUser -Identity "Test User1" -Enabled:$False
```

This command will ensure that a user can't log on to Lync but doesn't delete any settings or policy assignments.

To reverse the process, simply run the following command:

```
Set-CsUser -Identity "Test User1" -Enabled:$True
```

This command will bring the user back to life and ensure that they can log on to Lync again as before. These steps can be carried out from the Action drop-down using the Temporarily Disable For Lync Server and the Re-enable For Lync Server options. If instead you want to be more permanent, then you need to use the Action drop-down in the LSCP or the `Disable-CsUser` cmdlet in PowerShell. With the relevant user or users selected, move to the Action drop-down and select Remove From Lync Server. You will be prompted to click OK if you are sure. This action will remove the user entirely from the Lync server by removing Lync attributes on the user account and wiping out Lync user data such as buddy lists and policy assignments. It will not remove the Active Directory user object. To carry out the same action in PowerShell, use the following command:

```
Disable-CsUser -Identity "Test User1"
```

This will remove the user from Lync. At this point if you wanted to re-enable the user, you would have to go back and use the `Enable-CsUser` cmdlet or the LSCP process just described.

Bulk Changes

Using the GUI, it is possible to manage more than one user at a time. But unless you really enjoy repetitive tasks, if you need to manage tens or hundreds of Lync users, PowerShell is critical. We've covered some of the basics in this chapter, but take a look at Chapter 8 for more detailed information.

OTHER USER ACTIONS

The other options on the Action menu that we haven't covered are Assign Policies, the various PIN settings, and the Remove User Certificate setting. We will cover the Assign Policies option in the rest of this chapter, and the PIN settings are covered in the chapters in Part 4, "Voice," so the final element to cover is the Remove User Certificate option. As explained in Chapter 3, "Security," Lync allows users to be authenticated not only through traditional username and password combinations but also through the use of a certificate and PIN. This makes authentication from phone devices simpler because users only need to enter the numeric PIN. Of course, as an administrator, you may want a way to prevent a user from logging in this way. That is what the Remove User Certificate option does. Although it doesn't remove the certificates from the devices, it does remove them from the server, which prevents the user from logging on. Through PowerShell, the same thing can be carried out using the `Revoke-CsClientCertificate` cmdlet.

Understanding Lync Policies

The ability to control systems through the use of policies is critical to an enterprise. It is standard to have different groups of people carrying out different functions and to provide them with only the required tools to do the job. In this way, systems can be sized correctly and security can be maintained. In OCS 2007 and OCS 2007 R2 there were, of course, policies to enable control and management of the user experience. However, these policies could not always be applied in a way that provided the same experience for users no matter where they logged on. The policies were also applied in different ways and did not always allow enough granularity of control without significant effort. Thankfully, Lync Server 2010 brought in a completely different methodology for policies that Lync 2013 maintains. There are numerous policies that can be applied in very granular ways to give a single consistent experience to users and to ensure that Lync administrators can control Lync users without constantly needing the approval of other IT teams (as was the case when Group Policy was used). The remainder of this chapter looks in depth at just what you can do—and how—to keep order in your Lync environment.

In-Band Provisioning

In-band provisioning describes the application of policy to the client through information contained in SIP messages and passed to the client during usage so that settings apply immediately. For a really detailed description of how this works, see the TechNet article linked below. Note that it describes the process in Lync 2010, which is just as valid for Lync 2013:

```
http://blogs.technet.com/b/csps/p/cmgmtprovisioning.aspx
```

Because of the way policy is applied, different types of clients apply the relevant policy settings to the functionality they offer. Whatever the client, the user will have the same experience because this method of applying policy is as relevant to the browser client as it is to the PC that's not domain joined and even to the domain-joined PC. Another benefit is that administrators are not constrained to fit Lync policies around another policy engine, such as Group Policy in OCS. Almost all Lync policies can be created and applied either through the LSCP or through PowerShell (see "What about Group Policy?" later in the chapter for the exceptions). Not using group policies provides greater flexibility because policies can be applied at Global, Site, Service, and User levels, and these policies take effect immediately rather than having to wait for a Group Policy refresh cycle.

Understanding Where Policies Apply

One of the principal benefits of moving to the new Lync in-band provisioning model is that Lync policy can closely follow Lync architecture and users, allowing a high degree of granularity. As discussed in Chapter 5, "Planning Your Deployment," Lync has added to the architectural concepts of OCS 2007 R2 (the *organization* and the *pool*) and includes the concept of *sites*, which generally map to data centers. It is now possible to apply policy at all these levels. Default policies are applied at the Global level, but administrators can create certain types of policies at other levels, such as the site, service, or tag level. Tag-level policies are what allow policy to be assigned to an individual user or selection of users. (As you will see, the search skills you learned earlier can be used to locate users to apply policy to, thereby giving you the ability to specifically target users.)

Of course, all these different levels mean that you need to understand their precedence. The following rules apply:

- If a per-user policy is assigned to the user, then the per-user policy is used.

- If no per-user policy is assigned to the user, then the service policy is used.

- If there is no per-user or service policy, then the site policy is used.

- If there is no per-user, service, or site policy, then the global policy is used.

Simply summarized, the policy set closest to the user wins! Understanding this is important because it has a material effect on which settings are applied to users. For example, certain settings in a policy could be left blank by the administrator to allow the user discretion over how Lync works for them. For example, you could allow the user to choose whether to display a photo by leaving the DisplayPhoto section of the CsClientPolicy blank. But what would happen if you set the DisplayPhoto section of the CsClientPolicy to force the use of the AD stored photo on the global policy but then left that setting blank on a policy closer to the user (that is, site or user tag)? The user would still be able to choose. The whole policy is applied even if settings are blank, not just the settings that have an explicit value.

To understand the various levels more closely, you need to understand the difference between policy name and scope, which defines how policies are referenced using the `-Identity` parameter in PowerShell. Following are some examples of how different policies are referenced:

`Identity global` pulls back the global policy of whichever cmdlet is used.

`Identity site:PolicyName` reflects a policy that is assigned to a site.

`Identity registrar:server.domain.xyz` reflects a policy that is assigned to a specific service, in this case a registrar.

`Identity Tag:PolicyName` reflects a policy that is assigned to users.

You can see clearly the concept of policy name and policy scope. The element in the identity before the colon (:) is the scope; the element after the colon is the policy name. In the case of either site or service scopes, the policy name matches that of the site or service where the policy is to be assigned. In the case of the tag scope, the policy name should describe where the policy will apply. You will see how this works when you create and assign policies later in this chapter.

What about Group Policy?

We've mentioned that all policies could be created through LSCP or PowerShell; however, that is not quite true. When the Lync client starts up, it needs certain bootstrapping settings passed to it. For example, if you are not using autoconfiguration through DNS SRV records, the client would need to be provided the Lync server to log on to. Another such configuration is to enable or disable the welcome screen that pops up when the Lync client is launched for the first time. Clearly in-band provisioning won't work in these instances because the client hasn't logged on or been able to check settings. Therefore, the use of Group Policy is maintained for these client bootstrapping settings only.

In order to apply these Group Policy settings, you will need to obtain the relevant ADMX (.admx) template file. The Lync15.admx file is available as part of the pack of Office 2013 ADMX files. At time of writing it can be downloaded here:

www.microsoft.com/en-us/download/details.aspx?id=35554

You will see that there are 32-bit and 64-bit versions of the download. Don't worry about this. This is important when you are going to be doing custom installs of Office, but in this case, we will just download the 32-bit version.

The file you download will be called admintemplates_32bit.exe. On running the application, you will be prompted to extract the contents to a folder. In the folder where you extract the files, you will find that you have two more folders and a spreadsheet. The spreadsheet is called office2013grouppolicyandoctsettings.xlsx and contains details of every setting that the GPO can control. To locate the Lync settings that can be manipulated, go to the ADMX tab and filter the first column, File Name, to show Lync15.admx only. You will see all the settings that can be set. If you move back to the folder where you extracted the files, you will see the folder called admx. Inside is the Lync15.admx file. There is also a folder called en-us. In here you will find the Lync15.adml file, which is a language-specific file for the Lync GPO template file.

Once you have the template file, you will need to load it into a Group Policy object (GPO), which will then be applied at the level in AD where you want to control settings. This is subject to all the usual constraints, such as delays in policy propagation as mentioned earlier.

Since with Lync 2013 we are now dealing with ADMX templates rather than the older ADM templates that Lync 2010 used, the method of use has changed. Instead of manually importing the template into a specific GPO, we now have two options to load the new settings template. We can either add them locally on a single machine or load them centrally and have them replicated to any DC for multiple admins to access. Both processes are described in detail here:

www.petri.co.il/add-administrative-templates-to-gpo.htm

Given that this is Active Directory work, it is out of scope for this book, so we will stick to the simplest method, which allows you to test things out by using the local store on one machine. If you are rolling this out in production, then speak with your AD specialist to understand the best method for your network.

1. To load the template into a GPO, on a domain controller (or anywhere else you have the Group Policy Management tools installed), open the %systemroot%\PolicyDefinitions folder. Copy the lync15.admx file to this folder. Then open the en-US folder and copy the lync15.adml file in there.

2. Next open the Group Policy Management tool by clicking Start ➢ Administrative Tools ➢ Group Policy Management. On the left pane, drill down into the forest and domain and right-click Group Policy Objects. Select New, as shown in Figure 10.8.

FIGURE 10.8
Creating the new GPO object

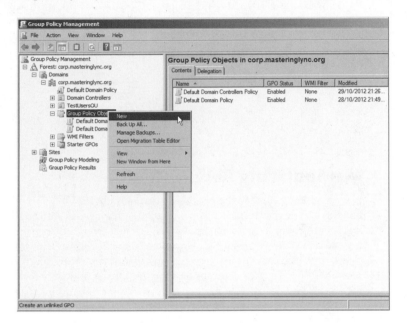

3. Give the policy a name, but don't select a starter GPO, and click OK.

4. Right-click the new GPO and click Edit. In the left pane, drill down to User Configuration ➢ Policies ➢ Administrative Templates: Policy Definitions (ADMX Files) Retrieved from the Local Machine. One of the folders you will find underneath is called Microsoft Lync 2013.

5. If you then drill down to the next level you will find Microsoft Lync Feature Policies, under which all the settings will be visible in the right pane. Each setting is fairly self-explanatory and comes with a useful help article built into the GPO, as shown in Figure 10.9.

6. After you set up the policy as needed, you can apply it to the relevant group of users by using the standard method.

FIGURE 10.9
The newly created
GPO with the Lync
settings imported

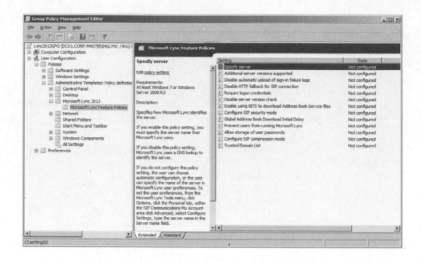

Manipulating Policies

You are getting close to the process of testing policies. As you will soon come to expect, Lync policies can be manipulated in the usual two ways: either through LSCP or through PowerShell. In general, though, most manipulation is done through PowerShell because the policies are very wide ranging. Because these policies must be manipulated using PowerShell, administrators must take the time to really think through what they were doing as they prepare and research the necessary commands. One final thing to note before you dive right in: Although the LyncUserAdmin account used in this chapter's examples so far can assign policies to users, it can't create them; therefore, to carry out the operations discussed next (except for the assignment of policies), you should be logged on as a member of the CSAdministrator RBAC role.

Viewing Policies

You will undoubtedly want to know what policies already exist before you create new ones. Lync comes with a global policy set up for each policy type available, and the default settings are hard-coded into the software. You will see this in action later in the chapter when we discuss what happens if you try to delete a global policy.

Because we discussed some of the policies earlier in this chapter, you already know several of the policy types. In LSCP, they are spread out in the various tabs to which they apply. For example, to see the available ClientVersionPolicies, you would navigate to the Client tab in LSCP; in the main pane under Client Version Policy, you would see all available policies. This is shown in Figure 10.10.

What you can see is not only the default global policy but also some other more focused policies, which you will create shortly. If you view one of the other policy sections, under the Federation and External Access tab, you can see the External Access policy. If you double-click the global policy, you will see the settings in Figure 10.11. Interestingly, this is one of those areas in the GUI that has changed from Lync 2010 to 2013 because external access now includes settings to configure XMPP, more of which is covered in Chapter 19, "Third-Party Integration."

To change any of the settings, simply check the relevant check box and then click Commit. You can see how easy it is to retrieve policy information and change settings in the LSCP. If you look carefully enough at all the possible options, you will also notice that some of the more wide-ranging policies like the CsClientPolicy are not visible through the LSCP.

FIGURE 10.10
Viewing the Client Version Policy tab in LSCP

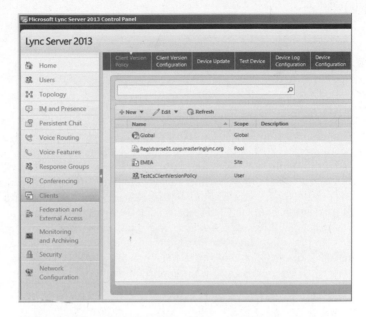

FIGURE 10.11
Viewing the settings of the default global External Access policy

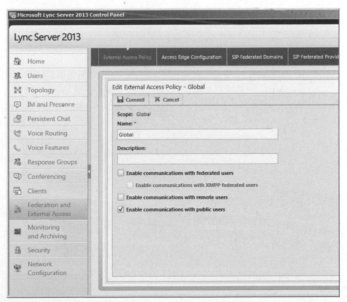

Given that some of the settings are not available through LSCP and in keeping with the rest of the book, let's take a look at how you would use PowerShell to view policies.

As we have already discussed, there are various default global policies. To retrieve one of them, the CsClientPolicy type, you would use a command such as this:

```
Get-CsExternalAccessPolicy -Identity global
```

Because you want to retrieve the default global policy, notice the naming convention. Also notice the output of this command, which shows the current settings that you saw in Figure 10.11:

```
Identity                          : Global
Description                       :
EnableFederationAccess            : False
EnableXmppAccess                  : False
EnablePublicCloudAccess           : False
EnablePublicCloudAudioVideoAccess : False
EnableOutsideAccess               : False
```

To get the remaining policies, you simply need to identify the relevant cmdlets. Sadly, this is not as simple as it could be because the developers didn't quite stick to a naming convention. Most of the cmdlets are formatted like the previous one, Get-CsXxxPolicy. However, there are a couple that stand out. First, note that although the Get-CsNetworkIntersitePolicy and Get-CsEffectivePolicy cmdlets follow the relevant naming format, the first actually works with Call Admission Control (CAC) and as such is not related directly to users, and the latter is a new cmdlet enabling administrators to see which set of policies applies to a user. We cover Get-CsEffectivePolicy later in this chapter. The other anomaly is the Get-CsDialPlan cmdlet; although it doesn't have Policy in the name, it retrieves dial plans related to Enterprise Voice that are applied to users and is targeted as the other policy cmdlets are, based on Global, Site, and User. Dial plans are covered in Chapter 13. With this knowledge, you can run the following command to get a list of all the relevant cmdlets:

```
Get-Command -Module Lync | Where-Object {($_.Name -like "Get-Cs*Policy" ↩
-or $_.Name -eq "Get-CsDialPlan")} | Where-Object ↩
{$_.Name -notlike "*Effective*"} | Where-Object {$_.Name ↩
-notlike "*Network*"} | Select-Object Name
```

This command will first get all the commands in the Lync module and then sort through them listing only those that fit the criteria of starting with Get-Cs and ending with Policy. It will omit the Get-CsNetworkIntersitePolicy and the Get-CsEffectivePolicy cmdlets and include the Get-CsDialPlan cmdlet. When it is run, you will see the following output:

```
Name
----
Get-CsArchivingPolicy
Get-CsClientPolicy
Get-CsClientVersionPolicy
Get-CsConferencingPolicy
Get-CsDialPlan
Get-CsExternalAccessPolicy
Get-CsHostedVoicemailPolicy
Get-CsLocationPolicy
Get-CsMobilityPolicy
Get-CsPersistentChatPolicy
Get-CsPinPolicy
Get-CsPresencePolicy
Get-CsUserServicesPolicy
Get-CsVoicePolicy
Get-CsVoiceRoutingPolicy
```

If you are familiar with Lync 2010, you will notice that we have a few new policies in Lync 2013. First, the `Get-CsMobilityPolicy` cmdlet is built in by default, having previously been added by the Mobility Service update in Lync 2010. It will be covered in Chapter 20, "Mobile Devices." Next we have the `Get-CsPersistentChatPolicy` cmdlet, which is used to get information about the policy that controls the Persistent Chat function now built into Lync 2013; it was previously called Group Chat and managed as a separate component in previous versions of OCS 2007 R2 and Lync. This is covered in Appendix C, "Using Persistent Chat Effectively." The `Get-CsUserServicesPolicy` cmdlet retrieves the policy that defines whether a user's contacts are stored in Lync 2013 or in the Unified Contact Store as part of Exchange w2013. This is covered in Chapter 17, "Exchange, SharePoint, and Group Chat." Finally, the `Get-CsVoiceRoutingPolicy` cmdlet is used to get information about the voice routing policies used when configuring Lync voice in a hybrid setup with Office 365. This is covered in Chapter 18, "Hybrid Deployments."

Now you have a useful list of all the cmdlets that can be used to retrieve policies. They all (even `Get-CsDialPlan`) take the same command structure as shown earlier to get the current global policy settings.

It's useful to see the current settings for each of the global policies, but sometimes you'll want to see the default settings. There are a few ways of doing this:

◆ Check the help file. This method doesn't require any discussion.

◆ Create a new, empty policy and retrieve it to display its settings. This method has a disadvantage we'll discuss next.

◆ Create a new policy but use the `-InMemory` parameter. This final way is rather clever.

As mentioned, creating a new policy with no parameters other than a name will create a policy using the default settings, as shown in this example:

```
New-CsClientPolicy -Identity TestDefaultSettings
```

This command would create a new client policy called TestDefaultSettings. However, you don't really want to have to create policies every time you want to see the default settings because it would be too easy to forget one and clutter up the system. Fortunately, another option is available. One of the parameters of the `New-CsXxxPolicy` cmdlets is `-InMemory`. When appended to the command just shown, it creates a policy but holds it in memory and never writes it to the configuration store. To see this parameter in action, run the following command:

```
New-CsClientPolicy -Identity TestDefaultSettings -InMemory
```

This will output the default settings of the client policy but not actually create the policy. Of course, this functionality is not provided just to let you see the default settings of a policy. It will also allow you to create a new policy in memory and assign it to a variable. You can then manipulate the policy settings as you need and then put the policy into action, thereby ensuring that the correct settings are applied immediately as shown in the following example:

```
$newpolvar = New-CsClientPolicy -Identity NewPolicy1 -InMemory
$newpolvar.DisableEmoticons = $True
$newpolvar.DisablePresenceNote = $True
Set-CsClientPolicy -Instance $newpolvar
$newpolvar = $NULL
```

What this does is set the variable $newpolvar to the default settings of the *NewCsClientPolicy* cmdlet creating in memory a policy called NewPolicy1. Next, you edit certain properties of that variable to disable emoticons, for example. Then you write back those setting with the Set-CsClientPolicy cmdlet, which actually creates the policy. Finally, you end by resetting the variable $newpolvar to Null so that it can't accidentally be used.

We've looked at how to retrieve the global policies and the default settings, but what about easily viewing the other policies of a specific type? The next command will list all policies of a certain type:

```
Get-CsClientVersionPolicy | Select-Object Identity
```

This command will list all the CsClientVersionPolicies, as in the output shown here:

```
Identity
--------
Global
Site:EMEA
Service:Registrar:se01.corp.masteringlync.org
Tag:TestCsClientVersionPolicy
```

This output nicely demonstrates the naming conventions showing scope and assignment. The Tag:TestCsClientVersionPolicy entry is ready to be assigned to users.

Creating and Assigning Policies

So far we've covered the basics of creating a policy using the New-CsXxxPolicy cmdlets. We know that simply using the cmdlet followed by an identity will create a new policy with the default settings. We've also discussed the basics of what the different identities for the policy mean to where they apply, but it will be useful to recap that here. This time we will use the New-CsClientVersionPolicy because it can be created against all of the various scopes available as follows:

```
New-CsClientVersionPolicy -Identity global
New-CsClientVersionPolicy -Identity Site:EMEA
New-CsClientVersionPolicy -Identity registrar:se01.corp.masteringlync.org
New-CsClientVersionPolicy -Identity TestDefaultSettings
```

These commands will create policies with the default settings. Of course, you can also create new policies through the LSCP. One of the benefits of this is that you get guidance in creating the policies of different, scope as shown in Figure 10.12.

Once you have selected the scope type, you will be presented with a search box to locate the relevant pool (registrar) or site, or you will be taken straight into the policy settings windows with a text box to name the policy if it is to be a user (Tag:) policy.

After policies have been created in LSCP or PowerShell, the next stage is the assignment of these policies. Global policies, site policies, and service policies don't need to be assigned; they just work immediately on creation because their identity specifically references an element of Lync architecture where they are to be active. That's why the name of a policy can be edited only with user policies. Of course, this means that you can't use one site policy on another site; you must create a new one because the naming format is specific to the site, such as Site:EMEA or Site:APAC. If you do need to do this, there is no simple method. It would be worth reviewing the article linked here, which details a possible workaround:

```
http://blogs.technet.com/b/csps/archive/2011/03/21/copypolicies.aspx
```

FIGURE 10.12
Creating a new
CsClientVersionPolicy
through LSCP, show-
ing the different policy
scopes available

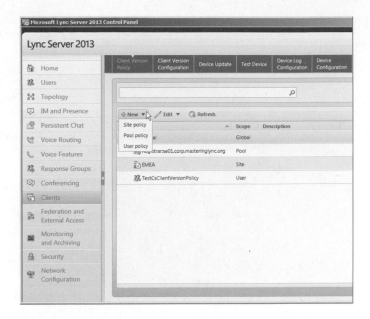

The user policy (sometimes called Tag level) will need to be assigned. This is where the `Grant-CsXxxPolicy` cmdlets come in. To assign the TestDefaultSettings client version policy to Test User 1, you would need to do the following:

```
Grant-CsClientVersionPolicy -Identity "Test User1" ↵
-PolicyName "TestDefaultSettings"
```

This will apply the policy to `Test User1`. But suppose you want to apply this policy to all members of a department or to those with a special custom attribute or specifically to members of an AD group.

Well, this is once again where PowerShell comes in. You can again utilize the searching skills you learned at the beginning of this chapter. You first locate the relevant group of users you need and then pipe the output to the relevant `Grant-CsXxxPolicy` cmdlet. Here is an example:

```
Get-CsUser -LdapFilter "Department=Marketing" | ↵
Grant-CsClientPolicy -PolicyName "TestCsClientPolicy"
```

This will first use an LDAP filter to get all the members of the Marketing department who are Lync enabled and then apply the TestCsClientPolicy to them. If you are using the LSCP to assign policy, things follow much the same format. You would use the search skills covered earlier to locate the relevant Lync-enabled users. Then you would select the users and, on the Action drop-down, click Assign Policies. This will open the window you see in Figure 10.13. You can assign the relevant policies to the users by using the relevant drop-down menus and clicking OK to apply.

Applying a policy to members of a specific AD group is unfortunately not quite so simple. Like many things, though, it can be achieved with a line of PowerShell.

You first need to get the members of the group. This can be done as follows:

```
Import-Module ActiveDirectory
Get-AdGroupMember -Identity TestGroup
```

FIGURE 10.13
Assigning policies
in the LSCP

Here, you are first importing the AD module so you can manipulate AD objects and then get the members of the group TestGroup. However, the output looks like this:

```
Get-ADGroupMember -Identity TestGroup
distinguishedName : CN=Test User5,Cn=users,dc=corp,dc=masteringlync,dc=org
name              : Test User5
objectClass       : user
objectGUID        : 1870d540-28f4-47eb-90fd-b98c339cd6d5
SamAccountName    : testuser5
SID               : S-1-5-21-97327702-4139054532-3539935471-1143
```

If you try to pipe that directly into the Grant-CsXxxPolicy cmdlet, you will get an error because the Grant-CsXxxPolicy cmdlet doesn't understand the input. So to work around this, you need to understand the type of input that the Grant-CsXxxPolicy cmdlet takes. You can get this from the help file, as shown here:

```
String value or Microsoft.Rtc.Management.ADConnect.Schema.ADUser object.
Grant-CsClientPolicy accepts pipelined input of string values
representing the Identity of a user account. The cmdlet also
accepts pipelined input of user objects.
```

This tells you that the cmdlet accepts pipelined user objects, as you proved when passing it output from Get-CsUser, and that it also accepts strings that represent user accounts. Therefore, what you need to pass the Grant-CsXxxPolicy cmdlet is something in the form of "Test User5."

As you can see from the output from the Get-AdGroupMember cmdlet, this particular format is found under the .name attribute. You can, therefore, use the following PowerShell command to grant policy to the membership of a specific AD group:

```
Get-ADGroupMember -Identity testgroup | ForEach-Object ↵
{Grant-CsClientPolicy -PolicyName testcsclientpolicy -identity $_.name}
```

This command first gets the members of the group and then for each member runs the `Grant-CsClientPolicy` cmdlet using the `.name` attribute for the identity.

 Real World Scenario

THE NEED TO AUTOMATE POLICY ASSIGNMENT

In many recent discussions with customers, a common scenario has arisen. As you have seen, assigning policy is a process that requires a command to be run. It is perhaps a slight disadvantage to the new way of doing things. With Group Policy, assuming a new user account fell under the scope of a GPO, that new user account would automatically get the new policy applied. In Lync this is not always the case. For example, suppose a new user is created in the Marketing department. Even if you have followed one of the earlier examples to assign a specific policy to all members of the Marketing department using the LDAP filter method, this new member of the Marketing department won't get the same policy as the rest of the department. Instead, they will get the nearest policy to it, following the normal inheritance method. This could either be a service (depending on which pool they register to), a site (depending on which site they are homed in), or the global policy, if none of the others apply.

What is required is a way to ensure that users get the policies they should get. At this point, there is really no good way that we have come up with for doing this. You could of course have scripts that are scheduled, but it would only be reasonable to run those, for example, at the end of each day. This means a user could be live on the system for a day without the correct policies. If this were an archiving policy, that could leave you open to some serious legal consequences!

All we can suggest in this case is to make the assignment of Lync policy part of your provisioning process. This could mean ensuring that assigning policy is added to the checklist of steps taken when creating a user. Or, you may have an automated method, given that PowerShell makes it so simple to assign policy based on user attributes. If so, you can ensure that when the user object is created by Forefront Identity Manager (FIM), which is a Microsoft meta directory and directory synchronization tool used in many provisioning systems, FIM will validate the relevant attributes based on user type (such as Marketing) and then run the relevant PowerShell commands to apply policy.

Finally, as part of operational management of Lync, you could report on Lync policies each month to double-check that people have the correct policies and no one has slipped through the net.

Realistically, you probably don't want to create all your policies with the default settings. After all, there would be little point in that because you could simply use the default global policies. So to create new policies with settings other than the default, you need to specify what settings you want in the `New-CsXxxPolicy`. As an example, creating a custom presence policy enables you to manage two important aspects of presence subscriptions: prompted subscribers and category subscriptions as shown here:

```
New-CsPresencePolicy -Identity MarketingPresencePolicy ↵
-MaxPromptedSubscriber 600 -MaxCategorySubscription 900
```

This would create a new presence policy using the settings entered. The `MaxCategorySubscription` parameter lets you control the maximum number of category subscriptions allowed at any one time. A category subscription represents a request for a specific category of information—for example, an application that requests calendar data. The MaxPromptedSubscriber parameter enables you to control the maximum number of prompted subscribers a user can have at any one time. By default, anytime you are added to another user's contacts list, a notification dialog appears onscreen informing you of this fact and giving you the chance to do such things as add the person to your own contacts list or block the person from viewing your presence. Until you take action and dismiss the dialog box, each notification counts as a prompted subscriber.

Creating a presence policy in this way is easy. However, what about a policy that has many more options you could set, like a client policy? In that case, you need to plow through them and set the ones you want. The options that you don't explicitly set will take on the default settings for that policy.

As you've seen, it is also possible to create policy using the LSCP. In this case, configuring the relevant settings is simply a case of using the GUI and then clicking Commit.

Editing Existing Policies

We have created several policies, but what about editing the existing ones? Editing policies is also a simple matter in PowerShell or LSCP. With PowerShell, you would use the relevant Set-CsXxxPolicy cmdlet and identify the policy using the naming conventions outlined previously (*Scope:Name*) and then use the relevant parameter to change the setting, as in the following example:

```
Set-CsPresencePolicy -Identity Tag:MarketingPresencePolicy ↵
-MaxPromptedSubscriber 200 -MaxCategorySubscription 400
```

There is at least one policy that works slightly differently than the others. That is the client version policy. This policy is made up of rules to allow or disallow certain versions, and it uses the CsClientVersionPolicyRule set of cmdlets to amend and create rules. They are covered in the final section of this chapter.

So having created and assigned all these policies, the last thing we will cover in this section is how to see which user has which policy assigned. After all, it could get rather complex with all those different levels in play!

To see the policies applied to a user, run the following command:

```
Get-CsUser -Identity "Test User5"
```

This will output something similar to the following:

```
Identity                  : CN=Test User5,CN=Users,DC=corp,DC=masteringlync,DC=org
VoicePolicy               :
VoiceRoutingPolicy        :
ConferencingPolicy        :
PresencePolicy            :
DialPlan                  :
LocationPolicy            :
ClientPolicy              : testcsclientpolicy
ClientVersionPolicy       :
ArchivingPolicy           :
ExchangeArchivingPolicy   : Uninitialized
PinPolicy                 :
ExternalAccessPolicy      :
```

```
MobilityPolicy          :
PersistentChatPolicy    :
UserServicesPolicy      :
HostedVoiceMail         :
HostedVoicemailPolicy   :
HostingProvider         : SRV:
RegistrarPool           : se01.corp.masteringlync.org
Enabled                 : True
SipAddress              : sip:testuser5@masteringlync.org
LineURI                 : tel:+445552222222
EnterpriseVoiceEnabled  : True
ExUmEnabled             : False
HomeServer              : CN=Lc Services,CN=Microsoft,CN=1:1,CN=Pools,CN=RTC Service,CN=Ser
vices,CN=Configuration,DC=corp,DC=masteringlync,DC=org
DisplayName             : Test User5
SamAccountName          : testuser5
```

Note that although some of the policies applied are shown, others are not! This is because the only ones shown here are the ones assigned specifically to the user; namely, the Tag: policies.

In the past with Lync 2010, to see all the policies that applied to a user required some fairly serious PowerShell. If you're interested in that, then take a look at the *Lync Server PowerShell* blog:

http://blogs.technet.com/b/csps/archive/2010/06/07/scriptuserpolicyassignments.aspx

However, in Lync 2013 we have been given a new built-in cmdlet to do exactly what we need. The Get-CsEffectivePolicy cmdlet will return all the policies applied to a user even if they are applied only at a global or site level. For example, if you run the following command, you will see the policies applied to Test User5:

```
Get-CsEffectivePolicy -Identity "Test User5"
```

The output looks like this:

```
Identity                : Test User5
ConferencingPolicy      : Global
PresencePolicy          : Global
LocationPolicy          : Global
VoicePolicy             : Global
LocationProfile         : Global
ClientVersionPolicy     : Global
ClientPolicy            : testcsclientpolicy
ImArchivingPolicy       : Global
UserPinPolicy           : Global
ExternalAccessPolicy    : Global
HostedVoicemailPolicy   : Global
MobilityPolicy          : Global
PersistentChatPolicy    : Global
VoiceRoutingPolicy      : Global
UserServicesPolicy      : Global
```

You can see that all the policies are applied at the Global level except for the ClientPolicy, which is defined at the user level.

Removing or Resetting Policies

With all the experimenting with policies you've done in this chapter, you have probably ended up with lots of policies you don't want! You also may well have changed the settings of the default global policies and, for that matter, other policies as well. So what can be done about that? Well, removing a policy at any of the levels other than global is simple. Use the relevant Remove-CsXxxPolicy cmdlet with the identity of the policy as follows:

```
Remove-CsClientVersionPolicy -Identity Site:EMEA
Remove-CsClientVersionPolicy -Identity registrar:se01.corp.masteringlync.org
Remove-CsClientVersionPolicy -Identity TestDefaultSettings
```

In LSCP, removing policies is just as simple; you simply select the relevant policy and then from the Edit drop-down, select Delete.

Interestingly, when you remove a policy, you remove the policy but not the assignment to the user. Of course, removing site and service policies automatically removes their assignment because the identity and assignment are intrinsically linked. It is different for user or Tag policies, as you will see if you run the following Get-CsUser command:

```
Get-CsUser -Identity "Test User5"
```

Assuming you have removed one of the previously assigned user policies, you will see that the user still has a reference to that policy although not by name:

```
Policy with identity X (Numerical value based on anchor) has been removed.
```

This essentially shows that the policy can't be found.

WHAT ARE ANCHORS?

An *anchor* is a unique value assigned to each policy of a certain type; the values increase by one each time a policy is created. If you had five policies, they will be anchored 1 through 5. If you delete number 3, then the next policy created will still take number 6, and number 3 will never be reused.

As discussed in the inheritance topic of the Creating and Assigning Policies section, what will happen now is that the next closest policy to the user will take precedence. Although this looks slightly messy, there is no need to take any further steps to clean up.

USER MOVING TO A NEW LOCATION

If a user moves from one place to another and therefore needs different policies, you don't need to first remove the policies from the user; you simply apply the new policies in the same way you did before (as discussed previously). The user—and for that matter, the site, service, and global levels—can have only one policy applied at any one time.

Interestingly, if you try to delete the default global policies, Lync won't let you! Essentially, all that happens is that any changes you have made to the global policy revert to the default settings. To try this for yourself, you would use a command like the following one:

```
Remove-CsClientVersionPolicy -Identity global
```

When you run this, you will reset the global CsClientVersionPolicy to its default settings. By way of warning, you will see the following output:

```
WARNING: Global configuration for "ClientVersionPolicy" cannot be removed. Instead of
removing it, the Global configuration for ClientVersionPolicy" has been reset to the
default value.
```

Choosing the Right Policy for the Job

We have looked at the policy architecture in Lync and have seen how policies operate, how they are targeted, and also where Group Policy is still needed. We have also looked at the basics of manipulating policies in Lync. Finally, we will dive in and look at the individual policies and the settings they control.

The first element of examining individual policies is knowing where to view and change those settings. Clearly, LSCP gives access to many policy elements, including the ability to edit and assign policies as well as create and delete them. However, not all policies can be accessed in this way. Table 10.1 lists the elements of LSCP that deal with policies (for example, assigning them to various scopes), and it shows how the settings in LSCP equate to PowerShell cmdlets; it also indicates which chapter of this book covers the related policies.

TABLE 10.1: A mapping of LSCP settings to PowerShell cmdlets

LSCP TAB	LSCP SETTING	POWERSHELL CMDLET	NOTES	CHAPTER COVERED
IM & Presence	File Filter	CsFileTransferFilterConfiguration		3
IM & Presence	URL Filter	CsImFilterConfiguration	Note that the IM Filter Configuration is different from the basic enabling and disabling of hyperlinks that is possible through the CsClientPolicy through the EnableURL setting.	3
Persistent Chat	Persistent Chat Policy	CsPersistentChatPolicy		C
Persistent Chat	Persistent Chat Configuration	CsPersistentChatConfiguration		C
Voice Routing	Dial Plan	CsDialPlan		13
Voice Routing	Voice Policy	CsVoicePolicy		13

TABLE 10.1:   A mapping of LSCP settings to PowerShell cmdlets   *(CONTINUED)*

LSCP TAB	LSCP SETTING	POWERSHELL CMDLET	NOTES	CHAPTER COVERED
Voice Routing	Trunk Configuration	CsOutboundTranslationRule CsTrunkConfiguration CsVoiceRegex		13
Conferencing	Conferencing Policy	CsConferencingConfiguration		16
Conferencing	Meeting Configuration	CsMeetingConfiguration		16
Conferencing	PIN Policy	CsPinPolicy	Note that this is the same policy defined in the Security tab and controls both Conferencing and Device access.	3, 16
Clients	Client Version Policy	CsClientVersionPolicy		3, 10
Clients	Client Version Configuration	CsClientVersionConfiguration	Allows you to modify the default action for clients not specifically mentioned in the active policy.	3
Clients	Device Log Configuration	CsUCPhoneConfiguration		4
Clients	Device Configuration	CsDeviceUpdateConfiguration		4
Clients	Mobility Policy	CsMobilityPolicy		20
Clients	Push Notification Configuration	CsPushNotificationConfiguration		20
Federation and External Access	External Access Policy	CsExternalAccessPolicy		4

TABLE 10.1: A mapping of LSCP settings to PowerShell cmdlets *(CONTINUED)*

LSCP TAB	LSCP SETTING	POWERSHELL CMDLET	NOTES	CHAPTER COVERED
Federation and External Access	Access Edge Configuration	CsAccessEdgeConfiguration	Note that this is a global-only setting.	4
Monitoring and Archiving	Call Detail Recording	CsCdrConfiguration		11
Monitoring and Archiving	Quality of Experience Data	CsQoEConfiguration		11
Monitoring and Archiving	Archiving Policy	CsArchivingPolicy		11
Monitoring and Archiving	Archiving Configuration	CsArchivingConfiguration		11
Security	Registrar	CsProxyConfiguration		3
Security	Web Service	CsWebServiceConfiguration		3
Security	PIN Policy	CsPinPolicy		3, 16
Network Configuration	Global Policy	CsNetworkConfiguration		14
Network Configuration	Location Policy	CsLocationPolicy		15

What you may notice in Table 10.1 is that there is no mention of the CsClientPolicy, CsPresencePolicy, PrivacyConfiguration, or UserServicesConfiguration. Some of the most far-reaching policies can be changed only through PowerShell. In the rest of this chapter, we will drill into the settings of these policies and any particular quirks of operation related to individual policies.

OTHER POLICY TYPES

There are, of course, many other policy types that we are not covering in this chapter. There are settings for conferences, voice, archiving, persistent chat, mobility, and simple URLs, among others. Although these policies can all be applied to users, they are applied in the context of specific areas of Lync functionality that are described in other chapters of this book, so we cover the relevant policies settings there too.

ClientPolicy

The client policy is manipulated using the `CsClientPolicy` cmdlets. It is this policy that replaces the vast majority of settings that would previously have been set using group policies in OCS 2007 R2. Client policies can be applied at the site or user scope.

It is the client policy that allows the configuration of such elements as these: `MaximumNumberOfContacts`, whether to add a disclaimer message to an IM with the `IMWarning` setting, whether to force saving of IMs in Outlook with the `EnableIMAutoArchiving` setting, and whether to display a photo with the `DisplayPhoto` setting.

Of course, there are many more settings available, which are all described in detail in the Lync help file. However, if the setting is not in the default scope, there is a way to make client policies even more flexible. You can use the `New-CsClientPolicyEntry` cmdlet to add additional areas of control to the Lync ClientPolicy. This functionality has to be used in conjunction with Microsoft, who would potentially add the relevant new element to control in a cumulative update as detailed here:

```
http://technet.microsoft.com/en-us/library/gg399046.aspx
```

In the past, this was used to add a method for providing a link to a feedback URL to capture client requests during the beta of Lync.

ClientVersionPolicy

The client version policy is set to ensure control over which different clients can register to a Lync pool. Client version policies are made up of rules that identify specific clients. These rules are defined using the `ClientVersionPolicyRule` cmdlets. Each SIP client sends identifying information in its SIP headers. This identifying information is then matched against the defined rules.

SPOOFING HEADERS

Because clients report their version in a SIP header, it is possible that given a correctly manipulated client, the header could be changed. This would allow a way around the policy. Therefore, you should not think of this as a top security policy—rather, think of it as something that can provide a good consistent service and as a line of defense against casual attackers.

These policies are used to ensure both a consistent user experience and security by making sure that old, unpatched clients cannot connect to the service.

Client version policies can be applied at the global, site, service (registrar), and user scope.

ClientVersionConfiguration

The `ClientVersionConfiguration` cmdlets allow you to control, at either the Global (default) or Site (new policy) level, what happens when clients attempt to connect to Lync. This is where you turn on or off the facility in Lync to check client version. If this policy is enabled, the ClientVersionPolicies apply. The other side to the ClientVersionConfiguration is what happens when Lync denies access to a client. You can use the settings to set the default action if a client version is not specifically noted in a ClientVersionPolicy. You can also configure whether to prompt the user with a URL to get an updated client if they have a client that is not compliant with the policy.

PrivacyConfiguration

Presence is a great resource; the ability to see whether someone is available can significantly streamline communication. However, some people are not eager to present this information. Lync 2010 introduces a new way of managing this situation, which Lync 2013 maintains, by applying Privacy Configuration settings. The fundamental aim of these settings is giving users control. It allows users to show their status to only those people on their contacts list.

Given that only allowing contacts to see your status is very restrictive, you can help users prepopulate their contacts list with their manager and direct reports using the AutoInitiateContacts setting. Other settings configure Lync to ensure that the user must specifically opt in to sharing photo and location information with others.

Policies can be configured at the global, site, and service scope. At the service scope, the policy can be applied only to the User Services service.

PresencePolicy

The presence policy controls two settings, the MaxCategorySubscription and the MaxPromptedSubscriber. Presence as a concept is all about providing information about whether someone or something (a group, for example) is available. However, the simple process of providing that information creates network traffic and database load because all the people who are tracking an object are communicated with and logged. Lync is a fairly efficient system and scales to hundreds of thousands of users; however, if all those users subscribed to a single object, then when it came online or changed status, that would generate hundreds of thousands of messages to let all those users know.

To mitigate this potential flood of network traffic, you can use the settings in the presence policy. The first setting, MaxCategorySubscription, controls the individual types of information that each user can subscribe to—for example, calendar information.

The MaxCategorySubscription property enables you to limit the number of category subscriptions a user can have.

The second setting is the MaxPromptedSubscriber setting. Each time you are added to another user's contacts list, the default Lync behavior is to prompt you with a pop-up that gives you the chance to reciprocate and add the user to your contacts list. Each of these prompts counts as someone subscribed to the requesting user's presence. It is common practice to limit the number of unacknowledged presence subscriptions; this can be done with the MaxPromptedSubscriber property. If a user were to reach the maximum number, they would not receive new contact notifications until some of the outstanding prompts have been acknowledged.

The CsPresencePolicy cmdlets can apply at the global, site, or per-user scope.

UserServicesConfiguration

User Services are the services that control the basic settings for maintaining presence for users and also some base meeting settings. The meeting settings cover the length of time an anonymous user can remain in a meeting without an authenticated user and the maximum time that any meeting can remain active. On the user side, you can set the maximum number of contacts each user can have and the maximum number of meetings that they can schedule.

The user services configuration policies are applied at site or service scope. You can also edit the global policy.

When the user services configuration settings and the client policy settings are in conflict (for example, when different maximum number of contacts per user has been set), the lower number wins.

The Bottom Line

Search for users in the LSCP and PowerShell.   Lync offers huge flexibility in what can be done to configure and control the Lync user experience. However, to work efficiently in Lync, being able to identify and retrieve information about different groups of users based on various criteria is critical. It is this skill that enables you to target specific groups with specific policies. As with most administration, you can search for users in both LSCP and PowerShell.

> **Master It**   You have been asked to run a report on two groups of users. How would you handle the following requests? Can you use two different types of search?
>
> Locate all users in Marketing.
>
> Locate all users who register to the se01.corp.masteringlync.org pool.

Perform basic user administration in the LSCP and in PowerShell.   As would be expected, most basic administration can be performed in LSCP and in PowerShell. New users can be created, deleted, enabled, and disabled in both. You can, of course, also change various Lync properties—in particular, things like the SIP URI of a user and the pool to which they register. User administration is generally carried out by a user who is a member of the CSUserAdministrator RBAC role.

> **Master It**   You have been asked to enable all users, except those who are in Marketing, for Lync. How would you do this? In addition, one of your colleagues, who is a domain administrator, has asked you to make some changes to his account. What problems might you face?

Understand Lync policies.   Lync has significantly improved the policy architecture since OCS 2007 R2. Although AD Group Policy still can have a role to play in getting the Lync client up and running, Lync enforces the majority of policy through in-band provisioning. It uses SIP messages to push policy out to the client instantly and ensures that there is no requirement for domain membership. Users get a consistent experience no matter where they log on. To apply Lync policies properly, it is important to understand the new scope model, in which policies can be applied at the global, site, service, and user levels and how inheritance works so that the policy closest to the user wins.

> **Master It**   You have been asked to explain to a new Lync administrator the different scopes at which a policy can be applied and how different scopes affect the identity of the policy. What would you tell her?

Manipulate Lync policies.   Lync policies are controlled and applied to users either through PowerShell or through LSCP. When in the shell, your search skills are critical to ensure that you can closely target relevant user groups. It is here that the piping capabilities of PowerShell are so useful. You can, of course, also apply policy through LSCP, which has a helpful Assign Policy page where you can apply applicable policies to one or many users from a single screen.

> **Master It**   You have been asked to create a new client policy for the APAC site. You first need to check the default settings for the policy and then customize it to limit the number of users a person can have on their contacts list to 300. How would you proceed?

Choose the right policy for the job.   There is a vast range of policy settings in Lync. One of the hardest things an administrator must do is understand where to make certain configurations. LSCP makes available many policy settings, but it is not always obvious which PowerShell cmdlet sets which setting, compared to what is presented in the LSCP. Equally, it is not possible to carry out all configuration through the LSCP, with some of the most wide-ranging policies being configured only through PowerShell.

> **Master It**   You have been asked to design a set of policies for your Lync organization. Where would you gather more information about specific settings?

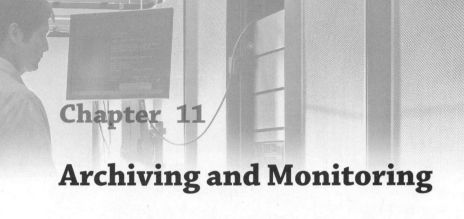

Chapter 11

Archiving and Monitoring

Any company facing the world of compliance will probably need to account not only for who is IM'ing with whom and when but also for the content of those messages. This is where the Lync Server 2013 Archiving role comes into play.

Its partner role is the Monitoring role. Monitoring is often associated with service availability up/down reporting capabilities, but the Lync Server 2013 Monitoring role is responsible for the quality-based call monitoring as well as the Call Detail Records capability normally associated with PBXs.

Server (and service) availability monitoring is the responsibility of System Center Operations Manager, and Lync Server 2013 has a management pack available to provide specific service alerting and reporting into System Center.

In this chapter, you will learn to:

◆ Understand the architecture of the Archiving and Monitoring roles

◆ Provide reporting on the data available from the Archiving and Monitoring roles

◆ Use the capabilities in the System Center Operations Manager management pack to report on the availability of the Lync Server 2013 service

Deploying the Architecture for Archiving and Monitoring

Live Communications Server (LCS) introduced the archiving and CDR capability; however, the Monitoring server role was not available until OCS 2007.

In both LCS (2003 and 2005) and OCS 2007, the Archiving database contained the IM logs as well as the CDR data. The monitoring database introduced with OCS 2007 contained only the Quality of Experience (QoE) data; however, with the move to OCS 2007 R2, the CDR data was removed from the Archiving database and included with the QoE data. This configuration was similar with both versions of Lync Server; archiving contained only the IM logs, and monitoring included both CDR and QoE data.

Lync Server 2013 has started to change the way in which archived data is maintained. When Exchange 2013 is also deployed in the environment, archiving can be directed to archive the data within the Exchange 2013 environment and make it subject to the same archiving configuration as Exchange. Specific information on this configuration can be found in Chapter 17, "Exchange and SharePoint."

Otherwise, Lync Server 2013 can continue to archive data to a SQL Server database.

In this chapter we'll focus on native Lync archiving. We'll look at the prerequisites required, the deployment architecture, and the policies required to enable the archiving and monitoring capability for users.

Prerequisites

Both Archiving and Monitoring roles have now been combined into the Front End role, so no additional hardware is required to deploy them; it's just a case of enabling them and publishing the topology. These roles both use SQL Server as a repository for their data. Only Archiving can use Exchange Server 2013 as an alternative.

Unlike in previous versions, neither role requires Microsoft Message Queuing (MSMQ) to be installed.

Installation

As with the previous version of Lync Server, Archiving and Monitoring are both defined within Topology Builder, but the big change with Lync Server 2013 is that they no longer require separate servers. Rather, they are installed as additional services on top of a Front End server.

Either the roles can be enabled as part of the New Pool Wizard, or they can be added later through editing and publishing the topology. Figure 11.1 shows the associations section of a pool being edited on a previously published pool.

FIGURE 11.1
Defining archiving and monitoring associations on a pool

As with other roles that are reliant upon databases, the act of publishing the topology will also prompt to allow for creation of the databases. You can leave it to Topology Builder to select the locations for the database files, or you can manually control these.

Database Support, Architecture, and Capacity

Microsoft recommends that you deploy separate instances for each of the archiving and monitoring installations; however, it does support sharing an instance between Archiving and Monitoring and even sharing within a Back End or Persistent Chat database instance.

While this is a supported configuration, it's not recommended because of the likely capacity of the Archiving database. Larger databases can need more maintenance time, potentially impacting the other databases. Typically, separate instances will be used when performance of SQL Server is critical.

In the case of a Standard Edition server, a separate SQL Server installation is still required. Archiving and Monitoring cannot use the SQL Express instance used by the Standard Edition server.

The Archiving instance creates a single database called LCSLOG, whereas the Monitoring instance creates two databases, LCSCDR, containing Call Data Record information, and QoEMetrics, containing Quality of Experience information.

Lync Server 2013 also provides a significant number of reports for accessing and reporting on the Quality of Experience data, allowing administrators to help diagnose and troubleshoot call quality problems. You'll see some of these later in this chapter.

Both roles require the 64-bit version of SQL Server to be used; the monitoring reports pack requires SQL Reporting Services. The following versions of SQL Server are supported (or later service packs):

◆ SQL Server 2008 R2 Standard

◆ SQL Server 2008 R2 Enterprise

◆ SQL Server 2012 Standard

◆ SQL Server 2012 Enterprise

High Availability

Lync Server 2010 and previous versions did not support high availability for Archiving or Monitoring. There was support for Critical Mode Archiving, meaning that if the solution was unable to archive a message for a given time period (which varied based on version, but was configurable), the Front End services would shut down, resulting in no message transfer possible, and indeed users would be logged out in earlier versions.

With the new changes to Lync Server 2013 and how it uses SQL Server, coupled with the fact that Archiving and Monitoring are services on the Front End servers, high availability is automatically achieved with an environment that includes the high availability components in the design and deployment—multiple Front Ends and a SQL Server instance in *mirrored* configuration for the Back End.

Policy Configuration

The configuration for both Archiving and Monitoring are defined in the same location within the Control Panel application, as shown in Figure 11.2.

FIGURE 11.2
The Archiving and
Monitoring con-
figuration menu

Both policies have the same scope configuration options:

◆ Global

◆ Site

◆ User (Archiving Policy only)

User policies will override both *site* and *global* polices, and *site* policies will override *global* policies. In the case of *archiving*, external and internal communications can be configured separately and can be overridden separately also; for example, if both external and internal archiving are enabled at the *global* level, and at the *site* level internal archiving of communications is disabled, then for users at that *site*, only archiving of external communications would occur.

Both Call Detail Recording and Quality of Experience data have the same options:

◆ Scope

◆ Enabled

◆ Purging

◆ Number of days for data to be kept (if purging is enabled)

In addition, Call Detail Recording can specify how long error reports are kept.

Archiving policy allows for control over internal and/or external enablement as shown in Figure 11.3.

To define the CDR policy using PowerShell, enter this command:

```
New-CsCdrConfiguration -Identity site:EMEA -EnableCDR $true -EnablePurging $true
-KeepCallDetailForDays 30 -KeepErrorReportForDays 30 -PurgeHourOfDay 3
```

To configure the QoE data, use the `New-CsQoeConfiguration` cmdlet.

The PurgeHourOfDay parameter allows you to customize when the old data will be purged. Common sense suggests that you define this outside normal office hours; however, other operations (such as backups) may occur at the default time (02:00 a.m.), and you may find it useful to change this.

FIGURE 11.3
Defining Archiving
Policy

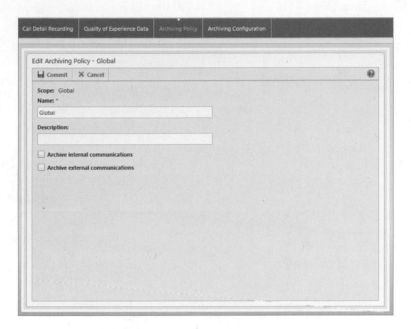

Archiving can be enabled for internal and/or external communications. You can define additional policies to allow this distinction to be made on a per-user or per-site basis if required.

The New-CsArchivingConfiguration cmdlet provides the options shown in Table 11.1 to configure the actual policy (using New-CsArchivingPolicy).

TABLE 11.1:   Archiving configuration cmdlet parameters

PARAMETER	DEFAULT	NOTES
ArchiveDuplicateMessages	True	Used when dealing with cross-pool messages. If set to True, the message will be archived once per pool of users involved. If False, it will be archived only once.
BlockOnArchiveFailure	False	If set to True, IMs will be refused if there are any issues with the archiving service. False enables message flow to continue in the event of problems.
CarchPurginInternal	24	Defines how often the system cache is purged of messages when none of the participants are enabled for archiving.

TABLE 11.1: Archiving configuration cmdlet parameters *(CONTINUED)*

PARAMETER	DEFAULT	NOTES
EnableArchiving	None	Specifies what is archived: None ImOnly ImAndWebConf
EnableExchangeArchiving	False	If set to True, archive data is stored in Exchange Server 2013 rather than SQL Server. If Exchange archiving is enabled, then Exchange archiving policies will be applied, not Lync policies.
EnablePurging	False	If set to True, messages will be removed from the database if older than the value specified in KeepArchivingDataForDays. If False, messages are not removed.
KeepArchivingDataForDays	14	Number of days that messages are kept (between 1 and 2,562, approximately 7 years).
PurgeExportedArchivesOnly	False	If True, only messages that have been exported will be purged (overrides KeepArchivingDataForDays value).
PurgeHourOfDay	2	Time value (hour only) when the data purging will occur.

A common archiving requirement is for compliance purposes, and typically it requires data to be kept for more than the default 14-day period. To create a new policy configuration with a one-year retention period, use the following command:

```
New-CsArchivingConfiguration -Identity site:EMEA -KeepArchivingDataForDays 365
-EnableArchiving ImAndWebConf
```

If the Archiving role has not yet been deployed, a warning will appear to remind the administrator that enabling archiving requires the Archiving server role to be deployed.

Using Get-CsArchivingConfiguration will return the following data for a new policy configuration:

```
Identity                  : Site:EMEA
EnableArchiving           : ImAndWebConf
EnablePurging             : False
PurgeExportedArchivesOnly : False
BlockOnArchiveFailure     : False
KeepArchivingDataForDays  : 365
PurgeHourofDay            : 2
ArchiveDuplicateMessages  : True
CachePurgingInterval      : 24
EnableExchangeArchiving   : False
```

To apply this configuration as a policy, you need to create an associated policy using the New-CsArchivingPolicy cmdlet; this will allow you to define whether the configuration applies to internal or external (or both) types of communication:

```
New-CsArchivingPolicy -Identity 1-year-external -ArchiveExternal $True
```

Here, you have created a user policy with only external archiving enabled.
Using Get-CsArchivingPolicy will display the following configuration:

```
Identity        : Tag:1-year-external
Description     :
ArchiveInternal : False
ArchiveExternal : True
```

Given that you created a site-based policy configuration and a user-based policy, when you assign the user-based policy to users (with the Grant-CsArchivingPolicy cmdlet), this specific site policy will take effect only when users are part of the EMEA site; for locations outside EMEA, the global policy is in effect with the default values.

Deploying the Reporting Pack

The Quality of Experience (QoE) data can be complicated, but Microsoft has provided a pack of built-in reports to help you understand the data captured. They range from simple usage and trending reports to detailed troubleshooting reports.

They are deployed into a SQL Reporting Services instance, using the Deployment Wizard setup application (shown in Figure 11.4).

FIGURE 11.4
The Deployment Wizard allows you to deploy Monitoring server reports.

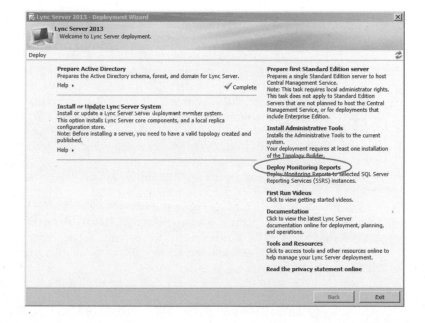

Once you select Deploy Monitoring Reports, the Deployment Wizard prompts you for the following information (although it is already completed with the SQL Server information from Topology Builder, as shown in Figure 11.5):

- Monitoring server

- SQL Server Reporting Services instance

- SQL Server account credentials (for use by the SQL Reporting Services)

- User group (to provide read-only access to the reports)

FIGURE 11.5
Deploying the
monitoring reports

By default in Lync Server 2010, the wizard attempted to create a secure web page on which to publish the reports (shown in the link on the home page of the Control Panel). However, the installation and configuration of the certificate was a manual process that wasn't really required. You don't have to install a certificate on this website, and you can access it without deploying a certificate if required.

Lync Server 2013 takes a more realistic approach by configuring the link as a standard HTTP link rather than HTTPS.

Unfortunately, the Reporting Pack covers only the Monitoring server databases (CDR and QOE); from an IM perspective, the best information that can be retrieved from this is the fact that two users had an IM conversation. The contents of that conversation (assuming archiving is enabled) are stored in the Archiving server database (LCSLog), which does not have any associated Reporting Pack.

Access to this data is via a SQL query, which, providing the user has the correct permissions, can be achieved using any product that supports Open Database Connectivity (ODBC) to retrieve and then manipulate the data. The actual IM conversation is held in Rich Text Format (RTF) and may require further manipulation before it is readable.

🌐 Real World Scenario

ARCHIVING FOR COMPLIANCE

Natively, the Archiving server role is not compliant with many of the regulatory compliance standards found throughout the globe, such as MoReq, UK Companies Act, Sarbanes-Oxley, HIPAA, FSA, and so on.

A copy of the IM data is stored in the SQL database. However, no further controls are in place to protect that data; any user with the appropriate permissions can get to the data and change it, with no record whatsoever of the access or change made. In addition, file transfers are not stored with the conversation transcript for easy recovery, and content from Group Chat channels is put in a separate repository.

Obviously with the updated feature set of Exchange 2013, some levels of "legal hold" capability are available.

To provide additional levels of compliance, you may be required to use a product such as Vantage from Actiance (`http://actiance.com/products/vantage.aspx`).

Vantage installs an agent on each Front End server, captures the data, and sends it to a Vantage server for processing and then onward to a SQL Server repository. This repository is tamperproof, ensuring message and conversation integrity.

As well as providing a compliant repository, Vantage has a built-in capability for IM reporting, both from a system administrator perspective (for policy setting) and a reviewer perspective (for eDiscovery and regulatory compliance reviews).

In addition to the compliance aspect of Vantage, it has other useful features, which either augment existing Lync features or provide new control capabilities:

- Central policy-based logging and analytics.
- Global, group, intergroup or user-based controls.
- Authentication and authorization. For example, ethical boundaries can be configured to stop users within the same organization from communicating with each other as well as provide granular control over federation.
- Antivirus and antimalware controls. For example, integration with several popular antivirus scanning engines is available.
- Keyword and regular expression triggers to block or alert on content.
- Granular SpIM (spam over IM) and URL blocking controls (including the ability to customize rules).
- Control over legal disclaimers (including the ability to customize disclaimers).
- File transfer capture—that is, it captures complete file data, not just the name.
- Comprehensive analytics engine to show, for example, the volume of Lync usage by users.

The following transcript search is an example of the reporting capabilities from Vantage.

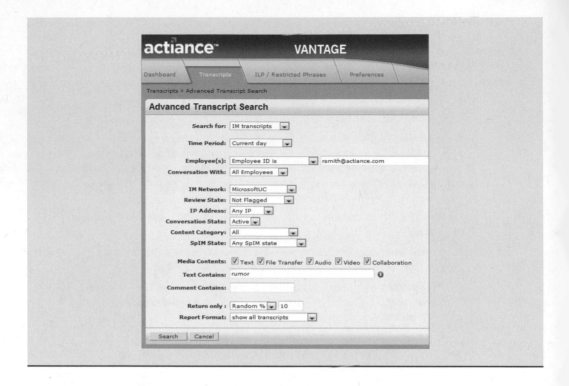

Interpreting the Monitoring Server Reports

Data is useless unless it can be interpreted and understood; the data provided by the Monitoring Reporting Pack is extremely rich and can be used in a number of ways:

◆ Troubleshooting

◆ Trend analysis for future capacity planning

◆ Usage analysis for return on investment (ROI) calculations

The following sections will cover the metrics used and how to interpret them as well as provide details on the reports available.

Understanding Voice Quality

Before delving into the details about the reports and how to interpret them, you really need to understand how voice quality is measured and what steps are taken to ensure that quality is retained throughout a call even when outside events impact that quality.

Some of the key metrics measured per call are listed here:

◆ Endpoint IP address

◆ Endpoint subnet

◆ Internal/external connectivity

- Codec used

- Network connectivity type (wired versus wireless)

- Link speed

- Any bandwidth restrictions applied (due to Call Admission Control)

- Signal level send

- Signal level receive

- Echo

- Device CPU

- Device driver/firmware versions

- Packet loss

- Round-trip time

- Latency

- Jitter

- Burst

- Network MOS

- Listening MOS

- Sending MOS

- Degradation MOS

- Audio healer metrics

Individually, these metrics may report values that would be considered "good." In spite of that, however, the call may still be considered poor quality because often it is the combination of many of the metrics that result in a poor call. For example, latency, jitter, round-trip time, and packet loss may individually be within tolerances, but the combination of packets being dropped along with packets that do arrive but are late will likely create problems on the call from which the healing metrics are unable to recover.

MEAN OPINION SCORE

Traditional telephony provides a subjective assessment of voice quality, based on a scale of 1 to 5, with 5 being perfect and 1 being very poor. A typical PSTN call will rate 2.95 on this scale.

The scoring is carried out by a group of testers listening to an output signal and rating it. This is where the subjective nature of the assessment comes in. It is up to the individual to mark the score, and the average is provided as the final rating.

Because this is a subjective rating, the results can vary from one test to another. Lync Server uses an objective approach, where the output signal is compared to a model to predict the perceived quality, in a way that's similar to the Perceptual Evaluation of Speech Quality (PESQ) standard.

There are four types of Mean Opinion Score (MOS) values.

Listening Quality MOS

This value is commonly used in VoIP deployments, but it does not consider bidirectional effects such as delay or echo. The following three metrics are wideband MOS-LQ scores:

Network MOS The Network MOS value takes into account only network-related factors (packet loss, jitter, and so on) and can be used to identify network conditions that impact audio quality.

Listening MOS The Listening MOS value is a prediction of the wideband quality of an audio stream being played to a user; it considers the output aspects of the device, as well as codec, transcoding, speech level, and background noise. Problems encountered with the sound output will be identified within Listening MOS.

Sending MOS Sending MOS is the counterpart to Listening MOS, and it is a prediction of the wideband quality of an audio stream being *sent* by a user. It deals with the input levels of the signal, considering the same aspects as Listening MOS. Both Listening and Sending MOS problems typically highlight device issues.

Conversational Quality MOS

This value considers the quality on both ends and includes bidirectional effects such as delay and echo. There is one narrowband MOS-CQ score in Lync Server:

Conversational MOS In addition to the aspects considered by Listening and Sending MOS, Conversational MOS also takes into account bidirectional aspects such as echo and delay.

MOS Values by Codec

Being able to understand the different areas of impact in a call will help you narrow down the problem; if one user reports problems hearing a call but another user reports all is well, it can suggest that you should start investigating the Listening MOS and the values associated there. What about comparing calls with each other?

Well, it's extremely difficult to replicate network conditions at any given time; starting with a comparison between the different expectations by codec is useful (shown in Table 11.2).

TABLE 11.2: MOS value by codec

CALL TYPE	CODEC USED	MAX NETWORK MOS
Media Bypass	G711	4.30
UC-UC	RTAudio (wideband)	4.10
UC-PSTN (non-media bypass scenarios)	RTAudio (narrowband)	2.95
UC-PSTN	SIREN	3.72
Conference Call	G722	4.30
Conference Call	SIREN	3.72

COMPARING CALLS BY CODEC

It is not feasible to compare two calls simply by the codec used to determine which was "better." Because both calls are inherently different, based not only on their own attributes but also the state of the network at the time of the calls, it is impossible to re-create the same conditions to allow any sort of comparison.

A much better approach to comparing calls is to evaluate how much each call has degraded, almost like determining the "least worst" call.

By taking this approach, you can determine which call has been impacted most by the network conditions and establish which has been degraded the most.

Viewing the Reports

Lync Server 2010 reporting offered several improvements to Office Communications Server 2007 R2, including an increase in the number of available reports, tooltips, and color highlighting. (Highlighted text is visible when the mouse is hovered over text, ensuring that potential issues are visible to the reader and easily understood.) Some diagnostic reports are generated only when there is enough data to be worthwhile. For example, problematic-server quality reports are available only on the dashboard when more than 30 data points have been captured.

Reporting in Lync Server 2013 is more of an incremental increase in capability. There aren't many new reports, but one dramatic change is the increase in the amount of data returned in each report; the number of records has been increased to 1,000.

By default the Reporting Pack is installed at the following location (reachable via a web browser):

```
Http:<SQL server name>:80/ReportServer_<SQL instance name>
```

There are two top-level report types:

Dashboard   Provides a weekly or monthly snapshot of the state of the environment, allowing an administrator to quickly see trends in both user usage and hotspots for problems. Each report is a hyperlink to the next level of detail. Figure 11.6 shows the weekly dashboard report.

DASHBOARD SUMMARY ERROR

On occasion when loading the dashboard, you may encounter the either of the following errors:

Report processing stopped because too many rows in summary tables are missing in the call detail recording (CDR) database. To resolve this issue, run dbo.RtcGenerateSummaryTables on the LcsCDR database.

Report processing stopped because too many rows in summary tables are missing in the Quality of Experience (QoE) database. To resolve this issue, run dbo.RtcGenerateSummaryTables on the QoEMetrics database.

To correct this, you must log in to the SQL Server instance and execute the specified procedure.

This will regenerate the summary tables. Only summary tables are affected; no data is lost.

FIGURE 11.6
Weekly dashboard report

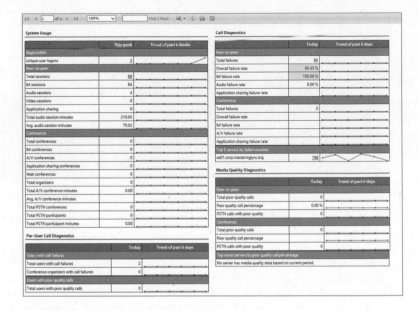

Reporting   Provides the same types of reports; however, they can be customized based on date ranges or targeted to specific pools or locations.

The reports here can be loosely grouped into four categories:

◆ System Usage

◆ Per-User Call Diagnostics

◆ Call Reliability Diagnostics

◆ Media Quality Diagnostics

Each of the reports can be further expanded by clicking the built-in hyperlinks in the report to drill further into the details behind the numbers. Figure 11.7 shows the Reporting page.

SYSTEM USAGE REPORTS

Within this section, you will find reports used for trend-based analysis, showing the number of connections and typical system usage.

User Registration Report   This report will provide an at-a-glance view of user login information broken into the following categories:

◆ Total Logons

◆ Internal Logons

◆ External Logons

♦ Unique Logon Users

♦ Unique Active Users

FIGURE 11.7
Reporting home
page

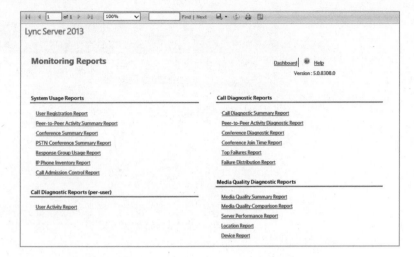

By default, this returns both tabular and graphical format broken down on a daily total for all pools; however, this breakdown and pool selection can be modified if required.

Peer-To-Peer Activity Summary Report The Activity Summary Report provides the total breakdown of sessions (the default is daily) for the following communications types:

♦ Total Peer-To-Peer Sessions

♦ Total Peer-To-Peer IM Sessions

♦ Total Peer-To-Peer IM Messages

♦ Total Peer-To-Peer Audio Sessions

♦ Total Peer-To-Peer Audio Minutes

♦ Average Peer-To-Peer Audio Session Minutes

♦ Total Peer-To-Peer Video Sessions

♦ Total Peer-To-Peer Video Minutes

♦ Average Peer-To-Peer Video Session Minutes

♦ Total Peer-To-Peer File Transfer Sessions

♦ Total Peer-To-Peer Application Sharing Sessions

Figure 11.8 shows a sample section of this report, with a breakdown of peer-to-peer sessions: total, audio, and IM only on the top graph; with video, file transfer, and application sharing shown on the bottom graph. At this level, you're simply looking at the trend, and as expected, there is minimal traffic over the weekend; however, the various modalities show different peaks.

FIGURE 11.8
Peer-To-Peer
Activity Summary
Report sample

Conference Summary Report Similar to the Peer-To-Peer Activity Report, the Conference Summary Report provides an insight into the conferencing statistics, with the following data reported (default daily):

- Total Conferences
- Total Participants
- Avg. Participants per Conference
- Total A/V Conferences
- Total A/V Conference Minutes
- Total A/V Conference Participant Minutes
- Avg. A/V Conference Minutes
- Total Unique Conference Organizers
- Total Conference Messages

Within these reports, drilling into the detail also shows the conference type, either Audio/Video or Application Sharing.

Figure 11.9 shows a snapshot of the more detailed Conference Activity Report, which is reached via the Conference Summary Report when you select a specific day to view the conference breakdown. This detailed report goes on to break down the different conference types, connection types, and connection locations.

FIGURE 11.9
Conference
Summary Report

PSTN Conference Summary Report   The PSTN Conference Report provides a view of the conferences that includes PSTN dial-in participants and shows the following:

◆ Total PSTN Conferences

◆ Total Participants

◆ Total A/V Conference Minutes

◆ Total A/V Conference Participant Minutes

◆ Total PSTN Participants

◆ Total PSTN Participant Minutes

◆ Unique Conference Organizers

Response Group Usage Report   This report provides a view of the number of calls being placed to the Response Group service and how they are being answered. The following fields are provided in the initial report:

◆ Received Calls

◆ Successful Calls

◆ Offered Calls

◆ Answered Calls

◆ Percentage of Abandoned Calls

◆ Average Call Minutes by Agent

◆ Transferred Calls

IP Phone Inventory Report   This report provides a view of the deployed phone hardware devices in the environment, specifically these:

◆   Manufacturer

◆   Hardware Version

◆   MAC Address

◆   User URI

◆   User Agent

◆   Last Logon Time

◆   Last Logoff Time

◆   Last Activity

Call Admission Control Report   This report (shown in Figure 11.10) provides a detailed view of how many calls are being rerouted or rejected based on the policy settings as well as a breakdown of the information per location.

A Diagnostic value of 5 indicates that a call has been rerouted via the PSTN.

FIGURE 11.10
Call Admission
Control Report

CALL ADMISSION CONTROL REPORTING

Over time, understanding the impact of Call Admission Control is important. If the values are set too high, then potentially the network is overspecified and costs may be reduced by decreasing the capacity. On the other hand, it's more likely that Call Admission Control will reject or reroute calls. If a significant number are reported, this may indicate that Call Admission Control is configured too low. In parallel to this, if the network is nearing capacity, it is an indication that the network is under pressure and bandwidth may need to be increased. See Chapter 14, "Call Admission Control," for more information.

CALL DIAGNOSTICS REPORTS (PER-USER)

This report is targeted at help desk staff, and it is used for analysis of activity based on a specific user. The following fields are provided:

◆   From User

◆   To User

- Modalities
- Response Time
- End Time
- Diagnostic ID

CALL RELIABILITY DIAGNOSTICS REPORTS

The diagnostics reports are most likely to be of interest to network and server administrators; these are the reports that tell you what is going wrong and what needs to be fixed. Within this section, you'll see values such as Expected Failures and Unexpected Failures. Expected failures are items such as a caller hanging up, or no answer. Unless there are a significant number of these events, they can typically be ignored. Unexpected failures are the ones that typically need to be investigated and corrected.

This is the section of reporting that has had the biggest change compared to Office Communications Server 2007 R2.

Call Diagnostics Summary Report   This diagnostics report covers both Peer-To-Peer sessions and conferences. A breakdown is provided showing the following data:

- Total Sessions
- Failure Rate
- Session Count by Modality (IM, app share, audio, video, file transfer)
- Failure Rate by Modality

Peer-To-Peer Activity Diagnostic Report   The Peer-To-Peer Diagnostics Report focuses only on the Peer-To-Peer aspect, and it provides a daily breakdown of sessions and failures further broken down by modality. The report shows the following data fields (summary and per modality):

- Date
- Success
- Expected Failures
- Unexpected Failures
- Total Sessions

Conference Diagnostic Report   Unsurprisingly, the Conference Diagnostic Report provides the same view as the Peer-To-Peer Diagnostic Report, but for conferences.

Conference Join Time Report   This report details how long (in milliseconds) it is taking users to join a conference.

Top Failures Report   This report covers the top failures based on reported sessions, also providing the number of users impacted and the weekly trend of a particular failure over the previous eight weeks. Each specific failure item provides the following data in the failure information field:

- Request Type
- Response

- ◆ Diagnostic ID

- ◆ Category

- ◆ Component

- ◆ Reason

- ◆ Description

This information provides the administrator with a great starting point to begin trouble-shooting. Figure 11.11 shows the failure information and trend volume graph for a specific failure item.

Based on this report, the admin would know that the gateway in question is suffering from a relatively steady number of failures before experiencing a sudden peak at the end of the week. This may correlate to a matching increase in call volume, suggesting that the actual failure rate is steady; however, the specific error shown in this case (Unexpected - 504 - Server Internal Error) suggests an issue that needs to be resolved by taking some action. Because it refers to a gateway, this may be faulty hardware or firmware. In this case, further investigation is needed on the gateway itself to determine the cause and resolution.

FIGURE 11.11
Top Failures Report

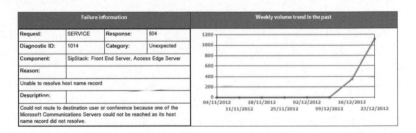

Failure Distribution Report   The Failure Distribution Report provides an overview of the top 10 items on each of the following lists:

- ◆ Session Distribution by Top Diagnostic Reasons

- ◆ Session Distribution by Top Modalities

- ◆ Session Distribution by Top Pools

- ◆ Session Distribution by Top Sources

- ◆ Session Distribution by Top Components

- ◆ Session Distribution by Top From Users

- ◆ Session Distribution by Top To Users

- ◆ Session Distribution by Top From User Agents

Figure 11.12 shows a sample section from this report. Based on this section, the admin would know that the majority of failures are due to issues with at least one gateway. This is a summary section showing the total of each error type; however, each diagnostic reason is a hyperlink to further break down the issues allowing specific gateways to be identified.

FIGURE 11.12
Session
Distribution by Top
Diagnostic Reasons
Report

MEDIA QUALITY DIAGNOSTICS REPORTS

The final section on the reports home page deals with call quality and diagnostics. These reports provide good information on how the individual components such as servers, devices, and network locations are coping in the environment.

Media Quality Summary Report   At a high level, the report is categorized into three sections:

◆   Audio Call Summary

◆   Video Call Summary

◆   Application Sharing Call Summary

Each section provides the quality view of the different endpoints, broken down by the following categories:

◆   UC Peer to Peer

◆   UC Conference Sessions

◆   PSTN Conference Sessions

◆   PSTN calls (non-bypass): UC Leg

◆   PSTN calls (non-bypass): Gateway Leg

◆   Other Call Types

Each of these categories is further broken down by specific software versions of the client or device.

For each combination entry, the following data is displayed:

◆   Endpoint Type

◆   Call Volume

◆   Poor Call Percentage

◆   Call Volume (Wireless Call)

◆   Call Volume (VPN Call)

◆   Call Volume (External Call)

◆   Round Trip (ms) (Audio Only)

◆   Degradation (MOS) (Audio Only)

◆   Packet Loss (Audio Only)

- Jitter (ms) (Audio and App Sharing Only)
- Healer Concealed Ratio (Audio Only)
- Healer Stretched Ratio (Audio Only)
- Healer Compressed Ratio (Audio Only)
- Outbound Packet Loss (Video Only)
- Inbound Packet Loss (Video Only)
- Frozen Frame % (Video Only)
- Outbound Avg. Frame Rate (Video Only)
- Inbound Avg. Frame Rate (Video Only)
- Inbound Low Frame Rate % (Video Only)
- Client Health % (Video Only)
- Avg. Relative One Way (App Sharing Only)
- Avg. RDP Tile Processing Latency (App Sharing Only)
- Total Spoiled Tile % (App Sharing Only)

Media Quality Comparison Report   The Media Quality Comparison Report provides a view to the number of calls on a per-day basis over the following items:

- Call Volume
- Degradation (MOS)
- Poor Call Percentage
- Round Trip (ms)
- Packet Loss
- Jitter (ms)
- Healer Concealed Ratio
- Healer Stretched Ratio
- Healer Compressed Ratio

Server Performance Report   The Server Performance Report provides insight into the performance of the individual server roles and gateways. It provides data similar to that of the Media Quality Summary Report (and is similarly broken into sections for audio/video/app sharing):

- Server
- Call Volume
- Poor Call Percentage
- Round Trip (ms) (Audio Only)

- Degradation (MOS) (Audio Only)

- Packet Loss (Audio Only)

- Jitter (ms) (Audio And App Sharing Only)

- Healer Concealed Ratio (Audio Only)

- Healer Stretched Ratio (Audio Only)

- Healer Compressed Ratio (Audio Only)

- Outbound Packet Loss (Video Only)

- Inbound Packet Loss (Video Only)

- Frozen Frame % (Video Only)

- Outbound Avg. Frame Rate (Video Only)

- Inbound Avg. Frame Rate (Video Only)

- Inbound Low Frame Rate % (Video Only)

- Client Health % (Video Only)

- Avg. Relative One Way (App Sharing Only)

- Avg. RDP Tile Processing Latency (App Sharing Only)

- Total Spoiled Tile % (App Sharing Only)

- Trend

In addition, an option to view the data trended for the previous week is provided for each server role or gateway.

CODEC HEALING

The implementation of the media codecs in Lync 2010 allowed healing aspects to be contained within them.

These healing capabilities enable the codec to recover from missed or delayed packets, in effect *healing* the media, so that in most cases the user will be unaware of the missing packets because the call will continue and the problems will be undetectable. The impacts of high values in each of these categories are described below:

- High values in *healer concealed ratio* will typically result in distorted or lost audio. This is typically due to packet loss or jitter.

- High values in *healer stretched ratio* will typically result in distorted or robotic-sounding audio. This is typically caused by jitter.

- High values in *healer compressed ratio* will typically result in distorted or accelerated-sounding audio. This is typically caused by jitter.

Location Report   Whereas the previous two reports look at the breakdown per endpoint, this report looks at the network viewpoint and shows per subnet (caller and callee).

The following data is provided:

- Caller Subnet
- Callee Subnet
- Call Volume
- Poor Call Percentage
- Round Trip (ms)
- Degradation (MOS)
- Packet Loss
- Jitter (ms)
- Healer Concealed Ratio
- Healer Stretched Ratio
- Healer Compressed Ratio

Device Report   The Device Report looks at the specific hardware device model or individual drivers used by the operating system to provide a view on the data. This can provide a useful view of which noncertified devices are being used in the environment, or more likely which calls are being made using built-in devices.

The following view is provided of the data:

- Capture Device
- Render Device
- Call Volume
- Poor Call Percentage
- Unique Users
- Ratio of Voice Switch Time
- Ratio of Microphone Not Functioning
- Ratio of Speaker Not Functioning
- Call With Voice Switch (%)
- Echo in Microphone (%)
- Echo Send (%)
- Calls With Echo (%)

The Call Detail Report

As mentioned, many of these reports link through to other reports, each of which reduces the scope and provides more detailed data resulting in the Call Detail Report, which provides a full breakdown of all the interaction and statistics of the call.

There is no direct method to access this report because it deals with a single call only and, therefore, the data must be filtered in some method first. The quickest route to get call details is to use the User Activity Report to filter on a specific user and then to select the detail of a specific call.

We will discuss the usefulness of this report in Chapter 12, "Troubleshooting"; however, an example section is shown in Figure 11.13 (note that the "Call Information" section is closed in the screen shot). This report is also known as the Peer-To-Peer Session Detail Report.

FIGURE 11.13
Peer-To-Peer
Session Detail
Report

This report contains almost 200 fields of information, broken down into the following sections:

Call Information   Here you will see information regarding the users (or PSTN numbers) involved in the call, the start time, and the duration along with client hardware and software version information.

Media Line (Main Audio)—MediaLine Information   The Media Line information section deals with the network identifiers such as network address information, internal/external connectivity, connection speeds, and whether any bandwidth controls are in place due to Call Admission Control.

Media Line (Main Audio)—Caller/Callee Device and Signal Metrics   Both caller and callee have separate sections here, providing device identifiers (including device driver versions), signal send and receive information, and any hardware (microphone/speaker) issues detected.

Media Line (Main Audio)—Caller/Callee Client Event   Again, this is repeated for both caller and callee, and this section provides reporting on the percentage of issues detected around the device hardware and signal.

Media Line (Main Audio)—Audio Stream (Caller ➤ Callee)/(Callee ➤ Caller)   This section deals with the specific audio stream in one direction. The following section provides the same data in the other direction. Here you see information regarding the codec used and network impacts (packet loss, jitter, and so on).

Typically, this is the most viewed section because it provides the summary impact due to the underlying network conditions.

Media Line (Main Audio)—Video Stream (Caller ➤ Callee)/(Callee ➤ Caller)   The final two sections provide the same information as the preceding except in dealing with the video stream. This is included only for calls that have a video aspect.

A massive amount of information is captured with every call. Some of the fields will be self-explanatory, but you will need more information to understand some of the other fields. In these cases, tooltips are provided, but not all fields have tooltips because they are presumed to be familiar.

Also, to help you understand which values are potentially causing problems, color coding is enabled on the reports. Yellow indicates a warning, and red indicates a high risk of problems.

CUSTOMIZING REPORTS

While the number of reports has increased dramatically with each version since the launch of Office Communications Server 2007, they still fall short of the requirements of many customers.

The database schemas for both QoE and CDR databases are detailed in the Lync Server 2013 help file and can also be viewed on Technet. The QoE schemas can be viewed at the following location:

```
http://technet.microsoft.com/en-us/library/gg398687.aspx
```

And the CDR schemas can be viewed here:

```
http://technet.microsoft.com/en-us/library/gg398570.aspx
```

Provided the correct permissions are assigned to a user, it is relatively easy to connect to those databases via ODBC and retrieve the data you'll need to provide customized reports. You can also use SQL Server 2008 R2 Report Builder to generate reports that can be added to the web page, enabling easy generation and a single storage/execution location for reports.

Service Monitoring with the Management Pack

The other aspect of monitoring is server or service monitoring, which is needed so that system administrators can alert their users when aspects of the Lync Server 2013 service fail (or begin to fail). Management packs provide a prepackaged set of rules and alert thresholds you can use to quickly set up and monitor the Lync Server 2013 environment. The Lync Server 2013 Monitoring Management Pack is available to download from the following location:

```
http://www.microsoft.com/en-gb/download/details.aspx?id=35842
```

MANAGEMENT PACK IMPROVEMENTS

In the feedback that Microsoft received about the previous management packs for Office Communications Server 2007 (specifically the R2 version), one of the most important findings was that the thresholds were set too low, resulting in a deluge of alerts almost upon installation of the management pack. This typically caused administrators to disable the alerts without coming back to tune and enable them at a reasonable level.

Based on this feedback, the management pack was included as part of the Lync Server 2010 beta code availability so that customers could provide further feedback and this was continued with the Lync Server 2013 beta program.

The management pack configuration should be tailored to each individual environment (baselined) to ensure that these thresholds do not produce inappropriate alerts. The last thing any administrator wants is to be paged at 1:00 a.m. for a problem that could wait until morning!

A good example of this scenario is in an Enterprise Edition pool with four Front End servers; if one server fails, the actual Lync 2013 services (registrar, routing, Address Book, conferencing, and so on) provided by the pool will continue to operate, and hopefully has been scaled to cope with a single server failure, so the impact will be minimal (quite possibly negligible) to the users. The server could wait until morning to be repaired.

Detailed steps on how to configure SCOM are beyond the scope of this book; however, assuming SCOM has been installed and configured with the Lync 2013 management pack deployed to discover the Lync servers, the next few steps will show how to change thresholds on alerts from the default. It should be noted that the Lync Server 2010 management pack leveraged the CMS to retrieve the topology, but with Lync Server 2013 a slightly different approach is used. The SCOM agents discover themselves and report their existence back to the SCOM server. This simplifies the discovery and administration of the Lync Server 2013 environment for SCOM.

From within the System Center Operations Manager (SCOM) 2012 console, select the Authoring tab, and within the management pack objects, select Object Discoveries, change the scope (using the button on the toolbar) and select View All Targets. Enter **ls** in the Look For box to filter for Lync Server objects (all Lync Server objects begin with LS). The results are shown in Figure 11.14.

FIGURE 11.14
Changing the scope within SCOM to show Lync objects

In this example, you will change the audio quality metrics for conferencing, so selecting LS Audio Quality for A/V Conferencing Server and clicking OK will take you back to the Object

Discoveries view, this time including the LS QoE Discovery entry under the selected type (LS Audio Quality for A/V Conferencing Server).

Right-click LS QoE Discovery and select Overrides ➤ Override The Object Discovery ➤ For All Objects Of Class: LS QoE Monitoring. See Figure 11.15.

FIGURE 11.15
Enable overrides on
Lync Server 2010
monitored values in
SCOM.

The Override Properties page then appears, and the Name column indicates the items queried from the database, and the description is provided in the Details window. Selecting an item in the Override column will enable the specific row to be modified at the necessary value, and clicking OK will apply the change.

The management pack raises alerts at different levels, ensuring the correct response based on the impact. The alerts raised provide relevant information to help identify the causes and help troubleshoot, hopefully resulting in a faster recovery time. In some cases, there will be links directly to the CDR or QoE record itself.

The management pack will leverage the information from the Central Management Store to determine the topology, which will help you accurately assign the rules to the server roles with limited administrative interaction. So, while Agent Discovery is used for the servers to report back, the CMS is still checked to ensure that the correct capability is assigned on each server—it's just no longer used to find the servers themselves.

End-to-end verification is provided through the use of *synthetic transactions*, which can test almost the complete range of functionality required from a client (including simulation of PSTN calling).

These synthetic transactions can be configured to run periodically (it is recommended to have dedicated accounts configured for this), and a failure can be used to generate a high-priority alert, which is automatically resolved if the command is successful on the next attempt. Synthetic transactions can be run without integration with SCOM; however, for full automated alerting and reporting, SCOM is required. Table 11.3 shows the full list of all synthetic transactions.

TABLE 11.3:   Synthetic transactions

SYNTHETIC TRANSACTION CMDLET	DESCRIPTION
Test-CsAddressBookService*	Tests the functionality of the Address Book service. This can be used to simulate an individual user.
Test-CsAddressBookWebQuery*	Similar to the Test-CsAddressBookService, except it tests the web query functionality.
Test-CsASConference	Tests Application Sharing using a pair of users.
Test-CsAudioConferencingProvider	Tests a connection to a third-party audio conference provider.
Test-CsAVConference*	Tests audio/video conference functionality using a pair of users.
Test-CsAVEdgeConnectivity*	Verifies connectivity using the AV edge component.
Test-CsCertificateConfiguration	Returns information on the certificates in use.
Test-CsClientAuthentication	Confirms whether a user can log on when using the Lync 2010–provided user certificate.
Test-CsComputer	Verifies that services are running, Active Directory groups have been configured correctly, and the firewall ports have been opened.
Test-CsDatabase	Tests configuration of the databases.
Test-CsDataConference*	Verifies user participation within a data collaboration conference session.
Test-CsDialPlan	Tests a phone number against a dial plan, returning the normalization rule, which will be applied, and the results of that normalization.
Test-CsExStorageConnectivity	Verifies that the Lync Server Storage Service is working on a Front End server.
Test-CsExStorageNotification	Verifies that the Lync Server Storage Service can subscribe to the Exchange Server 2013 notification service.
Test-CsExUMConnectivity*	Tests connectivity to Exchange UM.
Test-CsExUMVoiceMail	Verifies connectivity and that a voice mail message was left.
Test-CsFederatedPartner	Confirms the status of federation with an external domain.
Test-CsGroupExpansion	Confirms the functionality of the group expansion capability on the pool.
Test-CsGroupIM*	Tests the ability of two users to carry out an IM conference.

TABLE 11.3: Synthetic transactions *(CONTINUED)*

SYNTHETIC TRANSACTION CMDLET	DESCRIPTION
Test-CsIM*	Tests the ability of two users to carry out a Peer-To-Peer IM.
Test-CsInterTrunkRouting	Verifies routing and PSTN usage via a specific SIP trunk.
Test-CsKerberosAccountAssignment	Verifies that the assigned Kerberos account is working correctly.
Test-CsLisCivicAddress	Verifies address information against the Master Street Address Guide held by the E911 provider. This is the only test cmdlet that is not a synthetic test. It is capable of updating the LIS database.
Test-CsLisConfiguration	Confirms the address configuration when given a specific subnet (or other location identifier).
Test-CsLocationPolicy	Determines which location policy will be used.
Test-CsMcxConference	Tests three-user participation in a conference via the Mobility Service.
Test-CsMcxP2PIM*	Tests a Peer-Peer IM via the Mobility Service.
Test-CsMcxPushNotification	Tests that the push notification (Apple and Microsoft) service is working.
Test-CsOUPermission	Verifies that the permissions have been applied correctly within the Active Directory OU.
Test-CsP2PAV*	Tests audio/video functionality using a pair of users in Peer-To-Peer mode (rather than conferencing).
Test-PersistentChatMessage*	Verifies that a message between two users using the Persistent Chat service has been sent and received.
Test-CsPhoneBootstrap	Verifies that the environment is configured to allow Lync 2010 Phone Edition devices to connect and that a user can log on.
Test-CsPresence*	Confirms that a user can log on and publish presence information as well as receive presence updates from another user.
Test-CsPstnOutboundCall	Tests the ability of a user to make a PSTN call. A call will actually be placed and must be answered for this test to succeed.
Test-CsPstnPeerToPeerCall*	Similar to Test-CsPstnPeerToPeerCall, except the cmdlet places a call to another user via the gateway, and will answer the call on behalf of the user.
Test-CsRegistration*	Confirms whether a user can log on to Lync 2010.

TABLE 11.3:   Synthetic transactions *(CONTINUED)*

SYNTHETIC TRANSACTION CMDLET	DESCRIPTION
Test-CsReplica	Verifies the status of replica service on the local computer.
Test-CsSetupPermission	Confirms that Active Directory has been configured to allow Lync to be installed.
Test-CsTopology	Allows testing of the validity of a server or service.
Test-CsTrunkConfiguration	Confirms the operation of the trunk configuration when presented with a phone number.
Test-CsUcwaConference	Tests connectivity through the web service to a conference for two users.
Test-CsUnifiedContactStore*	Verifies whether the Unified Contact Store can access a user's contacts.
Test-CsVoiceNormalizationRule	Tests a phone number against a specific normalization rule and returns the resulting number after the rule has been applied.
Test-CsVoicePolicy	Tests a phone number against a specific voice policy and returns the determined route.
Test-CsVoiceRoute	Tests a phone number against a specific route pattern and returns success or fail based on whether the number is accepted by the route.
Test-CsVoiceTestConfiguration	Tests a combination of dial plan and policy to confirm that routing works as expected.
Test-CsVoiceUser	Confirms the route for a PSTN call from a specific user based on the voice configuration.
Test-CsWatcherNodeConfiguration	Verifies the watcher node configuration.
Test-CsWebApp	Verifies that authenticated users can use Web App to join a conference.
Test-CsWebAppAnonymous	Verifies that anonymous users can use the Web App to join a conference.
Test-CsWebScheduler	Tests whether a user can use the Web Scheduler to schedule an online meeting.
Test-CsXmppIM*	Tests sending of a message via an XMPP gateway.

* Indicates items that can be used by SCOM for continuous synthetic transaction testing.

For component monitoring (via SCOM), the alerts are separated into Key Health Indicators and non–Key Health Indicators. A Key Health Indicator is a service impacting issue (which is worth being paged about at 1:00 a.m.!), and non–Key Health Indicators are those aspects that do not impact service; for example, problems with components that have resiliency. These are automatically resolved if the service returns to health.

Chapter 12 provides more details (and examples) of running synthetic transactions from within PowerShell (without using SCOM integration).

DEPLOYING SYNTHETIC TRANSACTIONS WITH SCOM

While running the synthetic transactions from the PowerShell environment is a relatively straightforward task, configuring automatic transaction execution and monitoring within SCOM is a multistep process.

You'll need to define one or more watcher nodes. A *watcher node* is a server responsible for periodically executing synthetic transactions for a pool. If you have deployed multiple pools and want to have automatic synthetic transactions run on each of them, you will need one server per pool.

The server should have the following minimum specifications:

- 4 core processor 2.33GHz or higher

- 8GB RAM

- 1Gbps network adapter

- Windows Server 2008 R2 or Windows Server 2012

The additional software prerequisites for the watcher node are as follows:

- .NET Framework 4.5

- Windows Identity Foundation

- System Center Operations Manager (SCOM) Agent

- Lync Server 2013 core installation files (OCSCORE.msi)

- Unified Communications Managed API

In addition to having a SCOM Agent installed, the Lync Server 2013 core and Lync Server Replica MSI files need to be installed onto the watcher node. The easiest way to do this is to run the Lync Server 2013 setup.exe file with the /BootStrapLocalMgmt switch. Then verify the installation by opening the Lync Management Shell and running the Get-CsWatcherNodeConfiguration cmdlet.

If this command is being run for the first time, no response is expected because nothing is yet configured for the watcher node. If a response is received, it typically indicates an error.

Occasionally, I have seen the command line execution of setup.exe fail to enable the Lync services upon completion—be sure to check!

Once the core components are installed, the Watchernode.msi executable needs to be run to install the components specific to the watcher node. This executable is available from the same download location as the management pack itself.

Watcher nodes can be installed both inside and outside the enterprise to verify a large number of aspects of a Lync Server 2013 deployment.

A watcher node can use two types of authentication:

◆ Trusted server (using certificates)

◆ Credentials (using a username and password)

Because the watcher node is not directly part of the topology, a trusted application pool must be configured with the watcher node a member server of the application pool. Once the pool is created, a trusted application service is created.

Both of these tasks can be performed using PowerShell or Topology Builder. There are no options to configure trusted applications in the Control Panel.

To create a new Trusted Application pool, first, identify the site ID (`SiteId`) for the site to which the application pool will be associated. Figure 11.16 shows the output of `Get-CsSite`.

FIGURE 11.16
Output of
Get-CsSite

With the site ID, run the following command (where the `Identity` parameter is the FQDN of the watcher node):

```
New-CsTrustedApplicationPool -Identity watcher01.corp.masteringlync.org -Site 1
-Registrar se01.corp.masteringlync.org -ThrottleAsServer $True
-TreatAsAuthenticated $True -OutboundOnly $False -RequiresReplication $True
-ComputerFqdn watcher01.corp.masteringlync.org
```

The response will be similar to this:

```
Identity              : 1-ExternalServer-1
Registrar             : Registrar:se01.corp.masterinlync.org
FileStore             :
ThrottleAsServer      : True
TreatAsAuthenticated  : True
OutboundOnly          : False
RequiresReplication   : True
AudioPortStart        :
AudioPortCount        : 0
AppSharingPortStart   :
AppSharingPortCount   : 0
VideoPortStart        :
VideoPortCount        : 0
Applications          : {}
DependantServiceList  : {}
ServiceId             : 1-ExternalServer-1
SiteId                : Site:EMEA
PoolFqdn              : watcher01.corp.masteringlync.org
Version               : 6
Role                  : TrustedApplicationPool
```

`Get-CsPool` can also be run to verify that the application pool is configured.

The trusted application service is created using the following command:

```
New-CsTrustedApplication -ApplicationId "STWatcher-01"
-TrustedApplicationPoolFqdn watcher01.corp.masteringlync.org -Port 5061
```

The `ApplicationId` parameter can be any text entry. You can include the site name or ID so that it is easy to identify which application is dealing with which site. The `Port` parameter can be any unused port.

The result of this command will be similar to that shown in Figure 11.17.

FIGURE 11.17

New-
CsTrustedApplication

The `Enable-CsTopology` cmdlet needs to be run in order to apply these topology changes.

There is no output from this cmdlet, although status bars are displayed across the top of the PowerShell window.

To use certificate authentication, you'll need to request a certificate for the watcher node. You can use the same certificate wizard used in the rest of the Lync Server 2013 role setup processes, only this time, you can start it by using the Lync Server Deployment Wizard from the Start menu (or start screen if using Windows Server 2012). Once it's started, click Install Or Update Lync Server System ➢ Request, Install, Or Assign Certificate and follow the now-familiar certificate wizard to request and assign a default certificate.

Next you'll need to install the actual `Watchernode.msi` file, and because you're using certificate authentication, you must use the following command:

```
Watchernode.msi Authentication=TrustedServer
```

For some reason, Microsoft has made this command case sensitive!

If you wanted to use credential authentication, the watcher node computer network service account should be added to the RTC Local Read-only Administrators group on the local computer. The command for credential authentication is as follows:

```
Watchernode.msi Authentication=Negotiate
```

Once the `WatcherNode.msi` executable has completed, you need to restart the server for it to take effect.

You'll need to create and assign user accounts to the Health Monitoring Configuration entry, using the following command:

```
New-CsHealthMonitoringConfiguration -TargetFqdn se01.corp.masteringlync.org
-FirstTestUserSipUri sip:test1.lync@masteringlync.org
-SecondTestUserSipUri sip:test2.lync@masteringlync.org
```

The output will be as shown below:

```
Identity             : se01.corp.masteringlync.org
FirstTestUserSipUri  : sip:test1.lync@masteringlync.org
```

```
FirstTestSamAccountName   :
SecondTestUserSipUri      : sip:test2.lync@masteringlync.org
SecondTestSamAccountName  :
TargetFqdn                : se01.corp.masteringlync.org
```

The *health monitoring configuration* is the stored configuration that is used for the synthetic transactions. `Test-Cs*` cmdlets that require user accounts will use accounts from this configuration, if available; otherwise they will prompt for the account information. Obviously, for a noninteractive solution within SCOM, you'll need to use this stored configuration.

`Set-CsTestUserCredential` can also be used to define multiple user credentials for testing. This requires the storing of the user passwords in the Credential Manager Store on the machine in which it is run, so it must be run on the watcher node itself.

For machines outside the corporate network, this method must be used (do not use actual "live" user accounts for this!):

```
Set-CsTestUserCredential -SipAddress "sip:test1.lync@masteringlync.org"
-UserName "corp\test_lync1" -Password "Password1"
Set-CsTestUserCredential -SipAddress "sip:test2.lync@masteringlync.org"
-UserName "corp\test_lync2" -Password "Password1"
```

Up to this point, you have configured the watcher node and the user accounts, but you have yet to define the watcher node configuration; you do this by using the New-CsWatcherNodeConfiguration cmdlet as shown here. The output is shown in Figure 11.18.

```
New-CsWatcherNodeConfiguration -TargetFqdn se01.corp.masteringlync.org
-PortNumber 5061 -TestUsers
@{Add= "sip:test1.lync@masteringlync.org","sip:test2.lync@masteringlync.org"}
```

You can see from the output two entries for defined tests:

◆   `Tests`

◆   `ExtendedTests`

These entries allow you to configure the tests for each watcher node; you may have certain functionality you wish to test on a particular pool, for example. By default, the `ExtendedTests` entry is empty, and the `Tests` entry contains the following tests:

- ◆ Registration

- ◆ IM

- ◆ GroupIM

- ◆ P2PAV (Peer-To-Peer audio/video sessions)

- ◆ AvConference (audio/conferencing)

- ◆ Presence

- ◆ ABS (Address Book service)

- ◆ ABWQ (Address Book web service)

To create and enable an extended test, you must use the -ExtendedTests parameter, but first you must define the test and assign to a variable, as in the following example:

```
$extest = New-CsExtendedTest -TestUsers "sip:test1.lync@masteringlync.org",
"sip:test2.lync@masteringlync.org" -Name "PSTN Test" -TestType "PSTN"
New-CsWatcherNodeConfiguration -TargetFqdn "se01.corp.masteringlync.org"
-PortNumber 5061 -TestUsers "sip:test1.lync@masteringlync.org",
"sip:test2.lync@masteringlync.org" -ExtendedTests @{Add=$x}
```

Figure 11.19 shows the synthetic transactions in operation. In this case, the Front End server has been shut down, so you can see the synthetic transaction failure alerts. When the servers come back online, they will automatically clear (when the next synthetic transaction is successful).

FIGURE 11.19
Synthetic transaction failure alerts

Useful information is contained within the Alert Details section, providing initial suggestions on the problem and where to begin troubleshooting.

The Bottom Line

Understand the architecture for the Archiving and Monitoring roles.   Although related to different aspects of the data, the Archiving and Monitoring services are very similar in function, and they have similar Back End requirements. This allows them to be easily colocated and share the same database server or instance.

   Master It   What are the options available for enabling Archiving?

Provide reporting on the data available from the Archiving and Monitoring roles.   Lync Server 2013 provides a monitoring reports pack containing over 50 reports, which focus on the QoE data. Non-Microsoft vendors provide additional report capability for the other databases, and of course, you can always write your own reports.

   Master It   What options are available for creating customized reports?

Use the capabilities in the System Center Operations Manager management pack to report on the availability of the Lync 2013 service.   With the implementation of the Lync Server 2013 Monitoring Management Pack for System Center Operations Manager, administrators have a consolidated approach and location for collating and monitoring system (and service) uptime.

   Master It   Which synthetic transactions will confirm the status of the Address Book service?

Chapter 12

Troubleshooting

In an ideal world, every system would work perfectly as soon as it was installed and would continue to work until decommissioned. As we all know, this is never the case, and quite often the simple things (typically, the ones assumed to be correct) are what cause us problems. In this chapter we will explore the tools available to troubleshoot Lync.

There are some differences between Lync Server 2013 and its predecessor Lync Server 2010, but you still need to make sure the simple things are correct before you can progress to the complex areas—and with the many integration points that Lync provides with third-party hardware (gateways, devices, and so on), as well as its strong integration points with the underlying infrastructure, there are many areas to check when it comes to troubleshooting.

In this chapter, you will learn to:

◆ Confirm that the basics are in place from the infrastructure side

◆ Understand how to troubleshoot the client

◆ Know how to enable troubleshooting on the server

◆ Understand and use the troubleshooting tools available

Troubleshooting Basics

Let's say you receive a call from a user saying something is broken (can't log in, can't make calls, or the like). Where do you start?

First, always ask the usual questions:

◆ Did it ever work?

◆ What did the user change?

◆ What has an administrator changed?

NOTE   When we were working in support, we never had anyone admit making a change that broke something; however, as administrators we all knew it happened! When you're troubleshooting, always check to see if an administrative change could've caused the break.

First, you need to establish the scope of the problem. Is it related to a single user, a single location, or is the whole system down for everybody? The larger-scale impact issues tend to be easiest to troubleshoot, but they also tend to be the ones with the greatest amount of pressure.

When 10,000 users are without phone service, the problem can very quickly be escalated to the top!

When it comes to networking investigation, the usual suspects typically include the following tools:

◆ Ping

◆ Telnet client (not installed by default on Windows since Windows Vista was released)

◆ Nslookup.exe (don't forget to configure to check SRV records)

◆ The browser (for checking certificates, and so on)

◆ A network capture tool such as Network Monitor (Netmon.exe) or Wireshark

Confirming a Network Connection

Simply put, if a user can't log in, something is wrong with their connection to the server (assuming the account is enabled and not locked or there is a simple typo!).

Using automatic login on an internal network, the Lync 2013 Communicator client will attempt to discover the address of a pool (and therefore registrar) in the following order:

◆ _sipinternaltls._tcp.<sip domain>

◆ DHCP Option 120

◆ sipinternal.<sip domain>

◆ sip.<sip domain>

The Lync 2013 Phone Edition client will use the following methods:

◆ DHCP Option 120

◆ _sipinternaltls._tcp.<sip domain>

◆ sipinternal.<sip domain>

◆ sip.<sip domain>

The Lync 2013 Phone Edition device prefers to use Option 120 (in conjunction with Option 43 for certificate services) to allow the phone to be directed to a Lync Server 2013 server rather than a legacy OCS 2007 or OCS 2007 R2 server, which does not provide certificate (or PIN) authentication.

Using the Lync 2013 Communicator client, you can modify the connection type to be manual (see Figure 12.1) and enter the FQDN address of the pool to see if that connection is working. Using this test, you can confirm that the issue is within the DNS resolution of the automatic server discovery or the redirect from another pool.

To confirm the connectivity to a server, you can use ping; however, many network administrators will block ping on the firewall, especially when you're trying to communicate with the servers in the DMZ. To confirm communications on a specific port, you must use Telnet and provide the server (or pool) name and the port.

For example, to confirm SIP connectivity via a hardware load balancer, use this command:

```
telnet <pool name> 5061
```

FIGURE 12.1
Configuring a
manual server
connection

The result, rather confusingly, is a blank window. However, this shows that the Telnet client has successfully connected to the server. If there is a problem, the client will indicate that it cannot connect, and although the error may not be particularly descriptive, you should be able to determine whether it was a DNS issue (if you used the FQDN) or a network connectivity issue (routing or firewall). The potential DNS issue can be determined simply by repeating the test using the IP address in place of the FQDN.

Another useful tool to test this, and that can give a more meaningful output, is PortQry. This tool is available from

    www.microsoft.com/en-us/download/details.aspx?id=17148

and is currently in version 2. In Figure 12.2, you will see an example usage and output. PortQry also has the ability to work using UDP, whereas Telnet is limited to TCP only.

FIGURE 12.2
PortQry output

```
C:\PortQryU2>PortQry.exe -n sip.microsoft.com -e 5061

Querying target system called:

 sip.microsoft.com

Attempting to resolve name to IP address...

Name resolved to 65.55.30.130

querying...

TCP port 5061 (unknown service): LISTENING

C:\PortQryU2>
```

Using the client logs (enabled as shown in Figure 12.3), you can see the following entries, showing the failed DNS resolution for some of the automatic lookup addresses:

```
06/08/2011|21:43:25.361 2074:1E08 INFO  :: domainName:masteringlync.org:
serviceName:sipinternaltls: transportName:tcp:
06/08/2011|21:43:25.361 2074:1E08 INFO  :: domainName:masteringlync.org: serviceName:sip:
transportName:tls:
06/08/2011|21:43:25.372 2074:1E50 INFO  :: QueryDNSSrv - DNS Name[_sipinternaltls._tcp.
masteringlync.org]
06/08/2011|21:43:25.614 2074:1E50 ERROR :: QueryDNSSrv GetDnsResults query: _
sipinternaltls._tcp.corp.masteringlync.org failed 8007251d
06/08/2011|21:43:25.614 2074:1E50 ERROR :: DNS_RESOLUTION_WORKITEM::ProcessWorkItem
ResolveHostName failed 8007251d
```

```
06/08/2011|21:43:25.614 2074:1E50 INFO  :: QueryDNSSrv - DNS Name[_sip._tls.masteringlync.
org]
06/08/2011|21:43:25.614 2074:1E08 INFO  :: CUccDnsQuery::UpdateLookup - error
code=80ee0066, index=0
06/08/2011|21:43:25.614 2074:1E08 INFO  :: CUccDnsQuery::CompleteLookup
- index=0
06/08/2011|21:43:25.823 2074:1E50 ERROR :: QueryDNSSrv GetDnsResults query: _sip._tls.
masteringlync.org failed 8007251d
06/08/2011|21:43:25.823 2074:1E50 ERROR :: DNS_RESOLUTION_WORKITEM::ProcessWorkItem
ResolveHostName failed 8007251d
06/08/2011|21:43:25.824 2074:1E08 INFO  :: CUccDnsQuery::UpdateLookup - error
code=80ee0066, index=1
06/08/2011|21:43:25.824 2074:1E08 INFO  :: CUccDnsQuery::CompleteLookup
- index=1
06/08/2011|21:43:25.824 2074:1E08 INFO  :: Function: CUccServerEndpoint::OnDnsQueryComplet
ed
06/08/2011|21:43:25.825 2074:1E08 ERROR :: HRESULT API failed: 80ee0066 = hrStatus.
CUccDnsQuery::GetResults
```

The client logs provide extremely detailed information in terms of what is going on at the client end. You'll see a lot more of them in this chapter.

FIGURE 12.3
Enabling client logs

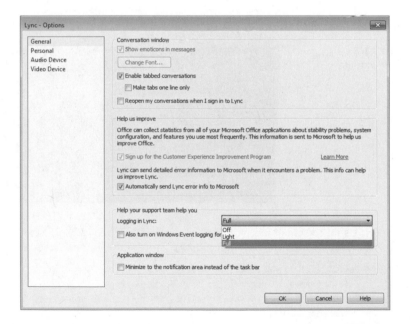

Confirming Secure Connectivity

Once you have the name resolution, routing, and firewall problems out of the way, the next part of the connectivity path is the certificate on the server. With the improvements made to the Lync Server 2010 Certificate Wizard (and this wizard has continued into Lync Server 2013), the task of configuring the certificates became a lot easier; however, changes can still be made and the certificates still might not be updated, which could lead to connectivity issues.

To test for the correct certificate configuration, you can use the following URL (similar to the successful Telnet connection, expect a blank screen, but this time white):

```
https://<poolname>/meet/blank.html
```

Figure 12.4 shows the result when the certificate is correctly configured (above) and incorrectly configured (below). Also notice the Lync icons on the address bar for the successful connection.

FIGURE 12.4
Confirming the correct certificate

This process can be repeated to confirm each of the expected subject alternative names (SANs) in the certificate simply by replacing the *<poolname>* entry with each of the SAN entries.

Checking for Audio/Video Peer-to-peer Connectivity

Now that you've established the basics for client connectivity to the servers, the next step is to confirm connectivity between clients when establishing a call. IM connectivity always flows through the server, whereas the clients must negotiate peer-to-peer connectivity between themselves. Where direct connectivity is not available, clients must connect via NAT or the Edge server. Figure 12.5 shows the connectivity options for a client, depending on the path available between them.

The client logs capture these IP addresses and ports negotiated (known as candidates) during the call initiation (audio, video, or desktop sharing). This Internet Connectivity Exchange (ICE) is shown here:

```
v=0
o=- 0 0 IN IP4 94.245.124.239
s=session
c=IN IP4 94.245.124.239
b=CT:53980
t=0 0
m=audio 56498 RTP/AVP 114 9 112 111 0 8 116 115 4 97 13 118 101
a=candidate:I0j2VRG1VNQG4cWj248JT8iqlOD42gmKoa8xdt4quqo 1 w4WZzoBiHwS3VeihjFFTuw
UDP 0.830 10.154.244.71 50028
a=candidate:I0j2VRG1VNQG4cWj248JT8iqlOD42gmKoa8xdt4quqo 2 w4WZzoBiHwS3VeihjFFTuw
```

```
UDP 0.830 10.154.244.71 50029
a=candidate:PZWZ6iscBZZ9TjL4kOKnxvcZDP4wODZKIklqiA/YLek 1 fCq9RqLw2pcibQlONAJULQ
TCP 0.190 94.245.124.238 53882
a=candidate:PZWZ6iscBZZ9TjL4kOKnxvcZDP4wODZKIklqiA/YLek 2 fCq9RqLw2pcibQlONAJULQ
TCP 0.190 94.245.124.238 53882
a=candidate:3aT5M3vcWbnE4FzWub2fX5CjNq6oDM61ZlcRKb0u5rQ 1 N9yLzNb17mpUVbCqNC2lAQ
UDP 0.490 94.245.124.239 56498
a=candidate:3aT5M3vcWbnE4FzWub2fX5CjNq6oDM61ZlcRKb0u5rQ 2 N9yLzNb17mpUVbCqNC2lAQ
UDP 0.490 94.245.124.239 55800
a=candidate:H46GRbUExoCxH7kQHprA5E2uVHxBroGV6aTGb56IowU 1 X1veRGhvsDShUEB8ND7GGQ
TCP 0.250 10.166.24.59 50004
a=candidate:H46GRbUExoCxH7kQHprA5E2uVHxBroGV6aTGb56IowU 2 X1veRGhvsDShUEB8ND7GGQ
TCP 0.250 10.166.24.59 50004
a=candidate:/fsTFKnb2oinetEHwrP5PkreyGP6dHnfhEsmI9V9xS8 1 fRqU3IuSWy2KXVF8MPZ7DA
UDP 0.550 195.226.18.36 50036
a=candidate:/fsTFKnb2oinetEHwrP5PkreyGP6dHnfhEsmI9V9xS8 2 fRqU3IuSWy2KXVF8MPZ7DA
UDP 0.550 195.226.18.36 50037
a=cryptoscale:1 client AES_CM_128_HMAC_SHA1_80
inline:kDgLmPIv2ufDNctJasF0KIkFq5w/6iXpUDMeWrDW|2^31|1:1
a=crypto:2 AES_CM_128_HMAC_SHA1_80
inline:s40wuCQ33Rw6SysXZs5f7C66IxsF/GdQRqiqcD3M|2^31|1:1
a=crypto:3 AES_CM_128_HMAC_SHA1_80
inline:SljnK0kFx6RtiWHywiCIVavo1SxLE/ztysYrFhZb|2^31
a=maxptime:200
a=rtcp:55800
a=rtpmap:114 x-msrta/16000
a=fmtp:114 bitrate=29000
a=rtpmap:9 G722/8000
a=rtpmap:112 G7221/16000
a=fmtp:112 bitrate=24000
a=rtpmap:111 SIREN/16000
a=fmtp:111 bitrate=16000
a=rtpmap:0 PCMU/8000
a=rtpmap:8 PCMA/8000
a=rtpmap:116 AAL2-G726-32/8000
a=rtpmap:115 x-msrta/8000
a=fmtp:115 bitrate=11800
a=rtpmap:4 G723/8000
a=rtpmap:97 RED/8000
a=rtpmap:13 CN/8000
a=rtpmap:118 CN/16000
a=rtpmap:101 telephone-event/8000
a=fmtp:101 0-16
a=encryption:optional
```

Each line beginning with a=candidate is an IP address/port/protocol combination on which the client can be reached, and the long, seemingly random text is the username/password combination, ensuring that this connection is secured. (This text string is exchanged via the SIP signaling path, which is already secured.)

FIGURE 12.5
Client connectivity options

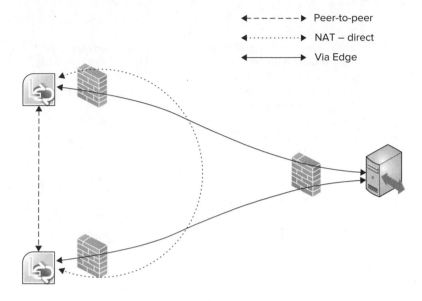

Let's look at a sample candidate entry:

```
a=candidate:I0j2VRG1VNQG4cWj248JT8iqlOD42gmKoa8xdt4quqo 1 w4WZzoBiHwS3VeihjFFTuw
UDP 0.830 10.154.244.71 50028
```

Broken down, it consists of the following elements:

`a=candidate:` is the session attribute.

`I0j2VRG1VNQG4cWj248JT8iqlOD42gmKoa8xdt4quqo` is the username.

`1` specifies that RTP is to be used (2 = RTCP).

`w4WZzoBiHwS3VeihjFFTuw` is the password.

`UDP` is the protocol.

`0.830` is the weighting (a higher number is preferred).

`10.154.244.71` is the IP address.

`50028` is the port number.

This same information is also provided in a previous ICE format, which is shown next (to ensure compatibility with legacy OCS clients):

```
v=0
o=- 0 0 IN IP4 94.245.124.239
s=session
```

```
c=IN IP4 94.245.124.239
b=CT:53980
t=0 0
m=audio 53046 RTP/AVP 114 9 112 111 0 8 116 115 4 97 13 118 101
a=ice-ufrag:hGFI
a=ice-pwd:cfwrCdU4lRuOe53ZFvWCSpJ4
a=candidate:1 1 UDP 2130706431 10.154.244.71 50020 typ host
a=candidate:1 2 UDP 2130705918 10.154.244.71 50021 typ host
a=candidate:2 1 TCP-PASS 6556159 94.245.124.238 57358 typ relay raddr
10.166.24.59 rport 50001
a=candidate:2 2 TCP-PASS 6556158 94.245.124.238 57358 typ relay raddr
10.166.24.59 rport 50001
a=candidate:3 1 UDP 16648703 94.245.124.239 53046 typ relay raddr
195.226.18.36 rport 50004
a=candidate:3 2 UDP 16648702 94.245.124.239 50913 typ relay raddr
195.226.18.36 rport 50005
a=candidate:4 1 TCP-ACT 7076863 94.245.124.238 57358 typ relay raddr
10.166.24.59 rport 50001
a=candidate:4 2 TCP-ACT 7076350 94.245.124.238 57358 typ relay raddr
10.166.24.59 rport 50001
a=candidate:5 1 TCP-ACT 1684797951 10.166.24.59 50001 typ srflx raddr
10.154.244.71 rport 50001
a=candidate:5 2 TCP-ACT 1684797438 10.166.24.59 50001 typ srflx raddr
10.154.244.71 rport 50001
a=candidate:6 1 UDP 1694234623 195.226.18.36 50004 typ srflx raddr
10.154.244.71 rport 50004
a=candidate:6 2 UDP 1694234110 195.226.18.36 50005 typ srflx raddr
10.154.244.71 rport 50005
a=cryptoscale:1 client AES_CM_128_HMAC_SHA1_80
inline:kDgLmPIv2ufDNctJasF0KIkFq5w/6iXpUDMeWrDW|2^31|1:1
a=crypto:2 AES_CM_128_HMAC_SHA1_80
inline:s40wuCQ33Rw6SysXZs5f7C66IxsF/GdQRqiqcD3M|2^31|1:1
a=crypto:3 AES_CM_128_HMAC_SHA1_80
inline:SljnK0kFx6RtiWHywiCIVavo1SxLE/ztysYrFhZb|2^31
a=maxptime:200
a=rtcp:50913
a=rtpmap:114 x-msrta/16000
a=fmtp:114 bitrate=29000
a=rtpmap:9 G722/8000
a=rtpmap:112 G7221/16000
a=fmtp:112 bitrate=24000
a=rtpmap:111 SIREN/16000
a=fmtp:111 bitrate=16000
a=rtpmap:0 PCMU/8000
a=rtpmap:8 PCMA/8000
a=rtpmap:116 AAL2-G726-32/8000
a=rtpmap:115 x-msrta/8000
```

```
a=fmtp:115 bitrate=11800
a=rtpmap:4 G723/8000
a=rtpmap:97 RED/8000
a=rtpmap:13 CN/8000
a=rtpmap:118 CN/16000
a=rtpmap:101 telephone-event/8000
a=fmtp:101 0-16
a=encryption:optional
```

Broken down, a sample entry in the legacy format

```
a=candidate:2 1 TCP-PASS 6556159 94.245.124.238 57358 typ relay raddr
  10.166.24.59 rport 50001
```

looks like this:

a=candidate: is the session attribute.

2 is the candidate ID.

1 specifies that RTP is to be used (2 = RTCP)

TCP-PASS is the protocol type (TCP-PASS = TCP Passive, TCP-ACT = TCP Active, UDP).

6556159 is the weighting (a higher number is preferred).

94.245.124.238 is the IP address.

57358 is the port number.

typ relay is the type of relay (direct = UDP only; relay = TCP-PASS, TCP-ACT, or UDP; srflx = self-reflective, TCP-ACT, or UDP).

raddr 10.166.24.59 is the remote IP address.

rport 50001 is the remote port number.

The clients both exchange a candidate (and codec) list and will try each address in order of preference. The logs will also show the address list provided by the remote client. Once you have this information, you can ensure manually that the clients can connect.

Once compatibility is confirmed via the IP address, port, and protocol selection, the remaining task is to establish a common codec. The previous listings include this codec map (a=rtpmap:); the clients will negotiate this and will continue to negotiate throughout the duration of the call, ensuring that the codecs adapt to any change in the network conditions. Later in this chapter, you'll see an excerpt from the media quality logs that shows the codec selection.

DEVICE CONNECTIVITY

Phone devices don't have the same requirements for connectivity as desktop clients, specifically the need for DHCP configuration.

To enable certificate-based authentication (making sure the phone can connect with no Active Directory available), you must make sure the phone connects to the certificate provisioning website on a Lync Server 2013 pool. This is provided via DHCP Option 43.

In addition, unless DHCP Option 120 is also configured (you need to provide the SIP registrar information), the phone will display an error to the user while it is performing a DNS query on the SRV records (although once the DNS records are discovered, it will connect as normal).

The dhcputil.exe tool (and DHCPConfigScript.bat file) provided in the C:\Program Files\Common Files\Microsoft Lync Server 2013 folder provides instructions for configuring a Microsoft-based DHCP server.

Real World Scenario

DEVICE ERROR FROM THE FIELD

A colleague recently reported a strange user experience from one of his customers—when the customer logged into the Lync 2013 client, everything functioned normally; however, when the customer was logged into a Lync 2013 Phone Edition client, the following functionality was missing:

◆ Voice mail

◆ Calendar integration

◆ Call logs

These functions are provided by Exchange Web Services (EWS), so we suggested troubleshooting EWS and verifying that it was operational. However, as our colleague pointed out, this was all functioning from the Lync 2013 client.

Next on the list was network routing and address resolution from the device (typically, phone devices are allocated to a separate VLAN). In this case, the device was on the same VLAN as the PC.

The end result was that EWS had been signed by a different certificate chain than the Lync Server 2013 Front End certificates had been. When the phone device connected to the Front End server to download the certificate chain, it had no way of downloading the chain for the Exchange server and, therefore, did not trust it.

There were two possible ways to resolve this certificate issue with the Exchange server:

Ensure that the Exchange server certificates came from the same certificate authority as the certificates user on the Front End servers

or

Use the New-CsWebTrustedCACertificate cmdlet to define the certificates used by the Exchange servers to be loaded onto the Front End servers and, therefore, trusted by the Lync Phone Edition client.

Because the Lync 2013 Phone Device will download the Front End server certificates (and root certificate authority certificate chain) anyhow, option 1 was the choice used. However, both have the same result, and in some cases it may not be possible to easily replace certificates in use by Exchange.

Another area to be aware of, especially when integrating with Exchange, is the use of web proxies. If you publish your web proxy via DHCP, this can affect clients connecting to EWS if the web proxies have not been configured to exclude internal traffic appropriately. You may see multiple attempts at authentication or integration issues because the web proxies are interfering with the traffic.

Sniffing the Network

After you've verified that name resolution, routing, and the firewalls are working and all appears to be fine, the next step is to better understand the actual traffic being sent and received on the network. The following tools are often used for network sniffing:

- Microsoft Network Monitor
- Wireshark

These tools intercept and provide a breakdown of the network traffic, including the protocol and meaning of the packets being transmitted or received. Figure 12.6 shows Microsoft Network Monitor examining generic network traffic.

Figure 12.6

Microsoft Network Monitor in action

Immediately, from the highlighted section in Figure 12.6, you can see the process (`communicator.exe`), so you know you're looking at the correct network traffic as well as the source and destination IP address information; this means that you are connecting to the server (or device) that you should be. You can also see the specific protocol (in this case TCP) and ports in use.

Although Network Monitor provides protocol parsers for SIP, it is normally much easier to enable logging on the server or client and import the log file into `snooper.exe` for analysis. Where Network Monitor comes into its own is in understanding the communications layer. There are two important scenarios:

- Understanding and establishing the certificate exchange (handshake)
- Understanding the hardware load balancer interaction

Certificate traffic analysis will indicate the names being provided by the certificate, ensuring that you can match those names with the ones you expect. It is really important in certificate analysis that you capture the initial handshake for the SSL session you are trying to decrypt. If you don't, all the useful data will be listed as application data in the network trace. By contrast, with the hardware load balancers, a common misconfiguration is the time-out values; here, you may capture a `TCP-RESET` packet showing that the time-out is configured incorrectly. `TCP-RESET` will cause the active session to reset and a new one to establish, which can confuse the troubleshooting process. When searching for `TCP-RESET` sessions, focus and limit your search to the TCP port. Doing this makes it far easier to locate an actual conversation.

Keep in mind these tips from the field when you're using network monitoring tools. Use aliases for naming the IP addresses so you can better track the flow. Use colors to highlight interesting trace information so when it is streaming in real time, you can better track what information you are looking for.

Now that we've looked at the methods of troubleshooting connectivity and introduced the snippets of the log files, we'll look at tracing.

Introducing Tracing

Both the server and the client provide a method to access what is happening "under the covers" by enabling logging. *Logging* enables the server and client to write detailed information to a text file to provide a means for an administrator or support engineer to understand what is occurring at any given time.

The server provides a means to enable subsets of components to log; on a busy server, there is too much information to simply log it all and then parse it. Next, you'll see how to enable and manage individual server components.

The client doesn't have as much information to log because it is dealing only with a single user's interactions, and therefore, everything is either Light, Full, or disabled.

Figure 12.3, earlier in the chapter, shows where you enable logging on the client; it can also be enabled via policy.

The log files are stored at the location

```
%USERPROFILE%\appdata\local\microsoft\office\15.0\lync\Tracing
```

and are named either `Lync-uccapi-0.UCCAPILOG` or `Communicator-uccapi-1.UCCAPILOG` (for the Communicator client).

These log files use *circular logging*, so there will always be a minimum of two files (occasionally there may be more—normally this would occur only when sustained traffic is being logged and not enough time has passed to close down the first file). Once the second is full, the first will be overwritten, and once the first is full, the second will be overwritten, and so on.

As mentioned, these are text-based log files and can be opened and viewed with any text viewer (such as `notepad.exe`); however, you'll see later in this chapter how a resource kit tool called `snooper.exe` makes reading and interpreting these log files much easier.

Under this directory you will also notice an Event Trace Log (ETL) file. This is a binary file that cannot be read by `notepad.exe`. These files are generally used by Microsoft support engineers to help provide further information to diagnose issues. To examine these files, you can use `OCSLogger.exe` from a Lync Server 2010 deployment.

Refer to the following location for more information:

```
http://blogs.msdn.com/b/leoncon/archive/2012/05/31/getting-amp-reading-the-
tracing-logs-for-a-lync-online-client.aspx
```

Using Centralized Logging

In Lync Server 2013 there is a new concept called centralized logging. It is designed to allow you to trace across multiple servers at one time, making it far easier to locate and troubleshoot a problem in order to resolve it. Previously, you had to run a trace individually and manually on every node you thought was involved in the communications flow as well as select the right components and flags to trace on.

In Lync 2013, each server runs a new service called Lync Server Centralized Logging Service Agent, as seen in Figure 12.7.

FIGURE 12.7

Lync Server
Centralized
Logging Service
Agent

NOTE   You can also monitor Lync Server Centralized Logging Service Agent via Task Manager under ClsAgent.exe.

There are global policies configured by default that control the behavior of this agent. These policies can be modified via the PowerShell cmdlet Get-CsCentralizedLoggingConfiguration (see Figure 12.8).

FIGURE 12.8

The Get-CsCentra
lizedLoggingCon-
figuration cmdlet

In Figure 12.8, you will see a list of scenarios that are configured, but more important, you'll see what is enabled. As you will see, a scenario called AlwaysOn is enabled by default. This in itself is a major leap forward in terms of troubleshooting because now there is the potential to capture the problem with this scenario. Although it does not monitor every component or flag, this scenario should allow you to reduce the time to resolution because you may not have to try to re-create an issue, which can sometimes be a challenge.

The central logging service can be controlled by ClsController.exe, which is located at C:\ Program Files\Common Files\Microsoft Lync Server 2013\ClsAgent\.

This tool needs to be launched from an elevated command prompt or elevated PowerShell environment.

The basic syntax of ClsController.exe is as follows:

```
ClsController <Command> [(options)] [(Scope)]
```

Here are the valid command options:

-start   Starts the trace session for a given scenario (-scenario becomes a mandatory option).

-stop   Stops the trace session for given scenario (-scenario is a mandatory option and the only valid one).

    -query   Queries for the list of scenarios being traced.

    -flush   Flushes the logs and makes them available to search.

    -update   Updates the duration of the active scenario that needs to be traced (-duration is mandatory option and the only valid one).

-search   Searches the logs. Results are returned in a text file. -starttime, -endtime, -components, -uri, -called, -phone, -ip, -loglevel, -matchany, -matchall, -keepcache, and -correlationids are valid options for searching.

The valid options are as follows:

-scenario   Lists valid scenario names.

-duration   Sets the duration (in minutes) to trace the given scenario. The default duration is 4 hours.

-matchall   Requires the search to match all criteria specified.

-matchany   Requires the search to match any criteria specified (this is the default).

-starttime   Sets a time stamp from which to start searching the log.

-endtime   Sets a time stamp to search the log to.

-loglevel   Sets the log level to search on (fatal|error|warn|info|verbose|noise).

-components   Lists the components separated by commas (i.e., siptack,s4).

-phone   Lists the phone number to search for. This must be an exact match.

-uri   Lists the URI to search for. This must be an exact match.

-callid   Lists the call ID to search for. This must be an exact match.

-ip   Lists the IP address to search for. This must be an exact match.

-skipnetworklogs   Bypasses using network logs (if using network logs is configured). This will improve the search performance.

The valid scope options are as follows:

-pools   List the pool FQDNs, separated by commas, of the pools from which you want to collect data.

-machines   List the machine FQDNs, separated by commas, of the machines from which you want to collect data.

Let's look at an example. Say you want to start the AlwaysOn scenario for a single machine in your deployment. You would type the following:

```
ClsController -start -scenario AlwaysOn -machine se01.corp.masteringlync.org
```

To stop this scenario, you would type this:

```
ClsController -stop -scenario AlwaysOn
```

Once the scenario is stopped, you need to flush the data so you can search the logs:

```
ClsController -flush
```

Finally, to search the logs you use the following command:

```
ClsController -search -components S4,Sipstack -loglevel verbose
-machine se01.corp.masteringlync.org
```

The list of scenarios and their components that are captured during tracing are exposed via the PowerShell cmdlet Get-CsClsScenario.

This will return all the scenarios currently available (see Figure 12.9).

FIGURE 12.9
Use Get-
CsClsSScenario
to display all
scenarios

If you want to show the providers that are being traced for in the AlwaysOn scenario, use the following PowerShell commands:

```
$scenario = Get-CsClsScenario -identity Global/AlwaysOn
$scenario.provider
```

This will return an entire list of all the components being traced on.

Now, if you want to return the flags where only one component is being traced, use the following command:

```
($scenario.provider |where {$_.Name -eq "SipStack"}).Flags
```

This will return only the flags that are enabled for the AlwaysOn scenario for the SipStack provider. You can modify the name for the components of your choice and determine their enabled flags.

Finally, if you wish to enable all flags for a provider, you can use the following command:

```
($scenario.provider |where {$_.Name -eq "SipStack"}).flags = "All_Flags"
```

Using *snooper.exe*

In a previous section, you viewed the log file snippets as text. The log file is a text-based file, but it can quickly grow quite large. Snooper is the tool that makes interpreting the logs extremely easy and straightforward. Snooper is shown in Figure 12.10 with a file loaded.

Previously, Snooper was part of the Lync (and OCS) resource kit; however, now the debugging tools have been separated to a download on their own, called Lync 2013 Debugging Tools, which can be found here:

```
http://www.microsoft.com/en-us/download/details.aspx?id=35453
```

FIGURE 12.10
The Snooper Trace tab

Immediately upon loading a file, Snooper will display the Trace tab (as shown in Figure 12.10) and provide an additional Messages tab (shown in Figure 12.11). If the file is too large (over 25MB), a prompt will appear asking if you want to load traces, messages, or both.

A new feature in Snooper provides the ability to switch between multiple logs with relative ease. Selecting LogSelector from the top menu (see Figure 12.11) will provide you with easy access to the logs you have opened, shown in Figure 12.12.

As you can imagine, this can be very useful when switching between multiple client logs or even multiple server logs.

As you will see, errors will be highlighted in red, allowing a quick and easy identification process. You may not always be interested in the errors on the Trace tab because they typically show the result of the problem rather than the cause.

FIGURE 12.11

The Snooper
Messages tab

FIGURE 12.12

The LogSelector
window

On the client, the component view shows UCCP (Unified Communications Client Platform API); however, server logs provide many different component options, shown here:

ABCommon	CLSAgent	LCCertHelper
ABServer	CLSCommon	LcsServer
ABServerIISModule	CLSController	LDM
ADConnect	CLSControllerLib	LocationInformationServer
AdminUI	CLSFormat	Lyss
AggregationScript	Collaboration	Mach
ApiModule	CpsDiagnostics	ManagementCore
ApplicationServer	CpsHostingFramework	MCUFactory
AppShareOoty	DataMCU	MCUInfra
ArchivingAgent	DataMCURunTime	McxService
ArchJournal	Deployment	Media_MMVR
AsMcu	DeviceUpdate	Media_PAL
AutoDiscover	DeviceUpdateHttpHandler	MediaStack_Audio_AGC
AvMcu	Dialin	MediaStack_Audio_DRC
AvMP	Dlx	MediaStack_Audio_EchoDT
BackupService	ExumRouting	MediaStack_Audio_FaxDT
CAAServer	HybridConfig	MediaStack_Audio_Healer
CASServer	IIMFilter	MediaStack_Audio_NoiseDT
CertProvisioning	ImMcu	MediaStack_Audio_VAD
ChatCommon	InboundRouting	MediaStack_Audio_VSP
ChatEndpoint	IncomingFederation	MediaStack_AudioCodecs
ChatRoomManagement	Infrastructure	MediaStack_AudioEngine
ChatSDK	InterClusterRouting	MediaStack_COMAPI
ChatWebService	InternalCommon	MediaStack_COMMON
ClientVersionFilter	JoinLauncher	MediaStack_Crossbar

MediaStack_Crypto	QueueDLL	ServerTransportAdapator
MediaStack_DebugUI	RDPApiTrace	SIPStack
MediaStack_DebugUI_AEC	RDPEncComTrace	StoreWeb
MediaStack_DEVICE	ReachJoin	TranslationApplication
MediaStack_MassConvertedTraces1	ReachPerf	UMCA_Workflow
MediaStack_MediaManager	RgsClientsLib	UCWA
MediaStack_PerFRame	RgsCommonLirary	UdcAgent
MediaStack_PerPacket	RgsDatastores	UserPinService
MediaStack_QualityController	RgsDeploymentApi	UserServices
MediaStack_RTCP	RgsDeploymentLibrary	WebInfrastructure
MediaStack_RTP	RgsDiagnostics	WebRelay
MediaStack_StreamingEngine	RgsHostingFramework	WebScheduler
MediaStack_TLS	RgsMatchMakingService	WPP_OC_RDP_APPSHAPI
MediaStack_Transport	Routing_Data_Sync_Agent	XDS_File_Transfer_Agent
MediaStack_VIDEO	RtcDbSyncAgent	XDS_Master_Replicator
MediaStack_VOICEENHANCE	RtcHost	XDS_Replica_Replicator
MediationServer	RTCSPL	XmppCommonLibrary
OutboundRouting	S4	XmppListener
OutgoingFederation	ServerAgent	XmppRouting
PowerShell	ServerConfiguration	XmppTGW

Many of these traces are typically of more use to Microsoft Product Support Services (PSS) than to the administrator.

The Messages tab is more useful to the administrator. Here, you can see the SIP flow of the client. Selecting a single message not only displays the associated content on the right, it also highlights all associated messages. For example, selecting a SIP INVITE message will display the content directly associated with that particular message, but it will also highlight the relevant message thread, all the way through to the BYE message.

However, where Snooper really comes into its own is the search capabilities, quickly allowing you to find the relevant parts of the log file that you are interested in. You can manually add entries into the search bar if you know the criteria to search for (simply type into the search bar)—typically, this starts with an error message or a username (or number) related to the problem.

The simple Search menu (shown in Figure 12.13) allows you to quickly build a search string from the text within the message to narrow down the content in the log file. This becomes more relevant when you are dealing with server-generated log files rather than log files from the client.

FIGURE 12.13
Searching with Snooper

```
/2.0/TLS 192.168.2.210:57116
orwards: 70

ith.lync@masteringlync.org>;tag=acef136chc;epid=5c2be4bde0
o:keith.lync@masteringlyn          Search
: 492bcd8ae23d4d76874da(
 REGISTER                           Copy
t: <sip:192.168.2.210:57116;transport=tls;ms-
:=ca7c4ecc04>;methods="INVITE, MESSAGE, INFO, OPTIONS, BYE,
L, NOTIFY, ACK, REFER, BENOTIFY";proxy=replace;
stance="<urn:uuid:5AE27C22-4127-5E1C-8A95-0D4F8DCD2AED>"
gent: UCCAPI/15.0.4420.1017 OC/15.0.4420.1017 (Microsoft Lync)
ted: gruu-10, adhoclist, msrtc-event-categories
ted: ms-forking
```

Selecting a text string and then choosing Search will simply replace the current search criteria with the selection.

Obviously, being able to understand the expected process (that is, a SIP call flow) makes the troubleshooting easier because you know roughly what to expect and can interpret deviations from this expected flow to troubleshoot.

In the latest version of Snooper, there is a new option on the menu bar that can provide the call flow sequence (shown in Figure 12.14). This gives you the ability to understand the call flow even if you are a complete novice.

FIGURE 12.14
Location of the Call Flow button

Call Flow

When you click the Call Flow button, the call flow diagram window will appear. As you will see in Figure 12.15, you now receive a graphical representation of the call flow for the particular conversation you have selected.

Pay close attention to the detail it can provide. For example, you will see the host IPs that are involved in the communication. You can also very easily see the direction of the response. In the screen shot in Figure 12.15, we are viewing the initial signing process.

An overview of the SIP call flow process is provided in Chapter 2, "Standards and Protocols."

Diagnostic Message Text

One more feature is worth mentioning in the context of tracing. Besides providing Snooper to help you narrow down a problem, Lync Server 2010 improved significantly on previous versions, and Lync Server 2013 has continued this work by including descriptive diagnostic text with all the messages. Some of these messages are shown here:

```
13004; reason="Request was proxied to one or more registered endpoints"
13014; reason="The routing rules did not result in a final response and callee
 is not enabled for Unified Messaging"
51004; reason="Action initiated by user"
51007; reason="Callee media connectivity diagnosis info"
```

FIGURE 12.15
The call flow diagram window

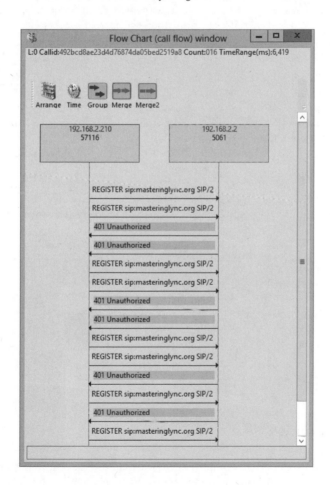

Other Troubleshooting Options

So far, we've covered only the server- and client-side logging of the Lync 2013 application itself. In the following sections, we'll look at some of the other areas where troubleshooting may be required, outside the central logging tool and the client logs.

We'll also touch on the performance counters available to provide a view into how the hardware is actually performing as well as the synthetic transaction capability to provide automated testing of the Lync 2013 environment. Ideally, this would be integrated with System Center Operations Manager 2007 R2/2012, providing the administrators with monitoring and alerting.

We'll have another look at the CDR report, this time in more detail, and you'll see which parts are of particular interest in troubleshooting.

Finally, we'll show how to capture the client configuration information, which will help confirm that the client is actually connecting to the correct servers!

Investigating Web Components

While most of the web components have specific scenarios within the central logging tool for debugging, they are still web based, so IIS logs will also need to be investigated.

There are two websites to consider, each with its own set of log files. (One website is for internal client connectivity and one is for external client connectivity. There are separate websites because the security configurations are different on each, and indeed some capability—such as administration—is only available internally.) These log files will capture every web-based interaction; in a large deployment, they can grow in size very quickly because every single client will make multiple web queries upon login (for Address Book updates, client updates, and so on).

Remember to turn IIS logging off after you have completed troubleshooting. These log files can grow extremely quickly and cause other issues from the space they consume.

FINDING THE IIS LOGS

First, you have to determine if the user is connecting to the internal website or the external one, and then you need to establish to which server the client is connecting. For a Standard Edition pool, this is straightforward, but you could be connecting to any Front End server in an Enterprise pool, and not only that, different connection types could be going to different servers!

Central Logging greatly simplifies this as you can now enable a scenario trace across the entire pool or specific machines if you are sure of the affected nodes.

CONTROL PANEL

The Control Panel is a Silverlight application, so any issues involving connectivity and loading this page are going to fall under IIS also. Often we have found that companies using a web proxy forget to configure it to exclude the Lync pools administration pages/websites.

DEVICE TROUBLESHOOTING

In the event of problems with devices (assuming the device has connected), there is a Send Logs option within the device menu itself, which will force the device to upload its log file to the web server to the following location:

```
\\servername\share\%Lync Pool WebServices Folder%\DeviceUpdateLogs\
```

NOTE   Use the PowerShell cmdlet `Get-CsService` to find the server name and file share you created in the topology.

These logs are in Windows CE log file format and require the use of the `ReadLog.exe` tool, which is part of Windows Embedded CE. This can be downloaded from the following location:

```
www.microsoft.com/windowsembedded/en-us/develop/windows-embedded-products-for-
developers.aspx
```

Performance Counters

Windows servers come with a tool called `PerfMon.exe`, which can display a detailed view of counters within the server and any applications installed. Figure 12.16 shows `PerfMon.exe` in action.

FIGURE 12.16
`PerfMon.exe`

The following counters are typically used to indicate generic server problems:

◆   Processor

◆   Disk (both LogicalDisk and PhysicalDisk)

- Memory

- Network

As can be seen in Figure 12.16, multiple counters can be viewed at the same time, allowing for correlation of conditions. For example, if both network and disk activity increased simultaneously, it could indicate that a file is being copied across the network to (or from) the server.

Most applications will install application-specific counters; Lync Server 2013 is no different and installs over 100. Listed here are some of the more common counter categories and specific objects within those categories:

- LS:USrv - DBSTORE\USrv - Queue Latency

- LS:USrv - DBSTORE\USrv - Sproc Latency

- LS:SIP - Load Management\SIP - Average Holding Time for Incoming Messages

- LS:SIP - Peers\SIP - Flow Controlled Connections

- LS:SIP - Responses\SIP - Local 504 Responses/sec

- LS:SIP - Peers\SIP - Sends Outstanding

These were originally detailed in a blog entry regarding server health determination for OCS, at

http://blogs.technet.com/b/nexthop/archive/2007/09/20/how-can-i-tell-if-my-server-is-healthy-in-less-than-10-counters.aspx

The counters and points in the blog are still relevant to Lync.

The full counter list can be found at www.sybex.com/go/masteringlync2013.

Each of the counter categories (for example, LS:SIP - Peers or LS:SIP - Responses) has a number of specific counters (for example, Flow Controlled Connections) associated with it. In most cases, they will provide rates of message flow—for example, success per second—and can be used to determine the rate of successful connections, or more likely in the case of troubleshooting, the rates (and count) of failures can be interesting.

SQL Server also installs counters, and because SQL Express is installed on every Lync Server 2013 role, these allow further in-depth visibility of the databases. (SQL-specific counters are beyond the scope of this book.)

Synthetic Transactions

Introduced in Chapter 11, "Archiving and Monitoring," the set of PowerShell cmdlets known as synthetic transactions are most useful when integrated with Microsoft System Center Operations Manager; however, they can be used effectively when troubleshooting because they simulate the activities carried out by the client. You can find the full list of cmdlets in Chapter 11. You'll only need a few of them for troubleshooting in this chapter.

Some of the cmdlets really are for onetime testing—for example, to test permissions prior to installation. The ones you are interested in, though, require a user ID as the parameter; this ensures that when a user reports a problem, an administrator can emulate all the correct policies that the user will be receiving, so the test is an accurate reflection of the settings applied to the user.

Before you can use the `Test-Cs` cmdlets that are based on user ID, you need to configure a health configuration. This consists of two test user accounts, typically disabled but enabled for Lync, that the `Test-Cs` cmdlets will use for their accounts to simulate traffic.

```
New-CsHealthMonitoringConfiguration -TargetFqdn se01.corp.masteringlync.org
-FirstTestUserSipUri sip:test1_lync@masteringlync.org
-SecondTestUserSipUri sip:test2_lync@masteringlync.org


Identity                 : se01.corp.masteringlync.org
FirstTestUserSipUri      : sip:test1_lync@masteringlync.org
FirstTestSamAccountName :
FirstTestUserSipUri      : sip:test1_lync@masteringlync.org
FirstTestSamAccountName :
TargetFqdn               : se01.masteringlync.org
```

Once the health configurations are configured for the pool, you can use the synthetic transactions to help troubleshoot.

For example, the command

```
Test-CsIm -TargetFqdn se01.corp.masteringlync.org
```

will return the following if there are no problems:

```
TargetFqdn : se01.corp.masteringlync.org
Result     : Success
Latency    : 00:00:00.0203802
Error      :
Diagnosis  :
```

Some of the `Test-Cs` cmdlets require authentication and will produce a lot of screen data prior to the results. For example, before an Address Book is created (by default 01:30 a.m. the morning after the pool has been installed), the command

```
Test-CsAddressBookWebQuery -TargetFqdn se01.corp.masteringlync.org
```

will return:

```
Connecting to web service : https://se.corp.masteringlync.org/webticket/webticketservce.svc
Using Machine certificate authentication
Successfully created connection proxy and website bindings
Requesting new web ticket
Sending Web-Ticket Request:
```

This is followed by lots of XML, which has been left out for brevity, and then, finally this:

```
Creating WebTicket security token request
TargetUri  : https://se01.corp.masteringlync.org/groupexpansion/service.svc
TargetFqdn : se01.corp.masteringlync.org
Result     : Failure
Latency    : 00:00:00
Error      : Address Book Web server request has failed with response code NoEntryFound.
Diagnosis  :
```

On the other hand, if the web server itself is not running, the same command will return the following:

```
TargetUri  : https://se01.corp.masteringlync.org/groupexpansion/service.svc
TargetFqdn : se01.corp.masteringlync.org
Result     : Failure
Latency    : 00:00:00
Error      : ERROR - No response received for Web-Ticket service.
Diagnosis  :
```

This response still provides the XML data; however, you can see that the error code gives a good indication of where the issue is located. Restarting the web service and allowing the Address Book to be generated (or using `Update-CsAddressBook`) gives the following response to the `Test-CsAddressBookWebQuery` command:

```
TargetUri  : https://se01.corp.masteringlync.org/groupexpansion/service.svc
TargetFqdn : se.corp.masteringlync.org
Result     : Success
Latency    : 00:00:20:5385645
Error      :
Diagnosis  :
```

Monitoring Reports

As mentioned in Chapter 11, the Call Detail Report provides an extremely detailed analysis of an individual call with almost 200 individual data points captured in an audio call alone!

Some of these data points help to set the scene (network address information and client hardware and software versions, for example). However, the ones of particular interest in identification of a root cause of a problem are in the Media Line (Main Audio)—Device and Signal Metrics, Client Events, and Audio Stream sections. Each of these sections reports in a single direction for the call (such as caller to callee); however, the CDR report includes both directions, so you can compare what is sent and what is received.

Figure 12.17 shows the three sections from the caller section of the report (intervening sections have been removed for brevity); each report will include the callee data as well.

DEVICE AND SIGNAL METRICS

The Device and Signal Metrics section of the report provides the hardware and software versions of the device in use, but more important from a troubleshooting perspective, it provides the Send and Receive sound levels.

By comparing the caller *Send* values with the callee *Receive* values (and vice versa), you can determine how much (if any) signal loss there has been due to the transmission.

Also included here is the amount of echo received by the microphone and the amount actually sent in the signal; this is a representation of how well (or badly) the echo cancellation in the device is working.

CALLER CLIENT EVENT

This section deals with the hardware associated with the device (including the PC if you are using built-in or USB-connected headphone and speakers).

Pay particular attention to the *time* values because they indicate how long the device has been malfunctioning; any value in the fields in this section indicates a problem with the call. Other sections of the report provide informational data, whereas any data in this section indicates a problem. You may need to refer to other sections to determine exactly what the problem is.

FIGURE 12.17

Using the CDR report

Caller Device and Signal Metrics			
Capture device:	Line 1 (Virtual Audio Cable)	Capture device driver:	EuMus Design: 4.12.0.4973
Render device:	Line 1 (Virtual Audio Cable)	Render device driver:	EuMus Design: 4.12.0.4973
Microphone glitch rate:	1133 per 5 minutes	Speaker glitch rate:	1933 per 5 minutes
Microphone timestamp drift:	0.01143217 %	Speaker timestamp drift:	4.26748991 %
Microphone timestamp error:	1.32751703262329 ms	Speaker timestamp error:	1.41965198516846 ms
Echo event cause:		Voice switch cause:	
Send signal level:	-16 dBov	Receive signal level:	-13 dBov
Send noise level:	-60 dBov	Receive noise level:	-59 dBov
Echo return:		Initial signal level RMS:	1144.60400390625

Caller Client Event			
CPU insufficient time:	0.00 %	Microphone not functioning time:	0.00 %
Speaker not functioning time:	0.00 %	Clipping time:	0.00 %
Echo time:	0.00 %	Glitch time:	0.00 %
Voice switch time:	0.00 %	Low SNR time:	0.00 %
Low speech level time:	0.00 %	Near end to echo time:	0.00 %
Device howling event count:	0	Device multiple endpoints event count:	0
Low network bandwidth time:	0.00 %	High network delay time:	0.00 %
Poor network receive quality time:	0.00 %	Poor network send quality time:	0.00 %

Audio Stream (Caller -> Callee)			
Codec:	x-msrta	Sample rate:	16000
Audio FEC:	False	Bandwidth estimates:	99012 Kbps
Packet utilization:	471		
Avg. packet loss rate:	0.00 %	Max. packet loss rate:	0.00 %
Avg. jitter:	3 ms	Max. jitter:	8 ms
Avg. round trip:	1 ms	Max. round trip:	2 ms
Burst duration:	0 ms	Burst gap duration:	7940 ms
Burst density:	0.00 %	Burst gap density:	0.00 %
Avg. concealed samples ratio:	0.00 %	Avg. stretched samples ratio:	1.00 %
Avg. compressed samples ratio:	1.00 %		
Avg. network MOS:	4.21	Min. network MOS:	4.21
Avg. network MOS degradation:	0.03	Max. network MOS degradation:	0.03
NMOS degradation (jitter):	0.00 %	NMOS degradation (packet loss):	0.00 %

AUDIO STREAM

The Audio Stream section covers the network impact to the call and provides information on the specific codec used for the call.

This section will help to determine if the network is causing any of the problems because this is where you can see information related to the packet loss, jitter, and round trip time. Also included here is information on how much healing was carried out on the call. Finally, the MOS values show how much impact the network conditions have had on the call quality.

INDEPENDENT MEDIA STREAMS

When troubleshooting audio issues, it's important to remember that each directional stream is completely independent. It's not unusual to have issues in one direction only. This may indicate a network issue, such as incorrect routing or router interface bandwidth issues.

Client Side

The connected client configuration can be determined by holding down the left Ctrl key and right-clicking the Lync 2013 icon in the system tray to bring up a menu from which you select the Configuration Information item. This will call up the screen shown in Figure 12.18.

The Lync 2013 client will cache a significant set of information, ranging from configuration items and search query results to photos and voice mails.

To ensure that the latest configuration information is being provided to the client and remove the possibility of stale cached information, the cache files in the following folder location should be deleted:

```
%USER PROFILE%\AppData\Local\Microsoft\Office\15.0\Lync\sip_<sip address>\
```

FIGURE 12.18
Configuration
information

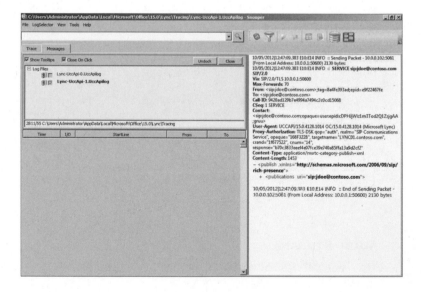

The Bottom Line

Confirm that the basics are in place from the infrastructure side.   Lync Server 2013 relies on a range of additional infrastructure to be able to provide its functionality—such as Active Directory, SQL, DNS, network, and so on. If any of these additional areas suffer interruptions or misconfigurations, it is extremely likely that Lync 2013 will begin to demonstrate issues also.

Master It   An internal Lync 2013 client is having difficulty connecting to its home pool when using automatic configuration. Describe the flow of DNS and connection attempts made for a client on the corporate network.

Understand how to troubleshoot the client.   The Lync 2013 client provides a lot of information in the configuration section as well as the log files to aid with troubleshooting, and this information should not be overlooked.

Master It   Where are the client log files stored?

Know how to enable troubleshooting on the server.   The Lync Server 2013 roles each have individual components that require logging and also provide performance counter objects that can be monitored.

By default, the logging scenario AlwaysOn is enabled on the servers. The default logging options and components can be configured to suit users' needs.

Master It   Which tool has replaced OCSLogger and is now used to enable logging on a Lync Server 2013 server?

Understand and use the troubleshooting tools available.   In addition to the built-in logging functionality of Lync Server 2013, more tools can (and should) be downloaded and installed on each of the servers to provide a better range of data, which is ready to be captured in the event of a problem.

Master It   Which tool is recommended for analyzing SIP logs or message traces? And where can it be found?

Part 4

Voice

Chapter 13

Getting Started with Voice

Lync Server 2010 on its release was seen as a match (and replacement) for most PBXs, providing what was considered to be fully fledged voice capability to the users via both the Lync Communicator client and the desktop phone device.

Lync Server 2013 builds upon that even further; we've seen how the clients have been updated, and also, as you'll see in an upcoming chapter, how the range of devices has been improved. Here we're going to be looking at the how the Enterprise Voice capabilities are managed, providing voice service to the user.

Because users' expectations for voice have increased to be on par with PBX, this is important. Can you remember the last time your company had a problem that caused the PBX to fail? In most cases, that's extremely rare! People expect to pick up a phone and just have it work. Lync Server 2013 builds upon this level of expectation, introduced in Lync Server 2010, with new high-availability capabilities.

In this chapter, you will learn to:

◆ Understand the voice capabilities

◆ Understand the voice architecture

◆ Configure voice policies and routing

The Back Story

In the early days of the Microsoft Unified Communications suite (before it was even called Unified Communications), Live Communications Server provided a feature called Remote Call Control, and while this feature is slowly being deprecated with each new version, it was the first way to integrate an instant messaging product with voice functionality (albeit through a traditional-style telephony system). Remote Call Control works by allowing the Communicator client to send signaling information to the PBX, via a dedicated server/interface, allowing control of the desk handset—you clicked (or typed) a number and then picked up the handset to talk.

Office Communications Server 2007 introduced the concept of Enterprise Voice, whereby the Communicator client itself was considered a phone (either hardware or software) and integrated via a media gateway device into a traditional (or IP) PBX or, indeed, directly to the PSTN. Office Communications Server 2007 R2 developed the voice functionality further and moved closer to being a PBX; however, there was still functionality that required the PBX—only in certain cases (typically, small companies or branches) could OCS 2007 R2 be considered capable of replacing a PBX.

Lync Server 2010 was the first true step in replacing a PBX (and for many enterprises it did), and as you'll see in the following pages, Lync Server 2013 is designed to close that gap and achieve the true PBX replacement capability.

Understanding the Voice Capabilities

As mentioned previously, Lync Server 2013 expands the voice capabilities previously developed in versions of Lync Server 2010 and Office Communications Server 2007 (and 2007 R2). Table 13.1 shows the feature set and when each feature was first introduced. These are all cumulative; if a feature is listed as OCS 2007, it is also available in OCS 2007 R2, Lync Server 2010, and Lync Server 2013 unless specifically indicated.

TABLE 13.1: Voice feature set

FEATURE NAME	FIRST AVAILABLE	SUMMARY
Inbound/outbound PSTN dialing	OCS 2007	Basic call functionality.
Call forward	OCS 2007	This is the ability to have incoming calls automatically forwarded to another contact or external number.
Simultaneous ring	OCS 2007	Similar to call forwarding, but instead of redirecting the call, it allows both the UC endpoint and the other endpoint to ring and the call can be answered at either endpoint.
Unified messaging	OCS 2007	Voice mail capability.
Single number reach	OCS 2007 R2	This is the ability to place a call from a mobile device and have that call routed via the OCS 2007 R2 infrastructure to enable the presentation of the OCS 2007 R2 user caller ID and the capture of Call Data Records (CDRs).
Delegation/team call	OCS 2007 R2	Allows others to handle calls on your behalf.
SIP trunking	OCS 2007 R2	Allows direct connection to a Mediation server without the use of a media gateway.
Dial-in audio conferencing	OCS 2007 R2	Provides audio-only conferencing to PSTN users.
Response group	OCS 2007 R2	Provides small-scale call center capability.
Call admission control	Lync Server 2010	Provides controls for the quality and quantity of calls on the network.
Call park	Lync Server 2010	Provides the capability to *park* a call from one Lync device and *retrieve* from another.

TABLE 13.1: Voice feature set *(CONTINUED)*

FEATURE NAME	FIRST AVAILABLE	SUMMARY
Unassigned number handling	Lync Server 2010	Allows for handling of incoming calls to numbers that have not been assigned to users.
Media bypass	Lync Server 2010	Endpoints can connect directly to another non-Lync endpoint (via G711) without the need to have the media transcoded by a Mediation server.
E911	Lync Server 2010	Support for the Enhanced 911 emergency services requirements to provide location information with an emergency call.
Analog devices	Lync Server 2010	Support for analog device integration, allowing for application of policy and capture of CDR information from non-Lync devices.
Common area phone	Lync Server 2010	Provides the ability to designate a device as a common-area device (for use in areas such as a lobby), allowing the device to be available for inbound and outbound calls under a generic policy, and provides the capacity to allow a user to log in and use the device as their own but be automatically logged out after a time period.
Private line	Lync Server 2010	Provides a user with a second number allowing the direct receipt of incoming calls.
Malicious call trace	Lync Server 2010	Allows a call to be flagged as malicious in the CDR database.
Caller ID Manipulation	Lync Server 2013	Enables the ability to display (or override) caller ID based on specific trunk calling information. Can be controlled for both caller and callee.
Voicemail Escape	Lync Server 2013	This feature can detect when a call has been routed to the user's mobile phone voice mail without giving the user the opportunity to answer the call. This scenario occurs when the user enables simultaneous ringing to their mobile phone and their mobile phone is turned off, out of battery, or out of range. Voicemail Escape detects that the call was immediately answered by the user's mobile phone voice mail and disconnects the call to the mobile phone voice mail.
InterTrunk routing	Lync Server 2013	This feature provides call control functionalities to downstream IP-PBXs. Lync Server can interconnect an IP-PBX to a PSTN gateway so that calls from a PBX phone can be routed to the PSTN and incoming PSTN calls can be routed to a PBX phone.

A number of these Lync Server 2013 capabilities are covered elsewhere in this book. Table 13.2 provides a cross reference to those chapters.

TABLE 13.2: Lync Server capability cross reference

CAPABILITY	CHAPTER
Call admission control	14
Call park	16
Unassigned number handling	16
E911	15
Analog devices	4
Common-area phone	4
Private line, malicious call trace, media bypass (covered in more detail in this chapter)	1

Private Line

A private line allows a user to have a second Direct Inward Dial (DID) number assigned to them, which will directly notify the user of an incoming call. As indicated by the name, it is intended to be for private calls only; therefore, the call does not follow any team-call or delegation-configured rules. It also ignores any presence-based rules such as Do Not Disturb, ensuring that it will always get through.

The private line can only be set via PowerShell, using the Set-CsUser cmdlet, as in this example:

```
Set-CsUser -identity "sip:keith_lync@masteringlync.org" -PrivateLine
"tel:+15557654321"
```

The number assigned to the private line does not appear anywhere within Active Directory (ensuring that it remains private) and indeed is even hidden within Lync Server. To view the number (and other hidden attributes), you must use the Get-CsUser cmdlet with the following syntax:

```
Get-CsUser -Identity "sip:keith_lync@masteringlync.org" | fl *
```

The resulting output looks like this:

```
SamAccountName             : keith_lync
UserPrincipalName          : keith_lync@masteringlync.org
FirstName                  : Keith
LastName                   : Lync
WindowsEmailAddress        : Keith.lync@masteringlync.org
Sid                        : S-1-5-21-51255695-3231353671-2943866482-78963
LineServerURI              :
OriginatorSid              :
```

```
AudioVideoDisabled              : False
IPPBXSoftPhoneRoutingEnabled    : False
RemoteCallControlTelephonyEnabled : False
PrivateLine                     : tel:+44666111122
AcpInfo                         : {}
HostedVoiceMail                 :
DisplayName                     : Keith Lync
ProxyAddresses                  : {eum:11122;phone-context=
LyncDP.corp.masteringlync.org, EUM:Keith_lync@masteringlync.org;
phone-context=LyncDP.corp.masteringlync.org, sip:keith.lync@masteringlync.org,
SMTP:keith.lync@masteringlyng.org....}
HomeServer                      : CN=Lc Services,CN=Microsoft,CN=1:1,
CN=Pools,CN=RTC Service,CN=Services,CN=Configuration,DC=corp,DC=masteringlync,
Dc=org
TargetServerIfMoving            :
EnabledForFederation            : True
EnabledForInternetAccess        : True
PublicNetworkEnabled            : True
EnterpriseVoiceEnabled          : True
EnabledForRichPresence          : True
LineURI                         : tel:+44555111122
SipAddress                      : sip:Keith_lync@masteringlync.org
Enabled                         : True
TenantId                        : 00000000-0000-0000-0000-000000000000
UserRoutingGroupId              : a7ba6e0a-bb11-5772-a075-fcc5f0adb0cc
TargetRegistrarPool             :
VoicePolicy                     :
ConferencingPolicy              :
PresencePolicy                  :
RegistrarPool                   : se01.corp.masteringlync.org
DialPlan                        :
LocationPolicy                  :
ClientPolicy                    :
ClientVersionPolicy             :
ArchivingPolicy                 :
PinPolicy                       :
ExternalAccessPolicy            : Allow No Access
HostedVoicemailPolicy           :
PesistentChatPolicy             :
UserServicesPolicy              :
ExperiencePolicy                :
HostingProvider                 : SRV:
ObjectId                        : 00000000-0000-0000-0000-000000000000
ExUmEnabled                     : True
Name                            : Keith Lync
DistinguishedName               : CN=Keith Lync,CN=Users,DC=corp,
DC=masterinlyng,DC=org
Identity                        : CN=Keith Lync,CN=Users, DC=corp,
DC=masterinlyng,DC=org
```

```
Guid                     : a64a9537-de65-4740-9198-9d83314fde96
ObjectCategory           : CN=Person,CN=Schema,CN=Configuration,
DC=corp,DC=masterinlyng,DC=org
ObjectClass              : {top, person, organizationalPerson, user}
WhenChanged              : 16/08/2011 09:01:02
WhenCreated              : 05/05/2011 15:09:24
OriginatingServer        : dc01.corp.masteringlync.org
IsByPassValidation       : False
IsValid                  : True
ObjectState              : Unchanged
```

Although Private Line can be configured without enabling Enterprise Voice, the user must be Enterprise Voice–enabled for Private Line to work.

The bold entries indicate the attributes that are not shown onscreen by default but that are returned by the Get-CsUser cmdlet. One attribute of significant note is the TargetServerIfMoving attribute. It is set to True if the user is in the process of moving pools. No other cmdlets will succeed for a user if this attribute is True.

Malicious Call Trace

Lync Server 2013 provides the ability for a user to flag the previous call as malicious immediately after hanging up the call. The data is flagged within a CDR record and, as such, requires the Monitoring server role to be deployed and configured. When a call is flagged, an entry is logged in the CDR database, allowing the administrator to identify the call as well as the associated information: calling number, gateways used, duration of call, and so on.

Figure 13.1 shows the user interface to flag a malicious call.

FIGURE 13.1
Flagging a malicious call

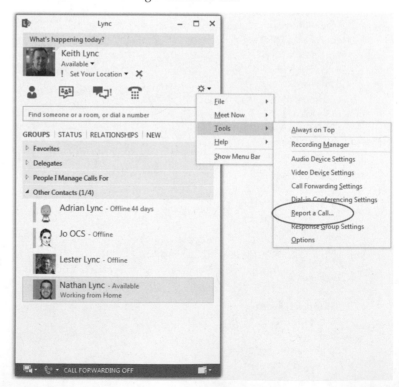

Malicious call tracing is enabled as part of the voice policy applied to users via the `Set-CsVoicePolicy` cmdlet or through the Control Panel ➤ Voice Routing ➤ Voice Policy page (see Figure 13.2).

FIGURE 13.2
Enabling malicious call tracing via the Control Panel

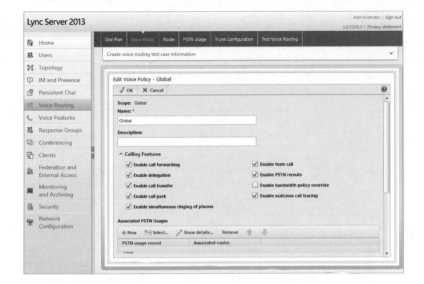

It is important to understand that aside from the entry being logged in the CDR database, there is no automated process to alert an administrator of a malicious call. You must monitor the database via System Center Operations Manager or other similar alerting system to enable some sort of automated alerting.

A manual query can be performed using the Top Failures Report from the Monitoring server report pack. To filter for malicious calls, you must select the following filter items:

◆ Category: Both expected and unexpected failures

◆ Diagnostic ID: 51017

Figure 13.3 shows an example of the filtered report.

Media Bypass

Lync Server 2010 introduced an important key feature called media bypass, which allows an organization to reduce the number of servers required (specifically reducing the load on Mediation servers).

So what's the big deal? Well, media bypass allows the Lync (2010 and 2013) clients to talk directly to non-Lync (or OCS) endpoints without transcoding the media stream by the Mediation server. Reducing the need for transcoding from native OCS codecs (such as RTAudio) to PSTN-style codecs (such as G711) improves the quality of the audio stream by reducing the number of network hops as well as reducing the loss when changing codecs.

OCS 2007 R2 introduced the capability for clients to use a G711 codec natively; however, the media stream still had to pass through the Mediation server (even though no transcoding occurred) when making a PSTN call.

The G711 codec uses more bandwidth but provides a better-quality signal than RTAudio; however, the RTAudio codec copes better on congested networks. Therefore, it is a better choice across WAN connections, and G711 is preferred on a LAN.

Where the media gateway (or compatible IP-PBX) is located on the same LAN, it makes more sense to use the higher-quality codec because it is likely the LAN will be able to cope with the (small) increase in traffic. Enabling media bypass allows this to happen and delivers the media stream directly to the gateway (or IP-PBX).

Signaling traffic (SIP) will continue to pass through the Mediation server. Figure 13.4 shows the path of each type of traffic for a PSTN call.

FIGURE 13.3
Malicious call reporting

FIGURE 13.4
Traffic flow in a Lync<>PSTN call

Removing the transcoding from a Mediation server dramatically increases the concurrent call capability of the server, and it allows the server role to be colocated with a Front End server, reducing the number of servers required in a voice deployment.

Understanding the Voice Architecture

Media bypass is a good context in which to look at the voice architecture within Lync Server 2010 (and 2013) and understand what is needed to provide Enterprise Voice capability to users.

Obviously, you need a pool (either Standard or Enterprise Edition) on which the users are to be homed. In addition, you need the Mediation server role to be installed and a certified integration device (media gateway, IP-PBX, or SIP trunk). These functions no longer have to be physical hardware because virtualization is fully supported. Figure 13.5 shows the minimum requirements for Enterprise Voice.

FIGURE 13.5

Minimum requirements for Enterprise Voice

Again, this configuration is the minimum required to provide Enterprise Voice. More realistically, we will be looking at additional configuration such as high availability and resiliency options, improved reporting and troubleshooting, expanded client (device) support, and increased configuration items such as E911 or Call Admission Control. This is where you'll start to get into the depths of the voice requirements for a design, not only hardware capability but configuration as well.

The full scope of Enterprise Voice interaction or requirements is shown in Figure 13.6.

With this view of the building blocks of Enterprise Voice, you can examine the role that each component will play:

UC Endpoints   This is the actual user device; it may be the softphone Communicator client or a desktop device running Lync Phone Edition.

Pool   This is the "heart" of the system. Clients register against a pool and receive a policy, which in turn will determine what calls can be made by each user as well as the feature set provided to each user. In addition, configuration items such as call routing, Call Admission Control, E911, Call Park, and Response Groups are all configured on the pool.

Mediation Server   This role may be colocated on the Front End servers and is responsible for all PSTN call-signaling information. In addition, it will transcode the media traffic when required.

IP-PBX   A certified device capable of media bypass. If not certified, it requires connectivity via a certified media gateway; if not capable of media bypass, it requires a Mediation server role to transcode the client media. A non-IP-PBX (legacy) may be connected via a certified media gateway.

Media Gateway   A certified device capable of media bypass. If not capable of media bypass, it requires a Mediation server role to transcode the client media. Also capable of supporting the connectivity of analog devices (such as a fax machine) and allowing Lync Server 2010 (and 2013) to manage these devices (via policy).

Monitoring Databases   Stores the CDR and Quality of Experience (QoE) information, allowing the reporting and troubleshooting of calls. This capability is not required but is strongly recommended when you're deploying Enterprise Voice to aid with troubleshooting. The Monitoring role itself is built into the Front End role.

Exchange Unified Messaging   Exchange 2007 SP1 (or higher) provides the voicemail capability for Lync Server 2013.

Trunk   A trunk is a unique combination of Mediation Server FQDN, Mediation Server SIP listening port, Gateway FQDN and gateway SIP listening port; it's not shown in the figure directly, and should be thought of as a virtual infrastructure element, made up of its components.

We've already covered a lot of these integration points in other chapters, so let's focus on the PSTN integration aspect now—Mediation servers.

Understanding Mediation Servers

In both versions of Office Communications Server 2007, the Mediation server had a one-to-one relationship with a media gateway (or IP-PBX). This meant that a large number of Mediation servers were required, and there was no flexibility for the supported hardware. It didn't matter how many calls your Mediation server was handling through the gateway on the other side; the same hardware was required for the server. In addition to this, a failure in either the Mediation server or the gateway would invalidate that route for calls.

With Lync Server 2010, that one-to-one relationship has gone away. Now there is no practical limit to the number of gateways a single Mediation server can service; but there is, of course, only the maximum number of concurrent calls a single Mediation server can handle! Even this maximum number is now variable based on the specifications of the hardware in use.

Not only that, but Mediation servers can be pooled in Lync Server 2013, giving a many:many relationship, providing an additional level of resiliency to the call flow.

Figure 13.7 compares the Office Communications Server (OCS) approach and the Lync Server 2013 approach to Mediation servers.

The Office Communications Server approach is still valid with Lync Server 2013 even if media bypass is not enabled. That is, the Mediation server will deal with not only SIP traffic but also the media transcoding.

In the SIP trunk scenario, a dedicated Mediation server is required to provide a termination point for the Lync 2013 endpoints.

FIGURE 13.6
Voice architecture within Lync Server 2013

FIGURE 13.7
The OCS 2007
approach versus
Lync Server 2013
Mediation server
approach

OCS 2007 R2 (and OCS 2007) Lync Server 2013

High Availability and Resiliency for Voice

When Lync Server 2013 replaces a PBX, the user's expectations don't change. Telephony has been around for decades, and the expectation of always being able to make a call when you pick up a handset is normal.

Right or wrong, user expectations about the uptime and availability of IT services are still very poor, based mostly on the early "Blue Screen of Death" experiences of Windows NT despite the massive steps forward since then. Previous chapters have covered resiliency in a general approach for user login; here the focus is purely on voice.

Lync Server 2013 has to overcome this preconception so that when there are challenges with the integrity of the IT infrastructure (whether networking or server related), the telephony service will continue and users will (hopefully) be unaffected. This is not possible in all cases, but Lync Server 2013 does a fantastic job of overcoming the majority of these cases to ensure that service continues.

We will consider the following failure scenarios:

- Individual server failure: Front End

- Individual server failure: Mediation

- Individual server failure: Back End

- Multiple server failure: Complete pool

- Multiple server failure: Complete data center

- Remote site: WAN failure

- Active Directory failure

In general, high availability is achieved by adding more servers of the same role to the configuration, either as stand-alone (using some sort of round-robin resource allocation) or as pool-based (using DNS or hardware load balancing) resources. If one of the servers fails, the others of the same role will take over the services of that server. In most cases, this is seamless; however, in a few cases, there may be a small impact.

Before you review each case, you need to understand the call flows involved in making an Enterprise Voice (PSTN) call. Although you'll review only a PSTN call in detail here, all of this applies equally to a peer-to-peer call, except for the Mediation server role. Figure 13.8 shows the anatomy of a call; the Mediation server role is broken out separately so you can better understand the call flow.

FIGURE 13.8
Call flow of an Enterprise Voice call

You can see the signaling traffic flows from the Lync 2013 client through the Front End server to the Mediation server and finally to the gateway, or IP-PBX. Media takes a more direct route, from the client through the Mediation server to the gateway—or, if media bypass is supported and enabled, directly from the client to the gateway itself.

INDIVIDUAL SERVER FAILURE: FRONT END SERVER

The failure of an individual Front End server in an enterprise pool does not have a significant impact on users logged in or to calls already in progress. If a user was logged in via the failed server, they will automatically reconnect to another Front End server in the pool (via either hardware or DNS load balancing). If the user is in a call at the time of their server failure, the call will continue unaffected (this functionality was introduced in Office Communications Server 2007 R2); however, signaling will be unavailable until the Lync 2013 client is signed into another Front End server. Figure 13.9 shows the user experience of the call in progress while the client is unable to connect to the Front End server.

The impact of signaling not being available is that although the media traffic continues, no changes can be made to it, such as call transfer or placing the call on hold. These functions will automatically become available again when the client (automatically) signs in to another Front End server or when the failed server is returned to service (whichever occurs first).

If a user is dialed into a conference hosted on the failed Front End server, they will be disconnected and will have to redial to rejoin the conference—which will be moved to an available server in the same pool.

FIGURE 13.9
User experience mid-call with a Front End failure

INDIVIDUAL SERVER FAILURE: MEDIATION SERVER

The loss of a Mediation server is very similar to the loss of a Front End server unless the Mediation server is performing media transcoding for a call, in which case the call will be dropped.

The call flow is as shown in Figure 13.8, and the user experience is as shown in Figure 13.9, with the exception that the client will remain signed in.

Once the Mediation server is in a failed state, the routing processes on the Front End servers are notified of the downed Mediation server and will route any calls being placed to other suitable Mediation servers.

For incoming calls, the gateway will be aware of the failure (because of the failed heartbeat SIP Options message exchange) and will redirect calls to another Mediation server.

INDIVIDUAL SERVER FAILURE: BACK END

Lync Server 2010 and previous version of OCS, as well as LCS, all relied upon SQL clustering to provide high availability for the pool, and in the early versions this included high availability for user login capability.

As mentioned previously, SQL clustering is no longer supported with Lync Server 2013; instead (some would say at long last), SQL mirroring is now the only supported topology. The changes to how the Front Ends store and replicate data has meant there is less reliance upon the Back End databases being available and up-to-date; this in turn means the bottleneck that was SQL has been effectively removed, and any SQL data writing is under a "lazy write" approach (similar to how Exchange has been for several versions) in that the data is written when the system has the resources to do so rather than how it was previously when the data had highest priority and *must* be written first; this has been simplified slightly as the detail is beyond the scope of this book.

Figure 13.10 shows the high-level architecture within SQL mirroring.

FIGURE 13.10
SQL Server mirroring architecture

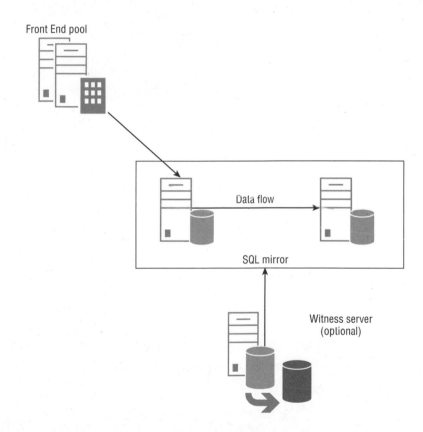

The *Witness server* is a SQL server that can be thought of as providing a quorum to the SQL mirror. It is stated as optional, and the difference is that if it is present, the failover is automatic, and if it is not present, the failover must be manually invoked.

It should be noted, from a pure voice perspective only, there is no impact to the users' capability to make and receive voice calls if a single Back End server is lost, or indeed the whole Back End "pool."

MULTIPLE SERVER FAILURE: COMPLETE POOL

With versions of OCS and LCS, when a user's complete pool failed, the user would be logged out and unable to carry out any tasks. A call in progress at this point would continue to operate with no signaling functionality available—assuming you're using Office Communications Server 2007 R2 rather than Office Communications Server 2007 (where it would be dropped).

Lync Server 2010 introduced the concept of a *backup* registrar; this is where the client will connect in the event of a failure in its primary registrar. A primary registrar failure comprises all the servers in the pool failing.

There are a few items that must be configured to achieve this. First, the topology of a pool must be configured (and published) to have a backup registrar assigned (shown in Figure 13.11). Associated with this configuration are some time-out values:

♦ Failover time-out (default 300 seconds)

♦ Failback time-out (default 600 seconds)

FIGURE 13.11
Configuring a backup registrar

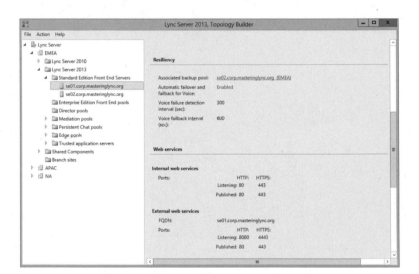

These default values are deliberately set slightly high to ensure that simple "blips" on the network do not cause all the clients to fail over to another pool and back again in quick succession.

Next, you are required to configure the DNS SRV record for automatic login to have multiple entries, possibly with different priorities (this will depend on the environment). If you are using a Director in the environment, this will have the highest priority for the SRV record, with the primary pool being next. The highest priority record is the one that all clients will attempt to connect to first. This setting is more important in a widely distributed deployment; you may not want European clients attempting to connect to a North American-based pool for their first attempt, even though the traffic is quite a small SIP request.

The use of multiple entries for the same SRV record ensures that if the first record directs to a pool that is unavailable, the client will try the next and so on until it finds an available pool to which to connect. Once connected, this pool will redirect to the correct pool (either primary or backup) if online.

The `SIP REGISTER` redirect request for the initial login will include a response like this:

```
07/09/2013|21:19:05.180 4D4:6F8 INFO  :: SIP/2.0 301 Redirect request to Home
Server
Contact: <sip:se01.corp.masteringlync.org:5061;transport=TLS>;q=0.7
Contact: <sip:eepool.corp.masteringlync.org:5061;transport=TLS>;q=0.3
```

This means that the client will attempt to register with the primary pool first, indicated by the q=0.7, and if that is unavailable will fail over to the pool indicated by the backup registrar, indicated by the q=0.3.

When the primary registrar has failed and the client has connected to the backup registrar, all functionality should continue to operate as normal.

However, if the client is connected to a Survivable Branch Appliance (SBA) or Survivable Branch Server (SBS) and if the primary pool fails, not all functionality will be available. Some of the built-in functionality is specific to a pool, such as the following:

◆   Response Groups

◆   Call Park

◆   Conferencing

◆   Buddy List

◆   Presence-based Routing (such as Do Not Disturb)

In this case the client goes into *Survivable* mode and displays a warning message to the user (see Figure 13.12). When the primary pool (SBA/SBS) comes back online, the client will automatically fail back; however, that does not happen immediately because it's based on the failback time-out value.

In summary, once the backup registrar is configured, in the event of failure of the primary pool, the client will automatically connect to the backup pool. If the primary registrar is a SBA or SBS, the client will continue in Survivable mode until the primary pool comes back online. In Survivable mode, the client will continue to be able to make and receive PSTN calls but will have limited pool functionality.

GEOGRAPHICAL POOL FAILURE

The primary and backup registrar functionality will work over a global network, but for the PSTN calling feature to be still available, the telephony capability must also be available globally. For example, a US-based pool could have its backup provided by a pool in Europe, but the users would still have a United States phone number. Although Lync Server 2013 fully supports this, the telecom provider must also support rerouting the calls globally in the event of failure.

Pools of the same type should be paired with each other: Enterprise Edition with another Enterprise Edition and Standard Edition with Standard Edition.

FIGURE 13.12
Client Survivable
mode

While failover is available in both Standard Edition and Enterprise Edition, automatic failover is available when using SQL Server mirroring and a Witness server; this is considered high availability. Using Standard Edition requires manual intervention to achieve failover, and therefore it's not classed as high availability.

There is no topology check to this effect, so it is technically possible to pair Enterprise Edition with Standard Edition (and vice versa), but it's not recommended. Scaling is a major concern when trying to match up pools of different types, as is the automatic failover capability.

The Survivable Branch Appliance (SBA) is a combination *primary* registrar (only), Mediation server, and gateway, and it works in conjunction with a pool. A Survivable Branch Server (SBS) is a combination *primary* registrar (only) and Mediation server; there is no gateway.

If a pool failure occurs in this scenario, even though the client is still connected to a *primary* registrar, it will go into Survivable mode as its connection to the main pool is lost.

MULTIPLE SERVER FAILURE: COMPLETE DATA CENTER

Now that you've considered the complete pool failure in the previous section, what about the next level up—the significant event of a loss of a data center?

Well, in many cases this is simply the same as the loss of a pool; there is a second data center with its pool configured as the backup registrar, and there are additional roles such as the Mediation server and gateways in this data center. In fact, this may be an active data center with the users split between both data centers, or it could be a standby ready and waiting for the disaster to happen. In this case, to be supported it must be active but with no users homed on it. Microsoft does not support having this as a "cold standby" pool.

The Metropolitan pool approach, where a single pool is *stretched* between both data centers, is not supported with Lync Server 2013. This was possible with Lync Server 2010 and required the data centers to be well connected and have a network latency of less than 20 milliseconds (ms); this requirement allows the SQL cluster (with synchronous data replication) to support the pool Back End database, which requires a stretched layer 2 VLAN to operate. As mentioned, SQL clustering itself is not supported with Lync Server 2013; the only supported approach to SQL high availability is SQL mirroring.

Using Lync Server 2013 and SQL mirroring for the database Back End as well as Distributed File System (DFS) for the file share provides a multi-data-center high availability approach. The architecture is as shown in Figure 13.13.

FIGURE 13.13
Cross data center architecture

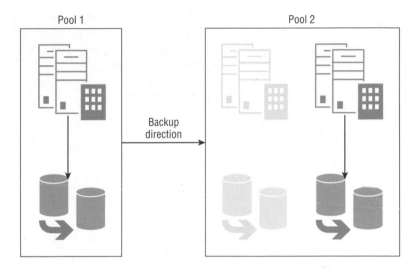

Pool 1 and Pool 2 are both live pools hosting users (although one could be empty if needed, but it must be on), and Figure 13.13 shows Pool 2 acting as a backup for Pool 1. In Figure 13.13, we've shown only one direction for clarity, however, they will back up each other.

Pool 2 holds a copy of the Pool 1 data (via replication through the fileshare) and is sized ready to take the load of the additional users if required.

Notice that the Front End servers are shown not connected to the database for the Pool 1 data. In reality, the Front End servers are active (taking the Pool 2 load); however, the Pool 1 database can be considered disconnected until a failure occurs.

Moving to a "replicate everywhere" type of model ensures that even when a full data center failure occurs, the users will continue to operate as if nothing has happened. In some cases, the users may be logged out but will log back in to the backup pool automatically. For a brief period some users may be in *Survivable* mode.

In an approach similar to that of a complete pool failure, users associated with a SBS/SBS for their *primary* registrar will fall into *Survivable* mode if their data center has failed.

When sizing this environment, it is important to size for the worst-case scenario—data center failure. Therefore, each data center should be sized to cope with a 100 percent load, which will significantly increase the number of servers required.

A complete data center failure introduces another concern for high availability: simple URLs. What do we do if the target FQDNs for the simple URLs are unavailable? Unfortunately, there isn't a simple answer to this, and it is almost always reliant on how DNS is implemented and managed in the environment.

One option is to *scope* simple URLs to each site. This introduces additional overhead in management but targets each site of users to a specific pool, and therefore a single data center will not impact the global deployment.

The second option is to implement some geographical DNS capability that will provide monitoring of the simple URLs to ensure their availability and return to clients the preferred DNS result based on availability; that is, the primary pool URL when the service is running, and the secondary pool URL when the primary is having an issue. The web services themselves will allow for redirection to the correct conference location in the event of an issue, and importantly, users will not be impacted.

A third option would be to manually control the DNS entries and update them in the event of a failure. This obviously introduces the manual overhead aspects but also requires DNS time to live (TTL) values to be set quite low, in turn adding overhead to the network in the form of additional DNS requests because clients will time out their DNS cache quicker.

REMOTE SITE: WAN FAILURE

The last few sections looked primarily at the data center and considered failures to individual servers and the complete data center. But what happens to those branch offices in the event of a network failure? Is there a solution for them? Well, as you've already seen, the Survivable Branch Appliance (SBA) has been designed to handle this scenario. Specifically, the SBA is designed for offices with between 25 and 1,000 users; different hardware versions of the SBA can handle different-sized workloads. The SBA, as its name implies, is an appliance device. The Lync Server 2013 aspects are centrally configured and will replicate to it when installed.

So what is an SBA? It's a hardened version of Windows Server 2008 R2, with only the registrar and mediation services installed from Lync Server 2013. Once joined to a domain and initialized, the Lync Server 2013 installation will replicate the configuration from the Central Management Store. Then the device will become an active part of the topology and will be able to host users. The SBA is configured through Topology Builder as part of the Branch Sites settings, as shown in Figure 13.14. Notice that the Resiliency options are configured by default for an SBA.

In addition to the Windows Server 2008 R2 and Lync Server 2013 installations, the SBA also includes a media gateway device; this is what will vary in size or type depending on number of users to be supported.

Users register in the same way with an SBA as they would with a pool; however, they are automatically associated with a backup pool as part of the SBA configuration. The SBA does not provide user services (conferencing and buddy list) capability, so the clients associate with the SBA for registration but continue to use the pool for conferencing and buddy lists.

In the event of an outage to the WAN (or the data center), the SBA will be unaffected because the client will go into Survivable mode and local PSTN calling will continue to operate (via the built-in media gateway).

Some customers will provide DHCP and DNS information from the data center, so a WAN outage will also affect these. To accommodate this scenario, the SBA can be configured to provide DHCP information to allow the clients to connect. This is not a full DHCP server; it will not provide IP address information, only DHCP option 43 (pool provisioning URL) and option 120 (SIP registrar), which would enable a client to connect in Survivable mode.

FIGURE 13.14
Configuring an SBA

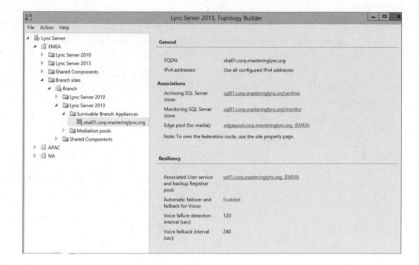

In the event of the pool failing, there is no additional failover capability provided to the users on an SBA; they are already connected to their *primary* registrar, and while users whose primary registrar is the pool itself will fail over to the backup pool for all modalities, the users hosted on the SBA will not be able to leverage the backup pool for conference capability.

Why would an organization deploy an SBA rather than a Standard Edition server? Well, really this comes down to the number of users at a location and cost. The SBA is expected to be cheaper to purchase and maintain than a full-blown server (even though to provide PSTN integration you would still need a gateway to purchase, configure, and deploy). Conferencing is also a consideration—should each branch host its own conferencing services? Will they all need high availability for this? If so, it may make more sense to centralize and provide that to everyone.

It is also possible to deploy a server-only version of the SBA. This is called the Survivable Branch Server (SBS) and will scale up to 2,500 users (similar to the Standard Edition server), but it only provides the functionality of the SBA (registration and mediation); a stand-alone media gateway is required to provide PSTN connectivity. This option may be suitable for customers who already have a number of gateways deployed as part of an OCS 2007 deployment (some gateways will need only a firmware update to be certified for Lync Server 2013).

ACTIVE DIRECTORY FAILURE

What happens if the previous section's WAN outage also removes your access to Active Directory? Perhaps you centralized the domain controllers, and while users can log on to their client PCs, how do they authenticate with Lync Server 2013? What about Lync Server 2013 Phone Edition? It doesn't have cached credentials, so how will users log in using it?

After being used to an "always on" telephony system for decades, the last thing users want is to lose access simply because they can't log in—especially if they can log into their computers. Well, unsurprisingly, Lync Server 2013 has a solution for this—a certificate-based login.

The first login attempt from a client will use NTLM (default) or Kerberos protocols to log in. and for this to be successful, you need Active Directory to be available. However, as part of this login process, the client will receive a Lync Server 2013 certificate and can present this certificate for any future login, bypassing the need to use Active Directory then.

It is important to understand that this certificate is available only for client-based authentication against the Front End server where the client is homed (not the pool). It cannot be used for any other purpose and is signed only by the Front End server.

This certificate is stored in the local user Certificate Store (see Figure 13.15) and by default is valid for 180 days. The validity period can be changed only by using the following PowerShell command:

```
Set-CsWebServiceConfiguration -DefaultValidityPeriodHours 4320
```

FIGURE 13.15
Certificate used for certificate-based authentication

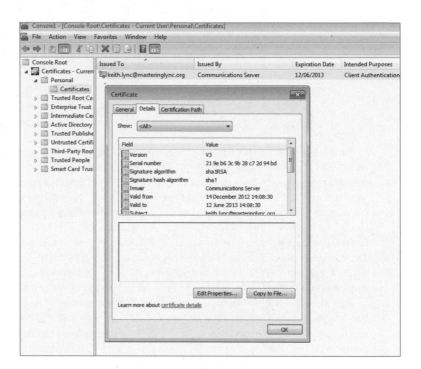

The value 4320 is the number of hours for which the certificate is valid; in this case, the default 4320 is equal to 180 days.

No additional PKI infrastructure is required for this functionality to operate. Figure 13.16 shows the login process for a client. Note that the Active Directory connections occur only on the first login for a particular client (not user).

Now that the client is logged in, the next thing to do is enable and configure the Enterprise Voice capability.

FIGURE 13.16
The client login process

DNS

Active Directory

DNS query/response

1st login – authenticate with AD
1st login – return authentication

Lync client

SIP register

Redirect to certificate provisioning

Https://<pool FQDN>/CertSvc

Download certificate

SIP register

Login succeed

Pool 1

Configuring Enterprise Voice

The configuration of Enterprise Voice is best approached in two distinct parts:

Client   This includes items such as the Address Book generation, dial plan creation, number normalization, and specific feature enablement (such as Call Forward) in the voice policy.

Server   Here you'll specifically look at the routing aspect of Enterprise Voice and how to configure and control it.

Once these two aspects have been defined, the user must be enabled for Enterprise Voice and should have a phone number assigned to them. If a phone number is not assigned, it is possible for the user to make PSTN calls but not receive them. Once enabled, the user will be assigned to a dial plan and a voice policy, and by default this would be the global dial plan and the global voice policy; however, an administrator would likely apply a specific dial plan and voice policy.

Configuring the Client Enterprise Voice Options

The Lync client is the interface between users and the back end of the system. As such, it is needed to translate what the user inputs to what the system expects. Not only that, but it needs to do that seamlessly to the user—without prompting!

The client also needs to adapt to the user's location if some specific configuration is required that may differ from location to location. A good example of this is emergency dialing; a US user who is traveling to Europe may dial 911 to access the emergency services, not knowing that the emergency services number is different in Europe (and indeed from one country to the next).

CONFIGURING NUMBER NORMALIZATION

Normalization means adapting the various internal, local, national, or regional phone number formats into a universal standard format. Although Lync Server 2013 can work without normalizing numbers, it is recommended (and much easier) if all numbers are normalized to E.164 format, a global standard that defines the format of telephone numbers and guarantees uniqueness globally. It is defined as such:

Country code = 1, 2, or 3 digits

Nationally significant number = 15 − length(country code digits)

The result is a maximum length of 15 digits, which in addition is prefixed with a + character, as shown in this example:

+15550123456

The United States country code is one digit (1), followed by the nationally significant area code and local number, with no spaces or other characters. A common misconception is that simply adding the + to the start of a number will make it E.164 compliant; this is not the case.

If all numbers were presented in E.164 format, Lync Server 2013 would have no issue, but this is not the case. Many numbers are stored without country codes, or only the internal extension may be stored, for example. In addition, this storage can be anywhere—Active Directory, local contacts, web pages, and so on.

To make this understandable and routable, Lync Server 2013 allows you to configure a set of rules that will manipulate the number entered and output as an E.164 format number. This number can then be presented to a gateway or PBX for further routing if required.

Number normalization is configured as part of the dial plan: users are assigned to a dial plan when enabled for Enterprise Voice (a user may be in only a single dial plan at any time).

A sample dial plan is shown in Figure 13.17; it has the following configuration items:

FIGURE 13.17
Configuring a sample dial plan

◆ **Name:** The name of the dial plan, used to reference the dial plan in policies.

◆ **Simple Name:** Used to match against Exchange Unified Messaging dial plans (versions prior to Exchange 2010 SP1 required the dial plans to match by name).

◆ **Description:** Description of the dial plan, used only for additional notes for the administrator

◆ **Dial-In Conferencing Region:** Creates an association with dial-in access numbers.

◆ **External Access Prefix:** Allows numbers to be dialed by users without an external access prefix. Completing this field will automatically add the prefix if listed

◆ **Associated Normalization Rules:** shows the list of normalization rules associated with the dial plan.

The command to create a dial plan from PowerShell looks like this:

```
New-Csdialplan -identity "LyncEnterpriseVoice" -description "default dial plan
for all users" -dialinconferencingregion "Birmingham" -ExternalAccessprefix 9
-simplename "LyncEnterpriseVoice"
```

Normalization rules are created using regular expressions (regex), and administrators already familiar with using regex will find this method quite easy. But if you are new to regex, you don't need to worry. Lync Server has improved significantly over Office Communications Server 2007 in this, and it provides a basic input system that will build the regex for you (see Figure 13.18). For detailed information on regex, see Chapter 8, "Introduction to PowerShell, the Lync Management Shell, and Regular Expressions."

FIGURE 13.18
Configuring a new normalization rule

Here you build out the following information for each rule:

◆ Name

◆ Description

◆ Starting digits

◆ Length

◆ Digits to remove

◆ Digits to add

Here's an example. In the United Kingdom, it is still very common to dial local numbers from a landline, so if someone is located in Birmingham (U.K.), where the national area code is 0121, they can dial the following Birmingham number in several different ways:

Birmingham Central Library: 0121 303 4511

Local dialing (from within the Birmingham area): 303 4511

National dialing (from within the U.K.): 0121 303 4511

International dialing (from outside the U.K.): +44121 303 4511.

In the case of international dialing from outside the U.K., the + symbol is introduced; this represents the international dialing access code. In the U.S., this will be 011. In France, it will be 00.

Configuring Lync Server 2013 to accommodate each of these formats allows users to continue to use their current (known) method to access numbers and reduces the extent of change they need to adjust to when using Lync 2013 (the less change for users, the more likely they are to accept it).

You can also create normalization rules using the `New-CsVoiceNormalizationRule` cmdlet, as in the following example:

```
New-csvoicenormalizationrule  -identity
"tag:LyncEnterpriseVoice/Prefix Local call without external prefix"
-Description "Local call without external line prefix"
-Pattern "^(\d{8})$" -translation "+44121$1"
```

So, let's take each of these formats and create a normalization rule to get to our target E.164 format.

Local Dialing

Here the input is seven digits and the output is going to include the +44121 prefix.

You will need the following information:

Starting digits: N/A

Length: Exactly 7

Digits to remove: N/A

Digits to add: +44121

Once you have added this information, scroll to the bottom of the tab. The pattern to match and translation rule will already be created for you (as shown in Figure 13.19).

FIGURE 13.19
Automatic regex
creation

National Dialing

Here your input is 10 digits and the output is going to include the +44 aspect.

So you need the following information:

Starting digits: 0

Length: Exactly 10

Digits to remove: 1

Digits to add: +44

With this combination of data, the pattern to match and the translation rule will be as follows:

Pattern to match: ^0(\d{9})$

Translation rule: +44$1

International Dialing

The dial plan is U.K. focused, so you probably won't be dialing the +44 aspect of a U.K. number; however, you might use the Click-To-Call functionality, which could already have the U.K. number defined. Here your input is not necessarily a defined length and the output is going to add only the +.

So you need the following information:

Starting digits: 001

Length: At Least 11

Digits to remove: 3

Digits to add: +

With this combination of data, the pattern to match and the translation rule will be as follows:

Pattern to Match: ^001(\d{7}\d+)$

Translation Rule: +$1

Internal Dialing

Of course, all of this is dealing with external number dialing, but what about calling other Lync users or internal PBX users? Well, assuming you have a four-digit extension range, you will need to normalize these numbers to E.164 too. The first thing Lync Server 2013 will do is attempt a reverse number lookup on the phone entered number to try to find a matching user—and because all of the TelUri information is expected to be in E.164 format, that is what you need to resolve to.

For this, you need to enter the following data:

Starting digits: N/A

Length: Exactly 4

Digits to remove: N/A

Digits to add: +44121555

With this combination of data, the pattern to match and the translation rule will be as follows:

Pattern to Match: ^(\d{4})$

Translation Rule: +44121555$1

ENABLING ADDRESS BOOK GENERATION

Once you have configured all the required normalization rules within the dial plan, you need to configure the Address Book in a similar fashion. The difference is that these rules will be used to map the entries from Active Directory into the E.164 format you need.

In an ideal world, Active Directory would be populated with E.164 format, and you would not have to do this at all, or a common format would already be applied to all the phone number entries, allowing you to keep the number of Address Book rules required to a minimum. Rarely is this the case, which results in a large number of normalization rules also being required for the Address Book generation.

These rules are stored in a file called Company_PhoneNumber_Normalization_Rules.txt, and this must be stored in the following directory:

```
\\<Lync file share>\<Server-id>\ABFiles\
```

Because one Address Book is generated per pool, this file must be duplicated for each pool too; it is important that when multiple Address Book files are in use, they are kept in sync. This unfortunately is a manual process.

This file is simply a text file and includes each of the normalization and translation rules on a separate line, as shown here:

```
^0(\d{9})$
+44$1
^001(\d{7}\d+)$
+$1
^(\d{4})$
+44121555$1
```

By default, the Address Book is generated daily at 1:30 a.m.; this can be changed by using the following PowerShell command:

```
Set-CsAddressBookConfiguration -RunTimeOfDay 01:30
```

If the Address Book needs to be updated immediately, the Update-CsAddressBook cmdlet is used (no parameters are required). It will take a few minutes to regenerate the Address Book. Clients will check for a new Address Book file only once every 24 hours.

 Real World Scenario

CORRECTING ACTIVE DIRECTORY DATA

When new Address Book data is generated, an output file listing all the incorrectly formatted phone number data can be generated too.

The error file can be found in the following location:

```
\\<Lync file share>\<server-id>\ABFiles\00000000-0000-0000-0000-000000000000\
00000000-0000-0000-0000-000000000000
```

and is called Invalid_AD_Phone_Numbers.txt.

The folder location shown is actually a GUID. If you are using Address Book segregation (see below), you will see differing values replacing the folder names (00000000-0000-0000-0000-000000000000) shown. The folder name will match the GUID used to group the users into an address book and each folder will have an `Invalid_AD_Phone_Numbers.txt` file.

From this error file, you can determine the accounts remaining in Active Directory that do not have a corresponding normalization rule associated and take one of the following appropriate actions:

◆ Correct the specific user account information in Active Directory.

◆ Create a new normalization rule to account for the number format.

ADDRESS BOOK SEPARATION

Some organizations may wish to provide separate address books for users as a way to segregate organizations or departments.

This can be achieved by allocating globally unique identifiers (GUIDs) to users under the `msRTCSIP-GroupingID` attribute, as shown here.

Users with a common value of this attribute will share an address book, and it's worth noting that users can only be in (and search) a single address book.

By default, all users and contacts created use the default GUID 00000000-0000-0000-0000-000000000000; however, assigning another (common) GUID to a group of users will create an additional address book. The default address book is located in the following location:

```
\\<Lync file share>\<server-id>\ABFiles\00000000-0000-0000-0000-000000000000\
00000000-0000-0000-0000-000000000000
```

And any additional address books will be created in a similar fashion. Specific folder IDs will be dependent upon the GUID used.

VOICE POLICY

Where the dial plan determines the rules used for each user to provide the number normalization capability, the Voice policy determines the features available to a user:

- Enable Call Forwarding

- Enable Delegation

- Enable Call Transfer

- Enable Call Park

- Enable Simultaneous Ringing Of Phones

- Enable Team Call

- Enable PSTN Reroute

- Enable Bandwidth Policy Override

- Enable Malicious Call Tracing

The Voice policy is also used to determine the PSTN usages assigned to a user. This can be considered similar to class of service in the legacy telephony world or, equally accurately, the type of call (such as local, national, or international) that the user is permitted to make.

Figure 13.20 shows the Voice policy creation screen.

FIGURE 13.20
Creating a new
Voice policy

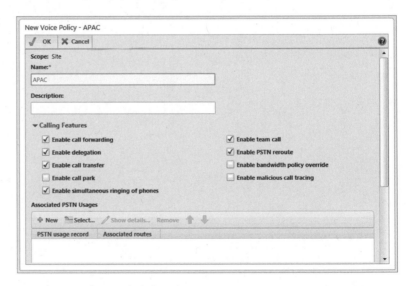

The following sample PowerShell command creates a Voice policy and associates it with some predefined PSTN usages; you'll see them in a later section:

```
New-CsVoicePolicy -Identity "standard" -AllowCallForwarding $true
-AllowSimulRing $true -Description "Default policy for all users"
-EnableCallPark $false -EnableCallTransfer $true
```

```
-EnableDelegation $false -EnableMaliciousCallTracing $true
-EnableTeamCall $true -Name "Standard" -PstnUsages
@{add="Internal", "Local", "National", "Mobile", "Emergency"}
```

A new capability within Lync Server 2013 is to be able to provide a different set of policies to deal with call forwarding and simultaneous ringing. This could be configured to allow users to only forward calls internally, or perhaps a user who can place calls internationally is restricted to only forwarding calls nationally (stopping potential toll fraud by forwarding calls to his great-aunt in Australia!).

Figure 13.21 shows the addition section of the Voice Policy window, with the options available; the PSTN usage table here is for the specific alternative PSTN usages if selected.

FIGURE 13.21
Alternative PSTN usage configuration for call forwarding and simultaneous ringing

Configuring the Server Enterprise Voice Options

Now that you have configured the user-side information, you need to configure the server side to route the call to the correct gateway as well as ensure that you have the correct permissions (PSTN usages) to place the call.

ROUTING

Because the server is expecting a normalized (E.164) number, basing the routing on E.164 numbering is the recommended approach to routing the call.

A global enterprise is likely to have at least one gateway in each country where an office is located. This provides the potential savings of least cost routing (LCR), where the call is routed internally across the company WAN to the in-country gateway; by contrast, in a traditional PBX the call would be long distance (or international) rate.

The definition of a route is similar to that of a dial plan; you need to define it using the regex notation shown earlier, although for this example you'll simply use the starting digits.

For instance, to define a route for calls to the United Kingdom (country code 44), you would use the following regex: \+44.

Notice that you do not define the number of digits, simply the starting digits of the normalized number. The more specific the definition (the more digits provided), the more granular the control over the target gateway you can have. For example, if you have multiple offices in the

United Kingdom, with a gateway in each office, you could use the following regex to specify regional dialing capability: \+44161 (Manchester), \+44121 (Birmingham), and so on.

Using the Control Panel to define the routing information is shown in Figure 13.22 (you need to scroll down to see the PSTN Usage section).

FIGURE 13.22

Creating a route with Control Panel

The equivalent PowerShell is as follows:

```
Set-CsVoiceRoute -Identity "LocalRoute"
-Description "local number routes"
-NumberPattern "^(\+44121{7})$"
-PstnUsages @{add="Local"} -PstnGatewayList
@{add="pstngateway:10.0.0.1", "pstngateway:10.0.0.2"}
```

PSTN USAGES

By defining the routes and associated PSTN usages, you tie the calling capability of the user to the permissions of the routes. When a user logs in successfully, the Voice policy is applied (containing the user-permitted routes), and when a PSTN call is placed, a check is performed against the matching routes to compare these against the permissions (PSTN usages) allowed.

An easy way to think of this is that it's the same way permissions to files are granted:

◆ Create a group (PSTN Usage).

◆ Assign the group to the file/folder (Route).

◆ Add the user to the group (Voice Policy).

TESTING CALL PATTERNS

Once the client and server configuration are defined, you need to be sure they work as expected. One option would be to apply the policy to a test account and confirm the operation; however, in a large environment, this is impractical. The solution to this is the Test Voice Routing option in the Voice section of the Control Panel.

Here you can provide the number dialed as well as the expected results when you run the test. Once the details are entered, you can save the option to run again in the future. This is where the benefits of scale come into play; once the numbers are saved, you can quickly rerun the tests anytime the environment is changed, ensuring that any changes work as expected prior to deploying to users.

Figure 13.23 shows a test case being defined.

FIGURE 13.23
Creating a voice test case

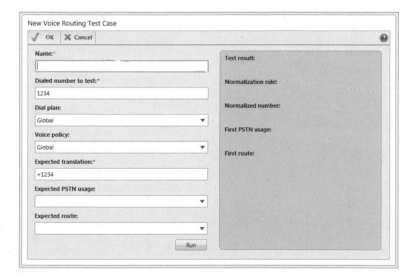

The Bottom Line

Understand the voice capabilities. Lync Server 2013 has dramatically expanded the capabilities provided by Microsoft in the Unified Communications space to be almost on a par with enterprise PBXs (and certainly equal to, if not better than, departmental PBX offerings).

Master It Describe the benefits of media bypass.

Understand the voice architecture.   With the introduction of media bypass and the support for virtualization, the architectural requirements to deploy voice have been consolidated into a smaller server footprint, and at the same time additional functionality has been included in the product. Significant investment has been made in the high availability and resiliency deployment models.

Master It   Describe the user experience when the user's home pool fails and only a backup registrar has been configured.

Configure voice policies and routing.   Aside from the architectural requirements, to enable Enterprise Voice requires configuration to be applied to users (policies) and Back End configuration to be applied to the servers (routing).

Master It   What configuration joins the user configuration to the server configuration and provides the permissions to enable (or block) a call?

Chapter 14

Call Admission Control

In the early days of OCS 2007, Microsoft made a big deal about how the codecs used were dynamic and could adapt to your network. A lot of people misinterpreted this to mean that you could simply install OCS 2007 and it would work, no matter how congested your network already was! As you know, introducing a new application onto a network also introduces network traffic. If your network is already saturated, introducing more traffic will only make matters worse, resulting in a poor user experience.

Lync Server 2010 provided an easy way to control the amount (and type) of traffic between users, allowing better understanding of the impact of this new application. If you are familiar with the implementation and management of Call Admission Control in Lync Server 2010, then you can skip this chapter because nothing has changed with the Lync Server 2013 implementation.

In this chapter, you will learn to:

- Identify Call Admission Control–capable endpoints
- Configure policy-based Quality of Service controls
- Design a Call Admission Control solution
- Configure Call Admission Control

Understanding Call Admission Control

In the legacy telephony world, Call Admission Control (CAC) was inherent in the infrastructure and not something that overly concerned people. Bandwidth was defined in *trunks* and *lines*. If you tried to make a call and there wasn't enough *bandwidth,* you would receive a *busy* tone because the system would be unable to route your call to the destination because it had no available capacity. Typically, you tried again sometime later. Advancements in PBX technology introduced a monitoring concept (*ring back*) that allowed the system to call you and connect your call when enough bandwidth was available.

The introduction of Voice over IP (VoIP) systems enabled these typically fixed-capacity trunks to become network links, which were much easier to change in size and therefore capacity. In addition, voice traffic could be routed across traditional network links, providing a potential cost saving to business by combining both voice and data links. In taking this approach, bandwidth control has become problematic. First, how do you ensure that there is enough bandwidth to cope with the calls that you want to allow? Second, how do you ensure that this traffic on a shared link does not impact other data traffic?

The early VoIP systems used a fixed-size codec, thereby ensuring that the required capacity per call was a known value (the number of concurrent calls times the codec size equals the required capacity). Then, however, Office Communication Server 2007 introduced RTAudio (see Chapter 2, "Standards and Protocols," for details), which added the complexity of a codec that changes dynamically (based on the network conditions) and attempts to calculate the bandwidth required.

You still know the number of concurrent calls; however, now you can't determine how much bandwidth is required per call, so you can't predict how much bandwidth is required. This can lead to unhappy users if the network is underprovisioned because the dynamic nature will reduce the quality of the call to ensure that all the calls can be completed.

Assuming the network link shown in the top half of Figure 14.1 is already saturated with calls, the impact of adding an additional call can be seen in the lower half of Figure 14.1.

FIGURE 14.1
A network link at capacity (a); a network link over capacity, with a fixed-rate codec (b)

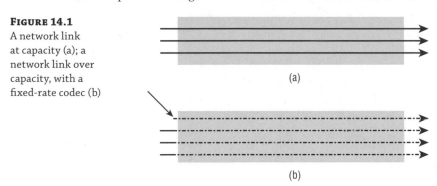

You can see that an additional call from a nondynamic codec will impact all other calls on the link. Because these are fixed-bandwidth calls, the only option is for some packets to be lost or delayed. The result is that all users will suffer a loss of quality.

On the other hand, using a dynamic codec would allow the situation shown in Figure 14.2. The calls in place (as well as the new one) would adapt and potentially use a lower-quality codec, but this means there would be no packet loss and, in many cases, no noticeable impact to users. Figure 14.2 shows all calls being impacted equally, but more likely only a few would be impacted.

FIGURE 14.2
A network link over capacity with a dynamic-rate codec

Having dynamic codecs does have a downside. Another call introduced would reduce the existing call quality again, as would another and another and another. Eventually, all calls would be operating at such low quality they would be either unintelligible or dropped. A dropped call would allow some "breathing space," but the cycle would continue. It is almost impossible to plan for or control.

With OCS and OCS R2, only three workarounds were available:

MaxAudioVideoBandwidth Registry Key   By setting this value, an administrator could determine the maximum bandwidth combined for audio and video; in most cases where this has been set, it results in video being unavailable. Because you don't have the capability to set the minimum value required, you can still continue to add calls to the network; all you are doing is restricting the maximum used by OCS.

Disable Video   By disabling the video capability, you reduce the functionality of the product; however, the benefit is that significant bandwidth is not being used for video and is available for use by audio or other applications.

Enable Diffserv   By enabling QoS on the network, you can provide a guaranteed bandwidth to OCS and in return provide a guaranteed bandwidth available to other applications.

None of these workarounds provide the capability to manage at the application (Lync) layer; typically, the results are the same as if the values were not enabled and the codec left to dynamically adjust.

Something had to be done to allow a business to accurately size the network and provision the correct amount of bandwidth for the number (and quality) of calls permitted on the network.

This something is Call Admission Control (CAC), which can be enabled as part of a Lync deployment with no extra hardware requirements (it is part of the front-end services) and requires no specific network hardware because it interacts at the application layer.

How Call Admission Control Works

The aim of Call Admission Control is to provide a guaranteed quality (user experience) for calls placed on the network. From a user perspective, a rejected call (clicking on the brief explanation will provide more detailed information), as shown in Figure 14.3, is usually a better experience than a call connected but of extremely low quality. From an admin perspective, CAC introduces a way to allow the network to be accurately architected and protected against unexpected spikes in call volumes.

FIGURE 14.3
A rejected call notification due to insufficient bandwidth

Lync configuration includes the definition of the network and details for the number of calls and quality permitted for each leg of the network. We'll implement this configuration later.

Each pool will replicate the number of current calls in place on the network; when a new call is attempted, a query is made to establish if enough bandwidth is available to handle another call and how much bandwidth is permitted for each modality use.

Within this query, the Lync client will provide the Policy Decision Point (PDP) with its IP address along with the IP address of the calling party client. From these two pieces of information, the PDP can determine the route and establish the current usage on that route.

IS LYNC INTEGRATED WITH THE NETWORK?

Lync's Call Admission Control operates purely at the application layer, so it is not integrated with the network. There are no ties to the underlying network infrastructure to reserve the bandwidth or ensure that it is actually available to handle the call.

The result of the query is one of the following:

Permitted   The call may be placed.

Rejected   The call may not be placed.

Rerouted   The call must take another route, which may be via Edge servers or via the PSTN.

For call rerouting, both modalities are handled together; therefore, it is not possible for the video portion of an audio and video call to be rerouted via the Edge servers and the audio portion to continue across the WAN, or even via the PSTN. If the call cannot be routed via the Edge servers, the video modality will be dropped and, assuming the user is permitted to make a PSTN call, the call will be attempted via a PSTN gateway.

As you can see in Figure 14.4, to enable routing via the Internet, you must make sure each pool (not shown) has an associated Edge server or, to connect via the PSTN, a Mediation server (or in the case of media bypass, a supported gateway).

FIGURE 14.4
Call Admission
Control rerouting

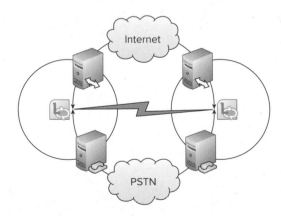

Rerouting is carried out in the following order:

1. Internet

2. PSTN

3. Voice mail (Voice mail routing is not subject to bandwidth controls.)

In Figure 14.5, the calling party will initiate the call. Without the recipient user being aware, the called-party Lync client will receive the request for call signaling and query the Policy Decision Point (PDP) of the site (only a single pool per site runs this process). The PDP will return a response based on the current (real-time) capacity of the link as defined within Lync. As noted, this will be permitted, rejected, or rerouted; based on this response, the calling-party Lync client will take appropriate action.

1. User places the call.

2. Receiving endpoint queries PDP.

3. Decision is made and returned to the called-party client.

4. The client will take appropriate action based on the response.

FIGURE 14.5
Signaling call flow for Call Admission Control, where the called party is local to the pool

In the scenario in Figure 14.6, the user is not in a location that has a pool. The subnet will be defined within Lync, and the client will query back to its home-pool (site) PDP, receiving the same responses as before. The scenario is the same for users who roam from site to site.

EMERGENCY CALL OVERRIDE?

Emergency calls do not override Call Admission Control. CAC is used to guarantee the quality of the calls placed on the network. If there is not enough capacity to accept another call, even if the call is an emergency call, it is not permitted. It would not be a good idea to connect an emergency call if the network is not capable of providing the capacity, because the call quality would most likely be poor. You'll find more details in Chapter 15, "E911 and Location Information Services."

Voice policy can be configured to override Call Admission Control and policies assigned to users or sites. This will allow Call Admission Control to be ignored for users assigned to the policy. Using this option should be an exception rather than the norm because it defeats the purpose of Call Admission Control.

FIGURE 14.6
Signaling call flow
for Call Admission
Control, where the
called party is not
local to the pool

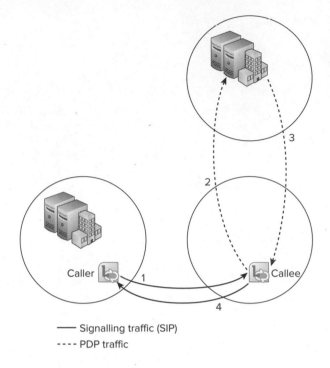

——— Signalling traffic (SIP)
- - - - PDP traffic

Where Call Admission Control Works

The endpoint will always query the pool on which it is associated; there is no requirement for a PDP role to be located in the same site as the endpoint. It is important to note that only one pool per central site should be enabled for Call Admission Control; having multiple pools enabled in the same site will prevent Call Admission Control policies from being applied on calls between some users. If the pool to which the endpoint is associated is not enabled for Call Admission Control, the request is simply proxied to the relevant pool.

The receiving endpoint always makes the query to the PDP, and the calling party never makes it (for reasons which will be explained shortly). Multiple Points of Presence (MPOP) are fully supported with each endpoint carrying out a separate query. This may result in a scenario in which a user is logged in with multiple endpoints and some users being able to receive the call and others not. In this scenario, only the endpoints capable of establishing the call will provide a toast/ringtone, and those not capable of call establishment will not.

If a call cannot be established, there is no indication to the intended recipient of a missed call. The user experience could be affected if someone saw a call attempt but was unable to do anything about it (except possibly start an IM conversation). On the other hand, the calling party will see a notification indicating that network issues are preventing the call from being established or that rerouting may cause a delay in establishing the call.

In Figure 14.7, where the recipient of the call is logged in on multiple devices, it is permissible that some devices will return a positive response, whereas others return negative following the PDP query stage.

FIGURE 14.7
Call Admission
Control in a
multiple-point-of-
presence scenario

—— Signalling traffic (SIP)
- - - - PDP traffic

For example, assume the recipient is logged in via both a desk phone and a laptop, which may be connected via wireless. The administrator has configured Lync to be aware of the wireless subnet and has restricted the number of calls available via the wireless LAN to ensure quality. In this case, the desk phone will return a positive response, and the laptop will return a negative one. As a result, only the desk phone device will ring.

Note that there is no indication of a call on the laptop device. This is to prevent the attempted establishment of a call where the network is not capable of delivering a quality call. If the desk phone is not answered, a single missed call notification will be generated and delivered as normal, or the call will be forwarded to Exchange Unified Messaging if configured.

Only a Lync (2010 or 2013) endpoint is capable of querying for Call Admission Control data, so when it is used in a legacy interoperability scenario, calls to pre-Lync clients (OCS 2007 or OCS 2007 R2) will always succeed. A call from a pre-Lync client to a Lync client will create a PDP query, and the result will obey the conditions imposed by the Call Admission Control policy.

In the case shown in the upper half of Figure 14.8, either endpoint will query the PDP for permission because both are Lync endpoints (an endpoint can be any Lync client or any Lync server role). However, as shown at the bottom of Figure 14.8, the legacy endpoint will not make a query.

When you're planning a migration, this scenario is extremely important to understand. When you're receiving a call on any legacy client, the call will be permitted to be placed, irrespective of policy.

Consider a remote branch office where you want to limit the number of calls being placed across the WAN link to the head office. If you delay the client upgrade at the site, leaving them on a legacy client, then any calls being made *from* the site will be subject to Call Admission Control policy; however, any calls being made *to* the site will not. This could cause potential degradation of calls for all parties using that link.

To ensure that each PDP in each topology site is fully aware of the state of the network—remember, the client will query only its home PDP—each PDP is required to synchronize the data containing its call information. This synchronization occurs via HTTPS.

FIGURE 14.8
Call Admission
Control Query
conditions for Lync
endpoints (top);
for combination or
legacy endpoints
(bottom)

—— Call Admission Control managed connectivity
---- Call Admission Control unmanaged connectivity

Underlying Network Requirements

Although Lync Call Admission Control does not *require* Quality of Service (QoS) to be configured on the network, to ensure that the bandwidth is properly reserved for Lync to manage, we *recommend* that you to apply QoS to the network.

Without QoS in place, you can define the maximum bandwidth used by Lync for each call modality as well as the maximum for the total concurrent calls of each modality. However, by not deploying QoS to guarantee the bandwidth when needed, you are in effect allowing other network traffic to eat into the Lync-defined bandwidth. As a result, the Lync codec will adapt dynamically to this lower bandwidth and likely reduce the quality of the call.

By configuring QoS, you ensure that Lync has the guaranteed bandwidth when needed, and any other network traffic will be required to adapt. This ensures that the quality and quantity of calls is as defined in Call Admission Control and enforced on the network by QoS.

Figure 14.9 shows configuration using only Call Admission Control to manage bandwidth. This will ensure that each individual call session will not increase above a given bandwidth value, shown here to be 40 percent, and subsequently change the codec type in use as well as ensure that the total will not increase above a total value. The other network traffic may increase past the 60 percent nominally allocated because there is no interaction between the network and Lync. If this increase does occur, the Lync traffic will dynamically decrease with a corresponding decrease in quality.

FIGURE 14.9
Impact of
configuring only
Call Admission
Control on the
network

Figure 14.10 shows the same configuration, this time enforced using QoS but with no Call Admission Control in place. In this scenario, you can again ensure that the Lync traffic will not

increase beyond the 40 percent value; however, you have no control over the number of Lync calls that can be placed or the codecs in use. This is the same situation you'll have when using OCS R2.

FIGURE 14.10

Impact of configuring only Quality of Service on the Network

The QoS value can be managed in either direction; assigning 40 percent to Lync will guarantee that 40 percent will be available when Lync needs it, and it will allow increases beyond 40 percent if there is available bandwidth, managing the other data to reduce to below 60 percent when needed.

On the other hand, you can configure the limit to be on the alternative data, ensuring that there is a minimum of 60 percent available for it and forcing Lync to adapt if the other data is deemed more important. To ensure voice quality, the guarantee should be configured on the Lync network traffic.

Figure 14.11 shows the ultimate goal, having both Call Admission Control and QoS complement each other on the network. Call Admission Control provides the application layer control over the network traffic placed on the network, and QoS provides the guarantee that traffic is prioritized when it is on the network.

FIGURE 14.11

Impact of configuring both Call Admission Control and Quality of Service on the network

Finally, Figure 14.12 shows a scenario where Call Admission Control has been configured to allow more calls than the network is capable of handling. Because the PDP is not aware of the underlying network capacity, in this situation calls will be permitted to be set up by Lync and the other calls on the network will be affected immediately. The codec bandwidth will be reduced dynamically, thereby reducing the quality of each call. Needless to say, the rest of the network will be impacted as well. This is not much different from not configuring Call Admission Control at all.

FIGURE 14.12

Impact of over-configuring Call Admission Control on the network

It's worth noting at this point that Call Admission Control works only with IPv4 configurations, not IPv6.

QoS Tagging

By default, Lync will use Differentiated Service Control Point (DSCP) tagging in the headers of the network traffic to allow the underlying network to control and route the traffic based on the configuration required. Table 14.1 shows the default QoS markings for Lync. These values may be changed if required; however, this should only be carried out in conjunction with the network management team of your organization because straying from the defaults could mean significant reconfiguration required on the network devices (switches, routers, firewalls).

TABLE 14.1: Default DSCP marking per modality

Media Type	Per-Hop Behavior	Queuing and Dropping	Notes
Audio	EF	Priority Queue	Low loss, low latency, low jitter, assured bandwidth. Pair with WAN bandwidth policies on constrained links.
Video	AF41	BW Queue + DSCP WRED	Class 4. Low drop priority. Pair with WAN bandwidth policies on constrained links.
SIP signaling	CS3	BW Queue	Class 3. Bandwidth allocation should be sufficient to avoid drops.
App sharing	AF21	BW Queue + DSCP WRED	Class 2. Low drop priority. Pair with end-user policy caps.
File transfer	AF11	BW Queue + DSCP WRED	Class 1. Low drop priority. Pair with end-user policy caps.

The Per Hop Behavior column indicates the DSCP tag applied to the packet (with a value providing further differentiation where listed):

EF: Expedited Forwarding

AF: Assured Forwarding

CS: Class

COMPARING LYNC CALL QUALITY

Before a full rollout of Lync (or any application for that matter), it is normal to pilot the new technology. When a pilot is running, it is extremely important that the same packet marking is used when comparing with another VoIP deployment.

We have had customers report that Lync is performing badly when compared to their existing deployment, and the reason has quite often been traced to the fact that they prioritize the existing VoIP packets.

In addition, the ports used for each modality can be defined both on the server side and the client, allowing control and prioritization of traffic based on port ranges. If the port range approach is taken, you should define the client range as a subset of the server range of ports; this will reduce the quantity of specific network configuration rules required, as in the following example:

Server port range = 50,001–55,000

Client port range = 50,001–50,100

Taking this approach, network administrators can configure the network devices to use the range 50,001 to 55,000 for the prioritizing of audio traffic rather than having to configure two ranges (one for the servers and one for the clients).

Here is a list of the configuration points for the client side, along with an example of port variation allowing for control at the network layer (ClientMediaPort and ClientMediaPortRange are values used by OCS R2 clients):

ClientMediaPortRangeEnabled	True/False
ClientMediaPort	Start port value; e.g., 5,000
ClientMediaPortRange	Number of ports. e.g., 20
ClientAudioPort	Start port value; e.g., 6,000
ClientAudioPortRange	Number of ports; e.g., 20
ClientVideoPort	Start port value; e.g., 7,000
ClientVideoPortRange	Number of ports; e.g., 20
ClientAppSharingPort	Start port value; e.g., 8,000
ClientAppSharingPortRange	Number of ports; e.g., 20
ClientFileTransferPort	Start port value; e.g., 9,000
ClientFileTransferPortRange	Number of ports; e.g., 20
ClientSipDynamicPort	Start port value; e.g., 10,000
ClientSipDynamicPortRange	Number of ports; e.g., 20

HOW MANY PORTS DO I NEED?

Some customers want to restrict the number of ports a client can open. For most users, we recommend that this be no less than 20 ports per modality. The reason for so many is that during call establishment, the ports are negotiated, and there may be several different ways to connect clients (peer to peer, via the Edge, and so on), so multiple ports are required during this phase. Once the call is established, two ports per modality are required. This is explained in detail at

http://technet.microsoft.com/en-us/library/dd572230(office.13).aspx

Although this is an OCS R2 document, the content also holds true for Lync 2013.

Users who handle more calls (such as personal assistants) will need a higher number, based on the number of calls expected.

With operating systems before Windows Vista, potential rogue applications could leverage this port prioritization; however, Vista (and newer OSs) provides policy-based control, allowing the tagging of packets based on the application itself, which reduces the risk of a rogue application introducing prioritized traffic onto the network.

DEFINING A POLICY-BASED CONTROL

Take the following steps to define a policy-based control:

1. In the Group Policy Management Editor, you'll see that the Policy-Based QoS option is available for both Computer Configuration and User Configuration policies. In this example, you'll use a computer-based policy, so click there and select Create New Policy, as shown in Figure 14.13.

FIGURE 14.13
Choosing to create a new QoS policy in the Group Policy Management Editor

2. Complete the configuration options on the Policy-Based QoS screen, shown in Figure 14.14. In addition to naming the policy and defining the bandwidth rate, notice that the

DSCP value is listed as a decimal value; this decodes to the values previously noted, as shown in Table 14.2.

TABLE 14.2: Decoding default DSCP values

PER-HOP BEHAVIOR	DECIMAL VALUE
EF	46
AF41	34
CS3	24
AF21	18
AF11	10

FIGURE 14.14
Entering a QoS policy value and throttle rate

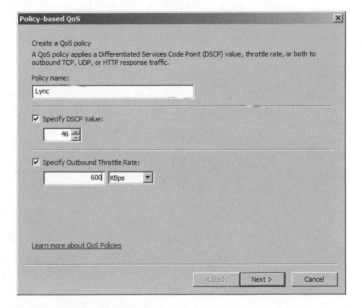

3. The next screen (Figure 14.15) is where you specify the application to which this policy will apply in the Lync case (and OCS); the filename is commun i cator . exe.

4. The next screen asks for source and destination information. This could be used to mark traffic specific to leaving a site, but in most cases it is likely this would be left as default.

5. Figure 14.16 shows where the port range and protocol can be specified. Choose Finish to complete the policy creation. From there the policy can be applied like any other Group Policy object.

FIGURE 14.15
Specifying application restrictions for the QoS policy

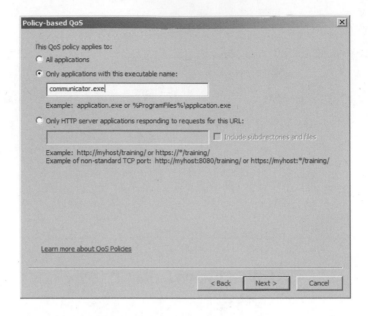

FIGURE 14.16
Specifying a protocol and port range for the QoS policy

Designing for Call Admission Control

The aim of designing the Call Admission Control policies is to ultimately associate IP subnets with locations and, with each location, to define the number of individual calls as well as the total number of calls permitted from (and to) each site. The association of IP subnets is how each client's location is determined for the PDP query.

The following example assumes a company with offices in the following locations, with available network bandwidth shown in brackets. Interregional links are from Chicago to London and from London to Sydney:

North America

    Chicago (100,000kbps)

    New York (50,000kbps)

    Washington, D.C. (50,000kbps)

    Seattle (5,000kbps)

    San Francisco (5,000kbps)

EMEA (Europe, Middle East, and Africa)

    London (10,000kbps)

    Dublin (5,000kbps)

    Paris (3,000kbps)

APAC (Asia and Pacific)

    Sydney (5,000kbps)

    Hong Kong (5,000kbps)

    Tokyo (5,000kbps)

To do this, you start by defining the network into regions, or central sites. Any addresses within a region are policy free—that is, they can establish any number of calls without being blocked or rerouted. You can include multiple physical locations in a single region (or site); in fact, this is recommended when you do not care to control the bandwidth between specific sites.

Next, you'll define the sites and associate each site with a region. Calls within a site are policy free; however, calls across sites or regions will have policy applied and controls put in place.

From the previous example data, you can see that Chicago, New York, and Washington, D.C. are well enough connected that you don't need to put any controls in place for calls between these locations. Table 14.3 shows the associations.

TABLE 14.3: Region, site, and bandwidth associations

REGION	SITE	AVAILABLE BANDWIDTH (KBPS)
North America	Chicago	100,000
North America	New York	50,000
North America	Washington, D.C.	50,000
North America	Seattle	5,000
North America	San Francisco	5,000
EMEA	London	10,000
EMEA	Dublin	5,000
EMEA	Paris	3,000
APAC	Sydney	5,000
APAC	Hong Kong	5,000
APAC	Tokyo	5,000

For each site, you need to define the bandwidth for the link to the central site or define a *cross-link* tying together two sites. Once you have the total bandwidth defined, you need to establish how much bandwidth will be assigned to total audio and how much bandwidth to total video. (In the example, Paris will be defined not to permit any video calls.)

Table 14.4 shows the required configuration.

TABLE 14.4: Site total session definitions per modality

REGION	SITE	AVAILABLE BANDWIDTH (KBPS)	TOTAL ASSIGNED TO AUDIO	TOTAL ASSIGNED TO VIDEO
North America	Chicago	100,000	Not controlled	Not controlled
North America	New York	50,000	Not controlled	Not controlled
North America	Washington, D.C.	50,000	Not controlled	Not controlled
North America	Seattle	5,000	2,000	1,200
North America	San Francisco	5,000	2,000	1,200
EMEA	London	10,000	Not controlled	Not controlled
EMEA	Dublin	5,000	2,000	1,200
EMEA	Paris	3,000	1,000	0
APAC	Sydney	5,000	Not controlled	Not controlled

TABLE 14.4: Site total session definitions per modality *(CONTINUED)*

REGION	SITE	AVAILABLE BANDWIDTH (KBPS)	TOTAL ASSIGNED TO AUDIO	TOTAL ASSIGNED TO VIDEO
APAC	Hong Kong	5,000	2,000	1,200
APAC	Tokyo	5,000	2,000	1,200

Chicago, New York, and Washington, D.C. will not have policy applied because they are well connected; London and Sydney will be defined as the central site in each region. It is important to note that the central site does not have to tie in with a physical location or indeed a data center. It can be considered a placeholder to which the other locations are connected. In most cases, it makes sense to associate with a location; however, in this example, three locations are being treated as one.

From these definitions, you define the maximum value for each modality that is permitted for a single call, as shown in Table 14.5.

TABLE 14.5: Site individual session definitions per modality

REGION	SITE	AVAILABLE BANDWIDTH (KBPS)	TOTAL ASSIGNED TO AUDIO	AUDIO SESSION LIMIT	TOTAL ASSIGNED TO VIDEO	VIDEO SESSION LIMIT
North America	Chicago	100,000	Not controlled	Not controlled	Not controlled	Not controlled
North America	New York	50,000	Not controlled	Not controlled	Not controlled	Not controlled
North America	Washington, D.C.	50,000	Not controlled	Not controlled	Not controlled	Not controlled
North America	Seattle	5,000	2,000	100	1,200	600
North America	San Francisco	5,000	2,000	100	1,200	600
EMEA	London	10,000	Not controlled	Not controlled	Not controlled	Not controlled
EMEA	Dublin	5,000	2,000	100	1,200	600
EMEA	Paris	3,000	1,000	60	0	0
APAC	Sydney	5,000	Not controlled	Not controlled	Not controlled	Not controlled
APAC	Hong Kong	5,000	2,000	100	1,200	600
APAC	Tokyo	5,000	2,000	100	1,200	600

Using Seattle as the first example, 2,000kbps was assigned for total audio sessions, and 100kbps was assigned for a maximum per audio session. This will permit a maximum of 20 concurrent calls (total sessions divided by individual session limit) on this connection (into the North America region). On the video configuration, 1,200kbps are assigned for the total sessions and 600kbps are assigned for each individual session, giving a maximum of two concurrent video sessions; HD video would not be permitted.

In the case of Paris, 1,000kbps are assigned for the total audio sessions, and 60kbps are assigned for each individual session, giving a concurrent call rate of 16 calls. For video traffic, none is permitted.

These two examples highlight the capability to control the quality of each individual call. Using Table 14.5, you can determine which codec will be used in the best case; you can also determine the capabilities to dynamically adapt if network issues are encountered during a call.

You can see that Seattle users can hold calls using the G711 codec, ensuring better call quality. However, if the network encounters issues, such as lost packets, and the codec requires the introduction of Forward Error Correction (FEC), then the Lync client cannot introduce FEC on G711 because that would require 156kbps. Instead, it must dynamically drop down to wideband RT-Audio and introduce FEC, using 86kbps.

You can find full details at

```
http://technet.microsoft.com/en-us/library/jj688118.aspx
```

The bandwidth used by each codec is listed in Table 14.6.

TABLE 14.6:   Codec bandwidth usage definitions

AUDIO/VIDEO CODEC	SCENARIOS	TYPICAL VALUE (KBPS)	MAX WITHOUT FEC (KBPS)	MAX WITH FEC (KBPS)
RTAudio Wideband	Peer-to-peer	39.8	62	91
RTAudio Narrowband	Peer-to-peer, PSTN	29.3	44.8	56.6
G.722	Conferencing	46.1	100.6	164.4
G.711	PSTN	64.8	97	161
Siren	Conferencing	25.5	52.6	68.6
Peer-to-Peer Main video (H.264)	Lync 2013 Endpoints	460	4010 (resolution 1920 × 1080)	N/A
Peer-to-Peer Main video (RTVideo)	Lync 2010 or OCS Endpoints	460	2510 (resolution 1280 × 760)	N/A
Conferencing Main video (H.264)	Receive	260	8015	N/A
Conferencing Main video (H.264)	Send	270	8015	N/A

TABLE 14.6:   Codec bandwidth usage definitions   *(CONTINUED)*

AUDIO/VIDEO CODEC	SCENARIOS	TYPICAL VALUE (KBPS)	MAX WITHOUT FEC (KBPS)	MAX WITH FEC (KBPS)
Panoramic video (H.264)	Lync 2013 Endpoints	190	2010 (resolution 1920 × 288)	N/A
Panoramic video (RTVideo)	Lync 2010 or OCS Endpoints	190	510 (resolution 960 × 144)	N/A
Panoramic video (H.264)	Sending bit-stream using multiple resolutions	190	2515	

Where multiple regions have been defined, you also need to establish the links between regions and permitted values of traffic across each, as in Table 14.7.

TABLE 14.7:   Interregion link definitions

NAME	REGION 1	REGION1	TOTAL ASSIGNED TO AUDIO	AUDIO SESSION LIMIT	TOTAL ASSIGNED TO VIDEO	VIDEO SESSION LIMIT
NA_EMEA	North America	EMEA	10,000	60	1,750	350
EMEA_APAC	EMEA	APAC	2,000	60	1,750	350

Finally, you need to associate IP subnets with each site, as shown in Table 14.8. As mentioned earlier, it is from these subnets that a client is able to determine which policy will apply.

TABLE 14.8:   Subnet associations per site

REGION	SITE	SUBNETS
North America	Chicago	10.0.1.0/24, 10.0.7.0/24, 10.43.23.0/24
North America	New York	10.0.2.0/24, 192.168.3.0/25
North America	Washington, D.C.	10.1.0.0/16
North America	Seattle	10.0.3.0/24, 10.0.54.0/24
North America	San Francisco	10.0.4.0/24
EMEA	London	10.25.1.0/24, 192.168.3.128/25

TABLE 14.8: Subnet associations per site *(CONTINUED)*

REGION	SITE	SUBNETS
EMEA	Dublin	10.25.2.0/24
EMEA	Paris	10.25.3.0/24
APAC	Sydney	10.0.9.0/24, 10.37.1.0/24
APAC	Hong Kong	10.37.2.0/24
APAC	Tokyo	10.37.3.0/24

The final Call Admission Control policy looks Figure 14.17.

FIGURE 14.17
Diagrammatic representation of Call Admission Control Configuration

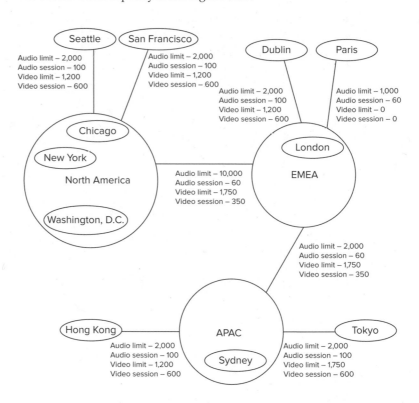

When a user in Seattle calls a user in Tokyo, Call Admission Control will assess the following connection links:

Seattle to North America Region

North America Region to EMEA Region

EMEA Region to APAC Region

APAC Region to Tokyo

If any of these links are saturated, the call will not proceed. If the call is established, the call details will be replicated to all PDPs in the topology to ensure that each is fully aware of the current network state.

In this example, we have not considered any rerouting capabilities. We will look at those in the section "Configuring Call Admission Control" later in this chapter.

 ## Real World Scenario

WHAT ABOUT MPLS?

MPLS networks can give the impression that all sites connected to the network are only one hop away from each other. This can cause confusion for anyone attempting to configure CAC in this type of scenario. You would normally have to configure a site link from each site to every other site—leading to a massive meshed network configuration, which would be extremely difficult to manage properly.

Taking the example from the section "Designing for Call Admission Control" and replacing the interregion links with a global MPLS network will give the configuration shown here:

Configuring Call Admission Control to manage this network could prove difficult. Following the logic shown, you would create regions and individual sites again; however, this would lead to misrepresentation on the network. It would be possible but extremely difficult to come up with a configuration where each site theoretically would have multiple links leaving the site but would not be represented as such from the network perspective, where there is only a single MPLS connection. The next illustration indicates how this might look.

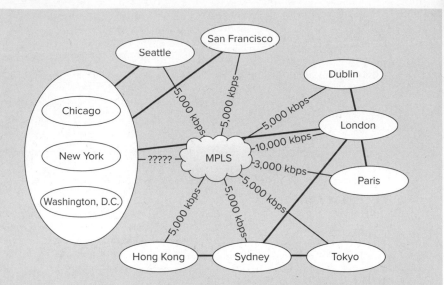

Taking London as the starting point, there are four connections: Dublin, Paris, APAC (Sydney), and North America; Call Admission Control would handle them individually, with no understanding of the underlying network where all the calls are actually following the same path. This could result in calls from London to North America being inadvertently impacted when the London-Dublin link is busy.

In addition, how would you manage the North America bandwidth?

A much cleaner approach is to treat the MPLS network *cloud* (MPLS networks are often referred to as *clouds* due to the way in which the actual network connections are abstracted from the user and appear as a single hop) as a Call Admission Control region in its own right. By taking this approach, you are back to the first diagram in this sidebar, but now you have control over each individual link; because all the links are to the cloud, the PDPs will be aware of the current concurrency rates on every link in the network and can efficiently manage the control of the call flow. This also allows multiple MPLS clouds to be managed easily.

By treating the MPLS mesh as a separate site and configuring links from each *actual* site to this imaginary site, you regain control over the network capacity used by Lync. Because you won't assign any network subnets to this imaginary site, no clients will be considered as if they are located within the mesh.

Configuring Call Admission Control

We'll keep using the original example to show how the configuration is built. To configure and enable Call Admission Control, you need to individually configure the following sections (the Control Panel view is shown in Figure 14.18, with the Global tab open):

◆ Global

◆ Location Policy (not related to Call Admission Control)

- ◆ Policy Profile

- ◆ Region

- ◆ Site

- ◆ Subnet

- ◆ Region Link

- ◆ Region Route

FIGURE 14.18
Using Control Panel
to configure Call
Admission Control

Although it is possible to configure all of Call Admission Control via a single Set-CsNetworkConfiguration command, that approach is extremely complex and not recommended. It is much easier to configure section by section.

Configuring the Global Setting

Because Call Admission Control is configured at the individual component level, the only setting on the policy in the Global tab is to enable or disable it.

Figure 14.19 shows Call Admission Control enabled in the Control Panel. The equivalent command in the Lync Management Shell would be either

```
Set-CsNetworkConfiguration -EnableBandwidthPolicyCheck $True
```
or
```
Set-CsNetworkConfiguration -EnableBandwidthPolicyCheck $False
```

Additional policies may be created and applied if Call Admission Control is not being controlled globally, or if the network setup does not allow a single global approach. Each policy can be enabled or disabled individually.

Using the `Get-CsNetworkConfiguration` cmdlet allows you to verify the state of each policy:

```
Identity                 : Global
MediaBypassSettings      : Enabled=False;InternalBypassMode=Off;EnternalBypassMode=Off;Alw
aysBypass=False;
BypassID=;EnabledForAudioVideoConferences=False
BWPolicyProfiles         : {}
NetworkRegions           : {}
NetworkREgionLinks       : {}
InterNetworkRegionRoutes : {}
NetworkSites             : {}
InterNetworkSitePolicies : {}
Subnets                  : {}
EnableBandwidthPolicyCheck : True
```

Figure 14.18 shows the Control Panel view of this command.

FIGURE 14.19
Enabling Call
Admission Control

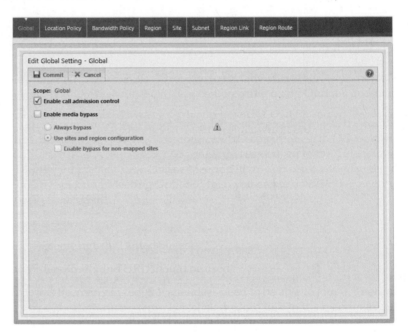

Defining the Policy Profile Settings

The Policy Profile page is where you define both the audio and video limits that will be assigned to the links between each site and region. Later you will link these policies to the relevant network sites. (Note that even though a policy may not allow audio or video across a link by setting the audio or video limit to 0, the individual session limit still requires a value to be added.)

Figure 14.20 shows the Control Panel input page and from the shell, the following command is used to create a bandwidth policy:

```
New-CsNetworkBandwidthPolicyProfile -Identity "Global Default Policy"
    -AudioBWLimit 2000 -AudioBWSessionLimit 100
```

```
-VideoBWLimit 1200 -VideoBWSessionLimit 600
-Description "Global Policy"
```

FIGURE 14.20

The New Bandwidth
Policy Profile page

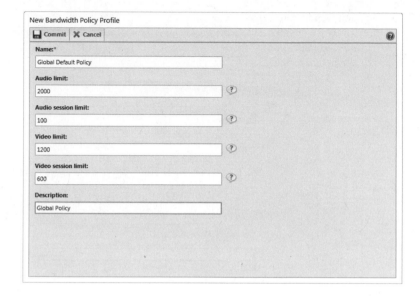

An interregion policy is simply a bandwidth policy applied to a region policy, so it is created
and configured in exactly the same way.

Once the profile is fully configured, you will see the following output:

```
Get-CsNetworkBandwidthPolicyProfile
Identity           : Paris Bandwidth policy no video
BWPolicy           : {BWLimit=0;BWSessionLimit=60;BWPolicyModality=Audio,
BWLimit=0;BWSessionLimit=100;BWPolicyModality=Video}
BWPolicyProfileID : Paris Bandwidth policy no video
Description        : No video permitted
Identity           : Global Default Policy
BWPolicy           : {BWLimit=2000;BWSessionLimit=100;BWPolicyModality=Audio,
BWLimit=1200;BWSessionLimit=600;BWPolicyModality=Video}
BWPolicyProfileID : Global Default Policy
Description        : Global Policy
Identity           : NA_EMEA Bandwidth Policy
BWPolicy           : {BWLimit=10000;BWSessionLimit=60;BWPolicyModality=Audio,
BWLimit=1750;BWSessionLimit=350;BWPolicyModality=Video}
BWPolicyProfileID : NA_EMEA Bandwidth Policy
Description        : NA-EMEA Bandwidth Policy
Identity           : EMEA_APAC Bandwidth Policy
BWPolicy           : {BWLimit=2000;BWSessionLimit=60;BWPolicyModality=Audio,
BWLimit=1750;BWSessionLimit=350;BWPolicyModality=Video}
BWPolicyProfileID : EMEA_APAC Bandwidth Policy
Description        : EMEA-APAC Bandwidth Policy
```

Defining Regions

Regions are the hubs of Call Admission Control, and calls within a region do not have any restrictions placed on them.

Each region is required to be assigned to a central site; this is as defined (and published) via the Topology Builder shown in Figure 14.21. (Topology Builder is a separate installation item, installed via setup.exe; however, it must be installed on at least one server to create and publish the initial topology.)

FIGURE 14.21
Central site representation in Topology Builder

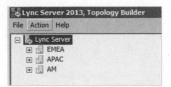

The Control Panel screen to define a region is shown in Figure 14.22 and requires the following items to be configured:

◆ Name

◆ Central Site

◆ Enable Audio Alternate Path

◆ Enable Video Alternate Path

◆ Description

◆ Associated Sites (you'll define the sites in the next section)

FIGURE 14.22
New region definition

Configuring the information for the remaining regions via the Lync Server Management Shell would look like this:

```
New-CsNetworkRegion -Identity EMEA -CentralSite EMEA -AudioAlternatePath $true
    -VideoAlternatePath $true -Description "EMEA Region"
```

Including -AudioAlternatePath and -VideoAlternatePath (and setting to $True) configures the region to reroute audio and video if Call Admission Control reports that not enough bandwidth is available on the links. This gives us with the capability to provide an alternate path for voice but not video if required:.

Get-CsNetworkRegion will return this output:

```
Identity         : North America
Description      : North America Region
BypassID         : 87961ca4-1fa6-4286-8e15-9de3ca47f4af
CentralSite      : Site:NA
BWAlternatePaths : {BWPolicyModality=Audio;
    AlternatePath=True,
    BWPolicyModality=Video;AlternatePath=True}
NetworkRegionID  : North America
Identity         : EMEA
Description      : EMEA Region
BypassID         : 13b075d8-fa32-4f21-8937-40e2d69e9934
CentralSite      : Site:EMEA
DWAlternatePaths : {BWPolicyModality=Audio;
    AlternatePath=True,
    BWPolicyModality=Video;AlternatePath=True}
NetworkRegionID  : EMEA
Identity         : APAC
Description      : APAC Region
BypassID         : e0a0a73a-ccfb-4cca-aa5b-46b8d2a74653
CentralSite      : Site:APAC
BWAlternatePaths : {BWPolicyModality=Audio;
    AlternatePath=True,
    BWPolicyModality=Video;AlternatePath=True}
NetworkRegionID  : APAC
```

Defining Sites

Sites are within and connected to regions. Lync clients are associated with sites, based on the actual subnet from which they are connecting. It is possible for a user to be connected with multiple Lync clients, each of which could be in a different site.

Figure 14.23 shows the Control Panel Configuration screen for a new site. This is where you can define the following items:

◆ Name

◆ Region (must be previously defined)

◆ Bandwidth Policy

- ◆ Location Policy (not Call Admission Control–related)

- ◆ Description

- ◆ Associated Subnets (subnets are being defined next)

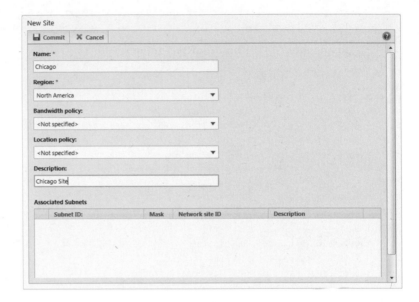

FIGURE 14.23
New site definition

Sites are defined using the `Set-CsNetworkSite` cmdlet:

```
New-CsNetworkSite -Identity "London"
   -NetworkRegionID EMEA
   -Description "London Site"
```

In the North America region, multiple sites are defined even though the example stated there will be no bandwidth controls. It is good practice to define *all* the sites in the environment because that will make them easier to match up and adjust in the future when—not if—the requirements change.

Not only will troubleshooting be easier when the complete environment is defined, but the fact that a site is defined but has no policy means the client will be correctly assigned within the logs, making them easier to follow when you're trying to understand a problem.

If this were a new site being introduced after Lync had already been deployed, it would make sense to fully populate the policy and location information sources at this point. Because this is the London site and we don't want to place any controls on the bandwidth usage for the example, we won't come back to assign a bandwidth policy; however, the subnets do need to be assigned. Location policy will be discussed in Chapter 15.

The full configuration of the defined sites looks like this:

```
Get-CsNetworkSite
Identity         : Chicago
```

```
NetworkSiteID     : Chicago
Description       : Chicago site
NetworkRegionID   : North America
BypassID          : 87961ca4-1fa6-4286-8e15-9de3ca474faf
BWPolicyProfileID :
LocationPolicy    :
Identity          : New York
NetworkSiteID     : New York
Description       : New York Site
NetworkRegionID   : North America
BypassID          : 87961ca4-1fa6-4286-8e15-9de3ca474faf
BWPolicyProfileID :
LocationPolicy    :
Identity          : Washington DC
NetworkSiteID     : Washington DC
Description       : Washington DC Site
NetworkRegionID   : North America
BypassID          : 87961ca4-1fa6-4286-8e15-9de3ca474faf
BWPolicyProfileID :
LocationPolicy    :
Identity          : London
NetworkSiteID     : London
Description       : London Site
NetworkRegionID   : EMEA
BypassID          : 13b075d8-fa-32-4f21-8937-40e2d69e9934
BWPolicyProfileID :
LocationPolicy    :
Identity          : San Francisco
NetworkSiteID     : San Francisco
Description       : San Francisco Site
NetworkRegionID   : North America
BypassID          : 87961ca4-1fa6-4286-8e15-9de3ca474faf
BWPolicyProfileID :
LocationPolicy    :
Identity          : Seattle
NetworkSiteID     : Seattle
Description       : Seattle Site
NetworkRegionID   : North America
BypassID          : 87961ca4-1fa6-4286-8e15-9de3ca474faf
BWPolicyProfileID :
LocationPolicy    :
Identity          : Dublin
NetworkSiteID     : Dublin
Description       : Dublin Site
NetworkRegionID   : EMEA
BypassID          : 13b075d8-fa-32-4f21-8937-40e2d69e9934
BWPolicyProfileID :
```

```
LocationPolicy      :
Identity            : Paris
NetworkSiteID       : Paris
Description         : Paris Site
NetworkRegionID     : EMEA
BypassID            : 13b075d8-fa-32-4f21-8937-40e2d69e9934
BWPolicyProfileID :
LocationPolicy      :
Identity            : Sydney
NetworkSiteID       : Sydney
Description         : Sydney Site
NetworkRegionID     : APAC
BypassID            : e0a0a73a-ccfb-4cca-aa5b-46b8d2a74653
BWPolicyProfileID :
LocationPolicy      :
Identity            : Hong Kong
NetworkSiteID       : Hong Kong
Description         : Hong Kong Site
NetworkRegionID     : APAC
BypassID            : e0a0a73a-ccfb-4cca-aa5b-46b8d2a74653
BWPolicyProfileID :
LocationPolicy      :
Identity            : Tokyo
NetworkSiteID       : Tokyo
Description         : Tokyo Site
NetworkRegionID     : APAC
BypassID            : e0a0a73a-ccfb-4cca-aa5b-46b8d2a74653
BWPolicyProfileID :
LocationPolicy      :
```

Defining Subnets

Each client will determine its site location and, therefore, policy restrictions based on its subnet. To enable this tie-up between site and subnet, you must first define the subnets in the environment and then assign them to the correct sites.

Figure 14.24 shows the Control Panel approach to define a subnet:

◆   Subnet ID

◆   Mask

◆   Network Site ID (must be previously defined)

◆   Description

The subnet ID must be the first address in the subnet range (known as the network address or *subnet-zero*). The mask must be in numeric format (e.g., 24), not the more common Classless Inter-Domain Routing (CIDR) format (e.g., /24).

FIGURE 14.24
New subnet
definition

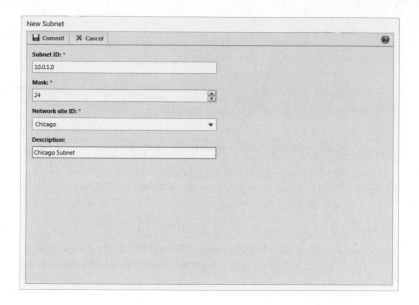

The cmdlet to use for this function is New-CsSubnet:

```
New-CsNetworkSubnet -Identity 10.0.7.0 -Mask 24
    -NetworkSiteID Chicago
    -Description "Chicago subnet"
```

Once fully populated, the environment looks like this:

```
Get-CsSubnet

Identity      : 10.0.1.0
MaskBits      : 24
Description   : Chicago subnet
NetworkSiteID : Chicago
SubnetID      : 10.0.1.0
Identity      : 10.0.7.0
MaskBits      : 24
Description   : Chicago subnet
NetworkSiteID : Chicago
SubnetID      : 10.0.7.0
Identity      : 10.43.23.0
MaskBits      : 24
Description   : Chicago subnet
NetworkSiteID : Chicago
SubnetID      : 10.43.23.0
Identity      : 10.0.2.0
MaskBits      : 24
Description   : New York subnet
```

```
NetworkSiteID : New York
SubnetID     : 10.0.2.0
Identity     : 10.0.3.0
MaskBits     : 25
Description  : Paris subnet
NetworkSiteID : Paris
SubnetID     : 10.0.3.0
```

The output has been cut for brevity because the definitions for subnets are the same for each and there really isn't a lot to configure.

Although the definition terminology is 'subnet', supernetting is also a supported method to define CAC subnets. Supernetting is the ability to combine multiple subnets into larger ranges, reducing the amount of data that needs to be input (which can be a very tedious process!). When a subnet if defined with a larger mask, CAC can still correctly determine which location a client is in, even if the client subnet mask differs from that used by CAC.

For example, in the Paris example highlighted earlier, the mask is 25, which resolves into the range 10.0.3.0–10.0.3.127. We could also define a France supernet of 10.0.3.0 with a mask of 24, which would include the Paris subnet as well as the remainder of the 10.0.3.128–10.0.3.255 range.

Defining Region Links

Now that you've defined the regions, sites, and associated subnets, you need to tell Lync Server 2010 how much bandwidth is available between regions. Region links are how you can do this. Region links also represent the logical connections from one region to the next.

Figure 14.25 shows the values required to create the region link between North America and EMEA. To do that, you need to configure the following items:

◆ Name

◆ Network Region #1 (must already have been defined)

◆ Network Region #2 (must already have been defined)

◆ Bandwidth Policy

To define a connection between EMEA and APAC, and assign the relevant bandwidth policy, use this command:

```
New-CsNetworkRegionLink -Identity EMEA_APAC
    -NetworkRegionID1 EMEA
    -NetworkRegionID2 APAC
    -BWPolicyProfileID "EMEA_APAC Bandwidth Policy"
```

Once all region links are defined, the environment will look like this:

```
Get-CsNetworkRegionLink
Identity             : NA_EMEA
BWPolicyProfileID    : NA_EMEA Bandwidth Policy
NetworkRegionLinkID  : NA_EMEA
NetworkRegionID1     : North America
NetworkRegionID2     : EMEA
Identity             : EMEA_APAC
BWPolicyProfileID    : EMEA_APAC Bandwidth Policy
```

```
NetworkRegionLinkID : EMEA_APAC
NetworkRegionID1    : EMEA
NetworkRegionID2    : APAC
```

FIGURE 14.25
New region link
definition

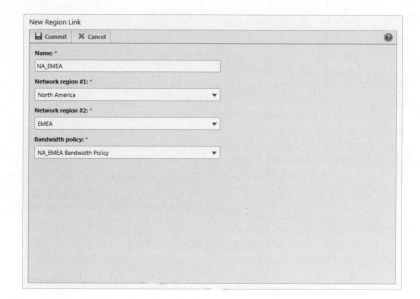

Assigning Region Routes

Once all the regions have been defined, Lync needs to understand how they are connected. The connections are defined in the Region Route section in the Control Panel. This is similar to the Region Link configuration, except that rather than defining the policy applied on a link, you are defining the routes to take between regions.

The actual network route taken by the data is not affected by this definition; it is used only internally within Lync Server 2013 to allow an understanding of the network within the Call Admission Control aspect of Lync Server 2013.

Figure 14.26 shows the Control Panel implementation, which requires the following items:

◆ Name

◆ Network Region #1 (must have already been defined)

◆ Network Region #2 (must have already been defined)

◆ Network Region Links (must have already been defined)

The equivalent PowerShell cmdlet is `Net-CsNetworkInterRegionRoute`. Here is an example:

```
New-CsNetworkInterRegionRoute -Identity EMEA_APAC
    -NetworkRegionID1 EMEA -NetworkRegionID2 APAC
    -NetworkRegionLinks EMEA_APAC
```

The fully configured environment will be like this:

```
Get-CsNetworkInterRegionRoute
Identity                   : NA_EMEA
NetworkRegionLinks         : {NA_EMEA}
InterNetworkRegionRouteID  : NA_EMEA
NetworkRegionID1           : North America
NetworkRegionID2           : EMEA
Identity                   : EMEA_APAC
NetworkRegionLinks         : {EMEA_APAC}
InterNetworkRegionRouteID  : EMEA_APAC
NetworkRegionID1           : EMEA
NetworkRegionID2           : APAC
```

FIGURE 14.26
Region route
definition

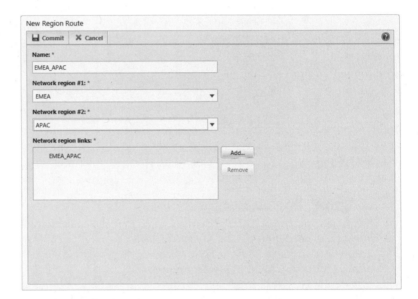

Assigning Policies

Now that the environment is fully populated, the final step in configuring it is to apply the policy controls. The previous two sections have shown how to assign policy to the region links; however, you also need to go back and assign the policy to a number of sites.

At this point, all calls within a region are uncontrolled; only the interregion calls have had policy applied to them. In the example, you want to control calls on a number of site links and leave the remaining as uncontrolled within region NA.

To assign policy to a specific site, use the Set-CsNetworkSite cmdlet:

```
Set-CsNetworkSite -Identity "Paris"
-BWPolicyProfileID "Paris Bandwidth policy no video"
```

You can also apply policies using the Control Panel; simply open the specific site (from the Site configuration tab in the Network Configuration section) by double-clicking the site entry. Once the site is opened, you will be taken to the Edit Site page (shown in Figure 14.27). From the defined Bandwidth Policy section there, you can choose which policy will be applied on this link.

FIGURE 14.27
Assigning a policy to an existing site

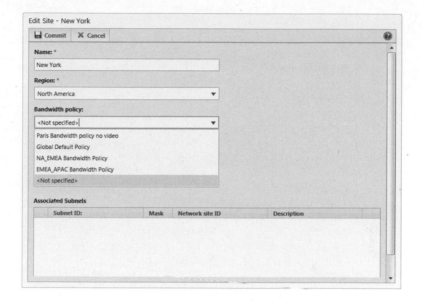

Finally, the fully configured site listing looks like this:

```
Get-CsNetworkSite
Identity          : Chicago
NetworkSiteID     : Chicago
Description       : Chicago site
NetworkRegionID   : North America
BypassID          : 6d278a1c-c994-4a28-b6de-a4a3773335ec
BWPolicyProfileID :
LocationPolicy    :
Identity          : New York
NetworkSiteID     : New York
Description       : New York Site
NetworkRegionID   : North America
BypassID          : 6d278a1c-c994-4a28-b6de-a4a3773335ec
BWPolicyProfileID :
LocationPolicy    :
Identity          : Washington DC
NetworkSiteID     : Washington DC
Description       : Washington DC Site
NetworkRegionID   : North America
```

```
BypassID            : 6d278a1c-c994-4a28-b6de-a4a3773335ec
BWPolicyProfileID :
LocationPolicy     :
Identity           : London
NetworkSiteID      : London
Description        : London Site
NetworkRegionID    : EMEA
BypassID           : ca72a529-277f-4757-aa8f-e13c681cc462
BWPolicyProfileID :
LocationPolicy     :
Identity           : San Francisco
NetworkSiteID      : San Francisco
Description        : San Francisco Site
NetworkRegionID    : North America
BypassID           : 86b36862-bd48-49de-a1d6-49561ce50bd9
BWPolicyProfileID : Global Default Policy
LocationPolicy     :
Identity           : Seattle
NetworkSiteID      : Seattle
Description        : Seattle Site
NetworkRegionID    : North America
BypassID           : 2049a6b0-02e1-4f71-b76b-db93aa7d130c
BWPolicyProfileID : Global Default Policy
LocationPolicy     :
Identity           : Dublin
NetworkSiteID      : Dublin
Description        : Dublin Site
NetworkRegionID    : EMEA
BypassID           : 1f0c441c-aac1-4ba4-b835-43b20fb95686
BWPolicyProfileID : Global Default Policy
LocationPolicy     :
Identity           : Paris
NetworkSiteID      : Paris
Description        : Paris Site
NetworkRegionID    : EMEA
BypassID           : 7c638937-4c0b-4a8f-9918-cebe7a7b7284
BWPolicyProfileID : Paris Bandwidth policy no video
LocationPolicy     :
Identity           : Sydney
NetworkSiteID      : Sydney
Description        : Sydney Site
NetworkRegionID    : APAC
BypassID           : d1b4c334-de17-40e8-950d-1ffe6bfd4c06
BWPolicyProfileID :
LocationPolicy     :
Identity           : Hong Kong
NetworkSiteID      : Hong Kong
Description        : Hong Kong Site
```

```
NetworkRegionID    : APAC
BypassID           : d6e14fc5-2082-4731-8973-8489cd4e6cde
BWPolicyProfileID  : Global Default Policy
LocationPolicy     :
Identity           : Tokyo
NetworkSiteID      : Tokyo
Description        : Tokyo Site
NetworkRegionID    : APAC
BypassID           : 4baa4383-c037-414e-b4dd-b780e4c88ee2
BWPolicyProfileID  : Global Default Policy
LocationPolicy     :
```

Identifying Calls on a Network

During the early stages of the beta program, customers had a question: "If the system knows what the current state of calls is throughout the network, where can an administrator find that information?"

A subsequent version of the beta (and released) code provided the following management shell command:

```
Set-CsBandwidthPolicyServiceConfiguration -EnableLogging $true
```

This enables CVS file logging to the following location

```
<file share>/1-ApplicationServer-1/AppServerFiles/PDP/
```

Several files are created:

PDP_<*servername*><*date*><*time*>_Links   This file is updated hourly, or when the Call Admission Control configuration is changed. It will contain one line per site or region and list the current permitted total and the current utilization for both audio and video traffic. It is a CSV format file.

PDP_<*servername*><*date*><*time*>_BwCheckFailure   This file is updated with every entry based on the local PDP failures and includes data such as the IP addresses of the clients involved as well as the minimum and maximum requested bandwidth values. This data does not get replicated to any other PDP in the topology. It is a CSV format file.

PDP_<*servername*><*date*><*time*>_Topology   This file is generated once per day at 00:01, as well as when any changes are applied to the Call Admission Control configuration. It is an XML format file.

Reporting on Call Admission Control

Over time, understanding the impact of Call Admission Control is important. If the values are set too high, then potentially the network is overspecified and costs may be saved by reducing the capacity. On the other hand, it's more likely that Call Admission Control will be rejecting calls, and if a significant number are reported, this may indicate that Call Admission Control is configured too low. In parallel to this, if the network is nearing capacity, it is an indication that the network is under pressure and may need to be increased.

From the reporting pack installed with the monitoring server, you can run the Call Admission Control report, which will provide a detailed view on how many calls are being rerouted or rejected based on the current policy settings. This is covered in Chapter 11, "Archiving and Monitoring."

The Bottom Line

Identify Call Admission Control–capable endpoints. Before designing and configuring Call Admission Control, you need to understand where it can be applied to ensure that the proper configuration is identified.

> **Master It** You are in the process of defining a migration from OCS R2 to Lync Server 2013. Users previously reported some issues with call quality due to the capacity on the network, so Call Admission Control is required. Which user endpoints can be restricted by the Call Admission Control policy?

Configure policy-based Quality of Service controls. Call Admission Control provides application-layer management of the call bandwidth; however, to truly provide this guarantee to clients, Quality of Service is required to operate on the network layer. Windows Vista introduced policy-based Quality of Service controls.

> **Master It** You have restricted the port range to be 5000 to 5999, and you will deploy Lync 2013 to your users. An application utilized in the finance department uses the port range 5500 to 5599. How can you ensure that only the Lync 2013 traffic is prioritized on the network?

Design a Call Admission Control solution. Call Admission Control can be complex in large interconnected networks. A properly designed solution will ensure that two important requirements of Call Admission Control are met: User call quality is high and the network is not saturated.

> **Master It** What special considerations should be given to an MPLS network?

Configure Call Admission Control. Once designed, Call Admission Control needs to be configured and applied to the Lync 2013 servers. The servers will keep each other constantly updated as to the number of the calls and bandwidth used on the network. By using the built-in logging functionality, it is possible to capture an hourly snapshot of the state, with more detailed reporting available via the monitoring server.

> **Master It** What needs to be defined and applied to configure Call Admission Control?

Chapter 15

E911 and Location Information Services

Being able to dial emergency services is probably the most critical requirement for any telephony system. Face it: If someone needs emergency services, something serious is probably happening.

Although Office Communications Server 2007 and R2 were both capable of calling emergency services, Lync Server 2010 and Lync Server 2013 are also compliant with the North American requirement to provide location-based data with calls, known as Enhanced 911, or E911.

If you have experience with configuring Lync Server 2010 for E911, then this chapter will be familiar to you. The only additional information included here is reference to Emergency Location Identification Number (ELIN) gateway support, which is also valid for Lync Server 2010 but was added significantly after release.

In this chapter you will learn to:

◆ Describe the E911 requirements for North America

◆ Configure Lync Server 2013 to meet E911 requirements

◆ Understand how Location Information services can be used by callers outside North America

Understanding E911

In the early days of telephony, each exchange could use a different number for contacting emergency services. Over 70 years ago, the United Kingdom was one of the first locations to introduce three-digit emergency service dialing. This informal standard has since spread worldwide, and almost all countries have three-digit dialing for the main emergency services: police, fire, and medical.

There is no common global number for emergency services; 911 is used in North America, 112 in Europe, and 999 in the United Kingdom, for example. Moreover, in many locations separate phone numbers are used for each of the emergency services, with no central public safety operator.

Where a central public safety operator is used, the safety operator establishes the specific emergency need and may route the call to the specific service or act as an intermediary and collect additional information such as the location, or they may provide verbal assistance and guidance until the emergency services arrive.

Figure 15.1 shows a typical interaction in a legacy telephony system.

FIGURE 15.1

Traditional interaction from an emergency operator

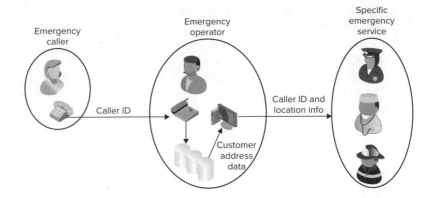

As phone systems developed, and in many cases became nationalized, it was possible to determine the phone's location based on the billing records for an individual line. In large organizations, the information was typically not detailed enough for this to occur; however, at least some of the address information could be discerned.

However, the introduction of cellular-based mobile devices removed this capability—in most cases, the caller was not at the billing address of the handset, rendering billing information useless.

Mobile handsets also introduced the concept of *roaming* and the complication of enabling users (when traveling out of country) to dial their home country's emergency number and have it translated to the local country number as well as being routed locally. Most devices accept 112, 911, and 999 as preprogrammed emergency service numbers. SIM cards may also have additional data programmed.

Mobile integration with the emergency services differs within each country, but there is normally a provision for the mobile carrier to provide the location information based on the cell tower details through which the handset is provided, as shown in Figure 15.2.

FIGURE 15.2

Cellular provision of location information

Including location information automatically ensures not only that emergency services are provided the information, saving valuable time, but also that the call is routed to the nearest Public Safety Answering Point (PSAP), guaranteeing that the emergency services in the vicinity of the emergency are notified.

Telephony has moved away from the traditional "fixed line" idea to the data network provision of Voice over IP (VoIP), and the copper lines to desks became network lines to anywhere. Continuing the trend is the concept of soft phone clients such as Lync, and you can see that the need for location-based information continues to become more apparent.

In the early implementations of VoIP systems, emergency calling was specifically excluded because of the flexibility of the potential location of the caller. Financial penalties imposed by governments over lack of emergency service calling provisions soon made this approach unreasonable.

Enhanced 911 (E911) is the provision of the emergency call as well as the location information associated with it. Lync Server 2013 implements E911, as shown in Figure 15.3.

FIGURE 15.3
E911
Implementation
within Lync Server
2013

The process is as follows:

1. A call is placed to emergency services.

2. The call is routed to the appropriate Mediation server, with Session Initiation Protocol (SIP) information that includes location details.

3. The call is routed via the emergency services service provider to the appropriate Public Safety Answering Point (PSAP). If at this stage the location information has not been validated via the Master Street Address Guide database, then an emergency services service provider operator will handle the call and verbally confirm location information prior to routing the call to the PSAP.

4. Optionally, the corporate security desk may be informed, via instant message (IM) and/or inclusion in a conference call.

When the Lync Server 2010 certification of ELIN gateways was achieved, the requirement to have a dedicated SIP trunk for E911 calling went away. An ELIN gateway provides a method to assign emergency response locations (ERLs) to specific telephone numbers, allowing the PSAP to identify the location from which the call is made. As would be expected, a single gateway is not as granular as an internal Lync Server 2013 database and would typically be used to define larger areas, such as a floor or building.

The ELIN gateway process uses the same infrastructure as shown in Figure 15.3, with the exception that a gateway sits between the Mediation server and the emergency services provider; a SIP trunk may or may not be used.

The calling number (from the user dialing 911) is cached on the gateway for a configurable time period, allowing for the emergency services to call back the "generic" number used in the location by the gateway, a reverse lookup is carried out on the cache to retrieve the original caller's Direct Inward Dial (DID) number, and the call is passed on to this cached number.

Current Legislation

As of May 2011, 16 states across North America have legislation requiring businesses, schools, and government agencies to provide E911 capabilities. Other states in North America and other countries throughout the world are considering similar legislation and approaches for provision of location information.

 Real World Scenario

The Consequences of Getting It Wrong

Providing location information to emergency services helps improve response times; however, in extreme cases, when this information is out of date or even wrong, it can lead to fatalities simply because the emergency responders are sent to the wrong location.

The first fatality due to failure to deliver the correct location for the caller's address happened in Canada in 2008.

A family moved from their home and, realizing the benefits of VoIP, continued to use the same telephony service provider and number at their new location. However, somehow the old street address was retained for the customer. Due to a miscommunication caused by language barriers, the emergency services operator was unable to confirm the address, and the emergency services were dispatched to the old (incorrect address).

This highlights the need to ensure not only that the technology is location aware but that the correct street address information reflects the actual location—addresses may still be valid but associated with an incorrect subnet or switch.

Configuring E911

Now that you understand why you need to configure E911 dialing and location services, how do you go about it?

Well, simply put, E911 calling is a voice route using a dedicated SIP trunk, so you'll need to define the following:

- PSTN usage
- Location policy
- SIP trunk
- Voice route

Configuring PSTN Usage

As described in Chapter 13, "Getting Started with Voice," the public switched telephone network (PSTN) usages are used to provide call authorization to users when they are attempting to place calls via the Lync Communicator client. A PSTN usage ties a voice policy to a user and also a route to a gateway, giving permissions for a user to use a particular route.

It is recommended that a separate usage be defined for emergency services dialing and that all users are permitted to use it.

The command to define a PSTN usage is as follows:

```
Set-CsPstnUsage -Identity global -Usage @{add="EmergencyUsage"}
```

Configuring Location Policies

The location policy contains the definition of the emergency services dialing implementation. Policies can be assigned to specific subnets or individual users. If neither of these is in place, the global policy takes effect.

Using the New-CsLocationPolicy or the Set-CsLocationPolicy cmdlet, the additional parameters shown in Table 15.1 provide the PowerShell method of configuration.

TABLE 15.1:   CsLocationPolicy parameters

PARAMETER	OPTIONAL?	EXAMPLE
Identity	Yes	Global
EnhancedEmergencyServicesEnabled	No	$True
LocationRequired	Yes	yes
UseLocationForE911Only	Yes	$True
PstnUsage	Yes	EmergencyUsage
EmergencyDialString	Yes	911
EmergencyDialMask	Yes	112
NotificationURI	Yes	Sip:security@masteringlync.org
ConferenceURI	Yes	Sip:+155512347890@masteringlync.org

TABLE 15.1: CsLocationPolicy parameters *(CONTINUED)*

PARAMETER	OPTIONAL?	EXAMPLE
ConferenceMode	Yes	TwoWay
Description	Yes	Global emergency location policy
EnhancedEmergencyServiceDisclaimer	Yes	"You are currently connecting from a location where location services are required for emergency dialing and your location has not been set. Do you wish to set your location now?"
LocationRefreshInterval	Yes	4

The parameters in Table 15.1 are described in more detail here:

Identity This defines the CsLocationPolicy to modify or create. If a policy is being scoped (tagged) to a specific site, the entry must be in the form site:*<site name>*—for example, site:UK.

EnhancedEmergencyServicesEnabled The EnhancedEmergencyServicesEnabled parameter tells the Lync client whether or not to retrieve and provide location information with an emergency call.

LocationRequired When the Lync client is logging, the LocationRequired parameter is used in the event that location information cannot be retrieved from the location configuration database. This parameter can take one of three options:

no The user will not be prompted for any location information, and location information will be unavailable for the emergency services call. The call will be answered by the emergency services provider, asking verbally for the location information before rerouting to the correct emergency services operator.

yes The user is prompted for location information; however, completion is not mandatory and the prompt can be dismissed. In this scenario, if the information is provided, the call is first answered by the emergency services provider to verify the location information before rerouting to the emergency services operator.

disclaimer Similar to yes, except that the prompt may not be dismissed without completing the location information. An emergency call can still be completed, following the no definition, but no other calls can be placed until this information is completed.

UseLocationForE911Only Other applications integrated with Lync Server 2013 may be able to leverage location information. For example, an application for booking conference rooms could prioritize available rooms closest to your current location; the UseLocationForE911Only parameter controls this capability.

PstnUsage The route associated with this PstnUsage parameter must already exist and should point to a SIP trunk dedicated to emergency calls.

EmergencyDialString   This value is the number dialed to reach emergency services. It will differ from country to country; for example, the United States uses 911, while most of Europe uses 112.

EmergencyDialMask   The EmergencyDialMask parameter allows multiple numbers to be used to dial emergency services. For example, suppose a user has traveled from Europe to the United States and needs to dial the emergency services without having to figure out what number to dial; they could continue to dial 112 and have this automatically translated to 911.

You can include multiple entries in this string, by separating each one with a semicolon:

```
EmergencyDialMask "112;999"
```

NotificationURI   In addition to providing location information to the emergency services, Lync Server 2010 provides the ability to notify SIP-based contacts through an instant message, which also includes the location information.

Multiple SIP URIs can be included by use of a comma-separated list:

```
-NotificationURI
"sip:security@masteringlync.org,sip:facilities@masteringlync.org"
```

ConferenceURI   As well as the NotificationURI parameter providing instant message notification, the ConferenceURI parameter allows a third party to be conferenced into the voice conversation between the initiator of the emergency call and the emergency service provider/operator. This is used in conjunction with the ConferenceMode parameter.

ConferenceMode   When the ConferenceURI is specified, the ConferenceMode parameter determines whether the third party can only listen to the conversation or can be an active participant. The values permitted are as follows:

oneway   Listen only

twoway   Actively participate

Description   As with all the cmdlets, the Description parameter allows descriptive text to be entered.

EnhancedEmergencyServiceDisclaimer   This parameter is new with Lync Server 2013. With Lync Server 2010, the emergency services disclaimer was set globally; however, now it can be set on a per-policy basis, allowing much more granular information. The dialog box presented provides a Yes/No option to the user, so be sure to word your disclaimer correctly. Selecting Yes will open the Location Definition dialog.

LocationRefreshInterval   By default, the client will request a service location update every 4 hours. This parameter allows for control of this refresh period.

The following command modifies the global policy:

```
Set-CsLocationPolicy -Identity Global -EnhancedEmergencyServicesEnabled $True
-LocationRequired "Yes" -PstnUsage "EmergencyUsage" -EmergencyDialString "911"
-ConferenceMode "twoway" -ConferenceURI "sip:+155512347890@masteringlync.org"
-EmergencyDialMask "112" -NotificationURI "sip:security@masteringlync.org"
-UseLocationForE911Only $True -LocationRefreshInterval 5
-EnhancedEmergencyServiceDisclaimer "You are currently connecting from a
location where location services are required for emergency dialing and your
location has not been set. Do you wish to set your location now?"
```

PstnUsage must be defined prior to running the CsLocationPolicy command. If LocationRequired is set to Disclaimer, the disclaimer test must be set using the -EnhancedEmergencyServiceDisclaimer parameter.

Lync Server 2010 allowed the following command:

```
Set-CsEnhancedEmergencyServiceDisclaimer
-Body "Text to display in the disclaimer window"
```

However, within Lync Server 2013, this will result in a warning informing you that this cmdlet has been deprecated and you must use the location profile instead. The default disclaimer is shown in Figure 15.4.

FIGURE 15.4
An emergency services disclaimer

NOTE   When you are configuring EmergencyDialMask, make sure you consider Call Park routing—doing so is extremely important. Call Park routing will take precedence, and as such, the numbers used in the EmergencyDialMask parameter should be excluded from the Call Park orbit.

Creating individual policies allows different policies to be applied directly to specific sites or even individual users. These policies show up with Tag: prefixed to their name and are also known as tagged policies. This strategy provides more granular control over routing of emergency services and certainly makes sense in globally distributed companies.

The Location policy information is provided via in-band provisioning and can be assigned by one of three different ways:

♦   Network Site associated

♦   User associated

♦   Global

This allows specific configuration for individual sites, perhaps to enable E911 or not, ensuring that any user, even visitors to a location, will provide the required location information when placing an emergency call.

Defining the SIP Trunk

The SIP trunk will be a dedicated trunk to the emergency services provider, and you need to enable support for the additional payload of the location information. This is provided via a Presence Information Data Format Location Object (PIDFLO) payload type within the SIP message.

To configure this support, use the following command (assuming the gateway address is gw01.corp.masteringlync.org):

```
Set-CsTrunkConfiguration Service:PstnGateway:gw01.corp.masteringlync.org
-EnablePIDFLOSupport $true
```

By default, EnablePIDFLOSupport on all trunks is False.

WHAT'S DIFFERENT WHEN USING AN ELIN GATEWAY?

The principle is very much the same when using an ELIN gateway rather than a SIP trunk.

The difference really comes down to defining a dedicated ELIN to each location—and the fact that a gateway may be providing location information for more than one location (a location other than where it is physically situated), very similar to the way in which the SIP trunk operates.

When you're using a gateway, the location information database also requires emergency response locations (ERLs) to be populated as well as the ELIN number. This number becomes the emergency number during the emergency call. This is achieved by assigning the ELIN number using the -CompanyName parameter within the LIS cmdlets.

There is also a responsibility on the PSTN carrier to upload the number assigned to its Automatic Location Identification database.

Configuring the Voice Route

As introduced in Chapter 13, voice routes define for Lync Server 2013 the path from client to destination for the defined number (in this case the emergency services number).

Once you have the PSTN usage, Location Policy setting, and SIP trunk defined, the last remaining step is to define the voice route itself:

```
New-CsVoiceRoute -Name "EmergencyRoute" -NumberPattern "^\+911$"
-PstnUsages "EmergencyUsage" -PstnGatewayList @{add="e911-gateway-1"}
```

This command defines the route to the emergency service provider via the dedicated SIP trunk. In addition to this, you should define at least one secondary route to use if the SIP trunk fails and an emergency services call needs to be placed via a "normal" PSTN connection (which may be via a separate SIP trunk or some other legacy-style connection). The command would look like this:

```
New-CsVoiceRoute -Name "LocalEmergencyRoute" -NumberPattern "^\+911$"
-PstnUsages "EmergencyUsage" -PstnGatewayList @{add="e911-local-gateway-1"}
```

The parameter NumberPattern defined here must use the number defined in the EmergencyDialString used in the CsLocationPolicy cmdlet. In addition, the + must be included because Lync Server 2013 automatically adds a + to emergency calls.

Location Information

The previous section covered how to enable Lync Server 2013 to provide the location information; however, it did not show how to configure the location information itself.

Configuring the Location Database

The Lync 2013 client can use a number of methods to establish its location, determined from one of the following:

- Wireless access point
- Subnet
- Port
- Switch
- Manual

Upon sign-in, the client requests its location information from the server. In order for the server to determine the location of the client, it must be provided with as much information as possible. The following is an example request where the subnet information is provided:

```
<GetLocationsRequest xmlns:xsi="http://www.w3.org/2001/XMLSchema-instance"
xmlns:xsd="http://www.w3.org/2001/XMLSchema">
<Entity>sip:keith.lync@masteringlync.org</Entity>
<RSSI>0</RSSI>
<MAC>00-15-5d-19-41-06</MAC>
<SubnetID>192.168.2.0</SubnetID>
<IP>192.168.2.107</IP>
</GetLocationsRequest>
```

The client provides the location identifier to the server, which in turn queries the LIS database to return the specific location information to the client, as can be seen in Figure 15.5.

FIGURE 15.5
Client, pool, and
LIS database
interaction

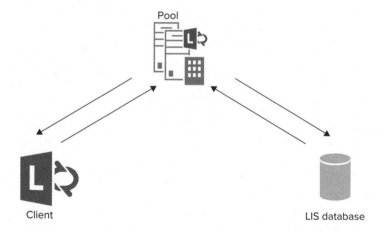

Pool

Client

LIS database

The server will return the response containing the address information:

```
<GetLocationsResponse xmlns:xsi="http://www.w3.org/2001/XMLSchema-instance"
xmlns:xsd="http://www.w3.org/2001/XMLSchema">
<ReturnCode>200</ReturnCode>
<presenceList>
```

```
<presence entity="sip:keith.lync@masteringlync.org
xmlns="urn:ietf:params:xml:ns:pidf">
<tuple id="_LIS:0">
<status>
<geopriv xmlns="urn:ietf:params:xml:ns:pidf:geopriv10">
<location-info>
<civicAddress xmlns="urn:ietf:params:xml:ns:pidf:geopriv10:civicAddr">
<country>UK</country>
<A1/>
<A3>Birmingham</A3>
<PRD />
<RD>MasteringLync Drive</RD>
<STS />
<POD />
<HNO>1</HNO>
<HNS />
<LOC>Birmingham</LOC>
<NAM>MasteringLync Organization</NAM>
<PC>AB12 3AB</PC>
</civicAddress>
</location-info>
<usage-rules>
<retransmission-allowed
xmlns="urn:ietf:params:xml:ns:pidf:geopriv10:basicPolicy">
true
</retransmission-allowed>
</usage-rules>
</geopriv>
</status>
<timestamp>2013-01-13T11:45:43.9369076Z</timestamp>
</tuple>
</presence>
</presenceList>
</GetLocationsResponse>
```

This is how the client would see the address:

MasteringLync Organization

1 MasteringLync Drive

Birmingham, AB12 3AB

UK

To ensure that this is a correctly formatted address, the LIS database entries must be verified against a public provider's address records.

Once connected and signed in, the Lync client will display the location field in one of three different modes (depending on the LocationRequired parameter as configured in the CsLocationPolicy command). The default view can be seen in Figure 15.6.

FIGURE 15.6
The Lync 2013
client displays the
default Location
field option.

The location information for the E911 location is stored in the LIS database, which is replicated to all servers along with the XDS (Configuration Management server) database in the RTCLOCAL instance. This ensures that there are no delays when location information is requested for emergency calls, and it also ensures that local server (or Survivable Branch Appliance) functionality can still provide this data in the event of a WAN outage to the data center.

Unfortunately for the administrator, this location information is separate from the location information provided for the Call Admission Control functionality (see Chapter 14, "Call Admission Control," for more information) and must be defined separately.

Locations can be defined independently using the Set-CsLisLocation cmdlets. Table 15.2 shows the parameters accepted by Set-CsLisLocation with a description of each.

TABLE 15.2: Set-CsLisLocation parameters

PARAMETER	DESCRIPTION
Instance	A location object
City	Maximum 64 characters
CompanyName	Maximum 60 characters
Country	Maximum 2 characters
HouseNumber	Maximum 10 characters
HouseNumberSuffix	Maximum 5 characters (additional information, such as *A*)
Location	Maximum 20 characters (the name for this location, such as *Suite* or *Office*)
PostalCode	Maximum 10 characters
PostDirectional	Maximum 2 characters (for example, the NW in 1st Avenue NW)
PreDirectional	Maximum 2 characters (for example, the NW in NW 1st Avenue)
State	Maximum 2 characters
StreetName	Maximum 60 characters
StreetSuffix	Maximum 10 characters (the *Street* or *Avenue* part of the address)

All the parameters are listed as "required"; however, blank entries are acceptable—because the address information is targeted to the United States, not all fields will be required, or indeed make sense, for other countries.

Each of the cmdlets used to input (and manage) the association of the location data has, as would be expected, a different dataset requirement for the determination of the location. Here are the cmdlets and the additional parameters required:

```
Set-CsLisPort
    ChassisID
    PortId
    PortIDSubType
Set-CsLisSwitch
    ChassisID
Set-CsLisSubnet
    Subnet
Set-CsLisWirelessAccessPoint
    BSSID
```

The associated `Get-` cmdlets will return the information about each type of location provision:

```
Get-CsLisPort
Get-CsLisSwitch
Get-CsLisSubnet
Get-CsLisWirelessAccessPoint
```

Determining which cmdlet is the correct one to use will be depend on a combination of the specific legal requirements in each location and the level of detail required as well as the current configuration of the network. For example, to be able to provide the location information down to the level of specific port configuration would require that port configuration to be in place; this can be a significant administrative overhead for the network's team. On the other hand, if the network configuration is a subnet per floor per building, that can be quite easily defined and imported to the database:

```
Set-CsLisSubnet -Subnet 192.168.2.0 -City Birmingham
-CompanyName "MasteringLync Organization" -Country UK -PostalCode "AB12 3AB"
-HouseNumber 1 -StreetName "MasteringLync Drive" -Location Birmingham
-Description "Birmingham Location"
```

The cmdlet `Get-CsLisCivicAddress` is used to view the address information specifically— that is, it does not return the company or location names, only the following fields:

```
HouseNumber
HouseNumberSuffix
PreDirectional
```

```
StreetName

StreetSuffix

PostDirectional

City

State

PostalCode

Country

MSAGValid
```

To return the additional information, the cmdlet `Get-CsLisLocation` is required and includes the additional fields shown:

```
Location

CompanyName
```

Once all the location information is defined, don't forget to publish it! Use `Publish-CsLisConfiguration` to achieve this task. (Note that there is no feedback from this cmdlet; even when you're using the `-Verbose` switch, the detail doesn't report anything useful, only that the cmdlet is being performed!)

If you have forgotten to publish the data, you can simply reopen a Lync PowerShell session and run the `Publish-CsLisConfiguration` cmdlet. it is not specific to location information posted in the PowerShell session; rather, it will publish any waiting location information.

Of course, there is also the `Unpublish-CsLisConfiguration`. Unfortunately, this isn't simply an "undo" but rather removes all of the LIS configuration information.

Using Secondary Location Databases

While Lync Server 2013 has an internal LIS database that will store the information for the location retrieval by the client, the database is required to be manually populated. In most cases, this will involve a lot of work. However, what if you already have that information in another database or, indeed, have another application that can provide the required data? Well, Lync Server 2013 can be configured to query other sources to retrieve the location information.

Lync Server 2013 allows for two methods of secondary location information retrieval:

◆ Simple Network Management Protocol (SNMP)

◆ Secondary Location Information Service

In both cases, configuration is via the `Set-CsWebServiceConfiguration` cmdlet.

If you have an SNMP application that can map MAC addresses to switch port information (also known as a *MACResolver*), the cmdlet is as follows:

```
Set-CsWebServiceConfiguration -MACResolveUrl "<app url>"
```

On the other hand, if you have a secondary database, the cmdlet is as follows:

```
Set-CsWebServiceConfiguration -SecondaryLocationSourceUrl "<app url>"
```

If both a location database and secondary source are configured, the location database is queried first, and only if no match is found is the secondary source queried.

Retrieving the Location Data by a Client

The client can be provided three types of address entry:

Validated   These addresses are defined by the administrator and are stored within the LIS database. They have been confirmed against a valid address from the Master Street Address Guide by an E911 service provider. This is achieved using the `Test-CsLisCivicAddress -UpdateValidationStatus $true` command. This in turn will update the `MSAGValid` attribute to `True`, as you can view in the output of the `Get-CsLisCivicAddress` cmdlet.

Suggested   These addresses are defined as are the *Validated* addresses; however, the `MSAGValid` attribute is `False` because they are not confirmed. This is how countries outside North America can leverage Location Information services.

Custom   These addresses are entered manually by the user, and up to a maximum of 10 are stored in the `PersonalLISDB.cache` file on the user's computer, in the `%userprofile%\ AppDate\Local\Microsoft\Communicator\<SIP URI>` folder.

In conjunction with the `LocationRequired` and `EnhancedEmergencyServicesEnabled` parameters, Table 15.3 shows the breakdown of the configuration options and the end result for the user (assuming `EnhancedEmergencyServicesEnabled` is True).

TABLE 15.3:   User experience based on configuration options

LOCATION REQUIRED	EXISTING LOCATIONS	USER EXPERIENCE
Yes	Validated location exists.	The location name is displayed automatically and cannot be changed unless `EnhancedEmergencyServicesEnabled` is `False`. If this is the case, then a new custom location can be created.
Yes	Single nonvalidated location exists.	The location name is displayed automatically and cannot be changed unless `EnhancedEmergencyServicesEnabled` is `False`. If this is the case, then a new custom location can be created.
Yes	Multiple nonvalidated locations exist.	The user is provided with a "Set Your Location" prompt, with a single suggested location entry. Note: Lync Server 2013 cannot provide multiple nonvalidated locations; however, a secondary source may.
Yes	Validated and custom locations exist.	The custom location is given preference.
Yes	Single nonvalidated and custom locations exist.	The suggested location is given preference.
Yes	Multiple nonvalidated and multiple custom locations exist.	The user is provided with a "Set Your Location" prompt in black text and may select other locations in the drop-down menu.
Yes	Custom location only.	The custom location information is automatically displayed.

TABLE 15.3: User experience based on configuration options *(CONTINUED)*

LOCATION REQUIRED	EXISTING LOCATIONS	USER EXPERIENCE
Yes	None	The user is provided with a "Set Your Location" prompt in red text to highlight the missing data.
No	None	The user is provided with a "Set Your Location" prompt in black text.
Disclaimer	None	The user is provided with a "Set Your Location" prompt in red text to highlight the missing data, along with a red X. It is not possible to dismiss the prompt, and the emergency services disclaimer is displayed if the user attempts to do so.

Other contact location information can be seen in the contact card shown in Figure 15.7. Nathan's office is defined as in the UK; his work and mobile numbers are defined, and his location is defined as Working from Home. In addition, time zone information is replicated here, so that you can see the local time for the user, which is extremely useful when you need to communicate globally.

FIGURE 15.7
Contact card location information

Roaming Users

Custom definitions allow users to store manually created entries for which the Lync 2013 client can automatically populate the location information field for frequently visited locations. When returning to a location for a second (or subsequent) time, the Lync 2013 client will not prompt the user; instead, it will read the data already entered into the cache file.

Figure 15.8 shows the blank custom location capture page—the user chooses which information to provide; not all of this information is required, even when the LocationRequired parameter is set to Disclaimer or Yes.

But what happens when multiple locations have the same subnet? It's not uncommon for the same private address range (192.168.0.0–192.168.0.255) to be used at multiple locations—for example, the local Starbucks and McDonalds could use the same private addresses. When that happens, the custom location cache file actually stores the MAC address of the network gateway as the identifier. This ensures that each location is globally unique even if the IP address range is shared.

Although you can still define an 11th custom location, it can only be used for the current Lync 2013 session and is not stored in the cache file.

Placing a Call

You've already seen the logs showing the exchange of information to determine the client location; Figure 15.9 shows the client feedback when placing a call.

The logs capture the PIDFLO data within the SIP INVITE traffic; here is the content of this log entry:

```
Content-Type: application/pidf+xml
Content-Transfer-Encoding: 7bit
Content-ID: <sip:keith.lync@masteringlync.org>
Content-Description: render; handling=optional
```

```
<?xml version="1.0" encoding="uft-8"?>
<presence entity="sip:keith.lync@masteringlync.org"
 xmlns="urn;ietf:params:xml:ns:pidf">
<tuple id="0"><status><geopriv
 xmlns="urn:ietf:params:xml:ns:pidf:geopriv10">
<location-info><civisAddress
 xmlns="urn:ietf:params:xml:ns:pidf:geopriv10:civicAddr">
<RD>1 MasteringLync Drive</RD><A3>Birmingham</A3>
<PC>AB12 3AB</PC><country>GB</country
></civicAddress></location-info>
<usage-rules><retransmission-allowed></usage-rules>
<method>Manual</method></geopriv>
<msftE911PidfExtn
  xmlsn="urn:schema:rtc.LIS.msftE911PidfExtn.2008">
<NotificationUri>sip:security@masteringlync.org</Notification>
<ConferenceUri>sip:+155512347890@masteringlync.org</ConferenceUri>
<ConferenceMode>two way</ConferenceMode>
<LocationPolicyTagID
 xmlns="urn:schema:Rtc.Lis.LocationPolicy TagID.2008">
<subnet-tagid:1></LocationPolicyTagID>
</msftE911PidfExtn></status></tuple></presence>
```

FIGURE 15.9
A client placing an
emergency call

Testing an E911 Call

Because there is special configuration needed for E911, it is wise to test. You certainly don't want to be relying on an untested phone routing and location information in an emergency.

Each country (and quite possibly each region within a country) is going to differ on the details of testing, but one thing is certain: No emergency services organization will appreciate the use of their resources for your test calls without some sort of prior notification and arrangement.

In some cases, it may be acceptable to place the call and explain to the operator that you are testing the phone system. However, be warned that this will not be tolerated for repeat testing! Of course, pick an expected "quiet" time, such as when your local major sports team is playing away or some large (nonlocal) event is being televised.

If using gateways, you can control the routing of calls to ensure that they do not leave your organization while testing, and this can allow you to capture logging to ensure that the location information is being transmitted correctly. Be sure to re-enable the emergency routing if you test using this method!

The Bottom Line

Describe the E911 requirements for North America.   Enhanced emergency services dialing provides location information to emergency services, enabling them to better respond in the event of an emergency.

> **Master It**   Is the provision of location information with emergency dialing compulsory?

Configure Lync Server 2013 to meet E911 requirements.   As a viable PBX, Lync Server 2013 is required to meet the E911 requirements to provide location information data and as such must have validated address information provided with each emergency call.

> **Master It**   Through what configuration items can location information data be delivered to the Lync 2013 client?

Understand how Location Information services can be used by users outside North America.   Although the actual requirements are only currently defined in locations in North America, beta program feedback from customers indicated that automatic Location Information services are extremely useful and desired worldwide.

> **Master It**   What specifically is required to enable Location Information services in North America, and what different requirements are in place for the rest of the world?

Understand how to query multiple sources of location information.   Lync Server 2013 allows for multiple sources of location information to be queried. Lync Server 2013 can be pointed to additional location databases or applications that can reduce the overhead in discovery and definition of all the network locations for an organization.

> **Master It**   Which cmdlet and parameters are used to configure secondary location information sources?

Chapter 16

Extended Voice Functionality

As organizations start to migrate their enterprise telephony to Microsoft Lync, they often require more functionality than is available within the core Enterprise Voice (EV) functionality. To fulfill the most common of these requirements, Microsoft has provided the following extended voice functions: dial-in conferencing, Response Groups, Call Park, and unassigned numbers.

For organizations that require additional functionality, a number of independent software vendors (ISVs) provide applications designed for Microsoft Lync; additional details of these and other third-party applications can be found in Chapter 19, "Third-Party Integration."

In this chapter, you will learn to:

◆ Understand dial-in conferencing

◆ Understand Response Groups

◆ Understand Call Park

◆ Understand unassigned numbers

◆ Design and implement solutions using extended voice functionality

Dial-In Conferencing

For years PBXs have had the ability to create conferences. In the early days, conferences were usually limited to three people and required using a dedicated key on the phone. Most people found this type of conference hard to set up and would usually end up cutting off people.

To provide a better solution, tools known as *conference bridges* were created. They allow participants to access their conference by calling an access number and then entering a conference ID and sometimes a passcode. These conference solutions usually come in two forms: ad hoc and scheduled.

Ad hoc conference bridges are often referred to as "meet-me" conference bridges because each user has an individual conference ID and can use it when desired. Because these conferences are ad hoc, even though users can use them when needed, there may be overall limits for the conferencing system in the number of people who can attend conference calls at any one time; these limitations can be in the form of license, hardware, or the number of available PSTN lines.

Scheduled conferences usually have to be booked, and a conference ID is assigned at the time of booking. One advantage of a scheduled conference is that resources are usually assigned to the conference, ensuring that if, for example, a conference is configured for four people from 15:00 to 17:00, then those resources will be available.

In addition to the type of conferencing bridge used, organizations have a choice of using either an on-premises system, usually integrated with their PBX, or a hosted solution. The recent trend has been for organizations to use hosted meet-me solutions. The move to hosted solutions has tended to be due to the cost of implementing on-premises solutions with organizations preferring monthly costs rather than upfront purchases.

Now that you have looked at what dial-in conferencing is, you can see how Lync handles it.

Understanding Dial-In Conferencing in Lync

In OCS 2007 R2, dial-in conferencing was a distinct feature with its own functionality, and when collaboration was required, the LiveMeeting client needed to be used. In Lync Server 2010, conferencing and collaboration have become a single feature called Online Meeting. The Online Meeting functionality removes the distinction between conferencing and collaboration, allowing all modalities to be used within a conference with a variety of access methods.

This section focuses specifically on the dial-in conferencing aspects that Online Meeting has to offer. Its approach falls within the meet-me category of conference bridges, with each allowed user (as defined by your policies) provided with their own conference ID. Dial-in conferencing provides the following functionality:

- PSTN access

- Roster of attendees

- Attendee management via roster

- Ability to secure conferences with a PIN

- Ability for Conference server to call attendees

- Meeting lobby

- Dual-tone multiple-frequency (DTMF) codes for management

- Name recording for anonymous users

- On-Demand Recording (client side)

- Built-in web scheduling

The last six items were new in Lync Server 2010 (although the built-in aspect of the web scheduler is new in Lync Server 2013; it was a separate download previously), and they addressed the limitations that prevented some organizations from migrating their dial-in conferencing facilities to OCS 2007 R2. In addition to the specific dial-in conferencing capabilities just listed, the following Online Meeting functions are also relevant:

- Scheduling via Microsoft Outlook 2010 is easy.

- Scheduling meetings via the Lync Web Scheduler allows non-Outlook users to set up meetings. Functionality can be restricted to a group of users.

- Clients can participate in meetings through a browser.

> ## ⊕ Real World Scenario
>
> ### CAN DIAL-IN CONFERENCING PAY FOR MY LYNC DEPLOYMENT?
>
> A number of organizations have been able to cover the costs of their entire Lync deployment purely on the basis of moving their conferencing away from a hosted solution to Microsoft Lync.
>
> Hosted conferencing solutions may appear to be cheap initially because there are no upfront capital expenditures; however, they can often become expensive due to the costs charged by the provider. These companies often provide the accounts for free but charge per minute, per participant for each conference call. There can also be additional charges for recording or for toll-free numbers. Let's take a look at the cost of a conference, based on the provider charging 5 cents per user per minute.
>
> A conference call with four participants for 30 minutes would cost $6.00 ($0.05 × 4 × 30). At these rates, an organization that has 10 people who perform 10 conferences a week for 52 weeks a year results in a cost of $31,200.00.
>
> Organizations often overlook these itemized costs when they are budgeting and performing cost analysis for Lync deployments. This is probably because IT departments often do not see these costs because they are assigned to individual departments, such as Sales. Although dial-in conferencing may not pay for the entire Lync deployment, it can certainly help defray the costs.

You'll see many of these functions later as you explore configuration, implementation, and client-side functionality, but for now let's look at the architectural and backend elements.

Architecturally, there are two main items to take into consideration when planning and setting up dial-in conferencing: the Audio/Video Conferencing service and server and the configuration of Enterprise Voice, which is discussed in Chapter 13, "Getting Started with Voice." With Lync Server 2010, it was possible to separate the A/V components of conferencing into a separate pool. This allowed for better scaling of conferencing, but this capability is no longer available with Lync Server 2013.

Architecturally, the only additional component needed for Lync Server 2013 is the Office Web Application (WAC) server. Without this additional server, meetings will be unable to host PowerPoint presentations (even with legacy clients).

Focusing specifically on the dial-in capabilities, a number of components depend on the Front End servers:

Web Components   These are used for the Dial-In Conferencing web page, allowing participants to look up conference access numbers and for users to set their PIN.

Conferencing Attendant Application   This accepts calls from the PSTN, prompts for conference details, and then routes the calls to the correct conference.

Conferencing Announcement Application   This is used once the participant has joined the conference; it plays announcements to callers and monitors and accepts DTMF tones for conference controls.

Web components also provide a Reach client option, which allows access to Online Meetings in the context of dial-in conferencing; the web components allow participants to specify a number for the conference bridge to call them (also known as "call me"), and participants can also view the meeting in a browser (including audio, if they do not wish to be called back, and also video). The ability for the conference bridge to call a Reach client participant can be restricted with a policy.

Although having the Lync Edge components deployed is not a requirement for dial-in conferencing, it does add another access method to conferences, and it allows federated users to access the conference the same way a user belonging to the organization would. This allows them to view the roster for the conference in the same way a user of the organization would and to bypass any costs associated with dialing access numbers.

Before you learn how to configure dial-in conferencing, it is worth briefly looking at the *meeting lobby*. This feature, new in Lync Server 2010, creates a "lobby" where users can be "parked" when they enter a meeting; the meeting presenter can then choose whether to allow them into the meeting. This provides a level of access control for the meeting. When creating the meeting, users can configure whether the lobby is to be used or not.

Configuring Dial-in Conferencing Features

Now that you know what dial-in conferencing in Lync can do, it is time to look at how it is configured. Configuration—most of it—can be performed either through the Control Panel or through PowerShell. That is, all of the required configuration to get conferencing up and running can be done through both interfaces, but PowerShell needs to be used to configure some of the more complex and custom features.

For dial-in conferencing to work, you need to configure the following components:

◆ Enterprise Voice

◆ Web components

◆ Conferencing policies

◆ Meeting configuration

◆ Access numbers

◆ PIN policies

Of these, all but the first two can be configured using the Control Panel as well as the related PowerShell cmdlets. For example, Figure 16.1 shows the Control Panel tab for configuring access numbers. In addition, the following optional components can be configured using PowerShell:

◆ Edge servers

◆ DTMF mappings

◆ Join and Leave announcements

◆ Conference directories

Chapter 6, "Installation," covers configuring web components and publishing them to the Internet as well as deploying Edge servers. In addition, setting up Enterprise Voice is covered in Chapter 13.

FIGURE 16.1
Configuring access
numbers via the
Control Panel

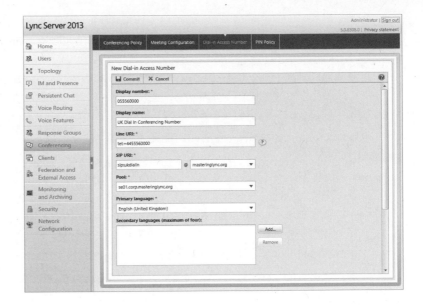

CONFERENCING POLICIES

Conferencing policies can be configured on a global, site, or user basis, depending on whether you require different users to have different settings. The global policy is created by default but can be modified as required.

The conferencing policy is used to control all aspects of conferencing, not just dial-in conferencing, but in this section we'll cover only the options that are either required or relevant to dial-in conferencing. In the following and similar definitions throughout the chapter, only the PowerShell parameters will be listed. Options equivalent to most of the cmdlets and parameters are available through the Control Panel.

When reviewing the PowerShell cmdlets, we'll focus on the creation cmdlets. They use the verb New, and for each of these cmdlets there are cmdlets for changing settings (Set), reviewing settings (Get), and deleting them (Remove), and although they are not explicitly discussed except as needed, they are available. Set and New cmdlets use the same parameters; the Get and Remove parameters are limited to the Identity parameter.

As mentioned previously, conferencing policies can be managed either through the Control Panel (Conferencing ➤ Conferencing Policy) or through PowerShell. To create a new policy through PowerShell, the New-CsConferencingPolicy cmdlet is used in conjunction with the parameters outlined here:

◆ Identity: This is the policy name, which is prefixed with site: if the policy is a site policy rather than a user policy.

◆ AllowAnonymousParticipantsInMeetings: This allows anonymous participants.

- `AllowAnnotations`: This allows participants to annotate slides and use the whiteboard.

- `AllowAnonymousParticipantsInMeetings`: This allows users to connect to a meeting without authenticating.

- `AllowAnonymousUsersToDialOut`: This allows anonymous users to dial out. It is the "call me" functionality covered earlier.

- `AllowConferenceRecording`: This allows the call to be recorded.

- `AllowExternalUserControl`: This allows external and anonymous users to record.

- `AllowExternalUsersToRecordMeeting`: This allows external users to record meeting content. This setting can be very important in restricted environments where data cannot be allowed to leave the site.

- `AllowExternalUsersToSaveContent`: This is similar to the preceding setting but it's for downloadable content rather than recorded.

- `AllowIPAudio`: This allows audio and covers PSTN audio as well.

- `AllowIPVideo`: This allows video to be used in the meeting.

- `AllowLargeMeetings`: This allows the meeting size to be greater than 250 attendees.

- `AllowMultiView`: This allows the multiple simultaneous video setting to be controlled.

- `AllowNonEnterpriseVoiceUsersToDialOut`: This allows participants to dial out of a conference even if their user settings do not normally allow for Enterprise Voice capability.

- `AllowParticipantControl`: This allows control of desktop sharing to be passed to other attendees.

- `AllowPolls`: This allows polls to be created.

- `AllowSharedNotes`: This allows the shared note capability of OneNote to be leveraged in a meeting.

- `AllowUserToScheduleMeetingsWithAppSharing`: This allows a user to create a scheduled meeting and leverage App Sharing within the meeting.

- `AppSharingBitRateKb`: This defines the maximum kilobits allowed for App Sharing.

- `AudioBitRateKb`: This defines the maximum kilobits allowed for audio.

- `DisablePowerPointAnnotations`: This disables the capability to annotate PowerPoint slides.

- `EnableAppDesktopSharing`: This allows for limited granular control of desktop sharing, either the full desktop or a single application (or none).

- `EnableDialInConferencing`: This allows participants to call into a conference using a PSTN access number.

- `EnableFileTransfer`: This controls the ability to transfer files within a meeting.

- `EnableMultiViewJoin`: This allows the user to join a conference with MultiView enabled.

- `EnableP2PFileTransfer`: This allows file transfer between individual users (outside of a meeting).

- `EnableP2PRecording`: This allows peer-to-peer recording (outside of meetings).

- `EnableP2PVideo`: This allows peer-to-peer video calls.

- `FileTransferBitRateKb`: This defines the rate for file transfers.

Once the policy has been created, it needs to be assigned to users. Global and site policies are assigned automatically as described in Chapter 10, "User Administration"; therefore, only user policies need to be assigned. You can do this through the Control Panel or through PowerShell using the `Grant-CsConferencingPolicy` cmdlet, as in the following example:

```
Grant-CsConferencingPolicy -Identity "corp\keith_lync"
-PolicyName "Std Dial In Policy"
```

This grants the "`Std Dial In Policy`" to the domain account with the username `corp\keith_lync`.

Meeting Policies

Meeting policies allow you to specify the types of meetings that can be created, and they can be created at a global, site, or pool level. They can be managed through the Control Panel (Conferencing ➤ Meeting Configuration) or through PowerShell. To create a new policy, use the `New-CsMeetingConfiguration` cmdlet.

The parameters for configuring meeting policies are as follows:

- `Identity`: Policy name.

  - For site policy, this needs to be prefixed with `site:`.

  - For a pool policy, this is be the pool FQDN prefixed with `service:UserServer:`.

- `AdmitAnonymousUsersByDefault`: This parameter permits anonymous users in the meeting by default.

- `AssignedConferenceTypeByDefault`: This parameter sets the conference default type. Set it to `True` for meetings to be public by default. Set it to `False` for meetings to be private by default.

- `CustomFooterText`: This defines the text footer applied when users join a meeting.

- `DesignateAsPresenter`: This parameter designates which users are automatically presenters. It can set to `None`, `Company`, or `Everyone`.

- `EnableAssignedConferenceType`: This parameter sets the conference type. If set to `True`, users can create public or private conferences, and setting it to `False` means only private meetings can be created. The only difference between them is that a different conference ID and access URL will be used for each private conference.

- `PstnCallersBypassLobby`: This bypasses the lobby for PSTN users.

- `RequireRoomSystemAuthorization`: This is used by Lync room systems, defining the requirement for someone to log in to the room system itself.

PINs

To authenticate when calling into a meeting via the PSTN, users need to set a PIN, which is used in conjunction with their phone numbers. This PIN is also used to allow users to log in to Lync IP phones. The policy for managing PINs can be configured on a global, site, or user basis.

If you are managing PIN policies using the Control Panel, they can be accessed under Conferencing ➢ PIN Policy; alternatively they can be managed through PowerShell using the New-CsPinPolicy cmdlet. The following options are used:

◆ Identity.

◆ Allow Common PIN Patterns (AllowCommonPatterns). Common patterns are defined as follows:

    ◆ Containing four or more consecutive digits—for example, 781234

    ◆ Repeating digits—for example, 114488

    ◆ Matching the user's phone number or extension

◆ Description.

◆ Maximum Logon Attempts (MaximumLogonAttempts).

◆ Minimum Password Length (MinPasswordLength). This is the minimum PIN length; it can be set to a minimum of 4 and a maximum of 24 digits.

◆ PIN History (PINHistoryCount). This can be set to 0 for no history and a maximum of 20.

◆ Days before the PIN must be changed (PINLifetime).

PIN lockouts work in two ways, based on the concept of *local logon failures* and *global logon failures*. The Local Logon Failures value is the number of failed attempts allowed within 30 minutes. If this is exceeded, the PIN is locked for 1 hour, at which time the Local Logon Failure count is reset. Global Logon Failures is the maximum number of PIN attempts allowed before the PIN is locked out and has to be unlocked by an administrator. This value is not reset when a user successfully logs in, and failed login attempts continue to be added to the Global Logon Failure counter. The counter resets only when an administrator unlocks a user's PIN.

The Local Logon Failure and Global Logon Failure values are predefined. Setting Maximum Logon Attempts in the PIN policy will only override the Local Logon Failure value. The global lockout value cannot be modified. As shown in Table 16.1, both limits depend on the number of digits in the PIN rather than the minimum password length specified in the policy.

TABLE 16.1:   PIN attempts

PIN LENGTH	LOCAL LOGON FAILURE LIMIT (UNLESS OVERRIDDEN)	GLOBAL LOGON FAILURE LIMIT
4	10	100
5	25	1,000
6 or more	25	5,000

The PIN policy is granted to users using the `Grant-CsPinPolicy` cmdlet.

CONFERENCE ACCESS NUMBERS

Some organizations have only one access number; others have numbers covering many countries. Before you can create access numbers, you'll need to take a quick look at Enterprise Voice dial plans because the access numbers you'll need depend on them.

Dial plans are used to provide a link between users and access numbers. When a user schedules a conference, the default numbers shown in the meeting request are the ones associated with the dial plan with which the user is associated. They are also used to translate extensions to full E.164 numbers. When users authenticate via DTMF, this allows them to enter their extension number rather than their full Direct Inward Dial number (DID).

To use a given dial plan, its dial-in conferencing region needs to be defined. You can do this when you create the dial plan or edit it; details on how to perform these actions are covered in Chapter 13. You can enter any text you wish in the dial plan region field, but it should be something that external participants can understand, such as a city or country. This will be shown on the dial-in web page so that participants can look for a number other than the one specified on the invitation to the conference. It is also used in Outlook, allowing the user to select a different region and thus change the access numbers shown in their invitation.

Once the dial plans are finished, you can create the access numbers, either through the Control Panel (Conferencing ➤ Dial-In Access Number) or through PowerShell (`New-CsDialInC onferencingAccessNumber`) using the following parameters:

- `PrimaryUri`: This is the contact URI, prefixed with `sip:`.

- `DisplayName`: This is the display name of the contact and how it should appear in Lync.

- `DisplayNumber`: This is how the number should be displayed in meeting requests and the dial-in web page.

- `LineURI`: This is the phone number prefixed with `tel:`.

- `Regions`: This is a comma-separated list of the regions the number is assigned to, such as US and Canada.

- `Pool`: This is the pool with which the access number is associated.

- `PrimaryLanguage`: This is the primary language used.

- `SecondaryLanguages`: This is a comma-separated list of up to four secondary languages, such as `en-US` and `fr-CA`.

Each access number can be configured with a primary language and up to four secondary ones. This option is often used when access numbers are defined for locations in which multiple languages are commonly spoken—for example, Montreal, Canada, where French is usually the primary language, followed by English.

A list of supported languages can be found by running this command:

```
Get-CsDialInConferencingLanguageList | Select-Object -ExpandProperty Languages
```

This command retrieves a list of the supported languages and restricts it to displaying only the language codes.

Once the access number has been created, users will be able to call it to access the conferences; they can also been seen on the Dial-In Conferencing web page, which is shown in Figure 16.2. In a change from Lync Server 2010, the In-Conference DTMF controls are also shown on this page.

FIGURE 16.2
Dial-In
Conferencing web
page

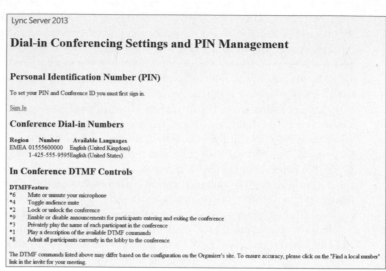

Lync Server 2013

Dial-in Conferencing Settings and PIN Management

Personal Identification Number (PIN)

To set your PIN and Conference ID you must first sign in.

Sign In

Conference Dial-in Numbers

Region	Number	Available Languages
EMEA	01555600000	English (United Kingdom)
	1-425-555-9595	English (United States)

In Conference DTMF Controls

DTMF	Feature
*6	Mute or unmute your microphone
*4	Toggle audience mute
*2	Lock or unlock the conference
*9	Enable or disable announcements for participants entering and exiting the conference
*3	Privately play the name of each participant in the conference
*1	Play a description of the available DTMF commands
*8	Admit all participants currently in the lobby to the conference

The DTMF commands listed above may differ based on the configuration on the Organizer's site. To ensure accuracy, please click on the "Find a local number" link in the invite for your meeting.

Before moving on, it is worth looking at the order in which the numbers are presented in the meeting requests and Dial-In Conferencing web page. By default, the order is alphabetical by region. If there are multiple numbers within the region, they are listed by comparing the first digit in each number. The lowest number is listed first, followed by the second lowest to the highest. If the first digit is the same, then the second number is compared. This process is continued as long as necessary to order the numbers. You may decide to reorder the numbers for a region for a number of reasons. For example, you may want a number with a higher capacity at the start of the list or a toll-free number at the end of the list. (Reordering regions isn't possible.) A specific order can be set using the Set-CsDialInConferencingAccessNumber cmdlet and its Priority and ReorderedRegion parameters, as in this example.

```
Set-CsDialInConferencingAccessNumber -Identity "sip:USdialin@masteringlync.org"
 -Priority 0 -ReorderedRegion "EMEA"
```

This will move the Toll Chargeable number to the top of the list for the U.S. region numbers.

GLOBAL ACCESS NUMBERS

Organizations often use hosted conferencing providers so that they can have global access numbers, which are usually required for organizations with a global presence. Such organizations do not need to be multinationals; many small businesses have customers in other countries.

Not having these numbers could be a potential roadblock to Lync migration conferencing for businesses that require them. Therefore, you may need to consider how to provide these numbers. Traditional PSTN providers can often provide global numbers, but setting them up is usually expensive and so is operating them.

One potential way around this is to work with a SIP trunk provider. These providers are often more competitive in their pricing for global access numbers and are often an excellent way to provide the number(s) required. While an organization may not want to move all of its PSTN access to the cloud, this approach is a good option for conferencing. And depending on how busy the conferencing system will be, it may also mean that you won't need additional PSTN bearers from the PSTN provider.

A list of certified SIP trunking providers for Lync can be found at `http://technet.microsoft`
`.com/en-us/lync/fp179863`.

ADDITIONAL CONFERENCING CONFIGURATION OPTIONS

The next three configuration items, entry and exit announcements, DTMF mappings for PSTN users, and conference directories, are not exposed through the Control Panel; they can be configured only through PowerShell.

Entry and Exit Announcements

Entry and exit announcements will be played only to people who access the bridge using the PSTN. It is assumed that announcements are not required for users who have access to the conference roster through one of the Lync clients. These settings are configured on either a global or site level. They are created using the `New-CsDialInConferencingConfiguration` cmdlet, and the following options are available:

- `Identity`, either `Global` for the global policy (only used when viewing or modifying the settings) or, if creating a site policy, the site name prefixed with `site:`.

- `EnableNameRecording` specifies whether users are able to record their names when they access a conference. If it is disabled, `EntryExitAnnouncementsType` needs to be set to `ToneOnly`.

- `EntryExitAnnouncementsEnabledByDefault`.

- `EntryExitAnnouncementsType` can be set to either `UseNames` or `ToneOnly`, depending on the announcement type needed.

DTMF Mappings

The next items to look at are the DTMF mappings for PSTN users that can be used during a conference call. Most of the options are limited to presenters, but two of the commands, Mute/Unmute and Private Rollcall, can be used by any participant.

These settings are configured on either a global or site level. The following options are available to create the `New-CsDialInConferencingDtmfConfiguration` cmdlet:

- `Identity`, either `Global` for the global policy (only used when viewing or modifying the settings) or, if creating a site policy, the site name prefixed with `site:`.

- `AdmitAll`: Admit all participants who are in the lobby.

- `AudienceMuteCommand`.

- `CommandCharacter`: Prefix for the commands, can be an * or #.

- ◆ `EnableDisableAnnouncementsCommand`: Play Entry/Exit announcements.

- ◆ `HelpCommand`.

- ◆ `LockUnlockConferenceCommand`.

- ◆ `MuteUnmuteCommand`.

- ◆ `PrivateRollCallCommand`: Play roll call.

Digits assigned to these commands need to be in the range from 1 to 9 and unique. The command prefix can vary or remain constant for each of the entries. If you need to disable any of these settings, you can do so by setting them to `$null`.

Conference Directories

The final item to look at is the conference directory; because Lync is based on SIP URIs, you need a way to map the numeric conference IDs that are required to access a conference to the relevant SIP URI. This is where the conference directories come into play.

By default, there is a single conference directory. This lone directory is sufficient for some organizations, but for larger organizations or for those who use different conference IDs for each conference, the conference ID number can grow rather long.

To keep the ID at a length that people will accept—usually no more than six to seven digits—multiple conference directories can be created. A new conference directory should be created for every 999 Lync users.

To create a conference directory (`New-CsConferenceDirectory`), the following parameters must be specified:

- ◆ `Identity`: This is a unique numeric number in the range from 1 to 999.

- ◆ `HomePool`: This is the Lync pool that hosts the conference directory. To get a list of the current conference directories, you can use the command

    `Get-CsConferenceDirectory | FT Identity, ServiceID`

    which will return a easy-to-read table listing each directory:

```
Identity                 ServiceId
---------                ------------
1                        UserServer:se01.corp.masteringlync.org
2                        UserServer:se02.corp.masteringlync.org
```

Implementing Dial-In Conferencing

Now that you've looked at the capabilities of dial-in conferencing, you need to see how to implement it. To do this, let's work through the following scenario:

Your organization is migrating away from its current hosting provider to Lync dial-in conferencing. Dial-in numbers are required in the following countries:

- ◆ *The United States*

- ◆ *The United Kingdom*

All users should be able to use the conference bridge. In addition, to match the current conference bridge, the Lock And Unlock Conference DTMF option needs to be set to *2.

After studying the requirements statement, you see that you need to complete the following steps:

1. Create two regions, each with its own access number.

2. Modify the DTMF mappings for Lock and Unlock.

In addition to the explicit requirements just detailed, you will need to configure some other options for dial-in conferencing to operate. You are going to set each of them to have a global scope. Some of the settings are configured by default, but you will set them in the PowerShell commands to make sure they are configured as required.

The first thing you need to configure is the global conferencing policy:

```
Set-CsConferencingPolicy –Identity Global -AllowAnonymousUsersToDialOut $true
-AllowAnonymousParticipantsInMeetings $true -AllowConferenceRecording $true
-AllowIPAudio $true -EnableDialInConferencing $true
```

This code modifies the global conferencing policy, allowing the required settings for all users who are not affected by a site policy or have a user policy assigned.

The next item to configure is the global meeting policy:

```
Set-CsMeetingConfiguration -Identity Global -AdmitAnonymousUsersByDefault $true
-AssignedConferenceTypeByDefault $true -DesignateAsPresenter Company
-EnableAssignedConferenceType $true -PstnCallersBypassLobby $true
```

This code modifies the global meeting policy, allowing the required settings for all users who are not affected by a site policy or who have a user policy assigned.

The final policy to configure is the global PIN policy:

```
Set-CsPinPolicy -Identity Global -AllowCommonPatterns $True -MinPasswordLength 5
```

This modifies the global PIN policy, allowing common PIN patterns and shorter PIN lengths for all users who are not affected by a site policy or who have an assigned user policy.

Now you can configure the access numbers; they will be assigned to two existing dial plans:

```
New-CsDialInConferencingAccessNumber
-PrimaryUri "sip:USDialIn@masteringlync.org" -DisplayNumber "1-425-555-9595"
-DisplayName "US Dial In Number" -LineUri "tel:+14255559595"
-Pool "se01.corp.masteringlync.org" -PrimaryLanguage "en-US" -Regions "US"
New-CsDialInConferencingAccessNumber
-PrimaryUri "sip:UKDialIn@masteringlync.org" -DisplayNumber "01555600000"
-DisplayName "UK Dial In Number" -LineUri "tel:+441555600000"
-Pool "se01.corp.masteringlync.org" -PrimaryLanguage "en-GB" -Regions "EMEA"
```

These two commands create the two dial-in conferencing numbers, the first for the United States with U.S. English and the second for the United Kingdom with U.K. English. When these two commands are run, the output for the U.S. access number will be similar to the following:

```
Identity           : CN={f50ac1dc-f9cb-412e-a612-6ff28bf1876f},
CN=Application Contacts,CN=RTCService,CN=Services,CN=Configuration,DC=corp,
DC=masteringlync,DC=org
PrimaryUri         : sip:USDialIn@masteringlync.org
DisplayName        : US Dial In Number
DisplayNumber      : 1-425-555-9595
```

```
LineUri            : tel:+14255559595
PrimaryLanguage    : en-US
SecondaryLanguages : {}
Pool               : se01.corp.masteringlync.org
HostingProvider    :
Regions            : {US}
```

The DTMF mappings are the last things to configure; to configure them, you will need to modify the existing global policy:

```
Set-CsDialInConferencingDtmfConfiguration -Identity Global
-LockUnlockConferenceCommand 2
```

This modifies the global DTMF mapping to use 2 as the unlock code for the conference; this will affect all conferences except where the conference is hosted in a site that has a site policy assigned.

This completes the dial-in conferencing configuration. To check the configuration, run the corresponding Get commands to view the settings just configured.

Using Dial-In Conferencing

Now that you have implemented dial-in conferencing, you need to take a look at how users will use it. Although a conference can be accessed from virtually anywhere, here you should concentrate on how an information worker will use dial-in conferencing using Outlook and their Lync client.

Although scheduling a conference call is not a requirement for a user to use the conference bridge, Microsoft has provided an easy way to populate a meeting request in Outlook with the required information, as shown in Figure 16.3. To access this screen, go to the Calendar view and select Online Meeting or create a new Online Meeting item. You can customize these settings for a conference; by selecting Meeting Options when you create or view the meeting, you can access the following settings:

◆   Who can access the meeting

◆   Who will be a presenter

◆   If a different conference ID and URL should be used

Once a conference has been organized, the attendees need to be able to join it. There are a few ways to do this: they could call the access number, click the Join link in the meeting request, or access it from the reminder for the meeting (shown in Figure 16.4).

The last two options launch the simple join process, in which the user's default web browser starts quickly, followed by the Lync client joining the conference. If the Lync client was not installed, the Lync 2010 Attendee client will start if it is installed; if not, by default, the Reach client will start. With Lync Server 2013, the preferred client (if the Lync client itself is not available) is the web client.

Once you've joined the conference, you can see the participants, as illustrated in Figure 16.5. On this screen, you can also control the Audio settings; for example, you can escalate the conference to a videoconference if video is enabled. Endpoints that do not support video will continue to access the conference using audio only.

FIGURE 16.3
Scheduling a conference

FIGURE 16.4
Joining a meeting from a reminder

FIGURE 16.5
A conference roster

From the roster, you can also control a participant's conference options. As shown in Figure 16.6, you do this by right-clicking the participant and choosing the required option from the context menu.

FIGURE 16.6
The conference context menu

The final option to look at in the Lync client is inviting people to an active conference. You can do this in the following ways: by dragging and dropping someone from the buddy list into the conference, by entering their name (retrieved via the address list) or phone number (as shown in Figure 16.7), or by sending them an email with the conference details. One thing to note is that for the first two of these options, the users will be added straight to the conference. If the invited person is using Lync, they will see that they are joining a conference; however, if they are joining from a cell phone, for example, it may come as a shock!

FIGURE 16.7
Adding users to a conference

The other element to consider is the Dial-In Conferencing web page, as shown in Figure 16.8. This interface is what users will use to configure their PIN to authenticate a conference with an access number. Additionally, this page lets participants look up more access numbers for Online Meetings.

In general, users will be want to authenticate using their extension and PIN rather than with their full number. You can enable this functionality and allow them to retain the ability to log in using the full number; when enabling users for Enterprise Voice, their TelURI should be defined with "**;ext=*xxxx***" appended to their number - where *xxxx* is the user's extension.

For example, assuming the user DDI number is 01234 567890 and the extension is 7890, when you enable this user, rather than simply enabling as TEL:+441234567890, you would enable the user as TEL:+441234567890;ext=7890.

Not only can you use the Lync client, but you can manage a meeting from the Aries IP phones. On these devices, you can add people to a conference, view the attendee list, remove people, and allow access to people waiting in the lobby. If extended features are enabled, you will also be able to join a conference from the Calendar view.

FIGURE 16.8
Setting a PIN on the Dial-In Conferencing web page

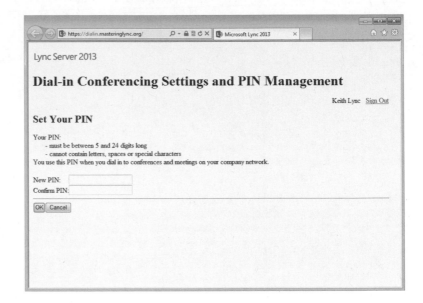

Response Groups

Hunt groups and basic Automatic Call Distribution (ACD) are provided by most PBXs. They allow calls to be distributed between multiple users, but their functionality varies between PBXs, and the majority provide a minimum level of functionality.

Hunt groups provide the most basic form of call distribution. For each hunt group, a list of numbers to which to route calls is defined. The PBX will route each incoming call according to the distribution method defined, which is usually one of the following:

Serial Always starts at the first entry. If there is no answer or the line is busy, it tries the second number and continues until someone answers. When the list is exhausted, it goes back to the beginning, effectively starting over.

Parallel Rings all of the numbers at the same time.

Round Robin For the first call, it starts at the first entry. If there is no answer or the line is busy, it tries the second number. If the second answers, then the next call starts at the third number. When the list is exhausted, it goes back to the beginning, effectively starting over.

Most Idle It starts at the number that has been idle the longest, and if there is no answer, it tries the next longest idle, and so on through the list.

Most PBXs allow the administrator to define the ring time on each number, along with a maximum wait time. Once the maximum wait time has been reached, calls will be either terminated or, more commonly, routed to a different number; this could be an overflow number or a voice mailbox.

Automatic Call Distribution (ACD) operates in a similar way to hunt groups in that calls are distributed to a range of numbers; the difference is that there tends to be more intelligence involved. With ACD, callers may be provided with a DTMF-based Interactive Voice Response (IVR), allowing them to choose based on a question. The call is then usually routed to a defined hunt group.

For example, the question could be "To which department would you like to speak?" This would be followed by a list of options, such as "Press 1 for Sales, press 2 for Support, press 3 for Customer Service." The customer would then select 1, 2, or 3 and then be routed to the correct set of numbers. Once they make a selection, depending on the PBX, they may hear ringing or music on hold (MOH) until their call is answered. The announcement will usually have to be provided in a certain format, which tends to be a very basic file type. In addition, there is usually a limit to the number of ACDs that can be defined. If the organization requires more complex call routing abilities, then a contact center is usually required. In Lync, hunt groups and ACD features are incorporated into the Response Group application.

Understanding Response Groups in Lync

To provide hunt group and basic ACD features for organizations, Microsoft created the Response Group application and its set of cmdlets. Response Groups match the functionality found in most PBXs and exceed it to a point that they can equal some basic call center offerings, although there are limitations that prevent this feature from being classed as a call center. Response Groups exceed the following capabilities in the majority of PBXs:

◆ Text-to-speech for announcements

◆ Voice along with DTMF IVR options

◆ Ability to specify working hours

◆ Ability to build custom workflows

Response Groups are made up of three main components:

Agent Groups   These are used to define whether the agents will need to sign in or not, the number of seconds that a call will wait for an agent to answer, the routing method, and which users are members of the group.

Queues   These are used to define which agent group will handle the call, along with the Timeout and Overflow settings.

Workflows   These are the initial entry points into the system. They provide the IVR functionality, which queues the call should be routed to, and other options such as working hours. In Lync as in OCS 2007 R2, there are predefined workflows. These are as follows:

◆ Hunt groups

◆ Interactive, up to two levels, up to four questions per level IVR

CONFIGURATION ORDER

When configuring Response Groups, whether you are using the Control Panel and Response Group web interface or the PowerShell cmdlets, you need to create the items in a certain order. You need to define the agent groups first, followed by queues, and then the workflows. If you do not create them in the correct order, you may end up not being able to complete the configuration of an item. This results in you needing to create the prerequisite item and then starting again to configure the item.

It you are using PowerShell, note that for queues and workflows, PowerShell commands usually need to be run before the main queue and workflow commands are run, as you'll see in the following sections. Creating queues and custom workflows through PowerShell can be a complex task, and it is a task that should be carefully planned and thoroughly tested to ensure that nothing is missed. After the following summary of the configuration tools and options, we'll go through a complete implementation of a Response Group, demonstrating the most important cmdlets and parameters.

RESPONSE GROUP CONFIGURATION OPTIONS

Only a couple of configuration options are available at the Response Group level, and they are set on a per-pool basis. These settings are automatically created by Lync during the pool-creation process; as such, there is no "New" cmdlet. The settings can, however, be modified and viewed using `Set-CsRgsConfiguration` and `Get-CsRgsConfiguration`, respectively. The following parameters are available:

- `Identity`: The Lync pool hosting the Response Group prefixed with `service:ApplicationServer:`.

- `AgentRingbackGracePeriod`: The ringback grace period is the period in which a call will not return to an agent if they declined it. This only really comes into effect when too few agents are available, and it is defined in seconds between 30 and 600.

- `DefaultMusicOnHoldFile`: The default MOH file used when no specific MOI I file is defined in the workflow.

- `DisableCallContext`: The call context consists of the details of the IVR responses and the wait time that is shown to the agent when it answers a call using the Lync client.

`Move-CsRgsConfiguration` is used when migrating from OCS 2007 R2 to Lync; it will migrate all of the Response Groups, not just the configuration settings.

Before looking at the rest of the Response Group cmdlets, you need to see how the `Set` cmdlets work because they operate in a slightly different way than most of the other Lync `Set` cmdlets. The difference is that the settings cannot be directly edited; instead, an instance of the setting first needs to be retrieved into a PowerShell variable, then the required updates need to be performed, and finally the instance needs to be fed into the `Set` command. Here's an example:

```
$variable = Get-CsRgsAgentGroup -Identity
service:ApplicationServer:se01.corp.masteringlync.org -Name "Attendant"
$variable.RoutingMethod = "RoundRobin"
Set-CsRgsAgentGroup -Instance $variable
```

You also need to use this method when you're creating queues and workflows because instances often need to be passed into these commands. Some of the PowerShell cmdlets are used only for populating a variable to pass into another cmdlet.

Agent Groups

Agent groups define a list of agents and their associated settings, such as call routing method and alert time. A single group can be assigned to multiple queues. Agent groups can be managed through the Control Panel (Response Groups ➤ Group) or through PowerShell. To create a new agent group, use the `New-CsRgsAgentGroup` cmdlet; the following parameters are available:

- Parent: This is the FQDN of the pool to host the agent group; it is prefixed with `service:ApplicationServer:`.

- `AgentAlertTime` (Ring time on Agent): This cmdlet is defined in seconds with a range from 10 to 600.

- `AgentsByUri` (Agent List): This cmdlet is a comma-separated list of agents. Each agent should be prefixed with `sip:`.

- `Description`: This is a description of the agent group.

- `DistributionGroupAddress` (Distribution Group Containing Agents): This is the email address associated with the distribution group.

- `ParticipationPolicy` (Participation Type): This is set to `Formal` if the agent needs to sign in to receive calls from the Response Group or `Informal` if they will always receive calls from the Response Group.

- `RoutingMethod`: The routing methods are as follows:

  - Longest Idle (`LongestIdle`)

  - Round Robin (`RoundRobin`)

  - Serial (`Serial`)

  - Parallel (`Parallel`)

  - Attendant (`Attendant`)

  Except for the Attendant routing method, all of these methods were discussed earlier in this section. As its name implies, the Attendant method is a new routing method in Lync used primarily for attendants. It operates like the Parallel method except that it ignores the user's presence state when routing a call. Normally, Response Groups will route a call to an agent only if it has a presence of Available or Inactive. When the Attendant routing method is used, the call will be routed to the agent irrespective of its presence state; the only exception to this is if the state is Do Not Disturb.

There are two ways to define which users are members of an agent group—either by defining a list of agents using their SIP URIs or by specifying a distribution group. Although specifying a distribution group can save having to specify a list of agents, you need to be aware of the following:

- Nested distribution groups will be ignored.

- Only a single distribution group can be defined.

◆ For the Serial and Round Robin routing methods, the calls will be routed to agents in the order listed in the distribution group. This can often cause issues when you want to use a different agent order.

When creating the agent group, you should specify only one of the two options, either AgentsByUri or DistributionGroupAddress. If you are creating a group in which you intend to use this agent group, you should store the result of the New command in a variable.

QUEUE AND WORKFLOW PRELIMINARIES

Once the agent groups have been created, you'll need to create the queues and then the workflows. To create these elements, you will need to pass into the respective cmdlets the results of a number of other cmdlets, which define various characteristics of the queue. The elements you need to configure first are as follows:

◆ Prompts

◆ Answers

◆ Questions

◆ Call actions

Prompts are either uploaded recordings or messages generated using text-to-speech, and they are used to read messages such as "Welcome to the Sales Department" or IVR questions. These prompts are not created in their own right; they are passed into a variable to pass into another cmdlet.

The New-CsRgsPrompt accepts two parameters: either TextToSpeechPrompt, which allows for up to 4,096 characters to be specified, or an audio file, using the AudioFilePrompt parameter.

If you use audio files rather than TTS, they needs to be either a WAV file (.wav) or a Windows Media Audio file (.wma). WAV files need to meet the following criteria:

◆ 8 or 16 bits

◆ Linear pulse code modulation (LPCM), A-Law or mu-Law

◆ Mono or stereo

◆ 4MB or less

For Windows Media Audio files, there are no specific limitations imposed by Lync. However, you should give some consideration to the bit rate because the higher the bit rate, the greater the load placed on the Lync servers.

The audio file containing the prompt is not directly uploaded; instead, the cmdlet requires a byte array representation of the file. This byte array is created using the Get-Content cmdlet; this array is used with the Import-CsRgsAudioFile cmdlet to upload the file. Here's an example:

```
$RGSPromptAF = Import-CsRgsAudioFile
-Identity "service:ApplicationServer:se01.corp.masteringlync.org"
-FileName "ResGroup1FirstPrompt.wav"
-Content (Get-Content C:\RGSPrompt.wav -Encoding byte -ReadCount 0)
```

This code imports the audio file to the Lync server. It first gets a byte array of the `RGSPrompt.wav` file, which is sent to the Lync servers and saved as `ResGroup1FirstPrompt.wav`. The `FileName` specified needs to be unique and does not need to match the name of the file you are uploading. That is because you are uploading the prompt to Lync as a byte array rather than the actual file; therefore, the original name is never uploaded.

The next cmdlet you need to look at is `New-CsRgsAnswer`, which is used to specify an answer for a question. This cmdlet does not create anything, and it is used only to populate a variable. It uses these parameters:

- `Action`: This parameter is used with the `New-CsRgsCallAction` cmdlet to specify the action that occurs when the response is chosen.

- `DtmfResponse`: The DTMF response can be *, #, or 0 through 9.

- `Name`: This is the name of the answer.

- `VoiceResponseList`: This is a list of voice responses this answer will match, separated by commas.

When creating the answer, either `DtmfResponse` or `VoiceResponseList` or both must be specified.

Now that you can create both the answer and the prompt, you can create a question using the `New-CsRgsQuestion` cmdlet. Like the previous two cmdlets, this one also needs to be passed into a variable. The `New-CsRgsQuestion` cmdlet uses these parameters:

- `Prompt`: This is the question to be asked. It should be a prompt object.

- `AnswerList`: This is a comma-separated list of answers. If the question allows two answers, at least two answer objects should be specified.

- `InvalidAnswerPrompt`: This is a prompt object that will be played if an invalid answer is entered.

- `Name`: This is the name of the question.

- `NoAnswerPrompt`: This is a prompt object that will be played if no answer is entered.

When a question with associated answers has been created, you need to look at the call action. To make Response Groups even more complicated, the `New-CsRgsAnwer` cmdlet requires that a call action already be created; therefore, to get to a stage where you have a question created, you will already have had to create a call action. But a call action can also be linked to a question if required and may require a prompt to be created.

A call action can do any of the following things:

- `Terminate`: This will end the call.

- `TransferToQueue`: This allows an agent to answer the call.

- `TransferToQuestion`: This transfers to a question.

- `TransferToUri`: Transfers to a SIP URI, such as another Response Group, specified in the `Uri` parameter.

◆ `TransferToVoiceMailUri`: Transfers to the voice mailbox, specified in the `Uri` parameter.

◆ `TransferToPSTN`: This transfers to a PSTN number specified in the `Uri` parameter.

To create a call action, use the `New-CsRgsCallAction` cmdlet. The following parameters are available.

◆ `Action`: This is one of the previously specified actions.

◆ `Prompt`: This is a prompt to play before the action is carried out. It should be a prompt object.

◆ `Question`: This is required only if the Transfer to Question action is chosen and should be a question object.

◆ `QueueID`: This is used if Transfer to a Queue is specified. It should be the identity of the queue that was previously created. If the queue is in a variable, this is retrieved using `$variable.Identity`.

◆ `Uri`: This is used if Transfer to a URI or PSTN is specified. It should be prefixed with `sip:`.

You'll see examples of all of these commands in action in the section coming up shortly.

QUEUES

Queues are used to define the actions once the caller has been processed by the workflow. This could be after an option is selected on an IVR, or callers could be routed straight to a queue as soon as they call the workflow if, for example, the workflow is configured as a hunt group.

With all of the preliminaries configured, you are ready to create a queue. Unlike the last few sets of cmdlets you've looked at, the `New-CsRgsQueue` cmdlet actually creates groups. It uses the following parameters:

◆ `Parent`: This is the FQDN of the pool to host the agent group, prefixed with *service*:*ApplicationServer*:.

◆ `Name`: The is the group name.

◆ `AgentGroupIdList`: This is a comma-separated list of agent groups. The groups will be worked through in order; if no agent in group 1 answers, then group 2 will be tried, and so on.

◆ `Description`: This describes the queue.

◆ `OverflowAction`: This is a call action object.

◆ `OverflowCandidate`: The Call to Overflow can be set to `NewestCall` or `OldestCall`.

◆ `OverflowThreshold`: The call count to overflow can be set between 0 and 1000. When the specified number of calls is in the queue, either the oldest or newest call will overflow.

◆ `TimeoutAction`: This is a call action object.

◆ `TimeoutThreshold`: This threshold is specified in seconds with a range from 10 to 65536. When the time-out is hit for a queued call, it will follow the time-out call action defined.

Queues can also be configured through the Control Panel. With this method, the preliminary configuration of items such as Overflow Action is not required because they are configured at the same time as the queue, which can be accessed at Response Group ➤ Queue. Once the queues and associated aspects have been created, you can move on to workflows and the additional cmdlets required.

WORKFLOWS

Workflows are the initial entry points. They define the phone number and contact URI associated with the workflow, the questions to be presented, whether it is an IVR, and the associated queues for the call to be routed to, along with settings such as opening hours and holidays.

Workflows can be configured through PowerShell, in which case there are a number of items that need to be configured before the actual workflow is created. If configuration is performed using the Response Group Configuration Tool, then all configuration is performed when the workflow is created. The Configuration tool (Figure 16.9) can be accessed through the Control Panel (Response Group ➤ Workflow ➤ Create Or Edit A Workflow) or through `https://poolfqdn/RgsConfig`.

FIGURE 16.9
The Response Group

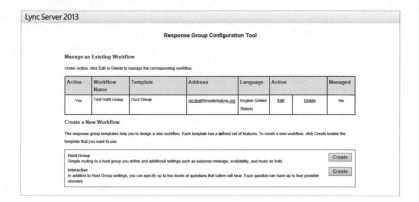

The first workflow elements to define are holidays; you do that using the `New-CsRgsHoliday` cmdlet. This cmdlet does not create anything and as such needs to be passed into a variable. It lets you specify a start date and time along with an end date and time. The following parameters are required:

- `Name`
- `StartDate`
- `EndDate`

Dates should be formatted as *MM/DD/YYYY HH:SS* AM|PM; as in this example, `12/25/2011 12:00 AM`.

When an individual holiday has been created, you need to add it to a holiday set. These are created and as such have associated `Get`, `Set`, and `Remove` cmdlets.

The `New-CsHolidaySet` cmdlet is used to create the holiday sets, which are linked to the workflows to indicate when the Response Group should be open. The following parameters are required:

◆ `HolidayList`: This is a comma-separated list of holiday objects.

◆ `Name`: This is the name of the holiday list.

◆ `Parent`: This is the FQDN of the pool to host the holiday set, prefixed with *service*:*ApplicationServer*:.

Now you need to define the business hours the Response Groups are open. To do that, you need to define time ranges to pass into the Hours of Business cmdlet.

Time ranges are defined using the `New-CsRgsTimeRange` cmdlet. This doesn't create anything, so its result needs to be passed into a variable. The cmdlet takes the following parameters:

◆ `Name`: This is the name of the time range.

◆ `OpenTime`: This is defined as *HH*:*MM* using a 24-hour clock.

◆ `CloseTime`: This is defined as *HH*:*MM* using a 24-hour clock.

If the business hours are the same for multiple days, such as Monday to Friday, only one time range needs to be defined for these hours.

Next, the business hours need to be defined using the `New-CsRgsHoursOfBusiness` cmdlet. Business hours are created and, as such, have associated `Set`, `Get`, and `Remove` cmdlets. `New-CsRgsHoursOfBusiness` allows two sets of hours to be specified for each day of the week, allowing it to close for lunch, for example. This cmdlet has the following parameters:

◆ `Name`: This is the name of the business hours.

◆ `Parent`: This is the FQDN of the pool to host the business hours, prefixed with *service*:*ApplicationServer*:.

◆ `MondayHours1` and `MondayHours2` through `SundayHours1` and `SundayHours2`: These are `TimeRange` objects.

Once all of the required objects have been created, you can finally create the workflows. Workflows link together all of the elements you've reviewed, and creating them is the final step required to complete a Response Group. They are created with `New-CsRgsWorkflow` cmdlets, using the following parameters:

◆ `Name`: This is the name of the workflow.

◆ `Parent`: This is the FQDN of the pool to host the workflow, prefixed with *service*:*ApplicationServer*:.

◆ `PrimaryUri`: This is the SIP address of the Response Group, prefixed with `sip:`.

◆ `Active`: This specifies whether the workflow is active. If it is not active, calls will not be accepted.

◆ `Anonymous`: If this is set to `True`, the agent's identity will be hidden.

◆ `BusinessHoursID`: This is a Business Hours object.

- ◆ `CustomMusicOnHoldFile`: This is an Audio File object, which is created using the `Import-CsRgsAudiofile` cmdlet.

- ◆ `DefaultAction`: This is the default call action to use when the workflow is open; it requires a Call Action object.

- ◆ `Description`: This is a text-based description for the workflow

- ◆ `DisplayNumber`: This is the number displayed when searched for, or calling, both incoming and outgoing calls.

- ◆ `EnabledForFederation`: This defines whether federated users can access the workflow via Lync. If `False`, federated users would be required to dial the actual number.

- ◆ `HolidayAction`: This is the call action to use during a holiday; it requires a Call Action object.

- ◆ `HolidaySetIdList`: This is the Holiday Set object to use.

- ◆ `Language`: This is used to specify the language to be used for Text-to-speech.

- ◆ `LineUri`: This is the PSTN phone number for the workflow, prefixed with `tel:`.

- ◆ `Managed`: This defines whether management of this workflow has been delegated.

- ◆ `ManagersByUri`: This is a collection of SIP addresses of the managers for the workflow.

- ◆ `NonBusinessHoursAction`: This is the call action to use outside business hours. It requires a Call Action object.

- ◆ `TimeZone`: This is the time zone for holidays and business hours.

As part of the workflow creation process, an application contact is created in the configuration partition in Active Directory. The contact stores the same information the Lync-enabled user would—for example, the display name and line URI. This contact is used for a number of tasks:

- ◆ When an incoming event occurs, such as a phone call, Lync will search both user and application contacts for a match. The application contact provides the application for the call to be routed to, in this case the Response Group application.

- ◆ It will be processed by the Lync Address Book service, allowing users to search for and add the contact to their Lync contacts list.

To view a list of application contacts in Lync, you can use the `Get-CsApplicationEndpoint` cmdlet.

ANONYMOUS RESPONSE GROUPS AND PRIVACY MODE

If an agent has Privacy mode enabled, the Response Group Presence Watcher can't see it because Response Groups have no additional privileges other than a standard user when it comes to presence.

In order for a Response Group to operate when Privacy mode is enabled, the RGS Presence Watcher contact needs to be in the agents buddy list.

Implementing Response Groups

Now that you've looked at what you can do with Response Groups, it's time to see how you can implement them. To do this, let's work through a fairly complete, realistic scenario.

Your organization requires a Response Group to be configured for routing calls to a group of three attendants. All attendants should see all of the calls, but they should be able to specify whether they will receive calls or not. The identity of all attendants should be hidden.

In addition, the callers should be told that they are being placed in a queue and hear music on hold while waiting. Outside business hours, calls should be routed to an Exchange mailbox along with calls that have been waiting for longer than 5 minutes. Callers should be told they are being transferred to voice mail.

After studying the requirements statement, you determine that you need to do the following:

◆ Create an agent group

◆ Create a queue with overflow settings specified for callers waiting in the queue

◆ Create a workflow with the announcement, working hours, and agent anonymity defined

To begin, you create the agent group:

```
$AGroup = New-CsRgsAgentGroup
-Parent "service:ApplicationServer:se01.corp.masteringlync.org"
-AgentsByUri "sip:keith.lync@masteringlync.org",
"sip:adrian.lync@masteringlync.org", "sip:lester.lync@masteringlync.org"
-ParticipationPolicy Formal -RoutingMethod Attendant -Name "Attendant Group"
```

With this command, you created the agent group. It is created as a formal group, with the three specified agents and routes using the Attendant routing method to ensure that calls are presented to agents irrespective of their state (except for Do Not Disturb).

Now you need to create the prompt to transfer the caller to voice mail on time-out:

```
$TimeoutPrompt = New-CsRgsPrompt -TextToSpeechPrompt "Unfortunately all of our
operators are busy, we are transferring you to voice mail."
```

This stores the prompt in $TimeoutPrompt, allowing you to pass it into the next command. Next, you need to create the call action for the time-out:

```
$TimeoutCallAction = New-CsRgsCallAction -Action TransferToVoiceMailUri
-Uri "sip:attendantMB@masteringlync.org" -Prompt $TimeoutPrompt
```

This stores the details into $TimeOutCallAction. The action transfers the call to the specified voice mailbox.

Now that you have created the required objects, you can create the queue:

```
$AQueue = New-CsRgsQueue -Parent "service:ApplicationServer:se01.corp.masteringlync.org"
-Name "Attendant Queue"
-AgentGroupIdList $AGroup.Identity -TimeoutAction $TimeoutCallAction
-TimeoutThreshold 300
```

This creates the queue and stores the details in the $AQueue. It also references the agent group you created earlier; because you need the Identity value out of $AGroup, you specify $AGroup.Identity.

Now you're ready to create the objects required for the workflow. The first step is to define the time range for the business hours:

```
$TimeRange = New-CsRgsTimeRange -Name "BusinessHours" -OpenTime 08:00
-CloseTime 18:00
```

This stores the time range, which is 08:00 to 18:00, in $TimeRange.
Now define the business hours:

```
$BusinessHours = New-CsRgsHoursOfBusiness -Name "Attendant Open Hours"
-Parent "service:ApplicationServer:se01.corp.masteringlync.org"
-MondayHours1 $TimeRange -TuesdayHours1 $TimeRange
-WednesdayHours1 $TimeRange -ThursdayHours1 $TimeRange
-FridayHours1 $TimeRange
```

This creates the business hours. Into this statement, you'll pass the $TimeRange several times because you require the same opening hours for each day that the business is open. Because the hours aren't specified for Saturday or Sunday, the Response Group will default to being closed on those days.

Now you need to create the prompt to transfer the caller to voice mail outside business hours:

```
$OBHPrompt = New-CsRgsPrompt -TextToSpeechPrompt "We are currently closed, we
are transferring you to voice mail."
```

This creates the Out of Business Hours prompt. Note that only a sort of "ghost object" is created at this point; the information is merely stored in the $OBHPrompt variable until the command to create the workflow is run.

Now you need to create the call action for outside business hours:

```
$OBHCallAction = New-CsRgsCallAction -Action TransferToVoiceMailUri
-Uri "sip:attendantMB@master1nglync.org" -Prompt $OBHPrompt
```

This creates the Out of Business Hours action. Again, at this point, the information is merely stored in the $OBHCallAction variable until the workflow is created.

Now that you have created the business hours, you need to create the default call action and associated prompt:

```
$DefaultPrompt = New-CsRgsPrompt -TextToSpeechPrompt "Thank you for calling
Masteringlync, please wait for an attendant."
```

This creates the default prompt. Again, at this point, the information is merely stored in the $DefaultPrompt variable until the workflow is created.

Next, you need to create the call action to route to the agents:

```
$DefaultCallAction = New-CsRgsCallAction -Action TransferToQueue
-QueueID $AQueue.Identity -Prompt $DefaultPrompt
```

This creates the default call action. Again, at this point, the information is merely stored in the $DefaultCallAction variable for use in the next command.

Now that you've created the required objects for the workflow, you can finally create the workflow:

```
New-CsRgsWorkflow -Name "Attendants" -Parent
"service:ApplicationServer:se01.corp.masteringlync.org"
-PrimaryURI "sip:AttendantRGS@masteringlync.org" -Active $true
-Anonymous $true -BusinessHoursID $BusinessHours.Identity
-DefaultAction $DefaultCallAction -DisplayNumber "1-425-555-1000"
```

```
-EnabledForFederation $true -Language "en-US" -LineURI "tel:+14255551000"
-NonBusinessHoursAction $OBHCallAction
```

This creates the actual workflow. Into this workflow you can reference the call actions created earlier. For the business hours, reference the `Identity` stored within `$BusinessHours`. The two action variables are not actually created in Lync; they are stored within the variables, so you don't need to specify a particular setting in them.

When this command is run, the output is similar to the following:

```
Identity                 : service:ApplicationServer:se01.corp.masteringlync.org
/6876ce92-7b33-450f-8a73-38fc7d5c1789
NonBusinessHoursAction : Prompt=We are currently closed, we are transferring you
to voice mail.
Action=TransferToVoicemailUri
Uri=sip:attendantMB@masteringlync.org
HolidayAction            :
DefaultAction            : Prompt=Thank you for calling, please wait for an
attendant.
Action=TransferToQueue
QueueId=dbaf6136-9386-4964-a49f-8610f0f761de
CustomMusicOnHoldFile  :
Name                     : Attendants
Description              :
PrimaryUri               : sip:AttendantRGS@masteringlync.org
Active                   : True
Language                 : en-US
TimeZone                 : GMT Standard Time
BusinessHoursID          : service:ApplicationServer:se01.corp.masteringlync.org
/6f7314e7-a88f-4f23-aa64-a9262404a050
Anonymous                : True
Managed                  : False
OwnerPool                :
DisplayNumber            : 1-425-555-1000
EnabledForFederation     : True
LineUri                  : tel:+14255551000
HolidaySetIDList         : {}
ManagersByUri            : {}
```

Now that the Response Group is configured, you can run the corresponding `Get` commands to check the configuration.

Using Response Groups

Now that you've implemented Response Groups, you need to see how network users work with them. As with dial-in conferencing and other Lync client features, admins may need to provide some level of training or support to their users. Here you are going to look at only the agent aspects of Response Groups.

If a user is assigned to a formal workflow, the first thing they need to do is log into the workflow by selecting Response Group Settings from the Lync client, which then loads the web page shown in Figure 16.10. Users will be presented with the queues to which they are assigned, and they will be able to check the queues they want to sign into.

Note that users are presented with the queues from only their home pool. If they are members of queues on another pool, they must manually direct their browser to the path to sign in on the other pool: `https:<pool fqdn>/RgsClients/Tab.aspx`.

FIGURE 16.10
Signing into a
queue

When the agent receives a call, the toast that appears to notify the agent of the call (Figure 16.11) will contain the name of the Response Group. By receiving this information, the agent knows, for example, what greeting to use when answering the call.

FIGURE 16.11
The toast for a
Response Group

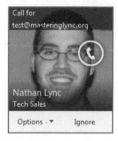

If the call is from a Response Group that uses an IVR, the agents will be presented with the IVR options that the caller selected along with their wait time, as shown in Figure 16.12.

With this information, the agent can handle the call as required. In addition, they can introduce additional modalities, as with a normal Lync call, and they can escalate to a conference if needed. The only time this is restricted is if the Response Group that they answered the call on is configured for Agent Anonymity, in which case they cannot do any of the following:

◆ Share individual applications, the desktop of a single display, or the entire desktop

◆ Transfer files

◆ Use whiteboard or data collaboration

◆ Escalate to a conference

What happens when the agent needs to make an outbound call? For the most part, making an outbound call is no different for a user configured as an agent than it is for a normal user. The only time this differs is if a user is a member of a Response Group that is configured for Agent Anonymity. In this case, as shown in Figure 16.13, the agent can choose whether they are making the call on behalf of themselves or the Response Group.

FIGURE 16.12
IVR details for a call

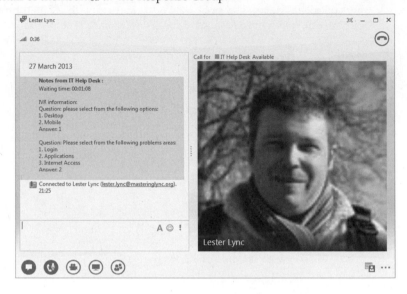

FIGURE 16.13
Choosing whether to make an anonymous outbound call

Call Park

Education, healthcare, warehousing, and retail are just a few of the organization types that take Call Park for granted. It is a feature they use every day and assume that it will be available on any PBX that they want to deploy. To fulfill the requirements of these organizations and others, Call Park was added as a voice application in Lync, removing a potential stumbling block for these organizations to migrate to Lync.

While you may not have heard of Call Park before, you have probably heard of it being used. If you have been in a store and heard "Call for Joe Blogs on extension 1023" over the public address system, they were probably referring to an incoming call for Joe Blogs that was "parked" on extension 1023. This allowed Joe Blogs to easily retrieve the call by calling 1023 from any of the store phones and be connected immediately.

Why would a store use Call Park rather than, for example, having the switchboard operator put the call on hold, page Joe Blogs to call them, and then transfer the call? The new technology has emerged due to the limitations of PBXs and the way they operate. The easiest way to understand this is to look at how a call flow would operate:

1. Customer calls the store.

2. Switchboard answers.

3. Customer asks to talk to the store manager.

4. Switchboard operator places the call on hold and pages the store manager.

5. Store manager calls the operator; if the operator is busy, it could take a while for the call to be answered.

6. Operator takes a note of the number the store manager called from and hangs up.

7. Operator takes the customer off hold and transfers it to the number the store manager called from; if by sheer chance someone else has called this number before the operator managed to transfer the call, then the operator will have to wait to transfer the call.

As you can see, this is a long process and includes a number of areas where issues can occur—for example, suppose the switchboard operator is busy. While that may not happen in a small retail store, in a busy hospital, the wait time could be tremendous. Some PBXs, including Lync, can shortcut part of this process by allowing calls to be *joined*, effectively removing the last two steps. However, there can be other limitations, such as the number of calls a person can put on hold at any one time.

In summary, Call Park allows a call to be parked on an extension number and retrieved by calling that extension number.

Understanding Call Park in Lync

Now that you understand what Call Park is, you need to examine how it works within Lync and the configuration options available. No separate installation is required for Call Park; it is installed as part of Lync. To use Call Park, you just need to configure it. You do that in the following stages:

◆   Voice policy configuration

◆   Call Park extensions

◆ Call Park Service configuration

◆ Call Park music on hold

In Lync, any user can retrieve a parked call by calling the extension on which it was parked. From a user standpoint, the only configuration option is whether the user can park a call. This is configured through the Voice policy assigned to the user, which was covered in Chapter 13.

CALL PARK EXTENSIONS

Call Park extensions are referred to in Lync as *orbits*, and they can be configured through the Control Panel or using PowerShell. These numbers have a lot of restrictions:

◆ The maximum number of orbits per range is 10,000.

◆ The maximum number of orbits per Lync pool is 50,000.

◆ They cannot be Direct Inward Dial numbers (DIDs).

◆ They must match this regular expression:

`([\*|#]?[1-9]\d{0,7})|([1-9]\d{0,8})`

The first two restrictions are not likely to cause an issue because most organizations usually require a small range of numbers to use. This range should be no larger than required; for most organizations this tends to be less than 100 extensions.

The requirement that the number not be a DID is fairly unusual for Lync, because most voice-related features require E.164 numbers to be assigned to them. A Call Park number cannot be a DID because retrieving calls from the PSTN is not supported, although retrieving calls from a PBX is supported.

The final requirement is for the number to match a specific regular expression. This breaks down as follows:

◆ It must start with a *, #, or one of the digits 1 through 9.

◆ If the number starts with a * or #, it must be followed first by a single digit in the range 1 through 9, and then followed by up to seven digits.

◆ If the number starts with a 1 through 9, it can be followed by up to eight digits.

Table 16.2 lists some sample orbit numbers.

TABLE 16.2: Sample orbit numbers

START NUMBER	END NUMBER
*1	*9
#100	#140
1000	1100
859000	859010

When assigning numbers to be orbits, you need to make sure they will not be affected by number normalizations, such as those found in the dial plans. If the number a user tries to call is converted to another number, they will be unable to retrieve the call.

This also applies to any normalizations that may be performed by a gateway linking to a PBX or by the PBX itself, if there is a requirement to retrieve calls from the PBX.

Orbits can be configured through the Lync Control Panel under Voice Features ➤ Call Park as well as via PowerShell. From the Call Park tab, shown in Figure 16.14, they can be created, edited, and deleted. To create the orbit using the New-CsCallParkOrbit cmdlet, you specify the following:

◆ Identity: This is the orbit range name.

◆ NumberRangeStart: This is the orbit range start number.

◆ NumberRangeEnd: This is the orbit range end number.

◆ CallParkService: This is the Application server to host the orbits.

For Call Park, the application server is a Lync pool FQDN prefixed with ApplicationServer:. This allows you to define which pool will host the parked calls. If you will be parking a large number of calls, this could be resource intensive because the pool needs to manage these calls and also stream music on hold if configured.

FIGURE 16.14
Creating an orbit
via Call Park

MANAGING THE CALL PARK SERVICE

The Call Park service configuration can only be managed through PowerShell. There are two configuration levels: global and site. The global level will apply to all Lync sites unless a site-level configuration exists. Both levels have the same configuration options; to create a new configuration, use the `New-CsCpsConfiguration` cmdlet:

- `EnableMusicOnHold`: A `True` or `False` option. This indicates whether music on hold (MOH) should be played. There is a default MOH file that ships with Lync; this can be replaced if required.

- `CallPickupTimeoutThreshold`: Defined as *HH*:*MM*:*SS*. This defines the length of time before the call recalls. This can be as little as 10 seconds or as long as 10 minutes. The default is 90 seconds.

- `MaxCallPickupAttempts`: The number of times the call will ring the person who parked the call before it will reroute to the Timeout URI. The default is 1.

- `OnTimeoutURI`: A SIP address to which the parked call will be routed if the call is not answered after the defined number of call pickup attempts. The SIP URI can be either a user or a Response Group.

MUSIC ON HOLD

A custom MOH file is uploaded to the Call Park service using a dedicated PowerShell command. Only one MOH file can be used per application server; when a new file is uploaded, the existing file will be overwritten.

The file needs to be in WMA 9 format, and it is recommended that it has the following characteristics: encoded at 44kHz, 16 bit, mono, with a constant bit rate (CBR) or 32kbps.

CONVERTING TO THE RECOMMENDED FORMAT

To convert audio files to the recommended format for music on hold, you can use Microsoft Expression Encoder, an application that allows existing files to be encoded to the correct settings, among other things. Expression Encoder is available in a number of versions; the free version, which can convert most audio formats, can be downloaded from here:

`www.microsoft.com/download/en/details.aspx?id=24601`

Expression Encoder is designed to do a lot more than convert audio files, so the conversion process can be confusing. The following steps will walk you through converting the file.

1. Select Transcoding Project.
2. Import the MOH file by choosing File ➤ Import.
3. Under the Encode tab on the right-hand side of the application, expand Audio and complete the settings as shown in the following screen shot.

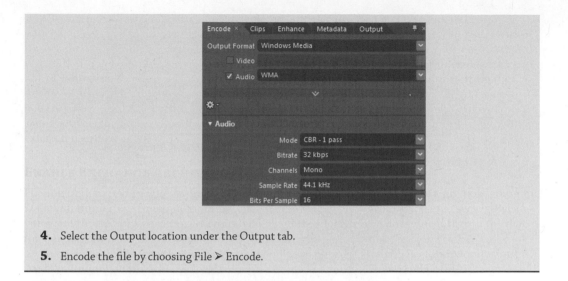

4. Select the Output location under the Output tab.

5. Encode the file by choosing File ➤ Encode.

The MOH file is not directly uploaded; instead, the cmdlet requires a byte array representation of the file. This byte array is created using the `Get-Content` cmdlet, which is combined with the `Set-CsCallParkServiceMusicOnHoldFile` cmdlet to upload the file. Here's an example:

```
$MoHFile = Get-Content -ReadCount 0 -Encoding byte "C:\music_on_hold.wma"
Set-CsCallParkServiceMusicOnHoldFile
-Service ApplicationServer:se01.corp.masteringlync.org -Content $MoHFile
```

These two commands create a byte array of the file `music_on_hold.wma` in the `$MoHFile` variable, then upload it to the Lync Server and set it as the Call Park service music on hold.

Implementing Call Park

Now that you know what you can and can't do with Call Park, let's look at how you can implement it. To do this, use the following scenario:

As part of the Microsoft Lync deployment, some of the staff members need access to the Call Park functionality. All other staff members should be able to retrieve calls but not park them. The staff members who should be able to park calls are the switchboard operators and the personal assistants. There should be capacity to park 30 calls at any one time; calls should recall after 30 seconds, and if a call is not answered when recalled, it should be directed to the switchboard.

After reviewing the given scenario, you determine that Call Park should be configured as follows:

◆ Only the switchboard and the PA require Call Park.

◆ Only 30 orbits need to be set up.

◆ The pickup time-out needs to be 30 seconds.

◆ The Timeout URI needs to be the switchboard Response Group.

◆ There should be only one recall attempt.

Although Lync does not require these tasks to be completed in any particular order, you don't want to enable the users until the rest of the configuration has been completed; therefore, you should work through the list in reverse order.

The first step is to configure the Call Park service, which can be performed only via PowerShell. Since there is only a basic setup, you will configure the service at the global level rather than on a per-site basis.

```
Set-CsCpsConfiguration -Identity Global -CallPickupTimeoutThreshold 00:00:30
-OnTimeoutURI "sip:switchboard@masteringlync.org" -MaxCallPickupAttempts 1
```

This sets the call pickup threshold, which specifies that a call reaching the time-out is routed to the switchboard after the call has rung back to the person who parked it once. This setting will apply to all users who are not covered by a site-specific policy.

Once the Call Park service is configured, you need to create the orbit numbers; although you could configure these through the Control Panel as shown earlier, you will continue to use PowerShell. Since you were not provided with specific extensions to utilize, you will use the range 1000 to 1029.

```
New-CsCallParkOrbit -Identity "CPO 1" -NumberRangeStart 1000
-NumberRangeEnd 1029 -CallParkService "se01.corp.masteringlync.org"
```

This creates the Call Park orbit, with a range of 1000 to 1029, allowing 30 calls to be parked; this pool is shared across all users in the pool. Its output will be similar to the following:

```
Identity          : CPO 1
NumberRangeStart  : 1000
NumberRangeEnd    : 1029
CallParkServiceId : ApplicationServer:se01.corp.masteringlync.org
CallParkServerFqdn : se01.corp.masteringlync.org
```

Almost everything is configured, but you still need to enable the users to park calls. To do this, you need to modify the Voice policies for the switchboard operators and personal assistants; because they already exist, you need to modify the existing policies:

```
Set-CsVoicePolicy -Identity Switchboard -EnableCallPark $true
Set-CsVoicePolicy -Identity PA -EnableCallPark $true
```

These two commands enable Call Park for the two Voice policies, one for PAs and the other for the switchboard.

This completes the Call Park configuration; run the corresponding `Get` commands to check the configuration.

Using Call Park

Now that you've implemented Call Park, you need to understand how network users can park and retrieve calls. Calls can be parked using the Lync client, the Attendant client, or Lync

Phone Edition. These clients operate in the same way; calls are parked by transferring the call to the parking lot, as shown in Figure 16.15.

FIGURE 16.15
Parking a call

When the call is transferred, you will see that the call has been placed on hold; this notification is then replaced with the number on which the call was parked, as shown in Figure 16.16.

FIGURE 16.16
A parked call extension

If there are no available extensions on which to park the call, the user will receive a notification like the one shown in Figure 16.17. Note that the call is left on hold to ensure that the caller being parked does not accidentally overhear anything they shouldn't.

FIGURE 16.17
Call park failure

If the parked call has not been retrieved, it will recall to the user who parked the call, as shown in Figure 16.18; this is to avoid a situation where a call is never retrieved. When the recall occurs, the user will be informed that it is a recall.

FIGURE 16.18
A call retrieved

To retrieve the call, the extension on which it was parked needs to be called. Once the call has been retrieved, it will operate like any other Lync call.

Unassigned Numbers

Organizations often have phone numbers that they do not use, for a variety of reasons. For example, they may be utilizing only part of the number range allocated to them, or staff may have left—but the organization may still receive calls to such numbers. Traditional PBXs have responded in the following ways:

◆ Presenting announcements, played to the calling party, for numbers that are not allocated to a phone or service

◆ Allocating multiple extensions to a single phone

◆ Leaving phones configured with Call Forward All set to route to a different number such as an attendant

These tend to be very blunt tools, using features within the PBX for purposes for which they were not intended. Although they may do what is required, the end result may not be the best solution. For example, the first of these methods would usually result in an announcement being played, followed by the call being terminated. For some organizations, this may be satisfactory; many others would prefer the call to be transferred to an attendant. The second and third methods will have similar results for the caller, who will be expecting to speak to Joe Blogs. Instead, their call will be answered by someone completely different, which can often lead to confusion or to the caller just hanging up.

There are also limits to the number of extensions that can appear on a single phone, often requiring more expensive phones or expansion modules to have more extensions configured. In addition, depending on the PBX type, the more expensive the phones, the more licenses required on the PBX. There are similar issues with leaving phones configured to forward calls.

From these scenarios, you can see that there is usually no ideal way to handle unassigned numbers, although some PBXs do provide a more complete features set for this. To provide a better solution than most and to ensure that organizations do not lose these features if they have them, Microsoft developed the Unassigned Number functionality in Lync.

Using Unassigned Numbers in Lync

In Lync, the Unassigned Number functionality works by defining number ranges and associated call treatments. The call treatments can send the call either to an Exchange Auto Attendant or to the Announcement Service.

The Announcement Service is used to play an announcement to the caller; the call can then be redirected to a SIP URI, voice mailbox, or telephone number. Alternatively, the call can be redirected without an announcement being played. The final option available with the Announcement Service is for it to play a busy tone to the caller. While this is better than the call just being disconnected, it does not provide any context. Using the Announcement Service allows an organization to tell the caller that a person has left the business, for example, and then redirect them to someone who can help them. For the majority of organizations, this is better than the call just being terminated after the announcement has been played.

The Announcement Service is a separate voice application within Lync, but it can be used only in conjunction with the Unassigned Number functionality. The announcements that are played to the caller can be provided either by providing an audio file or by using text-to-speech (TTS).

To TTS or Not to TTS

Text-to-speech provides a quick and simple way of generating announcements, although the drawback is that they may not sound perfect; this is usually most noticeable with company and employee names. Therefore, while TTS may be usable for a proof of concept and trial deployments of Lync or for emergency announcements, many organizations prefer to use prerecorded announcements, which allow more control and remove any potential issues found with TTS.

When configuring the Unassigned Number functionality, you need to perform the basic tasks in the following order:

1. Import Announcement Service audio files.

2. Create announcements and Exchange auto attendants.

3. Define Unassigned Number ranges.

Importing Audio Files

If you choose to use audio files rather than TTS, these audio files need to be in a specific format and must be uploaded to the Lync pool on which the unassigned numbers are defined. An audio file needs to be either a WAV file or a Windows Media Audio (WMA) file. For WAV files, the following characteristics need to be met:

◆ 8- or 16-bit file

◆ Linear pulse code modulation (LPCM), A-Law or mu-Law

◆ Mono or stereo

◆ 4MB or less

For WMA files, no specific limitations are imposed on the file by Lync. However, you should consider the bit rate, because the higher the bit rate, the greater the load placed on the Lync servers.

The announcement file is not directly uploaded; instead the cmdlet requires a byte array representation of the file. This byte array is created using the `Get-Content` cmdlet; this is used with the `Import-CsAnnouncementFile` cmdlet to upload the file. Here's an example:

```
$AnnFile = Get-Content ".\AnnouncementFile.wav" -ReadCount 0 -Encoding Byte
Import-CsAnnouncementFile -Parent ApplicationServer:se01.corp.masteringlync.org
 -FileName "AnnouncementFile.wav" -Content $AnnFile
```

This stores the contents of `AnnouncmentFile.wav` as a byte array in the `$AnnFile`. This is then imported using the second command and stored as `AnnouncementFile.wav`. The `FileName` specified needs to be unique and does not need to match the name of the file you are uploading.

When the file has been uploaded, the call treatments can be configured. Next, we'll discuss only the configuration of the Announcement Service, as Exchange Unified Messaging is covered in Chapter 17, "Exchange and SharePoint."

ANNOUNCEMENT SERVICE

When using New-CsAnnouncement, there are a number of ways to create new announcements depending on what is required. Each method, of course, has different configuration options. At a minimum all announcement will use these parameters:

- Identity

- Name

The Identity is the FQDN of the Lync pool on which the announcement should be created, prefixed with ApplicationServer:. Name is the name of the Announcement Service.

If an announcement is created with only these settings, the caller will hear a busy tone. If you need to create an announcement using an announcement file that you have previously uploaded, you will also need to use AudioFilePrompt.

If you want to create an announcement using TTS, then in addition to Identity and Name, you need to use the following:

- Language

- TextToSpeechPrompt

For each of these three options, you can add an additional parameter, TargetURI, which will transfer the caller to the SIP URI, telephone number, or voice mailbox specified. Each of these must be specified as a SIP URI, as in the examples shown in Table 16.3.

TABLE 16.3:   Transfer options examples

TYPE	EXAMPLE
SIP URI	sip:joe.bloggs@masteringlync.org
Telephone number	sip: +14255553250;user=phone
Voice mailbox	sip:joe.bloggs@masteringlync.org;opaque=app:voicemail

DEFINING UNASSIGNED NUMBER RANGES

When the call treatments have been created, you can define the Unassigned Number ranges. They can be created through the Control Panel (Voice Features ➤ Unassigned Numbers) or through PowerShell; no additional configuration options are exposed through PowerShell. To create a new number range, use the New-CsUnassignedNumber cmdlet, which has the following options:

- AnnouncementName: This is the announcement name.

- AnnouncementService: This is the Announcement Service used.

- ExUMAutoAttendantPhoneNumber: This is the Exchange Auto Attendant phone number.

◆ `NumberRangeStart`: This is the range start number.

◆ `NumberRangeEnd`: This is the range end number.

◆ `Priority`: This is used if number ranges overlap; if they do, the announcement with the highest priority will be used.

All of these parameters are required, except `Priority`, which is required only if you have overlapping number ranges. Note that when managing unassigned numbers through the Control Panel, there is no priority field; instead, priorities are managed by manipulating the order of the numbers using the Move Up and Move Down options, shown in Figure 16.19.

FIGURE 16.19
Managing unassigned numbers via Control Panel

The Announcement Service is the FQDN of the Lync pool on which the announcement should be created, prefixed with `ApplicationServer:`. If you are also using TTS, this should match the pool to which the audio file was uploaded.

The number range start and end numbers must comply with the following:

◆ The range must match this regular expression:

`(tel:)?(\+)?[1-9]\d{0,17}(;ext=[1-9]\d{0,9})?`

◆ The end number must be equal to or greater than the start number.

The regular expression breaks down as follows:

◆ The regular expression starts with a `tel:`—although if it doesn't, it will automatically be added.

◆ This can then optionally have a + following it.

◆ This is followed by a digit, 1 to 9.

◆ This is followed by up to 17 digits.

◆ This can then be followed by `;ext=`, 1 to 9, and then up to nine additional digits if the organization uses a single DDI and an extension range.

In addition to the requirements set out by the regular expression, when the extension field is used, the start and end number must be the same number because the extension field is used to define the number range in use. Table 16.4 lists some examples.

TABLE 16.4:   Sample unassigned number ranges

START NUMBER	END NUMBER
+18500	+18600
18500	18600
+18500;ext=8000	+18500;ext=8999

Now that you have seen how unassigned numbers operate and the options for configuring them within Lync, let's look at how you can implement them.

Implementing Unassigned Numbers

You're ready to build a configuration based on the following scenario:

No caller should receive an unknown number response when calling into your organization. Calls to all numbers will be answered and routed as appropriate. Where there is no specific requirement, calls will be routed to an auto attendant. Calls to any numbers that used to be assigned to a sales representative will be sent to the attendants after the caller has been told they are being redirected. The sales department has its own allocated range:

Organization DDI Range: +14255551000 to +14255559999
Sales Department DDIs: +14255553250 to +14255553299

From this scenario, you determine the following:

◆   You need to create an Unassigned Number range to cover all numbers.

◆   You need to set up an Exchange Auto Attendant.

◆   You need to create an Unassigned Number range for the sales departments.

◆   You need to set up an announcement for the sales team that will play a message to any caller who dials an unused number, such as a former salesperson's number, and then redirect the call to the Attendants Response Group.

As with other configurations, you need to make sure you perform these tasks in the correct order. The call treatments must be set up before the Unassigned Number configuration. Configuring the Auto Attendant in Exchange is outside the scope of this book, but for this example assume it exists and has an associated phone number of +14255551010.

In Lync Server, you first need to create the announcement for the sales team. This will be performed using the Announcement Service and can only be done via PowerShell:

```
New-CsAnnouncement -Identity "ApplicationServer:se01.corp.masteringlync.org"
-Name "Sales Team" -TargetURI "sip:AttendantRGS@masteringlync.org"
-TextToSpeechPrompt "Thank you for calling a member of the sales team, please
be patient while we redirect you to an attendant" -Language "en-US"
```

This creates a new announcement using text-to-speech and routes calls to the Attendants Response Group; it will also produce an output similar to this:

```
Identity              : Service:ApplicationServer:se01.corp.masteringlync.org
                        /07086c48-0bc5-4ce2-a6f4-f85c369a9
Name                  : Sales Team
AudioFilePrompt       :
TextToSpeechPrompt    : Thank you for calling a member of the sales team, please
                        be patient while we redirect you to an attendant
Language              : en-US
TargetUri             : sip:AttendantRGS@masteringlync.org
AnnouncementId        : 0786c48-0bc5-4ce2-a6f4-f85c369a91dc
```

Now that you've created the announcement, you can create the unassigned numbers. Although you can do this through the Control Panel, continue to use PowerShell for the example. Because of the requirement to overlap the number ranges, you need to ensure that the Priority field is specified, which will allow for the sales unassigned number to supersede the organization one. Here are the final commands:

```
New-CsUnassignedNumber -Identity "All Numbers" -NumberRangeStart "+14255551000"
-NumberRangeEnd "+14255559999" -Priority 2
-ExUmAutoAttendantPhoneNumber "+14255551010"
```

This creates an Unassigned Number configuration for all of the numbers the organization uses by specifying the entire number range, and it routes all calls to the Exchange Auto Attendant.

```
New-CsUnassignedNumber -Identity "Sales" -NumberRangeStart "+14255553250" -NumberRangeEnd
"+14255553299" -Priority 1 -AnnouncementService "ApplicationServer:se01.corp.masteringlync.
org" -AnnouncementName "Sales Team"
```

This creates the Unassigned Number configuration for the sales team number range and routes them to the announcement that was created earlier, thereby producing output similar to this:

```
AnnouncementServiceId  : ApplicationServer:se01.corp.masteringlync.org
AnnouncementServerFqdn : se01.corp.masteringlync.org
AnnouncementName       : Sales Team
AnnouncementId         : 07086c48-0bc5-4ce2-a6f4-f85c369a91dc
Identity               : Sales
NumberRangeStart       : tel:+14255553250
NumberRangeEnd         : tel:+14255553299
Priority               : 1
```

This completes the Unassigned Number configuration; to check the configuration, run the corresponding Get commands.

The Bottom Line

Understand the extended voice functionality.   Extended voice functionality provides additional voice applications that many organizations expect a PBX to have. Understanding what these applications can and cannot do is important so you can make the correct decisions when implementing them and know when a third-party solution is better.

> **Master It**   The manager for an internal help desk has been to a trade show and has been told he needs to have a full contact center to implement certain requirements. All he needs is to route calls to agents. He does not care about reporting or recording; he just needs to make sure that calls get to the right people. He is adamant that he needs a call center because this is what the experts have told him.

Design solutions using extended voice functionality.   Designing is usually seen as a boring, time-consuming task, when all you want to do is get your hands dirty and implement something. Although some of the extended voice functionality is straightforward, other elements are complex, and missing the design stage could cause you problems later. Design, design, design—and implement once.

> **Master It**   You need to implement a dial-in conferencing solution globally. You need to have global dial-in numbers and support at least 100 concurrent PSTN calls to the conferencing solution.

Implement extended voice functionality.   Lync's extended voice functionality is useless if you do not know how to implement it and use it to its fullest potential. To do that, you need to make sure that what you implement works and is fully tested.

> **Master It**   You have implemented Call Park but users are complaining about intermittent issues with parking calls. The complaints are coming from all user types, which is strange because not all users should be able to park calls.

Part 5

Integration

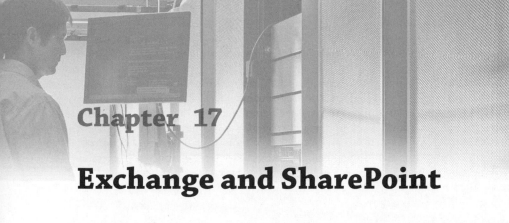

Chapter 17

Exchange and SharePoint

A huge amount of communication technology is built into Lync, but it is extended even further through tight integration with external systems. This chapter will explore Exchange and SharePoint integration. Lync relies totally on Exchange to provide voice mail capabilities; not only can Lync users receive voice mail, they also have full voice access to their mailboxes through tight integration into the Lync client. Exchange is also used to provide the Unified Contact Store and can be configured as the compliance archive for Lync interactions. Lync, in turn, provides Exchange with the ability to integrate presence and basic IM functionality into Outlook Web Access (OWA).

Lync and SharePoint together allow intelligent communications to be integrated into business processes. At its simplest level, presence is available in SharePoint, so there is quick and easy access to contact the author of documents; at a more complex level, it is also possible to integrate presence into workflow-related decisions—for example, to route documents to the most available manager for signoff. SharePoint also provides the search capabilities to enable Lync users to search for contacts by skill set.

In this chapter, you will learn to:

◆ Integrate Lync with Exchange

◆ Integrate Lync with SharePoint

Integrating Lync with Exchange

These days, it is rare not to come across an Exchange messaging platform in an organization. Exchange has become almost the de facto standard for carrying email. With the recent versions (2007, 2010, and 2013), Exchange broadened its role, becoming part of a unified communication platform through the provision of voice mail and unified inbox capabilities. As you have seen throughout this book, Lync is a fully functional communication platform; however, it relies on the unified inbox capabilities of Exchange to store conversation history and voice mail and with Lync 2013 to provide a compliance grade archive. Because Exchange is the standard calendaring platform, Lync utilizes this information to enhance presence and give visibility to out-of-office messages. Finally, Lync can bring some of its capabilities to Exchange through the provision of presence and basic IM functionality into Outlook Web App.

Lync 2013, when paired with Exchange 2013, brings a number of significant improvements in the way that it integrates with Exchange. Not only do we now have the ability to use Lync from any supported web browser, from any Internet location while checking our email, we now also have the ability to display high-resolution photographs instead of the standard 48×48 pixel format currently supported. That's definitely a move with the times in this HD era! We also now have the ability to choose where we store our Lync contacts and make full use of the search and litigation hold functionalities within Exchange for our Lync messages. As with the rest of the Office 2013 stack, Lync and Exchange should no longer be seen as separate products; they are slowly combining features to provide a truly unified experience for users.

This section of this chapter will focus upon Lync and Exchange integration. We will cover features already available with Lync 2010 and also the new elements added to Lync and Exchange 2013, as outlined here:

◆ Unified Messaging and voice mail for Enterprise Voice users

◆ IM and presence in Outlook Web Access

◆ Unified Contact Store (new to 2013)

◆ Exchange archiving (new to 2013)

◆ High-resolution photos (new to 2013)

DIFFERENT VERSIONS OF EXCHANGE

Throughout this chapter, we are focusing on integration with Exchange Server 2013. But what if you are running an older version, such as Exchange 2007 or Exchange 2010? Or indeed, what if you are in the middle of migrating from an older version and have users based on both platforms? In that case, all may not be lost because several features are still available. However, we would recommend that some serious testing is carried out and that potentially you leave features disabled until users are on the most modern platform to ease complexity.

As you will see, Lync makes extensive use of features in newer Exchange versions, such as voice mail and web services. That said, Lync can also integrate in some ways with versions as early as Exchange 2007 SP1.

The differences between Exchange 2007 and 2010 support are pretty small. Essentially, Exchange 2010 adds the ability to provide Message Waiting Indicator (MWI) information when used with Unified Messaging (UM) and also provides a contact sync feature, which allows Lync to create a personal contact in Outlook for each person on a user's Lync contacts list. Exchange 2013 provides the updated Unified Contact Store, Exchange archiving, and High-Resolution Photos support, which no previous versions support.

One other area for consideration is that it is now possible to deploy Exchange in the cloud using Microsoft Office 365. There are various supported scenarios for running parts of your organization in the cloud, including having either Lync Online or Exchange Online with its respective on-premises system.

Configuring Exchange Integration Prerequisites

Before we start to configure specific features, there are a number of prerequisites that need to be taken care of, on both the Lync and Exchange servers:

◆ Unified Communications Managed API 4.0 Runtime

◆ OAuthTokenIssuer

- Partner application

- Lync Storage Service (LYSS)

UNIFIED COMMUNICATIONS MANAGED API 4.0 RUNTIME

The Microsoft Unified Communications Managed API (UCMA) 4.0 is used primarily to build middle-tier applications that work with Microsoft Lync Server 2013. As such, it is required on the Exchange server. When integrating Exchange 2010 with Lync 2010, you had to specifically install UCMA 2.0 as a prerequisite on the Exchange server. Things are a little different with Exchange 2013. You now need version 4.0 of UCMA; however, given that the UM component on Exchange 2013 is installed on all Mailbox servers, UCMA 4.0 is a global prerequisite for any Exchange 2013 server and so will already be installed. UCMA plays its part in allowing Lync to communicate with UM (and also OWA) by adding the `Microsoft.Rtc.Internal.Ucweb.dll` in the `C:\Program Files\Microsoft UCMA\Runtime\SSP` directory.

Bottom line, there is no further work required for this prerequisite.

OAUTHTOKENISSUER

To provide the extensive integration between Exchange, Lync, and SharePoint 2013 server applications, the servers need to communicate with each other. To do so, they need a method of authentication, and this is provided by the OAuth protocol. OAuth is a standard authorization protocol based on the exchange of security tokens that grant access to resources for a specific period of time. The certificate is used for securing server-to-server communication and can be self-signed or issued by an enterprise certificate authority (CA). It is recommended that the same CA issue the certificates for all servers where possible because the issuing CA will be trusted by default. If this is not possible, then you must make sure each server trusts the issuer of all the certificates.

To support the OAuth protocol, Lync 2013 introduces a new certificate type, called OAuthTokenIssuer. This is also known as a server-to-server authentication certificate. You will find that the OAuthTokenIssuer certificate is one of the certificates you configure when running the Certificate Wizard during the installation of a Lync 2013 server, as shown in Figure 17.1.

FIGURE 17.1
The Lync Certificate Wizard showing the OAuthTokenIssuer

One thing to consider when configuring the OAuthTokenIssuer certificate is where it is stored. The default option, as shown in Figure 17.1, is Global, which means that the certificate is stored in the Central Management Store (CMS), thereby ensuring that the certificate is distributed to each Lync Front End server.

Exchange also has a similar authentication certificate, and when Exchange and Lync integration is configured, these certificates are exchanged using an authentication metadata document via web services. The authentication metadata document is provided through the /metadata/ json/1 (JSON = JavaScript Object Notation) directory. The specific web service URL can be configured using the command shell on both Lync and Exchange servers. This is achieved by running the `Configure-EnterprisePartnerApplication.ps1` command from the Exchange server and the `New-CSPartnerApplication` command from the Lync server, which are detailed in the next section, "Partner Application."

Another option, instead of using the default certificates, would be to use an existing certificate as your server-to-server authentication certificate. It must use at least a 2048-bit key, include the name of the SIP domain in the Subject field (not just as a subject alternative name), and the same certificate must be configured as the OAuthTokenIssuer on all Lync Front End servers. If you have multiple SIP domains, then providing that the primary SIP domain is registered in Lync, OAuth will continue to work with any other SIP domains associated with that primary domain. For example, if `masteringlync.org` is your primary SIP domain and you also use `admin.masteringlync.org` and `tech.masteringlync.org` as additional SIP domains, OAuth will require a primary certificate name only for `masteringlync.org`. Should you change your primary SIP domain, which differs from the default name in the Subject field, an additional OAuth certificate will need to be generated. In this case, you would need to reassociate the new OAuth certificate with the Lync server in the setup process.

The configuration of the OAuth certificate will propagate to all other Front End servers without any additional actions required. By having the same certificate on all Lync Front End servers, we are able to follow best practice and point Exchange to a load-balanced pool of Lync servers and have them all work together no matter which server Exchange talks to.

Partner Application

While the OAuth protocol allows for authentication between server applications, there is also a need to define what certain applications can do. This is where the partner application comes in. It is represented as a configuration entity on the both the trusted and trusting systems, Lync and Exchange in this case.

The applications are configured on both sides using PowerShell. On Exchange, this is done using the provided script `Configure-EnterprisePartnerApplication.ps1`, which can be found in the `Exchange Scripts` directory. When it is run, a disabled user account is created (LyncEnterprise-ApplicationAccount), and the UserApplication and ArchiveApplication management roles are assigned. This account is then associated with the /metadata/json/1 authentication document on the Lync server to create a partner application. This configuration gives Lync the ability to read and write data to Exchange mailboxes on behalf of users and is fundamental for us to be able to use the Message Archiving integration feature.

From the Lync side, instead of using a script, you simply run the `New-CSPartnerApplication` cmdlet and specify the URL where the authentication document can be found via Exchange Web Services (EWS), as shown in the following command:

```
New-CsPartnerApplication -Identity Exchange -ApplicationTrustLevel Full ↵
-MetadataUrl ↵
"https://autodiscover.corp.masteringlync.org/autodiscover/metadata/json/1"
```

We will put this into action and cover the details of the required configuration when setting up the Lync Storage Service (LYSS) in the next section.

Don't confuse the partner application with the Trusted Application pool, discussed later in the chapter. They are not the same thing even though they sound similar!

LYNC STORAGE SERVICE

Alongside OAuth, the Lync Storage Service (LYSS) is the other major new element of Exchange and Lync integration. LYSS is a storage framework in Lync Server 2013 intended to be used by different LYSS consumers to access storage platforms such as Message Archiving and the Unified Contact Store. LYSS is designed to provide access to multiple storage platforms. As we are writing this, SQL Server and Exchange Web Services (EWS) are commonly used. EWS supports the server-to-server authentication setup discussed previously.

To configure the LYSS, you must first ensure that the autodiscover service is correctly configured on Exchange. This is a hugely complex subject that is off topic for in-depth discussion here. We suggest a discussion with your Exchange team or that you consult the suitable Exchange documentation. However, if your Exchange 2013 is up and running and serving users, it is likely that this is configured.

In a nutshell, what is required is to make sure that `AutoDiscoverServiceInternalURI` has been correctly set up on all Client Access servers. For this to work successfully, you should ensure that a DNS A record has been created for `Autodiscover.corp.masteringlync.org` (of course, using your own domain here) and that it points to the Client Access server (CAS) or load-balanced CAS farm. The configuration can be carried out by running the following command:

```
Get-ClientAccessServer | Set-ClientAccessServer ↵
-AutoDiscoverServiceInternalUri ↵
"https://autodiscover.corp.masteringlync.org/autodiscover/autodiscover.xml"
```

This command will first get all the Client Access servers in your Exchange environment and then set `AutoDiscoverServiceInternalURI` to the URL specified. Be very careful doing this in production because getting it wrong will seriously break your Exchange client access!

Once this is completed, on the Lync server, you now need to point the Lync OAuthTokenIssuer certificate to the Exchange Autodiscover service, using the following command:

```
Set-CsOAuthConfiguration -ExchangeAutodiscoverUrl ↵
"https://autodiscover. corp.masteringlync.org/autodiscover/autodiscover.svc"
```

This command will point Lync to the Exchange farm at the URL specified.

As described in the earlier, in the section "Partner Application," on the Exchange server, you can now run the `Configure-EnterprisePartnerApplication.ps1` script to direct Exchange to the Lync authorization location. This script comes built in with Exchange and can be found in the following location (assuming you've used the default install directory): `C:\Program Files \Microsoft\Exchange Server\V15\Scripts`. The syntax for running this command is as follows:

```
.\Configure-EnterprisePartnerApplication.ps1 ↵
-AuthMetadataUrl "https://se01. corp.masteringlync.org/metadata/json/1" ↵
-ApplicationType Lync
```

You can see the output from the script here:

```
Creating User (LyncEnterprise-ApplicationAccount) for Partner Application.

Created User (corp.masteringlync.org/Users/LyncEnterprise-ApplicationAccount)
for Partner Application.

Assigning role (UserApplication) to Application User
(corp.masteringlync.org/Users/LyncEnterprise-ApplicationAccount).

Assigning role (ArchiveApplication) to Application User
(corp.masteringlync.org/Users/LyncEnterprise-ApplicationAccount).

Creating Partner Application (LyncEnterprise-b3abf3ae6e57403bb94d7bad382e70b1)
 using metadata (https://se01.corp.masteringlync.org/metadata/json/1) with
linked account (corp.masteringlync.org/Users/LyncEnterprise-ApplicationAccount).

Created Partner Application (LyncEnterprise-b3abf3ae6e57403bb94d7bad382e70b1).

THE CONFIGURATION HAS SUCCEEDED.
```

As you can see, the results of the script show that a new user has been created in the Users OU called LyncEnterprise-ApplicationAccount and an RBAC role has been assigned allowing that account to use UserApplication and ArchiveApplication roles within Exchange. A partner application with Lync has also been created at this point.

To ensure that the settings take hold, you now need to recycle the IIS service by running iisreset on your Exchange servers. Please bear in mind that this will affect any users currently connected to that server using web services, such as Outlook Web Access, ActiveSync, or Entourage clients.

Having configured Exchange, we now move across to the Lync server and create the partner application there. The process is similar to that for Exchange and is carried out using the following command:

```
New-CsPartnerApplication -Identity Exchange -ApplicationTrustLevel Full ↵
-MetadataUrl ↵
"https://autodiscover.corp.masteringlync.org/autodiscover/metadata/json/1"
```

The result of this command is that an AuthToken has been created on the Lync server pointing to the Autodiscover URL on the Exchange server. You should see verification of the properties created similar to the following example:

```
Identity                             : Exchange
AuthToken                            :
Value=https://autodiscover.corp.masteringlync.org/autodiscover/metadata/json/1
Name                                 : Exchange
ApplicationIdentifier                : 00000002-0000-0ff1-ce00-000000000000
Realm                                : corp.masteringlync.org
ApplicationTrustLevel                : Full
AcceptSecurityIdentifierInformation  : False
Enabled                              : True
```

You can now test that the partner application integration between Lync and Exchange was successful. The following command will create a test entry on the specified Exchange mailbox using TCP binding, which requires the name of the storage service to be included. Once completed, the command will delete the test entry:

```
Test-CsExStorageConnectivity -SipUri nathan@corp.masteringlync.org ↵
-Binding NetTCP -DeleteItem ↵
-HostNameStorageService se01.corp.masteringlync.org -Verbose
```

The -Verbose parameter is optional but is useful for troubleshooting any problems you may encounter. With verbose logging enabled, you will be able to see the Autodiscover location being looked up as well as the RequestMessage and ResponseMessage for the specified mailbox, as shown in the following output:

```
Test-CsExStorageConnectivity -SipUri Chris@contoso.com ↵
-Binding NetTCP -DeleteItem -HostNameStorageService lync.contoso.com -Verbose

VERBOSE: Successfully opened a connection to storage service at lync.contoso.com
using binding: NetTCP.
VERBOSE: Create message.
VERBOSE: Execute Exchange Storage Command.
VERBOSE: Processing web storage response for ExCreateItem Success.,
result=Success, activityId=e308d487-97d0-4bc1-aff8-022e769d3b39, reason=.
VERBOSE: Activity tracing:
2013/01/10 13:50:47.064 Lookup user details, sipUri=sip:Chris@contoso.com,
 smtpAddress=chris@contoso.com,
sid=S-1-5-21-114802761-1703574399-2147504919-1158, upn=chris@contoso.com,
tenantId=00000000-0000-0000-0000-000000000000
2013/01/10 13:50:47.226 Autodiscover, send GetUserSettings request,
SMTP=chris@contoso.com, Autodiscover Uri=https://autodiscover.contoso.com/autodiscover/
autodiscover.svc, Web
Proxy=<NULL> 2013/01/10 13:50:47.283 Autodiscover.EWSMA trace,
type=AutodiscoverRequestHttpHeaders, message=<Trace
Tag="AutodiscoverRequestHttpHeaders" Tid="47"
Time="2013-01-10 13:50:47Z">
POST /autodiscover/autodiscover.svc HTTP/1.1
Content-Type: text/xml; charset=utf-8
Accept: text/xml
User-Agent: ExchangeServicesClient/15.00.0516.004

</Trace>
2013/01/10 13:50:47.363 Autodiscover.EWSMA trace,
type=AutodiscoverRequest, message=<Trace Tag="AutodiscoverRequest"
Tid="47" Time="2013-01-10 13:50:47Z" Version="15.00.0516.004">
  <?xml version="1.0" encoding="utf-8"?>
  <soap:Envelope
xmlns:a="http://schemas.microsoft.com/exchange/2010/Autodiscover"
xmlns:wsa="http://www.w3.org/2005/08/addressing"
xmlns:xsi="http://www.w3.org/2001/XMLSchema-instance"
```

```
xmlns:soap="http://schemas.xmlsoap.org/soap/envelope/">
    <soap:Header>
      <a:RequestedServerVersion>Exchange2013</a:RequestedServerVersion>

<wsa:Action>http://schemas.microsoft.com/exchange/2010/Autodiscover/Autodiscover
/GetUserSettings</wsa:Action>

<wsa:To>https://autodiscover.contoso.com/autodiscover/autodiscover.svc</wsa:To>

    </soap:Header>
    <soap:Body>
      <a:GetUserSettingsRequestMessage
xmlns:a="http://schemas.microsoft.com/exchange/2010/Autodiscover">
        <a:Request>
          <a:Users>
            <a:User>
              <a:Mailbox>chris@contoso.com</a:Mailbox>
            </a:User>
          </a:Users>
          <a:RequestedSettings>
            <a:Setting>InternalEwsUrl</a:Setting>
            <a:Setting>ExternalEwsUrl</a:Setting>
            <a:Setting>ExternalEwsVersion</a:Setting>
          </a:RequestedSettings>
        </a:Request>
      </a:GetUserSettingsRequestMessage>
    </soap:Body>
  </soap:Envelope>
</Trace>


2013/01/10 13:51:01.213 Autodiscover.EWSMA trace,
type=AutodiscoverResponseHttpHeaders,
message=<Trace Tag="AutodiscoverResponseHttpHeaders" Tid="47"
Time="2013-01-10 13:51:01Z">
HTTP/1.1 200 OK
Transfer-Encoding: chunked
request-id: b357679c-be88-4f11-b5c6-81ae8ba495ec
X-TargetBEServer: exch.contoso.com
X-DiagInfo: EXCH
X-FEServer: EXCH
Cache-Control: private
Content-Type: text/xml; charset=utf-8
Date: Thu, 10 Jan 2013 13:51:01 GMT
Set-Cookie:
X-BackEndCookie=CN=Chris,OU=Contoso_Users,DC=contoso,DC=com
=u56Lnp2ejJqBmc3PzZ2ex5nSyZ6ezdLLnczN0p3Hms7Syc+enM7NzZ7Mzs+bgYHOz9DPztDNz87M38
7Lxc/Oxc/O; expires=Thu, 10-Jan-2013 14:01:01 GMT; path=/autodiscover; secure;
```

```
HttpOnly
Server: Microsoft-IIS/8.0
X-AspNet-Version: 4.0.30319
X-Powered-By: ASP.NET


</Trace>

2013/01/10 13:51:01.215 Autodiscover.EWSMA trace, type=AutodiscoverResponse,
message=<Trace Tag="AutodiscoverResponse" Tid="47" Time="2013-01-10 13:51:01Z"
Version="15.00.0516.004">
  <s:Envelope xmlns:s="http://schemas.xmlsoap.org/soap/envelope/"
xmlns:a="http://www.w3.org/2005/08/addressing">
    <s:Header>
      <a:Actions:mustUnderstand="1">http://schemas.microsoft.com/exchange/2010/
Autodiscover/Autodiscover/GetUserSettingsResponse</a:Action>
      <h:ServerVersionInfo
xmlns:h="http://schemas.microsoft.com/exchange/2010/Autodiscover"
xmlns:i="http://www.w3.org/2001/XMLSchema-instance">
        <h:MajorVersion>15</h:MajorVersion>
        <h:MinorVersion>0</h:MinorVersion>
        <h:MajorBuildNumber>516</h:MajorBuildNumber>
        <h:MinorBuildNumber>29</h:MinorBuildNumber>
        <h:Version>Exchange2013</h:Version>
      </h:ServerVersionInfo>
    </s:Header>
    <s:Body>
      <GetUserSettingsResponseMessage
xmlns="http://schemas.microsoft.com/exchange/2010/Autodiscover">
        <Response xmlns:i="http://www.w3.org/2001/XMLSchema-instance">
          <ErrorCode>NoError</ErrorCode>
          <ErrorMessage />
          <UserResponses>
            <UserResponse>
              <ErrorCode>NoError</ErrorCode>
              <ErrorMessage>No error.</ErrorMessage>
              <RedirectTarget i:nil="true" />
              <UserSettingErrors />
              <UserSettings>
                <UserSetting i:type="StringSetting">
                  <Name>InternalEwsUrl</Name>
                  <Value>https://exch.contoso.com/EWS/Exchange.asmx</Value>
                </UserSetting>
              </UserSettings>
            </UserResponse>
          </UserResponses>
        </Response>
```

```
            </GetUserSettingsResponseMessage>
        </s:Body>
    </s:Envelope>
</Trace>
```

```
2013/01/10 13:51:01.411 Autodiscover, received GetUserSettings response,
duration Ms=14154, response=NoError
2013/01/10 13:51:04.840 Lookup user details, sipUri=sip:Chris@contoso.com,
smtpAddress=chris@contoso.com, sid=S-1-5-21-114802761-1703574399-2147504919
-1158, upn=chris@contoso.com, tenantId=00000000-0000-0000-0000-000000000000
VERBOSE: Items choice type: CreateItemResponseMessage.
VERBOSE: Response message, class: Success, code: NoError.
VERBOSE: Item: Microsoft.Rtc.Internal.Storage.Exchange.Ews.MessageType,
Id:AAMkADY5OGNlMTFhLTg0ODEtNDBiYy1iMzA5LTUwZGUyMmVjYTY0YgBGAAAAAAD/2+5uKfB+TqB
/yCDIOxtJBwCkELsKI8wpSL+eEcs4L9z1AAAAAAQNAACkELsKI8wpSL+eEcs4L9z1AAAhlcypAAA=,
change key: CQAAABYAAACkELsKI8wpSL+eEcs4L9z1AAAhlOX0, subject: , body: .
VERBOSE: Is command successful: True.
VERBOSE: Delete message.
VERBOSE: Execute Exchange Storage Command.
VERBOSE: Processing web storage response for ExDeleteItem Success.,
result=Success, activityId=00000000-0000-0000-0000-000000000000, reason=.
VERBOSE: Items choice type: DeleteItemResponseMessage.
VERBOSE: Response message, class: Success, code: NoError.
VERBOSE: Is command successful: True.
Test passed.
```

If you do get errors, they will show up as follows, which is the important element of the error text:

```
Test-CsExStorageConnectivity : ExCreateItem exchange operation failed, code=5 reason=StoreC
ontext{traceId=1015445631], activityId=[4435392b-32b3-4195-b667-
4a53d2034ac1]}Access Denied, exception=System.ServiceModel.FaultException:
StoreContext{traceId=[1015445631], activityId=[4435392b-32b3-4195-b667-
4a53d2034ac1]}Access Denied
```

In this example, you will see the "Access Denied" message. This is most likely caused by the user running the test not being a member of the RTC Local User Administrators group on the server where the test is being run. Once you have the permissions set correctly, test again and you should find that you get the "Test passed" message displayed to confirm that the transaction was carried out successfully.

At this stage you have successfully introduced Lync to Exchange, created partner applications, and set permissions correctly. This is the underpinning of Lync and Exchange integration.

The Voice Mail Platform for Lync

Having worked through the prerequisite configuration steps, you can now move on to setting up voice mail. This is one of the most visible integration points for Lync and Exchange alongside the provision of presence in OWA. Given that in-depth coverage of Exchange Unified Messaging (UM) could be the subject of another book, we will here review the basics of Exchange UM integration with Lync so that you can provide Lync users with voice mail.

There are very few changes that have been made to the functionality of UM for Lync Enterprise Voice users between Lync and Exchange 2010 to 2013. The following are the biggest changes:

◆ The Unified Messaging service now runs as standard on all Exchange Server 2013 Mailbox role servers. Exchange 2013 has consolidated the once five roles into three. Therefore, the Mailbox server now runs components including Client Access, Hub Transport, UM, and Mailbox.

◆ There is a new service, the UM Call Router (UMCR) service, on Exchange Server 2013 Client Access role servers. The UM Call Router service uses the same principle as the mail routing service, where all inbound UM calls hit the UM Call Router service first and are then forwarded to the relevant UM backend server. This means that your setup for integration has an additional step: You use the `Set-UMCallRouterSettings` command to associate the Exchange certificate with the UM Call Router service and restart the service once you've applied security to it.

To configure Exchange UM, you carry out the following steps:

1. Ensure that the correct certificates are in place.

2. Configure the Exchange UM elements of the system (dial plan, policy, and auto attendants).

3. Ensure that Exchange knows about Lync as a gateway.

4. Confirm that Lync dial plans are configured correctly.

5. Configure Lync to utilize Exchange UM.

6. Enable users for UM.

CONFIGURING EXCHANGE CERTIFICATES FOR UM

To ensure that Exchange UM can operate in a secure manner, you need to verify that a suitable certificate is in place to protect communication between Lync and Exchange. In the Exchange documentation, you may notice a statement that a public certificate is required. This is in some ways correct but slightly ambiguous. What is needed is a certificate from a trusted certificate authority (CA) rather than a self-signed certificate. This could be an internal AD-based CA that both servers trust or one from a third party (DigiCert, for example). The key point is that an Exchange self-signed certificate is not going to cut it!

If you need help creating, importing, and assigning the Exchange certificate, you can find the details at this location:

`http://technet.microsoft.com/en-us/library/bb676409(v=exchg.150).aspx`

With the introduction of the UM Call Router service to the Client Access role in Exchange 2013, both the UM and UM Call Router services will need to be enabled for Dual or TLS mode in order for a certificate to be assigned. These steps can be carried out using the Exchange Management Shell and will be covered later.

CONFIGURING EXCHANGE UM

Once Exchange UM is configured with the relevant certificate, you can configure the UM components of Exchange for integration with Lync. The first required piece is a new UM dial plan. The UM dial plan provides Exchange with the following information:

◆ The number of digits that form the extension (as discussed in Chapter 13, "Getting Started with Voice"), which in this case will be four.

◆ The Uniform Resource Indicator (URI) type, which for communication with Lync must be SIP URI.

◆ The level of VoIP security required. Choose Secured so that both the SIP signaling traffic and the media will be encrypted. If you chose SIP Secured, only the signaling traffic would be encrypted. The other option, Unsecured, simply doesn't work—and if you are planning to deploy Lync Phone Edition you must use Secured, as in this example.

To create the UM dial plan, take the following steps:

1. Log into the Exchange Administration Console as an Exchange administrator—for example, https://mail.corp.masteringlync.org/ecp.

2. On the left side, select Unified Messaging; then on the UM Dial Plans section, click + to create a new dial plan. In this example, we used the following settings:

◆ Name: UMDialPlan (Ensure that there are no spaces!)

◆ Extension Length (Digits): 4

◆ Dial Plane Type: SIP URI

◆ VOIP Security Mode: Secured

◆ Audio Language: English (United States)

◆ Country/Region Code: 44

Figure 17.2 shows this configuration.

The SIP URI plan type allows the SIP protocol to be used for signaling messages, and using Secured for the VOIP security mode means that TLS can be used to encrypt the channel used by SIP.

3. Click Save, and then click the pencil icon to edit the dial plan.

4. Under UM Dial Plan, click Configure.

5. On the left side, select Dialing Rules, and create a new in-country/region dialing rule. We used the following settings:

◆ Dialing Rule Name: Anywhere

◆ Number Pattern To Transform: *

◆ Dialed Number: *

Figure 17.3 shows this configuration.

FIGURE 17.2
Configuring your
dial plan

FIGURE 17.3
Configuring the
dialing rules

6. Click OK. Within Dialing Authorization, click + to add the Anywhere dialing rule to Authorized In-Country/Region Dialing Rule Groups, as shown in Figure 17.4.

FIGURE 17.4
Configuring dialing
authorization

7. Click Save.

Of course, by this stage in the book, you may be getting into PowerShell! As you would imagine, all this can be set up from the command line as follows:

```
New-UMDialPlan -Name "UMDialPlan" -NumberOfDigitsInExtension 4 ↵
-URIType "SipName" -VoIPSecurity "Secured" -CountryOrRegionCode 44
```

The previous command creates the dial plan and configures the required options such as the VoIPSecurity and Extension length.

```
Set-UMDialPlan "UMDialPlan" -ConfiguredInCountryOrRegionGroups "Anywhere,*,*,*" ↵
-AllowedInCountryOrRegionGroups "Anywhere"
```

The previous command configures the dialing rules and authorization.

At this point, you will have a dial plan that has dialing rules and authorization configured. You are now ready to move on and configure a few other elements of UM.

First you will set the Outlook Voice Access (OVA) dial-in number and configure an auto attendant. Outlook Voice Access provides phone-based, voice, and touch-tone access to your mailbox, so among other things, mail can be read to you and calendar items can be manipulated. Second, you will configure an auto attendant, which is used to provide an access point for callers to be routed automatically to either a person or department. The UM auto attendant in Exchange is quite flexible and can be set up with personalized menus and audio recording. However, for the purpose of demonstrating Lync integration, you will simply create a basic auto attendant:

1. Using the Exchange Administration Console, within the properties for UMDialPlan, select Configure; then select Outlook Voice Access on the left side. Add the E.164 routing number for SIP, as shown in Figure 17.5. (Note that +441189098888 works for our environment, but you will need to choose a suitable free number in your pool of numbers.)

FIGURE 17.5
Entering the access number for Outlook Voice Access

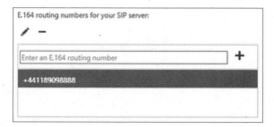

2. Click Save and scroll down to the bottom of the UMDialPlan settings.

3. Click + to create a new UM auto attendant called UMAutoAttendant.

4. Select Create This Auto Attendant As Enabled. Add the number (we added +441189098000, as shown in Figure 17.6). Then click Save and close the properties page.

As with setting up the dial plan earlier, the same configuration can also be carried out using the Exchange Management Shell, as shown here:

```
Set-UMDialPlan UMDialPlan -PilotIdentifierList "+441189098888" ↵
New-UMAutoAttendant -Name UMAutoAttendant -UMDialPlan UMDialPlan ↵
-PilotIdentifierList "+441189098000" -Status Enabled
```

FIGURE 17.6
Creating and
enabling the auto
attendant

Now that the dial plan, auto attendant and OVA numbers are set up, you need to configure the startup mode of the UM and UM Call Router services on Exchange to use TLS security so that all data flow is encrypted. You will also assign the dial plan to the required Exchange servers (those that are participating in the UM configuration) as follows:

1. To configure the UM service to use TLS and assign the dial plan, run the following command on the Exchange Mailbox server:

```
Set-UMService "exch.corp.masteringlync.org" -DialPlans "UMDialPlan" ↩
-UMStartupMode "Dual"
```

The use of UMStartupMode Dual in the previous command means that the UM service can accept both secure encrypted SIP communication and also standard unencrypted SIP messages. Another option for full security would be to enter TLS, which would require a certificate for all UM integration. Dual mode is especially useful in situations where you are migrating from a previous version of Exchange and may need to support unsecured conversations from some of your older servers.

On completion of the command, you should see the following message displayed, reminding you that because you have changed the UM service to start up in Dual or TLS mode, you will need to have a valid certificate associated with the UM service. You will do this in the next steps:

```
WARNING: Changes to UMStartupMode will only take effect after the Microsoft
Exchange Unified Messaging service is restarted on server EXCH. The
Microsoft Unified Messaging service won't start unless there is a valid TLS
certificate.
WARNING: To complete TLS setup, do all of the following:
(1) Create a new certificate using the New-ExchangeCertificate cmdlet
(2) Associate this certificate with the Unified Messaging server using the
Enable-ExchangeCertificate cmdlet
(3) For self-signed certificates, copy this certificate to the UM IP gateway
 and correctly import it. For CA-signed certificates, correctly import the CA
 certificate to the UM IP gateway.
```

2. Next you must apply the same settings to the UMCR service on the Client Access server using the following command:

```
Set-UMCallRouterSettings -Server exchcas.corp.masteringlync.org ↵
-UMStartupMode "Dual" -DialPlans "UMDialPlan"
```

3. Finally, you must ensure that Exchange uses the correct certificate to secure the connections to UM. This is done using the following commands. You first extract the thumbprint of the current certificate associated with the Mailbox server, then extract the one for the Client Access server. You then use these thumbprints to associate the UM and UMCR services with those certificates:

```
$certmbx = (Get-ExchangeCertificate | Where {$_.Subject ↵
-ilike  "*exch.corp.masteringlync.org*"}).Thumbprint
$certcas = (Get-ExchangeCertificate | Where {$_.Subject ↵
-ilike "*mail.corp.masteringlync.org*"}).Thumbprint
```

The $certmbx and $certcas values create a variable that will be used to capture the certificates from the output of the command. You can then use these variables to enter the thumbprint into the following command, which will ensure that the next time the UM and UMCR services are started, the correct certificates are used to secure them. This is done using the following commands:

```
Enable-ExchangeCertificate -Server exch.corp.masteringlync.org ↵
-Thumbprint $certmbx -Services "SMTP","IIS","UM"
Enable-ExchangeCertificate -Server exchcas.corp.masteringlync.org ↵
-Thumbprint $certcas -Services "IIS","UMCallRouter"
```

Note that these commands have been run against separated Mailbox and Client Access servers—for those of you running a collocated server, the process is simplified due to the fact that there is only a single certificate being used to publish the service and both the UM and UMCR services are running on the same server. You can use the following commands to achieve the same results for a collocated server:

```
$cert = (Get-ExchangeCertificate | Where {$_.Subject ↵
-ilike "*mail.corp.masteringlync.org*"}).Thumbprint
Enable-ExchangeCertificate -Server exch.corp.masteringlync.org ↵
-Thumbprint $cert -Services "SMTP","IIS","UM","UMCallRouter"
```

4. Restart the UM and UM Call Router services on both servers for these changes to take effect.

The final piece of Exchange-only configuration before we move on to introduce Exchange to Lync is the creation of a UM mailbox policy. The following command will create a new UM mailbox policy, which will be associated with the previously created dial plan:

```
New-UMMailboxPolicy "UMMailboxPolicy" -UMDialPlan "UMDialPlan"
```

It is worth exploring the UM mailbox policy so that you understand the settings that are configured there. In particular, you will find that there are policies that govern the length, complexity, and age of the PIN code that is assigned to users to enable them to easily authenticate with UM via a phone device. If you are simply testing UM, you may want to ease the default of six-character complex PINs to make them simpler to remember. Obviously, if this is a production environment, you will want to make sure the required PIN is suitably secure for your organization.

At this point, you've performed the bulk of the Exchange configuration. The next big thing to do is to introduce Exchange to Lync. This is done using a script provided with Exchange in the Exchange directory `Scripts` folder, which when installed in the default location will be at `C:\Program Files\Microsoft\Exchange Server\V15\Scripts`. This script is called `ExchUCUtil.ps1` and performs the following tasks:

◆ Grants Lync the required permission to read Exchange UM Active Directory objects, in particular the SIP URI dial plan objects you created previously by configuring the RTCUniversalServerAdmins and RTCComponentUniversalServices groups to read the UM dial plan.

◆ Creates a UM IP gateway object for each Lync pool or for each server running Lync Standard Edition that hosts users who are enabled for Enterprise Voice.

You must run this script from the Exchange Management Shell using the following command, which assumes that Exchange is installed as per default settings:

```
C:\Program Files\Microsoft\Exchange Server\V15\Scripts\ExchUCUtil.ps1
```

Once you have run the script, make sure to allow time for AD replication to occur. Once suitable time has elapsed, verify that the settings have been performed properly by running the script again, this time with a `-verify` parameter, as shown here:

```
C:\Program Files\Microsoft\Exchange Server\V15\Scripts\ExchUCUtil.ps1 -verify
```

This will run through and output the configuration as it stands, showing where permissions have been granted and which gateways have been created, as in the following:

```
Using Global Catalog: GC://DC=core,DC=masteringlync,DC=com


Configuring permissions for core.masteringlync.org\RTCUniversalServerAdmins ...
MasteringLync: The appropriate permissions haven't been granted for the Office
Communications Servers and Administrators to be able to read the UM dial plan
and auto attendants container objects in Active Directory. The correct
permissions are being added to the container objects.
UM DialPlan Container: The appropriate permissions haven't been granted for the
Office Communications Servers and Administrators to be able to read the UM dial
plan and auto attendants container objects in Active Directory. The correct
permissions are being added to the container objects.
UM AutoAttendant Container: The appropriate permissions haven't been granted
for the Office Communications Servers and Administrators to be able to read the
UM dial plan and auto attendants container objects in Active Directory. The
correct permissions are being added to the container objects.
Administrative Groups: The appropriate permissions haven't been granted for the
Office Communications Servers and Administrators to be able to read the UM dial
plan and auto attendants container objects in Active Directory. The correct
permissions are being added to the container objects.


Configuring permissions for core.masteringlync.org\RTCComponentUniversalServices ...
MasteringLync: The appropriate permissions haven't been granted for the Office
Communications Servers and Administrators to be able to read the UM dial plan
and auto attendants container objects in Active Directory. The correct
permissions are being added to the container objects.
```

```
UM DialPlan Container: The appropriate permissions haven't been granted for the
Office Communications Servers and Administrators to be able to read the UM dial
plan and auto attendants container objects in Active Directory. The correct
permissions are being added to the container objects.
UM AutoAttendant Container: The appropriate permissions haven't been granted for
the Office Communications Servers and Administrators to be able to read the UM
dial plan and auto attendants container objects in Active Directory. The correct
permissions are being added to the container objects.
Administrative Groups: The appropriate permissions haven't been granted for the
Office Communications Servers and Administrators to be able to read the UM dial
plan and auto attendants container objects in Active Directory. The correct
permissions are being added to the container objects.

Configuring UM IP Gateway objects...
Pool: se01.corp.masteringlync.org
A UMIPGateway doesn't exist in Active Directory for the Office Communications
Server Pool. A new UM IP gateway is being created for the Pool.
IsBranchRegistrar: False
MessageWaitingIndicatorAllowed: True
OutcallsAllowed: True
WARNING: The command completed successfully but no settings of 'lync' have
been modified.
Dial plans: UMDialPlan
Permissions for group core.masteringlync.org\RTCUniversalServerAdmins

ObjectName AccessRights Configured
---------- ------------ ----------
Contoso ListChildren True
UM DialPlan Container ListChildren, ReadProperty True
UM AutoAttendant Container ListChildren, ReadProperty True
Administrative Groups ListChildren, ReadProperty True

Permissions for group core.masteringlync.org\RTCComponentUniversalServices

ObjectName AccessRights Configured
---------- ------------ ----------
Contoso ListChildren True
UM DialPlan Container ListChildren, ReadProperty True
UM AutoAttendant Container ListChildren, ReadProperty True
Administrative Groups ListChildren, ReadProperty True

PoolFqdn UMIPGateway DialPlans
-------- ----------- ---------
se01.corp.masteringlync.org lync {(not found)}
```

At this point, you're ready to move over to the Lync server and perform the configuration needed there. The Enterprise Voice is already configured and set up, as covered in Chapter 13, but it is worth validating that the normalization rules on your Lync dial plans are configured to support the extension dialing configured in UM. (Remember the four-digit extension configured in the UM dial plan earlier?) You need to ensure that when someone on Lync dials the four-digit extension, Lync knows how to normalize the number to E.164 and route it correctly.

The normalization rules can be validated in the Lync Server Control Panel (LSCP, or simply Control Panel). Create a new voice testing routing case and enter the last four digits of the subscriber access number (**1234**) in the Dialed Number To Test box. In the Expected Translation box, enter the full E.164 subscriber access number (**+441189091234**) and then run the test. If it passes, you are ready to move on. If not, go back to Chapter 13 and configure the relevant dial plan settings to cope with 4-digit dialing.

Assuming your system is set up to pass the routing test, you can move on and introduce Lync to Exchange so that it knows where to route calls that need to go to voice mail. This is done using a utility called `OcsUmUtil.exe` (yes, that should be OCS; the name hasn't changed for a while!). The `OcsUmUtil.exe` will load the existing Exchange UM dial plans from AD and associate them with Lync contacts. In the event that a Lync user tries to access their voice mail, leave a voice mail for another user, or call the Outlook Voice Access attendant, there must be a way for Lync to be able to route the call to the appropriate voice prompt running on the Unified Messaging service.

You can find this utility in the `C:\Program Files\Common Files\Microsoft Lync Server 2013\Support\` directory.

When you run the utility, you will see the window shown in Figure 17.7.

FIGURE 17.7
The OcsUmUtil opening screen

Then follow these steps:

1. From the opening screen, click Load Data. The tool will contact AD to determine the forests available for configuration.

2. From the drop-down, select the relevant AD forest. The associated SIP dial plans for that forest will be displayed.

3. Click Add to start the process of creating the Outlook Voice Access (Subscriber Access) contact.

DIAL PLAN NAMING WITH EXCHANGE VERSIONS BEFORE EXCHANGE 2010 SP1

When working with either Exchange 2010 RTM or any flavor of Exchange 2007, you will need to ensure that you match up your dial plan names from Exchange UM and Lync, as described in the article here:

```
http://technet.microsoft.com/en-us/library/bb803622(office.12).aspx
```

You will see this requirement reflected in OcsUmUtil; the subscriber contact will show a warning red exclamation mark for any mismatch. The text in the lower pane explains the issue:

```
A location profile has not been created that matches this dial plan. Until a
location profile is created, the UM play-on-phone and call transfer features
may not work (ignore this error for Exchange 14 SP1 and above). This dial plan
has at least one auto-attendant that does not have a corresponding contact
object in Lync Server 2013.
```

When working with Exchange 2010 SP1 or higher, you can ignore the error.

---

4. In the window that opens, select the required organizational unit (OU) in which to create the object and name the contact. The name should be recognizable rather than something cryptic. The default settings can be used for the rest of the window as shown in Figure 17.8. To complete the process, click OK to exit to the original window.

FIGURE 17.8
Setting up the Outlook Voice Access contact

5. Click Add again to create a second contact, this time for the UM auto attendant. This time select Auto-Attendant as the contact type and then select the required OU. Give the contact a name, and then again opt for the default settings and click OK to complete.

6. Once you have created the contact objects, close the OcsUmUtil and the changes will automatically be written back to AD.

Now you can either wait for the Lync Address Book to update or force it by running the Update-CsAddressBook command on the Lync server. You will also need to restart the Lync Front End service (RTCSRV) for the changes to be applied to users logging into the Front End pool. Bear in mind that this will prevent any logged-on users from being able to access Lync services while the service restarts.

Within the Microsoft Exchange Security Groups OU container, there will now be two additional contact objects representing the subscriber access (Outlook Voice Access) and the auto attendant. Each will have the corresponding SIP URI number to enable Lync to route users to the correct Unified Messaging recipient.

At this point, you are ready to enable some users for Exchange UM. They should be users who are already configured for Lync Enterprise Voice as you set it up in Chapter 13. Enabling a user for UM is a simple process carried out either in the Exchange Administration Center (EAC) or in Exchange Management Shell. For the first user, you'll perform the configuration using the EAC:

1. Open EAC and select Recipients on the left side. Locate and select the user you want to enable, in this case Test User1. In the right Actions pane, click Enable for Unified Messaging.

2. In the window that opens, you will be able to select the UM mailbox policy you configured earlier and then click Next.

3. On the new screen, the settings apply to the user's SIP and extension settings. You should find that Exchange has picked up the user's SIP address and is using it as the predefined SIP address. If an extension number has already been defined for the user within their AD attributes, this will also appear; otherwise, it should be entered in the Extension Number field. Note that you will be prompted for the correct number of digits, as determined from the UM dial plan configured earlier. You'll be able to indicate whether the PIN should be automatically created or you will enter one manually, as shown in Figure 17.9.

4. Complete the wizard, and the user will be set up to use UM. The user will receive a welcome email giving them a subscriber number and PIN.
If you prefer the command line, use the following command:

```
Enable-UMMailbox -Identity "Test user1" -PinExpired $false ↵
-UMMailboxPolicy UMMailboxPolicy -Extensions 8123 ↵
-SIPResourceIdentifier testuser1@masteringlync.org
```

This command will enable Test User1 for UM as in the previous EAC steps. You have now completed the setup of UM integration with Lync. At this point, you test connectivity to UM from the Lync server using the following command:

```
Test-CsExUMConnectivity -TargetFqdn "se01.corp.masteringlync.org" -UserSipAddress ↵
"sip:testuser1@masteringlync.org"
```

From a Lync client logged in as the user you enabled for UM, you should now see the Call Voice Mail options and be able to dial into voice mail to set up your UM mailbox with a greeting. One final thing to note is that there are additional elements that can be configured to provide an even richer voice mail solution. The primary piece of functionality here is Play on Phone, which means that instead of listening to a voice mail on your PC speakers, you can reroute it to play over a phone device. This feature is completely configured in Exchange, so if you are interested in learning more about it, you should take a look at the following location:

http://technet.microsoft.com/en-us/library/jj150478.aspx

FIGURE 17.9
Setting the extension and PIN for the new UM user

Free/Busy, and Other Integration

Besides the obvious element of integration just discussed, Lync touches Exchange in a variety of other, more subtle but extremely useful ways. Like other programs that require access to Exchange data, Lync now predominantly utilizes Exchange Web Services calls to get that information. The types of information returned to Lync in this way are outlined here:

Access to Conversation History and Voice Mail Lync uses the Exchange mailbox for voice mail as previously described; however, when configured to do so, it also creates and uses the Conversation History folder in the user's Exchange mailbox. This allows a user to maintain a store of historical IM conversations, which is then searchable through normal Outlook methods. In Lync 2013, this conversation history also bubbles up into the Lync interface (the third tab in the main client) to provide information about all previous communication through Lync, including conference calls, phone calls, and of course, IMs. This process of saving the conversation detail relies on the conversation window being open long enough for the conversation to be picked up and saved. It is not a server-side process; the client must perform the operation, so if the window is closed too quickly, the information is not saved. This is different than the new Exchange-based archiving, which we cover shortly and is a fully compliant, server-based method of archiving.

Creation of Missed Call Notifications   Through integration with Exchange UM, users will be notified in their inboxes when they miss a voice or IM conversation.

Playback of Voice Mail Message   Again through integration with Exchange UM, the Lync client can be used to play back voice mail messages through the fourth tab in the main client. These can also be accessed through Exchange directly with Outlook or OWA or by dialing into the UM server with a standard phone.

Display Free/Busy Information and Working Hours for a User   As part of enhanced presence, Lync makes calls to Exchange to evaluate the logged-on user's calendar information, such as working hours, general availability, and Out of Office (OOF) status. Lync then publishes this information as part of the user's presence, which others can then query. Note that publishing is not triggered by someone querying a user's presence because a Lync user cannot access another user's calendar information directly. Instead, each user publishes the information about themselves in their presence.

Display a Meeting Subject, Time, and Location   Like the previous item, this is part of enhanced presence.

Display User's Out of Office Status and Note   Like the previous two items, this is part of enhanced presence. Lync shows the OOF message as the user's Lync note and publishes the information in the Lync activity feed for others who have subscribed to that user's presence.

Outlook Web App Integration

Having set up one of the most visible Lync and Exchange integration points, you can move on to the next, that of providing IM and presence capabilities in Outlook Web App (OWA). This functionality is particularly useful because in Lync there is no Communicator Web Access (CWA) server, which was used in OCS to provide IM and presence functionality through a web browser.

The configuration required is relatively straightforward and consists of the following major steps:

1. Ensure that Lync trusts the Exchange server.

2. Configure the OWA mailbox policy, OWA virtual directory, and Web.Config settings on the Exchange Client Access server.

3. Test functionality as an end user.

As with the Enterprise Voice and UM integration, there are not many differences in the way that IM and presence for Lync 2013 integrate with Outlook Web Access in Exchange 2013 compared to the functionality in the 2010 versions. The following changes are worth highlighting:

◆ There is a behavioral change around the use of Trusted Application pools in combination with Enterprise Voice.

◆ There is a requirement to enable IM in OWA via the OWA mailbox policy.

◆ Web.Config configuration is now required again. This was removed in Exchange 2010 SP1, although it was needed in Exchange 2010 RTM.

◆ Fewer prerequisite packages are required.

Out of these changes, the one major area that requires consideration is around the use or not of a Trusted Application pool. We will now take a moment to explain this before moving on to the configuration steps to get you up and running.

PREREQUISITE PACKAGES FOR IM AND OWA INTEGRATION

When integrating Lync 2010 and Exchange 2010, we had a list of prerequisite applications that were needed on the Client Access server for IM and presence integration to work correctly:

◆ CWAOWASSPMain.msi

◆ Vcredist_x64.exe

◆ UcamRedist.msi

◆ UcamRedist.msp

◆ CWAOWAASSP.msi

◆ CWAOWASSP.msp

The good news with Lync and Exchange 2013 is that none of these packages are required anymore!

UNDERSTANDING THE NEED FOR A TRUSTED APPLICATION POOL

For Lync to provide services to another server or service, that foreign system needs to be in something called the Known Servers Table (KST). The ability to add servers to this list is what enables Lync to talk to all sorts of third-party systems such as call center software and video-conference units. As far as Lync is concerned, Exchange is just another third-party system, and it therefore needs defining in the KST. However, there are a couple of ways that this can happen.

One such way is by creating a Trusted Application pool. Creating a Trusted Application pool to represent the Exchange Client Access server is required if no Exchange UM is configured. For integration scenarios where Lync Enterprise Voice has been configured to use Exchange UM, when the Lync Front End service starts it will request any Exchange servers hosting a SIP URI dial plan and add them to the KST. This replaces the need for creating a Trusted Application pool for those Exchange Client Access servers.

It is important to understand that if a Trusted Application pool is set up where you have UM already enabled, you will essentially have added the Exchange server to the KST twice. This will cause an error, which as an administrator you can see in the Lync Application event log when the Front End service starts. The sequence of events that will take place is as follows:

1. Creating a SIP URI dial plan in Exchange will add the server to the Known Servers Table (in this example, exch.corp.masteringlync.org).

2. Upon startup of the Lync Front End service, where a Trusted Application pool is in place, another entry for exch.contoso.com will be added to the Known Servers Table

3. The version number of the entry for the SIP URI dial plan (0) and Trusted Application pool (6) differ, meaning that Lync treats the entries as invalid, and removes them both from the Known Servers Table. This will generate event ID 14563.

4. As a result, integration for UM and OWA will both fail.

It is the logging of the error that is different behavior from Lync 2010. Previously, Lync 2010 didn't care if the servers ended up in the KST twice. If you do end up in this situation, when you restart the Lync Front End service, you will find that a further 14563 error is generated; however, after a few moments, event ID 14493 will be generated, stating that the Exchange server has been re-added to the Known Servers Table, and integration will continue to function as expected. All in all the simplest solution is to remove the Trusted Application pool you created that caused the error in the first place!

For a little more depth on the issue, take a look at the blog post here:

http://blogs.technet.com/b/jenstr/archive/2012/11/13/when-to-have-a-lync-trusted
-application-pool-for-exchange-owa-im-integration.aspx

Configuring Exchange

Now that you understand the choices to be made with regard to the Trusted Application pool, let's progress to setting up the integration. We will start by configuring the OWA virtual directory and OWA mailbox policy and then edit the Web.Config file.

For Exchange to utilize the IM and presence features of Lync, the first thing that is needed is to configure the OWA virtual directory on Exchange that is to be enabled for IM integration to point to a specific Lync server (or server farm). In previous versions of Exchange, we needed to extract information about the certificate being used on the Exchange server to secure the OWA virtual directory and associate the certificate with the service; however, because we will be modifying the Web.Config file to cater for this, the thumbprint is no longer needed.

To determine the correct OWA virtual directory to be configured, we run the following command:

```
Get-OwaVirtualDirectory
```

This will generate a list of all OWA virtual directories, which in this environment will be the one default instance:

```
Name                     Server            OwaVersion
----                     ------            ----------
owa (Default Web Site)   EXCH              Exchange2010
```

Note that despite this being an Exchange 2013 server, the output will still display Exchange2010.

Also, although a bit off topic for this book, Exchange 2013 has simplified its roles so that there are now only CAS and Mailbox servers. These can be collocated or installed on separate servers. On an Exchange server where the roles are collocated, it is important that you do not apply the settings to the Exchange backend virtual directory. This is not something you would do by accident, but it is important to understand that you need to apply these settings only to the CAS server OWA virtual directories. Using the command Get-OWAVirtualDirectory -ShowBackEndVirtualDirectories, you would pull back the OWA virtual directories on the mailbox server, not the CAS server, and these should *not* be configured.

WORKING WITH MULTIPLE EXCHANGE SERVERS

Exchange client access is a complex subject. You could have multiple Client Access servers (CASs) in a farm serving the same domain name or multiple virtual directories serving the different domains. If you follow best practices, you should use the same certificate for each of your Client Access servers and ensure that it contains all the names required to support the various domains for which you will host services. If this best practice is followed, you can simply export the certificate and import it on a new CAS, which means that the certificate thumbprint will remain the same even for multiple servers.

Assuming the same certificate is used across the board, you can progress with the commands discussed in the main text to configure integration. If you want to be more specific and work on only a single virtual directory, then instead of piping the output of Get-OwaVirtualDirectory to the Set-OwaVirtualDirectory command, don't run the Get-OwaVirtualDirectory command and simply use the -Identity parameter on the Set-OwaVirtualDirectory command to specify an individual virtual directory.

Getting back to the task in hand, once you have the name of your website, you can apply the instant messaging settings to both the website and the mailbox policy. The following commands will apply these settings to our OWA virtual directory in the Default Web Site. You also need to alter the existing mailbox policy to enable instant messaging features. This is done using the commands shown here:

```
Set-OWAVirtualDirectory "exch\owa (Default Web Site)" ↵
-InstantMessagingType OCS -InstantMessagingEnabled:$true

Get-OwaMailboxPolicy exch | Set-OwaMailboxPolicy ↵
-InstantMessagingEnabled $true -InstantMessagingType OCS
```

Note that the use of OCS here is not a typo, just a legacy command that is still in use from previous versions of Exchange! If the commands are successful, there should be no output from the Management Shell console. To verify that these settings have been applied, you can run the following commands to display the settings associated with each virtual directory, filtering on the InstantMessaging attributes:

```
Get-OwaVirtualDirectory |fl *instantmessaging*
Get-OwaMailboxPolicy |fl *instantmessaging*
```

You should see something that resembles the following:

```
InstantMessagingCertificateThumbprint :
InstantMessagingServerName            :
InstantMessagingEnabled               : True
InstantMessagingType                  : Ocs

InstantMessagingEnabled               : True
InstantMessagingType                  : Ocs
```

The last piece of configuration on Exchange is to edit the Web.Config file. You need to edit the Web.Config file on the Client Access server so that it contains the thumbprint of the certificate being used to secure OWA. The default location for the Web.Config file is in the `C:\Program Files\Microsoft\Exchange Server\V15\ClientAccess\Owa` folder. This file gives Exchange some key information about your web services, and by adding an additional couple of lines, you can tell the web service which Lync server or servers it should trust.

From the Exchange Management Shell, use the following commands to extract the thumbnail of the OWA certificate and display it on screen:

```
$cert = (Get-ExchangeCertificate | Where {$_.Subject -ilike "*mail.masteringlync.org*"}).↵
Thumbprint
```

This first command will populate the $cert variable with the thumbnail of the OWA certificate.

```
$cert
```

By typing $cert on its own, you will display the output to copy into the Web.Config file.

Having gotten the thumbprint of the certificate, open the Web.Config file and search for the <AppSettings> section. Within this section, insert the following two lines of code, replacing the following value with the $cert output from the previous command:

```
<add key="IMCertificateThumbprint" ↵
value="AFCAE30E305B57C5FE3A157A065D7830327B2B6F"/> ↵
<add key="IMServerName" value="se01.corp.masteringlync.org"/>
```

Close Web.Config and save the changes. Then run the following from the Exchange Management Shell:

```
C:\Windows\System32\Inetsrv\Appcmd.exe recycle apppool /apppool.name:"MSExchangeOWAAppPool"
```

This will refresh the OWA application pool in IIS to ensure that the changes made in the Web.Config are applied.

At this point, congratulations are due! You have completed the Exchange OWA virtual directory and OWA mailbox policy configuration.

Configuring Lync

With the Exchange side of things configured, you now move on to set up Lync to provide the IM and presence services to OWA. The first step, if required, is to create a Trusted Application pool to ensure that Lync trusts Exchange. Remember, this section is needed only if the Exchange CAS server to which Lync will be talking is not already in the KST via the automatic entry created when UM is run. Therefore, if you already have a SIP URI UM dial plan, the following steps are for information only:

To create the Trusted Application pool, take the following steps:

1. Log on to the Lync server as an administrator and open the Topology Builder.

2. Download the topology, navigate to the trusted application servers node, right-click it, and select New Trusted Application Pool.

3. In the Define the Trusted Application Pool FQDN window that opens, enter the name of the Exchange Client Access server (**exch.corp.masteringlync.org**, for the example), select Single Computer Pool, as shown in Figure 17.10, and then click Next.

FIGURE 17.10
Configuring the
FQDN for the
Trusted Application
pool

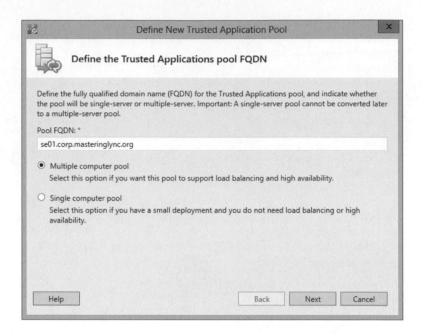

If you were to have multiple Client Access servers in an array, you would use the FQDN of the Exchange CAS array and select Multiple Computer Pool.

4. In the Select The Next Hop window, make sure SE01.corp.masteringlync.org is selected (or your own Front End pool) and click Finish.

Now you should publish the topology and then check to see whether the updates were successful.

The same configuration can also be carried out in the Exchange Management Shell using the following command:

```
New-CsTrustedApplicationPool -Identity exch.corp.masteringlync.org ↵
-Registrar se01.corp.masteringlync.org -Site EMEA
-RequiresReplication $False
```

To check that the settings applied correctly, open the Lync Management Shell and run the Get-CsTrustedApplicationPool cmdlet.

This will generate the following output:

```
Identity             : TrustedApplicationPool:se01.corp.masteringlync.org
Registrar            : Registrar:se01.corp.masteringlync.org
FileStore            :
ThrottleAsServer     : True
TreatAsAuthenticated : True
OutboundOnly         : False
RequiresReplication  : False
AudioPortStart       :
```

```
AudioPortCount       : 0
AppSharingPortStart  :
AppSharingPortCount  : 0
VideoPortStart       :
VideoPortCount       : 0
Applications         : {}
DependentServiceList : {}
ServiceId            : 1-ExternalServer-2
SiteId               : Site:EMEA
PoolFqdn             : exch.corp.masteringlync.org
Version              : 6
Role                 : TrustedApplicationPool
```

Next run the Get-CsTrustedApplicationComputer cmdlet to verify that you see the server FQDN you used during the creation of the Trusted Application pool, as shown here:

```
Get-CsTrustedApplicationComputer
Identity : exch.corp.masteringlync.org
Pool     : exch.corp.masteringlync.org
Fqdn     : exch.corp.masteringlync.org
```

Note that the previous command output would be blank if you have not set up a Trusted Application pool because of Lync being integrated with Exchange for UM.

You have now given Lync the ability to allow users within your pools to expose their status to others via your Exchange Client Access server.

The next step is to configure a trusted application. Essentially, the Trusted Application pool tells Lync it is okay to talk to a specific third-party system and the trusted application tells it how to communicate.

To create the trusted application, use the New-CSTrustedApplication cmdlet. The first thing you'll need for the application is a port on which Lync will listen. This can be any port that is not in use. You'll select port 5050 because it is similar to other Lync ports; however, this can be any free port over 1025.

It is critical that nothing else uses the port, so to verify that, open a Windows cmd.exe prompt as an administrator and run Netstat as follows:

```
Netstat -a | findstr 5050
```

The following output shows what it would look like if a conflict occurs because you selected a port (5070) on which Lync listens:

```
netstat -a | findstr 5070
   TCP    192.168.1.194:5070    Lync-SE01:0              LISTENING
```

When Netstat is run on the correct port, you won't see any output because there won't be any conflicts to show. Once a suitable port is chosen, set up the trusted application as follows:

```
New-CsTrustedApplication -ApplicationId ExchangeOWA ↵
-TrustedApplicationPoolFqdn exch.corp.masteringlync.org -Port 5050
```

This command will create a trusted application called ExchangeOWA in the Trusted Application pool set up earlier; it will listen on port 5050. The ApplicationID can be any unique string, but it makes sense to use a recognizable naming convention. When you run the preceding command, you will see the following output:

```
WARNING: The following changes must be made in order for the operation to be
complete.
Enable-CsTopology must still be run for all changes to take effect.
Identity                      : exch.corp.masteringlync.org/urn:application:
exchangeowa
ComputerGruus                 : {exch.corp.masteringlync.org
sip:exch.corp.masteringlync.org@masteringlync.org
;gruu;opaque=srvr:exchangeowa:_YHYY_tIL1qZQ_bFgC9FQAAA}
ServiceGruu                   :
sip:exch.corp.masteringlync.org@masteringlync.org;gruu;opaque=srvr:
exchangeowa:_YHYY_tIL1qZQ_bFgC9FQAAA
Protocol                      : Mtls
ApplicationId                 : urn:application:exchangeowa
TrustedApplicationPoolFqdn    : exch.corp.masteringlync.org
Port                          : 5050
LegacyApplicationName         : exchangeowa
```

Now all that remains is to run the Enable-CsTopology command as instructed, and OWA IM integration is complete and presence will light up in OWA.

Understanding and Configuring the Unified Contact Store

When Lync is deployed out of the box, all users have their own buddy list maintained and stored by Lync in its SQL database. However, now with Lync and Exchange 2013, it is possible, and makes more sense, to have those contacts in one location: the Unified Contact Store (UCS). This gives users the ability to manage their contacts from a single list and provides that single contact list to pick from across all Microsoft Office applications. At the backend, as with so much of the integration, Lync will talk to Exchange using Exchange Web Services (EWS), which has been previously configured using the OAuthTokenIssuer certificate in the prerequisite stage.

When configured, two folders are created in the Exchange Contacts folder for each user. The main contacts folder is visible by the user as a subfolder called Lync Contacts within their default Contacts folder. The second folder is a hidden subfolder that contains metadata used to communicate changes to contacts with Lync and is named using a GUID. Although this subfolder is hidden from the users, for troubleshooting purposes, you can easily access it using a folder exposure tool such as MFCMapi.

MIGRATING CONTACTS TO THE UCS

The process to enable the new method of storing Lync contacts in Exchange uses the New-CSUserServicesPolicy command on the Lync server. By setting the -UCSAllowed parameter to True, you can set this policy on a Global, Site, Service, or Tag level, as discussed in Chapter 10, "User Administration." The Grant-CSUserServicesPolicy command is then used to grant users access to the UCS.

Before we start the first step of migrating users from Lync to UCS, it is important to highlight that the default global policy is set to True, which would mean that any users that fall within the scope are automatically enabled for UCS. By running the following command, you ensure that only users who fall within the scope of the custom policy will be eligible for migration:

```
Set-CsUserServicesPolicy Global -UcsAllowed $False
```

To create a custom policy, you can run the following command from the Lync Management Shell:

```
New-CSUserServicesPolicy "UCSEnabled" -UCSAllowed $True
```

You can then assign the policy to your users as follows:

```
Grant-CSUserServicesPolicy corp\Nathan_lync -PolicyName "UCSEnabled"
Grant-CSUserServicesPolicy corp\Keith_lync -PolicyName "UCSEnabled"
```

The next time the user logs into Lync 2013, the scope of the policy created earlier will be pushed down to that user, and they will be included on the migration to UCS. The Lync client will use this information to send a "nudge" request to the Lync server to start migration of contacts to Exchange. The Lync Storage Service (LYSS) will then complete the migration. If the user is logged on when this completes, they will be prompted to sign out and back in again to start using UCS.

There are two ways you can check to see if the migration has been successful. From the server side, you can run `Test-CSUnifiedContactStore` as shown in the following command:

```
Test-CsUnifiedContactStore -UserSipAddress Nathan_lync@masteringlync.org ↵
-TargetFqdn se01.corp.masteringlync.org
```

The other verification method is to use the Lync client. You do this by holding down Control, right-clicking the Lync icon in the taskbar, and selecting Lync Configuration Information, which opens a page that will show you a range of configuration information including the contact list provider and UCS connectivity state properties. Prior to migration, the contact list provider will show as Lync Server and the UCS connectivity state will show as Exchange Connection Down. After migration, the values for Contact List Provider and UCS Connectivity State should be UCS and Exchange Connection Active, respectively, as shown in Figure 17.11.

FIGURE 17.11
A view of the configuration information showing UCS properties

At this point, the user should also be able to see a new contact folder in Outlook called `Lync Contacts`, as shown in Figure 17.12, and it contains the same contacts as those visible in the Lync client.

FIGURE 17.12
The new Lync Contacts folder in Outlook

> **UCS IN A PAIRED POOL SCENARIO**
>
> UCS is also protected in the new HA model for Lync 2013. If UCS is configured when a paired pool is set up, as the user/pool migration info is shared between paired pools, this will be available on any Front End server in the event of a failure. Therefore, users are unaffected if a Front End server fails because the information has already been replicated to another server.

ROLLING BACK THE CONTACTS FROM THE UCS TO LYNC

There may be circumstances in which it is necessary to roll the contacts from UCS back to Lync. This may be due to moving mailboxes from Exchange 2013 to Exchange 2010, which does not support UCS. The recommended way to do this is first to create a new policy where the -UCSAllowed value is set to $False using the following command:

```
New-CSUserServicesPolicy "NoUCS" -UcsAllowed $False
```

You then assign the new policy to the users:

```
Grant-CSUserServicesPolicy corp\Nathan_lync -PolicyName "NoUCS"
Grant-CSUserServicesPolicy corp\Keith_lync -PolicyName "NoUCS"
```

It is important to note that assigning a new policy to users will not remove their contacts from UCS. If the policy applied to the user has a -UCSAllowed value of $False, the server will take no further action; therefore, a further command will need to be run to move the contacts from UCS back to Lync.

The Invoke-CsUCSRollback command is used to mark the user for rollback and migrate the contacts back to Lync as follows:

```
Invoke-CSUCSRollback corp\Nathan_lync
```

Running this command will prevent any further migration to UCS being completed for a seven-day period, therefore meaning that rollback should not be invoked for a temporary server move. This is where the previous step of creating a new policy for rolled-back users comes in handy, because it can be set to exclude previously rolled-back users from accessing UCS. The result of not reassigning the users to a non-UCS-enabled policy is that after the seven-day period is over, the server will check to see if they should be assigned a policy, and they will then be reenabled for UCS.

Another reason for moving away from the UCS is when moving the Lync user to a non–Lync 2013 pool. In this case, you would run the `Move-CsUser` command, which will trigger an automatic rollback of the contacts from UCS to Lync and complete the pool move.

Integrating into Exchange for Compliance Archiving

In Chapter 11, "Archiving and Monitoring," we talked about how Lync can archive content to a SQL database. However, Lync 2013, when combined with Exchange 2013 and SharePoint 2013, provides a far more grown-up solution. It is possible for Lync to make use of the Exchange In-Place Hold functionality to store data in a compliance-suitable archive. Exchange archiving allows Lync archive messages to be stored in individual users' Exchange mailboxes rather than on the Lync SQL Archival database. Exchange provides various compliance functions, including the concept of In-Place Hold, where data is kept immutable either for a period of time or indefinitely. A set of hidden folders are created in the user's Exchange mailbox. One of these folders is called `Purges`, and this is the folder Lync stores its archive transcripts into. The contents of these hidden folders are indexed by Exchange and can later be used as part of an eDiscovery search either from EAC or from a combined Discovery Portal in SharePoint that enables administrators to search in a single location for all corresponding messages relating to that user whether the messages are in Lync, SharePoint, or Exchange.

Given that Lync provides many ways to communicate, it is important to understand which types of content can be archived. These are laid out as follows:

- Peer-to-peer instant messages

- Multiparty instant messages (within conferences)

- Conference content, including polls and whiteboards

The following types of content are not archived:

- Peer-to-peer file transfers

- Audio/video for peer-to-peer and conference conversations

- Desktop/Application Sharing content for peer-to-peer and conference conversations

ARCHIVE CONFIGURATION

As with many Lync settings, Exchange archiving is configured by policy, which is a concept we covered in depth in Chapter 10. The default scope for Exchange archiving is Global and it is set as disabled. As such, archiving is disabled for all users by default. An administrator can choose to enable the policy on a Global level by amending the existing default global policy or, if they want to choose a different scope such as Site or User level, they can do so by creating a new policy by running the `New-CsArchivingConfiguration` cmdlet.

Whether you're amending the existing policy or configuring a new one, two parameters define the major elements of the policy: `-EnableArchiving` and `-EnableExchangeArchiving`.

Here are some more details as to your options when running these commands:

- `EnableArchiving`: This has three possible settings:
  - `None`: This is the default value; no archiving is enabled.

- `IMOnly`: Instant messaging transcripts are enabled.

- `IMAndWebConf`: Instant messaging and web conferencing transcripts are enabled.

Both `IMOnly` and `IMAndWebConf` rely on the `EnableExchangeArchiving` setting being set to `$True` for message to be archiving in Exchange rather than Lync.

- `EnableExchangeArchiving`: This can either be `$True` for enabled or `$False` for disabled.

You will see these in action as you go through the process of configuring Exchange archiving in the following sections.

Because the Exchange archiving feature is available only for users whose mailboxes are stored on Exchange Server 2013, mailboxes on previous versions of Exchange that have archiving enabled within Lync will continue to use the standard Lync archiving. For example, when a user logs on to Lync, Lync will validate whether their mailbox is on Exchange 2013 or an earlier version. If the mailbox is not on 2013, then they are ineligible to use Exchange mailbox–based Lync archiving.

WORKING WITH OFFICE 365

It is worth noting that there are various scenarios in which Lync and Exchange could be split between on-premises deployments and cloud deployments. Thankfully, in most of these, Exchange mailbox–based Lync archiving still works as highlighted here:

- Lync Online and Exchange Online: Fully functional

- Lync Online and Exchange on Premises: Does not function

- Exchange Online and Lync on Premises: Fully functional

- Exchange on Premises and Lync on Premises: Fully functional

---

Another thing to take into consideration when archiving is where multiple AD forests come into play. As is often the case, this sort of configuration complicates things somewhat. For users where Exchange 2013 and Lync reside in the same forest, both Lync and Exchange look at the properties of a user in AD, and if the property to archive is set, Lync and Exchange will heed that. In the real world, this means that archiving is managed by the use of the `In-Place Hold` policy on the Exchange server. If `In-Place Hold` is configured on an Exchange user, Lync will automatically see that setting and turn on archiving of Lync data to Exchange (assuming the Lync policies do not block this as discussed earlier). However, for cross-forest deployments where Lync and Exchange are in different forests, the value of `ExchangeArchivingPolicy` on the Lync user object will determine where archiving takes place. There are four values for this parameter:

- `Uninitialized`: The In-Place Hold settings on the mailbox will determine the archive settings. If this has not been set, Lync will archive the messages.

- `NoArchiving`: No archiving will take place whatsoever.

- `UseLyncArchivingPolicy`: Archiving will take place on the Lync server.

- `ArchivingToExchange`: Archiving will take place on the Exchange server.

There is one final element to take into consideration before we get things up and running, which is the CsArchivingPolicy. As you know, Lync is able to communicate with users within the organization and also those external on Lync or other platforms. When Lync Server 2013 is installed, a default global archiving policy is created to determine whether internal, external, or both types of messages are archived. This is disabled for both by default. Setting the ArchiveInternal parameter on the CsArchivingPolicy will allow messages for AD users in your organization to be archived. Enabling the ArchiveExternal parameter will archive messages between an AD user and any other non-AD users (i.e., a local user communicating with an external user).

ENABLE EXCHANGE ARCHIVING

Having understood the theory and all the components that come into play, we are now going to walk you through redirecting Lync archiving for IM messages to your Exchange server. Because you want this to apply to all users, you will amend the global policy for Lync rather than creating a new policy.

To begin with, log into the Lync Control Panel as an administrator. Select the Monitoring And Archiving tab, and then select Archiving Configuration, as shown in Figure 17.13.

FIGURE 17.13
The Archiving Configuration area in LSCP

In Figure 17.13, you can see the default settings for the global policy, one of which is that archiving is disabled. At this point, you can choose whether to create a new policy with different archiving settings, depending on whether you want all users to have their messages archived in the same way.

As mentioned, you will simply edit the global policy because you are happy for all users to be archived in the same way. This is done by double-clicking the global policy to open it. Once it opens, you can then amend this to start archiving IM messages to Exchange by clicking the drop-down box under Archiving Setting, choosing Archive IM Sessions, and also selecting the Exchange Server Integration check box, as shown in Figure 17.14.

FIGURE 17.14
Configuring the
global archiving
policy for Exchange
archiving

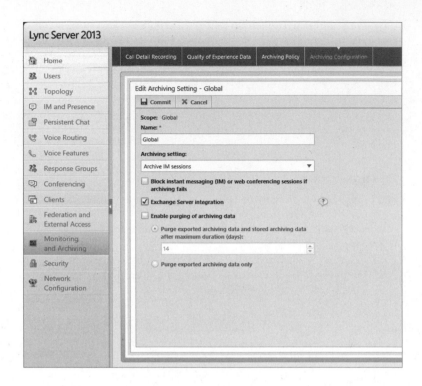

The same configuration can also be carried out in the Lync Management Shell using the following command:

```
Set-CSArchivingConfiguration Global -EnableArchiving IMOnly ↵
-EnableExchangeArchiving $True
```

Enable Internal and External Communication Archiving

You will now change the archiving policy to define which types of messages will be archived. You can choose to archive either internal communications only or those with users outside your domain.

In Lync Control Panel, select the Monitoring and Archiving tab, then Archiving Policy. Select Archive Internal Communications and Archive External Communications. This brings up the window shown in Figure 17.15.

In Figure 17.15, you can see that the default global settings do not have a scope defined. You'll enable both internal and external communication by double-clicking the global policy, and selecting both the Archive Internal Communications and Archive External Communications check boxes as shown in Figure 17.16.

The same configuration can also be carried out in the Exchange Management Shell using the following command:

```
Set-CSArchivingPolicy Global -ArchiveInternal $True -ArchiveExternal $True
```

FIGURE 17.15
The archiving policy window

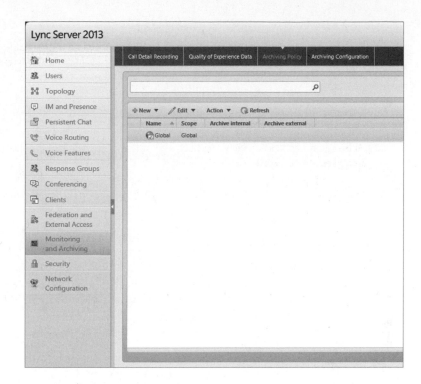

FIGURE 17.16
Setting the global policy to allow archiving of internal and external messages

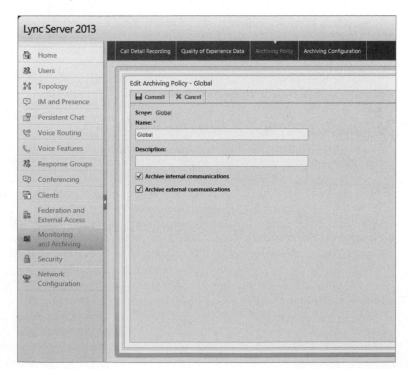

CONFIGURE EXCHANGEARCHIVINGPOLICY

As we touched on earlier, if the Exchange and Lync servers are in separate forests, you will need to simply tell Lync what it should do based on its own policy because it will not be able to make a decision based on the Exchange policy in place on the user object in the Exchange forest. In this case, the following command can be used to tell Lync where to archive for your user:

```
Set-CsUser corp\nathan_lync -ExchangeArchivingPolicy ArchivingToExchange
```

As a result, you've told Lync to use Exchange archiving for your user. This means that should your Exchange and Lync servers reside in separate forests, the policy applied to the user will take precedence. You would of course need to do this for all relevant users, so we come back to the search skills found in Chapter 10. You would use a filter to search for all users in a particular Lync pool and apply the settings to all users found using the following command:

```
Get-CsUser | Where-Object {[String]$_.Registrarpool -eq ↵
"se01.corp.masteringlync.org"} | Set-CsUser -ExchangeArchivingPolicy
ArchivingToExchange
```

You have now successfully applied Exchange archiving to your users in both single- and cross-forest environments. Those of you from an Exchange background can use the New-MailboxSearch command to create a new in-place hold and add a user to that hold, as shown in this example (we will not be covering Exchange In-Place Hold in detail in this book):

```
New-MailboxSearch "Hold-Ref123" -SourceMailboxes "Nathan.lync@masteringlync.org" ↵
-InPlaceHoldEnabled $true
```

As a result of enabling Exchange archiving for Lync messages, you have the ability to search content within the mailbox using the Exchange In-Place and Discovery features. The benefit of this is that if you are looking for a particular keyword (such as "SecretProject"), Exchange can now search the Lync archive as part of this search. This opens up the scope for administrators to be able to search for IM conversations as well as email messages. With the -ArchiveExternal parameter in use, you also have the ability to search conversations that have taken place with external parties. The scope for compliance teams to track down those elusive conversations taking place via Lync has definitely taken a step in the right direction!

Making Use of High-Resolution Photos in Lync

One of the things that has become more and more prominent over the last few years in all sorts of social or communication applications is user photos. Lync is no different! In Lync 2010, it was possible to use the thumbnailPhoto attribute from AD to display a photo representing a user. However, there were constraints for this, the biggest being the resolution of the photo, which could not exceed 48×48 pixels. This is a really tiny photo when you consider that most modern cameras are now capable of taking photos of at least 15 megapixels! In Lync 2013, things have been improved somewhat by using Lync integration to Exchange through Exchange Web Services (EWS). This enables us to store photos as large as 648×648 pixels (around 250KB). Cleverly, Exchange provides the ability to resize this photo depending on where it is needed (downscaling rather than upscaling). To provide the photos for scaling, users can upload their own using Outlook Web Access for Exchange 2013, or an administrator can do this using the Exchange Management Shell.

Using the scaling feature of Exchange, photos can be provided at one of three possible resolutions:

- ◆ 48×48 pixels (Thumbnail) : On creation of a high-resolution photo in Exchange, a 48×48-pixel photo will also be copied to the `thumbnailPhoto` attribute within AD for future use.

- ◆ 96×96 pixels (Default) : This is commonly used by applications such as Outlook 2013.

- ◆ 648×648 pixels (XXLarge2): This is used by the Lync client and Lync Web App.

Exchange will also create intermediate resolutions providing that the original photo had a resolution of at least 648×648 pixels. Although there are currently no applications that use these intermediate resolutions, they have been provided as an option for future use. In the event that a low-resolution photo is uploaded and an application such as the Lync client or Lync Web App requests a higher resolution, only the lowest-resolution photo will be returned. For example, if a user uploads a photo 120×120 pixels in size, and a Lync client user requests access to that photo, the default 96×96-pixel photo will be returned.

Table 17.1 illustrates the full range of photos stored by Exchange and the values that can be used to return photos using EWS.

TABLE 17.1: The range of photos stored in Exchange

PHOTO TYPE	WIDTH IN PIXELS	VALUE
Thumbnail	48×48	HR48×48
Small	64×64	HR64×64
Default	96×96	HR96×96
Large-1	120×120	HR120×120
Large-2	240×240	HR240×240
XLarge-1	360×360	HR360×360
XLarge-2	432×432	HR432×432
XXLarge1	504×504	HR504×504
XXLarge2	648×648	HR648×648

In terms of storage, we again find that we are making use of the hidden area of a mailbox to store the photo in the root of the user's mailbox. If you want to, the properties can be explored using a mailbox folder exposure tool such as MFCMapi. The benefit of having Exchange hold the photo as a central store is that it can be provided out consistently across the whole Office stack.

We will now walk through how a Lync administrator would enable high-resolution photos for a user. The scenario is that there can potentially be thousands of photos taken and you now need to import them all into the system. The process is carried out from the Exchange Management Shell by running the following commands and would import a photo for one user. You could of course expand on this to carry it out in bulk:

```
$photo = ([Byte]] $(Get-Content -Path "C:\Photos\Nathan.jpg" -Encoding Byte ↵
-ReadCount 0))
```

This first command will get the photo data and import it into the variable $photo:

```
Set-UserPhoto -Identity "Nathan Lync" -PictureData $photo -Confirm:False
```

The second command will take the photo and assign it to the user.

At this point you would likely go ahead and ask the user to log into the Exchange Control Panel through OWA and review the preview of the photo. At this stage, you have not actually saved the photo, so Exchange has only the preview; it has not yet processed all the various resolutions covered earlier. Once you are sure the user is happy with the photo, you run the next command:

```
Set-UserPhoto -Identity "Nathan Lync" -Save -Confirm:False
```

This will commit the photo and kick off the process of converting into the various required resolutions.

Of course, the other option for one-off changes is that the user logs into the Lync client and selects Options and then My Picture. They will be redirected to their Exchange Control Panel page in OWA, where they can upload the photo of their choice. Exchange will scale the photo to the maximum permitted resolution of 648×648. When the user clicks Save on the options page, the photo will be automatically committed.

If you then log out and back into the Lync client, you will notice that the new photo is now in use, and in the higher resolution of 648×648 pixels.

Finally, it is worth knowing that as an administrator, you can verify any user's photo within a web browser by navigating to the EWS page and using the size format (use Table 17.1 as a reference), as shown in this example:

```
https://mail.corp.masteringlync.org/ews/exchange.asmx/s/GetUserPhoto?email=
Nathan_lync@masteringlync.org&size=HR648x648
https://mail.corp.masteringlync.org/ews/exchange.asmx/s/GetUserPhoto?email=
Nathan_lync@masteringlync.org&size=HR96x96
```

The above URLs will pull back the 648×648-pixel photo and the 96×96-pixel photo for the user Nathan, respectively. As it happens, this is a good way to verify connectivity problems within Lync, especially if you can see the photo using the EWS link but not from the Lync client or Lync Web App.

Integrating Lync with SharePoint

SharePoint 2013 is a business collaboration platform for the enterprise. SharePoint allows the creation of web portals and sites (intranets, extranets, and websites) to centralize information and applications on a corporate network. Organizations use SharePoint to connect and empower users and facilitate collaboration among them.

Lync 2013 and SharePoint 2013 can be integrated to give users a rich in-context collabora-tion experience whether SharePoint is deployed on premises or as part of Office 365 in the cloud. Lync 2013 builds on what was provided in Lync 2010 and Office Communications Server (OCS) 2007 and OCS 2007 R2, which gave users the ability to access the instant messaging (IM), enhanced presence, telephony, and conferencing capabilities of Lync and Office Communicator from SharePoint. This basic communication functionality integration requires no complicated configuration for SharePoint or Lync Server. Should you wish to enable all those with access to SharePoint to have an associated Persistent Chat room, then there are third-party software tools that will allow you to add Persistent Chat to these intranets, extranets, and websites. This SharePoint integration section of the chapter is split into two main areas. First we will explore the available functionality and show you how to integrate Lync and SharePoint for things like presence and search and to provide user photos. We will then move on to focus on how you can extend Lync and SharePoint using UCMA by developing an automated communication bot.

Note that as with the Exchange section, you won't learn how to configure SharePoint. You'll simply be introduced to what is needed and any Lync-specific configuration; for the other ele-ments, you will need to see existing SharePoint documentation or your SharePoint team.

For guidance on installing and configuring SharePoint 2013, refer to the Microsoft TechNet articles at the following location:

```
http://technet.microsoft.com/en-us/library/cc262957.aspx
```

IM and Presence within Sites

Lync enables presence in SharePoint sites using the same presence indicator that is displayed in the Lync 2013 client, as shown in Figure 17.17.

FIGURE 17.17
SharePoint site showing presence indicators

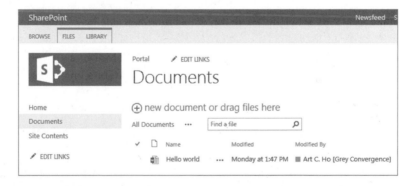

Wherever a username is displayed within SharePoint sites, their Lync 2013 presence indicator is displayed, based on the presence status set in Lync. With a single click, the contact card can be opened; it is the same contact card shown in the Lync 2013 client, as shown in Figure 17.18.

This enables full Lync functionality from within SharePoint. A user can initiate Lync com-munications from the contact card, such as sending an IM or starting a Lync audio call, so col-laboration is easy and intuitive. Presence is enabled by default in SharePoint, so there is no need for any special configuration on the server side for this to work.

To view presence in SharePoint sites, a user must have Office 2003 or Office 2007 with the latest service pack, Office 2010, Office 2013, or later. This is because when Office is installed, a dynamic link library called `name.dll` is installed. It can be found at `%Program Files%\ Microsoft Office\Office15` where Office 2013 is installed (lower-numbered versions refer to earlier Office versions). This DLL file is an ActiveX control that allows SharePoint to display a user's presence information. The ActiveX control actually leverages the Lync API to request the user's presence status so that it can be displayed within a SharePoint site. The required Lync API is installed automatically as a part of the Lync client installation. Note that when Firefox and other browsers are used, presence integration is not available.

FIGURE 17.18
The contact card experience accessible with a single click

Skill Search

SharePoint Search helps users in an organization find the information they need to help them in their everyday work. It provides a way to search the intranet for both content and people and to refine results by relevance. For example, you know there is a new employee named John in Finance. To find John, you could search for "John" in a SharePoint Search Center People search site and all the results with *John* would be returned. You could further refine that search to find John in Finance. Skill Search in Lync allows you to use the search term "John Finance" and get those filtered results immediately.

People Search requires that the following service applications be available:

◆ Search Service application (which is explained in the following text)

◆ User Profile Service application, which is a shared application within SharePoint 2013 and 2010 used to manage user profiles in an organization, synchronize profiles with Active Directory, and create My Sites for users

◆ Managed Metadata, which is used if you want to configure People Search and allow Search using a custom metadata property that is being populated into the user profiles from an external system such as a SQL or Oracle business system

People Search also requires that a Search Center site be created using the Enterprise Search Center template.

In SharePoint 2013 and 2010, Search is a service application. Service applications allow more granularity and control over how they work so that users can have a specific site collection that is associated with a specific service application. This means multiple indexes can be maintained, keeping information in separate indexes.

SharePoint Search can index all sorts of source content such as file shares, external websites (a partner's website, for example), SharePoint websites, Exchange public folders, databases, and a line of business applications (Oracle or SQL databases, product data, or customer data). This new architecture gives the user an experience that is highly efficient, effective, and personal.

With Lync and SharePoint 2013 (or SharePoint 2010 or 2007) integration, one exciting and useful new feature compared to OCS 2007 or 2007 R2 is the ability to perform a skill-based search within the Lync client. For example, if you need to find a Lync expert within your organization but you don't know exactly who or what kind of expert you need, you can simply type a keyword such as "Lync" into the search bar and then click the Skill button. The client will then display anyone with Lync in their job title or listed in the profile stored in their My Site on SharePoint.

WHAT IS MY SITE?

SharePoint's My Site feature provides a personal site that gives users in your organization a central location to not only store documents, links, and contacts but also populate and keep up-to-date with appropriate information about themselves. For example, users can list their skills, which can then appear as a result in other users' searches.

Once the results are returned, you can browse through them and find someone appropriate for what you need to know and send them a quick IM with your question. Because these results come from the SharePoint Skill Search component, a link is provided that opens the search results in SharePoint.

Skill Search is not enabled in Lync by default. For this feature to work correctly, the following components are required:

- **A full version of SharePoint:** Windows SharePoint Services (WSS) will not work with Skill Search.

- **SharePoint 2013 or SharePoint 2010 My Sites:** A My Site is a personal site that gives you a central location to manage and store your documents, content, links, and contacts and lets other see information about you.

- **The SharePoint User Profile service application:** This stores information about users in a central location and is where user My Sites are administered and configured.

- **A SharePoint Search Center site URL:** This is a feature introduced in Microsoft Office SharePoint Server 2007; it is a SharePoint site specifically configured for the search task. It includes certain fields, each responsible for a specific search task—for example, People Search.

In addition, you need to configure the following:

- SharePoint must be published to the Internet so external Lync clients can access it.

- Lync Server needs to be configured with the correct Search Center URL to provide to clients. The Search Center URL is provisioned to the Lync client through in-band settings as part of the CsClientPolicy, a topic discussed in Chapter 10.

Lync needs to be configured to provide the relevant URLs to clients. These are the URLs of the SharePoint Search Center; your SharePoint administrator should be able to give them to you. To provide this information, a client policy must be configured and applied so that the Lync clients are configured to use relevant SharePoint search URLs. To configure the client policy, you would run the following commands from the Lync Server Management Shell (LSMS):

```
Set-CsClientPolicy -SPSearchInternalURL https://<searchsite>/_vti_bin/search.asmx
Set-CsClientPolicy -SPSearchExternalURL https://<searchsite>/_vti_bin/search.asmx
```

Note that <searchsite> should be replaced by the full path to the SharePoint Search Center.

With these commands, you set not only an internal URL but also an external URL so that remote users (not connected to the internal LAN) can access the Skill Search feature. If you do not specify an external URL, then upon clicking Search, users working remotely will receive an error message telling them they won't be able to search, as shown in Figure 17.19. To provide external access to search, the SharePoint website must be made available to users working externally.

FIGURE 17.19
The error presented to users externally if the Lync Search URLs are not configured correctly

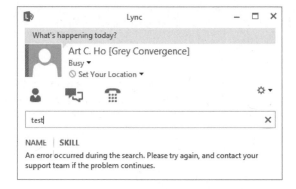

As previously mentioned, there is also the option to display a link to the Search Center, entitled "Display results in SharePoint," at the bottom of the Lync client once the search has finished. The user can click this link to see the results of the search displayed in a SharePoint web page. To enable this functionality, execute the following commands in the LSMS:

```
Set-CsClientPolicy -SPSearchCenterInternalURL https://<searchsite>/Pages/PeopleResults.aspx ↵
Set-CsClientPolicy -SPSearchCenterExternalURL https://<searchsite>/SearchCenter/Pages/ ↵
PeopleResults.aspx
```

Note that <searchsite> should be replaced by the full path to the SharePoint Search Center.

Once the in-band provisioning takes effect, you will be able to conduct a Skill Search through your Lync client:

1. In the search bar, type a keyword. You will be presented with the options Name and Skill.

2. Click Skill.

The query is sent to SharePoint, and the results are sent back to the Lync client. You can click the View Results In SharePoint link to see the search results in a SharePoint web page.

To see which URLs have been provisioned, you can use the Lync client Configuration Information tool. While holding down the Ctrl button, right-click the Lync icon in the system tray and click Configuration Information to display the window shown in Figure 17.20. The SharePoint URLs can be seen in the Configuration Information table. This area is a handy troubleshooting tool for many Lync client configuration issues.

FIGURE 17.20
The Configuration Information window can be used to troubleshoot client issues.

Lync Configuration Information	
DG URL Internal	https://lonsvm101:443/groupexpansion/service.svc
DG URL External	https://lonsvm101:443/groupexpansion/service.svc
Quality Metrics URI	
ABS Server Internal URL	https://lonsvm101:443/abs/handler
ABS Server External URL	https://lonsvm101:443/abs/handler
Voice mail URI	sip:art@art.local;opaque=app:voicemail
Exum URL	
MRAS Server	
GAL Status	https://lonsvm101:443/abs/handler
Focus Factory	sip:art@art.local;gruu;opaque=app:cont:focusfactory
Line	
Location Profile	
Call Park Server URI	
Server Address Internal	lonsvm101
Server Address External	lonsvm101
Server SIP URI	art@art.local
Exum Enabled	FALSE
Controlled Phones	TRUE
GAL or Server Based Search	GAL search
PC to PC AV Encryption	AV Encryption Enforced
Telephony Mode	Telephony Mode Disabled
Line Configured From	Auto Line Configuration
Configuration Mode	Manual Configuration
EWS Internal URL	
EWS External URL	
SharePoint Search Center U	http://lonsvm102/sites/Search/Pages/PeopleResults.aspx
Skill Search URL	http://lonsvm102/sites/Search/_vti_bin/search.asmx
Connected Lync Server	lonsvm101
Local Log Folder	C:\Users\art\AppData\Local\Microsoft\Office\15.0\Lync\Tracing

Photos

Another feature in the Lync client that immediately stands out is its ability to display photos, as shown in Figure 17.21. Having the ability to view another person's picture is very useful in large organizations that may have many employees with the same name, or in situations where you have "met" someone on Lync and you arrange to meet face to face; a picture makes it much easier to identify them.

FIGURE 17.21
A contacts list
showing photos

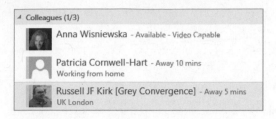

The photos come either from a basic web URL that was set in a Lync 2010 client or from AD. There are a couple of ways in which these get into AD. We have already covered the use of Exchange to do this import, but more relevantly for this section, the other way is from a SharePoint user's My Site via Active Directory integration. As with Skill Search functionality, certain components need to be set up first in order for photos to be displayed in the Lync client from SharePoint:

◆ SharePoint User Profile Service application and My Sites need to be set up and configured. Users must upload a photo to their My Site web page. To set up the User Profile service application, see the article at this location:

`http://technet.microsoft.com/en-us/library/ee662538.aspx`

◆ SharePoint AD needs to be synchronized. SharePoint must be configured to replicate pictures from the user profile to AD. A photo is loaded through this process into the attribute named `thumbnailPhoto` on a user object within AD. Lync uses the attribute to access photos for contacts. To set up AD synchronization, follow the instructions at this location:

`http://technet.microsoft.com/en-us/library/ee721049.aspx`

◆ A Lync client policy must be configured. If your organization allows pictures in Lync, you can provide users with a link from within the Lync client that allows them to change their default corporate picture on their SharePoint My Site. The link can be found in the My Picture options (accessed by clicking the photo in the Lync client), which allows the user to configure their picture without opening their My Site, instead allowing them to do it straight from the Lync client.

Once all of these components are set up and functioning correctly, a Lync client will receive pictures through in-band policies. The first two items in the preceding list cover SharePoint configuration, but the final item is on the Lync side. The required client policies are configured by using the `Set-CsClientPolicy` cmdlet.

The link to change the photo on My Site is not enabled by default. To add or remove it, use the following command to edit the existing global CsClientPolicy:

```
Set-CsClientPolicy -ShowSharepointPhotoEditLink $true
```

Users will be able to change their My Site picture directly through the Lync client.

As discussed in the Exchange section of this chapter, new with Lync 2013 and Exchange 2013 is the support for high-resolution pictures of up to 648×648 pixels and the scaling capabilities Exchange brings to the table. The recommended size in Lync 2010 and older is 96×96 pixels.

One important parameter is the picture size. By default in Lync, the maximum size setting for pictures is 30KB, whereas in AD it is up to 40KB. To enable clients to have pictures up to 40KB, you can modify the client policy using the following command:

```
Set-CsClientPolicy –MaxPhotoSizeKb 40
```

This command will set the Lync client policy to allow photos up to 40KB in size.

You may simply decide not to allow the use of photos in Lync. To do that, you must use the `Set-CsClientPolicy` cmdlet, specifically the `DisplayPhoto` parameter. The following example uses the `PhotosFromAdOnly` setting, which specifies that only the pictures uploaded to AD from SharePoint can be shown in the Lync client. This enables the maintenance of an element of control across the organization.

```
Set-CsClient –DisplayPhoto PhotosFromAdOnly
```

Once you have configured pictures, signing out and then back into Lync ensures that the client performs an Address Book web services query to the Lync server rather than possibly using cached values. Once the photo has been returned to the client, it caches it locally for 24 hours to prevent the client from unnecessarily downloading a photo it has already downloaded. After 24 hours, the client will send another query, and if the photo has changed in the SharePoint My Site and been synchronized to AD, it will receive and display it.

Converting Recorded Meetings into SP Asset Libraries

Now that Lync has integrated conferencing capabilities, one useful capability is to record meetings. Although these sound files can be saved to an individual's desktop machine, there is often huge benefit in sharing content, perhaps for training or catch-up purposes. With SharePoint integration, you can save and publish recorded Lync meetings to SharePoint asset libraries; this lets you quickly and efficiently share meeting content from one location with minimal effort. An organization can maintain and manage meeting recordings like other digital assets, for example, by setting retention periods on them.

To use this feature, you need to record a meeting in Lync. This can be done by simply selecting Start Recording from the menu shown in Figure 17.22.

FIGURE 17.22
Starting a recording of a Lync meeting

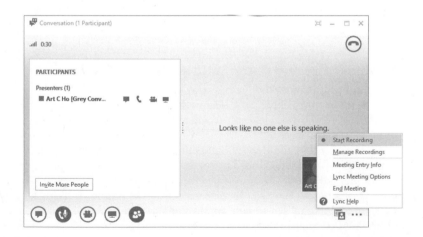

Once you have recorded your Lync meeting, open the Lync Recording Manager from Start ➤ Programs ➤ Microsoft Lync. From there, you can see your Lync recordings, as shown in Figure 17.23.

FIGURE 17.23
The Lync Recording Manager window with a saved recording

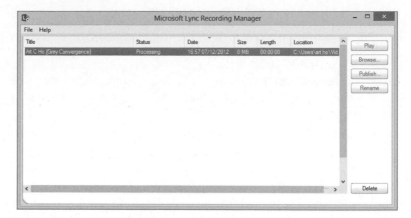

Select the recording to save to a SharePoint asset library and click Publish. A dialog box will open where you can type in the URL to the SharePoint asset library of your choice (if you do not know the URL, simply open the SharePoint site where you want to store the recording in IE and copy and paste the URL address from the IE address bar into the dialog box). As you can see in Figure 17.24, by default the user's Lync Recordings location is shown.

FIGURE 17.24
The Save And Publish dialog

Business Process Communication Workflows

Communications-enabled business process workflows (CEBPs) help organizations build workflows to enable Lync functions such as IM or calls within a workflow. Combined with SharePoint workflows, customized integration features between Lync and SharePoint 2013 can be achieved.

SharePoint 2013 and Lync 2013 together provide an extensible platform on which to build applications that are enhanced through the use of Unified Communications and collaboration technologies. Beyond the out-of-the-box integration features with SharePoint as previously discussed, businesses can use the Microsoft Unified Communications Managed API (UCMA) 4.0 to develop and deploy server-side applications hosted in SharePoint. UCMA can be combined with SharePoint communication workflows to enable the standard Lync communication functionality (such as presence or clicking to IM or call) within SharePoint. These workflows could include the ability to instantly contact those in an approval chain to make a decision, making the application more productive and efficient.

UCMA together with SharePoint can be used to create powerful applications that clearly impact business processes by enhancing them with communications, making them more efficient and collaborative.

The next sections cover development, including a working UCMA 4.0 SDK bot example.

Lync Development

Lync 2013 development broadly consists of two concepts: server-side and client-side development. Depending on your requirements, Lync provides different APIs and interfaces to control and extend both sides of the Lync solution. Used in combination, most requirements can be realized with less effort than traditional custom development scenarios.

There are three main areas of Lync development:

◆ The Unified Communications Managed API (UCMA) 4.0

◆ SPL

◆ The Lync 2013 API

Unified Communications Managed API 4.0

The Unified Communications Managed API (UCMA) 4.0 is the latest version of the API interface that accompanies Lync 2013. UCMA provides a rich set of libraries to manipulate Lync. The UCMA platform is a managed code endpoint API that is built on top of the Session Initiation Protocol (SIP). Where custom Lync functionality is required server side, developers will likely need to work with the UCMA.

Applications built using UCMA are able to harness unified communications capabilities such as voice, video, conferencing, instant messaging, and presence. The software-based approach enables developers to quickly code, test, and deploy UCMA applications. UCMA is written in Visual C#.

Here are some examples of UCMA solutions:

◆ Contact center, with interactive voice response (IVR), automated call distribution (ACD), call recording, and web chat

◆ IVR with VoiceXML support

◆ Connecting phones to online meetings using voice commands

◆ Integration with SharePoint to notify on events

◆ Text-to-speech readings of email from Microsoft Exchange

Using UCMA 4.0 to deliver trusted services offers many features for developers:

◆ Elevated permissions to impersonate users, participate in and control conferences invisibly, and control audio mixing.

◆ Ability to handle thousands of concurrent IMs on single instances.

◆ Scales up to multiple application hosts.

◆ Resilient to intermediate hop failures, good voice quality, speech recognition, text-to-speech, load balancing and failover.

◆ Integrates directly with most SIP PSTN gateways and IP-PBXs.

◆ New in UCMA 4.0, the support for Voice Extensible Markup Language (VoiceXML) 2.0. This provides an industry standard for developing applications supporting speech services.

◆ Built-in extensibility that enables you to develop bespoke custom media and call types.

There are two main components UCMA developers should familiarize themselves with: collaboration and signaling. Collaboration components provide access to presence, conferencing, contacts, and more. Signaling components provide access to the SIP/SIMPLE layer. They are given their respective namespaces:

◆ Microsoft.Rtc.Collaboration

◆ Microsoft.Rtc.Signaling

When setting up your projects, you should note that UCMA 4.0 is contained in the `Microsoft.Rtc.Collaboration.dll` assembly. In the exercise ending this chapter, we will be using Microsoft.Rtc.Collaboration and a Bot framework for Lync 2013 to build a working, intelligent IM bot.

Microsoft SIP Processing Language

The Microsoft SIP Processing Language (MSPL) script is a way to route and filter SIP messages. Used in conjunction with UCMA, advanced SIP processing and workflows can be created. MSPL scripts run server side.

As a sample, the following script provided with the Lync 2013 SDK filters incoming SIP responses and selects an endpoint.

```
<?xml version="1.0">
<lc:applicationManifest
 lc:appUri="http://www.contoso.com/DefaultRoutingScript"
 xmlns:lc="http://schemas.microsoft.com/lcs/2006/05">
  <lc:requestFilter methodNames="INVITE,MESSAGE,INFO,REFER,ACK,BYE,OTHER"
                    strictRoute="false"
                    registrarGenerated="true"
                    domainSupported="true"/ >
  <lc:responseFilter reasonCodes="NONE" />
  <lc:proxyByDefault action="true" />
  <lc:scriptOnly />
  <lc:splScript>
   <![CDATA[
   //
   // This script handles default routing of requests to Lync Server.  It
   // looks up all the registered endpoints for the To: user@host and tries
   // to pick the best endpoint to route based on:
   //   EPID
```

```
        //
        // Endpoints with no presence or an availability less than 100, or
        // no routing information (for example, set presence without
        // register) are not considered.
        //

        Log( "Debugr", 1, "we have a request - ", sipRequest.Method );

        //
        // Build the user@host from the To: header.
        //
        toUri = GetUri( sipRequest.To );
        toUserAtHost = Concatenate( GetUserName( toUri ), "@",
GetHostName( toUri ) );

        //
        // Determine whether this request is already asking for a specific EPID
        // through a parameter in the To: header.
        //
        requestEPID = GetParameterValue( sipRequest.To, "EPID" );

        //
        // Now loop over all the endpoints for the To: user@host.
        //
        bestEPID = "";
        bestAgeOfPresence = 0x7FFFFFFF;
        bestAvailability = 0;
        bestActivity = 0;
        bestContactInfo = "";
        Log( "Debugr", 1, "EPID - ", requestEPID );
        Log( "Debugr", 1, "toUserAtHost - ", toUserAtHost );
        foreach (dbEndpoint in QueryEndpoints( toUserAtHost, true )) {
            Log( "Debugr", 1, "     endpoint.EPID - ", dbEndpoint.EPID );
            Log( "Debugr", 1, "     endpoint.ContactInfo - ",
dbEndpoint.ContactInfo );

            //
            // First, determine whether this endpoint supports the method in the request.
            //
            if (!SupportsMethod( sipRequest.Method, dbEndpoint.StandardMethods,
dbEndpoint.ExtraMethods )) {
                //
                // Skip this endpoint because it cannot handle the method on this
request.
                //
                Log( "Debugr", 1, "        * skipped because of method" );
                continue;
```

```
            }

        if (requestEPID != "") {
            if (requestEPID == dbEndpoint.EPID) {
                //
                // The request is already targeted at a specific EPID that can
handle the method,
                // so use this endpoint.
                //
                Log( "Debugr", 1, "          * matched EPID" );
                bestContactInfo = dbEndpoint.ContactInfo;
                break;
            }
            else {
                //
                // The request is targeted at a specific EPID, but does not
match this endpoint.
                // Skip this endpoint.
                //
                Log( "Debugr", 1, "          * skipped because of EPID" );
                continue;
            }
        }

        bestEPID = dbEndpoint.EPID;
        bestContactInfo = dbEndpoint.ContactInfo;
        Log( "Debugr", 1, "          *** new best contact" );
        }

    //
    // See if an endpoint to proxy to was found.
    //
    if (bestContactInfo == "") {
        /* Uncomment this block of code and the two previous assignments to
sawAtLeastOneEndpoint
            if you want to run a UAC application before this one and have this
code
            route your messages to the correct home server.
        if (!sawAtLeastOneEndpoint) {
            homeServer = QueryHomeServer( toUserAtHost );
            if (!EqualString( homeServer, FQDN, true )) {
                Log( "Debugr", 1, toUserAtHost, " is homed on ", homeServer );
                newRequestUri = Concatenate( sipRequest.RequestUri, ";maddr=",
 homeServer );
                Log( "Debugr", 1, "Request is being routed to ", newRequestUri );
                AddHeader( "MS-LBVIA", FQDN );
                ProxyRequest( newRequestUri );
```

```
                return;
            }
        }
        */
        Log( "Debugr", 1, "Responding 480 - temporarily unavailable as no
suitable endpoint found" );
        Respond( 480, "Temporarily Unavailable" );
    }
    else {
        if (requestEPID == "") {
            Log( "Debugr", 1, "Adding missing EPID '", bestEPID,
"' to To header" );
            SetParameterValue( "To", "epid", bestEPID );
        }

        Log( "Debugr", 1, "Proxying request to - ", bestContactInfo );
        ProxyRequest( bestContactInfo );
    }

    return;
]]>
  </lc:splScript>
</lc:applicationManifest>
```

For more details about this script and MSPL syntax, see the MSDN article on MSPL:

`http://msdn.microsoft.com/en-us/library/lync/hh364805.aspx`

MSPL scripts are useful for processing SIP messages without heavy resource load on the server. MSPL can quickly filter and route SIP messages, passing them off to Lync trusted application endpoints in more advanced scenarios.

Lync 2013 API

UCMA and SPL are generally used to build middle-tier components that operate between the user and the Lync services to automate or enhance aspects of communication processes. For client-side development, the Lync 2013 API is provided.

The Lync 2013 API SDK is used to develop custom Lync 2013 applications or embed Lync functionality into other line-of-business (LOB) applications. Using the Lync API, IMs, voice, and video and conferencing capabilities can be presented from a custom client or LOB application.

The Lync 2013 API includes the following key new features:

◆ Resource sharing: Share applications, desktops, or attached displays.

◆ Persistent Chat: Client and add-in applications can be built that are attached to a Persistent Chat room.

◆ Online meeting content management: Manage the contents of meeting bins, the sharing stage, and video sources.

The Lync 2013 API is broadly split into three areas:

◆ Lync controls

◆ Lync API

◆ OCOM Unmanaged COM API

Lync controls provide a drag-and-drop method to enable existing applications with Lync features and user interface. Controls for all the functions are provided:

◆ Search

◆ Presence

◆ Instant messaging

◆ Calls

The controls provide a familiar Lync UI for each feature. Programming the Lync controls is done with XAML or with C#. Using a combination of controls, developers can simply drag and drop Lync components to integrate into existing applications.

The Lync 2013 API is used to launch or automate the Lync 2013 UI controls within your application. This client-side API could be used within a custom application to perform the following tasks:

◆ Add a contact.

◆ Associate line-of-business information with contacts.

◆ Join/start instant messaging and audio and video conversations.

◆ Join/start conferences.

◆ Add conversation participants.

◆ Automate scheduling conferences.

The Office Communicator Object Model (OCOM) API is a subset of the Lync 2013 API providing legacy support for Office Communicator. It lacks richer support such as conversations, but basic presence and contact list support is possible. This API may be useful for C++ developers who need contact or presence features.

What's New in UCMA 4.0?

The following list outlines some of the key new features in UCMA 4.0:

Bandwidth Management   Selectively decline and reroute calls based on network link consumption. Calls can also reroute through PSTN if bandwidth is oversubscribed.

Back-to-Back User Agents   Useful in help desk or call center scenarios, the user agent acts as the bridge between an incoming call and agents. Incoming communications are directly with the back-to-back user agent, enabling an agent's details to be hidden from callers. Supervisors can monitor calls to ensure quality control.

PSTN User Authentication   Users can be authenticated against Microsoft Lync Server 2013 or Exchange Server 2013 via a personal identification number (PIN). Users can also be authenticated separately, for trusted servers to take actions on behalf of authenticated users.

Industry-Standard VoiceXML 2.0 Support   IVR applications created in VoiceXML can be used. You can host local or remote VoiceXML applications with UCMA 4.0. Existing VoiceXML applications on other platforms can be migrated to UCMA 4.0.

Trusted Conferencing Users Mode   Enhance the communications experience using trusted users. They can join conferences invisibly and retain full control over conferences. This enables functions such as performing commands on behalf of other participants.

Trusted Service Discovery   Create distributed UCMA applications. UCMA communications-enabled business applications (CEBP) can discover and exchange information with one other. This allows distinct UCMA applications to interact, providing the ability for complex and distributed CEBP workflows.

Example Project: Grey Bot

This example project demonstrates how to use the Lync 2013 APIs to build a bot. Bots are quasi-intelligent information agents that can understand requests and respond with relevant information or actions. This bot runs server side, meaning it will be deployed against a Lync Trusted Application Server pool. For the purpose of this example, we will call our bot Grey Bot.

This exercise should be done in a lab environment. Doing this in a production environment may be a resume generating event (RGE).

To complete this example, you will need a 64-bit development machine with the following:

- Lync 2013 Server installed and part of the Trusted Application pool
- UCMA 4.0 SDK
- Visual Studio 2012
- Familiarity with C# and the Visual Studio IDE

You will need the following permissions:

- Lync Server 2013 Administrator:
    - Domain Admins security group
- Trusted Application Operator:
    - Administrator local group
    - RTCUniversalServerAdmins security group
- Trusted Application service account:
    - RTC Component Local Group local group

The steps we will take are as follows:

1. Configure Lync Trusted Application server/pool.
2. Configure Lync trusted application.
3. Configure Lync trusted application endpoint.
4. Create Grey Bot project in Visual Studio.
5. Set up Grey Bot project to use UCMA API.

6. Code the Grey Bot and test it.

7. Extend Grey Bot.

Step 1: Configure Lync Trusted Application Server/Pool

In order for Lync custom applications to run on servers, you need to define in the Lync pool one or more trusted application servers that form the pool. You can confirm whether you have an application server already configured either using Topology Builder or LSMS.

In Topology Builder, expand the site and check the Trusted Application Pool section for listed servers.

In LSMS, run the following command: Get-CsTrustedApplicationPool. This will list any configured pools, as shown later.

If no Trusted Application pools are available, you must create one, either using LSMS or via the Topology Builder.

You can use the following syntax from LSMS:

```
New-CsTrustedApplicationPool -Registrar <registrar pool>
```

Note that `<registrar pool>` should be replaced with the Registrar pool; for development environments you can simply use the Front End pool.

Upon successful completion of `New-CsTrustedApplicationPool`, you must run `Enable-CsTopology`.

Confirm that you have created the Trusted Application pool by running `Get-CsTrustedApplicationPool` and noting its output, as below. Note the `Applications` value because we will be using it in our C# project later.

```
PS C:\> Get-CsTrustedApplicationPool

Identity               : TrustedApplicationPool:lonsvm101
Registrar              : Registrar:lonsvm101
FileStore              :
ThrottleAsServer       : True
TreatAsAuthenticated   : True
OutboundOnly           : False
RequiresReplication    : True
AudioPortStart         :
AudioPortCount         : 0
AppSharingPortStart    :
AppSharingPortCount    : 0
VideoPortStart         :
VideoPortCount         : 0
Applications           : {urn:application:GreyBot}
DependentServiceList   : {}
ServiceId              : 1-ExternalServer-1
SiteId                 : Site:art.local
PoolFqdn               : lonsvm101
Version                : 6
Role                   : TrustedApplicationPool
```

Confirm that replication to all Management Stores have completed using Get-CsManageme ntStoreReplicationStatus. If you have issues replicating to the Trusted Application pool in a development environment, you may wish to disable replication. Note that some applications will require it; Grey Bot does not require replication. All servers listed in the command should show UpToDate as True, as shown here:

```
PS C:\> Get-CsManagementStoreReplicationStatus


UpToDate           : True
ReplicaFqdn        : lonsvm101
LastStatusReport   : 11/12/2012 15:55:35
LastUpdateCreation : 11/12/2012 15:55:33
ProductVersion     : 5.0.8308.0
```

Step 2: Configure Lync Trusted Application

Once you have a Trusted Application pool, you can create a trusted application and register it against the pool.

Use the following syntax in LSMS:

```
New-CSTrustedApplication -ApplicationId GreyBot ↵
-TrustedApplicationPoolFqdn <TAppPoolFqdn> -Port 10605
```

Note that <TAppPoolFqdn> should be replaced with the Trusted Application pool's FQDN, which you can confirm via the output of Get-CsTrustedApplicationPool. The port can be changed as desired.

Upon successful completion of New-CsTrustedApplication, you must run Enable-CsTopology.

Confirm that you have created the trusted application by running Get-CsTrustedApplication and noting its output, as shown here:

```
PS C:\> Get-CsTrustedApplication


Identity                    : lonsvm101/urn:application:GreyBot
ComputerGruus               : {lonsvm101 sip:lonsvm101@art.local;gruu;opaque=
srvr:Grey Bot:xxoQhdPFo1itXrfG_sfWwgAA}
ServiceGruu                 : sip:lonsvm101@art.local;gruu;opaque=srvr:GreyBot:
xxoQhdPFo1itXrfG_sfWwgAA
Protocol                    : Mtls
ApplicationId               : urn:application:GreyBot
TrustedApplicationPoolFqdn  : lonsvm101
Port                        : 10605
LegacyApplicationName       : GreyBot
```

Note these values because they will be used when creating an endpoint in the next step.

Step 3: Configure Lync Trusted Application Endpoint

Once you have a trusted application, you can create a trusted application endpoint and register it against the application.

Use the following syntax in LSMS:

```
New-CSTrustedApplicationEndpoint -ApplicationId <AppId> ↵
-TrustedApplicationPoolFqdn <TAPoolFqdn> -SipAddress sip:GreyBot@art.local ↵
-DisplayName "Grey Bot [Grey Convergence]"
```

Note that these values should be replaced with the output from the previous step:

◆ `<AppId>`: `ApplicationId`

◆ `<TAPoolFqdn>`: `TrustedApplicationPoolFqdn`

The SipAddress should not be in use: It must be unique. The DisplayName (and all other arguments) can be wrapped in quotes when needed, as shown in the preceding example.

If successful, the command will output the identity and details of the newly created application endpoint.

Confirm that you have created the trusted application endpoint by running `Get-CsTrustedApplicationEndpoint` and noting its output, as shown here:

```
PS C:\> Get-CsTrustedApplicationEndpoint

Identity                : CN={053b9c5b-752a-4472-b75d-551d89bccd4f},CN=
Application Contacts,CN=RTC Service,CN=Services,CN=Configuration,DC=art,DC=local
RegistrarPool           : lonsvm101
HomeServer              : CN=Lc Services,CN=Microsoft,CN=1:1,CN=Pools,CN=RTC Service,CN=Serv
ices,CN=Configuration,DC=art,DC=local
OwnerUrn                : urn:application:GreyBot
SipAddress              : sip:GreyBot@art.local
DisplayName             : Grey Bot [Grey Convergence]
DisplayNumber           :
LineURI                 :
PrimaryLanguage         : 0
SecondaryLanguages      : {}
EnterpriseVoiceEnabled  : True
ExUmEnabled             : False
Enabled                 : True
```

If during any of the Trusted Application pool, application, or endpoint steps you run into any difficulty, refer to the MSDN article on activating Lync applications:

`http://msdn.microsoft.com/en-us/library/lync/hh347291.aspx`

You are now ready to start coding!

Step 4: Create the Grey Bot Project in Visual Studio

To create the Grey Bot project, you will follow these steps:

◆ Start Visual Studio 2012.

◆ Create a new C# Console Application project.

◆ Name it Grey Bot, as shown in Figure 17.25.

FIGURE 17.25
Creating the Grey
Bot project

When you click OK, a new project should be created for Grey Bot. The Visual Studio IDE will open.

Step 5: Set Up the Grey Bot Project to Use UCMA API

Grey Bot makes use of the UCMA 4.0 SDK API and demonstrates how easy it can be to develop intelligent bots for Lync 2013. Before beginning, you will need to have downloaded and installed the UCMA 4.0 SDK. You can get it from here:

```
www.microsoft.com/en-us/download/details.aspx?id=35463
```

If you have not already built the BuildABot binaries and DLLs from the UCMA SDK samples, you need to do this first. If you are unable to find the DLLs when you add the references later, it is likely that you need to build them.

If UCMA 4.0 SDK was installed in its default location, open the following solution in Visual Studio:

```
C:\Program Files\Microsoft UCMA 4.0\SDK\Core\Sample Applications\Reference\
BuildABot\BuildABot.sln
```

Build the solution, and confirm that you now have the BuildABot DLLs. For example, the new DLLs should be created here:

```
C:\Program Files\Microsoft UCMA 4.0\SDK\Core\Sample Applications\Reference\
BuildABot\BuildABot.Core\bin\Debug\BuildABot.Core.dll
```

Return to the Grey Bot solution.

Add references for the following:

◆ `BuildABot.Core.dll` (Browse)

◆ `BuildABot.UC.dll` (Browse)

◆ `System.ComponentModel.Composition` (Assemblies ➤ Framework).

Note that the BuildABot DLLs can be found here:

```
C:\Program Files\Microsoft UCMA 4.0\SDK\Core\Sample Applications\Reference\
BuildABot\BuildABot.UC\bin\Debug
```

Your references list should now resemble Figure 17.26.

FIGURE 17.26

Grey Bot references
list

Next, set the startup object in the Grey Bot project properties to Grey Bot.Program as shown
in Figure 17.27.

FIGURE 17.27

Grey Bot project
properties and
startup object

The Grey Bot solution now has all the references to the UCMA SDK via BuildABot configured, and the project is set up to run.

Step 6: Code Grey Bot

Open `Program.cs`, noting that it may contain initial template code provided by Visual Studio.
Replace the default contents of `Program.cs` with the following code for Grey Bot:

```
using System;
using System.Diagnostics;
```

```csharp
using BuildABot.UC;

namespace GreyBot
{
    class Program
    {

        static void Main(string[] args)
        {
            Console.WriteLine("---[Grey Bot]---");

            // Send all Debug.WriteLine calls to the console.
            // Requires System.Diagnostics.
            Debug.Listeners.Add(new ConsoleTraceListener());

            String applicationurn = "urn:application:GreyBot";
            String applicationUserAgent = "Grey Bot";

            UCBotHost GreyBot = new UCBotHost(applicationUserAgent,
applicationurn);

            // SAMPLE: Hook into Replied event.
            // ucBotHost.Replied += new ReplyEventHandler(bot_Replied);

            GreyBot.Run();
        }

        // SAMPLE: Hook into Replied event.
        /*static void bot_Replied(object sender, ReplyEventArgs e)
        {
            foreach (ReplyMessage replyMessage in e.Reply.Messages)
            {
                Console.WriteLine("Grey Bot says: " + replyMessage.Content);
            }
        }*/
    }
}
```

Add a new class to the project, called MessageHandler.cs. Replace the template contents of this new file with the following code for Grey Bot:

```csharp
using System;
using System.ComponentModel.Composition;
using BuildABot.Core.MessageHandlers;

namespace GreyBot
{
    [Export(typeof(MessageHandler))]
    public class TimeMessageHandler : SingleStateMessageHandler
```

```
    {

        public TimeMessageHandler()
            : base("time", "Please wait while I get the current time...", true)
        {
        }

        public override Reply Handle(Message message)
        {
            Reply reply = new Reply();
            reply.Add("The current time is: " +
DateTime.Now.ToShortTimeString());
            reply.Add("The current date is: " +
DateTime.Now.ToShortDateString());
            return reply;
        }
    }

    // BEGIN: Optional code.
    [Export(typeof(MessageHandler))]
    public class HiMessageHandler : SingleStateMessageHandler
    {

        public HiMessageHandler()
            : base("hi|hello|hey|ahoy|avast|greeting")
        {
        }

        public override Reply Handle(Message message)
        {
            Reply reply = new Reply();
            reply.Add("Ahoy there!");
            return reply;
        }
    }
    // END: Optional code.

}
```

Grey Bot can now be built and run.

When Grey Bot starts, a console window will appear and you will be able to send IMs to the bot and receive replies. For debugging, output will be shown on the console:

```
---[Grey Bot]---
Collaboration Platform started.
The Application Endpoint owned by URI:
sip:GreyBot@art.local
 is now established and registered.
Call has changed state. The previous call state was: Incoming and the current
```

```
state is: Establishing
Call has changed state. The previous call state was: Establishing and the
current state is: Established
The call is now in the established state.
joe said: hi there!
Bot received: hi there!
Bot says:
Ahoy there!

The message has been sent.
joe said: hey dude!
Bot received: hey dude!
Bot says:
Ahoy there!

The message has been sent.
```

To test the bot, initiate an IM conversation with Grey Bot, and ask for the time, as shown in Figure 17.28.

FIGURE 17.28
Grey Bot conversation window showing natural language support

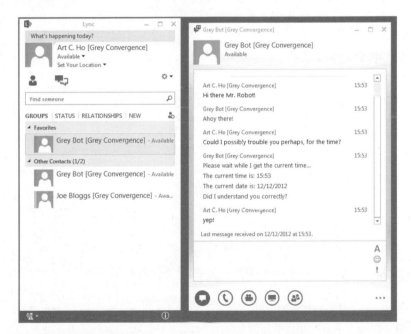

Note how Grey Bot can handle natural language. UCMA handles the complex language analysis and intent of the user and triggers the appropriate message handler. Complex regular expressions can be used to capture advanced user queries.

If you examine the TimeMessageHandler, you will find that it uses two additional arguments that the other message handlers do not. The second argument provides an initial reply string, and the third argument is a Boolean to specify whether to ask for feedback.

In the conversation shown in Figure 17.28, Grey Bot ends by asking the user whether it understood correctly. This is because the TimeMessageHandler's third argument is `true`, enabling feedback. This allows UCMA bots to build confidence based directly on user feedback, becoming smarter over time.

Step 7: Extend Grey Bot

Let's review the code.

`Program.cs` instantiates and runs the `UCBotHost` object, which is part of the UCMA 4.0 SDK. The `UCBotHost` inherits from the generic UCMA Bot class and features enhanced UC capabilities like presence and Lync support.

Commented out within `Program.cs` is a sample of hooking into the various events the `UCBotHost` will trigger during execution. By handling these events, we control Grey Bot's behavior.

The commented-out code shows how to run custom code when Grey Bot's `Replied` event is triggered. The `Replied` event triggers after every reply Grey Bot sends.

`MessageHandler.cs` provides logic and customized responses. As different messages come into Grey Bot, various events are triggered for the developers to handle. In our example, each class inheriting from `SingleStateMessageHandler` has an overriding `Handle()` class that provides Grey Bot with a `Reply` object to send back to the user.

Each class we create in here inherits from a `BuildABot.Core.MessageHandlers.SingleStateMessageHandler` class. `SingleStateMessageHandler` inherits from `MessageHandler`, which does much of the work behind the scenes to abstract messages for developers to handle.

For complex bots that need to handle multiple states within a conversation, a `SingleStateMessageHandler` will not be enough. Inheriting from the `MessageHandler` class can handle multistate conversations for these purposes. For more on handling various types of conversations and workflows with UCMA bots, please see the UCMA 4.0 SDK documentation on using bots:

```
http://msdn.microsoft.com/en-us/library/lync/jj728789.aspx
```

Looking under the covers at the code, you will find the API straightforward and easy to extend for most scenarios. As an exercise for the reader, one could extend Grey Bot with further features such as these:

◆ Advanced logic and workflows

◆ Integration with line-of-business applications like Microsoft Dynamics CRM, SharePoint, and Exchange

◆ Meaningful presence and contact list for Grey Bot

◆ Authorizing users against Active Directory to limit access

◆ Extending Grey Bot across the UC stack to allow interactive voice response access

Delving Deeper into Lync 2013 Development

The example project Grey Bot demonstrates one aspect of server-side Lync development: bots. While Grey Bot is a functional, extensible, and scalable Lync bot, there is more to the world of Lync development.

Client-side development, integrating Lync controls into line-of-business applications, contact centers, interactive voice response systems, and text-to-speech services are other examples of where Lync developers are assisted with rich APIs and frameworks to build upon.

We recommend that developers who want to explore further read the UCMA 4.0 SDK documentation, available here:

```
http://msdn.microsoft.com/en-us/library/lync/jj728784.aspx
```

The Bottom Line

Integrate Lync with Exchange.   Exchange provides a wide range of functionality to Lync, and Lync helps enhance Exchange. The most important integration points are for the provision of voice mail, where Exchange UM is the only supported voice mail platform for Lync. To enhance Exchange, Lync enables building presence and basic IM capabilities directly into OWA. There are also less obvious integration points because Lync utilizes Exchange Web Services to pull information about users' calendar entries and their contacts, providing enhanced presence information and a single view of a person as an entity with whom to communicate.

Master It   You company is rolling out Lync as its telephony platform, and you will be using Exchange 2013 as your voice mail platform. You have been asked to outline the process to the Exchange administrative team.

Integrate Lync with SharePoint.   SharePoint integration is both relatively simple and potentially complex! It is simple in that integrating presence capability is automatic, and it is complex in that you have the ability through application development to put together almost any piece of communication-enhanced workflow that you can think up. SharePoint integration also provides the Skill Search capability to Lync.

Master It   Your organization makes extensive use of SharePoint 2010 and already has OCS 2007 R2, which has been providing presence integration. Now you are moving to Lync 2013 and SharePoint 2013, and you have been asked to investigate the requirements for Skill Search integration between Lync and SharePoint.

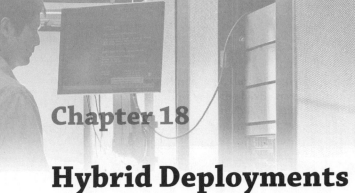

Chapter 18

Hybrid Deployments

With the advent of Office 365 and the first incarnations for Lync Online (based on Lync Server 2010), customers have been asking for the ability to host voice in the cloud as well as the ability to have some infrastructure on premises and some in the cloud (the *hybrid* model).

The Microsoft Office 365 Lync 2010 Online offering delivers the power of cloud productivity to businesses of all sizes, helping them free up valued resources by not having to maintain an on-premises Lync server infrastructure (in other words, patching, rack space, data center power, high availability, and disaster recovery planning). Lync Online provides cloud-based instant messaging, presence, and online meeting experiences with PC audio, videoconferencing, and screen sharing. It also works seamlessly with Microsoft Office and the other programs that business users already used every day.

In this chapter, you will learn to:

◆ Understand the Lync hybrid architecture model

◆ Understand the capabilities of a hybrid deployment

◆ Understand the call flow for media in different scenarios

◆ Understand the required steps to configure a hybrid deployment

The History of Lync Online

When Lync Online was first released, it did not offer an enterprise voice service, which is essentially the ability to call the public switched telephone network (PSTN); the only voice capability was for calling other Lync Online users. Eventually, for small businesses only, Lync Online was enabled to provide PSTN calling. The service is called Lync-to-Phone, and the SIP trunk infrastructure is provided by JaJah, which is part of the larger Telefonica organization. JaJah connectivity provides Lync Online users with the ability to have their enterprise voice capability hosted in the cloud.

As with an on-premises deployment of Lync, users also have the ability to receive calls and forward to other devices such as their computers or desk phones. At the time of this writing, provision of this service is available only with UK and US phone numbers. See http://platform.jajah.com/smbs/voice4lync for more information.

Figure 18.1 shows the high-level cloud architecture; each cloud is a separate entity, and an end customer has limited visibility into each.

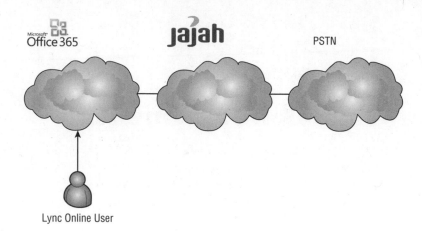

FIGURE 18.1
High-level Lync
Online enterprise
voice architecture

Lync Online User

Lync Online does not offer true Private Branch Exchange (PBX) replacement capabilities, which include features that require integration with on-premises networks and equipment. Businesses looking to take advantage of the full PBX replacement capabilities in Lync Server 2010 were advised to deploy Lync Server 2010 on premises (for all of the Lync workloads such as instant messaging, conferencing, and enterprise voice). They could, however, still utilize the online versions of Exchange and SharePoint Server provided by Office 365, including using Exchange Unified Messaging in the cloud to provide voicemail and missed call notifications to a Lync Server 2010 on-premises environment.

One of the new features of Lync 2013 is Hybrid Voice. Together with (at the time of this writing) Office 365 ProPlus or Enterprise options, organizations can now take advantage of an on-premises Lync Enterprise Voice infrastructure integrated with Lync Online.

Users who are hosted in the cloud using Lync Online can now leverage the on-premises Enterprise Voice infrastructure as if they were on-premises enterprise voice users.

In this chapter the following terminology is used:

Lync Online　An environment where everything is hosted in the cloud.

Lync Online user　A Lync user who only has access to cloud-based infrastructure. This may be part of a wider Hybrid infrastructure configuration; however, this user will not have access to Enterprise Voice capability.

Lync Hybrid (or Hybrid Voice)　A Lync environment which leverages some Lync Online (in the cloud) infrastructure, but also has some on-premises infrastructure, both of which share the same SIP domain.

Lync Hybrid Voice user　A user whose account is located in the cloud, but leverages some on-premises infrastructure for making PSTN calls.

Lync on-premises　A Lync infrastructure wholly deployed on-premises for an organization. (This may also be a hosted infrastructure; however, the distinction then becomes that it is a dedicated hosted environment and not share—in other words the servers are the same as they would be if the organization deployed them, simply in another location.)

Lync on-premises user　A user whose account is located on on-premises infrastructure— whether this infrastructure is part of a wider Lync Hybrid deployment or not.

What Is Hybrid Voice?

Many organizations are seeking to actively move enterprise services such as Exchange Server, SharePoint Server, and Lync Server to the cloud. With Lync Server 2013, the move is made much easier with the option to support a Hybrid Voice environment.

Hybrid Voice allows organizations to take advantage of any investments they have already made with their on-premises enterprise voice environment, such as deploying PSTN media gateways or integrating with PBX/IP-PBX deployments, but still move users to the Lync Online environment to take advantage of all the benefits of cloud-based infrastructure (such as no capital purchase costs, paying only for capacity that has been used, and so on).

This means they can "sweat" their existing assets and not lose any prior investment made but still take advantage of the cloud offering. Lync Hybrid users can use the on-premises voice infrastructure as though they were on-premises enterprise voice users. Their inbound and outbound calls are routed through the PSTN infrastructure that forms part of the on-premises Lync Server deployment.

Figure 18.2 shows a typical Lync Hybrid Voice infrastructure.

FIGURE 18.2
Typical Lync Hybrid Voice Infrastructure deployment

In Figure 18.2, Alice is a Lync-enabled user who is configured as on premises; in other words, her SIP registrar is a server that is part of the Lync on-premises pool. Bob and Charlie are Lync-enabled users who are configured as Lync Hybrid users; in other words, their SIP registrar server is part of a Lync pool in the Lync Online cloud. Bob is signed on from within the corporate network, and Charlie is working remotely. Both the on-premises and online environments have Lync Edge Servers deployed.

The other exciting development that facilitates Hybrid Voice is that on-premises and online users can now share the same SIP domain and users can be in both infrastructure locations.

Hybrid Voice is configured and kept in sync with the on-premises Active Directory by using Active Directory synchronization. A typical Hybrid Voice deployment will consist of an on-premises Lync Server 2013 pool (Standard or Enterprise Edition) with collocated Mediation Server role (or possibly, a stand-alone Mediation Server pool dedicated to call routing), an on-premises Lync Server 2013 Edge Server (or pool), and some on-premises PSTN infrastructure, such as PSTN gateway(s).

The organization will have an Office 365 tenant with Lync Hybrid users signing in from the corporate network or the Internet. For organizations that are planning to migrate from Lync Server 2010 to Lync Server 2013 and will be using the Lync Online service, it is possible to use the on-premises Lync Server 2010 Edge Server, provided it is updated with Cumulative Update 5 or later.

Table 18.1 compares the features that are available between Lync Server 2013 on-premises and Lync Hybrid users who are configured for Hybrid Voice.

TABLE 18.1: Comparison of Lync 2013 on-premises deployment with a Lync Hybrid Voice deployment

LYNC FEATURES AND FUNCTIONALITY	LYNC 2013 ON-PREMISES	LYNC HYBRID VOICE
Putting calls on hold/retrieving calls	Yes	Yes
Transferring calls	Yes	Yes
Forwarding calls	Yes	Yes
Voice mail	Yes	Yes
USB devices	Yes	Yes (yes for headsets, "soon" for phone devices)
Mobile-Outside Voice	Yes	Yes
Team call, call delegation	Yes	Yes
On-premises PBX integration	Yes	Yes
Remote call control (RCC)	Yes	No
Private line	Yes	Yes
Voice resiliency	Yes	No
E911	Yes	Yes (only if available on premises)
Unified Communications devices	Yes	Yes
Response group services	Yes	No
Call Park	Yes	No
Analogue devices	Yes	Yes
Media bypass	Yes	Yes (only if available on premises)
Common Area Phone	Yes	Yes
On-premises call center integration	Yes	No

Features such as Call Park, response group, and remote call control are not available for Lync Online users enabled for Hybrid Voice. Organizations that require all users to be able to use these features must go with Enterprise Voice on-premises. If an organization requires a contact center solution, this will have to be on premises, and Hybrid Voice users will not be able to act as agents for it if it relies upon deep Lync server integration or indeed the response group functionality.

Voice resiliency refers to the lack of backup SIP registrar capability and survivable branch appliance support for Hybrid Voice users. If the network connection between the organization and the Lync Online service is unavailable, the Lync Online service will be unavailable to users who are enabled as Hybrid Voice users, even if they are accessing Lync Online from the Internet (e.g., outside the corporate network).

The advantage of Lync Hybrid Voice is that it removes many of the barriers to cloud adoption, allowing organizations to more rapidly move users to Lync Online in a controlled, phased manner. Once the users are moved, they can then validate the features, functionality, security, quality, and reliability of Lync Online as Hybrid Voice users.

How Does Lync Online Work?

One of the steps for setting up Lync Hybrid Voice is to federate the on-premises Lync Edge servers with the Lync Online Edge servers. This important step is explained in the following sections. The Edge federation is used to explain many of the scenarios discussed in the next sections of the chapter.

We will look at how Lync Hybrid Voice works and how it is configured. We'll also look at some call flow examples as well as how advanced features such as Media Bypass and E911 work when a user is enabled for Hybrid Voice.

Sign-In/Registration Process

The registration process for a Lync Hybrid Voice user is essentially the same as for on-premises Lync Server. When a user is moved from on-premises Lync Server to Lync Online, the Deployment Locator attribute of their Active Directory user account is updated to reflect that they are hosted in the cloud. Figure 18.3 shows this attribute on an Active Directory user.

When a user who is a member of the masteringlync.org domain signs in to Lync and is using automatic configuration, the Deployment Locator attribute allows the on-premises Lync server to redirect the user to their correct Lync Online pool for registration.

Figure 18.4 shows this process.

In Figure 18.4, Bob logs into his computer, and his Lync 2013 client is configured to automatic configuration. For automatic login, there will be an SRV record created on the internal DNS for this purpose, such as _sipinternaltls._tcp.masteringlync.org. Then the following occurs:

1. Bob's Lync client performs a DNS SRV record lookup.

2. Because Bob is accessing from inside the corporate network, the internal DNS SRV record will be returned. This resolves to the on-premises Lync Server 2013 deployment. Bob will then authenticate to the on-premises Lync Server 2013 pool.

3. The Lync Server 2013 on-premises pool will redirect Bob with a SIP 301 to the Lync Online service. It knows to do this because Bob's Active Directory user account is stamped with the Deployment Locator attribute.

4. Bob will then register against the Lync Online environment.

FIGURE 18.3
Deployment
Locator attribute

FIGURE 18.4
Lync Online user
registration process

For Bob to successfully register with the Lync Online service, he needs to have access to the Internet so that he can reach the service.

If Bob was accessing Lync Server 2013 from outside the corporate network (such as from the Internet because he was working remotely), his client would find the DNS SRV record that had been created in the organization's external DNS, which resolves to the Access Edge service of the on-premises Lync Server 2013 Edge server. His client would then follow the same process and would be redirected to the Lync Online service.

Call Flow Scenarios

To get a good understanding of the various possible call flows, we'll take a step-by-step look at a number of different scenarios:

Scenario 1: Two Hybrid Voice users logged on to the corporate network (peer to peer)

Scenario 2: Two users logged on to the corporate network, one on-premises user and one Hybrid Voice user

Scenario 3: Incoming PSTN call to Lync Hybrid Voice user (peer to peer)

Scenario 4: Incoming PSTN call to Lync Hybrid Voice user who is logging in remotely (from the Internet)

Scenario 5: Lync Hybrid Voice user making an outgoing PSTN call while logged on from the internal corporate network

Scenario 6: Lync Hybrid Voice user making an outgoing PSTN call while logged on remotely (from the Internet)

Remember, in all these cases, registration has already occurred and the users are logged in. We're not considering complex cases where local firewalls restrict direct traffic and media has to flow via an Edge server.

SCENARIO 1

In this scenario, two Hybrid Voice users are logged on to the corporate network (peer to peer). See Figure 18.5.

FIGURE 18.5
Two Hybrid Voice users logged on to the corporate network (peer to peer)

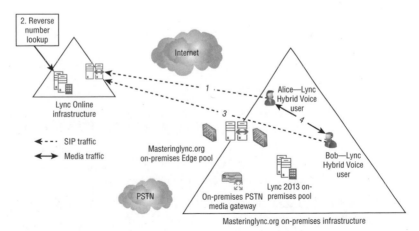

Scenario: Alice is a Lync Hybrid Voice user, in the office.

Bob is a Lync Hybrid Voice user, in the same office.

1. Alice initiates a call to Bob by dialing his extension or clicking Work in the Lync client.

2. The Lync Online infrastructure, on which both Alice and Bob are registered, will perform a reverse number lookup that determines that the number Alice dialed resolves to Bob.

3. All the SIP signaling flows through the Lync Online infrastructure. A SIP INVITE is sent to Bob's endpoint.

4. When Bob answers the call, the media flows directly between the two clients (peer to peer) because they are both on the corporate network.

SCENARIO 2

In this scenario, two users are logged on to the corporate network, one on-premises user and one Hybrid Voice user (peer to peer). See Figure 18.6.

FIGURE 18.6
Two users logged on to the corporate network, one on-premises user and one Hybrid Voice user (peer to peer)

Scenario: Charlie is a Lync on-premises user, in the office.

Bob is a Lync Hybrid Voice user, in the same office.

1. Charlie, who is a Lync on-premises user, initiates a call to Bob, who is a Lync Hybrid Voice user, by dialing his extension or clicking Work in the Lync client.

2. The Lync on-premises infrastructure knows that Bob has an Active Directory object on-premises. The reverse number lookup can look at Bob's on-premises object and determine that Bob is in the federated Lync Online infrastructure.

3. The SIP signaling (the call) is then routed over the federation route via the Edge server up to the Lync Online infrastructure.

4. The SIP signaling returns from the Lync Online infrastructure to Bob's endpoint.

5. When Bob answers the call, the media flows directly between the two clients (peer to peer) because they are both on the corporate network.

SCENARIO 3

This scenario details an incoming PSTN call to Lync Hybrid Voice user. See Figure 18.7.

FIGURE 18.7
Incoming PSTN
call to Lync Hybrid
Voice user

Scenario: Bob is a Lync Hybrid Voice user, in the office.

1. A PSTN call is placed to Bob's phone number; the call is received on the on-premises PSTN media gateway.

2. The on-premises media gateway directs the call to the Lync Mediation server, which is collocated on the on-premises Lync 2013 pool.

3. The Lync on-premises infrastructure knows that Bob has an Active Directory object on premises. The reverse number lookup can look at Bob's on-premises object and determine that Bob is in the federated Lync Online infrastructure.

4. The SIP signaling (the call) is then routed over the federation route via the Edge server up to the Lync Online infrastructure.

5. The SIP signaling is sent from the Lync Online infrastructure to Bob's endpoint.

6. When Bob answers the call, media is established and flows between the on-premises mediation server/PSTN infrastructure and Bob's client. This could be using Media Bypass if configured, or the media may flow via the Mediation server if Media Bypass is not configured.

SCENARIO 4

In this scenario, there is an incoming PSTN call to a Lync Hybrid Voice user who is logging in remotely (from the Internet). See Figure 18.8.

Scenario: Bob is a Lync Hybrid Voice user, working remotely.

1. A PSTN call is placed to Bob's phone number. The call terminates at the on-premises PSTN media gateway.

2. The on-premises media gateway directs the call to the Lync Mediation server, which is collocated on the on-premises Lync 2013 pool.

3. The Lync on-premises infrastructure knows that Bob has an Active Directory object on premises. The reverse number lookup can look at Bob's on-premises object and determine that Bob is in the federated Lync Online infrastructure.

4. The SIP signaling to set up the call is then routed over the federation route via the Edge server to the Lync Online infrastructure.

5. The SIP signaling is sent from the Lync Online infrastructure to Bob's endpoint.

6. When Bob answers the call, media is established and flows through the on-premises Lync Edge server through to the next hop, which is the Lync on-premises pool. Media Bypass cannot happen because the user is working remotely and therefore is not on the same subnet as the media gateway.

FIGURE 18.8
Incoming PSTN call to Lync Hybrid Voice user who is logging in remotely (Internet)

SCENARIO 5

In this scenario, a Lync Hybrid Voice user is making an outgoing PSTN call while logged on from the internal corporate network. See Figure 18.9.

FIGURE 18.9
Lync Hybrid Voice user making an outgoing PSTN call while logged on from the internal corporate network

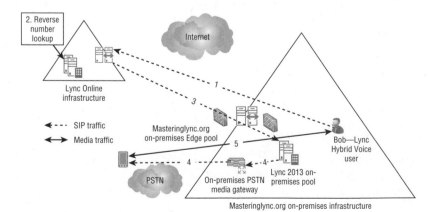

Scenario: Bob is a Lync Hybrid Voice user, in the office.

1. Bob places a PSTN call. The SIP INVITE with the dialed PSTN telephone number is sent to the Lync Online infrastructure. Lync Online is synchronized with user and contact objects from the on-premises AD. This means that reverse number lookup will work for all on-premises- and online Enterprise Voice–enabled objects.

2. Reverse number lookup will take place on the online infrastructure and will fail because the telephone number is an external PSTN number and not associated with any objects within the on-premises or online infrastructure.

3. The SIP INVITE will be routed to the on-premises Lync infrastructure. The call routing and authorization decisions will be made on premises.

4. Bob's voice routing policy is examined, and based on this, a PSTN media gateway on premises is selected and the call is allowed to proceed.

5. Media is established and flows using the optimal path between the on-premises Mediation server/PSTN infrastructure and the PSTN device. This could be using Media Bypass if configured, or the media may flow via the Mediation server if Media Bypass is not configured.

SCENARIO 6

In this scenario, a Lync Hybrid Voice user is making an outgoing PSTN call while logged on remotely (from the Internet). See Figure 18.10.

FIGURE 18.10
Lync Hybrid Voice user making an outgoing PSTN call while logged on remotely (Internet)

Scenario: Bob is a Lync Online user, working remotely.

1. Bob places a PSTN call. The SIP INVITE with the dialed PSTN telephone number is sent to the Lync Online infrastructure. Lync Online is synchronized with user and contact objects from the on-premises AD. This means that reverse number lookup will work for all on-premises- and online Enterprise Voice–enabled objects.

2. Reverse number lookup will take place on the online infrastructure and will fail because the telephone number is an external PSTN number and not associated with any objects within the on-premises or online infrastructure.

3. The SIP INVITE will be routed to the on-premises Lync infrastructure. The call routing and authorization decisions will be made on premises.

4. Bob's voice routing policy is examined, and based on this, a PSTN media gateway on premises is selected.

5. Media is established and flows through the on-premises Lync Edge server through to the next hop, which is the Lync on-premises pool. Media Bypass will not happen because the user is working remotely and therefore is not on the same subnet as the media gateway.

E911 and Media Bypass

For a Lync Hybrid Voice user to be able to use advanced features such as Media Bypass and E911, an on-premises Lync Server 2013 pool must be deployed.

Media Bypass essentially works in the same way for Lync Hybrid Voice users as it does for Lync on-premises users. Media Bypass occurs when the Lync Hybrid Voice user and PSTN media gateway are in the same network location and have matching Bypass IDs. How the client discovers its Bypass ID in a Hybrid Voice scenario is the only difference (shown in Figure 18.11).

FIGURE 18.11
Lync Online client discovery of Media Bypass ID

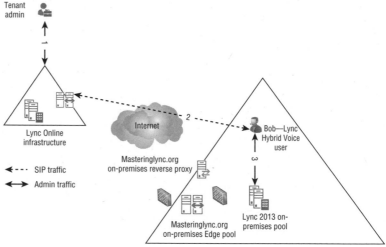

Scenario: Bob is a Lync Hybrid Voice user, logging in from the office.

1. The Office 365 tenant administrator is responsible for configuring an internally and externally accessible URL that resolves to the provisioning web service, which is hosted on the on-premises Lync Server 2013 pool.

2. This URL is passed to the Lync 2013 client via in-band provisioning during sign-in.

3. The client will perform an HTTP POST to the URL and in return receives its Bypass ID, location policy, and LIS URL.

4. This allows the Lync 2013 client, when logged in to by a Lync Hybrid Voice user, to identify which network site it is in because site and subnet definitions are not configurable using Lync Online in Office 365.

Note that the previous steps assume the user is signing in from the organization's corporate network, not the Internet. Media Bypass will not work across the Internet. Although the user client will still follow the process defined and the user will resolve the URL via the reverse proxy, the Media Bypass ID will not match the subnet ID.

E911 works the same way as for an on-premises Lync user. The location information and policy of Lync Hybrid Voice users is automatically retrieved by the Lync client via the Provisioning Web Service (described earlier) and transmitted during an emergency call. When an E911 call is placed, the Lync Online infrastructure routes the request through to the on-premises Lync Server infrastructure. The on-premises Lync Server infrastructure then routes the E911 call to the E911 provider.

If a Lync Hybrid Voice user is logged on remotely (e.g., from the Internet) and makes an E911 call, the location cannot be automatically determined; in this case the user will be prompted to enter an address manually. This address is then passed to the E911 provider.

Conferencing

Once a user is moved to Lync Online, their conferencing data, meeting content, and scheduled meetings are not migrated with their user account. These users must reschedule their meetings after their accounts have been moved to Lync Online.

Users homed on-premises or online can join each other's Lync meetings as before; if a user is enabled for Hybrid Voice, there are some different requirements, and also how the meeting location is determined is different from how it's determined for an on-premises user.

Once a user has been enabled for Lync Hybrid Voice, they can no longer use the on-premises infrastructure for dial-in conferencing. Lync Hybrid Voice users who require dial-in and dial-out access for Lync meetings that they organize must be set up with dial-in conferencing accounts with an audio conferencing provider (ACP). ACPs provide dial-in conference capability for the cloud solution. This is because once a user is moved to the online service, they will be using the online Lync pools for hosting their conferences, and these pools do not have native dial-in and dial-out capabilities.

Figure 18.12 shows how a conference that is hosted online is located.

In Figure 18.12, the first *getConference* SIP/C3P request goes to the on-premises Lync Server pool, which checks Bob's Deployment Locator attribute on his AD user account object. This identifies Bob as a Lync Hybrid Voice user, so the SIP/C3P request gets proxied from the on-premises Lync Server pool, via the Edge, to the cloud to find Bob's conferencing pool.

Configuring Lync Hybrid Voice

The next sections will take you through the different stages of configuration for a Lync Hybrid Voice environment. This time you're not only concerned about installation of the on-premises environment (see Chapter 6, "Installation") but also the prerequisites for the online environment.

FIGURE 18.12
Online confer-
ence discovery and
connectivity

Prerequisites and Configuring the Environment for Hybrid Voice

Hybrid Voice is not enabled in Lync by default. Before configuring the infrastructure for
Lync Online integration, it is a good idea to verify that the on-premises Active Directory
infrastructure is ready for synchronization with Office 365 (Online). You can use the Office
365 Deployment Readiness Tool to check (http://community.office365.com/en-us
/forums/183/p/2285/8155.aspx).

To set up Hybrid Voice to work correctly, you require the following components and
configuration:

- You must set up the internal corporate network for Lync Online. For users who are Lync
  Online enabled to access the service, various ports and access to various domains need to
  be allowed.

- Users enabled as Hybrid Voice need to have Internet access in order for them to reach the
  Lync Online infrastructure.

- You must create and configure a tenant in Lync Online before you can configure your Lync
  environment for hybrid. Your domain also needs to be verified.

- Active Directory Federation Services (ADFS) 2.0 must be configured. ADFS 2.0 enables
  federation between the Lync Server 2013 on-premises deployment and the Lync Online
  tenant.

- You need to create DNS records for ADFS.

- You need to create certificates for ADFS.

◆ Install the Microsoft Online Services Sign-In Assistant and Microsoft Online Services Module for Windows PowerShell onto the ADFS server.

◆ Install and configure an ADFS proxy (can be Threat Management Gateway (TMG) 2010 reverse proxy also). A proxy to the ADFS in the perimeter network is required so that users logging on remotely can access the service.

◆ Set up directory synchronization, which allows you to manage Active Directory in your environment and then synchronize the changes with Office 365.

◆ Install and configure on-premises Lync Enterprise Voice deployment.

◆ Enable users for Enterprise Voice.

◆ Configure remote PowerShell, which is used to connect to the Lync Online infrastructure to manage Hybrid Voice users.

◆ Configure the on-premises Lync Edge server for federation with Lync online.

SETTING UP THE INTERNAL CORPORATE NETWORK FOR LYNC ONLINE

For users to be able to access Lync Online from within the corporate network, specific ports and URLs need to be allowed via firewalls or forward-facing proxies. Table 18.2 shows the required ports on the corporate reverse proxy servers and external firewalls.

TABLE 18.2:   Required firewall ports and protocol configuration

PORT	PROTOCOL	DIRECTION	USAGE
443	STUN/TCP	Outbound	Audio, video and application-sharing sessions
443	PSOM/TLS	Outbound	Data-sharing sessions
3478	STUN/UDP	Outbound	Audio and video sessions
5223	TCP	Outbound	Lync Mobile push notifications (if Lync Mobile is deployed)
50000–59999	RTP/UDP	Outbound	Audio and video sessions

Configure an exception for Microsoft Online Services URLs and applications from the proxy or firewall. Create these rules/exceptions on the external firewall that apply to all users on the organization's network:

◆ Allow outgoing connections to `*.microsoftonline.com`.

◆ Allow outgoing connections to `*.microsoftonline-p.com`.

◆ Allow outgoing connections to `osub.microsoft.com`.

◆ Allow outgoing connections to `*.outlook.com`.

◆ Allow outgoing connections to *.lync.com.

◆ Allow TCP and HTTPS.

◆ Set HTTPS/SSL time-out to 8 hours.

If the firewall being used does not accept URLs such as *.lync.com, then exclude the IP address ranges that are used by Lync Online. The following Technet article lists the IP ranges:

http://technet.microsoft.com/en-gb/library/hh372948.aspx

Also ensure that the host firewalls allow Microsoft Online Services Sign-In Assistant traffic through (msoidsvc.exe).

Any Internet proxy access needs to be unauthenticated so that the sign-on process is seamless.

LYNC ONLINE TENANT (PREPARING ONLINE SERVICES)

When you create an online tenant, you will be assigned a domain such as, for example, masteringlync.onmicrosoft.com; you will then need to add your vanity domain, which is actually your on-premises domain name (such as masteringlync.org).

To create an online tenant, you will need to visit the Office 365 online services website:

www.microsoft.com/office/preview/en/office-365-proplus

These are the next high-level steps:

1. Enter your email address, physical address, and contact telephone number.

2. Create an administrator account in the online domain; it will be automatically populated—for example admin@masteringlync.onmicrosoft.com.

3. Add your vanity domain (e.g., masteringlync.org).

4. You will then have to verify your domain.

5. Enable federation for Lync Online.

6. Activate Active Directory synchronization online (this step must be completed before installing the Directory Synchronization Tool).

 Real World Scenario

WHY USE HYBRID DEPLOYMENTS?

There are several reasons for moving to a hybrid deployed model; the most popular is to remove the local server footprint of a highly available Lync deployment. For small organizations, Lync can be expensive to deploy because of the number of servers needed. Although a single Standard Edition server will support up to 2500 users, voice is typically a business-critical function, so high availability is a requirement. Suddenly two Front End servers (it truly should be three) are needed along with multiple SQL Server machines.

Perhaps this company has only a few hundred users and now the potentially six servers required equates to a massive investment.

> Moving to hybrid allows all the high-availability aspects—as well as administration, patching, and so on—to be taken care of by someone else. In addition, there is the flexibility to grow the number of users dramatically in a short period of time.
>
> All that is needed from the organization perspective is the minimal local infrastructure to connect to the PSTN and Internet.
>
> And, of course, to pay the phone bills!

Installing and Configuring Active Directory Federation Services 2.0

Active Directory Federation Services (ADFS) is a service that provides web single sign-on (removing the need for users to repeatedly enter credentials) to authenticate a user to multiple web applications (such as Lync Online) over the life of a single online session.

In ADFS, the federation service is a Security Token Service (STS). STS is a web service that issues security tokens. Specific detailed guidance on how to configure ADFS for Office 365 is beyond the scope of this book; however, we've listed the high-level guidance steps required.

Follow these steps from the Office 365 help guides:

1. Prepare for single sign-on.

   http://onlinehelp.microsoft.com/en-US/office365-enterprises/ff652540.aspx

2. Plan for and deploy AFDS 2.0 for use with single sign-on.

   http://onlinehelp.microsoft.com/en-US/office365-enterprises/ff652539.aspx

3. Install the Microsoft Online Services Module for Windows PowerShell.

   http://onlinehelp.microsoft.com/en-US/office365-enterprises/ff652560.aspx

4. Add your domain to Office 365.

   http://onlinehelp.microsoft.com/en-gb/Office365-enterprises/ff637620.aspx

5. Verify the domain.

   http://onlinehelp.microsoft.com/en-gb/office365-enterprises/gg584188.aspx

6. Install Active Directory Synchronization with Dirsync.

   http://onlinehelp.microsoft.com/en-US/office365-enterprises/ff652543.aspx

7. Manage Directory Synchronization.

   http://onlinehelp.microsoft.com/en-US/office365-enterprises/ff652533.aspx

8. Verify single sign-on.

   http://onlinehelp.microsoft.com/en-US/office365-enterprises/ff652538.aspx

Configuring On-Premises Lync Edge Servers for Federation with Lync Online

Log on to a Lync on-premises Front End server with an account designated CsAdministrator privileges and open the Lync Management Shell.

Type the following command and then press Enter:

```
New-CsHostingProvider -Identity LyncOnline -ProxyFqdn "sipfed.online.lync.com"
-Enabled $true -AutodiscoverUrl "https://webdir.online.lync.com/
Autodiscover/AutodiscoverService.svc/root" -EnabledSharedAddressSpace $true
-HostsOCSUsers $true -VerificationLevel UseSourceVerification -IsLocal $false
```

Moving Users to Lync Online

You need to ensure that all user data is backed up before moving them to Lync Online. The user should also be licensed for Lync Online using the tenant administrator portal user interface.

1. To move a user to Lync Online, use the on-premises Lync Management Shell, using the administrator credentials of the tenant.

2. Type the following command and then press Enter:
   ```
   $creds=Get-Credentials
   ```

3. In the Windows PowerShell Credential Request window, enter your Microsoft Online Services tenant administrator username and password, and then click OK.

4. Back in the Lync Management Shell, type the following command and then press Enter:
   ```
   Move-CsUser -Identity keith.lync@masteringinglync.org -Target
   sipfed.online.lync.com -credentials $creds -HostedMigrationOverrideUrl
   "https://admin0b.online.lync.com/HostedMigration/hostedmigrationservice.svc"
   ```

5. Type Y to confirm and then press Enter.

6. To verify that the user was successfully moved, you can use a Get-CsUser command in the on-premises Lync Management Shell and look to make sure the output shows that HostingProvider is set to sipfed.online.lync.com (shown in Figure 18.13).

FIGURE 18.13
User data for a Lync Hybrid user

CONFIGURING USERS FOR HYBRID VOICE

Once you've finished the previous steps to create an online tenant and you've moved the users identified to be enabled for Hybrid Voice to Lync Online, you can configure them for Hybrid Voice.

This assumes you already have an on-premises Lync deployment with users enabled for Enterprise Voice and you have an on-premises PSTN infrastructure such as a PSTN media gateway configured as a peer with your Lync deployment.

1. Create a Hybrid PSTN usage for the Hybrid Voice users. This step uses the on-premises Lync Management Shell.

   a. Log on to the Lync Front End as a member of the RTCUniversalServerAdmins group, or as a member of the CsVoiceAdministrator, CsServerAdministrator, or CsAdministrator role.

   b. In the Lync Server Management Shell, type the following commands:
   ```
   Set-CsPstnUsage -Usage @{add="HybridVoiceUsage"}
   ```

2. Create a Hybrid Voice routing policy. Note that you can assign an existing voice routing policy to the Lync Hybrid Voice users if preferred. This step uses the on-premises Lync Management Shell; it is not available in the Lync Control Panel.

   a. Log on to the Lync Front End as a member of the RTCUniversalServerAdmins group, or as a member of the CsVoiceAdministrator, CsServerAdministrator, or CsAdministrator role.

   b. In the Lync Server Management Shell, type the following command:
   ```
   New-CsVoiceRoutingPolicy -Identity "tag:HybridVoiceUser"
   -Name "Hybrid Voice Policy" -PstnUsages @{add="HybridVoiceUsage"}
   ```

3. Create a dial plan for Hybrid Voice users. Note you can apply an existing dial plan to Hybrid Voice users if you prefer. This step uses the on-premises Lync Management Shell.

   a. Log on to the Lync Front End as a member of the RTCUniversalServerAdmins group, or as a member of the CsVoiceAdministrator, CsServerAdministrator, or CsAdministrator role.

   b. In the Lync Server Management Shell, type the following command:
   ```
   New-CsDialPlan -Identity "tag:HybridVoiceDialplan"
   -Description "Hybrid Voice Dial Plan"
   ```

4. Create normalization rules for the dial plan. If you decided to use an existing dial plan, then you will not have to run this step.

   a. Log on to the Lync Front End as a member of the RTCUniversalServerAdmins group, or as a member of the CsVoiceAdministrator, CsServerAdministrator, or CsAdministrator role.

   b. In the Lync Server Management Shell, type the following command to create a normalization rule, for example, that translates a six-digit dialed number from 123456 to +441344 123456:
   ```
   New-CsVoiceNormalizationRule -Identity tag:HybridVoiceDialplan/6Digit
   -Pattern '^(\d{6})$' -Translation '+441344$1'
   ```

5. Assign a voice routing policy. Assign an existing voice routing policy as discussed in step 2, or assign the new one created specifically for the Hybrid Voice users.

   a. Log on to the Lync Front End as a member of the RTCUniversalServerAdmins group, or as a member of the CsVoiceAdministrator, CsServerAdministrator, or CsAdministrator role.

   b. In the Lync Server Management Shell, type the following command:
   ```
   Grant-CsVoiceRoutingPolicy -Identity "Bob" -PolicyName HybridVoiceUser
   ```

6. Assign a dial plan. Assign an existing dial plan or one that you created specifically for the Hybrid Voice users.

   a. Log on to the Lync Front End as a member of the RTCUniversalServerAdmins group, or as a member of the CsVoiceAdministrator, CsServerAdministrator, or CsAdministrator role.

   b. In the Lync Server Management Shell, type the following command:
   ```
   Grant-CsDialPlan -Identity "Bob" -PolicyName HybridVoiceDialplan
   ```

7. Assign a Lync Online voice policy. An existing voice policy can be used if preferred.

   a. This next step requires the use of remote PowerShell. The tenant administrator must assign the voice policy to the Lync Online users. Import the LyncOnlineConnector Module, open PowerShell on the Lync Front End, and type the following:
   ```
   Import-Module LyncOnlineConnector
   ```

   b. Create the credential object for the tenant admin user. For example, to create credential object for admin@masteringlync.org, do the following:
   ```
   $cred=Get-Credential admin@masteringlync.org
   ```

   c. When prompted for password, enter the password.

   d. Create the session using the Admin Pool FQDN and passing in the credential object created in the previous step:
   ```
   $CsSession = New-CsOnlineSession -TargetServer admin0b.online.lync.com
   -Credential $cred
   ```

   e. Import the session created:
   ```
   Import-PsSession -Session $CsSession
   ```

   f. Assign Lync Online users the Lync Online voice policy by running the remote Windows PowerShell cmdlet:
   ```
   Grant-CsVoicePolicy -Identity Bob@masteringinglync.org -PolicyName HybridVoice
   ```

Once all the previous steps have been run, you can test that users can make and receive PSTN calls from their Lync clients.

Note that both a Hybrid Voice Policy and a Voice Policy are required to be assigned to the user.

Troubleshooting Lync Hybrid Voice

Ensuring that you have prepared your network for Lync Online will enable you to sign in without issues (see the section "Setting Up the Internal Corporate Network for Lync Online" earlier in this chapter). However, you may still experience some.

If your users are unable to sign into Lync Online, there is a handy tool available called the Lync Online Transport Reliability IP Probe. The tool tests your connection to the Microsoft Lync Online service.

Follow this link to run the test (Java is required):

    http://support.microsoft.com/kb/2409256

Choose the appropriate URL that is the closest region to the user who is having the problem (see Figure 18.14).

FIGURE 18.14
Test URLs for Microsoft Lync Online data centers

> **How to verify that all network requirements for Lync Online are met**
>
> In a web browser, browse to one of the following Office 365 Lync Online Transport Reliability IP Probe (TRIPP) tool URLs. (Browse to the URL that is closest to the user's physical location.)
>
> - Amsterdam, NL: http://trippams.online.lync.com
> - Blue Ridge, VA: http://trippbl2.online.lync.com
> - Dublin, IE: http://trippdb3.online.lync.com
> - Hong Kong: http://tripphkn.online.lync.com
> - San Antonio, TX: http://trippsn2.online.lync.com
> - Singapore: http://trippsg1.online.lync.com
>
> Then, click **Start Test**.

In addition to testing your connection, individual port tests are carried out as well as a route and speed test (we're not reproducing them here because samples are included in the KB article mentioned earlier).

It is important to have the affected users carry out the test because the test is carried out from the PC on which it is run; there's no point in testing from a help desk location because it's likely to be in a different location than the user reporting the issue, especially so if the user is connected via the Internet and is not an office user.

The following support article also can assist you with troubleshooting sign-in issues to Microsoft Lync Online:

    http://support.microsoft.com/kb/2541980

Please note that authenticating proxies are not supported for Lync 2013:

    http://technet.microsoft.com/en-us/library/jj205120(v=ocs.15).aspx

Finally, you can install Snooper to troubleshoot sign-in issues (see Chapter 12, "Troubleshooting," for more details on Snooper):

    http://community.office365.com/en-us/wikis/lync/485.aspx

The Bottom Line

Understand the Lync hybrid architecture model.   Lync Server 2013 introduces the new capability of a hybrid model that allows hosting some users of an organization on premises in the traditional way of having on-premises infrastructure deployed but also hosting other members of the organization in a cloud solution.

Master It   Lync Server 2013 (and previous versions) provides support for multiple SIP domains in the same Lync deployment within an Active Directory forest. What change to this model does the hybrid deployment require?

Understand the capabilities of a hybrid deployment.   Users can be hosted either online in the cloud, or on premises on a local infrastructure. Each location provides a common set of features, but not all are available when users are using Lync Online.

Master It   Which features are only available in an on-premises deployment?

Understand the call flow for media in different scenarios.   Lync can be a very complex product when it comes to understanding signaling flows and media flows. Using Edge servers adds additional complexity, and having an additional pool hosted in the cloud adds a level of complexity beyond simple Edge servers!

Master It   Describe the call flow path between two users, Alice and Bob. Alice is calling from a cell phone to Bob's Lync phone number. Bob is a Lync Online user and is located currently on the corporate network.

Understand the required steps to configure a hybrid deployment.   Introducing a hybrid scenario to a local Lync Server 2013 environment requires a number of additional configuration items to be carried out. Some are as basic (and expected) as firewall port configuration, while others are significantly more complex, such as ADFS configuration.

Master It   You are configuring your organization for Hybrid Voice and need to configure rules for the proxy exceptions list. What do you need to configure?

Chapter 19

Third-Party Integration

The previous chapter discussed how Lync can be enhanced through integration with other Microsoft products; this chapter discusses how Lync can integrate with third-party systems to perform as the center of a much broader communications platform. By using the standards and protocols covered in Chapter 2, "Standards and Protocols," Lync can integrate with many systems and gateways to provide translation to other devices and systems. For example, Lync can talk directly to a SIP trunk provider for PSTN connectivity, but it can also communicate via more traditional methods using standard ISDN lines through a PSTN gateway. Likewise, Lync can integrate with existing PBX systems to provide elements of control over handsets from the PC through a technology called Remote Call Control (RCC). Lync is, of course, not limited to talking only to PBXs or the PSTN. It is perfectly capable of sitting at the center of a videoconferencing system, utilizing its superb native external connectivity functionality to link hardware and software video endpoints from the likes of Radvision and Polycom. Lync's external connectivity can also be extended. While Lync can federate natively with other Microsoft communications platforms and with Internet IM clouds like AOL and Yahoo!, other platforms require another type of gateway to enable communication. Microsoft includes an XMPP gateway, which translates the protocols used by Lync into the XMPP standard to enable communication with the likes of Google Talk and IBM Sametime. Finally, because Lync is a software platform, a software developer can extend and integrate applications into Lync to provide enhanced functionality that is not available by default.

In this chapter, you will learn to:

◆   Connect to telephony systems via a gateway

◆   Integrate with your PBX

◆   Use RCC to integrate with your PBX

◆   Deploy a Survivable Branch Appliance

◆   Connect to other external systems via an XMPP gateway

◆   Utilize third-party software enhancements

Connecting to Telephony Systems via a Gateway

Gateways have been referred to throughout this book, but what *is* a gateway and what does it do in the Lync environment? Fundamentally, a gateway is a hardware device from a third-party vendor that enables voice integration between your Lync deployment and other external voice elements, such as a PBX (Private Branch Exchange), the PSTN, DECT phones (digital handsets), and analog devices as represented in Figure 19.1.

FIGURE 19.1
Gateway connecting various voice components together

While Lync can potentially talk directly to certain PBXs or SIP trunk providers, the PBXs that support this ability are limited. Even some IP PBXs don't talk the correct variety of SIP, and SIP trunks may not be suitable to your particular environment, especially if you have a significant investment in ISDN lines. Implementing a gateway to integrate to the telephony world brings distinct benefits, including security and flexibility in manipulating traffic, which are two of the most important. Session border controllers (SBC) can also be considered gateways; they specifically are dealing with SIP trunks and have a separate section on the Open Interoperability Program but often provide similar functionality as a gateway.

In the following sections, you'll explore the various benefits of using a gateway, look at some of the gateway options available in the market today, and review some of the more advanced features being implemented on the latest generation of gateways that make Lync integration and user migration easier and more robust. First though, let's take a look at some of the typical voice elements that you have to integrate with and at the challenges that lie ahead.

Public Switched Telephone Network (PSTN)

The public switched telephone network is a worldwide telephony infrastructure that is hosted and supported by various carriers in different countries all over the world. Similar to the World Wide Web, this infrastructure gives global reach and enables users to make a voice call to anywhere in the world. Figure 19.2 shows many of the typical PSTN interconnect standards and devices that exist around the world today.

FIGURE 19.2
The PSTN showing various endpoints

In contrast to the World Wide Web, which is ultimately based on a common protocol—IP—the PSTN network has many different interfaces, protocols, and standards associated with it. This is driven by differences in local country standards, evolution of voice services over the years, and adoption of different technology by different carriers. What this means for you is that for a global Lync deployment, you may be facing a slightly different interface or protocol in each location where a connection to PSTN is required. It is in this situation that it's important for a gateway to offer a wide range of interfaces, protocols, and standards. It is also important that the gateway device is acceptance-tested (*homologated*) by the carrier in a country for direct connection to its PSTN service.

Traditional PSTN connectivity (known as *legacy PSTN*) is generally presented to an enterprise over a digital service known as ISDN (Integrated Services Digital Network) or an analog line, such as you may have at home. The digital services are presented as BRI (*Basic Rate*), which gives two voice channels and one for signaling, or PRI (*Primary Rate*), of which there are two variants—T1 and E1.

T1 is used in North America and Japan and provides 23 channels of voice and one channel for signaling. E1 is used in Europe and Australia and is fairly widespread across the rest of the world. E1 provides 30 channels for voice and one for signaling.

Internet Telephony Service Provider (ITSP)

Another option for connecting to the PSTN network, to provide external voice services to your Lync users, is to implement a SIP trunk service from an Internet telephony service provider (ITSP). A SIP trunk service is much more flexible and dynamic than the traditional PSTN services delivered by local carriers because it uses VoIP technology in much the same way that Lync does for delivering voice services over IP. In fact, some providers offer certified services that can be directly connected to your Lync infrastructure. However, these services are not available in all locations, and there are still very good reasons to consider using a gateway device between your Lync infrastructure and a Microsoft Open Interoperability Program (OIP)–certified SIP trunk service.

MICROSOFT OIP CERTIFICATION—OPEN INTEROPERABILITY TESTING

As with any third-party device connecting into Lync, it is very important that the device interface, protocols, and features are fully tested and compliant with Lync to ensure a smooth implementation and to avoid any unexpected issues. The OIP program instigated by Microsoft ensures that any gateway or PBX equipment undergoes a full and extensive interoperability test suite before being supported and listed on the OIP web page, at this address:

    http://technet.microsoft.com/en-us/lync/gg131938

A good SIP gateway can provide an additional layer of security and flexibility by acting as a session border controller. The gateway sits on the edge of your IP network, terminating the SIP trunk service, and is able to provide stateful SIP firewall services, session management, and connection admission control. Also thanks to its location, it provides topology hiding and failover to traditional PSTN connectivity in the event of a failure or congestion on the SIP trunk.

Securing the voice traffic at the edge of your enterprise network is important. You must remember that voice traffic over IP is just like your regular Internet data. It is subject to the same security concerns and considerations that you apply to your data traffic. Various secure protocols and methods can be used to protect your voice traffic. The SBC device is key to their implementation. You'll explore these protocols in detail later, and you'll see how both the signaling and voice traffic itself can be protected against unlawful intercept or eavesdropping by unwanted parties.

Your SIP trunk will be delivered over the Internet or your virtual private network (VPN). The SBC will be the *voice firewall* between your SIP trunk provider and your internal Lync voice network; it will provide security and session management to make sure you don't oversubscribe your SIP trunk connection with excessive voice calls. This session management can include the ability to manage peak call periods by overflowing calls to traditional PSTN trunks when your SIP trunks are at capacity.

SIP trunk providers are growing in number and popularity right now; the flexibility and cost savings offered by some of these services are attractive, but there are differences in signaling protocols and codecs used for media encoding. This again creates a need for a flexible and capable gateway device to interface with these services; such an interface might be in parallel to your "traditional" ISDN connection as well, thereby presenting a common and known secure interface to your Lync deployment via the gateway.

Typically, an ITSP will implement the UDP protocol for signaling transport, the RTP protocol for media transport, and the G.729 codec for the media encoding itself. By contrast, a Lync enhanced gateway will use the TLS encrypted protocol for signaling transport, SRTP encrypted protocol for media transport, and G.711 codec for the media encoding toward the Lync pool Mediation role, as shown in Figure 19.3.

FIGURE 19.3
The protocols and codecs used between the gateway and provider in a typical SIP trunk setup

The gateway must be capable of translating between the secure and nonsecure protocols used for both signaling and media, and it must be able to transcode between the different audio codecs used on either side.

Take note of that last point; audio transcoding is becoming a key factor in today's Unified Communications (UC) telephony environment. Whereas the traditional telephony environment used in the PSTN carries the voice traffic as uncompressed audio, within the IP world it is common to encode and compress the audio data to reduce the bandwidth required to transport it end to end. With SIP, the endpoints trying to establish a voice call must agree on a common codec to use in order to transport the audio stream between them. As mentioned, many ISTP providers like to deliver the voice using the G.729 codec, which is able to compress the audio data from 64Kbps to 8Kbps while still maintaining reasonable voice quality.

Within Lync, the clients are able to support two codecs. The default used for all PC-to-PC calls is Microsoft's proprietary RTAudio codec, which is a high-fidelity wideband codec that is able to dynamically adjust the compression rate to the available bandwidth. The second codec available is G.711, which is 64Kbps voice and is comparable to uncompressed voice used on the PSTN. G.711 is used toward the gateway for calls out to the PSTN or PBX. For interfacing with Lync, the gateway must be able to transcode this G.729 audio traffic presented by the ITSP carrier to G.711 data, which is passed on toward the Lync client.

As mentioned, this direct SIP-to-SIP audio transcoding is becoming a commonplace requirement for Lync deployments where a SIP trunk connection is involved, either to an ITSP or an IP-PBX. The gateways available on the market vary greatly in their capability and capacity to perform this task. As you can imagine, this task of completely changing the voice compression technique on either side of a gateway is resource intensive. The voice must be processed by the gateway dynamically and without introducing noticeable latency to the voice traffic. Imagine a gateway processing a few hundred calls simultaneously, each call generating hundreds of packets of audio data that require decoding and re-encoding, and you can see that audio transcoding is no trivial task. Within a gateway, this task is performed by a hardware element known as a Digital Signal Processor (DSP) chip. When looking at your gateway requirements, pay particular attention to this capability. With the increasing move toward SIP trunking, this requirement is only set to grow.

Private Branch Exchange (PBX)

Another common voice element that most organizations need to interface with is the PBX. This is typically an on-premises device that delivers the existing voice capability to users; it usually hosts internal phones and fax machines and connects to the PSTN, as described previously. PBXs are proprietary; they come from an array of vendors and have different features, models, and software versions that affect their capabilities. You may have heard a PBX vendor talk about the 100-plus features that a PBX is capable of, and that a software VoIP platform cannot deliver. The question is, in any given installation, how many of those features are in fact licensed, configured, used, or even known? Maybe five or six!

Three main types of PBX technology are deployed: traditional analog/digital PBX, IP-PBX, and a combination of the two, generally known as an *I-enabled* PBX.

Traditional PBX: This describes the majority of PBX equipment deployed. It is typically very old—15 to 20 years old is not uncommon—and usually has proprietary analog or digital handsets. It is low on features.

IP PBX: Full IP VoIP PBX systems tend to be much newer and feature rich and have VoIP endpoints, although these endpoints may run a proprietary version of SIP.

IP-Enabled PBX: Some traditional PBX systems can be upgraded with an IP card to enable them to interface with VoIP platforms such as Lync. However, when SIP is implemented on these systems, it often has some proprietary extensions, making interoperability and certification to Lync a challenge.

Achieving Connectivity

In order for Lync to integrate with external elements to establish a voice call, the gateway must be able to understand and translate various signaling and transport protocols. They fall under two key areas: signaling transport, which sets up the call, and media transport, which facilitates the passing of the audio stream encoded with whichever codec is being used. In addition, the media codec is responsible for the interchange of actual audio content. These areas are outlined here and shown in Figure 19.4.

FIGURE 19.4
The connectivity components through a gateway

Signaling transport: For a voice call to be established, information, including the number dialed and the number of the caller, must be passed between devices. This process is known as the *call signaling*. With SIP, this information can be transported using the UDP, TCP, or secure TLS transport protocols. UDP is obviously connectionless and is often used by ITSP providers for SIP trunk signaling. It is lightweight, fast, and suited to the ITSP needs. TCP is a connection-oriented protocol that provides guaranteed data transport. Lync uses TLS for all signaling transport to avoid any unwanted data interception. TLS is based on the TCP protocol but adds a layer of encryption and security.

Media transport: The standard protocol for transporting the voice traffic over IP is Real-Time Transport Protocol (RTP). RTP is widely used as a transport protocol for both voice and video traffic. A later extension to this protocol was the addition of security to eliminate the risk of interception and eavesdropping. It is known as Secure RTP (SRTP), and the endpoint devices encrypt any voice traffic within a secure payload before transmitting over the IP network. Lync employs SRTP for communication to the gateway.

Media codec: As mentioned earlier in the ITSP section, the encoding and compression of the voice traffic element is achieved using one of the voice codecs, such as G.711, G.729, or Microsoft RTAudio. The codec used must be agreed upon by both voice endpoints during the signaling negotiations to establish the call. If no common codec is available on the devices, the call will not be established. The gateway device in your Lync deployment should be capable of changing the audio between different codecs, a process known as *transcoding*. The different gateways on the market today have different technical implementations to achieve this functionality, and they vary in capability and capacity!

SIP and ISDN Gateways

A number of gateways available on the market today are certified for Lync integration. They range from very small, low-cost analog devices to high-end data-center-type devices that can handle multiple E1 circuits, thousands of users, and high call volumes. Various vendors provide different platforms, including Dialogic, NET, Cisco, Ferrari, and AudioCodes. Again, the gateway offerings differ in interfaces, features, and capability, so be sure to research your needs carefully.

In the following sections, we'll take a closer look at one of the gateways available for Lync integration, the AudioCodes MSBG range, including the Mediant 1000 and the Mediant 800 designed for smaller office locations. This is the latest range of gateway and Survivable Branch Appliance (SBA) platforms from AudioCodes; it has been designed specifically with Lync in mind and provides a flexible and high-performance way of connecting Lync to other platforms.

First, let's look at some of the models available and the typical interfaces and features that you can configure for voice integration to Lync, and then we'll review some of the GUI configuration items of the platform.

FEATURES

The 1000 shown in Figure 19.5 is a mid-point modular platform allowing for growth. If you look closely you can see that each of the modules is screwed in and can be easily replaced. Indeed, one of the modules can be an SBA or CPU module, allowing for the easy upgrade of older versions (perhaps purchased for use with OCS 2007 R2) to provide more functionality for Lync.

FIGURE 19.5

The AudioCodes
Mediant 1000

Courtesy of AudioCodes,
www.audiocodes.com

It provides the following features:

♦ Mix and match interfaces to allow the connection of digital (PRI) and analog (FXS/FXO) devices directly to the gateway. Multiple interface slots enable analog and digital connectivity in the same platform.

♦ High-capacity DSP resources that enable direct SIP-SIP transcoding of many codecs, as described in the previous section. This transcoding scales with extremely low latency and no loss of capacity or performance.

♦ Router/firewall/VPN to enable SBC functionality, giving security for your voice traffic.

- Optional branch survivability with fully integrated SBA. Lync users in a branch have the ability to register directly to the gateway, providing full voice survivability in the event of a WAN outage.

- AD integration for advanced call routing, enabling smooth staged migration of users from your PBX to Lync.

- SIP phone registration. By allowing the direct registration of existing SIP phones to the gateway, the device eliminates the need for an additional registrar server. By using this feature on the gateway, SIP phones can become tightly integrated with your Lync and PBX environment.

The Mediant 800, shown in Figure 19.6, uses the same configuration interface and code set as its larger brother, the Mediant 1000.

FIGURE 19.6

The AudioCodes Mediant 800 MSBG

Courtesy of AudioCodes, www.audiocodes.com

This similarity can make managing a solution easier when different gateway types are used. An organization can benefit from the advanced features and hardware components of the 1000 (and indeed there are larger-capacity models as well: Mediant 2000 and Mediant 3000) by using it at a central office and providing suitable capacity and functionality with the 800 at small office locations. The 800 has the following features:

- Mixed interfaces, enabling the connectivity of analog phones (FXS/FXO), and digital interfaces, either Basic Rate (BRI) or Primary Rate (PRI)

- High-capacity DSP resources that enable direct SIP-to-SIP transcoding

- Router/firewall/VPN to enable SBC functionality, giving security for your voice traffic

- Optional branch survivability with fully integrated SBA, giving branch office Lync users total voice survivability

- AD integration for advanced call routing, enabling smooth staged migration of users from an existing PBX to Lync

- Network interfaces (both Gb and FE) capable of Power over Ethernet (PoE)

Some of the advanced features now being implemented on voice gateways are specifically intended to assist in Lync deployments and migrations; one such feature is Active Directory integration, which is provided on the platform. This capability enables many different dynamic routing scenarios. For example, the gateway can route incoming calls to either the Lync environment or the legacy PBX, depending on whether the user's Direct Inward Dial (DID) number has been moved to Lync or not as provisioned in AD, shown in Figure 19.7. Although this may not seem hugely significant, it plays a major factor in the migration of users from the PBX to Lync because without this feature, an awful lot of manual routing table reconfiguration is needed. With AD integration on the gateway, the process is totally automated, enabling you to migrate users at your own pace and with ease.

FIGURE 19.7
AD-based intelligent call routing

CONFIGURATION

Now that we've covered the main features of the gateways, let's look at some of the gateway configuration areas that pertain to Lync deployments. As you will see, the configuration interface is HTTPS based and allows wizard-style configuration as well as full parameter configuration and manipulation. There is also are monitor windows that displays all calls, alarms, and events on the system.

By browsing to the default admin port IP address 192.168.0.1 (or 192.168.0.2), you can access the configuration screen. From there you configure the IP address that you want on the gateway along with the DNS servers, default gateway, and user credentials to log in and start your configuration. You then cable the gateway into your network and begin the configuration by browsing to the IP address just configured. From this point on, the unit is secured by the credentials you have just entered.

One core element required is the set of signaling groups. These groups are a way to logically group and route voice traffic through the gateway, providing flexibility in the handling of different types of signaling, protocols, and codecs. They are used for both ISDN and SIP interfaces from the gateway, and they enable custom configuration of specific parameters related to the device to which the gateway will interface. You can have multiple SIP and ISDN signaling groups, each with its own associated device (Lync Front End, PBX, PSTN circuit, ITSP SIP trunk, and so on). Figure 19.8 shows a SIP signaling group ready for configuration. The IP address of the Lync server is the only address able to send SIP traffic into this signaling group, and it is only the configured signaling ports that will listen for SIP traffic from the Lync mediation service, which can be either TLS or TCP (the gateway also supports UDP); in addition, the port number used can be customized.

FIGURE 19.8
Signaling group
setup page

Another very common task that a gateway needs to perform is name and number manipulation; this needs to be done for the Dialed Number, Calling Number, and Diversion headers. Diversion headers are commonly used when a call goes unanswered by the end user and the PBX is sending the call to a voice mail server. The Diversion header is used to identify which user's extension the call was originally intended for so that the voice mail server can identify the call and send it to the correct user's mailbox. The recommended format to which Lync will normalize numbers as it sends calls to the gateway is E.164. Typically, a PSTN carrier will not accept the dialed or calling number if it starts with + (country code). Therefore, in the gateway it is necessary to strip off the + and replace it with a preceding zero or maybe two zeros depending on whether it is a national or international call. Figure 19.9 shows an example in which national numbers from Lync are normalized from +1xxxxxxxxxx to 00xxxxxxxxxx.

FIGURE 19.9
Number normaliza-
tion in the gateway

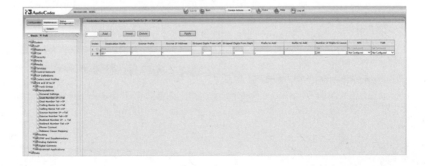

Another common translation that many gateways will need to perform is for calls from Lync to internal PBX users. Most deployed PBX systems employ a four- or five-digit dialing plan internally; therefore, the E.164 number presented by Lync needs to be stripped down to four or five digits, but *only* for internal calls. Active Directory can again help the gateway determine what numbers are internal to that location. By using the information in Active Directory, you can see in the gateway which DID numbers are assigned to users within the enterprise; these numbers can be treated as internal, stripped down from E.164 format, and sent to the PBX. Any number that is *not* found in the AD database, therefore, does not belong to the enterprise and can be correctly formatted and sent to the PSTN for onward routing.

MONITORING

Monitoring capability is important. You need to be able to get an idea of what traffic is passing through your gateway and see the statistics of call volumes over a particular link. In Figure 19.10, you can see the live monitor aspect of the gateway.

FIGURE 19.10
The monitoring capabilities of the gateway

Figure 19.11 shows the statistics capabilities of the gateway; you can see that there are many different views available, giving information about traffic over the particular links. You can see at a glance the current number of calls over this link and the total number of calls both inbound and outbound, including any calls rejected or refused. You can also see statistics on the SIP messages sent in and out over this link, along with any error messages; this enables you to quickly and easily diagnose issues or capacity problems on a particular link.

FIGURE 19.11
The Statistics and
Diagnostics menu

Integrating with Your PBX

Many organizations will need to enable interoperability between their legacy PBX and Lync environment. This may be for a short period during migration from a telephony platform to Lync or for an extended time as existing telephony assets are deprecated. In this part of the chapter, we will go through the different options that are available to you and offer some advice about which is best for your organization.

When you're interfacing a Lync deployment to an existing PBX infrastructure, a big challenge you'll face is the wide array of PBX devices located in different offices and the general lack of knowledge about how to configure them. Enterprises grow over time and acquire and upgrade their PBX equipment at different times in different locations. Even if all PBX equipment is supposed to be replaced with Lync Enterprise Voice, the approach may well be a staggered process across locations over a period of months.

The following factors will also affect your integration strategy:

◆ **The age of the existing telephony platform:** Consider the capabilities of the existing platform and whether its cost has been written off as an asset.

◆ **The number of users and sites:** For example, a single location of one hundred people could be migrated in a single weekend, while multiple locations might be best migrated in separate phases.

◆ **The telephone number ranges in use:** Does everyone already have a direct-dial-inward (DDI) (also known as DID—Direct Inward Dial) number, or will new numbers be required? If needed, these new numbers could be independent of the existing telephony platform, thus negating the need for integration.

◆ **The number of circuits:** The number and location of circuits and the way in which inbound numbers are presented across the circuits will influence whether you migrate numbers gradually or support parallel running of the PBX and Lync.

LEGACY PSTN CIRCUITS

If your telephony circuits (connections to the PSTN) are extremely old, the specific type of circuit may have been discontinued for new products and, as a result, may need to be upgraded. For example, in the United Kingdom, DASS circuits are a UK-specific form of ISDN that was used before Euro ISDN was standardized. It has been discontinued for new installations but can still be found in use. Although DASS circuits can be supported with some gateways, it is worth considering whether these circuits should be upgraded to ISDN Q.931 Primary Rate Interface (PRI) circuits or even replaced with SIP trunks.

A fundamental difference from the way legacy telephony has been provided is that Lync is deployed in a far more centralized manner. For example, it is customary for users to have a single identity and for there to be a single Active Directory forest across an entire organization, in contrast to the physical location boundaries that most legacy telephony deployments followed.

With Lync, a user can receive their phone calls wherever they log on to the network, including remote locations. Telephony deployments have traditionally been based on a single number provided to a single physical location, such as a desk, with little relationship to the end user beyond an entry in the phone list. More recent deployments may support hot-desking, but they often have limitations in a multiple-location organization where hot-desking may work only within a single office or country.

As part of your planning, you should make sure you fully understand the existing telephony in use. You may need to consider the following scenarios:

Emergency phones: They are sometimes found by emergency exits. These phones automatically dial either a central security point or the local emergency services. They often can dial only a preset list of numbers and may have to be operational even when all power has been lost to the building.

Gatehouse or security barrier points: In this scenario, a handset or push-button speaker and microphone dials a predetermined number to allow access. These are often provided over long runs of copper cabling through existing duct work. Newer solutions utilize Wi-Fi or mobile networks to provide similar functionality without the cabling requirements.

Elevator phones: Similar to emergency and gatehouse phones, these phones must work when no other building services are functioning so that someone stuck in an elevator can call for assistance. They are provided over long lengths of copper cabling, which typically run from a PBX room to the roof elevator machinery room and then down the elevator shaft with the internal elevator power cables.

Rugged or explosion-proof phones: Most industrial areas require special handsets. They may need to be ruggedized, water resistant, or dust resistant; have an Ingress Protection (IP) rating; be designed to restrict any chance of electrical sparks (such as in grain stores or chemical plants), or meet any combination of these requirements.

Wireless or DECT handsets: Typically, these phones are used in large areas with only a few people, such as a warehouse, but also where users are very mobile, such as hospitals or airports.

Devices integrated with public address systems: These allow people to dial an extension and make building-wide announcements, such as fire alarm test warnings.

All these scenarios, and many more, can be supported by Lync. You need to understand your environment and know what is required from the outset. It's important so that you can plan accordingly to maximize performance. Failure to plan properly will certainly be exposed during migration and coexistence.

Integration Options

There are two basic approaches to Lync and PBX coexistence. The first is where the two platforms exist and calls are routed between them but there is no integration at a user level between them. A user can have extensions on both the PBX and Lync, but they are independent of each other.

The second is where the user's PBX phone is connected to their Lync identity and they are able to control their PBX phone from within Lync. This is called Remote Call Control (RCC) and is covered later in the chapter.

Where you logically place Lync in relation to the PBX gives you different options for call routing, as discussed next.

LYNC BEHIND PBX

When Lync resides logically behind the PBX (as in Figure 19.12), all incoming and outbound calls still route via the PBX. The connection to Lync can be via an E1/J1/T1 connection from the PBX to a Lync-approved gateway and then on to Lync, or you can use Direct SIP. The latter method is the least intrusive and allows your telephony team to remain in control of the call routing. It is, therefore, normally the easiest to deploy, so can be popular for proof-of-concept or pilot deployments.

If the PBX supports SIP IP trunks, it may be possible to connect the PBX and Lync directly using a SIP trunk across your internal network so long as it is listed as supported in the OIP. This removes the need to add any interfaces to your PBX, but not having a gateway removes a point of demarcation between the PBX and Lync. Some organizations still prefer to use a gateway with SIP trunks. For example, if your PBX is not supported, a gateway can translate between the PBX and Lync to give you a supported environment. Quite often, a demarcation device has unexpected benefits during the project because additional functions or devices are involved in the migration and can be supported by the gateway.

SIDE BY SIDE

In this scenario, the existing PBX and Lync sit logically alongside each other with a gateway sitting in front of them terminating the PSTN or SIP trunks, as shown in Figure 19.13. This could be a gateway such as the those discussed in this chapter, or in very large environments, it may be carrier-class equipment working with SS7 signaling directly with the PSTN. The importance of this gateway is that it exists at the very edge of the voice network. This gateway allows a point of control over the call routing before the call reaches the PBX, Lync, or the PSTN. In this position, it can reroute calls intelligently using an AD lookup.

FIGURE 19.12
Lync behind the PBX

FIGURE 19.13
The side-by-side arrangement of PBX and Lync with a gateway in front

With Active Directory–based routing, the gateway constantly queries AD for relevant user configuration, usually based around the population of the msRTCSIP-Line attribute, and routes a call based on this information. If the inbound call destination is found to match the number in the msRTCSIP-Line attribute, the calls to that user are routed only to Lync. This provides for very easy migration of users and rollback if required, all from within common management tools. There is no need to change the gateway or PBX configuration to alter inbound call routing. Figure 19.14 shows how to set this on the AudioCodes gateway.

FIGURE 19.14
Configuring AD integration on the gateway

PBX: THE ROUTE OF LAST RESORT

Sometimes it is possible to configure the PBX to route to Lync as the route of last resort, in a similar way that IP routers are able to have a route (the default route, typically to your ISP) that says, "If I don't know where to route this address, route it to this upstream gateway for resolution." Some PBXs can be configured in a similar way, so when the phone extension is migrated to Lync and removed from the PBX, the PBX passes the call to another device to resolve. In the side-by-side scenario, the gateway resolves the routing; when Lync resides behind the PBX, then Lync resolves.

LYNC IN FRONT OF PBX

Placing the PBX behind Lync (Figure 19.15) is similar in approach to placing Lync behind the PBX, although this is rarely done because the PBX is more established within your environment. The advantage of this approach is that from day one you establish Lync as the point of control to the PSTN and you minimize any disruption from decommissioning the PBX, compared to placing Lync behind the PBX initially. However, this approach requires all the effort, and more, of a side-by-side deployment (as well as the possibility of additional gateway hardware) without the advantages of dual-forking. Think through your objectives carefully before adopting this method.

FIGURE 19.15
Lync in front of the
PBX

RECOMMENDATION AND TIPS

Wherever possible, it is generally preferable to use the side-by-side method with the gateway truncating the PSTN connections and routing calls to either Lync or PBX as needed. This involves minimal disruption initially because the PSTN circuits can be configured to effectively pass straight through the gateway to the PBX. During migration, the side-by-side method gives the best flexibility of call routing options, and when all users are migrated, the PBX can be decommissioned without impacting the production environment.

Placing Lync behind the PBX is normally an approach used in proof of concepts or small pilots because there is zero impact to the PBX other than configuration (of course, this assumes the PBX has suitable connectivity available).

Whichever logical deployment approach you choose, there are two items you need to be conscious of during the period of coexistence.

The first is link capacity and call routing. On the first day of coexistence, the majority of users will remain on the PBX and very few calls will be terminating on Lync. As your migration progresses, more calls will terminate on Lync until a point when half your traffic is on Lync and half is on the PBX. From this point on, the amount of traffic on the PBX will decline. Think of this as a set of scales with the load gradually transferring from one side to the other. As the traffic patterns change, you must make sure the connections between the systems are sized to handle the appropriate level of traffic. There will also be a certain amount of tromboning, which is acceptable as long as it is managed. *Tromboning* occurs where a call from one system, say the PBX, is transferred to the other, Lync, and then transferred back to the PBX—like a trombone going out and in again. This can happen if users divert their extensions, or sometimes it happens through misconfiguration. A certain amount of tromboning is to be expected during migration, but it must be managed so it does not become excessive. Worse still, it can lead to circular routing of calls, where a call passes back and forth between the two systems until there are no free channels or system resources to route more calls.

The second important thing to be aware of is the number of translation patterns available on the PBX. Subject to the way you deploy Lync and the specific functionality on the PBX, each extension or range of extensions will require entries on the PBX to reroute the extension number to Lync. Although this is rarely a problem early on, it can quickly become an issue as you progress through your deployment. Once it is encountered, often the only way around this is either an expensive PBX software upgrade, which is what you are trying to avoid by deploying Lync, or changing your coexistence method during your project. Note that while the number of translation patterns supported by a PBX can be found, they often get used in seemingly mystical ways, and the limit can be reached unexpectedly soon!

Using RCC to Integrate with Your PBX

Remote Call Control (RCC) allows you to control your PBX phone from the Lync client and thereby continue using your PBX as the voice transport while using the Lync client to provide features such as click-to-call and address lookup. RCC as a feature is available with a variety of PBX systems. This section will discuss RCC in general so you may find specific features; how they behave will depend on your specific PBX and how it is configured. To begin, let's take a look at the features that RCC provides. The user can do any of the following:

◆ Make an outgoing call.

◆ Answer an incoming call; the PBX handset will generally answer in hands-free mode.

◆ Answer an incoming call with an instant message. (This will be available only if the calling number can be matched with an IM address in the global address list (GAL) or in the receiving party's Lync contacts list.)

◆ Transfer a call.

◆ Forward an incoming call.

◆ Place a call on hold.

◆ Change the active call between concurrent calls, placing the nonactive call on hold.

◆ Answer a call while already in a call—i.e., answer a waiting call.

◆ Dial dual-tone multiple-frequency (DTMF) digits.

In addition to these features, when a call comes in, Lync will try to resolve calling numbers to names at the client using the Exchange GAL, Lync contacts list, and Outlook contacts. Entries in the Conversation History folder in Outlook for made and received calls and missed call notifications will be created if Lync is signed in when the missed call occurs.

VIDEO AND RCC

In OCS 2007 R2, there was the scenario where you could make an OCS video call but the audio portion went over the PBX voice system. With the initial release of Lync Server 2010, this was not the case. A significant amount of customer feedback encouraged Microsoft to re-introduce this functionality in a later Cumulative Update (CU).

A user enabled for RCC cannot be enabled for Lync Enterprise Voice. They will, however, be able to make and receive Lync PC-to-PC voice calls using the Lync client and join the audio content of a conference created by an enterprise voice user, assuming they have the relevant headset. An RCC-enabled user can also dial into a conference via their PBX handset.

If you're going to enable the Lync client to control the PBX handset, the RCC feature requires a SIP/CSTA gateway between Lync and the PBX. Computer Supported Telecommunications Applications (CSTA) is a standard managed by Ecma International. The SIP/CSTA gateway connects to Lync using TCP/IP and typically connects to the PBX using TCP/IP also. There are two main aspects to configuring Lync and RCC. The first is the configuration of the Lync backend, and the second is the configuration of the end user.

Configuring the Lync Infrastructure

Because of the differences in how each particular vendor's SIP/CSTA gateways are configured, this section will not cover the installation of that piece of RCC. Instead, you should refer to the documentation supplied by the relevant vendor to understand how it should be configured. Once the SIP/CSTA gateway is installed, you can progress with the Lync configuration elements.

Lync must be configured to forward CSTA requests to the SIP/CSTA gateway. Each Lync pool can have its own CSTA route, and you can configure a global static route that will be used if an individual pool has not been configured. Note that the relationship of one CSTA server per Lync pool may influence your pool design based on where your PBXs are deployed and if they are from the same vendor. For example, if you have different PBXs with their own SIP/CSTA gateways in two locations, each SIP/CSTA gateway will require its own Lync pool.

The route you create can use either TCP or TLS protocols. Note that sometimes using the TLS protocol can resolve routing and trust issues, even though the gateway has been configured as trusted within Lync. Because it is also more secure as a result, this is the preferred deployment option.

If you have migrated from Office Communications Server, you must ensure that any previously entered routes or application entries for RCC are first deleted. You can use the `Get-CsStaticRoutingConfiguration` and `Get-CsTrustedApplication` PowerShell commands without any parameters to view these settings and then use the related `Remove` cmdlets to get rid of any unneeded entries.

To create a new route, you must use the `New-CsStaticRoute` PowerShell cmdlet from within the Lync Server Management Shell. The format of the command for a TCP-based route is as follows:

```
New-CsStaticRoute –TCPRoute –Destination <gateway IP address or FQDN>
-Port <gateway SIP listening port> –MatchUri <destination domain>
```

Use the following syntax for a TLS route:

```
New-CsStaticRoute –TLSRoute –Destination <gateway FQDN>
-Port <gateway SIP listening port> -UseDefaultCertificate $true
-MatchUri <destination domain>
```

The `MatchUri` parameter supports wildcards—for example, `*.mydomain.com`—to minimize the number of routes you must add. This domain name matches the domain configured for the CSTA gateway. When adding a TLS route, you must use an FQDN as the destination, while a TCP route can use either an FQDN or an IP address. Note that if you set `UseDefaultCertificate` to False, the `TLSCertIssuer` and `TLSCertSerialNumber` parameters must be specified for the certificate you are using. These parameters set the issuing CA name and the TLS certificate serial number.

When the `New-CsStaticRoute` command is issued, the default values of the following parameters shouldn't be changed: `Enabled = True`, `MatchOnlyPhoneUri = False`, and `ReplaceHostInRequestUri = False`. These parameters allow for certain complex scenarios that are unlikely to be needed when using RCC.

Once you've created the static route, a trusted application entry must be created for RCC. This entry allows Lync to use the route that was just created. To create this entry, use the `New-Cs-TrustedApplicationPool` cmdlet.

If the static route you created uses TCP, use the following command syntax to create the trusted application entry:

```
New-CsTrustedApplicationPool
-Identity <IP address or FQDN of the SIP/CSTA gateway>
-Registrar <Service ID or FQDN of the Registrar service>
-Site <Site ID for the site where the trusted application pool is to be created>
```

Here's an example:

```
New-CsTrustedApplicationPool -Identity 192.168.0.200
-Registrar se01.corp.masteringlync.org -Site EMEA
```

Then add the trusted application to the pool using the `New-CsTrustedApplication` command:

```
New-CsTrustedApplication -ApplicationID <application name>
-TrustedApplicationPoolFqdn <IP address or FQDN of the SIP/CSTA gateway>
-Port <SIP gateway listening port> -EnableTcp
```

Here's an example:

```
New-CsTrustedApplication -ApplicationID CSTAGatewayApp
-TrustedApplicationPoolFqdn 192.168.0.200 -Port 5060 -EnableTcp
```

If the static route you created uses TLS, use the following command syntax to create the trusted application entry:

```
New-CsTrustedApplicationPool -Identity <FQDN of the SIP/CSTA gateway>
-Registrar <Service ID or FQDN of the Registrar service>
-Site <Site ID for the site where the trusted application pool is to be created>
```

Here's an example:

```
New-CsTrustedApplicationPool -Identity cstagw.corp.masteringlync.org
-Registrar se01.corp.masteringlync.org -Site EMEA
```

Then add the trusted application to the pool using the `New-CsTrustedApplication` command again:

```
New-CsTrustedApplication -ApplicationID <application name>
-TrustedApplicationPoolFqdn <FQDN of the SIP/CSTA gateway>
-Port <SIP gateway listening port>
```

Here's an example:

```
New-CsTrustedApplication -ApplicationID CSTAGatewayApp
-TrustedApplicationPoolFqdn cstagw.corp.masteringlync.org -Port 5061
```

Once the trusted application is created and added to the pool, make your changes active by publishing the topology using this command:

```
Enable-CsTopology
```

If the SIP/CSTA gateway uses TCP, its IP address must be defined in Topology Builder. This is not required if the SIP/CSTA gateway uses TLS. To complete this task, start Topology Builder and download the existing topology. Once it is downloaded, expand Trusted Application Services in the site where you are configuring RCC, right-click the application pool that you created, and choose Edit Properties. Uncheck the Enable Replication Of Configuration Data To This Pool check box. Then choose Limit Service Usage To Selected IP Address, and in the Primary IP Address text box, enter the IP address of your SIP/CSTA gateway. You must then publish these changes to the topology. To do so, click Lync Server 2010 and choose Actions and then Publish.

User Configuration

RCC can be configured using in-band provisioning policies on the server or by using client-side settings within Lync. For RCC to work, a line server URI and line URI must be specified for each user. The syntax of these settings must match the syntax expected by your SIP/CSTA gateway. Check the supplied documentation for your gateway for further information.

The domain that you specify in the line server URI must match the domain specified in the MatchURI parameter in the static route you created in "Configuring the Lync Infrastructure." The line URI specifies the phone number assigned to the user in E.164 format with a tel: prefix—for example, tel:+12121234567. If you want to add an extension number to the line URI, the format becomes tel:+12121234567;ext=4567.

To configure these settings with the Management Shell, use the Set-CsUser cmdlet as follows:

```
Set-CsUser -Identity <User ID> -EnterpriseVoiceEnabled $false
-LineServerUri <SIP URI of the SIP/CSTA gateway>
-LineUri <TEL URI of the user> -RemoteCallControlTelephonyEnabled $true
```

To configure these settings in the Lync Control Panel, take the following steps:

1. Start the Lync Control Panel and choose Users.

2. Find and select the user you want to configure using the Search tool. Choose Edit ➢ Modify and then choose the Telephony section.

3. To enable Remote Call Control of the PBX phone from Lync 2010 and to allow the user to make PC-to-PC audio calls and PC-to-phone calls, click Remote Call Control. Enter the telephone number of the user in the Line URI field, and in Line Server URI field, enter the SIP URI of the SIP/CSTA gateway.

4. If you want to enable RCC but not allow PC-to-PC calls, click Remote Call Control Only. Enter the telephone number of the user in the Line URI field, and in Line Server URI field, enter the SIP URI of the SIP/CSTA gateway.

5. When you have completed the changes, click Commit.

Phone Number Normalization

At this point, you've configured the basics of RCC and set up a user to utilize the feature. However, there is one more important area to take into account, which will dramatically affect the usefulness of RCC. That is *number normalization*, which converts numbers Lync finds in AD or user contacts into numbers that Lync and the SIP/CSTA gateway can dial.

When a network uses Remote Call Control, phone number normalization rules are applied to inbound and outbound calls. These rules are downloaded as part of the Address Book service.

When an inbound call is received for an RCC-enabled user, the calling line ID (CLID), which is the number of the person making the call, must first be normalized to E.164 format by either the PBX or the SIP/CSTA gateway. This enables Lync to perform a reverse number lookup (RNL) on the number when the call is received against the Outlook contacts list of the user receiving the call and against the GAL. If this lookup resolves a name, the name is presented within Lync rather than the calling number.

For outbound calls, the phone number normalization rules are applied before the called number is passed to the SIP/CSTA gateway.

It is generally best practice to keep all numbers within the Lync environment in E.164 format. However, reverse number lookup can rapidly become complicated, subject to the specific environment. It is sometimes necessary to configure phone normalization rules so that an alternative dial plan is maintained. This is especially true in large environments that may not have unique DDIs assigned to everyone or where routing codes are needed in conjunction with extension numbers.

ADDRESS BOOK MIGRATION

If you have previously used RCC with Office Communications Server 2007 R2 or Lync Server 2010 and you customized the phone normalization rules, you will need to perform some manual steps as part of your migration to Lync.

1. In the root of the Address Book shared folder, find the file `Company_Phone_Number_Normalization_Rules.txt`. Copy this file to the root of the Address Book shared folder for your Lync Server 2013 pool.

2. The file will need to be edited using a text editor—for example, Notepad—to change some entries that are no longer supported with Lync. Any entry containing strings that include required white space or punctuation will cause normalization rules to fail because these characters are stripped out of the string that is input to the normalization rules. If you have strings that include white space or punctuation, these must be modified.

3. In addition to normalization rules, if you set the `PartitionbyOU` WMI (OCS 2007 R2 only) property to `True` to allow address books to be created for each OU within Active Directory, you must use the `msRTCSIP-GroupingId` Active Directory attribute on users and contacts if you want to continue grouping Address Book entries—for example, to limit the scope of Address Book searches.

4. Use the `msRTCSIP-GroupingId` attribute within a script to assign a value for each common group. For example, for each user within an OU, set their `msRTCSIP-groupId` to the OU's name.

Deploying a Survivable Branch Appliance

A key feature of Lync over previous versions of OCS is the ability to deploy Remote Site Survivability so that if a WAN link back to the central Lync pool goes down, local PSTN connectivity is maintained. To implement such functionality, an appliance known as a Survivable Branch Appliance (SBA) must be deployed at the branch location.

Once the SBA is deployed, Lync users in the branch office will register to it as their primary registrar; they will have full Lync features provided by both the SBA and the main Lync Front End pool. In the event of a WAN outage, the Lync users remain registered to the local SBA and will still have full outbound and inbound calling capability via the SBA.

The SBA combines a gateway device capable of performing media bypass, security, and all the other features associated with an enhanced Lync gateway device, with an embedded server running the Lync SBA software element. The whole idea of having a third-party appliance for this role simplifies the branch deployment, and it avoids having dedicated servers and their associated IT management and maintenance, which often become a problem in small branch locations.

As with the enhanced gateway devices, a range of vendors and appliances is available for SBAs. A list can be found on the OIP page discussed earlier in the chapter.

Preparing Lync for the SBA

The process of deploying a branch site SBA device is relatively simple. First, you must prestage the SBA in the central site. This requires the following:

- A reverse lookup must be performed on the DNS server for the SBA.

- DNS *A* records must be available for the gateway and SBA.

- The SBA should be added as a computer before the deployment, and RTCUniversalSBATechnician should be in the default group as described in the following discussion.

- A service principal name needs to be applied to the SBA computer in `ADSI.edit`, as discussed shortly.

- The account used within the gateway to deploy the SBA (for example, the Administrator) should be a member of the RTCUniversalSBATechnician group.

- The SBA should be configured in the correct branch site from Lync Topology Builder and successfully published to the CMS.

To begin the configuration, make sure that DNS *A* (address) records for both the SBA and gateway IP address, resolving to their relevant FQDN, are in place.

Once the DNS records are in place, you can add the SBA into Active Directory. Make sure you do this *before* making any changes in the Lync Topology Builder.

1. Log on to a machine with the Active Directory Management Tools using an account that can create computer accounts in Active Directory.

2. Open Active Directory Users and Computers. In an organizational unit where you store computer objects, right-click and select New ➢ Computer.

3. In the window that opens, enter a name for the SBA. Note that this should be just the hostname, not the FQDN. Under User Or Group, click the Change button, enter **RTCUniversalSBATechnicians**, and then click OK. Click OK again to close.

After completing these steps, you need to add a service principal name (SPN) to the computer account; this is done using ADSI Edit.

To run ADSI Edit, take the following steps:

1. Click Start ➢ Run, enter **adsiedit.msc**, and then click OK. Once the program opens, right-click the root node and select Connect To.

2. Leave all the parameters at their defaults and click OK; then expand the default naming context.

3. Under the location where you created the computer object in step 2 of the previous list, locate the SBA computer account. Right-click it, select Properties, and then scroll down and highlight the servicePrincipalName entry. Click Edit, enter **HOST/<SBA FQDN>**, and click Add. Click OK twice to complete.

Now that you've created the computer account for the SBA in AD, you can move on to configuring the Lync topology.

1. Open Topology Builder and download the topology from the CMS.

2. Under the central site where this branch site will be linked (EMEA in this case), expand the tree and drill down to the Branch Site folder. Right-click it and select New Branch Site.

3. Enter the location of the site for the name and click Next. Enter a city and country/region, and click Next and then Finish.

4. At this stage, the Survivable Branch Appliance Wizard opens to let you configure the SBA. Enter the FQDN of the SBA (which is the host name of the computer you created plus the domain suffix) and then click Next.

5. Select the appropriate Front End pool, in this case Se01.corp.masteringlync.org, and then click Next.

6. Select the appropriate Edge server (assuming you require external connectivity for the branch users), which is edgepool.corp.masteringlync.org in this case, and then click Next.

7. On the Define New Survivable Branch Appliance window, shown in Figure 19.16, enter the FQDN of the gateway and modify the root trunk name if appropriate (by default it will follow the FQDN of the PSTN gateway). Make sure the port is set for 5067 and the transport protocol is set for TLS, and then click Finish.

8. Once it is complete, publish the topology.

If you do not have a Director in place between the SBA and Edge, you also need to allow TCP port 5061 traffic from the Edge server to the SBA (and vice versa).

Once the main Lync topology and AD changes have been made to accommodate the new branch site, you can begin working on the SBA itself. The following general steps are required:

1. Install and physically cable the SBA at the branch site.

2. Configure an IP address for the SBA.

3. Join the domain.

4. Prepare the SBA and replicate against the Front End pool.

5. Assign the required certificates to enable security.

6. Start the services.

7. Verify the operational status.

8. Start to migrate users in the branch to the SBA.

FIGURE 19.16
Configuring the
gateway FQDN and
listing port for the
SBA

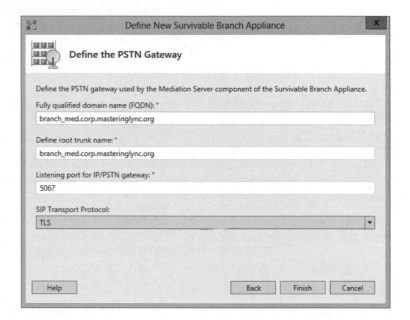

How these steps are achieved will vary from one vendor to another, and there are key differences in how the SBA and gateway integration is done by each vendor, including the security model and deployment method employed. Figure 19.17 shows the different SBA implementation methods used by different vendors. On the top, the gateway and server are hosted in the same physical chassis, but there is no communication between the elements internally. The SBA is deployed using the standard server interface, while the gateway is configured using a separate interface. On the bottom, you see a fully integrated example where the embedded server and SBA software are tightly integrated to the gateway element, with a single network interface for all traffic and a single user interface to configure the gateway and deploy the SBA. This model is highly secure and much easier to deploy in the field.

Let's review the AudioCodes SBA integration, which follows the true appliance high-security model, giving a single user interface to perform both the gateway configuration and the SBA configuration and deployment steps.

The first step is to apply an IP address and name to the SBA device so that it can communicate with the Lync Front End pool. You must ensure that there is IP connectivity from the

SBA to the Lync Front End. Next, the SBA must be joined to the domain, using the FQDN that you have already configured in the DNS server. Both of these tasks are performed on the SBA using the Deploy Survivable Branch Appliance Wizard within the main gateway GUI interface. Depending on your network configuration, you may also have to set the date and time on the SBA; this is to ensure that the security information can be correctly exchanged with the domain controllers.

FIGURE 19.17
The different SBA security models

Once the SBA has been joined to the domain (Figure 19.18), the next step is to prepare the SBA, replicate the configuration against the Front End server, and activate the SBA device against the Lync Front End. Again, ensure that there is IP connectivity between the SBA and Lync Front End for this step.

FIGURE 19.18
Joining the SBA to the domain

Figure 19.19 shows the GUI interface displaying the first of four steps to install, configure, and enable replication and activate the SBA. All four show similar screens, so we haven't shown them all.

FIGURE 19.19
Preparing the SBA using gateway management web interface

The next step is to configure the certificates required by the SBA to enable TLS secure signaling to the Front End server and Lync clients in the branch. Again the web interface makes this task a simple process; Figure 19.20 shows the screen that performs all of the certificate steps for the SBA.

FIGURE 19.20
Configuring certificates for the SBA

Once all of the preceding steps have been completed, the SBA services need to be started, and then it should be fully operational. You can easily verify the SBA processes and status from within the web interface; Figure 19.21 shows a deployed and activated SBA, with all SBA processes stopped and showing a red cross.

FIGURE 19.21
Verifying SBA system status via the web interface

You may notice that each of the services has a Start button beside it and that there's a Start All (and corresponding Stop All) button. These buttons provide the ability to start each service individually or start them all at once.

Also on this screen are the Restart Server and Shutdown Server buttons.

Connecting to Other External Systems via XMPP Federation

XMPP stands for the Extensible Messaging and Presence Protocol. Both XMPP and SIP are standards supported by the Internet Engineering Task Force (IETF). XMPP can be compared to the Session Initiation Protocol for Instant Messaging and Presence Leveraging Extensions (SIMPLE).

XMPP is used to provide presence, messaging, and collaboration features by platforms that include Cisco, Jabber, and Google. By providing the XMPP gateway, Microsoft enables interoperability with both open-source and competitors' platforms. The gateway supports presence and instant messaging only. Voice, video, and desktop or application sharing are not supported.

Previously (for OCS 2007 R2 and Lync Server 2010) the XMPP gateway software had to be downloaded from the Microsoft download site:

    www.microsoft.com/download/en/details.aspx?id=8403

There is also a single hotfix required for the XMPP gateway relating to OCS 2007 R2:

    www.microsoft.com/download/en/details.aspx?id=12722

Lync Server 2013 includes the XMPP functionality natively; it needs to be enabled on an Edge pool in Topology Builder (see Figure 19.22), and the XMPP Translating Gateway runs as a service on each Edge server as well as each Front End.

The XMPP integration can be used to connect to both external and internal services. For example, you may have a client or partner who uses Jabber or you may need to connect to GoogleTalk to extend public IM connectivity.

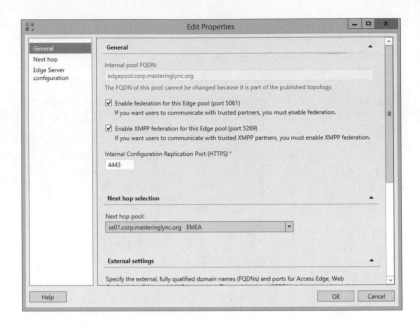

CONFIGURATION

Figure 19.22 showed how to enable XMPP in the topology; however, it still needs to be configured for your users.

For that, first you need to enable a federated partner, and then you need to create and/or enable a policy.

To set up XMPP federation with Google, select New from the XMPP Federated Partners tab in the Federation and External Access menu within Lync Control Panel to get the screen shown in Figure 19.23, and complete the relevant sections.

You can also enter the following PowerShell command:

```
New-CsXmppAllowedPartner gmail.com -TlsNegotiation NotSupported
-SaslNegotiation NotSupported -EnableKeepAlive $false
-SupportDialbackNegotiation $true
```

Information on specific supported configuration required for connecting to Google can be found here:

```
https://developers.google.com/talk/open_communications#realtime
```

Obviously, there is an assumption that federation has been enabled, or will be. Figure 19.24 shows where to enable it.

FIGURE 19.24
Enabling federation

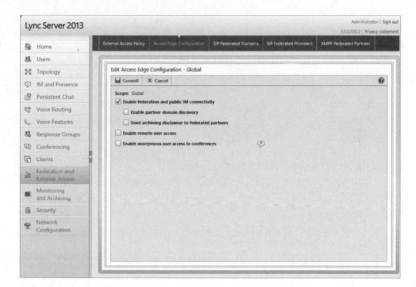

Or, again, you can use PowerShell:

```
Set-CsAccessEdgeConfiguration -AllowFederatedUsers $true
```

Finally, you need to enable the policy for users. When enabling a policy, it's not enough to specify Enable Communications With Federated Users. XMPP must be set explicitly (see Figure 19.25) and then applied to users (if the global policy is not changed).

Or, once again, you can use PowerShell:

```
New-CsExternalAccessPolicy -Identity XMPP -EnableFederationAcces $true
-EnableXMPPAccess $true
Get-CsUser | Grant-CsExternalAccessPolicy -PolicyName XMPP
```

DNS CONFIGURATION

This section assumes that you have already configured the Edge server and that external access, federation, and public IM are all working correctly as discussed in Chapter 6, "Installation." To add the XMPP gateway to your environment, you must create a DNS service record (SRV). The XMPP gateway requires a TCP service record and one for TLS if it is being used. For example, _xmpp-server._tcp.masteringlync.org and _xmpp-server._tls.masteringlync.org would work for the internal systems. These records should be created in the DNS domain that the gateway supports and for each XMPP domain, or namespace, that you want to support within your organization. For public IM purposes, these service records will be created in your public DNS along with your _sipfederationtls._tcp.masteringlync.org record for the Lync Edge.

FIGURE 19.25
Defining external access policy

Lync Edge Configuration

Any XMPP domains you want to federate with must be configured within the Lync Server Control Panel. Under Federation And External Access, choose XMPP Federated Partners and add each of the XMPP domains that you have. For each XMPP domain, the expectation is that it can be discoverable via DNS. Once you've added all your domains, click Commit to apply your changes.

User Configuration

Support for federation, XMPP, and public IM must be enabled for Lync at the forest level, and individual users must be enabled for public IM connectivity and again specifically for XMPP. Users must be enabled for public connectivity even if connecting to a system that is inside your organization, because all traffic will route via the Edge.

Lync and XMPP have different presence states, and the gateway maps these differences as shown in Table 19.1.

TABLE 19.1:   Lync and XMPP presence states

LYNC	XMPP
Available	Available
Available	Free To Chat

TABLE 19.1:   Lync and XMPP presence states   *(CONTINUED)*

LYNC	XMPP
Away	Away
Away	Extended Away
Be Right Back	Away
Busy	Do Not Disturb
Do Not Disturb	Do Not Disturb
Offline	Unavailable

Using Third-Party Software Enhancements

As mentioned at the beginning of this chapter, Lync provides an open platform on which organizations can build their own products and services to extend Lync's core functionality. There have long been add-ons for legacy PBX phone systems to provide capabilities such as call billing and call recording, and their availability for Lync reflects the maturity of the Lync platform for voice services. Of course, because it is a software platform, the ability to build products around Lync is vastly greater than that of legacy PBXs. As you will see from some of the options described next, many varied and useful offerings are available.

THIRD-PARTY SOFTWARE UPDATES

The remainder of this chapter talks about released third-party software applications integrating with or building on Lync Server 2010, not Lync Server 2013. As we are going to press so early in the release cycle with Lync Server 2013, there are not yet a wide range of specific Lync Server 2013 applications available. Some of the applications mentioned will continue to work with Lync Server 2013 as they have with Lync Server 2010; others will need updating before being compatible. Please check first with each vendor for compatibility and release information prior to committing a design!

Reusing SIP Handsets

Even in deployments where headsets are the predominant form of interface with the voice system, there will often be the need for physical handsets, and where there is a large investment in handsets, you may want to reuse them.

NET SmartSIP allows a range of phones to be reused with Lync, using SIP phone loads rather than its own proprietary protocols. It does this by acting as a proxy, or more specifically a SIP back-to-back user agent (B2BUA), allowing phones running third-party SIP stacks to sign into SmartSIP, which then registers the phone with Lync, acting as a broker between the phones and Lync SIP stacks, as shown in Figure 19.26. SmartSIP provides not only telephony support between the SIP handsets and Lync, but also presence status to Lync users to show when the SIP phone is registered/online or in a call.

FIGURE 19.26
An overview of
the SmartSIP
architecture

In this way phones from Aastra, Avaya, Cisco, Linksys, and Polycom can be reused with Lync. The SmartSIP server includes a TFPT server, which allows it to act as a central provisioning server. Phones can easily be correlated to a user by entering the MAC address of the phone handset within the user's AD record. As the phone registers to SmartSIP, it is automatically provisioned with all the necessary user information, and the user's presence is updated within Lync.

Call Recording

Two types of call recording are typically used: trunk-side and line-side. Trunk-side recording typically records all calls that include a participant from inside and outside the organization, both for inbound and outbound calls. Line-side recording allows calls between internal extensions, and also those external to the organization, to be recorded; this approach gives greater flexibility by allowing any call to be recorded.

Trunk-side recording equipment normally sits between the PBX and the carrier's customer premises equipment. This equipment can continue to be used with your Lync gateway. Note, however, that external calls may also exit the organization over a federated connection via the Lync Edge server role and that they may still need to be recorded subject to your organization's regulatory and compliance needs.

If you need to record line-side while using Enterprise Voice, then a third-party application is required. Using Lync APIs, the recording applications either will monitor the call or will add a call recording agent to the call, turning it into a conference, and will then record the call as shown in Figure 19.27, using the Geomant recording application. This screen shot is from an OCS client, but you can clearly see the recording server user, which would be the same approach used in Lync.

If line-side recording is used a lot in your organization, you need to reflect the increased use of audio conferencing in your capacity planning.

From the discovery perspective—in other words, the investigation of who called who, when, and/or the content—Actiance provide a very capable solution called Vantage. Figure 19.28 shows the call summary information, and Figure 19.29 provides the interaction screen, where the content of the call can be played back.

FIGURE 19.27
Conversation with recording server participant

FIGURE 19.28
Actiance Vantage call interaction record

FIGURE 19.29
Actiance Vantage call recording playback

Call Center

Lync includes basic call distribution and Response Group services, but they are not intended to provide a complete call or contact center solution. However, the APIs within the Lync platform allow independent software vendors to create full-featured contact center solutions.

Typical contact center products allow agents to have multiple subject skills and ratings. This can also reflect which languages an agent speaks. A contact center typically has to support a matrix of competencies, language expertise, and call routing rules; the latter can include timers to decide how long a call waits before being routed to a lower-skilled agent.

Contact or call center products are deeply integrated with business processes and often have links with line-of-business applications to prepopulate information to an agent's screen.

Call center software is its own specialty, often sitting alongside a PBX running, effectively, as its PBX for the agents. Microsoft, by providing the APIs to Lync that software developers require, enables call center software to be developed with all the UC functionality of Lync while also including call-center-specific functionality.

Geomant Contact Expert is one of many call center products available for Lync. When selecting your Lync call center platform, be aware of how the product performs call control. Some applications use Lync for all call control functionality, such as connections to the PSTN and signaling to make or receive a call. Others have their own call control and integrate with Lync presence separately.

Products that use Lync for call control are generally preferred because this reduces complexity and cost, but there can be scenarios where the call center product may need to have its own call control. For example, you might need to provide call center functionality to agents, some of whom use Enterprise Voice while others use the PBX. As always, plan carefully and understand both the likely and worst-case scenarios for where call signaling and media traffic will route, paying attention to any circular routing or tromboning.

Call Billing

Call billing is a traditional PBX requirement. It provides for call costs to be calculated and then billed to internal departments. It also allows you to monitor costs and take action where required. For example, if a particular extension has very high usage, that may imply excessive personal calls or out-of-business-hours calls.

With Lync and unified communications, the environment you need to monitor includes more ways to communicate, including instant messaging and conferencing. In addition to calls to the public network, you may want to monitor usage of the entire unified communications environment. This can help show return on investment by reduced travel or call spend and also allow you to calculate reduced carbon footprint.

PhonEX ONE from MindCTI is an example of a call-billing platform that has been updated to reflect unified communications. It collects the raw information provided by the Lync Monitoring server role and creates easy-to-understand graphical reports of usage.

Figure 19.30 shows a sample report detailing outbound calls by carrier in the top-left panel, number of calls by device type in the top-right panel, and usage of different roles during the day across the bottom.

Used with thought, these reports can help you plan the server hardware capacity and link capacity as you deploy. PhonEX ONE can also connect to your existing PBX, giving you a single view of usage during your migration from a telephony platform to Lync unified communications.

FIGURE 19.30
The MindCTI PhonEX ONE system dashboard

Combining Presence with Location

You already have the option in the Lync client to show your location based on network mapping or an entered location. This is, however, fairly static information and is used either as information within the interface, like a status update, or for enhanced emergency services requirements such as E.911 in North America, as discussed in Chapter 15, "E911 and Location Information Services."

What if you were able to make your location real time and updated with GPS or mobile network location triangulation and integrate that with your availability? This would allow you to tightly integrate availability and location for field-based services, which would be useful to a wide range of organizations, from those concerned with public safety, such as the police, to those with traveling sales staff.

Geomant Presence Suite provides such an extension, as shown in Figure 19.31, where you can see where people are across the city and their current availability.

This information can be used by agents to make job allocation decisions or it can be extended further. For example, you could extend this for lone-worker protection, so if a field-based employee didn't change their status after the expected appointment duration they could be contacted by phone using Lync to verify that they are safe and well.

Presence Suite is a great example of how Lync provides out-of-the box functionality that can then be extended to deliver significant added value using published APIs and development tools.

FIGURE 19.31
Geomant Presence
Suite client

The Bottom Line

Connect to telephony systems using a gateway. Gateway devices enable Lync to connect to a wide range of different telephony platforms in a uniform way, providing intelligent routing and security.

Master It When connecting to telephony systems, three main components come into play. What are they?

Integrate with your PBX. Connecting Lync to telephony systems need not be hard; however, there are many areas you must consider to ensure that you make the correct deployment choices. Lync can connect directly to an ITSP or a PBX or in both cases can utilize a gateway device to provide security, control, and intelligent routing of traffic.

Master It Your PBX is five years old and capable of being upgraded to talk to Lync directly. You want to deploy Lync for Enterprise Voice and need a way out to the PSTN. What must you consider in your decision about connecting Lync to the PSTN?

Use RCC to integrate with your PBX. Remote Call Control (RCC) allows you to use the Lync software client on your PC to control your physical phone handset from PBX vendors like Cisco, Mitel, and Avaya. It allows you to maintain your PBX as the audio transport mechanism while enhancing the functionality of the PBX with click-to-call and Address Book lookup features of the Lync software client. Each vendor has a slightly different way of hooking up Lync with its PBX because they each provide the SIP/CSTA gateway that allows communication.

Master It You have been asked to look into why your company might use RCC. What are the key points about which you would report?

Deploy a Survivable Branch Appliance. The Lync SBA is one of the great additions that make Lync a fully viable voice platform for the enterprise. It provides the capability for branch offices to maintain the ability for PSTN breakout even if the WAN to the central Lync site is down.

Master It You have been asked to roll out an SBA to a branch location. What are the main prerequisite and deployment steps to which you should adhere?

Connect to other external systems via an XMPP gateway. The XMPP gateway is now integral to Lync Server 2013 and gives you the capability to connect Lync to other IM platforms, both internally (in the case of an internal Jabber or Sametime system) or externally to public clouds like Gmail. It is deployed on a separate server and interacts with Lync through the Edge server.

Master It You need to install and configure the XMPP gateway. What do you need to do?

Utilize third-party software enhancements. As a software UC platform, Lync is infinitely extendable. This gives rise to the possibility for third-party developers to create products that enhance the native functionality in key ways, such as call recording and call billing. Equally, it enables in-house development teams to incorporate Lync communications functionality directly into line-of-business apps in your organization.

Master It Call recording is one of the available add-on applications for Lync. Name the two locations where call recording can be carried out and describe the difference this makes to the types of calls that can be recorded.

Part VI

Mobile Devices

Chapter 20

Mobility

Mobility has very much been a buzzword in the last few years, especially since the launch of the iPhone and the various "app" stores that have the ability to make your mobile phone be so much more than just a phone device.

The early days had texting; then the next big development was the BlackBerry, providing very usable email on the go. Then came the iPhone, and finally we're seeing tablets. With tablets, the first to have mass uptake in the consumer market was Apple with the iPad. The iPad was then joined by the Android versions and more recently Windows 8. In between, we had variations and attempts to add additional functionality to each device with varying degrees of success.

The past few iterations of Lync (and OCS) have seen a similar development cycle of initial release through adding more and more capability across more and more platforms.

The focus was obviously on the Microsoft platforms initially, with wider development on later releases of Lync on the more popular platforms (Android and iOS). BlackBerry has a history of developing its own Lync (and OCS) clients, typically leveraging the BlackBerry Enterprise Server (BES).

We're going to focus first on the mobile phone clients and then on the tablet clients. The Windows 8 Store App client (for use whilst using the Windows 8 Modern UI) was covered in Chapter 4, "Clients."

In this chapter, you will learn to:

- ◆ Understand the different capabilities of each mobile client (including tablets)
- ◆ Understand the policies available to manage mobile clients
- ◆ Understand the infrastructure configuration required for enabling mobile devices

Mobile Client Capability

Lync Server 2013 has the ability to connect mobile clients across the following mobile platforms:

- ◆ iOS (iPhone and iPad)
- ◆ Android
- ◆ Windows Phone

The Lync 2010 mobile client is used to connect to these platforms. (In addition, the Nokia Symbian platform also had a Lync 2010 client; however, this wasn't actively stated as supported when using Lync Server 2013 as the infrastructure.)

Table 20.1 summarizes the features available for each mobile device when using the relevant client.

TABLE 20.1:   Feature summary per mobile device for Lync 2010 mobile clients

FEATURE	WINDOWS PHONE 7.5	NOKIA SYMBIAN	IPHONE (IOS 4)	IPAD (IOS 4)	ANDROID 2.3+
Instant messaging	Yes	Yes	Yes	Yes	Yes
Presence colors and status	Yes	Yes	Yes	Yes	Yes
Photos	Yes	Yes	Yes	Yes	Yes
View Lync contacts list	Yes	Yes	Yes	Yes	Yes
Search corporate directory	Yes	Yes	Yes	Yes	Yes
View contact card	Yes	Yes	Yes	Yes	Yes
Multiparty IM	Yes	Yes	Yes	Yes	Yes
Distribution list expansion	Yes	Yes	Yes	Yes	Yes
Send Bing map location data via IM	No	No	Yes	Yes	No
Contact management	No	Yes	No	No	No
Join conference	Yes	Yes	Yes	Yes	Yes
Conference callback	Yes	Yes	Yes	Yes	Yes
Conference calendar information	Yes	Yes	No	No	No
URL-based join	No	No	No	No	Yes
Meeting pane join	No	No	Yes	Yes	No
Single-number reach	Yes	Yes	Yes	No	Yes

TABLE 20.1: Feature summary per mobile device for Lync 2010 mobile clients *(CONTINUED)*

FEATURE	WINDOWS PHONE 7.5	NOKIA SYMBIAN	IPHONE (IOS 4)	IPAD (IOS 4)	ANDROID 2.3+
Dial pad	Yes	Yes	Yes	No	Yes
Call from contact card	Yes	Yes	Yes	No	Yes
Call from conversation window	Yes	Yes	Yes	No	Yes
Call via work	Yes	Yes	Yes	No	Yes
Call forwarding control	Yes	Yes	Yes	Yes	Yes
Visual voicemail	No	No	Yes	Yes	No

The Lync Conference in San Diego (February 2013) saw the launch of the latest mobile clients, this time specifically targeted for Lync Server 2013. These clients require Lync Server 2013 Cumulative Update (CU) 1 to be installed on the servers. You can find the latest Lync Server 2013 update here:

```
www.microsoft.com/en-us/download/details.aspx?id=36820
```

This time there is no client for Nokia Symbian.

Table 20.2, Table 20.3, and Table 20.4 show the feature set comparison between versions for the new client broken down by major feature. We've included the Windows 8 Modern UI client for a comparison.

We don't have a direct comparison available for Table 20.1, and because the clients are not "live" at the time of going to press, we can't provide a direct test feedback, unfortunately. Upon release, more complete comparison data will be available here:

```
http://technet.microsoft.com/en-us/library/hh691004.aspx
```

TABLE 20.2: Feature summary for presence and IM using the Lync 2013 mobile client

FEATURE	WINDOWS 8 MODERN UI	WINDOWS PHONE	ANDROID	IPHONE	IPAD
Lync and Lync Online connectivity	Yes	Yes	Yes	Yes	Yes
New UI	Yes	Yes	Yes	Yes	Yes
Presence colors and status	Yes	Yes	Yes	Yes	Yes

TABLE 20.2: Feature summary for presence and IM using the Lync 2013 mobile client *(CONTINUED)*

FEATURE	WINDOWS 8 MODERN UI	WINDOWS PHONE	ANDROID	iPHONE	iPAD
Photos	Yes	Yes	Yes	Yes	Yes
View Lync contacts list	Yes	Yes	Yes	Yes	Yes
View contact card	Yes	Yes	Yes	Yes	Yes
Multiparty IM	Yes	Yes	Yes	Yes	Yes
Distribution list expansion	Yes	Yes	Yes	Yes	Yes

TABLE 20.3: Feature summary for Lync Meetings using the Lync 2013 mobile client

FEATURE	WINDOWS 8 MODERN UI	WINDOWS PHONE	ANDROID	iPHONE	iPAD
Join Lync Meetings with a single touch	Yes	Yes	Yes	Yes	Yes
Voice and Video over IP (3g/4g/Wi-Fi)	Yes	Yes	Yes	Yes	Yes
Multi-party video	Yes	No	No	No	Yes
View shared Lync Meeting content	Yes	No	No	No	Yes

TABLE 20.4: Feature summary for Enterprise Voice using the Lync 2013 mobile client

FEATURE	WINDOWS 8 MODERN UI	WINDOWS PHONE	ANDROID	iPHONE	iPAD
Single-number reach	Yes	Yes	Yes	Yes	Yes
Voice and Video over IP (3g/4g/Wi-Fi)	Yes	Yes	Yes	Yes	Yes
Call via Work	No	Yes	Yes	Yes	No

At this point, we expect a lot of readers to be surprised (and quite possibly excited) at the Voice and Video over IP (3g/4g/Wi-Fi) row in both Table 20.3 and Table 20.4. This can cause confusion because on first read it may lead you to believe that the Lync client can hand off calls from a Wi-Fi network to a mobile operator network (for example, if you walk from your office, connected to Wi-Fi, and go outside where there is no Wi-Fi signal); however, this is *not* a capability provided by the client today.

The client will provide voice and/or video over the network on which the call is initiated. If the call begins on Wi-Fi and the Wi-Fi signal is lost, then the call is dropped. Equally, if the call begins on a mobile operator network and a Wi-Fi signal is received, the call will continue on the mobile network. We hope this "handover" functionality will come in a future release!

As mentioned previously, Lync Server 2013 has significantly improved the high-availability capabilities across the majority of features. Mobile clients are now included in that list. Previous versions of the mobile Lync (and OCS) client were unable to reconnect to other servers if the server to which they had logged in with was unavailable. Now it's seamless to the user. If the expected server is unavailable, the Lync 2013 mobile client will try another and then another until the client can connect.

The clients now also include support for the high resolution (HD) photo that is stored in the Exchange mailbox of the user. As with the traditional clients, if this is unavailable, the photo will be taken from SharePoint or Active Directory, but these will be lower-definition photos.

Table 20.5 shows the connection experience depending on which client/server combination is used.

TABLE 20.5: Client/server interoperability

CLIENT	LYNC SERVER 2010 WITH MOBILITY SERVICES	LYNC SERVER 2013 RTM	LYNC SERVER 2013 CU1, MOBILITY ENABLED	LYNC SERVER 2013 CU1, MOBILITY DISABLED
Lync 2010	Yes	Yes	Yes, prompt to upgrade to Lync 2013	Error, not configured for Lync 2013
Lync 2013	Error, please install Lync 2010 mobile client	Error, please install Lync 2010 mobile client	Yes	Error, not configured for Lync 2013

Table 20.6 shows the version requirements for the OS on each device.

TABLE 20.6: Mobile device OS version requirements for running Lync 2013

CLIENT	MINIMUM OS VERSION
Microsoft Lync 2013 for Windows Phone	Windows Phone 8
Microsoft Lync 2013 for iPad	iOS 6.0 or later
Microsoft Lync 2013 for iPhone	iOS 6.0 or later
Microsoft Lync 2013 for Android	Android 4.0 or later (phone only, not tablet devices)

Enough talk about what the client can do; we'll now show what the mobile client looks like on Windows Phone and Apple iOS (unfortunately, Android screen shots were unavailable at press time).

Figure 20.1 shows the account setup screen, Figure 20.2 shows the 'My Info' screen, Figure 20.3 shows the contacts screen, Figure 20.4 shows the incoming call screen, Figure 20.5 shows the IM conversation screen, and Figure 20.6 shows the video screen.

FIGURE 20.1
Account setup screen

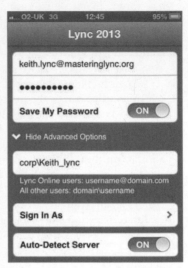

FIGURE 20.2
My Info screen

Figure 20.3
Contacts screen

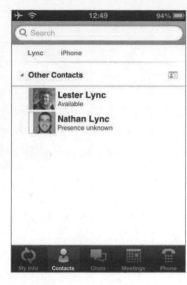

Figure 20.4
Incoming Call
screen

FIGURE 20.5
IM conversation
screen

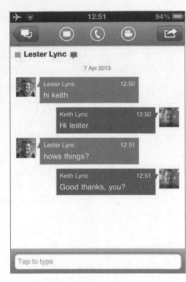

FIGURE 20.6
Video calling screen

As you can see from the screenshots, the user experience on each device is very similar—this ensures a consistent look and feel from one device to the next. Users do not need to be retrained if their device is changed.

Managing Mobile Clients

Configuring mobility for Lync Server 2013 requires configuration of the backend server capability as well as the mobility policy for users. You'll see how to deploy and configure the server later in this chapter; here we'll focus on the user policy capability.

The cmdlets to define and manage the mobility policy are as follows:

◆ New-CsMobilityPolicy

◆ Set-CsMobilityPolicy

◆ Grant-CsMobilityPolicy

◆ Remove-CsMobilityPolicy

These cmdlets are available prior to the installation on Lync Server 2013 CU1, although they have been updated for CU1.

Prior to CU1, the New-CsMobilityPolicy cmdlet had the following parameters:

◆ Identity: Used to provide a unique name for the policy.

◆ Description: Allows provision of administrative text describing the policy.

◆ EnableIPAudioVideo*: When False, prevents any use of IP for voice and video calling; any calls will be forced through the mobile network operator.

◆ EnableMobility: Must be set to True to allow users to connect using mobile devices.

◆ EnableOutSideVoice: When set to True, allows users to use Call via Work functionality.

◆ RequireWIFIForIPAudio*: When set to True, allows users to place audio calls via the Wi-Fi network rather than via the mobile operator network.

◆ RequireWIFIForIPVideo*: When set to True, allows users to place video calls via the Wi-Fi network when available rather than via the mobile operator network.

Although the cmdlet had all these parameters prior to installing CU1 being installed, those parameters labeled * have no effect until Lync Server 2013 clients can connect; this functionality is available only with the CU1 update.

Here's an example command that defines a mobility policy:

```
New-CsMobilityPolicy -Identity "WiFi Voice Enabled" -EnableMobility $True
-EnableIPAudioVideo $True -RequireWIFIForIPAudio $True
-RequireWIFIForIPVideo $False
```

This would define a policy named WiFi Voice Enabled, which would allow users to use the Wi-Fi network for voice calls but not for video calling.

Once the policy is created, it must be granted, using the Grant-CsMobilityPolicy cmdlet:

```
Grant-CsMobilityPolicy -Identity "sip:keith.lync@masteringlync.org"
-PolicyName "WiFi Voice Enabled"
```

Now, the user will be able to log in and will have the policy applied, be unable to place video calls, but be able to place audio calls when connected via Wi-Fi.

Figure 20.7 shows the Mobility Policy tab in the Control Panel.

FIGURE 20.7
Configuring a
mobility policy in
Control Panel

Users can configure the following properties on their own devices:

◆ Require Wi-Fi for Voice

◆ Require Wi-Fi for Video

◆ Require Wi-Fi for sharing (iPad only)

◆ Push notifications on/off for VoIP and IM (Windows Phone only)

◆ Phonebook access on/off

◆ Photos on/off

◆ Define Outside Voice mobile number

◆ Accessibility - TTY on/off

Deploying and Configuring Mobility on Lync Server 2013

The tools used in Chapter 5, "Planning Your Deployment," include consideration for mobility clients, so assuming that you completed the questionnaire sections correctly when planning, your server specifications and numbers will be able to cope with the additional load incurred by hosting mobile clients.

If not, we advise you to revisit the planning tools shown in Chapter 5 and adjust the server counts and/or specifications as advised. Incorrectly specified environments are likely to introduce bottlenecks, ultimately appearing as a poor experience to end users. In a lot of cases, the bottlenecks introduced will be felt by all users, not just on the underspecified client types. It's always worth bearing this in mind if you start to experience issues; see Chapter 12, "Troubleshooting," for more information.

Deploying the Update

As previously mentioned, Lync Server 2013 will work from the RTM version with the older Lync 2010 mobile clients. However, to enable the more feature-rich capability introduced with the Lync 2013 mobile clients, you need to install CU1.

Like any Lync Server update, CU1 can be downloaded as a series of nine individual files or a single cumulative file (called LyncServerUpdateInstaller.exe). Figure 20.8 shows LyncServerUpdateInstaller.exe being run on a server prior to being updated; if we ran it again after the update was complete, we'd see green tick marks rather than the red cross marks.

FIGURE 20.8
LyncServerUpdate
Installer.exe

KB #	Description	Update Version	Installed Version	Latest Installed?
2781550	Update for Core Components	5.0.8308.291	5.0.8308.0	✕
2781555	Update for Core Runtime 64-bit	5.0.8308.291	5.0.8308.0	✕
2781549	Update for Call Park Service	5.0.8308.291	5.0.8308.0	✕
2787570	Update for Web Conferencing Server	5.0.8308.291	5.0.8308.0	✕
2796554	Update for Mediation Server	5.0.8308.291	5.0.8308.0	✕
2781551	Update for Conferencing Server	5.0.8308.291	5.0.8308.0	✕
2781547	Update for Lync Server 2013	5.0.8308.291	5.0.8308.0	✕
2781564	Update for Web Components Server	5.0.8308.291	5.0.8308.0	✕

UPDATING LYNC SERVER

Personally, we don't see any benefit in downloading and applying individual files. The single-file installer will detect the current version of each file and apply any updates needed, saving any administrative overhead of detecting and applying only specific files.

Once CU1 is installed, the server will need to be updated before the database updates can be carried out. It's important to note that Lync will not start until the databases are updated. Not all CUs will require a database update.

For a Standard Edition server, this command is straightforward:

```
Install-CsDatabase -ConfiguredDatabases -SqlServerFqdn
<standard edition server fqdn>
```

Enterprise Edition servers will be more complicated because both the Front End and the Back End databases need to be updated, and any SQL mirroring configuration will need to be stopped and removed prior to updating and reconfigured once the databases are completely updated.

We're not going to repeat all the commands required here for every variation of Enterprise Edition configuration. Fortunately, these will always be included with the release notes for the CU, located here:

```
http://support.microsoft.com/kb/2809243
```

Once the main databases have been updated, the Central Management Store (CMS) database then needs to be updated, using the following command:

```
Install-CsDatabase -CentralManagementDatabase
-SqlServerFqdn <server FQDN where the cms is hosted>
-SqlInstance <instance name of SQL hosting the cms>
```

Once the update is deployed, the next steps are to configure the infrastructure to support mobility. (It will need to be deployed on all servers interacting with mobile-enabled users. It's recommended practice to update all servers in your environment to the same level.)

Configuring for Mobile Access

For any Enterprise Edition deployments, the load balancer (hardware or software) should be configured to *not* use cookie persistence because this was used for the legacy mobile clients (Lync 2010), and for high availability to work correctly, this feature must be disabled on the load balancers.

Chapter 4 introduced the `Autodiscover` service concept, used by clients to automatically determine the correct connectivity points to access the Lync infrastructure. This was first introduced with the mobility service in Lync Server 2010. It should not be confused with the Exchange Autodiscover capability used by Outlook.

Lync clients will look for one of two DNS records:

LyncDiscover.<sipdomain>

LyncDiscoverInternal.<sipdomain>

These records can be either A records (pointing to IP addresses) or CNAME records (pointing to other FQDNs).

When a client connects to one of these records (they ultimately resolve to web locations on a Front End pool), the data returned will provide all the web service URLs required for the user's home pool.

Once the data is received, the mobile client parses it to determine the mobility server URL and will then connect via that location.

INTERNAL VS. EXTERNAL MOBILITY CONNECTIONS

The mobile client will use `LyncDiscover` for external connectivity and `LyncDiscoverInternal` for internal (on the corporate network) connectivity; however, both of these will resolve to the external web services FQDN, ultimately through the external reverse proxy.

The point behind this is to ensure that clients are not disconnected when moving from the Wi-Fi network to the external mobile operator network. If a client were to switch between the internal and external web services, they would be forced to disconnect and log in again, losing the cached data connection.

Configuring the Autodiscover service DNS entries and the reverse proxy to ensure that the traffic is forwarded to the pools (and Directors if deployed) allows your mobile clients to connect, log in, and initiate communications. What about for communications initiated by someone else and terminating on your mobile device? Well, the answer to this is the push notification service or, for Android devices, the P-Get event channel (no configuration required!).

Configuring the push notification service requires a command run with a parameter for the Apple push notification service as well as one for the Microsoft push notification service. Enabling this capability allows users to receive incoming content such as IMs or invitations to conferences.

This is simply the following:

```
New-CsPushNotificationConfiguration
```

And the parameters are as follows:

```
-EnableApplePushNotificationService
```

```
-EnableMicrosoftPushNotificationService
```

Each of these can be to `True` to enable or `False` to disable. This cmdlet can be scoped to sites, allowing for different policies to apply to users in different locations if required. Configuration is required to allow push notifications to work. First, configure a new hosting provider (the target for the notification):

```
New-CsHostingProvider -Identity "LyncOnline" -Enabled $True
-ProxyFqdn "sipfed.online.lync.com"
-VerificationLevel UseSourceVerification
```

Next, allow federation to the push service:

```
New-CsAllowedDomain -Identity "push.lync.com"
```

Now notifications will leave the environment to the hosted service, which will then in turn forward them to the mobile devices as required. The Lync Online service is responsible for forwarding notifications to the Apple push notification service.

APPLE PUSH NOTIFICATIONS

The iOS devices (iPad and iPhone) do not require the Apple push notification service parameters to be configured in a pure Lync 2013 mobile client infrastructure. The push notification cmdlets and configuration is used for backward compatibility with the Lync 2010 mobile clients.

Windows Phone 8 devices do require the Microsoft push notification service to be configured for both Lync 2010 and Lync 2013 mobile clients.

Confirming the Mobility Service

Once you've followed all the steps to this point, you can use the following test cmdlets to test and confirm the installation and configuration.

- ◆ Test-CsMcxConference

- ◆ Test-CsMcxIM

- ◆ Test-CsMcxPushNotification

Chapter 12 covers the use of the Test-Cs cmdlets in detail; however, these three are specifically used to test the mobility feature set, as their names suggest: conference capability, IM, and the push notification service.

How Does Mobility Work?

The mobility clients have a set of unique call flow scenarios, not only through the push notification service but also in terms of discovery. Here we'll cover each of the flows in detail.

Let's start with connectivity; Figure 20.9 shows the process for discovery and then connectivity. We've included both internal and external clients because only the initial steps have a different approach.

FIGURE 20.9
Mobile client connectivity call flow

Here are the steps:

1. The client carries out a DNS query for `LyncDiscover.<sipdomain>` as well as `LyncDisco verInternal.<sipdomain>`.

2. The IP address of the mobility web services is returned. This is resolved to the external address of the reverse proxy.

3. The reverse proxy translates the request to the mobility web service on a pool (or Director). This is the mobility service (MCX) running on the "external" website.

4. The response to this initial request will include all the web service URLs for the user; these will be specific to their home pool.

5. The client will make another request to the specific mobility service URL provided.

6. The reverse proxy translates the request to the specific mobility web service on the user home pool. This is the mobility service (MCX) running on the "external" website.

In a hybrid scenario (both on-premises and in-cloud deployment), the addresses returned in step 4 will be for the online service.

FIGURE 20.10
Push notifications

Now, let's take a look at how push notifications work (see Figure 20.10):

1. The user (the callee) is logged in using the process listed earlier (not shown).

2. The caller places a call, which is sent to the registered endpoints for the recipient.

3. The recipient's home pool will forward the request to the push notification service, via the Edge (using federation).

4. The Lync Online push notification service will send a push message to the device, using the Microsoft push notification service.

5. The Microsoft push notification service will forward the message to the device, the device will display the incoming call details, and the user will accept the call.

6. Signaling information is relayed via the reverse proxy to the user's home pool as determined during the discovery process and on to the caller.

7. Call is connected; details of how will be down to the specific policy and device capability at the minute (Wi-Fi enabled/allowed/preferred, and so on).

Step 7 raises an interesting point. What if the user has configured a preference to require Wi-Fi for VoIP calls?

Well, in this case, the call routing information is actually contained within the message via step 6. The pool will determine that a "failback to PSTN" is required, and the call will proceed as if it were a PSTN call. This assumes the caller is permitted to make PSTN calls to mobile devices, of course.

Specifically, How Does Presence Work?

Traditionally, presence on devices was an up-to-date view of the status of a user. If the user logged into a mobile device and navigated to another app on the device, then presence may or may not be accurate. Especially with the older phones that had only a single channel for data and voice, there were easily reproducible situations where the mobile client was showing as available but the user was actually on a call, simply because the device could not send a data packet to update the status since the channel was being used for voice.

Current devices don't have this particular problem. Multiple apps are common and so is the scenario where the user in logged in on the mobile device but then stays logged in when the device is put into a pocket or bag.

FIGURE 20.11
Mobile presence
with Lync 2010

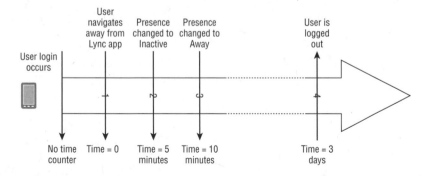

Figure 20.11 walks you through the scenario of how this is dealt with within the Lync 2010 app:

1. The user logs in as described previously, then navigates away from the Lync 2010 app.

2. After 5 minutes, the Lync 2010 app will change the presence state to Inactive.

3. After a further 5 minutes, the Lync 2010 app will change the status to Away.

4. After 3 days of inactivity on the Lync 2010 app, the user is logged out.

Here we are covering only the mobile client app; obviously if the user is signed in on other devices, the presence is aggregated and the most recent presence is provided to other users. If at the end of the three-day period only the mobile device is registering presence, then when the user is logged out, the presence will show as Offline.

At this point, if you get another user trying to place a call to your mobile user, they will receive a User Unavailable message and not be able to place the call. So, what changes with Lync 2013, and why do you have a better experience? Figure 20.12 walks you through this scenario. Steps 1 through 3 are the same, with one subtle difference; when we sign in, a static registration is created.

FIGURE 20.12
Mobile presence with Lync 2013

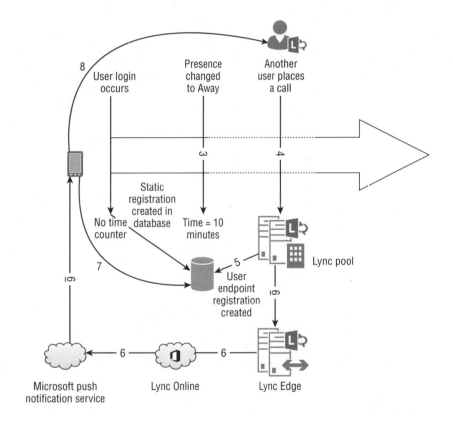

Here are the steps:

1–3. The user signs in as with Lync 2010 client, except this time a static registration is created; this static registration is valid for 15 days.

4. At some point before the 15 days expiry, another user tries to call.

5. This time the call gets "forwarded" to the static registration. The Lync Server 2013 pool understands this is for a mobile device and creates a user endpoint registration for the device; at this point, you won't know the IP address, but push notification will work.

6. A push notification is sent to wake up the device and notify it of the incoming call.

7. During the "wake-up" process, the user endpoint is updated with the connectivity information.

8. The call will connect as expected.

With Lync 2013, you can see immediately that the experience will be a lot better, both for the caller and for the callee, because presence is available for longer as well as the ability to wake up the device and get the call notification received for the caller to accept (or not!).

The Bottom Line

Understand the different capabilities of each mobile client (including tablets).   Lync Server 2013 released with the capability to allow Lync 2010 mobile client connectivity. However, since the release of CU1 in February 2013, Lync 2013 mobile clients are natively available and are able to bring new mobility features to the environment.

Master It   What capabilities are not available on phone devices but are available on the Windows 8 Modern UI and iPad?

Understand the policies available to manage mobile clients.   With another client available to connect to Lync Server 2013, it's important for the administrator to be able to manage the feature capabilities as well as they would do with any other device client.

Master It   Name the three settings new to the Lync 2013 mobile client, which can be managed via the `*-CsMobilityPolicy` cmdlets.

Understand the infrastructure configuration required for enabling mobile devices.   Not only is an update (CU1) required, but specific additional configuration is needed to enable the mobility clients, and of course, consideration must be given to the specification of the hardware (and number) servers needed. Capacity planning for mobility is built into the capacity planning tools, but the configuration still requires the administrator to take a hand!

Master It   What is required to configure push notifications for Apple iOS and Microsoft Windows Phone devices?

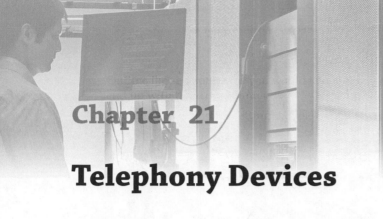

Chapter 21

Telephony Devices

Lync is a software platform, and without hardware devices to bring it alive, communications wouldn't be the same. Voice would be limited to tiny devices built in to desktop and laptop PCs, and video would be restricted to those web cams that are now standard parts of any laptop.

However, there is a massive devices business from which Lync reaps huge rewards. The list of devices includes USB-connected devices (such as headsets and handsets), stand-alone IP phone devices, and devices that provide full-room immersive video experiences.

Many devices are capable of providing audio (and also video); however, for this chapter we will be covering only devices that are certified for use with Lync. These devices are tested and proven to give a high level of audio (and video) quality of experience when used with Lync. See http://technet.microsoft.com/en-us/lync/gg236602 for information on the Open Interoperability Program (OIP) certification of devices.

There are multiple usage scenarios in which these devices can be used, and we'll take a look at them here.

In this chapter, you will learn to:

◆ Understand the range of devices available

◆ Understand how to choose which device suits which purpose

◆ Configure a network environment for IP phone devices

USB Devices

There are so many types of device and connectivity methods it's hard to truly categorize them, but we've tried! First up are USB devices, which are typically headset or handset-style devices. They are "dumb" in the sense they simply plug into a PC (or Mac) and are recognized by the operating system (OS), which in turn presents them to Lync as a "communications device." Figure 21.1 shows a number of connected devices. Note that the final device is shown as a "default communications device," which means that any Lync sounds will be directed though it.

FIGURE 21.1
Sound devices
in the operating
system

It's also worth highlighting here that the default device (in this case speakers, Conexant 20672 SmartAudio HD) will play normal OS sounds such as music, audio from applications or websites, OS alerts and so on, and Lync is smart enough to reduce these sounds when a call is in progress. Figure 21.2 shows the configuration settings available to control audio devices in Lync. The Secondary Ringer option is extremely useful because users aren't always wearing their headset when a call comes in. This allows another device to play the ringing alert.

You might ask yourself, "Why don't I just use the built-in 3.5-mm jacks for headphones and microphones rather than a USB device?" Well, aside from the USB devices being tested and qualified for Lync, the built-in jacks are classed as system devices (or "default devices"), so they will play the default operating systems (OS) alerts, prompts, and so on, potentially disrupting your conversations. USB devices will be classed as communications devices, and the OS allows for a default device setting as well as a default communications device setting.

Headsets

Probably the most obvious device type with a USB connection is a headset. These typically fall into one of the following categories:

◆ Wired

◆ Bluetooth

◆ Digital Enhanced Cordless Technology (DECT)

Each of these types will have USB connectivity of some sort; even the "wireless" ones will have a USB dongle. The reason for this is primarily that the Bluetooth stack within the OS is not certified as part of the Lync OIP; therefore, a device using this connectivity method would not itself be certified, ultimately meaning that vendors have to provide their own (certified) implementation of Bluetooth for their devices.

Headsets will typically offer a range of sound enhancement features:

◆ Automatic gain control

◆ Echo cancellation

◆ Noise canceling

A point often forgotten when specifying devices is that wireless devices need charging. This is the main reason one of the authors continues to carry a wired device in his laptop bag; he is rather forgetful when it comes to charging devices!

FIGURE 21.2
Lync audio device options

WIRED

Wired headsets are typically going to be used by users who are at a fixed desk type of location. They are not going to be moving much, and the USB connection can simply be flexible in their localized environment. Wired headsets are the cheapest of the three types available; there's no additional technology required to make them work.

Multiple variations and styles of headsets are available (indeed, some headsets are flexible enough to offer all three in the same package!):

◆ Over the head

◆ In, on, or behind ear

◆ Around the neck

In addition to these form factors, they will have variations on the number of "ears" covered: monaural (one ear) or binaural (two ear).

Figure 21.3 shows the Sennheiser SC30 USB ML, also available as a binaural device (SC60). On the cable itself is a control unit allowing for some noncomputer controls such as the following:

◆ Answer/end call

◆ Volume up/down

◆ Mute

◆ Redial last call

FIGURE 21.3
Sennheiser SC30
USB ML

BLUETOOTH

Bluetooth headsets have the same styles as their wired counterparts but have more flexibility in terms of their location usage because they're not tied to the USB cable.

One massive advantage Bluetooth devices have over both wired and DECT is the ability to connect also to a cell phone device, enabling a user to answer calls on either Lync or their cell phone without having to make any configuration changes. Indeed, some of the newer Plantronics devices allow for signaling capability from the device itself into Lync, changing the user status to "in a call" even if the call is on their cell phone. These devices have built-in intelligence capability (Plantronics SmartSensor), allowing them to "know" their state, to the extent that picking up the device itself will answer the call and moving the device away from your ear will hang up a call in progress. Figure 21.4 shows the Plantronics Voyager Legend UC, which has the following key features:

◆ Triple mic with noise cancellation

◆ Three layers of wind noise protection

◆ Voice controllable to management of calls via voice

◆ Voice alerts to inform of connection status, talk time remaining, and so on

◆ SmartSensor, which allows for intuitive user experience

FIGURE 21.4
Plantronics Voyager
Legend UC

The more "office-based" devices have a docking station, which will typically also allow for connection of a traditional telephony device.

DECT

DECT devices provide even more range than their Bluetooth brothers, up to 400 feet in some cases. One of the authors has the Sennheiser Office DW ML (see Figure 21.5), which provides the same clarity of audio whether he is sitting at his desk in the basement, in the garden, or in the loft! This particular device has headset controls to allow for answering (or hanging up) a call as well as volume (and mute).

The built-in battery allows for easily a full day's talk time or almost a week on standby.

The Sennheiser Office DW also allows for connection to both Lync and a desk phone, allowing for receipt of calls from either device to the headset and easy selection from the base station as to which device is connected by pressing a switch for either the computer (Lync) or the phone.

DECT devices are likely to be more office based because of the inability to natively connect to cell phone devices. They can connect to the traditional telephony devices, enabling ease of transition from a PBX environment to Lync.

FIGURE 21.5
Sennheiser Office
DW

Handsets

Next on the list of USB devices are handsets. In the early days of OCS 2007, we had a device (Polycom CX200) that was simply a phone-shaped microphone and speaker system connected via USB (see Figure 21.6). Yes, it had a few buttons, but these were volume, answer, and speakerphone mode buttons. (It also had the OCS icon that changed color based on your presence state.)

These devices turned out to be quite popular, simply because people are used to having a phone device on their desk. They didn't appreciate fully changing to a softphone client with a headset; they still were looking for the familiarity of the handset, and the Polycom device (along with a few others) allowed organizations to meet this need. (There were devices that were slightly more developed in that they had a number pad!)

At the same time, we also had devices that were shaped and sized more like a cell phone yet still connected via a cable.

In this range, not a lot has truly changed with the ongoing development of OCS R2 and Lync 2010 and 2013.

Where we see the most developments are with IP handsets that are covered later in this chapter.

FIGURE 21.6
Polycom CX200

Personal Speakerphones

One device range that sits in among the "great idea implementations" in our minds is the personal speakerphone. This is a device, typically no larger than an ice-hockey puck, that acts as a Lync speakerphone when connected via its USB cable. There is a wide range of devices available from a number of different manufacturers. Some of the newer ones use Bluetooth (via the dongle) to connect, so they have another level of portability. Figure 21.7 shows the latest device from Plantronics in this category, the Calisto 620.

FIGURE 21.7
Plantronics Calisto
620

This device has the following features:

◆ Battery length of up to 7 hours talk time

◆ Bidirectional 360-degree microphones that activate in the direction of the speaker

◆ Background noise cancellation

It's a great comfort to be able to quickly have a Lync call between a number of people via the speakerphone in any environment. Gone are the days when you had to book a conference room that had the speakerphone already in place. These are small enough that you can keep one in your laptop bag and simply whip it out when needed.

IP Desk Phones

IP desk phones for Lync Server 2013 come in two flavors:

◆ Lync Phone Edition

◆ Third-Party IP Phone (3PIP)

Lync Phone Edition devices run a version of Windows CE and have a native Lync client installed and configured on them. While these devices are still supported running against Lync Server 2013, they are slowly being phased out in favor for the more generic 3PIP devices.

In the following sections, we'll cover both of these types of devices and the configuration required to enable them to integrate into a Lync Server 2013 environment.

Lync 2010 Phone Edition

It is correct that 2010 appears in the name—no new client has been developed for Lync Server 2013.

A number of Lync Phone Edition devices are available from a small number of vendors, including Polycom, Aastra, and HP. You can download a complete list of certified devices from here:

http://technet.microsoft.com/en-us/lync/gg278172

Each of these phones has its own look and feel, but they run the same software, which is Lync 2010 Phone Edition. This software is provided by Microsoft and has the same user interface and functionality regardless of who makes the device.

The IP phones are split into three categories: common area phones, information worker phones, and conference phones. Table 21.1 shows the relevant model numbers for Aastra, Polycom, and HP.

TABLE 21.1: Lync 2010 IP phone models

PHONE TYPE	AASTRA	POLYCOM	HP
Common area phone	6720ip	CX500	4110
Information worker phone	6725ip	CX600	4120
Conference Phone	N\A	CX3000	N\A

In addition to these phone models, the Polycom CX700 and LG-Nortel 8540 are supported and can be updated to Lync 2010 Phone Edition, but they operate with a reduced feature set. Figure 21.8 shows the Polycom CX500 common area phone, and Figure 21.9 shows the HP 4120 information worker phone.

FIGURE 21.8
Polycom CX500
Common Area
Phone

FIGURE 21.9
HP 4120
Information
Worker Phone

COMMON AREA PHONES

Common area phones are designed to be deployed in areas where there is no single user, such as reception areas, warehouses, and so on. Compared to the information worker phones, these phones have a reduced feature set, which is referred to as *basic mode*, and also a reduced hardware configuration. Basic mode offers the following functionality:

◆ Contacts

◆ Photos

◆ Message waiting indicator

◆ Local call logs

◆ Remote usage (after intranet provisioning)

◆ Conference call control

Although referred to as common area phones, they can be used by standard users—for example, in a hot-desking configuration where they are configured as common area phones and also enabled to allow users to log into them. The phones can also be used without common area configuration by a single user.

INFORMATION WORKER AND CONFERENCE PHONES

From a Lync Phone Edition standpoint, the information worker and conference phone types provide the same functionality, which builds on that of the common area phone and implements what is commonly referred to as *Enhanced mode*.

This Enhanced mode is made possible by connecting the phone to a PC using a USB cable, a technique referred to as *USB tethering*, which is possible to do with these phones. If a user decides to log in using their extension and PIN instead, they will be restricted to Basic mode. Enhanced mode adds the following functionality: Exchange Calendar including Join Conference, Exchange integrated call logs, and visual voice mail. When a user decides to use USB tethering, they will be prompted to reenter their password when they connect their PC and phone together, as shown in Figure 21.10.

FIGURE 21.10
Login for USB tethering

These devices, unlike the common area phones, can also be set up from remote locations without needing to be on the corporate network. This allows organizations to drop-ship the devices without needing to preconfigure anything. Users will be required to log in using USB tethering rather than log in with their extension and PIN.

CX700 AND 8540 PHONES

The CX700 and 8540 phones are upgradable to Lync 2010 Phone Edition but operate with a reduced feature set. The features that are supported are in line with those offered in OCS 2007 R2. The features that are not supported are the ability to operate as a common area phone, PIN authentication, and contact photos. For users, the most noticeable change is that they can view their calendar and join Lync Online meetings from the phone.

Configuring IP Phone Prerequisites

A number of elements need to be configured to allow Lync IP phones to operate within your organization so people can use them. The requirements vary depending on how the phone is going to be initially configured. Phones can be configured either through USB tethering or directly on the phone using PIN authentication. USB tethering doesn't depend on the network as much as the method because the required certificates, SIP URI, and authentication information are synced through the USB cable. The main thing you need is Network Time Protocol (NTP); however, depending on your requirements, you may also need Link Layer Discovery Protocol (LLDP) and Power over Ethernet (PoE). For PIN authentication, the phone needs to locate information about the Lync setup; it needs information in DHCP to provide this.

Irrespective of the method used for the initial configuration, DHCP is needed to provide basic information to the phone, such as the IP address, subnet, and default gateway along with the DNS domain name and server.

Dynamic Host Configuration Protocol

Dynamic Host Configuration Protocol (DHCP) is used to provide the information you need for Lync Phone Edition to connect to the Lync server; this information cannot be manually entered into the phone, making the DHCP configuration a requirement for deployment. DHCP provides the following information as part of the in-band provisioning process:

◆ Lync registrar address, which could be a Director pool or a Lync pool

◆ URL of the web services

◆ Relative URL of the certificate provider on the Lync server

◆ Protocol for the certificate provider (HTTPS by default)

◆ Port for the certificate provider (443 by default)

The Lync registrar address is provided in Option 120; the other settings are provided under Option 43, using a vendor-specific MS-UC-Client setting. Both of them are provided as hexadecimal strings.

Two methods are available to provide the required DHCP settings. The first is to use the DHCP server that is provided as part of the Lync registrar. This DHCP server is very limited in functionality and is used to provide the required information. It will only respond to a DHCP request that contains a Vendor Class ID of MS-UC-Client and asks for Option 120 or 43. A fully functional DHCP server is still required to provide an IP address, subnet, and default gateway along with the DNS domain name and server for the phone. This DHCP server can be useful for labs or for small installations, but once a network becomes segregated by VLANs or WAN connections are used, this method is not usually feasible. To enable the DHCP server, use the following PowerShell command:

```
Set-CsRegistrarConfiguration –EnableDHCPServer $true
```

The second method is to use existing DHCP servers to provide the required configuration settings. This way, you do not have to configure the network to route DHCP requests to the Lync registrar, and you can also use it to deliver additional configuration information to the device.

To help you configure DHCP servers, Microsoft provides a configuration tool that will generate the required DHCP entries. While this tool is mainly aimed at Windows DHCP, the information it generates can be used to configure third-party DHCP servers. The utility, called DHCPUtil, is provided as part of the Lync installation and is located in the C:\Program Files\ Common Files\Microsoft Lync Server 2013 directory, assuming the default installation path. This tool works in conjunction with a batch file called DHCPConfigScript.bat, which configures the DHCP server. The DHCPUtil application generates the DHCP configuration, emulates the client to check the DHCP configuration, and finally, removes the DHCP configuration.

To create the DHCP configuration, at a minimum the batch file needs to be run on the DHCP server with the required settings passed into it as command-line arguments. These settings are generated by the DHCPUtil application and are created from three parameters:

-SipServer, which is the FQDN of the Director or Lync pool

-WebServer, which is the FQDN of the web services

-CertProvUrl, which is the URL of the certificate provider

For a Standard Edition installation, only the FQDN of the SIP server needs to be specified because it is the same as the web server FQDN. This is also the case for an Enterprise Edition installation in which the SIP server and the web server share the same FQDN, and it's usually the case when a hardware load balancer is used. It is usually not necessary to specify the certificate provider URL.

For example, to configure DHCP for a Standard Edition installation with an FQDN of se01. corp.masteringlync.org, use the following syntax:

```
DHCPUtil.exe -SipServer se01.corp.masteringlync.org
```

This will produce an output detailing the configuration (shown in Figure 21.11), along with the syntax required for the DHCPConfigScript batch file.

FIGURE 21.11
Output for
DHCPUtil.exe

Copy the DHCPConfigScript file to the DHCP server and run the previous command to create the DHCP configuration. These configurations are created as server options, and they will be applied to every DHCP scope on the DHCP server. If scope-specific options are required rather than server options, you will need to write your own configuration script. You can use the batch file as a basis for this. If you need to remove the DHCP configuration, run the following command from the DHCP server:

```
DHCPConfigScript.bat -Cleanup
```

The DHCPUtil command can be used to test the DHCP configuration; it sends a DHCP INFORM packet, displaying its contents, and also displays the contents of the DHCP ACK packet it receives along with the decoded settings. If the ACK is not received or the decoded settings appear to be wrong, this indicates a configuration issue. You can run the test using the following command and you should receive the output shown in Figure 21.12:

```
DHCPUtil.exe -EmulateClient
```

Figure 21.12

Output for
DHCPUtil.exe
-EmulateClient

Remember, the output from DHCPUtil.exe will be dependent upon the network location from which it is run; it is advisable to run this from each network location (and possibly even each VLAN) to ensure full coverage!

The final DHCP-related item you need to look at is how to get the IP phone to switch to a specific VLAN. This is often required in scenarios where a PC is connected via a phone and the two devices need to be on separate VLANs. Using DHCP to do this should always be seen as a fallback option; the preferred method is to use Link Layer Discovery Protocol (LLDP).

The VLAN configuration is provided through Option 43 in a similar way to the configuration of the actual phone, but it is provided under a different vendor-specific class, CPE-OCPHONE. During the boot stage, the phone will try to retrieve a VLAN ID from LLDP; if this fails, it will perform a DHCP request, looking for a VLAN ID. If it receives one, it will release the IP address it was issued and perform another DHCP request; this is tagged with the VLAN ID it just received. If a VLAN ID is not retrieved, the second DHCP request is still performed to retrieve the server details because two different vendor class IDs are being used.

Although you could populate DHCP with the server details, there is no utility to populate the VLAN information, so it must be manually created or scripted. The following method is an example of how it can be scripted.

```
netsh dhcp server add class CPEOCPHONE "Lync Phone Edition VLAN Tagging"
"CPE-OCPHONE" 1
netsh dhcp server add optiondef 10 VLANID Word 0 vendor=CPEOCPhone
```

```
comment="Lync Phone VLAN"
netsh dhcp server set optionvalue 10 Word vendor=CPEOCPhone "250"
```

This script creates the vendor class, assigns it the VLAN suboption 10 under Option 43, and adds it as a DHCP server option, applicable to all scopes. To use these commands, replace 250 with the voice VLAN you need.

Once DHCP has been updated, the phones will discover the VLAN the next time they are restarted and begin using it. If you ever need to change the VLAN once the phones have been configured, each phone will need to be hard-reset because the VLAN information is cached.

Caching the VLANs does potentially create an issue for one scenario: If an organization requires IP phones to be used remotely via the Edge servers, a cached VLAN can potentially cause problems. If the IP phone is attached to a switch that honors and routes based on the VLAN tag applied by the phone, there is the possibility that the packets will be placed into a VLAN that may not have a DHCP server configured or Internet access, or they may be dropped by the switch completely if the VLAN does not exist. Therefore, if phones need to be configured on site before being used off site, scope-specific options should be used for the VLAN configuration rather than server-wide options, and the phone should be connected to switch ports on the correct voice VLAN.

The final item to consider is the actual switch configuration. Because two VLANs are used on a single port, the primary VLAN needs to be set to the VLAN that the computer will use, while the voice VLAN should be set to a supported VLAN for the port.

Link Layer Discovery Protocol

Link Layer Discovery Protocol (LLDP) allows Phone Edition to discover which VLAN it should use. This is the preferred VLAN Discovery method, but it requires network switches that support LLDP-MED, the protocol's Media Endpoint Discovery extension. The configuration varies depending on the switch make and model. The following is a sample Cisco configuration:

```
!-- Enter configuration mode
configure terminal
!-- Enable LLDP
lldp run
!-- Configure Ethernet port 1
interface FastEthernet 1/1
!-- Set Data VLAN to 100
switchport access vlan 100
!-- Set Voice VLAN to 101
switchport voice vlan 101
!-- Configure as Access Port
switchport mode access
```

This configuration instructs Phone Edition to use VLAN 101, and all network traffic will be tagged with this VLAN, ensuring that the correct DHCP scope is used and the traffic is prioritized correctly.

Power over Ethernet

Power over Ethernet (PoE) allows a Lync phone to be powered by the network switch rather than requiring a local power supply for the phone. This often simplifies the deployment because it does not require power sockets local to the phone or additional cables.

The available phones support both 802.3AF and 802.3AT standards for Power over Ethernet; it is important to check that any existing switches support these IEEE standards. If you are upgrading from an existing IP telephony system, the current switches may not support these standards. For example, older Cisco switches use a proprietary PoE implementation that is not compatible with these phones.

Network Time Protocol

Because Phone Edition does not allow any configuration on the device, Network Time Protocol (NTP) is used to retrieve the current date and time. This lets you check items, such as the certificates, for validity. Phone Edition discovers the NTP server using DNS; the following two DNS records will be tried in order:

- The SRV record, `_ntp._udp.<SIP domain>` (port 123)

- `time.windows.com`

If there is no SRV record, Phone Edition will fall back to `time.windows.com`. If this is used, the phone will need to be able to access the Internet using UDP on port 123.

If you do not have an internal NTP server and do not want to use `time.windows.com`, then the Windows Time Service, which runs on every Windows server, can be configured to act as an NTP server. You can enable this through a Group Policy change. The group policy can be applied to any existing server, and a new policy can be used or an existing one can be changed. The settings that need to be changed can be found at Computer Configuration ➤ Policies ➤ Administrative Templates ➤ System ➤ Windows Time Service ➤ Time Providers.

To enable the Time server on the server to which the group policy applies, set Enable Windows NTP Server to Enabled in the Group Policy Management Editor, as shown in Figure 21.13. This will allow the server to respond to NTP requests.

FIGURE 21.13
NTP Group Policy change

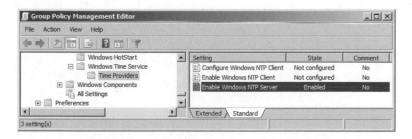

Once this has been enabled, the SRV record should be created in DNS Manager with the server FQDN specified as the server configured to offer this capability.

DEVICE CONFIGURATION

Device configuration is performed in two parts; the first part is performed through in-band configuration and is configured through the Lync Control Panel (Clients ➤ Device Configuration) and PowerShell using the CsUCPhoneConfiguration cmdlets (New, Set, Get, and Remove).

These settings are available on either a global or a site basis. The following settings are available:

♦ Identity, which is set to global for the global configuration or the Lync site name prefixed with Site:

♦ SIPSecurityMode, which is the SIP Signaling Security level for devices

♦ LoggingLevel, which indicates the depth of logging on the device

♦ VoiceDiffServTag, which is the DSCP value for marking voice packets

♦ EnforcePhoneLock, which locks the phone when the time-out occurs

♦ PhoneLockTimeout, which is the length of time until the phone is locked

♦ MinPhonePinLength, which is the minimum length of the device PIN

♦ CalendarPollInterval, which is the interval at which EWS will be polled for changes

♦ Voice8021p, which is the 802.1p value for marking voice packets

The last two settings are exposed only via PowerShell.

Of these settings, the ones most commonly modified are DSCP and Device Lock. The other settings can be left at the factory defaults for most deployments, unless you need to troubleshoot, which requires logging to be turned on. If, for example, you needed to modify the global policy to change the device time-out to 5 minutes, the following PowerShell command would be used:

```
Set-CsUCPhoneConfiguration -Identity global -PhoneLockTimeout "00:05:00"
```

The second part of device configuration is done on the devices themselves; it is performed as part of the user sign-in process and allows the following information to be configured:

♦ Time zone

♦ Date and time format

♦ Ringtone

♦ Phone lock code

Unfortunately, there is no method to configure these settings centrally, and configuring them on a per-user basis in large deployments can be a time-consuming process.

CLIENT CONNECTION PROCESS

Lync Phone Edition connects to the Lync servers in a different way than a Lync client. Phone Edition at a high level goes through the following steps for internal clients:

1. Tries to locate a VLAN to use.

2. Issues a DHCP request looking for an IP address.

3. Checks for device updates.

4. Downloads certificate chains.

5. Authenticates.

6. Receives and publishes the client certificate.

7. Registers with Lync.

The first three steps were covered earlier in this chapter, so we'll focus on the remaining four steps now.

In order for Lync Server 2010 Phone Edition to trust the certificates used for web services, the root certificate needs to be downloaded and verified. This process happens only if a root certificate has not already been downloaded. The certificate is downloaded using a standard HTTP query, containing the web services details retrieved from DHCP. Once it is downloaded, an HTTPS request to the web services is performed; this check ensures that the root certificate is valid.

In scenarios where the certificates used are not from the same root CA as those used for the Lync Server 2013 servers, or trusted by those default certificates in the Lync Phone Edition OS, then it is possible to use web services on the Lync Server 2013 pool to provide additional trusted root certificate information. See Chapter 12, "Troubleshooting," for an example of how to do this.

Authentication for first-time logins is performed using either the user's extension and PIN or NTLM details to the Lync web service, which checks to see if they are valid. If the details are valid, a certificate is returned to the client; the certificate is also published into the data store in the user's home pool. If the phone already has a user certificate, it is used to perform the authentication, and the client can then automatically log in after a restart.

Once the authentication is complete, the phone needs to register with the Lync pool to which the client is allocated. To locate the correct pool to connect to, the Lync 2010 Phone Edition client uses DNS and DHCP to locate the initial connection pool. It will try to locate the Lync pool address, using the following order:

- DHCP address using Option 120 (Option 43 is used for certificate services discovery.)

- Internal DNS SRV using TLS (`_sipinternaltls._tcp.masteringlync.org`)

- Internal DNS SRV using TCP (`_sipinternal._tcp.masteringlync.org`)

- External DNS using TLS (`_sip._tls.masteringlync.org`)

- DNS using an A record (`sip.masteringlync.org`)

This differs from a PC client in that the DHCP option is first. This is to ensure that the Lync 2010 Phone Edition client does not connect to an OCS 2007 R2 pool first because it would be unable to sign in. Once it has connected to the initial pool, for single pool deployment or where the user is allocated to this pool, the client will proceed. If this initial pool is a Director or the client is hosted on a different pool, the client will be redirected to the correct home pool.

Once the client has connected to the home pool, it will connect to the registrar. For Standard Edition deployments or single-server Enterprise deployments, there is only one registrar, so it will be used. Where there are multiple registrars in a pool (each Front End server contains a registrar), the client will be redirected to the registrar to which the user has been allocated.

This allocation process is defined when the user is created or moved to the pool. It cannot be changed by an administrator.

At this stage, the client is registered to Lync, and the registrar address is cached to be used for future connections. Should the registrar become unavailable, the process is started again.

While this may seem like a complicated process, it is not seen by end users and is exposed to administrators only when they're troubleshooting. The change to using items such as certificates was necessary to support new functionality in Lync, such as the Survivable Branch Appliance.

For external clients, the process is different. The phones must first be logged in internally; once this has occurred and they are taken external, the following process occurs on the phone:

1. Request an IP address from DHCP.

2. Check for device updates.

3. Authenticate.

4. Register with Lync.

These steps are similar to that of an internal client, but at this stage the user certificate already exists. Instead of connecting directly to a Lync pool, all requests are relayed through an Edge server. In addition, only DNS is used to locate the address to connect to the following records:

- DNS SRV using TLS

- DNS SRV using TCP

- SIP *A* Record from DNS—i.e., `sip.masteringlync.org`

DEPLOYING PHONE EDITION UPDATES

As with OCS, updates for Lync 2010 Phone Edition are managed and distributed by Lync Server 2013. This allows updates to be rolled out in a managed way, with the ability to configure test devices and to roll back to a previous version if necessary.

For the most part, you can manage any updates through either PowerShell or the Lync Control Panel. The only thing you must do through PowerShell is upload the update files.

Update files are published on the Microsoft download site and are released periodically. One update file is released for each hardware vendor, so a separate update file is released for the Polycom CX700 and LG-Nortel 8540 devices.

Organizations do not usually need to download all of them because they commonly standardize on a single vendor; however, for an upgrade from a previous version, you may need to also download the update for CX700 and 8540 devices.

These update packs have the same filename, `UCUpdates.exe`, so if you are downloading files for multiple vendors, you need to be careful not to overwrite another update file. The downloads are executable files and will extract to the same location, which is the `%userprofile%` path. Likewise, they all extract with the same filename, which is `ucupdates.cab`, so make sure that you do not overwrite an existing update file.

Once downloaded and extracted, the update files need to be uploaded to the Lync web services. The following PowerShell command can be used to perform this task; it will upload the file to each web services server. This assumes that the ucupdates.cab file is located on the root of the C: drive.

```
Get-CsService -WebServer | ForEach-Object {Import-CsDeviceUpdate
-Identity $_.Identity -FileName c:\UCUpdates.cab}
```

Once the updates have been uploaded, they will appear as *pending versions*. When updates are pending, they will be deployed only to test devices. They will not be deployed to other devices until they have been approved.

Device testing, update approval, and version restoration can be managed through either PowerShell or the Lync Control Panel. Test devices are identified using either their MAC address or serial number; both of these should be globally unique, so using either should not cause a problem. In addition, the test devices can be created on either a site or global basis.

To create a test device, use the New-CsTestDevice cmdlet, which requires four parameters:

-Name, which is the name of the test device

-Parent, which is defined as global or site:<sitename>

-Identifier, which is the MAC address or serial number of the device

-IdentifierType, which is set to either MACAddress or SerialNumber

To create a test device at the EMEA site using an Identifier value of AB37_679e, for example, use the following PowerShell command:

```
New-CsTestDevice -Name "EMEA Test Phone 1" -Parent Site:EMEA
-Identifier "AB37_679e" -IdentifierType SerialNumber
```

Once this command has been run, any future uploaded updates will be deployed to this device for testing. You can use the following cmdlets to manage test devices:

Get-CsTestDevice

Set-CsTestDevice

Remove-CsTestDevice

When planning your test devices, choose at least one of each device to test. You should not use mission-critical devices or high-profile users such as C-level executives; they should be users who use the most of their device's functionality.

Once the updates have been tested, they can be approved to be deployed to all the remaining devices. Updates can be approved using either the Control Panel or the Approve-CsDeviceUpdateRule cmdlet. This cmdlet takes a single input, which is the unique identity of the update, and it could look like this:

```
Approve-CsDeviceUpdateRule -Identity service:WebServer:se01.corp.masteringlync.
org/d5ce3c10-2588-420a-82ac-dc2d9b1222ff9
```

To retrieve the identities of updates, use the Get-CsDeviceUpdateRule cmdlet, which retrieves all available updates and can be filtered as needed. If you want to approve all pending updates after you've tested the update, use the following command:

```
Get-CsDeviceUpdateRule | Approve-CsDeviceUpdateRule
```

If you need to restore to a previous version of Lync 2010 Phone Edition, use the `Restore-CsDeviceUpdateRule` cmdlet. If you want to remove a pending update completely, you can use `Reset-CsDeviceUpdateRule`. Both of these cmdlets use the same syntax as `Approve-CsDeviceUpdateRule`.

Now that you've seen how updates are managed, you need to see how the device updates itself. Updates are handled differently, depending on both the state and the location of the phone. Therefore, we'll look at three different update processes: the process for nonprovisioned devices, for internal devices, and for external devices.

Nonprovisioned devices are ones that do not have a user signed into them. These devices can be updated only if they are on the corporate network because access to the updates website is blocked for anonymous users. The update process is as follows:

1. Send a DNS request for `ucupdates-r2.<DHCPIssuedDomainName>`.

2. Send an HTTPS request asking if an update is available.

3. If `NumOFFiles = 0` is returned, no update is available.

4. If an update is available, the download path will be provided.

5. The phone downloads the updates, installs them, and after 5 minutes of inactivity, reboots the device.

The main issue with this process is that because an HTTPS request is used, the phone needs to trust the certificate that is returned. At this stage, the phone will not trust internal certificates because the root certificate isn't installed; therefore, it will reject it. To work around this, you can use an externally issued certificate, or you can have a user sign in because this process will download the root certificate.

The update process for internal and external devices is similar with one difference—for external access, the anonymous request is rejected and the phone retries using credentials. The process is as follows:

1. On startup, user login, or every 24 hours, a check for updates using the in-band provisioned URL is performed.

2. If `NumOFFiles = 0` is returned, no update is available.

3. If an update is available, the download path will be provided.

4. The phone downloads the update, installs it, and after 5 minutes of inactivity, reboots the device.

When the updates have been applied and the device rebooted, the phone will automatically be logged in as the same user.

PHONE EDITION LOGS

To troubleshoot Lync Phone Edition, the log level needs to be specified, and the logs need to be uploaded from the phone to the server and converted. Once at this stage, you can begin analyzing the logs to troubleshoot the issue. This may sound like a cumbersome process, but it is relatively straightforward. The logging level is set through the phone in-band provisioning process, either through the Control Panel or through PowerShell.

To enable logging on a global basis, you can use the following PowerShell command:

```
Set-CsUCPhoneConfiguration -Identity Global -LoggingLevel High
```

To disable logging, change `High` to `Off`. The phone will start logging once the settings have been updated. This will be done through the in-band provisioning periodically, but the quickest way is by rebooting the phone.

Since the phone has logging enabled, you can re-create the issue that you are experiencing, and once this is completed, the log files need to be sent to the server. To do this, if the phone is logged in, use the phone's Settings menu and select Set Log Settings ➢ Send Logs. If the phone is not logged in or locked, use System Information.

Once the log files have been uploaded, they can be found in `DeviceUpdateLogs\Client\CELog` on the File Store for the pool. At a minimum, there will be a file with a `.clg` extension. There could also be a *Dr. Watson* log file if one has been created; this file is created in case of a crash and is automatically uploaded. It is the CLG file you want. It needs to be converted to a readable format using Readlog; the following syntax can be used:

```
readlog.exe -v logfile.clg logfile.txt
```

Now that you have a log file in plain text, you can begin the analysis.

HOW TO GET YOUR HANDS ON READLOG

Readlog is part of the Windows CE Platform Builder; it is not freely available but you can use it for a 180-day-trial period. Once you have installed the trial, you can find Readlog here: `C:\WinCE600\Public\Common\Oak\Bin\I386`

Readlog does not depend on any other files, and the executable can be copied to the machine on which you want to convert the files. To install the trial, you will need a trial license key. You can request one at the following location:

> `www.microsoft.com/windowsembedded/en-us/downloads/download-windows-embedded-ce-6-trial.aspx`

You will need to log in with your Windows Live ID and complete the registration process. The 180-day trial can be downloaded from the following location:

> `www.microsoft.com/downloads/en/details.aspx?FamilyID=7e286847-6e06-4a0c-8cac-ca7d4c09cb56`

CONFIGURING COMMON AREA PHONES

To use common area phones, you need to create accounts for each phone. These accounts exist only within Lync, but they are represented as contacts within Active Directory and allow users to search for them in the Lync Address Book and call them.

You can create a common area phone through PowerShell using the `New-CsCommonAreaPhone` cmdlet, and you can manage it using the equivalent `Set`, `Get`, and `Remove` cmdlets. There is also a `Move` cmdlet, allowing you to move the phone from one pool to another.

Once you've created the common area phone, you can assign client, voice, conferencing, and PIN policies to it in the same way you assign them to a user. You should create specific policies for these phones so they can be locked down more than a standard user would be. For example, if you want to create a common area phone for the headquarters reception area, you can use the following PowerShell command:

```
New-CsCommonAreaPhone -LineUri "tel:+4455577777"
-RegistrarPool "se01.corp.masteringlync.org"
-DisplayName "HQ Main Reception Phone"
-SipAddress sip:hqmainreception@masteringlync.org
-OU "ou=Common Area Phone,DC=corp,DC=masteringlync,DC=org"
```

This will create the common area phone with a phone number of +4455577777 on the se01.corp.masteringlync.org pool with a display name of HQ Main Reception Phone. You can also set a SIP address; this is an optional setting, but if you set the phone to an address that is easy to remember, it will make it easier to grant policies. If it is not set, a SIP address based on the default domain name and GUID is used.

Once the phone has been created, the necessary policies can be assigned to it; this is performed in the same way as assigning policies to a normal user using the Grant cmdlets.

The voice and conferencing policies should be configured as follows; these settings will suffice for the majority of requirements. The following voice policy is recommended:

- Call forwarding disabled
- Team call disabled
- Delegation disabled
- Call transfer disabled

The following conferencing policy is recommended:

- Audio conference disabled
- File transfer disabled

The following is not a conferencing policy setting but is set within the conference policy:

- Peer-to-peer file transfer disabled

Once the policies have been granted, a PIN needs to be set for the common area phone. Without this, it is not possible to log in to the phone. The PIN is set using the Set-CsClientPin cmdlet. To set it on the common area phone you just created, use the following PowerShell command:

```
Set-CsClientPin -Identity "HQ Main Reception Phone" -Pin 165643
```

Note that the PIN specified must comply with the PIN policy that covers the common area phone. This could be a specific policy or a site or global one. Once the PIN has been set, you can log in to the common area phone using the phone number and PIN.

Enabling Hot-Desking

Hot-desking allows a user to sign into a common area phone, and the phone will become theirs until they sign out or their login times out. This is often useful in conference rooms and offices that have hot-desking or touch-down areas. Users sign into the phone using their phone number and PIN or through USB tethering if the phone supports it.

Hot-desking is enabled through the client policy using the EnableHotdesking and HotdeskingTimeout options. The EnableHotdesking option is set to either True or False, and HotdeskingTimeout is set in an HH:MM:SS format, such as 00:05:00 for 5 minutes. The time-out can be set to a minimum of 30 seconds, with a default of 5 minutes. For most organizations this is too low because it is common for a user not to use a phone for a period of time but still be using the hot desk; a setting of at least 60 minutes is usually required.

If you want to enable hot-desking for an existing client policy and set a time-out of 90 minutes, use the following PowerShell command:

```
Set-CsClientPolicy -Identity SalesHotDeskPhone -EnableHotdesking $true
-HotdeskingTimeout 01:30:00
```

This change will become active once the settings on the phone have been refreshed, either through rebooting the phone or through the regular configuration updates.

3PIP

In addition to phones running Lync 2010 Phone Edition, which are referred to as "Optimized for" devices, there are phones that are designed to work with Lync but that do not run Lync 2010 Phone Edition. One vendor of these phones is SNOM. These devices are tested to work with Lync but may not offer the same features as the "Optimized for" devices, and they are configured differently.

Lync 2013 has opened the door wider to 3PIP devices in that Lync Phone Edition has not been further developed specifically for Lync Server 2013, and therefore the focus will shift more to these third-party devices and their capabilities.

Of course, the downside of using 3PIP devices is they will likely provide support and capability beyond what Lync Server 2013 can enable, such as a message waiting indicator or specific button capability such as transfer or directory lookup.

In the following sections, we will show how to configure the SNOM 821 device (see Figure 21.14) for working with Lync Server 2013, and we will be using firmware version 8.8.1.1.

FIGURE 21.14
SNOM 821 VoIP
Handset

This particular firmware version provides a significant number of Lync-capable features:

◆ Native Lync Software Update

◆ Sign in with extension and PIN

◆ Call Park

◆ Support for Survivable Branch Appliances

◆ Music on Hold

◆ Boss/Admin

◆ Assigning contacts to buttons for quick presence updates

◆ Additional language support

SETUP AND LOGIN

Upon first boot (assuming DHCP is in place to provide network address information), the device will prompt for the language, time zone information, and sounds (Tone Scheme). Once these have been completed, you'll see the welcome screen (Figure 21.15).

FIGURE 21.15
SNOM 821 device
welcome screen

The SNOM 821 device supports up to 12 concurrent identity logins, each one being a separate user, which is ideal for hot-desking scenarios where a single phone is shared on a desk.

Figure 21.16 shows the sign-in process:

◆ SIP-URI

◆ Domain\User

◆ Password

Once you're signed in, the phone will display presence information as you would expect (see Figure 21.17), and the buttons along the bottom of the screen can be used for the following functionality:

◆ Contacts

◆ Call History

◆ Call Forward

◆ Set Presence

FIGURE 21.16
Sign-in process

FIGURE 21.17
Logged-in presence
state

The SNOM 821 device also has a number of feature buttons alongside the numeric keypad:

◆ DND: Quick setting for Do Not Disturb

◆ Directory: Access to directory search (see Figure 21.18)

◆ Menu: Access to the phone menu settings

◆ Transfer: Quick transfer of calls

◆ Hold: Quick setting to put calls on hold

FIGURE 21.18
Searching the
directory

When placing a call, the display shows both the callee and caller identities (or indeed phone numbers), as shown in Figure 21.19.

FIGURE 21.19
Placing a call

When you receive a call, the screen is a similar to the screen you see when placing the call (Figure 21.19), but it has a button enabled on the bottom row to allow forwarding of calls without answering.

Once a call is answered, it can be parked (assuming the user has the ability to park calls as defined in their voice policy) by selecting the P button from the bottom row; see Figure 21.20 for the in-call display.

FIGURE 21.20
In-call display

DEVICE UPDATING

From version 8.7.3.1 onward, the SNOM devices support "native" Lync Server 2013 device firmware management (in other words, the same as with Lync Phone Edition) using the ucupdates-r2.<domain name> DNS record or via in-band provisioning (see Figure 21.21). Prior to this version (and potentially with other vendor versions), this would have to be managed directly for each phone or through the vendor-specific update provision.

Prior to firmware version 8.8.1.1 for this device, the upgrade capability was managed direct via the web interface, either set to poll for updates to a specified URL (by default to the SNOM provisioning page at http://provisioning.snom.com/) or set to be manually uploaded; see Figure 21.22 for the web interface.

If a firmware update is pending (discovered during in-band provisioning), you'll see a countdown timer in the bottom left of the screen (see Figure 21.23). If the phone device is left untouched for 5 minutes, the update will be applied, causing the phone to reboot. Any interaction with the device will reset the counter.

ASSIGNING PRESENCE TO KEYS

One of the features in the SNOM devices is the ability to assign users to the "line" buttons. Not only does this give a quick method to contact the user, it also provides an immediate visual as to their presence state because it changes color in line with their presence.

Figure 21.24 shows the screen overlay. When users are assigned to each button (there are four), their name and status are displayed in the dark area on the right side, and a button indicating their presence is colored according to their present state.

FIGURE 21.22
Configuration of firmware updating on legacy 3PIP devices (or firmware)

FIGURE 21.23
Countdown timer

FIGURE 21.24
Presence buttons

Boss/Admin Scenario

The SNOM devices are the first non–Lync Phone Edition devices to support the Boss/Admin scenario. Here, the admin and boss can share line status and call retrieval on a button.

Sharing Presence Capability

With Lync Server 2010, a new presence publication category needs to be defined within the backend database. This is achieved by running the following command in the osql utility:

```
osql -E -S <pool fqdn>\RTC -Q
"use rtc;exec RtcRegisterCategoryDef N'dialogInfo'"
```

Lync Server 2013 already has this in place, so it is not required.

The supported scenarios are as you would expect on a normal Lync client:

◆ Monitor line state

◆ Call pickup

◆ Call on behalf of

◆ Safe transfer

◆ Join conference call

To enable the Boss/Admin scenario, the delegates need to be first configured as normal in the Lync client.

For the boss, you'll see the Delegates group, and for the admin, the group is called People I Manage Calls For. Figure 21.25 shows this configured in the Lync client.

On the SNOM 821 device, these contacts need to be assigned to the relevant button. Figure 21.26 shows a number of these having been assigned.

From the top the first item (Nathan Lync – Boss/Admin) was configured as a Boss/Admin line item. This shows the Boss/Admin relationship, and when the button is selected, allows calls to be made on behalf of the boss, who in this case is configured as Nathan.

The second item down simply shows Boss/Admin. As a boss, you can assign all your administrators to a single button. There is an M:N relationship permitted with the Boss/Admin configuration: not only can one boss have one or many admins, an admin can be responsible for one or many bosses. Selecting this button will bring up the next display, which will show each of the individual admins and their status.

The third item from the top simply shows the presence status of the delegate, in this case Keith Lync. There is no special relationship flowing from the boss to the admin.

FIGURE 21.25
Delegation setup in
the Lync client

FIGURE 21.26
SNOM 821 showing
Boss/Admin setup

Meeting Room Devices

With the introduction of common area phones in Lync 2010, a new type of device was also
enabled: the Lync speakerphone. Figure 21.27 shows an example, the Polycom CX3000. This is
essentially a common area phone device optimized with microphones and speakers to cover a
wider area than the front of the device, as would be seen on a traditional handset-style device.

As well as providing this style of devices for the audio aspects of a call, since OCS 2007 there has also been the RoundTable device (also known as the Polycom CX5000), allowing the display of the "panorama room" style view as well as having active microphones to focus on the current speaker.

FIGURE 21.27
Polycom CX3000

For Lync Server 2013, the RoundTable device has been upgraded to cater to HD video streams.

The observant among you will have noticed a number of new cmdlets focused on meeting room capability:

```
Disable-CsMeetingRoom
Enable-CsMeetingRoom
Move-CsMeetingRoom
Set-CsMeetingRoom
```

These cmdlets focus on a new generation of Lync video solutions: the Lync Meeting Room System (LMRS).

These systems are similar to common area phones in that they have a dedicated account for each device; however, they are targeted at the full-room videoconference solutions, although not as high end as a "telepresence" room. Because an individual account will exist for each device (or "room"), they can be invited to meetings as a normal user would be, either scheduled or ad hoc.

Announced at the Lync Conference in San Diego, February 2013, LMRS is expected to be developed by a number of manufacturers:

- Polycom
- LifeSize
- SMART Technologies
- Cestron

The feature set is expected to remain relatively consistent across manufacturers:

◆ Single or dual touch high-definition displays

◆ HD camera

◆ Interactive whiteboard capability

◆ Ability to email the whiteboard content to participants

◆ Auto-join to scheduled meetings

◆ Desk-based control panel

Figure 21.28 shows the conceptual design for the SMART Technologies device. SMART Technologies will be releasing devices in three variations depending primarily on the size of the room. (Table 21.2 shows a high level feature breakdown.)

FIGURE 21.28
SMART
Technologies
Meeting Room
System

TABLE 21.2: SMART Technologies device selection

	SMART ROOM SYSTEM FOR MICROSOFT LYNC SMALL	**SMART ROOM SYSTEM FOR MICROSOFT LYNC MEDIUM**	**SMART ROOM SYSTEM FOR MICROSOFT LYNC LARGE**
Room Size	Up to 6 people, 100 sq ft	Up to 12 people, 180 sq ft	Up to 16 people, 300+ sq ft
Panel Size	80"	84"	2 x 70"
Camera	1 (audio on)	1 (audio off)	1 (audio off)
Table Mics	0	2	2

Video Endpoints

At the most basic level, a video endpoint is a web cam either built in to the PC or connected via USB, going up the scale. However, we have devices from Polycom (such as the HDX 4500 shown in Figure 21.29) and LifeSize as the two main players in this space.

FIGURE 21.29
Polycom HDX 4500

These devices can register directly with Lync with a username and password, either as a conference room itself or directly as a user. Presence can be provided (typically In a Call or Available) and interactions are as would be expected with any other Lync client device.

Integrating with Hardware Video Conferencing Platforms

Lync provides for videoconferencing natively and can accommodate sessions ranging from a peer-to-peer call to up to 250 participants in a video conference. Although this desktop video capability is useful and gaining traction in organizations, there are already many deployments of room-based and other hardware video platforms. Thankfully, Lync has the capability to integrate with these systems to provide enhanced capability. For example, not only can a hardware video endpoint dial a Lync desktop video user and hold an audio and video call, but equally a Lync user can be dialed into a conference hosted on a hardware video Multipoint Control Unit (MCU), a device to mix and distribute channels of audio and video, to participate in a conference that also includes those on the high-end video system in the board room. It's also possible to use the external access capabilities of Lync to allow remote or federated users to dial into conferences held on hardware systems; such systems can provide connectivity to a wide range of legacy video standards and also different ways of displaying end users so that all video participants can be seen at once.

Before we dive into configuration, it is important to note that Lync can interoperate with a wide variety of video systems, including those from Polycom, LifeSize, and Radvision. In this section, we'll cover some of the points of integration with the Polycom range of devices.

Polycom devices have two main areas of integration with Lync: endpoints and conference units. They have their HDX systems, which are essentially endpoints of different scales and sizes, ranging from simple desktop video units to room-based systems. They also have telepresence systems that are fitted in an entire room to give the experience of actually sitting around a table with those at the other end of the call. Polycom also has its RMX range; these devices are video MCUs. They provide the ability to host conferences and can tie into a wide range of video systems via various protocols, including ISDN, H.323, and SIP. For more information about the devices available, see the Polycom website at www.polycom.com.

Polycom is working very closely with Microsoft to ensure that its products integrate closely with Lync, and it is frequently adding new functionality. Two main scenarios are possible. The first is simply enabling one of the endpoint HDX devices to dial into Lync, which is a relatively straightforward process. Assuming that the device has the latest software, it is simply a case of creating an identity for it and letting it register to Lync. This identity could be either that of an end user, if the system is a personal desktop video unit, or one created for a conference room, if the unit is a room-based system. The second scenario we'll cover allows integration between Lync and an RMX unit so that Lync users can internally or externally participate in conferences hosted on the RMX unit.

Given the complex nature of the configuration and the fact that new versions of the Polycom software add features and occasionally change setup steps, we won't cover the step-by-step configuration here. We'll look at the Lync and HDX integration from the Lync perspective. Then you can refer to resources that will provide up-to-date and detailed information about how to configure integration between Lync and the Polycom systems.

Configuring Lync and HDX Integration

As mentioned, having a Polycom HDX system sign on to Lync is relatively straightforward. There are a couple of prerequisites that must be checked before you try, though. First, you must confirm that NTLM authentication is enabled on the registrar, as of course the server itself is configured to permit it. This can be checked in the Lync Server Control Panel on the Security tab under the registrar policy, as shown in Figure 21.30.

As long as NTLM is enabled, you are ready to create the required users. It is, of course, possible to have any Lync user who has Enterprise Voice enabled (although it doesn't need a number assigned) log on to the HDX, so creating specific users is needed only if this is a room system that you need to specifically identify rather than a personal one.

To refresh your memory, here are the required commands to enable the user for Lync and Enterprise Voice:

```
Enable-CsUser -Identity "Test User1"
-RegistrarPool se01.corp.masteringlync.org
```

```
-SipAddressType UserPrincipalName
Set-CsUser -Identity "Test User1" -EnableEnterpriseVoiceEnabled $True
```

FIGURE 21.30
Checking the authentication types available on the registrar policy

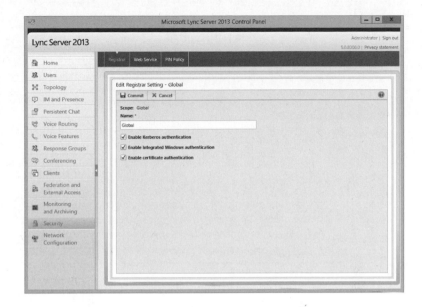

This command will enable the user Test User1 for Lync and Enterprise Voice. The user that is now enabled will fall under any relevant Lync policies, so make sure that if you need external access, you have the relevant policies in place as covered in Chapter 10, "User Administration."

The HDX systems have an address book, which should be populated with the entries from the Lync user's buddy list. To populate the list, log on to a PC Lync client with the Lync user and populate the list in the normal way.

Finally, you must ensure that the Lync encryption settings are configured to match those configured on the HDX. The HDX supports the Lync default settings on RequireEncryption; however, the HDX can also be configured to not use encryption. In that case, you will need to configure Lync to accept such connections using the following command:

```
Set-CsMediaConfiguration -EncryptionLevel supportencryption
```

This will allow Lync to accept unencrypted media connections.

You must follow the steps in the *Polycom Unified Communications Deployment Guide for Microsoft Environments* document at the following link to configure the HDX:

http://support.polycom.com/global/documents/support/setup_maintenance/products/
video/UC_Deploy_Guide_MS.pdf

FURTHER REFERENCE MATERIAL

Although we have limited space to discuss the connectivity options in this chapter, the following resources provide useful information about the integration of Polycom and Lync systems.

This is a Polycom website with configuration material:

```
http://support.polycom.com/PolycomService/support/us/support/strategic_partner_
solutions/microsoft_software_download.html
```

This is a direct download link for the *Polycom Unified Communications Deployment Guide for Microsoft Environments* document:

```
http://support.polycom.com/global/documents/support/setup_maintenance/products/
video/UC_Deploy_Guide_MS.pdf
```

Here are some other blog sites that are worth viewing:

```
http://blog.schertz.name/category/polycom/
http://mikestacy.typepad.com/mike-stacys-blog/rmx/
http://blogs.technet.com/b/meacoex/archive/2011/05/26/lync-with-polycom-rmx-
integration.aspx
```

The Bottom Line

Integrate with hardware video conferencing platforms.   Lync can integrate with several hardware video platforms to provide control and connectivity through Lync to room-based and high-quality video networks.

> **Master It**   You are trying to configure Lync integration with a Polycom HDX unit, but it won't connect. What might be causing an issue?

Configure prerequisites for IP phones.   Lync IP phones are designed to be as simple as possible to deploy and receive all of their configuration settings automatically. For this to occur, a number of items need to be configured, such as network configuration and DHCP.

> **Master It**   You have deployed Lync IP phones, but you are unable to log in to the phones when using extension and PIN authentication; however, logging in using USB tethering works as expected.

Appendix A

The Bottom Line

Each of The Bottom Line sections in the chapters suggest exercises to deepen skills and understanding. Sometimes there is only one possible solution, but often you are encouraged to use your skills and creativity to create something that builds on what you know and lets you explore one of many possible solutions.

Chapter 1: What's in Lync?

Describe the features of the client.   The Lync 2013 client is designed to achieve three core goals: connect, communicate, and collaborate. This new client makes it is much easier to find people and verify identity, initiate communications (typically, with a single click), and collaborate with full-blown information sharing. Device integration and call management have been greatly simplified, removing the need to run through wizards constantly.

Master It   You are assembling a new product-development team. The new product will be similar to a previously released product, and you want to ask members of the previous team for guidance. How can you find people associated with the previous product team?

Solution   Use the key-skills search feature integrated with SharePoint to return the names of the appropriate people.

Describe the features of the server.   Lync Server 2013 provides most of the server roles included in Office Communications Server and introduces the Survivable Branch Appliance (or Server) to help in the high-availability scenarios. The management approach has changed through the introduction of the Topology Builder application and role-based access control to limit administrative access to defined users and scopes as required. PowerShell and Silverlight combine to provide the day-to-day administration of the environment.

Master It   When deploying high availability, which of the following roles can be a primary registrar?

- Director
- Enterprise Edition Front End
- Standard Edition Front End
- Survivable Branch Appliance
- Survivable Branch Server

Solution   The Front End servers (Enterprise and Standard Edition) and the Survivable Branch Appliance (and Server) can be primary registrars. Only the Front End servers (Enterprise and Standard Edition) can be backup registrars.

Describe the voice features.   Significant investment and development have gone into Lync Server 2013's voice feature set. The new set has allowed it to become a match for a large portion of the PBX workload and, in many cases, a viable replacement for a PBX.

New functions (such as Private Line, Call Admission Control, Call Park, E911, and Common Area Phones) provide welcome additions to the user experience. By contrast, behind-the-scenes features (such as Media Bypass, routing improvements, resiliency improvements, and analog device management) provide a more integrated and available solution for the administrator while they help reduce the number of servers required.

Master It   As the network and telephony administrator for your company, you want to invest in SIP trunks rather than legacy PBX-style PSTN connectivity using media gateways.

How should you configure media bypass and deploy mediation servers?

Solution   When SIP trunks are used, separate, physical mediation servers are recommended, and media bypass should be disabled. A SIP trunk does not have a termination point to allow the client to connect directly; instead, the client will connect to the Mediation server. The client can still use G711, and the Mediation server may not be required to transcode the codec.

Chapter 2: Standards and Protocols

Understand the basics of SIP for signaling.   SIP originates from an extensive background of telephony signaling. Although knowing that background is not strictly required for Lync administration, understanding how we have gotten to where we are today will help you overcome some of the challenges you'll face when integrating with legacy telephony environments.

Master It   For what is a jitter buffer used?

Solution   By buffering incoming data prior to playback, a jitter buffer is used to help smooth out the delay that occurs when packets are transmitted across a network.

Understand how SIP has been extended to provide additional functionality for Lync Server 2013.   In its plainest form, SIP provides session-based signaling; however, with some of the extensions for SIP, you can extend this session-based signaling approach to incorporate additional functionality within the SIP request itself, such as IM and presence information.

Master It   Assuming a user is not yet logged in, describe the SIP requests required to log in and establish an IM session with another user.

Solution   REGISTER—Provide the login and registration information.

SUBSCRIBE—Request presence information.

NOTIFY—Receive presence information.

> `INVITE`—Initiate the session.
>
> `ACK`—Acknowledge the `INVITE`.
>
> `MESSAGE`—Send the instant message.

For completeness, the session should be terminated with a `BYE` request.

Identify additional protocols used by Lync Server 2013. Lync Server 2013 uses many different protocols for its various modalities as needed by the user. It can also tie many of these modalities together, providing an integrated solution running on top of SIP. Microsoft has also been able to successfully (and securely) extend this functionality to the Internet.

Master It What is the new codec used in video calling and conferencing?

Solution H264 AVC/SVC.

Chapter 3: Security

Secure external access. Lync utilizes the Edge server and supporting components to provide external access to communications modalities. The Edge server sits in the DMZ and is a proxy between internal and external users. Many layers of security are in place to ensure that communicating externally won't cause security breaches.

Master It Describe the role the Director plays in external access. Why would you use one?

Solution The Director role sits in front of the Front End servers and carries out both authentication and redirection. When external connections are passed on to the Director through the Access Edge role, the Director acts as the point of authentication and as such will shield the Front End servers from potential DoS attacks using malformed authentication traffic. In its redirection role, the Director server will route traffic intelligently where one central site has multiple pools, thereby helping to keep the load on the Front End server to a minimum.

Understand core security. Lync is designed to be secure by default. It does this in many ways, not least of which is by encrypting all traffic and using certificates as part of mutual authentication of connections.

Master It In different circumstances, Lync can use five different authentication mechanisms. What are they and where are they used?

Solution Kerberos authentication is used for clients who are domain joined and inside the LAN.

NTML authentication is used for clients accessing Lync through the Edge server.

Digest authentication is used by anonymous clients participating in conferencing.

Certificate-based authentication is used in conjunction with a PIN by those signing in on IP phone devices.

Certificate authentication is used following a successful initial login using either Kerberos/NTLM/PIN.

Provide security administratively. No matter how secure a product is by design, an administrator can easily open up holes in its defenses. Lync provides many ways in which administrators can participate in tightening or relaxing security. Numerous policies are available to control users, including the clients they are allowed to use and the length and complexity of PINs. Equally, you can configure Lync to block links in IMs and prevent the transfer of files. Finally, Lync can be set up to add disclaimers to messages so that regulatory issues can be managed.

Master It You have been asked to ensure that users in the EMEA site can send only files with extension .txt in IM messages and that any links in the messages will be prefixed with an underscore character so they must be copied into a browser manually. How would you do this?

Solution To achieve the required results, you need to use two different cmdlets. The first is the New-CsFileTransferFilterConfiguration cmdlet, which should be used as shown here:

```
New-CsFileTransferFilterConfiguration -Identity site:EMEA -Extensions .txt
```

This cmdlet will create a new policy assigned to the EMEA site, which will allow files with extension .txt.

The second cmdlet needed is New-CsImFilterConfiguration, which should be used as shown here:

```
New-CsImFilterConfiguration -Identity site:EMEA -Prefixes https: -Action Allow
  -enabled $true
```

Chapter 4: Clients

Understand usage scenarios for each client. Each of the Lync clients discussed in this chapter is designed for a specific usage scenario. For example, Lync 2013 allows IM and presence with other users.

Master It You have been engaged by a graphic design company to design and deploy Microsoft Lync Server 2013. The company already has Lync Server 2010 and will be migrating to Lync Server 2013 over the next six months. The company has 300 employees who are split almost 50/50 between Apple Mac computers and Windows PCs running Lync 2010. All users need to be able to participate in meetings with partners and customers during this coexistence phase.

Solution Lync Web App in Lync Server 2013 has been significantly redesigned to support a number of different platforms, including Windows and Mac. Due to the native support for audio and video in Lync Web App, it is the preferred client for joining meetings hosted on Lync Server 2013, even if users already have the Lync 2010 desktop client installed. Lync 2010 Attendee is no longer supported for joining Lync Server 2013 meetings.

Understand changes in Group Chat. In Lync 2013, Group Chat has been built into the main products and called Persistent Chat.

Master It You are working with a large financial services company that is in the process of migrating from Lync Server 2010 to Lync Server 2013. The company's employees are heavy users of Group Chat in Lync Server 2010. What benefits do Lync Server 2013 and Lync 2013 introduce in this area?

Solution   The feature previously called Group Chat is now called Persistent Chat and is built in to the Lync 2013 client. You no longer require a separate Group Chat client to be installed in parallel. You can interact with a Persistent Chat room in the same way as you would another user.

Chapter 5: Planning Your Deployment

Use the available planning tools.   Lync Server 2013 is an extremely complex application, even when only some of the modalities are being used. Being able to plan for capacity, not just the number of servers but also bandwidth, is extremely critical.

Master It   Which of the planning toolsets would you use to determine the required bandwidth on the network?

Solution   The Bandwidth Calculator.

Determine when virtualization is appropriate.   Lync Server 2010 introduced support for all modalities when virtualized. Lync Server 2013 has increased the performance capabilities and supported options. In certain cases, this enables administrators to reduce the server footprint, giving a better "green computing" deployment.

Master It   What virtualization support improvements have been introduced with Lync Server 2013?

Solution   Support for client-side virtualization using Virtual Desktop Infrastructure (VDI).

Understand the prerequisites.   Like most applications, Lync Server 2013 has a number of prerequisites that must be met prior to installation. These range from Active Directory requirements to individual server role requirements, at both the OS level and the component level.

Master It   Which operating systems are supported for deployment of Lync Server 2013?

Solution   The following systems are supported:

- Windows Server 2008 R2 Standard (with SP1)
- Windows Server 2008 R2 Enterprise (with SP1)
- Windows Server 2008 R2 Datacenter (with SP1)
- Windows Server 2012 Standard
- Windows Server 2012 Datacenter

Only the 64-bit version of the OS is supported.

Chapter 6: Installation

Configure Windows Server for a Lync installation.   Installing Lync is relatively simple, but many steps are involved. One of the most important is the preparatory work needed. If you get this wrong, it will slow down your installation and you may find that certain features will not work later on down the line.

Master It   Lync can be installed on several subtly different operating systems. You have been asked to lay out which OS requires the least amount of preparatory work and what the main preparatory stages are before Lync can be deployed.

Solution   Lync Server 2013 can be installed on Windows Server 2008 R2 SP1 and Windows Server 2012. Windows Server 2012 requires no additional downloads to be installed above the standard components.

Those components are split into a few categories: the .NET Framework, the web components, and the supporting software installed with Setup, such as the Visual C++ software. Finally, for certain roles, the Windows Media Format Runtime is needed, as are the Active Directory remote server administration tools (RSAT-ADDS).

Prepare Active Directory for Lync installation.   Like many Microsoft server applications, Lync has tight ties with AD. Lync Server 2010 was the first version of Microsoft's real-time communications product to start moving away from the reliance on AD, but nevertheless, with both Lync Server 2010 and Lync Server 2013 there are still hard requirements and preparatory steps that must be carried out, which include schema, forest, and domain prep.

Master It   You are working in a large corporation with a single forest and multiple domains. You have been instructed to work with your directories team to help them understand the changes that need to be made to the schema as part of setup.

Solution   Lync schema prep is run once per forest. It will create new classes and attributes and requires Schema Administrator rights to be carried out. Setup can be run from the GUI tools, which need to be run from a 64-bit server, or from the command line through PowerShell using the Lync cmdlets. If the directories team wants to maintain tight control over the installation, they can import the four LDF files into the directory manually using the LDIFDE tool. The LDF files are readily available to be inspected in the \Support\schema folder on the installation media. A great deal of detailed information about the exact changes required to AD is contained in the Lync help file.

Install your first Standard Edition server.   A Lync Standard Edition server is a complex environment requiring careful deployment. It has numerous prerequisites that need to be installed. Once you have completed the installation of prerequisites, setup is relatively straightforward, following a standard process.

Master It   You have been tasked with installing the first Standard Edition Lync server in your network. What is one of the unique preparatory steps required for this Standard Edition, and why? Following that, what are the standard steps that setup takes?

Solution   When installing the first Standard Edition server in a network, the topology needs to be published to the CMS, which first needs to be created. Because Standard Edition uses a local SQL Express deployment, you need to run Prepare First Standard Edition in the setup GUI tool to create the SQL Express instance locally, which will then allow the topology to be published and setup to continue.

The setup steps that follow are pretty standard:

1. Deploy Local Configuration Store.

2. Install Lync components.

3 Configure certificates.

4. Start services.

5. Install Windows Updates and the latest Lync Cumulative Update.

6. [Optional] Configure accounts for Kerberos use.

Get your first users up and running.   Getting the first users on Lync is slightly more involved than it first sounds. Of course, you need a couple of users with which to test. Enabling them for Lync is straightforward, especially if they already have an email address defined that matches the SIP uniform resource identifier (URI) you want the user to have. The more interesting challenge is getting the client deployed. Of course, this can be done manually, but once things scale out that won't be feasible.

Master It   You are rolling out the Lync client to thousands of users. How would you do this, and what are some of the considerations you need to make?

Solution   Rolling out Lync to many users is possible either using a logon script with the command-line setup tool or by using the MSI file. The MSI file is included as part of the Office 2013 media, both x86 and x64 versions.

Implement external access through the Director, Edge, and reverse proxy servers.   There are many elements that come together to provide external access. The Edge server and reverse proxy server sit in the perimeter network and provide access to media and web components, respectively. The Director sits on the LAN and acts as a routing and security buffer between the external users and the Front End pools. The deployment of the Director is very similar to the deployment of Standard Edition or Front End servers and requires similar prerequisites.

Master It   You are deploying an Edge server as part of providing remote access to your network. What is different about the install compared to the Standard Edition and Director installs?

Solution   The Edge server sits in the perimeter network. As such, it can't automatically pull the config from the CMS during setup. You must, therefore, export the config from the CMS to a file and import it manually as part of installing the Local Configuration Store on the Edge server. Once installation is complete, push synchronization is carried out from the CMS out to the Edge, which allows centralized management.

Understand the differences in an Enterprise Edition installation.   There are many differences when working on an Enterprise deployment of Lync compared to a Standard Edition install. For example, there is the potential for a complex directory to be present, which requires close cooperation with a directories team. Another change is that SQL is installed separately from Lync and does not coexist with the Lync server as it does with Standard Edition. Finally, there is the challenge of scalability and branch offices to overcome.

Master It   You have been asked to work with the database team to ensure that everything is in place for the Lync installation. What do you need to explain and how would you instruct the database team to create the databases?

Solution   Lync requires both a CMS database and a general database for config and user information. Once Lync AD prep is complete, the databases can be installed from the command line. This is done using the `Install-CsDatabase` cmdlet. First, ensure that the server where the command is to be run has the following prerequisites installed:

- Lync Server 2013 Core components (`OCSCore.msi`)

- SQL Server 2012 Management Objects (`SharedManagementObjects.msi`)

- SQL Server 2012 Native Client (`sqlncli.msi`)

- System CLR Types for SQL Server 2012 (`SQLSysClrTypes.msi`)

Next, ensure that the PowerShell execution policy is set to RemoteSigned and then run the relevant `Install-CsDatabase` command to first install the CMS database and then later during setup to install the individual SQL stores per pool.

Chapter 7: Migration and Upgrades

Understand migration considerations.   The process of migrating to Lync involves many aspects of an organization, not the least of which are the end users who will have new functionality to exploit and skills to learn. It is very important to thoroughly evaluate all the phases of a migration and communicate clearly and efficiently to the staff. This is particularly true for any phase of coexistence where some users will be on Lync and others on OCS, potentially with different versions of the client in place.

Master It   You have been asked to prepare a short presentation covering the key elements of the migration. List areas you would cover.

Solution   During a migration to Lync Server 2013, only one other version of OCS or Lync can exist in the organization. Either OCS 2007 R2 or Lync Server 2010 is supported, but not both. Equally, migration from LCS or OCS 2007 is not supported; instead, you must step up to OCS 2007 R2 first. The migration is a side-by-side process where you introduce Lync Server 2013 into the organization and then gradually move services and users across, testing as you go. There is no direct upgrade path. It is important to fully understand the way Lync interacts with legacy components. For example, OCS clients cannot pass traffic through a Lync Mediation server; equally, Lync cannot host UCMA 2.0–based apps. These limitations must be understood and mapped out so the migration progresses smoothly. Finally, communication is critical to ensure that users understand how the migration will affect them.

Consider client pain points.   During Lync migration, your primary concern should be for your users. Throughout the migration users will face a changing environment. How you deal with this and control the changes both through careful process and configuration of policy will have a large impact on the successful completion of the migration.

Master It   You have been asked to prepare a short presentation covering the key difficulties faced by users during migration. List the areas you would cover.

Solution   The major factor in migration is client compatibility. The Lync client cannot talk to the OCS server, so where possible users should remain on OCS until the end of the migration process. This approach means that users will not be able to use Lync functionality, and in a large deployment where the start and finish are separated by months, this may not be acceptable. Therefore, rollout of the Lync client may progress before all users are off OCS. This causes challenges with coexistence. The key challenges are around policy settings. You must ensure that all OCS policies are documented and the correct Lync policies put in place so settings are maintained. Another key area of concern is that of meetings. Lync has a new meeting infrastructure both at the client functionality level and at the server level. You must ensure that users on OCS are properly trained to conduct the new Lync meeting join experience. To help in this regard, it makes sense to roll out the Lync attendee client so that even users on the OCS client can make full use of Lync meeting features when they are invited to a Lync meeting.

Migrate to Lync.   Migrating to Lync is a complex set of processes that will move you from a stable OCS environment to a stable Lync environment with minimal downtime.

Master It   You have been asked to lay out the steps to migrate to Lync. What are they?

Solution

1. **Prepare for the migration:** This stage includes ensuring that all documentation is up-to-date and that the latest patches are installed on all systems.

2. **Deploy the first Lync pool:** Here you create the Lync topology and install Front End (or Standard Edition) servers.

3. **Merge OCS and Lync topology:** With Lync installed, you must ensure that Lync knows about the OCS organization by using the Merge OCS 2007 R2 Topology Wizard.

4. **Configure the first Lync pool:** At this point, you must configure the Lync pool to communicate properly with OCS, in particular the Edge and Mediation Server roles.

5. **Test and migrate pilot users:** Here you move the first test users over from OCS to Lync and test coexistence functionality.

6. **Add Lync Edge and Director roles:** Introduce the Lync Edge and Director roles to give Lync its own route to the outside world.

7. **Move the Lync pool from pilot to production:** This step involves migrating the remaining services required to take the Lync pool from pilot to production, including the Edge federation route, Response Group services, and Exchange UM contact objects. Once it is complete, all users are on Lync.

8. **Complete postmigration steps:** At this point all users are on Lync, so you can migrate any remaining services across to Lync, such as conferencing directories, the Mediation server, and dial-in conferencing numbers.

9. **Decommission legacy systems:** Finally, you must remove OCS from the organization and rerun the Lync Merge OCS 2007 R2 Topology Wizard to remove OCS from the Lync topology.

Chapter 8: Introduction to PowerShell, the Lync Management Shell, and Regular Expressions

Use the PowerShell command syntax.   PowerShell is an easy-to-use command-line interface that provides more control over the manipulation and configuration of Lync (as well as other Microsoft and third-party products).

PowerShell cmdlets consist of a verb, indicating the process (New, Enable, Set, and so on), and a noun, indicating the object (CsUser, CsPool, CsExternalAccessPolicy, and so on).

Master It You need to assign a conference policy to a user. Which is the correct cmdlet to use?

◆ `Grant-CsConferencePolicy`

◆ `Set-CsUser`

◆ `New-CsConferencePolicy`

Solution

`Grant-CsConferencePolicy`

Employ tips and tricks to get more out of PowerShell. PowerShell has many built-in capabilities, and extensions such as Lync provide the specifics to manage an application environment.

One of its most powerful features is the ability to pipe output from one command to another. This ability lets you easily and quickly perform repetitive tasks.

Master It You want to enable all users for Enterprise Voice. How would you do this?

Solution

`Get-CsUser | Set-CsUser EnterpriseVoiceEnabled $True`

Get help using PowerShell. The ability to get detailed help information on any cmdlet, as well as use case examples, without leaving the PowerShell environment is an invaluable time-saver.

Master It You need to manipulate some conference configuration items but you can't remember which cmdlet to use. How can you identify possible cmdlets to use?

Solution

`Get-Command *conference*`

Understand PowerShell remoting and scripting. PowerShell provides a wealth of scripting capability, allowing relatively easy automation of everyday tasks which previously could be very complex.

Remoting extends PowerShell even further. Now you don't need to install individual administration toolsets for every application on an administrator's workstation; simply connect remotely to a PowerShell session and you can use the cmdlets.

Master It You want to administer the Lync Server 2013 configuration from your local workstation without installing any local administration tools and without using Remote Desktop. How would you connect to a remote PowerShell?

Solution

```
$session = New-PsSession -ConnectionUri https://se01.corp.masteringlync.org
/ocspowershell -Authentication NegotiateWithImplicitCredential
Import-PsSession $session
```

Understand regular expressions. Regular expressions are used to help manipulate user dialing habits, to ensure that the correct numbers (from a Lync Server perspective) are provided to the gateway. In the majority of cases, this regex approach is hidden by the Lync Control Panel GUI; however, it may be required to manipulate regex in some complex scenarios (as well as to implement the address book normalization file).

Master It You want to create an entry that will match only upon a six-digit entry, starting with 12. Which is the best approach from those shown?

^12\d{6}

\d{6}

^12\d{4}$

^[12|\d{4}]$

[12]\d{4}$

Solution

^12\d{4}$

Chapter 9: Role-Based Access Control

Use PowerShell to list the standard RBAC groups. RBAC in Lync 2013 is administered through the Lync Server Management Shell (LSMS). There are 11 standard roles that ship with Lync; they provide an organization with the ability to delegate administration with a reasonable degree of granularity.

Master It You are in the middle of planning your enterprise Lync deployment and have been asked by the senior architect to research the available options for administrative delegation. You have been asked to provide a list of standard RBAC roles.

Solution To list the standard roles, you would run the following PowerShell command:

```
Get-CsAdminRole | Where-Object {$_.IsStandardRole -eq $True} | fl Identity
```

Understand the permissions available to each role. There are 11 RBAC roles in Lync. These roles range from granting high-level administrative access using the CSAdministrator role to granting read-only access with the CSViewOnlyAdministrator. To use them properly, you need to know what each role does and understand any overlaps where different roles provide the same capability.

Master It As part of an investigation into how to make the best use of RBAC, you have been asked to identify a list of cmdlets each role grants access to so that it can be analyzed to see which RBAC role best fits the way your administrative teams work.

Solution To provide a list of the cmdlets assigned to an RBAC role, use the command in the following example. It lists the cmdlets assigned to the CSArchivingAdministrator role.

```
Get-CsAdminRole -Identity CSArchivingAdministrator |BREAKHERE Select-Object –
ExpandProperty Cmdlets |BREAKHERE Out-File c:\csarchivingadminrolecmdlets.txt
```

Undertake planning for RBAC roles. Your implementation of RBAC roles should relate to the way your organization is set up for administration. Some organizations are centralized and others are distributed. You must understand your organizational structures and take them into account when planning RBAC roles. It is also important to follow the principle of least privilege, granting only the rights necessary for an administrator to do the job. This may mean utilizing custom roles and targeted scopes at either user OUs or Lync sites.

Master It You are in the middle of planning your enterprise Lync deployment and have been asked by the senior architect to plan the RBAC deployment in your organization. What should you consider?

Solution You must take into account many factors:

◆ The nature of administration in your organization. Is it centralized or distributed?

◆ How many levels of administrators do you have? Are there help desk staff who need basic permissions, or are there a handful of senior administrators who do everything?

◆ Are there separate telephony teams that sit outside the server department but need access to maintain the telephony functions of Lync?

◆ Do your Lync administrators also manage Exchange? If so, how do the roles in Exchange correlate to Lync roles?

◆ The principle of least privilege. Should you grant administrators rights to do their job by using scopes both for site and user?

◆ Are all the existing roles too permissive or restrictive? In that case, consider creating a role with a custom list of cmdlets or scripts assigned.

Create custom RBAC roles and assign them to administrators. Lync allows the creation of custom RBAC roles. These are not as flexible as in Exchange because you cannot grant access to specified single cmdlets. When creating a custom RBAC role, you must specify a template role from one of the eleven standard roles and then set an appropriate scope.

Master It Having carried out a planning exercise, you have decided that the standard Lync roles are not adequate for your organization. Because you have a separate site supported by a separate team of junior admins who only need to manage users in one site, you need to be more specific about the areas that certain administrators can manage. How would you create an RBAC role to ensure that the junior admins don't have too many permissions?

Solution First, you would identify the relevant standard role to use as a template for the custom RBAC role. In this case, you would use the CSUserAdministrator role. Next, consider a suitable name for the role—in this case, RemoteSite-CSUserAdministrator.

Next, you would create the Universal security group in AD with the same name as the new role. Finally, you would create the actual role and, while creating the role, scope it to the Lync site and also to a specific OU that holds the users for the site as follows:

```
New-CsAdminRole -Template CSUserAdministratorBREAKHERE -Identity RemoteSite-CSUserAdmin
-ConfigScopes "Site:RemoteSite"BREAKHERE -UserScopes "OU:ou=RemoteSiteUsersOU,dc=corp,dc
=masteringlync,dc=org"
```

Manipulate the cmdlets assigned to a role. One of the new capabilities of Lync 2013 is the ability for RBAC to be far more flexible that it was in 2010. We can now manipulate roles right down to the cmdlet level, enabling far greater granularity of permissioning.

Master It You have an existing RBAC role created called MinimalRole1. Holders of the role need to be allowed to use only the `Get-CsUser` and `Get-CsAdminRole` cmdlets.

Later on you decide that the role should be expanded to include the use of the `Get-CsAdminRoleAssignment` cmdlet.

Finally, you realize that allowing the `Get-CsUser` cmdlet was a mistake.

Outline the separate steps you would take to carry out each configuration. You should end up with three commands.

Solution   You start by setting the role only to use the `Get-CsUser` and `Get-CsAdminRole` cmdlets:

```
Set-CsAdminRole -Identity MinimalRole1 -Cmdlets "Set-CsUser",Set-CsAdminRole"
```

Next you want to add the `Get-CsAdminRoleAssignment` cmdlet:

```
Set-CsAdminRole -Identity MinimalRole1BREAKHERE -Cmdlets @{Add="Get-
CsAdminRoleAssignment"}
```

Finally, you need to remove the `Set-CsUser` cmdlet:

```
Set-CsAdminRole -Identity MinimalRole1 -Cmdlets @{Remove="Get-CsUser"}
```

Carry out general administration, including granting and removing RBAC roles.   There are a few cmdlets that allow management of RBAC roles in Lync 2013 and most use the `CsAdminRole` verb. All PowerShell roles are assigned through the membership of a linked Active Directory Universal security group.

Master It   A colleague who administered Lync has moved to a new role, and his replacement starts on Monday. You have been asked to ensure that the new staff member has the appropriate rights to do his job.

Solution   Adding and removing RBAC roles from a user is as simple as ensuring membership in the related AD security groups. In this instance, you would first check which roles the colleague who has left was a member of using the following command:

```
Get-CsAdminRoleAssignment -Identity "Useralias"
```

Next, you would add the new administrator's user account to the relevant AD groups and remove the old administrator's account at the same time.

Report on the use of RBAC roles.   Given that the purpose of RBAC is to provide people with administrative access to a system, there will always be a need to review and provide reports to management on who has what access. Reporting on RBAC takes various forms but can all be done through LSMS.

Master It   You have been asked to provide details on which roles have access to the APAC site and list the membership of those roles. How would you proceed?

Solution   First, you would identify the roles that have access to the APAC site using the following command:

```
Get-CsAdminRole | Where-Object {$_.ConfigScopes -match "site:APAC"}
```

Next, to enable searching in AD groups, you would load the Active Directory module into PowerShell:

```
Import-Module ActiveDirectory
```

Finally, for each of the roles that the previous command returns, you would run the following command to list the membership:

```
Get-ADGroupMember -Identity Rolesfromlist | Select name
```

Discuss what is new in RBAC in Lync 2013.   Lync 2010 provided the first iteration of RBAC in the Lync product range. Now Lync 2013 adds some key new capabilities that start to bring the Lync RBAC implementation closer to that of Exchange in flexibility.

Master It You have been asked to produce a short report on what Lync 2013 brings to the table in new RBAC functionality. What would you cover?

Solution Lync 2013 adds the ability to create custom roles that have either a fully user-defined set of cmdlets or the ability to add to an existing template set of cmdlets. It also allows scripts to be specifically added to a role and allow holders of the role to run that script.

There are also two new standard roles, CsPersistentChatAdministrator and CSResponseGroupManager, which give management rights to persistent chat features and a specific response group queue, respectively.

Chapter 10: User Administration

Search for users in the LSCP and PowerShell. Lync offers huge flexibility in what can be done to configure and control the Lync user experience. However, to work efficiently in Lync, being able to identify and retrieve information about different groups of users based on various criteria is critical. It is this skill that enables you to target specific groups with specific policies. As with most administration, you can search for users in both LSCP and PowerShell.

Master It You have been asked to run a report on two groups of users. How would you handle the following requests? Can you use two different types of search?

Locate all users in Marketing.

Locate all users who register to the se01.corp.masteringlync.org pool.

Solution In PowerShell, run the following command:

```
Get-CsUser -LDAPFilter "Department=Marketing"
```

This will get all the Marketing users enabled for Lync using an LDAP filter.

Another type of search is carried out by piping the results of Get-CsUser to the Where-Object cmdlet as demonstrated in the following command:

```
Get-CsUser | Where-Object {[String]$_.Registrarpool
-eq "se01.corp.masteringlync.org"}
```

This command gets all users registering to the pool se01.corp.masteringlync.org.

Perform basic user administration in the LSCP and in PowerShell. As would be expected, most basic administration can be performed in LSCP and in PowerShell. New users can be created, deleted, enabled, and disabled in both. You can, of course, also change various Lync properties—in particular, things like the SIP URI of a user and the pool to which they register. User administration is generally carried out by a user who is a member of the CSUserAdministrator RBAC role.

Master It You have been asked to enable all users, except those who are in Marketing, for Lync. How would you do this? In addition, one of your colleagues, who is a domain administrator, has asked you to make some changes to his account. What problems might you face?

Solution You first need to search for the users and then pipe the output to the Enable-CsUser cmdlet. Remember that until a user is enabled for Lync, you must use the Get-CsAdUser cmdlet to find them:

```
Get-CsAdUser -LDAPFilter "!(Department=Marketing)" | Enable-CsUser
-RegistrarPool se01.corp.masteringlync.org SipAddressType EmailAddress
```

This will get all the users who are not members of the Marketing department (note the use of the ! wildcard to signify NOT). It then enables them for Lync on the se01.corp. masteringlync.org pool using their email addresses for SIP URIs.

For your colleague, you can administer domain administrator Lync users from PowerShell only when you are logged on as a domain administrator yourself.

Understand Lync policies.   Lync has significantly improved the policy architecture since OCS 2007 R2. Although AD Group Policy still can have a role to play in getting the Lync client up and running, Lync enforces the majority of policy through in-band provisioning. It uses SIP messages to push policy out to the client instantly and ensures that there is no requirement for domain membership. Users get a consistent experience no matter where they log on. To apply Lync policies properly, it is important to understand the new scope model, in which policies can be applied at the global, site, service, and user levels and how inheritance works so that the policy closest to the user wins.

> **Master It**   You have been asked to explain to a new Lync administrator the different scopes at which a policy can be applied and how different scopes affect the identity of the policy. What would you tell her?
>
> **Solution**   Lync policies can apply at several levels. By default, there is a global policy that contains the default settings for each policy type. As an administrator with the CSAdministrator RBAC role, you can create policies at the Site, Service, and User level. The identity of the policy is defined by the level at which it is assigned, as shown in this example:
>
> ```
> Site:PolicyName
> Registrar:se01.corp.masteringlync.org
> ```
>
> Site and service policies are assigned automatically when they are created because they are specifically linked by name to a certain object. However, user policies have to be assigned. The identity of a user policy is Tag:PolicyName, which is why they are sometimes called Tag policies.

Manipulate Lync policies.   Lync policies are controlled and applied to users either through PowerShell or through LSCP. When in the shell, your search skills are critical to ensure that you can closely target relevant user groups. It is here that the piping capabilities of PowerShell are so useful. You can, of course, also apply policy through LSCP, which has a helpful Assign Policy page where you can apply applicable policies to one or many users from a single screen.

> **Master It**   You have been asked to create a new client policy for the APAC site. You first need to check the default settings for the policy and then customize it to limit the number of users a person can have on their contacts list to 300. How would you proceed?
>
> **Solution**   To see the default settings for a policy, you can always create a new policy without specifying any settings, but that would leave you with a leftover policy. Instead, a cleaner way is to use the -InMemory parameter as follows:
>
> ```
> New-CsClientPolicy -Identity TestDefaultSettings -InMemory
> ```
>
> This creates an object in memory and prints the default settings. Used in this way, it is never committed to disk.
>
> To create the policy you require, you would use the following command:
>
> ```
> New-CsClientPolicy -Identity Site:EMEA -MaximumNumberOfContacts 300
> ```

Choose the right policy for the job. There is a vast range of policy settings in Lync. One of the hardest things an administrator must do is understand where to make certain configurations. LSCP makes available many policy settings, but it is not always obvious which PowerShell cmdlet sets which setting, compared to what is presented in the LSCP. Equally, it is not possible to carry out all configuration through the LSCP, with some of the most wide-ranging policies being configured only through PowerShell.

Master It You have been asked to design a set of policies for your Lync organization. Where would you gather more information about specific settings?

Solution The list of cmdlets available to create Lync policies and set Lync functionality is long, so you would use the help file to identify what each individual parameter would do. Also, searching in the help file for cs*policy and cs*configuration will bring back a raft of cmdlets to review.

Chapter 11: Archiving and Monitoring

Understand the architecture for the Archiving and Monitoring roles. Although related to different aspects of the data, the Archiving and Monitoring services are very similar in function, and they have similar Back End requirements. This allows them to be easily colocated and share the same database server or instance.

Master It What are the options available for enabling Archiving?

Solution Exchange Integrated, requiring Exchange Server 2013

Traditional SQL archiving to a SQL Server instance within the Lync Server 2013 environment.

Provide reporting on the data available from the Archiving and Monitoring roles. Lync Server 2013 provides a monitoring reports pack containing over 50 reports, which focus on the QoE data. Non-Microsoft vendors provide additional report capability for the other databases, and of course, you can always write your own reports.

Master It What options are available for creating customized reports?

Solution You can connect via ODBC from any data manipulation software (such as Excel), or you can use SQL Server Report Builder to create and publish reports to the SQL Reporting Services server.

Use the capabilities in the System Center Operations Manager management pack to report on the availability of the Lync 2013 service. With the implementation of the Lync Server 2013 Monitoring Management Pack for System Center Operations Manager, administrators have a consolidated approach and location for collating and monitoring system (and service) uptime.

Master It Which synthetic transactions will confirm the status of the Address Book service?

Solution `Test-CsAddressBookService`

`Test-CsAddressBookWebQuery`

Chapter 12: Troubleshooting

Confirm that the basics are in place from the infrastructure side.   Lync Server 2013 relies on a range of additional infrastructure to be able to provide its functionality—such as Active Directory, SQL, DNS, network, and so on. If any of these additional areas suffer interruptions or misconfigurations, it is extremely likely that Lync 2013 will begin to demonstrate issues also.

Master It   An internal Lync 2013 client is having difficulty connecting to its home pool when using automatic configuration. Describe the flow of DNS and connection attempts made for a client on the corporate network.

Solution   First, automatic configuration will attempt the following DNS queries:

```
_sipinternaltal._tcp.<sip domain> (A DNS SRV record)
sipinternal.<sip domain>
sip.<sip domain>
```

The SRV record will return a CNAME record, which will require a further DNS lookup to return the IP address. All other requests will return the IP address of the pool.

The client will attempt to connect and register with this pool; if this is a Director pool, the client will receive a redirect to the home pool.

A further DNS lookup will be carried out due to the redirection, and the client will attempt to register with a server from this pool; if this server is not the home server itself, the final redirect will occur with the client being sent to the home server.

If the SRV record is not available, the remaining DNS records are resolved in order, with the client attempting to connect to the returned addresses.

Understand how to troubleshoot the client.   The Lync 2013 client provides a lot of information in the configuration section as well as the log files to aid with troubleshooting, and this information should not be overlooked.

Master It   Where are the client log files stored?

Solution   In the following folder:

```
%USER PROFILE%\Appdata\Local\Microsoft\Office\15.0\Lync\Tracing
```

Know how to enable troubleshooting on the server.   The Lync Server 2013 roles each have individual components that require logging and also provide performance counter objects that can be monitored.

By default, the logging scenario AlwaysOn is enabled on the servers. The default logging options and components can be configured to suit users' needs.

Master It   Which tool has replaced OCSLogger and is now used to enable logging on a Lync Server 2013 server?

Solution   ClsController.exe and ClsAgent.exe. Generically called the Central Logging Tool under the Common Files\Microsoft Lync Server 2013 folder structure.

Understand and use the troubleshooting tools available.   In addition to the built-in logging functionality of Lync Server 2013, more tools can (and should) be downloaded and installed on each of the servers to provide a better range of data, which is ready to be captured in the event of a problem.

Master It   Which tool is recommended for analyzing SIP logs or message traces? And where can it be found?

Solution   `snooper.exe`. It is part of the Lync 2013 Debugging Tools download.

Chapter 13: Getting Started with Voice

Understand the voice capabilities.   Lync Server 2013 has dramatically expanded the capabilities provided by Microsoft in the Unified Communications space to be almost on a par with enterprise PBXs (and certainly equal to, if not better than, departmental PBX offerings).

Master It   Describe the benefits of media bypass.

Solution   Media bypass allows the media flow to bypass the Mediation server and connect directly to the gateway or remote endpoint. This removes potential delays introduced by transcoding the media, resulting in less chance of call quality degradation. In addition, when this transcoding requirement is removed from the Mediation server, it allows the Mediation server to scale up the number of concurrent calls it can handle as well as provide the capability to colocate the Mediation server on a Front End, reducing the deployed server footprint.

Understand the voice architecture.   With the introduction of media bypass and the support for virtualization, the architectural requirements to deploy voice have been consolidated into a smaller server footprint, and at the same time additional functionality has been included in the product. Significant investment has been made in the high availability and resiliency deployment models.

Master It   Describe the user experience when the user's home pool fails and only a backup registrar has been configured.

Solution   The user's clients will be disconnected from the server, and it will automatically log in to the backup registrar. This is known as Survivable mode and it provides limited functionality—the ability to make and receive voice calls as well as to search for users.

A user who has a call in progress will be able to continue this call with no impact (the client will transfer to Survivable mode seamlessly in the background).

If a user is joined to a conference hosted on the failed pool, they will lose connection to the conference and be unable to rejoin. If the conference is hosted on a different pool, they will remain connected.

Configure voice policies and routing.   Aside from the architectural requirements, to enable Enterprise Voice requires configuration to be applied to users (policies) and Back End configuration to be applied to the servers (routing).

Master It   What configuration joins the user configuration to the server configuration and provides the permissions to enable (or block) a call?

Solution   PSTN usages are attached to both the Voice policy and the routes, and a user must have the PSTN usage as part of their Voice policy to enable them to use a route associated with the same PSTN usage.

Chapter 14: Call Admission Control

Identify Call Admission Control–capable endpoints.   Before designing and configuring Call Admission Control, you need to understand where it can be applied to ensure that the proper configuration is identified.

Master It   You are in the process of defining a migration from OCS R2 to Lync Server 2013. Users previously reported some issues with call quality due to the capacity on the network, so Call Admission Control is required. Which user endpoints can be restricted by the Call Admission Control policy?

Solution   All Lync endpoints can be restricted by the Call Admission Control policy:

◆   Lync (2010/2013) Communicator client

◆   Lync 2010/2013 Phone Edition

◆   Lync Server 2010/2013 roles (Edge, Mediation, and Front End server roles)

Configure policy-based Quality of Service controls.   Call Admission Control provides application-layer management of the call bandwidth; however, to truly provide this guarantee to clients, Quality of Service is required to operate on the network layer. Windows Vista introduced policy-based Quality of Service controls.

Master It   You have restricted the port range to be 5000 to 5999, and you will deploy Lync 2013 to your users. An application utilized in the finance department uses the port range 5500 to 5599. How can you ensure that only the Lync 2013 traffic is prioritized on the network?

Solution   Define a policy-based QoS group policy, which specifies the port range to prioritize and sets the application to `Communicator.exe`.

Design a Call Admission Control solution.   Call Admission Control can be complex in large interconnected networks. A properly designed solution will ensure that two important requirements of Call Admission Control are met: User call quality is high and the network is not saturated.

Master It   What special considerations should be given to an MPLS network?

Solution   The MPLS cloud should be defined as a region, with each network link defined as a connection to a site. No site should be associated directly with the region. If multiple MPLS clouds are used (for example, one in Europe and one in America), then each should be a separate region, and region links (and routes) will be required too.

Configure Call Admission Control.   Once designed, Call Admission Control needs to be configured and applied to the Lync 2013 servers. The servers will keep each other constantly updated as to the number of the calls and bandwidth used on the network. By using the built-in logging functionality, it is possible to capture an hourly snapshot of the state, with more detailed reporting available via the monitoring server.

Master It What needs to be defined and applied to configure Call Admission Control?

Solution

◆ Regions

◆ Sites

◆ Policy profiles

◆ Subnets

If multiple regions are defined, you also need region links and region routes.

Chapter 15: E911 and Location Information Services

Describe the E911 requirements for North America. Enhanced emergency services dialing provides location information to emergency services, enabling them to better respond in the event of an emergency.

Master It Is the provision of location information with emergency dialing compulsory?

Solution Providing location information is required only in certain states in North America, and even then the requirements differ from state to state.

Configure Lync Server 2013 to meet E911 requirements. As a viable PBX, Lync Server 2013 is required to meet the E911 requirements to provide location information data and as such must have validated address information provided with each emergency call.

Master It Through what configuration items can location information data be delivered to the Lync 2013 client?

Solution Any of the following methods can be used:

◆ Subnet

◆ Switch chassis

◆ Switch port

◆ Wireless SSID

◆ Manual configuration

◆ Secondary location services such as a MACResolver or Secondary Location Source database

Understand how Location Information services can be used by users outside North America. Although the actual requirements are only currently defined in locations in North America, beta program feedback from customers indicated that automatic Location Information services are extremely useful and desired worldwide.

Master It What specifically is required to enable Location Information services in North America, and what different requirements are in place for the rest of the world?

Solution   Inside North America, address validation against the Master Street Address Guide provides the address validation. Outside North America, the requirement is to have installed at least Cumulative Update 1 to provide a suggested address automatically.

Understand how to query multiple sources of location information.   Lync Server 2013 allows for multiple sources of location information to be queried. Lync Server 2013 can be pointed to additional location databases or applications that can reduce the overhead in discovery and definition of all the network locations for an organization.

Master It   Which cmdlet and parameters are used to configure secondary location information sources?

Solution   An SNMP application is configured as follows:

```
Set-CsWebServiceConfiguration -MACResolveUrl "<app url>"
```

A secondary location source application is configured as follows:

```
Set-CsWebServiceConfiguration -SecondaryLocationSourceUrl "<app url>"
```

Chapter 16: Extended Voice Functionality

Understand the extended voice functionality.   Extended voice functionality provides additional voice applications that many organizations expect a PBX to have. Understanding what these applications can and cannot do is important so you can make the correct decisions when implementing them and know when a third-party solution is better.

Master It   The manager for an internal help desk has been to a trade show and has been told he needs to have a full contact center to implement certain requirements. All he needs is to route calls to agents. He does not care about reporting or recording; he just needs to make sure that calls get to the right people. He is adamant that he needs a call center because this is what the experts have told him.

Solution   Response Groups can fulfill these requirements because items such as reporting and recording are not required. Although it can be difficult to dissuade people from accepting what an expert has told them, showing them what can be done is usually the best way. Find out what they need to do and create the Response Groups; then show them that they can do what they want at a fraction of the cost.

Design solutions using extended voice functionality.   Designing is usually seen as a boring, time-consuming task, when all you want to do is get your hands dirty and implement something. Although some of the extended voice functionality is straightforward, other elements are complex, and missing the design stage could cause you problems later. Design, design, design—and implement once.

Master It   You need to implement a dial-in conferencing solution globally. You need to have global dial-in numbers and support at least 100 concurrent PSTN calls to the conferencing solution.

Solution   Dial-in conferencing may seem easy. You already have Enterprise Voice deployed. You just need to add some access numbers and away you go. Usually, this is not the case. Although you may have designed for Enterprise Voice in terms of PSTN capacity and bandwidth, dial-in conferencing adds more load, in this case the requirement for 100 concurrent calls PSTN. This requires not only additional PSTN capacity but also sufficient capacity on the Mediation and Conferencing servers.

Never assume that an existing voice design will be able to cope with additional requirements. If you are changing the dynamics of an element, in this case Enterprise Voice, you need to go back to the drawing board and update the design to cope with the new requirements.

Implement extended voice functionality. Lync's extended voice functionality is useless if you do not know how to implement it and use it to its fullest potential. To do that, you need to make sure that what you implement works and is fully tested.

Master It You have implemented Call Park but users are complaining about intermittent issues with parking calls. The complaints are coming from all user types, which is strange because not all users should be able to park calls.

Solution The first step is to determine why these users are able to park calls. To do this, you can use PowerShell to query the Voice policies to see which ones have Call Park enabled. To do that, issue the following command:

```
Get-CsVoicePolicy | select Identity, EnableCallPark | fl
```

This will return all the Voice policies and indicate if Call Park is enabled or not. In this case, the following was returned:

```
Identity       : Global
EnableCallPark : False
Identity       : Tag:Attendants
EnableCallPark : True
Identity       : Tag:IWs
EnableCallPark : True
```

From this, you can see that the IWs policy has `EnableCallPark` set to `True`, allowing all information workers to park calls. Setting this to `False` will prevent them from using Call Park:

```
Set-CsVoicePolicy -Identity IWs -EnableCallPark $false
```

Now only the attendants will be able to park calls. At this stage, you can wait to see if the attendants report any issues. The intermittent issue probably occurred because Call Park ran out of orbits because it was sized only for the attendants and not for everyone.

Chapter 17: Exchange and SharePoint

Integrate Lync with Exchange. Exchange provides a wide range of functionality to Lync, and Lync helps enhance Exchange. The most important integration points are for the provision of voice mail, where Exchange UM is the only supported voice mail platform for Lync. To enhance Exchange, Lync enables building presence and basic IM capabilities directly into OWA. There are also less obvious integration points because Lync utilizes Exchange Web Services to pull information about users' calendar entries and their contacts, providing enhanced presence information and a single view of a person as an entity with whom to communicate.

Master It You company is rolling out Lync as its telephony platform, and you will be using Exchange 2013 as your voice mail platform. You have been asked to outline the process to the Exchange administrative team.

Solution   Integration of Lync into Exchange UM takes the following major steps:

1. Ensure that the correct certificates are in place for the Exchange UM service. It is important that the Exchange UM service is bound to a certificate that is trusted by Lync and has the FQDN of the Exchange UM server as its subject name.

2. Configure the Exchange UM elements of the system (dial plan, policy, and auto attendants). Exchange dial plans are used to set major configuration points such as the security of communications and the length of the phone extension number. Make sure your PIN access policy is set up suitably for your organization.

3. Ensure that Exchange knows about Lync as a gateway. You will use the `ExchUCUtil.PS1` script to set the correct permissions and to set up the Exchange VoIP gateway object to represent the Lync server.

4. Check to see that Lync dial plans are configured correctly. Lync must be able to understand the dialing setup in the Exchange dial plan.

5. Configure Lync to use Exchange UM. You will use the `OcsUmUtil.exe` application to set up the contact objects so that Lync knows how to route calls to Exchange voice mail and auto attendants.

6. Enable users for UM. Each user will need to be enabled for Exchange UM through either the Exchange Management Console or PowerShell.

Integrate Lync with SharePoint.   SharePoint integration is both relatively simple and potentially complex! It is simple in that integrating presence capability is automatic, and it is complex in that you have the ability through application development to put together almost any piece of communication-enhanced workflow that you can think up. SharePoint integration also provides the Skill Search capability to Lync.

Master It   Your organization makes extensive use of SharePoint 2010 and already has OCS 2007 R2, which has been providing presence integration. Now you are moving to Lync 2013 and SharePoint 2013, and you have been asked to investigate the requirements for Skill Search integration between Lync and SharePoint.

Solution   SharePoint-based Skill Search is not enabled in Lync by default.

For this new feature to work correctly, the following components and configuration are required:

◆ A full version of SharePoint is required; Windows SharePoint Services (WSS) will not work with Skill Search.

◆ SharePoint 2013 My Sites.

◆ The SharePoint User Profile service application; this stores information about users in a central location and is where users' My Sites are administered and configured.

◆ A SharePoint Search Center site URL; a feature introduced in Microsoft Office SharePoint Server 2007, it is a SharePoint site specifically configured for the search task. It includes certain fields, each responsible for a specific search task—for example, People Search.

◆ SharePoint must be published to the Internet so that external Lync clients can access it.

◆ Lync Server needs to be configured with the correct Search Center URL to provide to clients. The Search Center URL is provisioned to the Lync client through in-band settings, as discussed in Chapter 10.

Chapter 18: Hybrid Deployments

Understand the Lync hybrid architecture model.   Lync Server 2013 introduces the new capability of a hybrid model that allows hosting some users of an organization on premises in the traditional way of having on-premises infrastructure deployed but also hosting other members of the organization in a cloud solution.

Master It   Lync Server 2013 (and previous versions) provides support for multiple SIP domains in the same Lync deployment within an Active Directory forest. What change to this model does the hybrid deployment require?

Solution   The hybrid deployment allows a single SIP domain to be shared with both on-premises and cloud infrastructures, in a way "federating" with itself in the cloud.

Understand the capabilities of a hybrid deployment.   Users can be hosted either online in the cloud, or on premises on a local infrastructure. Each location provides a common set of features, but not all are available when users are using Lync Online.

Master It   Which features are only available in an on-premises deployment?

Solution

Remote call control

Voice resiliency

Response group services

Call Park

Integration with an on-premises call center

In addition, E911 and Media Bypass are available only with a local infrastructure but can be used by Lync Online users.

Understand the call flow for media in different scenarios.   Lync can be a very complex product when it comes to understanding signaling flows and media flows. Using Edge servers adds additional complexity, and having an additional pool hosted in the cloud adds a level of complexity beyond simple Edge servers!

Master It   Describe the call flow path between two users, Alice and Bob. Alice is calling from a cell phone to Bob's Lync phone number. Bob is a Lync Online user and is located currently on the corporate network.

Solution

1. Alice places a PSTN call to Bob's DID (Bob is an Hybrid Voice user). The call is received on the on-premises PSTN media gateway.

2. The on-premises media gateway directs the call to the Lync Mediation server, which is collocated on the on-premises Lync 2013 pool.

3. The Lync on-premises infrastructure knows that Bob has an Active Directory object on premises. The reverse number lookup can look at Bob's on-premises object and determine that Bob is in the federated Lync Online infrastructure (the Deployment Locator attribute).

4. The SIP signaling (the call) is then routed over the federation route via the Edge server up to the Lync Online infrastructure.

5. The SIP signaling is sent from the Lync Online infrastructure to Bob's endpoint.

6. When Bob answers, the call media is established and flows using the optimal path between the on-premises Mediation server/PSTN infrastructure and Bob's client. This could be using Media Bypass if configured or the media may flow via the Mediation server if Media Bypass is not configured.

Understand the required steps to configure a hybrid deployment. Introducing a hybrid scenario to a local Lync Server 2013 environment requires a number of additional configuration items to be carried out. Some are as basic (and expected) as firewall port configuration, while others are significantly more complex, such as ADFS configuration.

Master It You are configuring your organization for Hybrid Voice and need to configure rules for the proxy exceptions list. What do you need to configure?

Solution

- Allow outgoing connections to `*.microsoftonline.com`.
- Allow outgoing connections to `*.microsoftonline-p.com`.
- Allow outgoing connections to `osub.microsoft.com`.
- Allow outgoing connections to `*.outlook.com`.
- Allow outgoing connections to `*.lync.com`.
- Allow TCP and HTTPS.
- Set HTTPS/SSL time-out to 8 hours.

Chapter 19: Third-Party Integration

Connect to telephony systems using a gateway. Gateway devices enable Lync to connect to a wide range of different telephony platforms in a uniform way, providing intelligent routing and security.

Master It When connecting to telephony systems, three main components come into play. What are they?

Solution Signaling transport is a way of passing information about the communication between systems, such as the calling number and called number. SIP is the protocol used with Lync, which can be carried over TCP (as Lync uses) or UDP (as some SIP trunk providers use).

A media codec is the method used to encode the audio (or video) stream for transport. It is agreed to by both parties as part of the signaling traffic when the call is set up.

Different systems support different codecs: Lync uses RTAudio natively, while G.711 is common on the PSTN. The gateway performs a process called transcoding, which is the process of converting audio encoded with one codec into audio encoded in another codec to help two different systems communicate.

Media transport is the process of actually getting the encoded audio from one system to another. The standard protocol for transporting the voice traffic itself over IP is Real-Time Transport Protocol (RTP). A later extension to this protocol, known as Secure RTP, or SRTP, added security to eliminate the risk of interception and eavesdropping. The endpoint devices encrypt any voice traffic within a secure payload before transmitting over the IP network. Lync employs SRTP for communication to the gateway.

Integrate with your PBX. Connecting Lync to telephony systems need not be hard; however, there are many areas you must consider to ensure that you make the correct deployment choices. Lync can connect directly to an ITSP or a PBX or in both cases can utilize a gateway device to provide security, control, and intelligent routing of traffic.

Master It Your PBX is five years old and capable of being upgraded to talk to Lync directly. You want to deploy Lync for Enterprise Voice and need a way out to the PSTN. What must you consider in your decision about connecting Lync to the PSTN?

Solution While your PBX could be upgraded, if you are deploying Lync for voice, it is unlikely that spending additional money on a piece of legacy hardware you plan to replace makes sense. Therefore, you have to consider either operating Lync as an entirely separate entity to the PBX with a separate numbering scheme or, far more likely, utilizing a gateway to connect the two systems. You have a choice about where you position the gateway in the system. Placing the gateway in front of the PBX and Lync is highly recommended; the gateway will take the place of the PBX in terminating the inbound lines. This gives the most flexibility in the way calls can be routed and means that the PBX hardly has to be reconfigured at all, leaving the gateway to intelligently route calls between the systems.

Use RCC to integrate with your PBX. Remote Call Control (RCC) allows you to use the Lync software client on your PC to control your physical phone handset from PBX vendors like Cisco, Mitel, and Avaya. It allows you to maintain your PBX as the audio transport mechanism while enhancing the functionality of the PBX with click-to-call and Address Book lookup features of the Lync software client. Each vendor has a slightly different way of hooking up Lync with its PBX because they each provide the SIP/CSTA gateway that allows communication.

Master It You have been asked to look into why your company might use RCC. What are the key points about which you would report?

Solution RCC is useful in that it extends the capability of an existing PBX. It enables the Lync client to be used to control the phone and provides integration with the PC for elements like name lookup, call logging, and simple by-contact (rather than number) dialing. If you have a heavily entrenched PBX system, this may be an integration point that is worth considering. However, RCC is a challenging technology to implement, given that each vendor has its own SIP/CSTA gateway. It also ties you into a legacy PBX technology, which by definition cannot provide the fully integrated experience that Lync embraced completely as a voice communication platform can provide. Finally, RCC users cannot make video calls, which is a massive limitation for some.

Deploy a Survivable Branch Appliance.   The Lync SBA is one of the great additions that make Lync a fully viable voice platform for the enterprise. It provides the capability for branch offices to maintain the ability for PSTN breakout even if the WAN to the central Lync site is down.

Master It   You have been asked to roll out an SBA to a branch location. What are the main prerequisite and deployment steps to which you should adhere?

Solution   First, you should prestage the SBA in the central site. This requires the following steps:

1.   A reverse lookup must be created on the DNS server for the SBA.

2.   DNS *A* records must be available for the gateway and SBA.

3.   The SBA should be added as a computer before deployment, and RTCUniversalSBATechnician should be in the default group.

4.   A service principal name needs to be applied to the SBA computer in `ADSI.edit`.

5.   The account used within the gateway to deploy the SBA (for example, Administrator) should be a member of the RTCUniversalSBATechnician group.

6.   The SBA should be configured in the correct branch site from Lync Topology Builder and successfully published to the CMS.

Once the prerequisites are met, the deployment should proceed as follows:

1.   Install and physically cable the SBA at the branch site.

2.   Configure an IP address for the SBA.

3.   Join the domain.

4.   Prepare the SBA and replicate against the Front End pool.

5.   Assign the required certificates to enable security.

6.   Start the services.

7.   Verify the operational status.

8.   Start to migrate users in the branch to the SBA.

Connect to other external systems via an XMPP gateway.   The XMPP gateway is now integral to Lync Server 2013 and gives you the capability to connect Lync to other IM platforms, both internally (in the case of an internal Jabber or Sametime system) or externally to public clouds like Gmail. It is deployed on a separate server and interacts with Lync through the Edge server.

Master It   You need to install and configure the XMPP gateway. What do you need to do?

Solution   Enabling XMPP in the Lync infrastructure requires the following steps:

◆   Enable XMPP in Topology Builder.

◆   Define XMPP federated partners.

◆   Enable federated user access.

◆ Define a policy that allows XMPP.

◆ Apply the policy to users.

Utilize third-party software enhancements.   As a software UC platform, Lync is infinitely extendable. This gives rise to the possibility for third-party developers to create products that enhance the native functionality in key ways, such as call recording and call billing. Equally, it enables in-house development teams to incorporate Lync communications functionality directly into line-of-business apps in your organization.

Master It   Call recording is one of the available add-on applications for Lync. Name the two locations where call recording can be carried out and describe the difference this makes to the types of calls that can be recorded.

Solution   Two types of call recording are typically used: trunk side and line side.

Trunk-side recording typically records all calls that include a participant from inside and outside the organization, for both inbound and outbound calls.

Line-side recording allows calls between internal extensions and also those external to the organization to be recorded, thereby giving greater flexibility by allowing any call to be recorded.

Chapter 20: Mobility

Understand the different capabilities of each mobile client (including tablets).   Lync Server 2013 released with the capability to allow Lync 2010 mobile client connectivity. However, since the release of CU1 in February 2013, Lync 2013 mobile clients are natively available and are able to bring new mobility features to the environment.

Master It   What capabilities are not available on phone devices but are available on the Windows 8 Modern UI and iPad?

Solution   Meeting capabilities are enhanced for the Windows 8 Modern UI and iPad clients when compared to phone devices, with support for content sharing as well as the multiparty video feature.

Understand the policies available to manage mobile clients.   With another client available to connect to Lync Server 2013, it's important for the administrator to be able to manage the feature capabilities as well as they would do with any other device client.

Master It   Name the three settings new to the Lync 2013 mobile client, which can be managed via the `*-CsMobilityPolicy` cmdlets.

Solution   The three settings new to the Lync 2013 mobile client are as shown below:

◆ `EnableIPAudioVideo` for enabling IP to be used for audio and video

◆ `RequireWIFIForIPAudio` for allowing users to place audio calls via Wi-Fi

◆ `RequireWIFIForIPVideo` for allowing users to place video calls via Wi-Fi

Understand the infrastructure configuration required for enabling mobile devices. Not only is an update (CU1) required, but specific additional configuration is needed to enable the mobility clients, and of course, consideration must be given to the specification of the hardware (and number) servers needed. Capacity planning for mobility is built into the capacity planning tools, but the configuration still requires the administrator to take a hand!

Master It What is required to configure push notifications for Apple iOS and Microsoft Windows Phone devices?

Solution Federation must be in place with the Lync Online push notification service. This service will take a message and distribute to Apple or Microsoft as necessary.

```
New-CsHostingProvider -Identity "LyncOnline" -Enabled $True
-ProxyFqdn "sipfed.online.lync.com"
-VerificationLevel UseSourceVerification
New-CsAllowedDomain -Identity "push.lync.com"
```

The mobility configuration must also be configured to use push notification; each Apple iOS (for Lync 2010 mobile client only) and Microsoft Windows Phone device is configured using separate parameters.

```
New-CsPushNotificationConfiguration -Identity "Enable push"
-EnableApplePushNotificationService $True
-EnableMicrosoftPushNotificationService $True
```

Chapter 21: Telephony Devices

Integrate with hardware video conferencing platforms. Lync can integrate with several hardware video platforms to provide control and connectivity through Lync to room-based and high-quality video networks.

Master It You are trying to configure Lync integration with a Polycom HDX unit, but it won't connect. What might be causing an issue?

Solution There are a couple of common errors when configuring the HDX platform to talk to Lync. You should double-check that the Lync user logging into the HDX for Enterprise Voice is enabled, and you should also check that you have matching encryption settings on both sides so you don't have one platform requiring encryption while the other one will only send in the clear.

Configure prerequisites for IP phones. Lync IP phones are designed to be as simple as possible to deploy and receive all of their configuration settings automatically. For this to occur, a number of items need to be configured, such as network configuration and DHCP.

Master It You have deployed Lync IP phones, but you are unable to log in to the phones when using extension and PIN authentication; however, logging in using USB tethering works as expected.

Solution This issue usually occurs when the Lync phone cannot reach an NTP server. An indication of this is that it takes more than 30 seconds to retrieve the time during the login process. In a network trace, you can see the phone performing DNS queries for the NTP server, trying to connect to them, and failing.

This often occurs when the NTP DNS records weren't created and/or the NTP server is not responding. Lync will attempt to fall back to time.windows.com, but if the organization's firewall blocks access to UDP port 123, this will also fail.

Ensure that the DNS records are created. You should see a successful response in a network trace and verify that the NTP server is working.

You can't use logging on the IP phone at this stage because the in-band provisioning stage has not been reached to enable logging or to set the upload location.

Appendix B

Adoption

Throughout this book, we've discussed a wide range of topics, explored details of the Lync product, and even delved into integration with third-party products. However, all this technical information is not enough to ensure that you have a successful experience with Lync.

Lync is a unified communications platform and, as such, has the potential to radically change a business. In particular, it changes the way people communicate. There are so many potential benefits of unified communications that it has become one of the top chief information officer (CIO) priorities in recent years. However, unless this radical change is managed correctly within a business, it can easily cause anxiety and resentment, which hinder the implementation of the technology and slow the pace at which a business sees a return on its investment. After all, a business is simply a bunch of people who know things, and without them all you have is a shell, perhaps a brand. You need to take these people with you on your journey with Lync. This appendix aims to show you how!

Understanding the Power of UC

Unified communications (UC) is one of the big buzz phrases in IT, rivaled only by *the cloud* and *virtualization*. It is notoriously hard to define, and people have various understandings of its meaning. For us, *unified communications* is all about providing customers—both end users and more widely the companies they work for—with the ability to work efficiently by communicating and collaborating through whatever means necessary, wherever and whenever they need to work. This communication might be either one to one or multiparty, either internal or across organizations. Communication should be woven tightly into an organization and integrated with the business process to drive productivity and efficiency. In that sense, UC could be thought of more as ubiquitous communication.

Of course, that utopian vision requires a fair amount of work in the background. There is the technical challenge of integrating and providing communication modalities such as voice, video, instant messaging (IM), email, voice mail, SMS, and fax, which we have covered in depth in this book. However, in many ways, the technical challenge is far simpler than changing the culture of a business, making information about people and process freely available, and changing the way people work and communicate. Any company that embarks on a unified communications project needs to clearly identify why they are doing so, what they must achieve, and how they will bring this change to users.

The Promise

As you can see, UC has immense power. It can allow people to communicate more efficiently than ever before, potentially saving companies millions in hard cash in several ways. For example, instead of spending money on a cents-per-minute basis with third-party conferencing services, with Lync you can bring this bridge functionality in house. In large companies, this has regularly shown savings on the order of millions or even tens of millions of dollars per year. Even in small companies of a few hundred people, it can save several thousand dollars a year, which is enough to contribute significantly to the deployment costs. Another significant savings possibility is that of travel reduction. Although we are in no way advocating stopping travel altogether, there might be chance to cut back, by perhaps sending only one person to meet a customer while the other dials in using voice and video to a meeting. Similarly, instead of senior managers all traveling to meet each other on a regular basis, some of these meetings could be held using solely Lync or Lync in conjunction with a third party like Polycom, thereby saving travel costs and time, not to mention reducing the company's carbon footprint, which is so important these days. Other significant reductions in cost can be made through the flexibility Lync brings—for example, enabling people to work from home or from various locations without necessarily coming into the central office all the time.

Other benefits are harder to quantify. Lync brings people together; as we've said, a business is only a bunch of people who know things working together. In that capacity, if these people cannot communicate quickly and efficiently, then you are simply not allowing them to work to their fullest potential. Enabling efficient communication can speed up business processes—for example, by allowing automated document signoff through routing to the most suitable person based on availability—and it can make resorting to voice mail a rarity because presence makes a person's availability known. Finally, all these examples can easily be extended outside a single company to a wide ecosystem of partners and customers, allowing even wider savings and better customer service.

The Pitfalls

Unified communications products often challenge organizational structure. Lync is no different. In fact, given that it is so successful as a true UC product bringing together IM, voice, video, and conferencing, it is perhaps even more disruptive. Traditionally, companies have had a networking team and a server team. Often there has also been a telephony team, which potentially in recent times has merged or coexisted with the networking team. Lync, of course, doesn't fit nicely into these boundaries. One of the major challenges many organizations will face is how to fit Lync into this structure. For some companies, this can stall the project to roll out Lync; other companies have to take a serious look at why they want Lync and then work out what the future looks like. In many senses that could be a combined working party or a complete restructuring, as the server team takes on board the new technology and brings in elements of the telephony and networking teams to make this work.

What is important is to be aware of the broader goal of deploying Lync and not to get bogged down in all the politics that inevitably occur as change happens within a business. Clarity of communication is important, so that people know what is happening, why it is happening, and what it means to them. Leadership is essential; projects sponsored by a strong CIO have far more chance of success than something led by a team from IT (often the server team), who inevitably end up fighting battles with networks and telecoms.

People react strongly to change, and not usually in a positive way. Of course, there are some who embrace change, but more often than not, people shy away from something different. This is simple human nature. However, in situations where you have placed your reputation on driving a successful rollout of new technology, it is something that needs significant thought to overcome. Much of the reticence can be overcome by explanation and user training. All the elements outlined in "The Promise" earlier, when combined, offer huge potential; it is critically important that these messages are understood not just by the CIO who signs off on the project but by the business as a whole. People need to be shown how this new technology makes their working lives easier.

Introducing Lync to Your Business

Now that we've looked at the power of UC and some of the human-related pitfalls that can befall deployments of this nature, let's move on to how best to address the rollout of Lync in your business. There are two major elements: One is to pilot Lync and the other is to ensure adequate training for users. However, there are also surrounding efforts that can be undertaken to play roles in a successful deployment.

Rolling out a new technology can be seen very much as launching a new product. As such, it is sensible to mount a marketing campaign. Many companies, for example, create posters and ads for display in prominent locations and on intranet portals. They help communicate key messages about the features of the new technology, such as the ability to create conference calls with ease; they also communicate why the business is deploying the technology, such as work flexibility and cost savings.

The most successful examples of this type of campaign that we've been involved with created excitement before deployment, gradually enforced the messaging, added new information about features and functions, and highlighted where users could get support and learn more at their own pace. This type of prelaunch marketing campaign should utilize all the media types available, including items such as posters, websites, email messaging, and videos, perhaps from the CEO or other senior managers.

LYNC IS MORE THAN JUST A TELEPHONE SYSTEM

Although Lync can replace a telephony system or conferencing platform, it is really important that you fight the widespread assumption that Lync is simply a replacement for whatever was previously in place. Simply put, it isn't! Yes, Lync takes over many functions provided by other communication platforms in the past; however, as we've mentioned many times, Lync is much more. It is a unified platform that allows not only communication in its own right but communication as part of the business process.

It is absolutely essential that this mindset is positioned correctly at the highest levels of the company. This is not always a problem; sometimes people just "get it." But if your senior personnel think of Lync as "just another phone system," you will be limited because the messages coming down from them will not be positive and will not have the changing effect that Lync can have. Be aware of this possibility and use all the resources available from Microsoft and the partner community to demonstrate the wider benefits and uses of Lync to ensure that your organization gets the most out of it.

Clearly not all of these and the following ideas will work for everyone because every company is different; however, these suggestions have been tried and tested in several different scenarios and have been found to be useful.

Piloting Lync

Once you have made the decision to roll out Lync, running a pilot is essential. This may take a couple of different forms. You may find that running a proof of concept (PoC) is necessary to evaluate specific Lync features and functionality. The PoC would likely have very specific success criteria and look at only a handful of features. It would be carried out to prove that Lync can meet the stated requirements. It is important to make sure the PoC isn't confused with a full pilot. The full pilot program should take place once the production deployment of Lync is completed. That way, people participating in the pilot would be running on the actual systems, which would be taken live if the pilot succeeds.

When starting up the main Lync pilot, the first thing to undertake is to set out the success criteria. Without this, you will never know whether you have succeeded in your aim and can continue with a Lync rollout. Success criteria can be very simple, such as that you have run with Lync for two weeks across a broad range of users and received notification of issues that have been resolved. It could also be more specific, encompassing the uptime of the service and the number of minutes of voice, video, and conference calls completed. Either way, it is important to lay out these criteria and understand how you will monitor results, either through existing monitoring tools, such as System Center Operations Manager, or through Lync-specific tools, such as the Monitoring server reports, or perhaps even through your in-house help desk tool.

We have found that a pilot should take various steps. It will probably start as an evaluation by IT staff. This enables testing of all the main functionality without exposing it to the wider staff. It also enables IT to make sure they are comfortable monitoring and supporting the service and that they have hit the most common issues users are likely to experience. This is important because part of the process of rolling out a new technology is to maintain a positive user experience. There is nothing worse than rolling out something to a wide audience too early when IT doesn't know how to support it and when there are still major issues. Doing so causes negativity, and people won't want to use the technology, which is exactly the opposite of what is required for a successful rollout. This IT phase of the pilot is complete once any functionality issues are ironed out and the service has been running for a couple of weeks.

Of course, tech-savvy IT professionals are unlikely to use the new technology in the same way that the business users will; they can probably work around or fix most issues. Therefore, the next phase of the pilot is to broaden the scope of users. Throughout this phase, communication is key. It is very important to prepare pilot users for what they should expect, giving them clear and focused instructions rather than bombarding them with messages that will not be read! Pilot members should be made aware of the status of the program, the way to get support, and how to give feedback. It is this feedback that will enable the project team to fully evaluate how Lync is performing for users and to tweak systems or policies as necessary to enable a wider rollout to commence.

One element of the pilot is particularly important—the choice of pilot users. The users must be chosen from various areas of the business. It is important to identify areas where different working practices are found and make sure these areas are represented. Given that Lync is a tool for communication, it often makes sense to enable a whole project team. It is, of course, also important to choose users who understand the importance of providing feedback; without feedback, it is hard to gauge the status of the deployment.

Don't make the mistake of a partial pilot group, where you have some users enabled for Lync but not their key coworkers. You'll encounter problems reported by these groups of users, mostly in the areas around usability as Lync actually prevents them from doing their job. An example here is enabling the assistants of senior managers but not enabling the managers. If you can't involve the complete interaction group, you're better not involving anyone.

CHOOSING THE RIGHT USERS

It's important to choose users who will test the functionality you are rolling out. One customer we worked with chose its IT department for the pilot phase of the project; with more than 100 IT staff members, this seemed a good choice. However, once the two-week pilot had concluded and no data was captured, it turned out that the members of the pilot user group used their cell phones as their main phones!

Evaluation of the pilot is important. This can take several forms. You can generate reports from systems to evaluate based on your acceptance criteria, and you'll also want human input. As such, it makes sense to invite representative pilot users to a project board meeting to discuss issues and experiences. Although it may not be possible to directly quantify ease of use as a success criterion, the human feedback you get based on ease of use will help you guide the future rollout and will help you tweak the settings and policies. Furthermore, these individuals are likely to be chosen not only because they will give valuable feedback but also because they will become points of contact going forward as the technology is rolled out more widely in their areas of the business. If you like, these people will become the superusers, or champions.

Once you have properly met the criteria set out at the beginning of the pilot, you are ready to deploy more broadly. Be aware that it may take time to reach this stage and that it is far better to spend time understanding issues, getting the support desk up to speed, and reconfiguring systems at this stage than it will be after you have rolled out more broadly. Even if you need to make significant changes, do so now. Then reevaluate the success criteria and pilot again until you are sure that your Lync deployment is solid, is fit for purpose, and meets business requirements.

THE ROLLOUT AND ADOPTION SUCCESS KIT

The Rollout and Adoption Success Kit (RASK) is a collection of tools and documentation to help organizations ensure the success of the pilot phase. Some of it we covered earlier; however, the RASK provides all of this in easy-to-use documentation such as project plans as well as task checklists. The RASK can be downloaded from the following location:

    www.microsoft.com/en-us/download/details.aspx?id=37031

Training Your Users

As with any new technology, training users is necessary if you want to ensure that the rollout is smooth and the benefits to the business are maximized. Given the type of technology Lync is, this is all the more important because otherwise, people can be left floundering and significantly slowed down. That is not to say that training needs to be extensive. Lync is a very easy-to-use technology; however, many people simply will have no idea of its capabilities. As part of your rollout, you can address this in many ways.

The first suggestion would be to carry out "Buzz Days." These events can take varying forms and should be carried out either during or near the Lync rollout. The general premise is that you make Lync available somewhere so people can come and play with it. These sessions can be scheduled, whereby you identify a group of users and get them all down at once, or perhaps you can just set up timeslots and allow people to sign up themselves. Or you could simply set up machines with access to Lync in a common area with experts on hand so people passing can come and spend a few minutes getting the key points and having a go. The important thing with a Buzz Day is to identify the key messages you want to get across. Make sure you show people the functionality that is most important to them and then make sure they know how to back it up when they get stuck.

We believe that, beyond simply covering tasks, etiquette should be covered. Over the last 10 to 15 years, people have gotten used to how email works and learned the customs associated with it, such as replying to all, using a signature, and out-of-office messages; however, Lync provides entirely new ways to communicate. Central to these is the concept of presence. It is important to discuss how you want people to use presence within your business. For example, frequently someone may be in a meeting and their presence will show as much, but they could take a quick IM. Equally, if someone doesn't want to be contacted, then they should set themselves to Do Not Disturb. A nuance to this is that people should be trained to put contacts into the relevant level of access group so that only those who they want to be able to break through the Do Not Disturb state can do so. All these subtle differences are worth discussing as part of the pilot and then feeding into your training so that users become accustomed to starting an IM with "Have you got a moment to talk?" rather than barging in with a direct call immediately.

It is likely that a combination of the training types previously outlined will be needed. While it will be fine for some users to come by and play with Lync, others with more specialized needs will need more extensive training. In general, this applies to two particular groups. First, those people identified as local area champions or superusers should be given training. Often this will take an hour or perhaps an hour and a half to take these people through Lync features in detail. They can be taught about common questions and user mistakes, which you will have picked up both from the training materials (discussed next) and also from your experiences in your pilot. Another important group is the executive assistants. This group is critical, because they have the ear of both the senior management and the wider staff in general. They also have a specific role that involves using Lync like few other people in that they must be able to manage and make communications on behalf of others. The final group that warrants special training consists of the switchboard operators or receptionists. Again, they have a specific method of using Lync, usually via the Attendee Console, which provides the ability to handle and route multiple calls. Again, any loss in productivity here will be noticed quickly at high levels within the business, so this group must be given priority and have a clear method of escalation should problems occur.

Once you've conducted the training, one element that is perhaps useful is some form of accreditation. Many companies give users credit for completing training, and Lync training should be no different. This could range from online quizzes on a company portal to a specific test after the training. What you choose depends on the culture of your company, but in any case, finding a method to measure capability and rewarding new education is valuable.

TRAINING MATERIALS

Now that we've discussed the training that should be conducted, this final section describes some of the materials already available to assist you with putting together your training. While the content of these downloads and this section refers to Lync Server 2010, Microsoft is in the process of updating it for Lync Server 2013, and hopefully by the time this book is on the shelves, the updated content will be available. The screen shots and descriptions may refer to Lync 2010, but the concepts are equally valid for Lync 2013.

Microsoft has put together a collection of different materials that are downloadable here:

www.microsoft.com/downloads/en/details.aspx?FamilyID=f01a17e2-bec0-42c7-b1ce-fd4842ab1c91&displaylang=en

They are also available in online format along with a lot of useful additional material, like sample client application add-ins, here:

http://lync.microsoft.com/Adoption-and-Training-Kit/Pages/default.aspx

After downloading and extracting the 65MB ZIP file, you will find the following types of content:

QuickStarts The content enables users to get up to speed quickly with a variety of tasks, including using IM and presence, using the various Lync clients, working with voice and video modalities, and sharing their desktop or programs.

ShortVideos The videos show users a walk-through of common tasks such as forwarding calls, sending an IM, and sharing their desktop, among others.

Training slides These slides provide a useful starting point for structured classroom training on topics such as conferencing and collaboration, working with delegates, working as an agent on a response group, and manning the switchboard using the Attendant Console.

WhatsNew This material is in both HTML and video format, and it highlights some of the key elements new in Lync 2013.

WorkSmarts This material covers slightly more advanced topics and is focused on developing smarter working practices, such as making presence work for you and how to schedule conferences and customize them at the same time.

CUSTOMIZING TRAINING MATERIALS

In the QuickStarts and WorkSmarts folders, the material is in HTML format and includes a folder containing style sheets and images related to the page. You have the option to customize these web pages and either publish them on an intranet or make them available to others for local download. Alternatively, they could be cut up and distributed via Word documents or inserted into regular quick-tip emails. In this way, the material can be repurposed for structured training or self-help.

Also at your disposal are a couple of resources for driving adoption. The first set of materials is aimed at helping you promote Lync and communicate with users as you move through the process of pilot and rollout of Lync. It is accessible here:

www.microsoft.com/download/en/details.aspx?id=8737

There are templates for posters, T-shirts, and perhaps even more usefully a variety of emails, as laid out in Table B.1.

TABLE B.1:   The template emails provided by the adoption kit

EMAIL TEMPLATE NUMBER	TIMING	SUBJECT	AUDIENCE	PURPOSE
1	1 month before rollout	Join the Microsoft Lync Rollout	All users	Builds awareness and sign up users for the pilot
2a	Several weeks before rollout	Thanks for joining the Lync Pilot Rollout	Users accepted to the pilot	Notifies user of acceptance to pilot
2b	Several weeks before rollout	Thanks for your interest in the Lync Rollout	Users rejected from the pilot	Notifies user of rejection from pilot
3	1 week before rollout	Migration Warning	Users accepted to the pilot	Builds awareness of upcoming migration
4a	1 week before rollout	More Information Needed for Delegate Account	Users who will be delegates	Collects necessary information for delegate accounts
4b	Rollout day	Welcome and Installation Instructions	All users	Announces account migration/installation instructions
5	Weekly after rollout	Scenario Spotlight— Highlights a common scenario each week and asks for feedback	All users	Provides a timely way to expose users to high-productivity scenarios and offers a way to collect targeted feedback

The second set of adoption materials is a custom intranet site that pulls together much of the information in the various forms previously laid out—including the HTML help pages and videos—into a website ready for deployment on the intranet in your organization. This custom site is shown in Figure B.1, and it can be downloaded at the following location:

www.microsoft.com/download/en/details.aspx?id=3063

FIGURE B.1
The custom intranet site for assisting user adoption

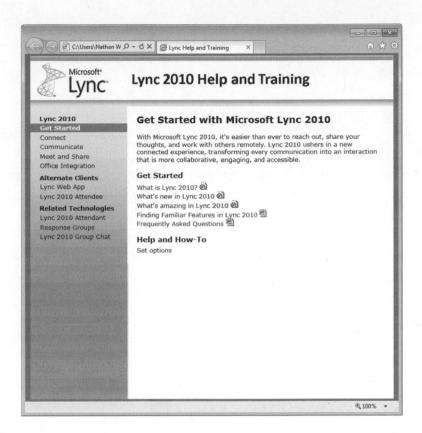

In the end, these resources are a great starting point. Likely, you will want to customize them for your company's needs. Thankfully, they were designed with that in mind!

In summary, our experience shows that having a controlled process such as the following for the PoC and pilot stages as well as choosing the correct users for the pilot will make the project more successful.

1. Deploy proof of concept to prove functionality.

2. Expand proof of concept to pilot with IT staff.

3. Provide constant communications.

4. Expand Pilot to include business users.

    a. Ensure that the users have realistic opportunity to use the functionality.

    b. Include the users in feedback.

    c. Provide extra training for these users.

5. Provide easily accessible training for the users during the rollout.

Using Persistent Chat Effectively

Combining the immediacy of instant messaging with multiparty outreach, Persistent Chat, now a fully fledged component in Microsoft Lync Server 2013, is transforming how groups and individuals communicate by facilitating real-time discussion, changing the way teams work.

You learned how to install Persistent Chat in Chapter 6, "Installation"; however, with functionality potentially as complex as Persistent Chat, this isn't enough. This appendix will look at some use case examples of how Persistent Chat can be used along with some channel deployment approaches, as well as how the technology can be used effectively in the global business environment to share knowledge, communicate more efficiently, save time, and keep abreast of up-to-date news that can impact the business.

You'll also be able to see how, with the use of some third-party applications from Formicary Collaboration Group, conversations can take place on a desktop or mobile device, a tablet, or the Web from any location using a multitude of clients.

Completing the entire communication spectrum, Persistent Chat cannot be altered or deleted, ensuring compliance for those in heavily regulated industries or those organizations that adhere to self-governance policies.

Introduction to Persistent Chat

In our fast-paced and highly global world, various modes of communication exist, email being the most often used. Email's downside, however, is that conversations end up taking the shape of "reply-all" email threads, clogging up people's inboxes and making it difficult to find the latest information or filter out irrelevant updates from urgent messages. Email conversations contain a wealth of expertise that is often lost in the "black hole" of employee inboxes.

Cross-functional projects and teams are a commonality in the business world. Internal processes and workflows are ever more important and can be the linchpin to a competitive edge. This puts further emphasis on ensuring that communication is widely shared among team members. Regardless of the amount of planning or foresight, these processes and workflows encounter exceptions. Moreover, emails between teams are a necessary but imperfect solution that often leads to siloed knowledge and information bottlenecks.

Persistent Chat can contribute to knowledge sharing in a structured and filtered way, all in real time. Conversations can be organized according to teams, topics, projects, geographies, categories, and so on. Users can be invited to join relevant groups and participate and engage in those conversations.

All conversations on Persistent Chat are stored and cannot be altered or deleted, allowing knowledge to be retained as an organizational asset. Others not partaking in the conversation at the time can refer back to the information and easily get up to speed. All past information is easily searchable.

To help put all of this together and graphically illustrate how Persistent Chat can help, the following use cases are examples of how Persistent Chat can be used across a variety of functions and industries. While not an exhaustive list (and there are many, many, others), these examples will showcase how Persistent Chat can better advance efficient communication and productivity:

- Persistent Chat for project managers
- Persistent Chat for lawyers
- Persistent Chat for consultants
- Persistent Chat for banking
- Persistent Chat for software companies
- Persistent Chat for operations

Table C.1 breaks these into the two categories of role-based and industry-based examples.

TABLE C.1: Role-based and industry-based Persistent Chat examples

ROLE-BASED EXAMPLES	INDUSTRY-BASED EXAMPLES
Project managers	Banking
Lawyers	Software companies
Consultants	Operations

Roles in project management, operations, and consulting can be applicable across various industries. While not wholly isolated from other departments, these roles generally focus on a particular product or project and around the sharing of intellectual capital.

In contrast, industries such as banking, technology, and operations are heavily dependent on multiple departments working together in coordination.

Both rely on effective communication to achieve goals and drive the business forward.

Examples of Role-Based Solutions for Persistent Chat

The roles in these examples center on the sharing of intellectual capital.

Project Managers

A company consists of several hundred people who are constantly traveling or working from home, with their only connection to the office being their laptops or phones. The project team consists of a core group of 20 business users at subsidiary headquarters and regional offices, technical leads at global headquarters, and their external consultants. The team is functionally, geographically, linguistically, culturally, and chronologically dispersed. In addition, stakeholders include members of the senior leadership team such as the CIO, CTO, and CFO. The challenge is keeping everyone involved, interested, and up-to-date on the latest status or changes.

Throughout the project life cycle (discovery, development, test, and rollout), communications among team members can take on a variety of forms including onsite visits, videoconferences, and teleconferences, but email typically becomes the go-to communications method due to time, language, and geographical differences. The dependence on email throughout the project life cycle not only promotes ineffective communication but also reinforces siloed knowledge, which may derail the project. Persistent Chat allows real-time interaction and a more streamlined but highly transparent approach while still empowering users with the ability to filter the right information to the right people, reducing communication bottlenecks and information overload.

For example, a separate channel for each stage of the cycle can be created (see Figure C.1). The groups would be used to discuss ideas, clarify issues, and answer specific questions around functionality requirements. Each new revision of the functional specification document or test results would be posted into the group so all users would be confident they're looking at the latest one. Updates from the document management system could be integrated into the channel, alerting all users of a new version. During rollout, a group can be created to foster a self-help community where users would post questions or comments. If users had specific questions, they could first search the history to see if the question was previously asked and answered; instead of just the project manager and a few help desk resources being inundated with questions, other users could also provide answers. A separate group would also be set up for the management team and the key stakeholders, providing a filtered set of information to upper management throughout the project.

FIGURE C.1

Project life cycle
project rooms

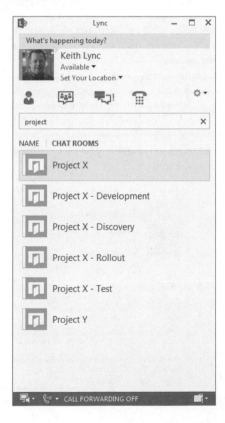

These are examples of how Persistent Chat enables real-time interaction for project managers and a more streamlined but highly transparent collaboration foundation while still empowering users with the ability to filter the right information to the right people, reducing communication bottlenecks and information overload. Persistent Chat allows real-time interaction and becomes an indispensable part of the workflow and integrates into other applications.

Lawyers

In a law firm, there can be a myriad of senior partners, partners, associates, contract lawyers, "Of Counsel" lawyers, law clerks, paralegals, legal assistants, and legal secretaries. Although the majority are law practitioners, larger law firms may specialize in different kinds of law, such as, for example, mergers and acquisitions (M&A), corporate, environmental, Internet, biotech, and aviation. This could mean potential overlaps between practice areas and could influence the outcome of cases. Additionally, lawsuits are often complicated and involve many different parties. Within a "single" lawsuit, there can be any number of claims and defenses between multiple plaintiffs or defendants, each of whom can bring any number of cross-claims and counterclaims against each other. Managing both clients and teams can be complex and overwhelming and extremely time consuming, especially with ineffective communications practices.

Persistent Chat can help all members of a firm within and across different practice areas align their cases to ensure the best outcome for their clients as well as for the firm. Gathering expert knowledge and data and connecting with peers in the firm to share information, experience, advice, or particulars on past cases allows a case to be built better and faster within binding, designated timeframes. This can be a matter of winning or losing a case, especially when time is of the essence. All information transmitted is secure, ensuring that confidential information is not improperly leaked.

For each case, a channel can be created (see Figure C.2) to track progress from the senior partners to legal secretaries. If a case crosses multiple practice areas, additional users may be given access to certain channels. Future assignments can benefit as channels enable expert knowledge of predecessors. This creates a valuable asset to the firm by providing insight into the thought processes associated with decisions, creating advantages or setting up for when a case is handed over from one to another. This also helps elevate a good client relationship to one of utmost confidence and trust.

FIGURE C.2
Creating a chat room

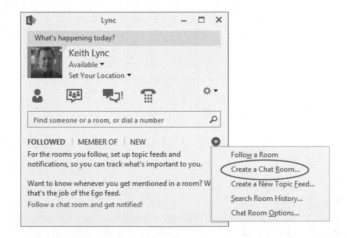

All of these information streams and associated functionalities can be accessed via mobile devices, perfect for those times in between traveling, trials, or meetings. Additional filters can be added, as well as instant messaging, which can be helpful for a discreet inquiry in a public place.

Persistent Chat enables firms to reduce their dependence on email for mass communication and improve dialogue among legal teams by creating a real-time platform to efficiently share knowledge and update each other on progress, flag potential problems, or brainstorm solutions, thereby transforming how legal teams operate by extracting the most valuable asset of all—knowledge sharing—for driving cases or assignments forward and increasing productivity and time management for success.

Consultants

A consultant's time is mostly spent in the air, airport lounges, cabs, trains, client meeting rooms, hotel rooms, and finally, in the office or home. While a consultant constantly travels to meet clients to identify their needs and find other potential ways to help their business, it's their imperative to make sure the firm's team delivers first-rate work to meet these needs. At the most senior levels, it is not uncommon to oversee 20-plus clients, each with its own dedicated team of 10 to 50 people consisting of directors, senior managers, managers, senior consultants, consultants, and analysts. The teams are functionally, geographically, linguistically, culturally, and chronologically dispersed, making it extremely difficult to connect and collaborate on project status, issues, and business decisions needing attention.

Managing clients and the internal teams is a complex and demanding part of the job, while equally challenging is communicating with peers in the firm to share knowledge, experience, advice, or particulars on past projects. The professional peer network is just as far-flung and nomadic, and reliance on email to communicate clogs up inboxes. To make matters worse, it is not readily obvious who would be the best resource, so an email is sent to the most logical choice to see what result that will yield. This step often creates the dreaded email chain, which often gets deleted.

While everyone shares the common goal of providing the best work to the client, ineffective communication practices through email can negatively affect the quality of work to the client or cause delays. To help cope, consultants have learned to be disciplined in the habit of scanning, absorbing, deleting, filing, and remembering the information read in email. Often, this exercise is completed in between client meetings on the mobile phone.

The contrast to email, Persistent Chat can help ensure smoother communication. A channel can be created for each client to allow internal team members to efficiently share knowledge and update each other on progress, flag potential problems, or brainstorm solutions. This allows consultants to review these goings-on for each project when it is convenient and not be a prisoner to email alerts. Clear communication to the entire team is as amazingly simple as a post. Important or urgent messages to the team can be highlighted as an alert. To counteract the anxiety of searching through countless emails and scrolling through email chains, a simple search function displays the data in context, reducing the amount of information that needs to be filtered through to find the answer.

Not only can this information help the firm be more informed, it can also better help the firm help the client. Up-to-date news can potentially impact the assignment; taking quick action to mitigate risks could elevate a good client relationship to one of utmost confidence and trust.

Among peers, separate streams can be set up to share knowledge and expertise in particular practice areas or topics. Queries will be broadcast to a wide audience, eliminating the need to send untargeted emails. Not only would this mean a reduction in multiple emails with the same response, it benefits the group and the firm as a whole since knowledge is shared and stored as an organizational asset. This will help other consultants who face the same challenge, those unaware of the situation, or others who need a reference at a later point in time. Persistent Chat ensures that questions will not be lost in the inbox "black hole."

All of these information channels and associated functionalities can be accessed via mobile devices, perfect for those little chunks of time in between traveling time or meetings. Additional filters on the mobile device can be added to ensure alerts only for the most important information. An additional benefit is being able to quickly ask a question or clarify an issue with the team via instant message; this can be helpful for discreet inquiries.

Persistent Chat creates a collaborative platform, easily integrating itself into the business workflow and supporting the mobile nature of consulting in an efficient, easy, simple way in real time.

Examples of Industry-Based Solutions for Persistent Chat

The industries in the following examples are heavily dependent on cross-functional coordination.

Banking

Broadly speaking, in an investment bank there exist two divisions that work closely together, although they can't always communicate directly. Traders rely on the work of the research department to help them make decisions on various financial instruments being traded on the floor. This information is vital to the job of the trader and impacts the cash flow and bottom line of the institution. The research department can be seen as the nerve center for a bank. Not only do the findings from the research department need to get to the traders, the information may also be shared with third parties such as hedge funds and private equity clients who do not have the same in-house capabilities. Moreover, to ensure that the output is as accurate as possible, up-to-the-minute news on various topics must be included into the models. The research scope is separated into several verticals, or sectors, such as Fast Moving Consumer Goods (FMCG), energy, transportation, and commodities. Each of these groups has a team of managers, senior analysts, and analysts who focus on different aspects of the sector, such as pricing, news trends, consumer reports, corporate purchasing trends, and marketing analysis. The analysts and senior analysts communicate with their peers within the same sector but also with peers in other sectors, depending on their specialization.

The interdependencies, communication, and information flows are highly intricate and complex; the addition of regulations that impose "ethical" or "Chinese" walls between research and trading makes this elaborate arrangement even more challenging.

Persistent Chat can reduce dependence on emails for communication and minimize accidental information sharing between internal banking groups and external clients. For example, a separate channel for each sector can be created to update the different analysts on the progress of the reports. Another channel could be created for all team leaders across the sectors to share knowledge and align internal initiatives. Communications within the channels are secure and users can be restricted to certain channels.

Persistent Chat is a form of electronic communication and is therefore subjected to compliance regulations. All information communicated through Persistent Chat cannot be altered or deleted by end users, adhering to compliance guidelines. Communication through Persistent Chat can be captured and transferred to a preexisting archive.

For banks, Persistent Chat can seamlessly integrate with other technological applications as well as outside news sources and business workflows. This information can be shared in a secure and compliant environment with internal and external stakeholders.

Software Company

A software company consists of 250 employees and occupies office space in two different locations. The 50-person-strong sales force travels extensively to meet clients and channel partners, logging important details in Customer Relationship Management (CRM) software. The marketing department is just as mobile, engaging with potential customers, affiliates, media, and other networking events to keep track of outreach activities in their own marketing automation software. The development team, although it's in-house, has multiple projects for each product running concurrently and relies on development tracking tools. Last, the customer support team fields suggestions for improvement and issues encountered by customers.

Although highly disjointed technology-wise, the departments are interdependent and serve as critical touch points for the customer experience. The challenge is keeping everyone involved, interested, and up-to-date on the latest status or changes despite these siloed and "department-centric" tools used. Persistent Chat can extensively organize the company's internal management, sales, marketing, development, and customer support.

For example, the sales team can have channels for each major prospect providing up-to-the-minute information on prospects and their respective industries. For the development team, a channel can be set up for every product to log exceptions or progress. Customer support can provide the clients with the opportunity to access its portal in addition to the normal support tools. Everything that happens with each client happens within one of those channels. This provides a clear view of activity or issues and means that support can be given 24/7. All the information is auditable and provides fast and easy search facilities. One of the biggest benefits is that it allows people who are unfamiliar with the issue or client to quickly come up to speed. Across all departments, alerts from each of the "department-centric" tools can be set up to show new cases, updates, and edits.

Persistent Chat can greatly enhance and enable efficient communication in real time within departments and across the entire organization as well as integrate siloed systems.

For software companies, Persistent Chat provides a collaborative foundation. It can seamlessly integrate other technological applications and outside news sources, external clients, and business workflows and allow employees to access information.

Operations for Multinational Enterprise (MNE)

Multinational enterprises (MNEs) run mission critical, global, real-time operations with distributed teams that need to stay tightly coordinated in response to incidents and provide highly effective shift handovers. Developing, manufacturing, and delivering goods to the consumer can touch upon teams in a broad range of functions, from R&D to manufacturing, logistics, distribution, warehouse, and merchandising. Seamless transitions need to occur at every functional shift in the journey to the consumer, otherwise delays, mix-ups, and worst of all, lack of product for consumers will negatively impact the MNE's bottom line and reputation.

Because the vertical chain is so complex, so can be the technology being deployed in this process. Users in those teams are very often using a mix of different desktop technologies, such as, for example, Windows, Mac, Linux, and mobile devices. The challenge is not only to ensure that all parties are kept up-to-date on the latest shipment but also to consolidate all modes of communication. You'll see later in this appendix how third-party products can help here. As can be seen in Figure C.3, membership of each category can be defined in many ways:

- Organizational units

- Distributions groups

- Domains

- Individuals

FIGURE C.3
Defining allowed members in a category

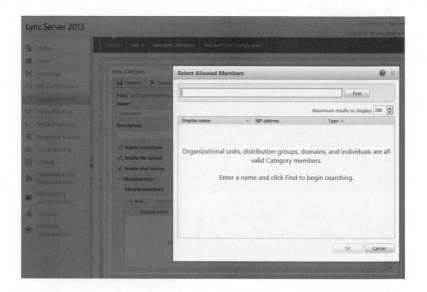

Persistent Chat enables both real-time and near-real-time communications across platforms and incorporates relevant external feeds; that is, users can conversations in real time, have access to the recent chat history, and join or rejoin a channel and quickly come up to speed on the latest information and discussions. A separate channel can be created for the "internal" departments (R&D, manufacturing) to flag any quality issues for each product and "external" departments (logistics, distribution, warehouse, and merchandising) to pinpoint where legal liabilities for each shipment change hands along with other transportation issues. The history forms valuable input into postmortems and acts as a knowledge base for recurring issues.

As opposed to the use of telephone or conference calls, the use of written real-time communications is very helpful for users who are not native speakers of their company's preferred business language. The ability to lock down channels means that communications can be limited on a "need to know" basis.

This collaborative foundation seamlessly integrates into the business workflow and unites teams using disparate systems while providing access only to those who need the visibility. Persistent Chat can provide further efficiencies in time-sensitive operations that could have a huge impact on the bottom line by providing a collaborative foundation and integrating this into the business workflow.

Better "Unification" of Data

We talk a lot about unified communications. Using a product such as MindLink from Formicary Collaboration Group (`www.fcg.im`) allows multiple data streams from many sources to be truly unified and presented within the Persistent Chat channels. Equally, data can be taken from the channels and presented in other formats for consumption in other ways. For example, in almost all of the examples in this appendix, RSS connector feeds could be created to summarize channel content and present via Outlook or an RSS aggregation application, similar to newswire-type data.

How about the lawyer example? We can further aggregate data channels into the relevant SharePoint workspace, ensuring that all the communications for a particular case are in one place.

What about configuring connections that provide alerts to financial traders of relevant news to a particular industry? You could pick up data feeds and provide the information to the channel as necessary. In turn, the trader is alerted to new data and can read it and take the necessary actions as required to buy or sell.

Clients to support Lync 2013 aren't yet available on the Mac platform, and who's to say whether it'll support Persistent Chat? Enabling access to channel content via other methods (RSS, email, web, mobile) allows the user base to significantly increase, resulting in a much more informed (and hopefully more capable) workforce.

What Is MindLink?

The use cases detailed earlier demonstrate how Persistent Chat can greatly enhance and enable efficient communication in real time within departments and across an entire organization as well as integrate siloed systems. Not only can Persistent Chat be used on the desktop, it also offers communication and access to vital information while traveling.

The MindLink platform puts your team's objectives first, and it achieves this by balancing confidential group discussions and public social interactions, delivering your information the way you require it and allowing you to decide which information you would like to receive in your customizable streams.

MindLink is an enhancement to Persistent Chat and turns the Persistent Chat, presence, and instant messaging components of Lync into an all-around enterprise collaboration platform. It extends Lync Server 2013 beyond the Microsoft solutions to gain further efficiencies in the collaborative processes, and it comes in different versions:

- MindLink Anywhere makes the environment more inclusive. It works for employees using MAC, Linux, and iOS as well as employees wanting to work from home on personal devices and external users using the Web.

- MindLink Mobile is for an increasingly mobile workforce. It provides the ability to filter subsets of content on the go using Apple iPhone, Apple iPad, and BlackBerry Playbook.

◆ MindLink Connectors integrates with existing business applications and processes, bringing information and communications together.

◆ MindLink Compliance is for regulated industries already using an email archiving store.

These enhancements to the Persistent Chat platform provide real business value as they translate this little-known, yet extremely powerful technology into viable solutions for the business. Specifically, Persistent Chat and its enhancements yield benefits that email alone fails to provide:

◆ A collaborative foundation

◆ Seamless technology assimilation into the business workflow

◆ Easy integration into other applications

◆ Mobilization of the workforce

◆ Communication extension to external clients

MindLink Anywhere provides web access to presence, instant messaging, and persistent chat functionality on all major web browsers, allowing access through desktop and laptop computers as well as tablet devices. MindLink Anywhere is essential for engaging Mac and Linux users as well as remote workers. MindLink Anywhere's state-of-the-art design is optimized for touch-enabled devices including Apple iPad. MindLink Anywhere builds upon Microsoft OCS 2007 R2, Lync Server 2010, and Lync Server 2013 and offers the following additional features and benefits:

◆ It unifies presence and instant messaging with Persistent Chat so users don't have to switch between client experiences. (Note that in OCS 2007 R2 and Lync Server 2010, Persistent Chat [then known as Group Chat] is accessed through a separate desktop client that is independent of the client used to access presence and instant messaging functionality. In Lync Server 2013, the Lync client brings together Persistent Chat with IM and presence in a single client.)

◆ Multiple groups are displayed in a single interface so users can participate in several conversations at once.

◆ MindLink Anywhere allows users to filter what's important and what's not and prioritize a personal view of messages.

◆ LiveStream provides a real-time universal update across all subscribed groups. Users can use Quick-Reply to respond to a group without having to navigate to the group itself.

◆ MindLink Anywhere has the same features as Microsoft's Persistent Chat client, including chat history, search function, sharing of attachments, links, and story and alert capabilities.

◆ MindLink is a Section 508–compliant solution.

MindLink Mobile brings Persistent Chat capabilities combined with IM and presence for mobile users. It keeps mobile workers in touch with teams when they are on the move. It allows users to prioritize chat rooms to follow and users to connect to. The only mobile client to bring Persistent Chat capabilities to mobile users, MindLink Mobile provides the following additional benefits:

◆ Advanced filtering capabilities allow users to select a subset of their groups and contacts for their mobile experience, helping them stay on top of the most critical information and ignoring irrelevant chatter.

◆ Users can switch seamlessly between Persistent Chat and instant messaging.

◆ Custom push notification preferences let users decide when to be notified of new messages in selected groups or from selected contacts.

◆ LiveStream provides a snapshot of the latest updates from a further filtered set of groups. Users can use Quick-Reply to respond to a group without having to navigate to the group itself.

◆ Presence information can be set to keep colleagues updated.

◆ It is optimized to conserve battery life.

MindLink Add-In for Outlook creates a unified experience by enabling real-time team collaboration within the familiar email client. The Add-In for Outlook activates Persistent Chat channels within Outlook, allowing users to keep track of Persistent Chat and email simultaneously. The add-in retains the Outlook look and feel, which encourages user adoption because it offers familiarity. Because it's an add-in to Outlook, users have the option to choose the best medium to communicate with teams, minimizing the number of nonurgent and one-line emails.

MindLink for SharePoint brings a new dimension to your Microsoft Office SharePoint Server implementation by integrating presence, instant messaging and Persistent Chat capabilities. If your teams are already using Microsoft Office SharePoint Server to collaborate on projects or files, MindLink for SharePoint allows them to interact in real time from within the context of the SharePoint site. Users can use the same environment to store or retrieve information as well as discuss the information with other team members. MindLink for SharePoint can be configured to show a single channel within a Team Site or allow users to access all their subscribed channels from their My Site.

MindLink Compliance offers a simple, cost-effective transfer mechanism allowing you to keep using your usual eDiscovery tool. Whether you are regulated by a governing body or simply want to store all communications for compliance and security, ideally you want all data stored on a single device. It moves Microsoft Lync communication data (Persistent Chat and IM) into a nonrepudiation store of your choice, which could be Microsoft Exchange Hosted Archive, Symantec Enterprise Vault, EMC Centera, or others.

MindLink Connectors and API is a simple RESTful API that allows content to be fed into or read out of MindLink streams. Using MindLink Connectors and API, you can bring relevant content into active discussions by connecting to your existing systems (such as email or JIRA for issue tracking) or external systems (RSS newsfeeds) as well as developing your own integrations using any technology of your choice.

Figure C.4 shows the connectivity paths available into Lync.

FIGURE C.4
MindLink connec-
tivity capability

Microsoft®
Lync™

MindLink

Email
connector

REST
API

Social
connector

Microsoft
Outlook

CRM, ERP, document management,
order management, trading,
monitoring, issue tracking, risk

RSS feeds,
Twitter, etc.

Index

Note to the Reader: Throughout this index **boldfaced** page numbers indicate primary discussions of a topic. *Italicized* page numbers indicate illustrations.